S0-BHR-795

VOLUME

3

GATHERING
STRENGTH

REPORT
OF THE ROYAL COMMISSION
ON ABORIGINAL PEOPLES

Canadian Cataloguing in Publication Data

Canada. Royal Commission on Aboriginal Peoples.
Report of the Royal Commission on Aboriginal Peoples.

Issued also in French under the title:
Rapport de la Commission royale sur les peuples autochtones.

Contents: v. 1. Looking forward, looking back –
v. 2. Restructuring the relationship –
v. 3. Gathering strength –
v. 4. Perspectives and realities –
v. 5. Renewal: a twenty-year commitment
ISBN 0-660-16413-2 (V. 1);
ISBN 0-660-16414-0 (V. 2);
ISBN 0-660-16415-9 (V. 3);
ISBN 0-660-16416-7 (V. 4);
ISBN 0-660-16417-5 (V. 5).
Cat. no. Z1-1991/1-1E (V. 1);
Cat. no. Z1-1991/1-2E (V. 2);
Cat. no. Z1-1991/1-3E (V. 3);
Cat. no. Z1-1991/1-4E (V. 4);
Cat. no. Z1-1991/1-5E (V. 5).

1. Native peoples – Canada.
2. Native peoples – Canada – Social conditions.
3. Native peoples – Canada – Economic conditions.
4. Native peoples – Canada – Politics and government.
I. Title.

E78.C2R46 1996   971'.00497   C96-980078-9

Available in Canada through
your local bookseller
or by mail from
Canada Communication Group – Publishing
Ottawa, Canada K1A 0S9

Cat. no. Z1-1991/1-3E
ISBN 0-660-16415-9

Cover: Jim Logan, "The Visit", 1987, acrylic on canvas,
72 x 48 centimetres.
Endpapers: Mireille Siouï, "Dans la maison d'Handiaouich, la petite tortue",
intaglio, watercolour on paper, 50 x 32.5 centimetres.
Both, collection of the Indian Art Centre, Department of Indian Affairs
and Northern Development. Photographer, Lawrence Cook.
Photograph facing page 1: Fred Cattroll.

Canada	Groupe
Communication	Communication
Group	Canada
Publishing	Édition

VOLUME

3

GATHERING STRENGTH

CONTENTS

3 ◾ Health and Healing   107

4 ◾ Housing   365

6 Arts and Heritage   585

A Note About Sources

Among the sources referred to in this report, readers will find mention of testimony given at the Commission's public hearings; briefs and submissions to the Commission; submissions from groups and organizations funded through the Intervener Participation Program; research studies conducted under the auspices of the Commission's research program; reports on the national round tables on Aboriginal issues organized by the Commission; and commentaries, special reports and research studies published by the Commission during its mandate. After the Commission completes its work, this information will be available in various forms from a number of sources.

This report, the published commentaries and special reports, published research studies, round table reports, and other publications released during the Commission's mandate will be available in Canada through local booksellers or by mail from

> Canada Communication Group – Publishing
> Ottawa, Ontario
> K1A 0S9

A CD-ROM will be published following this report. It will contain the report, transcripts of the Commission's hearings and round tables, overviews of the four rounds of hearings, research studies, the round table reports, and the Commission's special reports and commentaries, together with a resource guide for educators. The CD-ROM will be available in libraries across the country through the government's depository services program and for purchase from

> Canada Communication Group – Publishing
> Ottawa, Ontario
> K1A 0S9

Briefs and submissions to the Commission, as well as research studies not published in book or CD-ROM form, will be housed in the National Archives of Canada after the Commission completes its work.

A Note About Terminology

The Commission uses the term *Aboriginal people* to refer to the indigenous inhabitants of Canada when we want to refer in a general manner to Inuit and to First Nations and Métis people, without regard to their separate origins and identities.

The term *Aboriginal peoples* refers to organic political and cultural entities that stem historically from the original peoples of North America, not to collections of individuals united by so-called 'racial' characteristics. The term includes the Indian, Inuit and Métis peoples of Canada (see section 35(2) of the *Constitution Act, 1982*).

Aboriginal people (in the singular) means the individuals belonging to the political and cultural entities known as Aboriginal peoples.

The term *Aboriginal nations* overlaps with the term Aboriginal peoples but also has a more specific usage. The Commission's use of the term nation is discussed in some detail in Volume 2, Chapter 3, where it is defined as a sizeable body of Aboriginal people with a shared sense of national identity that constitutes the predominant population in a certain territory or collection of territories.

The Commission distinguishes between local communities and nations. We use terms such as *a First Nation community* and *a Métis community* to refer to a relatively small group of Aboriginal people residing in a single locality and forming part of a larger Aboriginal nation or people. Despite the name, a First Nation community would not normally constitute an Aboriginal nation in the sense just defined. Rather, most (but not all) Aboriginal nations are composed of a number of communities.

Our use of the term *Métis* is consistent with our conception of Aboriginal peoples as described above. We refer to Métis as distinct Aboriginal peoples whose early ancestors were of mixed heritage (First Nations, or Inuit in the case of the Labrador Métis, and European) and who associate themselves with a culture that is distinctly Métis. The more specific term *Métis Nation* is used to refer to Métis people who identify themselves as a nation with historical roots in the Canadian west. Our use of the terms Métis and Métis Nation is discussed in some detail in Volume 4, Chapter 5.

Following accepted practice and as a general rule, the term *Inuit* replaces the term *Eskimo*. As well, the term *First Nation* replaces the term *Indian*. However, where the subject under discussion is a specific historical or contemporary nation, we use the name of that nation (for example, Mi'kmaq, Dene, Mohawk). Often more than one spelling is considered acceptable for these nations. We try to use the name preferred by particular nations or communities, many of which now use their traditional names. Where necessary, we add the more familiar or generic name in parentheses – for example, Siksika (Blackfoot).

Terms such as Eskimo and Indian continue to be used in at least three contexts:

1. where such terms are used in quotations from other sources;
2. where Indian or Eskimo is the term used in legislation or policy and hence in discussions concerning such legislation or policy (for example, the *Indian Act*; the Eskimo Loan Fund); and
3. where the term continues to be used to describe different categories of persons in statistical tables and related discussions, usually involving data from Statistics Canada or the Department of Indian Affairs and Northern Development (for example, status Indians, registered Indians).

1

NEW DIRECTIONS IN SOCIAL POLICY

ABORIGINAL PEOPLE IN CANADA endure ill health, insufficient and unsafe housing, polluted water supplies, inadequate education, poverty and family breakdown at levels usually associated with impoverished developing countries. The persistence of such social conditions in this country – which is judged by many to be the best place in the world to live – constitutes an embarrassment to Canadians, an assault on the self-esteem of Aboriginal people and a challenge to policy makers.

1. SOCIAL POLICY IN CONTEXT

The challenge to the Commission to investigate social and cultural issues, and to propose solutions to problems that compromise the quality of life of Aboriginal people, was placed squarely before us in the terms of reference recommended by former Chief Justice Brian Dickson.[1]

All the items in our mandate have social and cultural dimensions. The subjects addressed specifically in this volume include

- social issues, including poverty, ill health, substandard housing, and family violence;
- cultural issues, including languages, spirituality, child care patterns, and traditional ways of life; and
- educational issues, including primary, secondary and post-secondary education, protection of cultural identity, and education in Aboriginal communities and settings where Aboriginal students are a minority.[2]

Justice issues – including relations with police, respect for Aboriginal culture in the justice system, incarceration rates, and elaboration of Aboriginal justice systems – form a closely related set of concerns that were addressed in our report on justice released early in 1996.[3] The concerns of women, youth, elders, Métis people, and Aboriginal people who live in the North and in rural and urban settings naturally encompass social and cultural issues as well. While the perspectives of these groups are addressed to some extent in this volume, a more integrated review can be found in Volume 4.

Our comprehensive mandate allowed us to look beyond the individual policy sectors that numerous commissions and task forces have studied over the past 25 years.[4] Consequently, we were able to examine current evidence of social dysfunction in the context of historical experience and to consider solutions that are not merely social.

This broader perspective has shown us that we are living with the painful legacy of displacement and assimilation policies that have undermined the foundations of Aboriginal societies. With the problems seen in this light, the solution is redistribution of power and resources so that Aboriginal people can pursue their social and economic goals and regain their health and equilibrium through means they choose freely.

2. Confronting
a Painful Legacy

In Volume 1 we described the process by which Aboriginal peoples were systematically dispossessed of their lands and livelihood, their cultures and languages, and their social and political institutions. We showed how this was done through government policies based on the false assumptions that Aboriginal ways of life were at a primitive level of evolutionary development, and that the high point of human development was to be achieved by adopting the culture of European colonists. We argued that these ethnocentric and demeaning attitudes linger in policies that purport to work on behalf of Aboriginal people while actually withholding from them the power to work out their own destiny. We proposed that the way of the future be to put behind us all notions of wardship, assimilation and subordination and to develop a new relationship based on mutual recognition, mutual respect, sharing, and mutual responsibility.

In Volume 2 we set out the means by which this new relationship can become a reality. These include honouring historical treaties and concluding new ones, implementing the right of Aboriginal peoples to self-determination and self-government, effecting a more just distribution of lands and the wealth those lands generate, and developing economic policies to revitalize Aboriginal nations and communities and enhance their self-reliance.

The Commission believes that the inherent right of Aboriginal self-government is recognized and affirmed in section 35(1) of the *Constitution Act, 1982* as a protected Aboriginal and treaty right and is now entrenched in the constitution (see Volume 2, Chapter 3 for a fuller discussion).

Constitutional recognition of the inherent right of self-government intro-duced a new dynamic into the relationship between Aboriginal and non-Aboriginal people. It will, however, take time for both sides to recognize the full implications of partnership. Building institutions to translate the concept of part-nership into reality will be a lengthy and demanding process.

In the meantime, pressing problems facing Aboriginal people must be addressed. Children's lives are being stunted by violence in the home and fail-ure at school. Communities are suffering the soul-destroying effects of inadequate housing, unsafe water and rampant unemployment. Young people are subjected to racist taunts because they are marked as members of a devalued underclass.

Solutions cannot wait until self-government becomes a reality. Problems will not disappear with the recognition of the inherent right of self-government. Federal, provincial and territorial governments, along with Aboriginal leaders and organizations, must act now to erase the disparities between Aboriginal and non-Aboriginal opportunity in Canada. Aboriginal nations need a strong and durable foundation upon which to build self-government. That foundation is the people – healthy, educated individuals, strong in body, soul, mind and spirit. That is why we entitled this volume *Gathering Strength*. As our recommendations are implemented, individuals and communities will gain the strength needed to make their nations viable, so that they will be able to seize the opportunities opened up by the structural changes recommended in Volume 2.

The subjects addressed in this volume – family life, health and healing, housing, education and cultural policy – all fall within what we identified (in Volume 2, Chapter 3) as the core jurisdiction of Aboriginal self-government. These core matters have a direct impact on the life, welfare, culture and iden-tity of Aboriginal peoples. Therefore, Aboriginal nations are free to proceed with policy making in these areas without waiting for agreements to be worked out with federal, provincial or territorial governments. They can start now.

In the next five chapters we explore current problems in particular sectors, the barriers to resolving the problems, solutions that are being implemented in some quarters, and action required on the part of governments – federal, provin-cial, territorial and Aboriginal – to achieve positive change. Recommendations are not directed to governments alone. We point out often what Aboriginal and non-Aboriginal citizens and their organizations can do to promote and com-plement policy makers' actions.

3. LOOKING AHEAD

We begin with a discussion of Aboriginal families in Chapter 2 because we are per-suaded that restoring stable, nurturing families, in their diverse contemporary forms, is essential to achieving the social goals of Aboriginal people. We examine briefly the place of families in traditional cultures and the interventions that have undermined their continuity and effectiveness. We propose that Aboriginal people be in charge of family service institutions that emphasize rebuilding mutual-aid networks within communities and protecting vulnerable persons from violence. Enacting family law that incorporates Aboriginal customs will help remove some of the gaps and contradictions in the current application of federal and provincial law.

We examine health and social services together in Chapter 3 because Aboriginal people advised us consistently that the health of body, mind, emotions and spirit must be understood holistically. Seen in this light, the current fragmentation of services is a major obstacle to supporting and enhancing whole health – that is, a state of well-being in the individual and harmony with social and environmental systems that are themselves functioning in a balanced way. We probe selected aspects of health and well-being to illuminate the source and nature of the factors that contribute to troubling statistics on life expectancy and quality of life. We conclude that Aboriginal concepts of health and contemporary research on the determinants of health converge. Together they point to a plan in which services play a significant but not the only role. The following constitutes the core of our proposed health and healing strategy:

- reorganization of health and social services under Aboriginal control;
- a human resources strategy to prepare Aboriginal people to design and staff services;
- reform of mainstream institutions to make them more responsive to Aboriginal people; and
- urgent action to achieve minimum standards of safe housing, water supply and waste disposal.

Political empowerment and economic development must complement this health strategy.

Chapter 4 focuses on ways to correct serious problems in housing, water supply and waste disposal in Aboriginal communities. We analyze the extent of current deficiencies in the housing supply and community infrastructure, as well as the impediments to devising a policy to address these deficiencies. We propose that community services be brought up to public health standards for a safe water supply over a five-year period. We outline a 10-year plan to raise housing conditions to at least a minimum level of health and safety on First Nation territories and to provide access to affordable housing in areas where a housing market operates. This would be achieved through a combination of mortgage and income subsidies, householder contributions, and community investment. The 10-year schedule is proposed so that Aboriginal governments, as they assume responsibilities now carried by federal, provincial and territorial governments, will not be saddled with the consequences of years of neglect and ineffective policies. To maintain an adequate and affordable housing supply, individual and community incomes must increase through economic development.

In Chapter 5, we consider the statistics on Aboriginal educational achievement, the recommendations made by commissions and task forces since 1966, and the advice we received in hearings and briefs, and we conclude that educational reform is not achieving the needed breakthrough. As an alternative, we set out a proposal to implement lifelong, holistic learning that includes strategies to engage children, young people, adults and elders in accessible, culturally appropriate education. Key elements of the strategy are

- institutions at all levels under the control of Aboriginal people
- greater recognition of Aboriginal culture and identity in provincial and territorial education systems; and
- full participation of Aboriginal people in educational governance.

A strategy to prepare people to implement self-government is given prominence in setting educational goals.

Finally, in Chapter 6, we address cultural policy. Mutual respect between Aboriginal and non-Aboriginal people in Canada can be achieved only with knowledge of one another. However, the opportunities for Aboriginal people to contribute to authentic knowledge – by representing themselves in their own languages, with reference to their own symbols, in their own literature, radio, movies and television – have been, and continue to be, severely restricted. The result is that stereotypes and distorted images, based on historical and current misconceptions, are widespread. In this chapter we set out ways for Aboriginal people to gain more equitable representation in the arts, literature, and communications media and to have their history portrayed more accurately in museums and historical displays. We suggest how public policy can contribute to conserving and restoring languages threatened with decline or disappearance.

While intercultural relations demand attention, relations within and between Aboriginal nations are also an urgent priority. The nation building over the next generation will require access to the various media and the skills to use them. Transmitting cultural traditions between generations with radically different life experiences will require innovative means of communication; so will the challenge of maintaining a shared identity among Aboriginal people dispersed in rural and urban settings. Our recommendations address both dimensions – intercultural communication and communication within and among Aboriginal nations and cultures.

4. FROM DEPENDENCY TO STRENGTH

Current social problems are in large part a legacy of historical policies of displacement and assimilation, and their resolution lies in recognizing the authority of Aboriginal people to chart their own future within the Canadian federation. Specific policies we recommend assume that this framework of authority will be put in place and that lands and resources will be redistributed to make self-government workable. Institutions to serve social needs will be established by Aboriginal governments and will reflect the cultural priorities of the population being served. Distinct Aboriginal institutions will play an important role in demonstrating how traditional wisdom can be applied to contemporary problems. These will take time to develop, however, and even when fully operational they will not occupy the whole field of Aboriginal services.

We anticipate that the transition to self-government will proceed quickly in some Aboriginal nations and more slowly in others. Therefore, our recommendations for policy and institution building are formulated to involve Aboriginal people in decision making in existing jurisdictions and to accommodate easily a transition to Aboriginal jurisdiction when self-government is accomplished. The challenge will be to ensure there is dialogue between policy makers and managers of new initiatives and emerging Aboriginal governments, so that momentum, efficiency, and continuity are maintained throughout the transition.

Even when self-government is fully operational, large numbers of Aboriginal people will continue to participate in non-Aboriginal society as a result of living in urban areas, encountering the justice system, attending schools and universities, being admitted to hospitals, watching television, reading newspapers, working for the public or private sector, or simply interacting with others. Aboriginal people need to be recognized and accepted for what they are and for what they can offer non-Aboriginal society. Assimilationist and racist policies and attitudes must be eliminated. That is why so many of our recommendations are aimed at making governments, policies, school curricula, public institutions, and professional organizations more aware of the Aboriginal presence in Canada and more receptive to what it can contribute to society.

Immediate threats to health must be removed. Living conditions that undermine morale and well-being must be improved to match prevailing Canadian standards. Equal opportunities to acquire the skills needed to participate in the social, political and economic life of Canada must be made available to Aboriginal people. As our examination of past efforts at policy reform has demonstrated, however, Aboriginal life will not be transformed by the continuation of paternalistic policies designed and administered outside the control of Aboriginal people.

Recommendations in this volume thus have three interrelated objectives:

1. to address urgent social concerns through institution building and program development congruent with the emergence of self-government;
2. to pave the way for Aboriginal self-government by enhancing the capacity of Aboriginal citizens to engage in nation building; and
3. to stimulate adaptation of mainstream institutions to provide services in a manner that recognizes and affirms Aboriginal identity, involves Aboriginal

people in governance and decision making, and assumes a complementary and supportive role in the development of Aboriginal service institutions.

Past social policy, based on false assumptions about Aboriginal people and aimed at their colonization and assimilation, has left a heritage of dependency, powerlessness and distrust. Establishing a new relationship based on mutual recognition, mutual respect, sharing and mutual responsibility in an era of Aboriginal self-government is the challenge of the twenty-first century. Aboriginal people are anxious to put the past behind them and work with governments in Canada to meet that challenge. They are gathering strength for the task ahead.

NOTES

1. Report of the Special Representative respecting the Royal Commission on Aboriginal Peoples, 2 August 1991.

2. The Commission's terms of reference are set out in Volume 1, Appendix A.

3. Royal Commission on Aboriginal Peoples [RCAP], *Bridging the Cultural Divide: A Report on Aboriginal People and Criminal Justice in Canada* (Ottawa: Supply and Services, 1996).

4. A search revealed close to 900 commissions and task forces sponsored by federal, provincial and territorial governments or Aboriginal and other organizations over the past 25 years. More than 200 of these reports were reviewed and analyzed in *Public Policy and Aboriginal Peoples, 1965-1992*, a four-volume study conducted for RCAP by the Centre for Policy and Program Assessment, School of Public Administration, Carleton University (Ottawa: Supply and Services, 1993-1996).

2

The Family

We believe healthy individuals ensure healthy families, communities, and nations. This is the foundation for any of the successes we are to have now and in the future, be it in settlement of land claims or in self-government.

Eric Morris
Teslin Yukon
26 May 1992*

WE BEGIN OUR DISCUSSION of social policy with a focus on the family because it is our conviction that much of the failure of responsibility that contributes to the current imbalance and distress in Aboriginal life centres around the family. Let us clarify at the outset that the failure of responsibility that we seek to understand and correct is not a failure of Aboriginal families. Rather, it is a failure of public policy to recognize and respect Aboriginal culture and family systems and to ensure a just distribution of the wealth and power of this land so that Aboriginal nations, communities and families can provide for themselves and determine how best to pursue a good life.

Volume 2 of our report focused on restructuring political and economic relations between Aboriginal people and the rest of Canadian society. The need for structural change forms a backdrop to our discussion of Aboriginal family life and, indeed, all the chapters in this volume. In this chapter, we are concerned principally with the Aboriginal vision of family well-being, the forces that have compromised the attainment of that vision, and the practical steps that can be

---

* Transcripts of the Commission's hearing are cited with the speaker's name and affiliation, if any, and the location and date of the hearing. See *A Note About Sources* at the beginning of this volume for information about transcripts and other Commission publications.

taken to restore health and efficacy to Aboriginal families struggling to maintain a sense of cohesion and balance.[1]

For many Aboriginal people who spoke about the family at our hearings, families are at the core of the process of renewal in which they are engaged. These witnesses compared their present experiences of family life – of the all-too-common threats of violence and experiences of family breakdown – with the stories, passed down to them in the oral tradition, of a different order that prevailed in previous generations. The first part of this chapter begins with some brief sketches of what life used to be like as told in these stories.

In the following section, "Our Children Are Our Future", we explore the impact of residential schools, the relatively recent history of interventions by child welfare authorities, and current efforts to create children's services that are supportive of Aboriginal family life.

Many Aboriginal people consider family violence so pervasive a problem that it is preventing nations and communities from achieving their political and economic goals. Some presenters maintained that community healing from the scourge of internal violence is a prerequisite for self-government. All Aboriginal people would agree that the goals of re-establishing norms of mutual respect and caring for injured spirits must be pursued in concert with that of self-government. Further on in this chapter, we explore avenues to address family violence.

The authority of Aboriginal nations and their communities to exercise jurisdiction is central to specific strategies for protecting children, restoring balance in relations between men and women in families, and establishing ethical standards of respect for vulnerable persons. In the final part of this chapter, we consider aspects of family law that might reasonably fall within the jurisdiction of Aboriginal nations under self-government, the need to harmonize Aboriginal law making with provincial authority in particular, and the internal consultations necessary to the process of framing Aboriginal laws affecting the family.

We conclude the chapter with some observations about the role of public policy in regulating family life, an area considered in Canadian law and policy, as well as by many Aboriginal people, to be a private domain and one in which government intervention should be limited.

1. THE CENTRALITY OF
FAMILY IN ABORIGINAL LIFE

1.1 Views from our Hearings

Two themes stand out in presentations by Aboriginal people at our public hearings: the overwhelming concern for the well-being of children, and the belief that families are at the crux of personal and community healing.

Aboriginal interveners described in vivid terms their hopes for their children: that education would open opportunities they had never enjoyed; that children would learn their Aboriginal languages and histories; that they would be safe from violence; that they would not have to endure racist insults; that they would gain control over their lives and life conditions; and that they would be able to live with dignity as Aboriginal people in the land of their ancestors.

Detailed presentations on the Aboriginal family were more likely to focus on evidence of distress and breakdown, except when the revitalization of culture and the renewal of community were at issue. Then, family appeared repeatedly as part of a formula for transforming reality, where individual, family, and community are the three strands that, when woven together, will strengthen cultures and restore Aboriginal people to their former dignity. We saw that sometimes individuals undergo healing and strengthen families, while sometimes families nurture healthier individuals, but families consistently occupied the central position between individual and community. We heard that land reform, self-government and social institutions that deal fairly are all important, but it was the vision of restoring the vitality of individuals, families and communities *in concert* that mobilizes the energy of the vast majority of Aboriginal people who spoke to us. The following excerpts from our hearings illustrate this.

> The family is the foundation of Inuit culture, society and economy. All our social and economic structures, customary laws, traditions and actions have tried to recognize and affirm the strength of the family unit....Only positive constructive action by community governments and families and individuals can help recover our vision and zest for life.
>
> Henoch Obed
> Labrador Inuit Alcohol and Drug Abuse Program
> Nain, Newfoundland and Labrador, 30 November 1992

> We believe that the Creator has entrusted us with the sacred responsibility to raise our families...for we realize healthy families are the foundation of strong and healthy communities. The future of our communities lies with our children, who need to be nurtured within their families and communities.
>
> Charles Morris
> Executive Director, Tikinagan Child and Family Services
> Sioux Lookout, Ontario, 1 December 1992

1.2 Family Life in Various Traditions

To Aboriginal people, family signifies the biological unit of parents and children living together in a household. But it also has a much broader meaning. Family also encompasses an extended network of grandparents, aunts, uncles and cousins. In many First Nations communities, members of the same clan are considered family, linked through kinship ties that may not be clearly traceable, but stretch back to a common ancestor in mythical time.

Under the rules of clan membership, individuals are required to marry outside the clan to which they belong. Over generations, this resulted in every family in a community being related by descent or marriage to every other family in the community. Indeed, in rural communities whose membership has remained stable over time, family and community represent the same network of persons.

The layers of relationship built up over generations are described in a study of traditional life among the Caribou Inuit who live in the area west of James Bay.

> According to Caribou Inuit belief, the best marriages were those of first cousins, and the very best arrangement of all was a brother-sister exchange (*akigiik*) between two sets of cousins; thus a brother and sister of one family would marry a sister and brother of another, the two sibling pairs being cousins to begin with. When a cousin marriage occurred, people who started life as siblings, cousins, nieces, and nephews, suddenly would become spouses and in-laws of various kinds as well, thus building one layer of kin relations upon another.[2]

The practice of marriage between cousins, with restrictions against marriage within the same clan, has been found in other Aboriginal societies as well.[3] The problems of intermarriage with close kin were evidently known historically to Aboriginal people. Elders report that raids on neighbouring nations to steal wives, as well as large seasonal gatherings where marriages of persons from different communities were contracted, were methods used to broaden the gene pool of small communities.

Aside from descent and marriage, Aboriginal people became kin or like kin in other ways as well. For example, adoption was a common practice in most communities. Some nations, such as the Iroquois, adopted captives taken in war, giving family names and full membership privileges to these persons, who replaced a member lost to war or misfortune. It is still common practice in many communities for parents to give a child to another family in the community. In some cases, a fertile couple would agree to have one of their children adopted at birth by a childless couple; in so doing the two families would contract a special bond with each other for life. As well, many traditionalists, having retained their knowledge of Aboriginal language, bush skills and medicine practices, consider it a privilege to have been reared by grandparents within these customary adoption arrangements.

Other forms of bonding within a community included hunting partnerships whereby kin groups or friends would share hunting territories to reduce the impact of the harvest on the land. The entire group would use the territory of one part of the partnership one year, then shift to another partner's territory the following year. These partnerships also often entailed certain obligations to distribute meat from the hunt.

The effect of these diverse, overlapping bonds was to create a dense network of relationships within which sharing and obligations of mutual aid ensured that an effective safety net was in place. As Ernest Burch observed regarding the Caribou Inuit:

> A Caribou Inuit society was entirely lacking in politically, economically, or other specialized institutions, such as governments, businesses, churches or schools. Almost all of the functions required to sustain life were performed within the extended family context. Indeed, to a degree that most Canadians could scarcely comprehend, the life of a Caribou [Inuk] revolved around the family – from the moment a person was born until the time one died.[4]

As is the case in contemporary society in Canada, among Aboriginal peoples traditionally it has been the responsibility of the family to nurture children and introduce them to their responsibilities as members of society. However, the extended family continued to play a significant role throughout the lives of its members. When a young man went out on the hill to seek a vision of who he was to be and what gifts were uniquely his, it was not because he was preparing to go out into the world and seek his fortune. Rather, he would come back to the camp or the village to obtain advice from his uncles or his grandfather on the meaning of his experience, and his 'medicine', or personal power, was to be exercised in the service of family and community.

A clear division of labour along sex lines prevailed in most Aboriginal societies. For example, among the Anishnabe (Ojibwa),

> ...there was a clear distinction made between male and female roles, and public recognition went almost exclusively to the activities of men. The exploits of the hunter, warrior and shaman were celebrated in stories told in the lodge. The legends recording encounters with the supernaturals deal with the affairs of men. The role of women was to send men on their journeys with proper ceremony, to welcome them back with appropriate mourning or rejoicing, to hear and applaud the accounts of their achievements.
>
> Ojibwa women were more, however, than passive complements to the life of their men. They were essential economic partners in the annual cycle of work. They were needed to perform the normal domestic chores of cooking, sewing and child care, but their skills were also essential to weave the fish nets and paddle the canoe during the duck hunt, to construct protective fur robes and roof the birchbark wigwam, to tan the hides and harvest the rice and maple sap.[5]

Métis families similarly divided responsibilities between men and women as they ranged on extended hunting expeditions from permanent settlements, such as Red River. A woman from a Montana Métis settlement, who lived a mobile lifestyle with a group that migrated from Manitoba to Montana following the buffalo, recalled camp life in the early part of the twentieth century:

> Our men did all the hunting, and we women did all the tanning of the buffalo hides, jerky meat making, pemmican and moccasins. For other supplies, we generally had some trader with us...who always had a supply of tea, sugar, tobacco and so on.[6]

In many Aboriginal nations, women could become warriors, hunters, healers or bearers of chiefly names and titles. But their contribution to the well-being of the community was typically through responsibilities specific to women, including marriage and child rearing. The fact that women did so-called women's work did not necessarily mean that they had minor influence or low status.

Thelma Chalifoux, a Métis woman of senior years who has been honoured for her community service, spoke at our hearings about her experience in a Métis extended family:

> I would like to make a couple of little comments here on the role of women.
>
> I was not a product of the Mission school. I was a product of a very strong Métis extended family that lived between the City of Calgary and the Sarcee Reserve.
>
> I went to a public school and was discriminated against there because we were dirty halfbreeds. But the role of women, as I mentioned yesterday, was to take care of the elderly people in our community. We each had a role.
>
> My mother's role was equal to my father's. My mother's role, my aunt's role and my grandmother's roles were that they looked after the whole family, the children, the garden, the berry picking, the food, because the men were away working most of the time. So they had total control and roles.
>
> The man's role in the family was to make the living and bring home the money. When times were hard, everybody stuck together. When my grandmother or my aunts were out of food, everybody joined together and helped them out. We were a very, very proud extended family. There was relief in those days, but we never took it because that was just gifts and we weren't about to take it.
>
> The role of the woman...was an equal role....The women's role within the Elders, my grandmother's role and my aunt's roles we were almost like hidden leaders, as we used to learn in community development days.

Everybody that needed advice went to my mother, went to my aunts, went to my grandmother. Even the men, when they went to the meetings and organizing, they never went before we always had a meeting and a gathering of the total family unit, the total community unit, and the women told the men what to say. It was a consensus of the total family unit.

When I went into community development and went into northern Alberta, I was amazed. It was like another total world, the way the women were treated; it was normal to be beaten every Saturday night. It was normal to have sexual abuse from young children to older children. And when we looked at it and we studied it, it was the demise of the Native culture that caused that. That never happened before.

There was no alcoholism in our community. There was no sexual abuse. I can remember old George _____ hit his wife and it was my dad and my uncles and the men in the community that went after him, and he never touched his wife again. It was a justice system that was fair and hard, but it was a good justice system in those days.

And when I went up North and I saw women, for survival, had to dress like men, it was a sad, sad state of affairs....The demise of the Métis and the Indian cultures, a lot of it is the result. Alcoholism and sexual abuse and physical abuse are only symptoms of a much larger problem.

Senator Thelma Chalifoux
Metis Nation of Alberta
Winnipeg, Manitoba, 22 April 1992

Senator Chalifoux's comments point to another feature of Aboriginal families that prevailed even in urbanized settings until recent times: families were the seat of both economic and political activities.

In Thelma Chalifoux's generation, the pursuit of the buffalo had given way to waged employment. Métis people continued to be mobile, but the maintenance of community life then fell to the women.[7] Sharing within the extended family helped ease the effects of economic ups and downs. Women were the decision makers and practical nurses, and they were secure in their skills and knowledge. Decisions in organizations, presumably political, were reached by consensus within the family.

Clearly, Métis culture in the framework of a strong extended family was a source of life skills and confidence for Senator Chalifoux. Many other presentations in the transcripts of our hearings document the vitality of Aboriginal families and their effectiveness in fostering a strong sense of identity and extraordinary resourcefulness in individuals, particularly those who are now elders (see especially Volume 4, Chapter 3).

In Volumes 1 and 2, we described how, in traditional Aboriginal societies, the family was responsible for passing on the skills necessary for the varied round of economic activities, in which each member was expected to fulfil a specific role with competence and self-discipline (see Volume 1, Chapter 15, and the introductory sections of Volume 2, Chapter 5). People were expected to know what was required of them, as failure to learn and practise the lessons of survival could bring dire consequences.

Paulus Maggo, an Inuit hunter from Labrador who shared his life history as part of a research project conducted for the Commission, gave a terse commentary on hunters who neglected the basic necessity to apply knowledge specific to a situation. In one case, Maggo was part of a search party looking for two hunters who failed to return to camp; in another case, he described how the wrong choice of footwear contributed to a hunter's death:

> We found that they had fallen through the ice and gone into the water....Where they fell through the ice was the kind of hazard my father used to tell me about. A thin layer of frozen ice, with water below but not touching it, creates an air pocket between the ice and the water beneath it. This is called a Kauk and it can form at inlets and outlets of any lake, large or small. It's visible if you know what to look for. They had gone straight over it when they could have avoided the dangerous spot by going around it....
>
> It was sad to hear that one of them froze to death but thankfully the other one lived. S. also froze to death when he was lost in the country after having been separated from his hunting party....It was only after he reached the treeline and was travelling along the brook that he froze his feet. It was said that he would have been fine if he was wearing sealskin boots because apparently he was wearing caribou skin moccasins with cotton leggings. He got his feet wet somewhere along the brook when he walked over some freshly fallen snow which covered shallow water underneath. By the time he realized this it was too late to turn back. He got wet and froze to death.[8]

Women's knowledge and proficiency also made essential contributions to survival. As Martha Flaherty explained:

> If a woman was a sloppy sewer, her husband might freeze; a man who was a poor hunter would have a hungry family. Everyone in the camp worked hard and everyone had a specific role based on their age, gender and capabilities.

Martha Flaherty
President, Pauktuutit
Ottawa, Ontario, 2 November 1993

Among the historical Métis people, entire families participated in buffalo hunting expeditions. As there were large numbers of participants to organize, some of the activities within family units were supplemented by a quasi-military organization in the camp as a whole. Alexander Ross, in an 1856 account, described the discipline enforced during a buffalo hunt involving 1,210 Red River carts and 1,630 men, women, boys and girls. The movement of the camp was under the direction of 10 captains, among whom a senior was named. Under the captains were 10 soldiers and 10 guides, the latter taking turns bearing the flag used to signal directions to move or to stop the entourage. While the flag was up, the guide was chief of the expedition and in command of everyone. The moment the flag was lowered, the captains and soldiers were on duty. They policed violations of the camp rules, for example, "No party to fork off, lag behind, or go before without permission....No person or party to run buffalo before the general order".[9] As with the more informal rules governing the Inuit hunting party, these injunctions ensured success in the hunt as well as the survival of the group.

As discussed at some length in Volume 2, Chapter 3 on traditions of governance, families and clans were also the principal avenue for political representation in Aboriginal societies. The decision-making forum might be a circle of elders assigning hunting grounds, a formal chiefs' council to decide on the nation's business, or a potlatch to formalize succession to a title and accord territorial rights.

The terms 'institution' and 'social institution' are used throughout this chapter to refer to the social functions of the family. An institution is a social structure that reflects the values of a society and is recognized as the appropriate agency for fulfilling certain purposes within the collective. Institutions such as the family, the education system, and the police force socialize or influence members of the group to conform to group values. The family as a social institution fulfils in some measure all the various roles of social institutions: it performs a mediating or bridging function, helps the individual understand the world and respond appropriately to society's expectations, and helps society recognize and make a place for the individual.

From the earlier discussion in this chapter, it is evident that the family has fulfilled many functions. It has been co-extensive with the community in many cases, it has provided protection and security for individuals, and it has been the principal avenue for participation in the social, economic and political life of the nation and the local community. In short, the family can be said to be an all-purpose social institution.

1.3 The Family as a Mediating Institution

The family in Aboriginal societies stood between the individual and the larger society, playing an interpretive or mediating role. It helped individuals understand and respond to society's expectations, and it helped Aboriginal society engage individuals in constructive ways and discipline them should they venture on a course that conflicted with prevailing social values and expectations of behaviour.

In urban societies, individuals are involved in many activities not directly related to each other – working, studying, shopping, selling and playing. Numerous social institutions have been created, therefore, to play the mediating role that families continue to fulfil in many Aboriginal societies. In urban centres, families are also counted as mediating institutions, alongside neighbourhoods, schools, unions, churches and voluntary associations.[10]

If an Aboriginal person has been socialized in a situation where the family is the all-encompassing mediator between the individual and the social, economic and political spheres of the larger society, and that family is subsequently lost or disrupted, then the individual has lost not just one support, but also the principal agency that helps him or her make sense of the world. In effect, the person is set adrift. Such individuals can join a church or a union or a club, as many city dwellers do to deal with isolation. But since a process of deep communication is involved, the language of these formal groups may not satisfy individuals' need to understand what is expected in a new situation and may do little to help them interpret who they are and what they have to offer in an unfamiliar environment.

Aboriginal families have undergone all the stresses that any hunter-gatherer or agricultural institution undergoes as it is plunged into an urbanized, specialized and industrial or post-industrial world. There are huge demands on its adaptability. In addition, Aboriginal families have been subjected to disruption and loss at the instigation of the Canadian state.

Several experiences of massive loss have disrupted the Aboriginal family and resulted in identity problems and difficulties in functioning. First is the historical experience of residential schooling in which children, some as young as six, were removed from their families for 10 months of the year or even years at a stretch. They were prevented from speaking Aboriginal languages and taught to reject their 'savage' ways (see Volume 1, Chapter 10 on residential schools, in particular the discussion concerning the vision and policies of residential school education). They lived without intimate contact with adults whom they could trust to make sense of their environment, trapped in a world with other equally confused and deprived children. In their testimony, former residents of these schools stated that their development had been arrested by the experience and it would take years for them to complete their maturation, if they succeeded at all in growing into socially and emotionally mature adults.[11]

A second experience of loss involves children whose parents have relinquished their responsibility to interpret the world for their children. In a study of education among the James Bay Cree, for example, John Murdoch describes a place referred to as "dress-up creek". It was there that the Cree used to stop to remove their bush clothing and get dressed in European clothes before proceeding to the trading post. Murdoch observes that "While a well-dressed Cree might influence a better bargain in trade, the habit of 'dressing up' was also a social high point of the year." He goes on to suggest, from the vantage point of many years of experience living in the James Bay Cree community and working in the education system, that schools are still predominantly Euro-Canadian institutions in which Cree competence is undervalued:

> Consequently, success at school for Cree children has required them to assume or 'dress-up' in behaviours and attitudes, many of which are not part of Cree competence....The children have generally been urged by their parents to 'act properly' and 'try hard', often in fashions not seen as proper or normal at home.[12]

Children in this situation have the world interpreted to them by two institutions, school and family, that may well present contradictory messages. The younger children are when confronted with such contradictions, the less likely they are to succeed in sorting out the confusion or to gain the appropriate life skills required to survive in a complex world.

The third situation in which children suffer from identity confusion and impairment of learning is when they are reared by parents who are insecure in who they are, what their responsibilities are, and how they should fulfil them. Their lack of confidence and life skills may stem from their own deprivation in residential schools. It may be the result of having relocated to an unfamiliar environment where nothing the parent knows is useful, or it may be the result of repeated experiences of failure in a colonial school environment where the demands communicated in a foreign language made no sense to them. This situation, in which parents had difficulty fulfilling their responsibilities, brought thousands of Aboriginal children into foster care and adoption in non-Aboriginal agencies in the past two generations.

Thus arises a fourth situation generating stress on people's personal and family lives. Foster placement outside the Aboriginal community has compounded the identity confusion of children, while their physical characteristics ensure that they will be perceived as 'Indians'. If separation from families and communities occurs after several years of cultural patterning have taken place, the adjustment they are required to make is all the more traumatic. If they are removed while very young, they never learn how to behave and respond in an Aboriginal manner. Yet if their appearance marks them as Aboriginal in a society that makes much of racial difference, the social expectation that they should be Aboriginal would present them with a constant dilemma. Individuals whose childhood socialization was disrupted by foster home placement outside their culture face enormous challenges in assuming nurturing roles as adults.

Evidence of the extent of the damage done to the development of children removed from dysfunctional families is contained in reports such as those we heard from inmates at the correctional facility at Prince Albert, Saskatchewan, where it was reported that 48 per cent of the inmate population was Aboriginal at the time of our visit.

> A couple of years ago, the Prince Albert Native Awareness Group took a little survey amongst the Aboriginal prisoners here and we found that over 95 per cent of our people came from either a group home or a foster home. Of course, the survey was by no means scientific. It was based on common sense. We just asked: Were you ever in a group home or in a foster home?
>
> Ken Noskiye
> Prince Albert, Saskatchewan
> 27 May 1992

A final situation resulting in stress on family life is the migration out of close-knit communities where individuals have experienced social support from a network of kin. Migration to urban centres gained momentum following the Second World War. The first generation of migrants maintained close ties with their communities of origin, being described in some studies as "commuters".[13]

There is some statistical evidence that migration in search of education, employment and an improved standard of living has had some success, since the educational and economic status of urban Aboriginal people tends to be higher than that of persons who continue to live in reserve and northern settings. However, our research indicates that while many of these people are intent on retaining their Aboriginal culture and identity, they find few institutional supports to sustain their identity and many impediments to building a sense of community. (Aboriginal cultural identity in urban settings is discussed in Volume 4, Chapter 7.) They experience considerable personal alienation and family stress in settings where they encounter the same expectations as immigrants do – that they should adapt themselves in a one-way process of integration into a predominantly secular, francophone or anglophone, European-based institutional culture.

If disruption of the family and its capacity to mediate between individuals and their world invariably stunted individuals' development and destroyed their capacity to regulate their own behaviour, there would be few healthy Aboriginal people alive today. However, there is plenty of evidence that the extended family has provided a safety net for many.

> I was a victim of a certain amount of abuse within my original home...I don't feel that I'm unique in terms of those abuses. My home was a battleground because of alcoholism. And with that I've carried on that search and questions that I had and went to my elders in my community and I asked my elders different questions as to why my family was different.
>
> My elders became my parents. They were the ones who raised me, because my parents were not parents for me as a young girl.

In being raised with elderly people around you and them being your parents I realized that I was taught the equality of human beings within our nation.

We were equal and I was given a lot of rights at a very young age. I was given a lot of independence and that independence has carried me through.

> Karen Pine-Cheechoo
> Moose Factory, Ontario
> 9 June 1992

The concept of the family as a mediating institution helps to clarify why people become less vulnerable to disruptions of personal development as they mature and why elders are able to apply their life skills to complex intercultural situations. If the mediating structure functions well, children feel secure in the world. They gain confidence that they are knowledgeable and capable, and they are secure in taking risks to learn more. As they mature, children learn the codes for interpreting the world at large, and their dependence on the family to do the mediating work for them gradually decreases. Finally, they are able to mediate meaning for themselves.

Unlike children who have never internalized the codes and skills to interpret the world on their own terms, individuals with a secure identity and good problem-solving skills are open to new experiences. They can interact in relationships with strangers without being thrown off balance. These qualities of being in balance, of relating to all of life as a learning adventure, of accepting all sorts and conditions of people as they present themselves, make the character of elders attractive to Aboriginal and non-Aboriginal people alike. One such person is Merle Beedie, an elder who spoke to the Commission at Orillia:

> One elder, an Anishnawbe-kwe [Ojibwa woman], said, "The next 500 years are for Native people." That is so encouraging. And they say, "Promote talking circles, teaching circles, healing circles to the Native and the non-Native communities. Promote healing lodges in our territories, develop all forms of teaching materials for the schools, TV programs, plays for the theatres, movies, et cetera, et cetera. Educate all the community about our history, what our history was and is. Invite non-Native people to add to this history because some non-Native people out there know about our history and the part they played in this and they have to match roles, and we did survive together. Get our women into politics of our communities and nations and support women's groups whenever and wherever in our communities because they are our life givers, they are our peace keepers, they are our faith keepers."

> Elder Merle Assance Beedie
> Barrie and Area Native Advisory Circle
> Orillia, Ontario, 13 May 1993

Aboriginal families have been at the centre of a historical struggle between colonial governments on one hand, which set out deliberately to eradicate the culture, language and world view of the First Nations, Métis and Inuit children over whom they assumed control, and Aboriginal parents on the other hand, who believe wholeheartedly that they have a sacred responsibility to maintain balance in the world for their children and others not yet born. Many Aboriginal adults have lived through this struggle and come out as whole human beings. Others, however, are serving time in a dead end from which they see no way out.

We quote here two young men who were inmates at the Prince Albert correctional institution at the time of our visit. Victims of family breakdown and multiple foster home placements, they did not plead for themselves, but rather for the children who can and must be kept from walking the path they have walked.

> As I heard about this Commission, what was on my heart was the kids....I wondered what I might say to you people today. I wrote some things out here. I said, I don't know the number of people in this institution, but I know it's high, who have gone through that road, that pattern through child welfare....I hear this voice and I hear them pleading for someone to come and help. As we speak, there are children all across this country who need to come home to their people. So I said a prayer that this Commission would help them.
>
> Pat McCormick
> Prince Albert, Saskatchewan
> 27 May 1992

> What I would like the Commission to do, if possible, is try to have the Native children who are very young to live with their own parents, instead of putting them in a place where there are white people who will molest them. I grew up hating white people because of this and I still kind of resent them, but I've been thinking about this a lot and I wanted to get it out. I hope what I say will be heard a bit....
>
> I hope the people will start paying more attention to the Native children and help them by making sure that they stay with their own families, their own blood families, because when they are separated from their families they just grow up and they end up in places like this. Thanks for listening.
>
> Arthur Darren Durocher
> Prince Albert, Saskatchewan
> 27 May 1992

Healing the wounds of Aboriginal families is absolutely essential to achieving the rest of the Aboriginal agenda of self-reliance and self-determination. The family is the mediating structure, the bridge between the private world of the vulnerable child and the unfamiliar, too often hostile world of non-Aboriginal society.

In the next sections of this chapter we take the reader through the harsh realities of family dysfunction, evident in the high rate of children in care outside their biological families and in widespread violence. We examine the limitations and failures of interventions by agencies outside the Aboriginal community and the responses currently gaining ground in Aboriginal communities.

2. Our Children Are Our Future

Today we are in a time of healing for our children, our families, our communities and Mother Earth.

Judy Gingell
Teslin, Yukon
27 May 1992

We believe our children are our future, the leadership of tomorrow. If you believe in that, then you have to believe also that you must equip your future with the best possible tools to lead your community and lead your nation into the twenty-first century.

Grand Chief Joe Miskokomon
Union of Ontario Indians
Toronto, Ontario, 26 June 1992

2.1 The Special Place of Children in Aboriginal Cultures

Children hold a special place in Aboriginal cultures. According to tradition, they are gifts from the spirit world and have to be treated very gently lest they become disillusioned with this world and return to a more congenial place. They must be protected from harm because there are spirits that would wish to entice them back to that other realm. They bring a purity of vision to the world that can teach their elders. They carry within them the gifts that manifest themselves as they become teachers, mothers, hunters, councillors, artisans and visionaries. They renew the strength of the family, clan and village and make the elders young again with their joyful presence.

Failure to care for these gifts bestowed on the family, and to protect children from the betrayal of others, is perhaps the greatest shame that can befall an Aboriginal family. It is a shame that countless Aboriginal families have experienced, some of them repeatedly over generations. Here we examine the genesis of that shame, the efforts to erase it, and the role of public policy in restoring the trust of children, parents and grandparents in their future.

2.2 Historical Overview

Our children are our future, a maxim of many Aboriginal nations, underscores the great value attached to children. The maxim was adopted as the title of a film that etched in unforgettable images the devastation wrought upon the lives of Aboriginal children by the workings of the child welfare system, a social institution created expressly to protect 'the best interests of the child'.[14] The film has three story lines. We see the numbed consciousness and aimless violence of a young man who, adopted as a child into a non-Aboriginal family, has lost his way since becoming a teenager. We observe the efforts of an Aboriginal counselling service to help a troubled mother communicate with a court determined to protect her children from neglect. And we see a sign of hope for the future as a young child is restored to health through nurturing by his First Nations foster family, which introduces him to the ceremonial traditions of his people.

The film was one in a series of actions, beginning in the 1980s, aimed at drawing attention to the misdirected and destructive effects of government-sponsored interventions in Aboriginal family life. Another was the assertion of control over child welfare by the Spallumcheen First Nation Community near Vernon, British Columbia. Chief Wayne Christian, who himself had been in foster care, was moved to action following the suicide of his brother, who had tried unsuccessfully to become re-integrated into the community after a period in foster care. Chief Christian led his community in passing a child welfare by-law in 1980 under the authority of the *Indian Act*. The federal government was persuaded to refrain from overturning it, and the government of British Columbia agreed to co-operate, under pressure from the Aboriginal community. Spallumcheen remains the only First Nation community to have achieved this degree of autonomy in child welfare administration.[15]

The 1983 publication of *Native Children and the Child Welfare System*, prepared for the Canadian Council on Social Development by Patrick Johnston, sent shock waves through child welfare and government systems, particularly those involved in First Nations child welfare.[16] It presented documentary evidence that First Nations people had good grounds for protesting against the massive involvement of child welfare agencies in removing children from their families and communities.

Johnston adopted the phrase 'Sixties Scoop' to describe a phenomenon that emerged in the years preceding his study. For example, he reported on the significant increase in the percentage of Aboriginal children in care in the province of British Columbia:

> In 1955 there were 3,433 children in the care of B.C.'s child welfare branch. Of that number, it was estimated that 29 children, or less than 1 per cent of the total, were of Indian ancestry. By 1964, however, 1,446 children in care in B.C. were of Indian extraction. That

number represented 34.2 per cent of all children in care. Within ten years, in other words, the representation of Native children in B.C.'s child welfare system had jumped from almost nil to a third. It was a pattern being repeated in other parts of Canada as well.[17]

The term 'in care' refers to children in the care of child welfare agencies for the purpose of protecting them from neglect or abuse. Care may be provided in foster homes, adoption placements, or in group or institutional settings. Johnston gathered data from the federal department of Indian affairs and from provincial and territorial ministries responsible for social services. Despite some problems of comparability of data, his analysis showed consistent over-representation of Aboriginal children in the child welfare system across the country, the percentage of children in the care of the state being consistently higher than the percentage of Aboriginal children in the total population. Comparisons were done using two criteria:

- the proportion of Aboriginal children in care was compared to the proportion of Aboriginal children in the total child population; and
- the number of children in the care of the state, as a percentage of all Aboriginal children, was compared to the total number of children in care as a percentage of the total child population of Canada.

Within the general picture of over-representation there were wide regional variations. In 1981-82 the percentage of Aboriginal children in care, as a percentage of all children in care in various provinces ranged from a low of 2.6 per cent in Quebec to a high of 63 per cent in Saskatchewan.[18] Child-in-care rates in the Maritime provinces were in the lower range: New Brunswick, 3.9 per cent; Nova Scotia, 4.3 per cent; and Prince Edward Island, 10.7 per cent. An estimate of the number of Aboriginal children in care in Newfoundland and Labrador placed the rate at around 8 per cent. Ontario's overall rate of 7.7 per cent masked the fact that in northern Ontario child welfare agencies the proportion of Aboriginal children in care was extremely high – an estimated 85 per cent in the Kenora-Patricia agency, for example. Intermediate ranges were found in other western provinces: Manitoba, 32 per cent; Alberta, 41 per cent (including delinquent children on probation and children with disabilities receiving special services); and British Columbia, 36.7 per cent. The Yukon, with 61 per cent, still had over-representation of Aboriginal children despite the higher proportion of Aboriginal children in the general population.[19] The Northwest Territories, with First Nations, Métis and Inuit children making up 45 per cent of children in care, was the only jurisdiction where the representation of Aboriginal children was not disproportionate.

When the number of Aboriginal children in care is considered as a proportion of all Aboriginal children, the percentage of children in care ranged from a low of 1.8 per cent in the Northwest Territories to a high of 5.9 per cent in British Columbia.[20] Across Canada, on average, 4.6 per cent of Aboriginal children were in agency care in 1980-81, compared to just under 1 per cent of the general Canadian child population.[21]

Information on where children in care were placed, whether in Aboriginal homes or non-Aboriginal foster and adoption homes, was not available for all provinces. In most provinces, however, placements in non-Aboriginal homes typically ranged from 70 per cent to 90 per cent, with the exception of Quebec, where Cree and Inuit child placements, reported separately, were almost entirely in Aboriginal homes, usually in the children's home communities. Approximately half the other Aboriginal children in care in Quebec were placed in non-Aboriginal homes.

Increased activity on the part of child welfare agencies corresponded with the federal government's decision to expand its role in funding social welfare services and phase out residential schools, which in the 1960s had increasingly assumed the role of caring for children in 'social need'.[22]

It was already accepted at the time in the professional community that apprehension should be strictly a last resort in protecting children from harm and that Aboriginal children were particularly vulnerable to its harmful effects.[23] Johnston explains:

> Many experts in the child welfare field are coming to believe that the removal of any child from his/her parents is inherently damaging, in and of itself....The effects of apprehension on an individual Native child will often be much more traumatic than for his non-Native counterpart. Frequently, when the Native child is taken from his parents, he is also removed from a tightly knit community of extended family members and neighbours, who may have provided some support. In addition, he is removed from a unique, distinctive and familiar culture. The Native child is placed in a position of triple jeopardy.[24]

Later analysts echoed Johnston's criticism that the interventions of social agencies reflected colonial attitudes and attempts to assimilate Aboriginal children and continue the work begun by residential schools.[25] Hudson and McKenzie argued that the child welfare system devalued Aboriginal culture by not recognizing and using traditional Aboriginal systems of child protection, making judgements about child care based on dominant Canadian norms, and persistently using non-Aboriginal foster and adoption placements.[26]

In a research report prepared for this Commission, Joyce Timpson, a social worker with extensive experience in northwestern Ontario, suggests that the colonialist and assimilationist explanation of the 'Sixties Scoop' may underplay the reality that Aboriginal families were dealing with the severe disruption caused by social, economic and cultural changes. In many communities they were also coping with the stress of relocation. Timpson presents strong evidence suggesting that the federal government's willingness to pay child-in-care costs,

An Instance of "a System Gone Awry"

When Cameron Kerley was eight years old he witnessed his father being beaten to death. Cameron and three sisters were apprehended by the Children's Aid Society and placed in foster homes. His mother died two years later as a result of heavy drinking.

Cameron was placed for adoption with Dick Kerley, a bachelor who had previously adopted another Aboriginal boy. Cameron soon began to display social problems, skipping school and getting into trouble with the law.

When he was 19 years of age he murdered his adopted father with a baseball bat. Cameron pleaded guilty to second degree murder and was sentenced to life in prison with no eligibility for parole for 15 years. After being sentenced, Cameron alleged that he had been sexually abused by his adoptive father since shortly after he was placed.

Cameron's appeal for a reduced sentence in January 1985 was denied, but his request to be returned to Manitoba to serve his sentence was granted with the consent of the Canadian government.

Source: Review Committee on Indian and Metis Adoptions and Placements, *No Quiet Place: Final Report to the Honourable Muriel Smith, Minister of Community Services* (Winnipeg: Manitoba Community Services, 1985), p. 246.

along with federal and provincial governments' resistance to supporting preventive services, family counselling or rehabilitation, were major factors in making apprehension and permanent removal of children the treatment applied most often in problem situations.[27] (For a discussion of the extent and consequences of relocation of Aboriginal communities, see Volume 1, Chapter 10.)

Another milestone in the history of Aboriginal child welfare was the 1985 report of an inquiry by Justice Edwin C. Kimelman on adoptions and placements of First Nations and Métis children from Manitoba. The inquiry was prompted by protests from the Aboriginal community against placement of First Nations and Métis children in adoptive homes in the United States. Justice Kimelman found that the highly publicized case of Cameron Kerley (see box) was only one instance of a system gone awry.

At our hearings in Kenora, Josephine Sandy, who chairs Ojibway Tribal Family Services, explained what moved her and others to mobilize for change:

> Over the years, I watched the pain and suffering that resulted as non-Indian law came to control more and more of our lives and our traditional lands. I have watched my people struggle to survive in the face of this foreign law.

Nowhere has this pain been more difficult to experience than in the area of family life. I and all other Anishnabe people of my generation have seen the pain and humiliation created by non-Indian child welfare agencies in removing hundreds of children from our communities in the fifties, sixties and the seventies. My people were suffering immensely as we had our way of life in our lands suppressed by the white man's law.

This suffering was only made worse as we endured the heartbreak of having our families torn apart by non-Indian organizations created under this same white man's law.

People like myself vowed that we would do something about this. We had to take control of healing the wounds inflicted on us in this tragedy.

> Josephine Sandy
> Chair, Ojibway Tribal Family Services
> Kenora, Ontario, 28 October 1992

Justice Kimelman's report validated for the people of Manitoba and Canadians at large the pain and suffering being inflicted on First Nations and Métis families and children. To First Nations people, his report constituted an indictment of child welfare services:

The failures of the child welfare system have been made known many years after the fact in the statistics from correctional institutions, psychiatric hospitals, and as former wards of agencies became neglectful and abusive parents themselves....

In 1982, no one, except the Indian and the Métis people really believed the reality – that Native children were routinely being shipped to adoption homes in the United States and to other provinces in Canada. Every social worker, every administrator, and every agency or region viewed the situation from a narrow perspective and saw each individual case as an exception, as a case involving extenuating circumstances. No one fully comprehended that 25 per cent of all children placed for adoption were placed outside of Manitoba. No one fully comprehended that virtually all those children were of Native descent....

Children who entered the [child welfare] system were generally lost to family and community – or were returned with there having been little input to change the situation from which they were taken in the first place....

Every facet of the system examined by the Commission revealed evidence of a program rooted in antiquity and resistant to change.

An abysmal lack of sensitivity to children and families was revealed. Families approached agencies for help and found that what was described as being in the child's "best interest" resulted in their families being torn asunder and siblings separated. Social workers grappled with cultural patterns far different than their own with no preparation and no opportunities to gain understanding. It was expected that workers would get their training in the field.

The agencies complained of a lack of adequate resources, and central directorate staff complained of a lack of imaginative planning for children by agencies....

The funding mechanisms perpetuated existing service patterns and stifled, even prevented, innovative approaches. There was little statistical data and, what there was, was next to useless for program planning purposes. There was no follow-up on adoptions and thus no way to gather the data upon which any kind of evaluation of the adoption program could be based....

The appalling reality is that everyone involved believed they were doing their best and stood firm in their belief that the system was working well....The miracle is that there were not more children lost in this system run by so many well-intentioned people. The road to hell was paved with good intentions and the child welfare system was the paving contractor.[28]

2.3 Child Welfare Reform

Some things have changed as a result of efforts begun in the 1980s. Since 1981, when the first agreement was signed authorizing a First Nation agency to deliver child welfare services, responsibility for delivering child welfare services has been delegated progressively to agencies administered by First Nations and some Métis communities. Emphasis is being placed on supporting increased Aboriginal control of the development, design and delivery of child and family services. In 1990-91, DIAND funded 36 Aboriginal child and family agencies covering 212 bands. Also in 1990-91, a total of $1.5 million was allocated to First Nations, over a period of two years, for the development of Aboriginal child and family service standards.[29]

Most Aboriginal child care agencies have adopted placement protocols specifying the following placement priorities: first, with the extended family; second, with Aboriginal members of the community with the same cultural and linguistic identification; and third, other alternative Aboriginal caregivers. As a last resort, placement is considered with non-Aboriginal caregivers.[30] Some work has been done to develop culturally appropriate standards for selecting Aboriginal foster caregivers; however, as discussed later, it has been hampered by funding constraints and limited policy support for developmental work in new Aboriginal agencies.

The following summary illustrates the developments in child welfare in Aboriginal communities:

• Agencies established under the tripartite agreement with the Four Nations Confederacy of Manitoba, signed in 1982.
• Agencies authorized to administer child welfare, particularly in northern and northwestern Ontario under the 1984 *Child and Family Services Act.*
• Child welfare prevention services sponsored jointly by bands and the provincial government in southern Ontario.
• Agreements signed with single bands such as the Blackfoot at Gleichen, Alberta, and the Métis and Cree community of Sandy Bay, Saskatchewan, to provide services under provincial mandates.
• Regional Aboriginal services developed, including Mi'kmaq Family and Children's Service of Nova Scotia and Nuu-chah-nulth Community and Human Services in British Columbia.
• Child welfare and other human services, in regions where land claims agreements have been concluded, delivered through boards under Aboriginal control, such as Kativik Regional Social Services and Cree Regional Health and Social Services Board in Quebec.
• Social services in the Northwest Territories decentralized to increase community control.

Aboriginal child and family services have been established in metropolitan centres such as Toronto and Winnipeg. They report significant success in recruiting Aboriginal foster homes. For example, Native Child and Family Services of Toronto reported that 62 per cent of the agency's placements in 1993-94 were customary care arrangements, signifying voluntary involvement of parents and placement in Aboriginal homes.[31]

Alberta has the distinction of sponsoring the only Métis-specific child welfare agency yet established. Metis Child and Family Services of Edmonton provides foster care placements and emphasizes traditional values as a component of the assessment process in home studies to screen potential caregivers. According to information provided to Brad McKenzie, who conducted a research study for the Commission,

> An orientation training program and ongoing support meetings for foster parents are provided. As a private agency [Metis Child and Family Services] did not qualify for a 1994 increase of 5 per cent paid to foster parents providing service within the provincial system. Barriers to the recruitment and retention of Aboriginal foster care identified by this agency respondent included limited funding, an inadequate training program for foster parents, limitations in the number of potential families who are able to foster, and a failure on

the part of the social service bureaucracy to involve foster parents as meaningful partners in meeting the needs of children in their care.[32]

In the study McKenzie notes that such agencies, administered by Aboriginal people, have achieved considerable success in expanding the number of Aboriginal foster home providers, even though provincial agencies in diverse locations acknowledge difficulties in locating a sufficient number of homes.

Several provinces have moved to make their legislation more sensitive to Aboriginal identity in making plans for children. For example, Alberta specifies that an Aboriginal child must be informed of his or her status and that the chief and council of an Aboriginal child's community must be consulted before permanent wardship hearings.[33] Newfoundland's legislation specifies that "the child's cultural and religious heritage" must be considered in determining a child's best interests.[34] In the Northwest Territories, the objective of the 1994 *Aboriginal Custom Adoption Recognition Act* is "without changing aboriginal customary law, to set out a simple procedure by which a custom adoption may be respected and recognized".[35] The adoptive parent or parents simply provide identification papers along with a written statement from the interested parties that an adoption took place in accordance with Aboriginal custom. Once the custom adoption commissioner is satisfied that the information provided is complete and in order, a certificate of adoption is issued and the adoption is registered in appropriate vital statistics files. Records of the adoption are not sealed.[36] The Yukon provides that the child's "own cultural background" and "lifestyle in his home community" be considered in adoption cases.[37] Quebec's *Youth Protection Act* stipulates that "Every person having responsibilities towards a child under this Act, and every person called upon to make decisions with respect to a child under this Act shall, in their interventions, take into account the necessity...of opting for measures in respect of the child and the child's parents...which take into consideration...the characteristics of Native communities".[38]

Ontario has the most extensive provisions in relation to Aboriginal child welfare in its *Child and Family Services Act (1984)*. The act seeks to include both status Indian people and others of Aboriginal ancestry by using the term 'Native'. Special provisions for all children's aid societies serving Aboriginal communities recognize 'Indian' and 'Native' status as a 'best interests' category over and above the obligation to consider cultural background. The act devotes an entire section to Aboriginal child and family service agencies. It also recognizes customary care and permits these agencies to seek exemptions from the application of any part of the law.[39]

Alberta and Manitoba have created a child advocate office to provide impartial investigations into complaints concerning services rendered to children. About 20 years ago Quebec created a youth protection commission with a similar mandate. This commission was recently merged with Quebec's human rights commission to become the province's human rights and youth rights commission. Its mission is "to ensure...that the interests of children are protected, and that their rights recognized by the Quebec youth protection act are respected".[40]

In many jurisdictions, exceptions are permitted to culturally inappropriate requirements that might screen out Aboriginal people applying to foster or adopt Aboriginal children. Such exceptions may be explicit, as in Ontario's *Child and Family Services Act*; or implicit, as in the practice of agencies that encourage Aboriginal families to provide care for Aboriginal children.

Expenditures to improve the coverage and quality of Aboriginal-specific child welfare services have been increased substantially for services to registered Indians ordinarily resident on-reserve and Indian child-in-care costs charged back to the federal department of Indian affairs. In 1992-93 the department allocated $159.8 million to child and family services, representing 78 per cent of the welfare services budget, which also includes services to enable adults with functional limitations to maintain their independence. The welfare services budget increased from $38.7 million in 1981-82 to $204.8 million in 1992-93 – an annual increase of 16 per cent. Expenditures per child in care increased at an average annual rate of 17 per cent in the same period, rising from $6,754 in 1981-82 to $28,260 in 1991-92.[41]

Despite these welcome reforms, and modest successes in placing children in Aboriginal foster homes, which have stemmed the flow of Aboriginal children out of their communities and nations, it is evident that services to care for neglected and abused children are insufficient to repair the ills plaguing Aboriginal families.

In 1992-93, about 4 per cent of First Nations children living on-reserve were in agency care outside their own homes, a reduction from the highs of between 6 and 6.5 per cent in the 1970s.[42] During the same period, however, child welfare agencies serving the general population made an effort to keep children in their own homes, a move that reduced the general child-in-care rate to 0.63 per cent. The percentage of First Nations children in care is six times that of children from the general population in the care of public agencies. This disparity has increased since the 1970s, when First Nations children were placed in care at five-and-a-half times the rate of children in the general population.[43] As with most statistics on social services, only data on First Nations services provided directly or funded by the federal government are available. The extent of service to Métis people cannot be discerned from existing sources.

A November 1994 publication of Alberta's Commissioner of Services for Children states that "While only nine per cent of all children in Alberta are Aboriginal, nearly 50 per cent of the children in care are Aboriginal".[44] The terminology used would seem to imply that Métis and non-status Aboriginal children are included in the figures, despite the prevailing scarcity of data on the Métis population.

In a more localized study prepared for this Commission in 1994, an Aboriginal child and family service agency in southern Manitoba reported an on-reserve child population (0-18 years) of 2,238 and an in-care figure of 257 at 31 March 1994, which translates to an in-care rate of 11.5 per cent.[45]

Child welfare agencies are set up to protect the interests of children at risk of neglect or abuse. The continued high rates of children in care outside their homes indicate a crisis in Aboriginal family life. In the next section, we explore the sources of stress in family life and the role of child welfare agencies in alleviating distress.

2.4 Current Issues

In our hearings, the nature and intensity of concern about child welfare issues varied across the country. In northern Ontario and the western provinces, concern about Aboriginal control of child welfare services predominated. In the north, strong traditions of custom adoption have helped Inuit to keep their children in their communities. Some interveners expressed concern about the encroachment of more formalized procedures of child placement, which they see as interfering with customary placements. Others maintained that informal checks to protect the interests of children in custom adoptions are insufficient and that young mothers may feel pressured by family members to make inappropriate placements.[46] Clusters of youth suicide cause serious concern, and awareness of child sexual abuse is being brought into the open, particularly by the action of Inuit women.[47]

Presentations to the Commission and research conducted for us confirmed the reality that reforms to child welfare services have effected only modest improvements in the well-being of families, chiefly by maintaining the cultural, community and family ties of children in care. We heard reports that in some places Aboriginal people have overcome alcohol abuse and its effects in their communities and instituted more culturally appropriate services, only to find that in a more supportive environment new layers of pain and abuse are revealed.

In *Choosing Life*, the Commission's special report on suicide, we recorded the experience of Canim Lake, B.C., where the people uncovered the widespread experience of sexual abuse in residential schools and the repetitive cycle whereby the abused became abusers. We also reported the collective response of the Canim Lake community in confronting this new challenge.[48]

Joan Glode, executive director of Mi'kmaq Family and Children's Services, was quoted in a research report prepared for the Commission as saying that

The development of an agency is not a happy ending because it is neither happy nor an ending. In our fourth year of operation a flood of disclosures of family violence and child sexual abuse have begun to surface. Many of these happened years ago and were masked by misuse of alcohol and drugs, social and health problems and mental illness. New skills and knowledge are needed, but as a community we have learned that the process involves looking back to our values and traditions and outward to current therapy and practice.[49]

The catalogue of problems and the limitations of current services in resolving them, as revealed in our public hearings and research reports, reads eerily like that presented in Judge Kimelman's analysis in 1985.[50] Among the current issues explored later in this chapter are the following.

- Intergenerational effects. The consequences of past errors continue to be felt in successive generations of Aboriginal families.
- External control of services and inappropriate funding. Child welfare policy is set in provincial institutions and is based on a non-Aboriginal value system and world view.
- The need for community healing. Families are losing their young less frequently to distant non-Aboriginal foster homes and adoption, but they still suffer the effects of highly dysfunctional families and community turmoil.
- Inadequate follow-up and evaluation, as illustrated by the problem of repatriating children seeking to re-establish their Aboriginal identity.
- Marginal and insufficient urban services, despite the increase in the urban Aboriginal population.
- Systemic resistance to change.
- Crisis orientation. Resources are inadequate to go beyond crisis response.
- Inappropriate training of social work personnel.

Intergenerational effects

As Justice Kimelman did in 1985, presenters at our hearings linked current child welfare issues with the history of interventions by non-Aboriginal government in the affairs of Aboriginal families.

Most of our clients – probably 90 per cent of them – are, in fact, victims themselves of the child welfare system. Most of our clients are young, sole support mothers who very often were removed as children themselves. So we are dealing with perhaps the end product of the child welfare system that was apparent in the sixties scoop. Actually the sixties scoop lasted well into the '70s and we are seeing the reality of that on our case loads....We take the approach in our agency that it is time to break that cycle. The other interesting note is that while the mother may have been in foster care the grand-mother – I think we all know where she was. She was in residential school. So we are into a third generation.

Kenn Richard
Executive Director, Native Child
and Family Services of Toronto
Toronto, Ontario, 2 November 1992

The intent of the residential school policy was to erase Aboriginal identity by separating generations of children from their families, suppressing their Aboriginal languages, and re-socializing them according to the norms of non-Aboriginal society (see Volume 1, Chapter 10). The repercussions of the often brutal enforcement of measures to achieve assimilation are still being felt in the lives of former students:

I stayed in that residential school for 10 years. I hurt there. There was no love there. There was no caring there, nobody to hug you when you cried; all they did was slap you over: "Don't you cry! You're not supposed to cry". Whipped me when I talked to my younger brother. That's my brother, for God's sake. We were not supposed to talk to these people.

Jeannie Dick
Canim Lake, British Columbia
8 March 1993

I was one of the fortunate ones in the residential school, but the boy who slept next to me wasn't very fortunate. I saw him being sexually abused. As a result, he died violently. He couldn't handle it when he became of age.

Wilson Okeymaw
Hobbema, Alberta
10 June 1992

I have heard people who have said, "I left that residential school, and I have been like a ship without a rudder". I have heard people say, "I have left that place, and I left there just like a robot, with no feel-ings, with no emotions".

Elmer Courchene
Fort Alexander, Manitoba
29 October 1992

Chief Cinderina Williams of Spallumcheen recounted the events in her community leading to the take-over of child welfare. She writes:

With the absence of this caring and nurturing environment, [chil-dren] lost their identity, their feeling of self-worth, their self-esteem, their place within their own society and their whole reason for being. Some children harboured great resentment toward their parents, grandparents and their whole community for subjecting them to the horrors of the residential schools and found they could trust no one, not even themselves, for self-betrayal was common in order to survive. They had to cheat, lie and steal to avoid punishment, get food to eat and obtain special favours, or avoid hard labour.

Later when these children returned home, they were aliens. They did not speak their own language, so they could not communicate with anyone other than their own counterparts. Some looked down on their families because of their lack of English, their lifestyle, and some were just plain hostile. They had formed no bonds with their families, and some couldn't survive without the regimentation they had become so accustomed to....

Many, after years of rigid discipline, when released, ran amok, created havoc with their new-found freedom and would not listen to their parents, elders or anyone else in a position of authority. Perhaps the greatest tragedy of this background was the unemotional upbringing they had. Not being brought up in a loving, caring, sharing, nurturing environment, they did not have these skills as they are not inbred but learned through observation, participation and interaction.

Consequently, when these children became parents, and most did at an early age, they had no parenting skills. They did not have the capability to show affection. They sired and bred children but were unable to relate to them on any level. This is still evident today.[51]

The family dysfunction of today is a legacy of disrupted relationships in the past, but the effects are broader and more diffuse than can be traced in a direct cause-and-effect relationship. There are entire communities whose members are imbued with a sense of violation and powerlessness, the effect of multiple violations having reverberated throughout kin networks. The treatment of individuals is only part of the healing process that needs to take place. Bonds of trust and hope must be rebuilt within whole communities as well.

External control of services

As mentioned earlier in the chapter numerous child welfare services have been instigated by Aboriginal people. These are authorized under provincial or territorial legislation, even when they are funded by the Department of Indian Affairs and Northern Development (DIAND) and established through federal, provincial and Aboriginal tripartite agreements or as voluntary agencies.

Under the constitutional division of powers, jurisdiction over child welfare is provincial. Authority is delegated by provincial legislation to local agencies of the province or, in the case of Ontario and southern Manitoba, to private agencies chartered locally with boards of directors appointed by members of the local community.

The agencies have the power to apprehend children who are neglected or in danger of being neglected and to bring the matter before a family court, which can transfer guardianship or parental rights to the agency. Usually after two years of temporary care, if the parents are unable to provide for the child, the court grants an order transferring guardianship permanently to the agency. Agencies can also make voluntary arrangements to care for children with the consent of the parents. Agencies use foster homes that have been screened and approved. They may operate group homes for older children or children with relationship problems and foster homes for children with physical or developmental disabilities. They also use treatment facilities operated by health institutions or private organizations. Agencies have the authority to arrange adoption placement of children placed permanently in their care.

While children are in the care of the agency, per diem rates for maintenance are charged to the province, or in the case of registered Indians, to the federal government. Rates are set by the province or the local agency. These per diem fees usually constitute the bulk of an agency's budget and cover payments to foster parents, clothing and other expenses for children in care, a portion of agency workers' salaries, as well as operating costs. Per diem fees are paid directly in proportion to the days of child care provided and are not subject to an upper limit.

A much smaller portion of agency budgets is allocated to working with families to prevent apprehension, improving the conditions that lead to neglect so that children can return home, or planning adoptions. The budget for preventive and rehabilitative work with families is established with some degree of negotiation, but basically it is set at the discretion of the funder. Since more resources are available for child care, more effort goes into this portion of agency work.

The federal government historically has declined to introduce services (other than education) on Indian reserves in parallel with provincial institutions. The provinces have been reluctant to extend services to reserves principally because of the costs involved, but also because many First Nations have not welcomed provincial involvement, fearing that engaging in a relationship with the province might compromise their relationship with the federal government and their entitlements under treaties. A revision of the *Indian Act* in 1951 provided that all laws of general application in force in a province apply on-reserve unless they conflict with treaties or federal laws. This did nothing, however, to make the federal and provincial governments any less reluctant to work with Aboriginal governments in planning social services on reserves. The federal government has denied responsibility for services to Indians off-reserve, although post-secondary education assistance and non-insured health benefits have been available to some registered Indians off-reserve and Inuit living outside their traditional territory. Provincial governments historically maintained that funding of all services for Indian people, regardless of where they lived, was a federal responsibility. (For a discussion of the policy vacuum affecting urban Aboriginal services, see Volume 4, Chapter 7.)

A major review of government policy on First Nations, led by Harry Hawthorn and published in 1966, criticized both orders of government for their hands-off policy and argued that Indian people were eligible to receive services from both.[52] Federal-provincial dialogue on cost sharing of social welfare programs in general had been going on for several years. The federal government was now pushing for agreement on cost sharing of Indian welfare services. In 1965, it signed a welfare agreement with Ontario, which extended numerous Ontario social services, including child welfare, to Indian people on reserves, with provision for charge-backs to the federal government. Child-in-care costs for Indian children living off-reserve were also eligible for charge-back under the new agreement.

The Canada Assistance Plan (CAP) was introduced in 1966 to ensure that all citizens of the provinces received basic services. It provided 50/50 cost sharing of social welfare costs between federal and provincial governments. Indian people off-reserve were to be covered by programs supported by CAP. Part II of CAP provided for a separate agreement to clarify off-reserve costs of services to Indian people, but apart from Ontario, no other provinces signed such agreements.[53] Money remained the stumbling block. While the provinces maintained that the federal government was entirely responsible for services to Aboriginal people, the federal government held that since it reimbursed 50 per cent of social program costs under CAP, Aboriginal people should be covered by provincial programs.[54]

CAP funding and the rules of program accessibility incorporated in the plan's guidelines did help to resolve the problem of eligibility for off-reserve Indians, who routinely had had difficulty accessing municipal social services when they moved off-reserve. Non-status Indians, Métis people and off-reserve Indian people were clearly within the ambit of provincial services.

Except on an emergency basis, child welfare services were generally not available to Indian people living on-reserve. The federal government purchased some services, but they were usually for children already in care, and none of the agencies was willing to get involved. Perhaps it was because of the post-war mobility of Indian people moving off-reserve, or perhaps it was because problems were ignored and allowed to deteriorate until apprehension was necessary. Whatever the reasons, the number of Aboriginal children in care continued to grow. The Canadian Council on Social Development sponsored an investigation of Aboriginal child welfare in two studies.[55] Patrick Johnston's study, quoted earlier in this chapter, was highly critical of child welfare practices and helped to fuel the fires of change being lighted elsewhere in the country.

Beginning in 1981, DIAND began to enter into tripartite child welfare agreements with provincial governments and tribal councils or regional groups representing First Nations. As a condition of these agreements, the federal government insisted that child and family services established under the agreements and operating under delegated authority from the province must adhere to provincial regulations.[56] The federal government was entirely responsible for financing on-reserve services and child-in-care costs.

Charles Morris, executive director of Tikinagan Child and Family Services in northwestern Ontario, described the consequences of placing child welfare in his region under provincial control.

> Tikinagan Child and Family Services is mandated under the *Child and Family Services Act* to provide service in child welfare, community support and young offender categories....
>
> It was our misfortune to have received our mandate when we did, in April of 1987, because of what has subsequently transpired. A five-year organizational review was conducted in 1990, and it showed the extent of our unpreparedness. We became, for all intents and purposes, a children's aid society which was indistinguishable from other white-operated children's aid societies, and to this date we continue to emulate the practices of these traditional children's aid societies. We adopted a system without question, we became incorporated to this system, and today we perpetuate the practices of such a system. This is despite our efforts to not do so....
>
> During our second-last annual assembly in Muskrat Dam, our elders directed us to seek more authority and autonomy in the child welfare field based on our natural and treaty rights as the First People of this land. Their rationale was that the Creator bestowed upon us the inherent authority to govern our own relationships amongst ourselves in our communities, and to structure our family support services in accordance with our unique culture and customs and in a manner which respects the genuine needs and priorities of our people.
>
> We state categorically that the above is not possible within the present framework.
>
> Charles Morris
> Executive Director, Tikinagan Child and Family Services
> Sioux Lookout, Ontario, 1 December 1992

The need for community healing

Conventional treatment services provided under provincial child welfare legislation typically treat children's needs for protection and care on a case-by-case basis, viewing each incident of neglect as though it were a discrete and exceptional occurrence rather than a localized eruption that is symptomatic of more generalized disorder in the organism of extended family and community.

Casework or therapy with a nuclear family is consistent with the western cultural perception that individuals are members of nuclear families that provide economic support and affection and can turn to specialized institutions for problem-specific help. Aboriginal people, on the other hand, often perceive themselves as members of family networks in which everyone is obliged, to the extent of their ability, to share their resources and assist all other members. In rural communities with stable membership over generations, the family and the community may be virtually the same group.

These different concepts of family, community and social obligations can lead to very different notions of how to conduct a helping interaction, as described by an Anishnabe social worker and his colleagues.

Figure [2.1] attempts to illustrate and compare the two distinctly different environmental contexts in which an Aboriginal worker functions. Figure [2.1A] depicts the Aboriginal community as a network. One immediately striking characteristic of this context is the high number and complexity of the interrelationships. Both the worker and the individual (or family) who is the focus of concern...are deeply and equally embedded in this community network. Members of the Aboriginal community potentially (and normally do) play multiple roles in relation to one another – friend, neighbour, relative, and community service volunteer, as well as job-related service giver and receiver roles. All of these roles are reciprocal, each (at least potentially) being played by each person in relation to all others in the community.

Figure [2.1B] illustrates the Aboriginal worker and his or her client seeking human service outside the Aboriginal community. The individual or family who is the focus of concern assumes the role of 'client' [in the] system – a more dependent and generally stigmatized role. In like manner, the community member functioning in the job of human service worker is cast in the role of 'worker' – a more powerful and generally more expert role. The worker is not seen by formal human service agencies as an individual simply fulfilling an expected role in the mutual aid system of the Aboriginal community. In the formal system, the worker-client role relationship becomes single faceted rather than multiple, and uni-directional (helper-helped) rather than reciprocal. Both worker and client become removed and isolated from the interpersonal network that gives their needs and behaviour meaning and that will ultimately provide the support and resources, or obstacles, to satisfaction of those needs.[57]

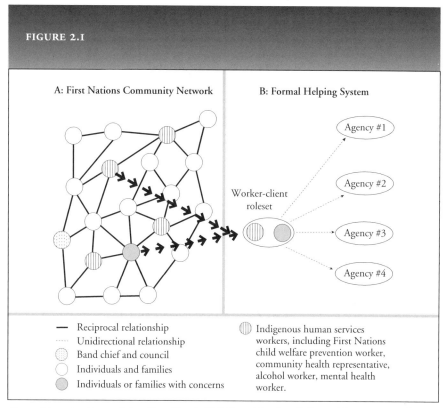

FIGURE 2.1

A: First Nations Community Network

B: Formal Helping System

Agency #1

Agency #2

Worker-client
roleset

Agency #3

Agency #4

— Reciprocal relationship
······ Unidirectional relationship
⬤ Band chief and council
◯ Individuals and families
⬤ Individuals or families with concerns

▥ Indigenous human services
workers, including First Nations
child welfare prevention worker,
community health representative,
alcohol worker, mental health
worker.

Source: Adapted, with permission, from Connie H. Nelson, Mary Lou Kelley and Dennis H. McPherson, "Rediscovering Support in Social Work Practice: Lessons from Indian Indigenous Human Service Workers", *Canadian Social Work Review* (1985), pp. 233-235.

The differences between culturally conditioned Aboriginal ways of helping and services delivered in the conventional manner of professionalized social services are even more pronounced when the worker is also an outsider to the community. Aboriginal workers typically try to modify the mode of service in an ad hoc manner, risking being seen by both the community and the sponsoring agency as acting inappropriately.

Applying this model of helping, in which many members of the community network are conditioned or required to turn to outside agencies for help, weakens internal bonds of mutual aid. Community members are unable to contribute to the agencies that are the source of help, and they begin to doubt that they have the resources to help one another. Such a situation fosters dependent relationships.

External aid may well be required, however, given the poor economic situation of many Aboriginal communities. And Aboriginal nations will undoubtedly choose to respond to some community needs through service institutions similar to agencies operating elsewhere in Canada. We do not wish to imply that either external aid or formal agencies are inappropriate or unnecessary vehicles for meeting needs. We do wish to emphasize that services should be diligent about strengthening the capacity for mutual aid and using local resources, practices that, by all accounts, mainstream child welfare agencies have been slow to adopt.

In Chapter 3 of this volume we discuss the problems created by a multiplicity of agencies offering help within the confines of narrow bureaucratic regulations and divorced from community influence. At our hearing in Hobbema, Alberta, Wilson Okeymaw described the conflicts he experienced:

> When we try to act as white people we have problems. We try to sit behind a desk, and wear a tie and a shirt. That's fine, but in the whole process we run into some difficulty....There is a real strong connection among people in this community, all the extended families. When something happens to an individual, everybody goes over there. And the funding agencies come back to me and say, "You're spending too much time over there. You have to be inside one 10 x 10 office." And [they] stack me with some more papers. There's an underlying family structure that the system has a hard time understanding.
>
> Wilson Okeymaw
> Director, Nayo-Skan Healing Centre
> Hobbema, Alberta, 10 June 1992

Our proposals in Chapter 3 for reorganizing health and social service delivery systems under Aboriginal control will naturally encompass child and family services. We expect that services developed in community healing centres and regional healing lodges will address the need for community healing and mutual support networks, and at the same time acknowledge that professional services and resources from outside the community may still need to be deployed strategically in some circumstances.

Inadequate follow-up and evaluation

The foster care and adoption practices that removed thousands of Aboriginal children from their families and communities and placed hundreds of them outside Canada disrupted Aboriginal families to an appalling degree. Each situation was seen as an exceptional case, and no steps were taken to evaluate and adjust the larger picture. Many of the cross-cultural adoptions broke down, setting the adoptee adrift in the process. When these lost children attempt to search for their roots, they are often thwarted by agency rules of confidentiality. Even when adoption placements have been successful, some adoptees are still interested in establishing an identity that encompasses their Aboriginal culture and origins. It is a priority of Aboriginal communities and family service agencies to repatriate Aboriginal children who lack stable family ties and Aboriginal youth who have no community connections, and to help rootless adults find their way home. But it is a priority that the mainstream service system has failed to recognize in a systematic way. In the words of an administrator of a Manitoba child welfare agency:

> Since 1982, First Nations leaders have continuously requested that the federal and provincial governments demonstrate their support for resolving the historical injustices against Indian children, families and communities by assisting in the search for adoptees and by facilitating the repatriation for those who wish to return to their families and communities.
>
> The Government of Manitoba provides repatriation assistance only on a case-by-case basis and only to those adoptees under the age of 18. Due to long years of government inaction, many of these children are now over the age of majority, 18, and are once again victims of a system that previously failed them.
>
> The Manitoba Child and Family Services Department will attempt to reunify families only when both parties have registered with the post-adoption registry, a system that is relatively new and largely unknown to Aboriginal people who have lost their children. The Canadian government has failed to accept any responsibility and has refused to release documents critical to the search for adoptees....
>
> Over the past decade, a number of adoptees have found their way home. All of the returning adoptees are searching for a cultural identity and many of them incorrectly perceive that they have been rejected by their own people. Although some of these adoptees have been happy in their adoptive homes, a much larger number were victims of emotional, physical, and sexual abuse....
>
> First Nations child and family service agencies are doing their best to search for adoptees and assist those who are returning home. They have been left with the responsibility of picking up the pieces caused by inhumane child welfare policies of the provincial and federal governments....
>
> No government has recognized responsibility and, consequently, the monumental care and treatment that is required for these adoptees is not available.
>
> Morris Merick
> Director, Dakota Ojibway Child and Family Services
> 10 December 1992

At another hearing, a young person who had lost touch with her family of origin described her perspective:

Proposals to Support Repatriation of Adoptees

1. Immediate release of any documents that would assist in the search for adoptees.
2. Financial assistance for those adoptees who wish to return home.
3. Immediate access to essential support services for those adoptees returning to Canada.
4. Appropriate funding for First Nations to allow for the development of a central registry office that would search, track and refer Native adoptees to appropriate agencies.
5. Appropriate funding for First Nations agencies to allow for the establishment of a repatriation home [program] that would provide a temporary shelter for returning adoptees, in addition to services related to developing cultural awareness and identity, preparing for life on the reserve, integrating with the community, counselling for alcohol, drug, sexual, physical, and emotional abuse, coping and life skills.
6. A public apology to the First Nations people of Manitoba and, in particular, Native adoptees and their families.
7. Monetary compensation to Native adoptees and families for the pain and suffering they have endured.

Morris Merick
Director, Dakota Ojibway Child and Family Services
Brandon, Manitoba
10 December 1992

I come from a family that was somewhat dysfunctional and I am a product of the other Child Welfare Services. That Child Welfare Service said that my grandmother was too old and too poor to keep us children, although she wanted us. I met my sister, who managed to miss that system somehow and lived with my grandmother. What she said to me when she met me was: "I have to tell you this because my grandmother and your grandmother wanted me to if ever I found you. That was that she tried for years and years and years to find you – there were two others of us – and bring you back to the family."

Linda Nicholson
Orillia, Ontario
12 May 1993

Morris Merick presented a proposal to support repatriation of adoptees to their families and communities (see box). We urge that the important role of

Aboriginal family and children's services in facilitating repatriation be recognized and assisted by appropriate adaptations of regulations in provincial agencies.

Establishing service standards and evaluation procedures will devolve more fully upon Aboriginal governments and service agencies as they gain more autonomy from federal and provincial governments.

Aboriginal agencies currently acknowledge the need to set standards of practice and monitor the effectiveness of their operations, but the history of external assessments, which were often seen as a threat to funding and often imposed inappropriate criteria, has left a legacy of distrust and resistance to assessments. Policy making and evaluation, therefore, are part of the set of skills that will be required in future even more than they are now. In a self-government context, with jurisdiction exercised at the level of the Aboriginal nation, communication skills to foster co-operation, as well as evaluation skills, will be essential. Accountability to members of the Aboriginal nation served will likely be through nation and regional structures, staff and board committees of community members, service agency and government personnel – whether the responsible government is Aboriginal, federal, provincial or territorial.

In our hearings, a number of presenters called for Aboriginal-specific legislation at the federal level in the field of child welfare. We do not discount the need for collaboration across Aboriginal nation boundaries and among networks of sectoral agencies to develop standards of practice. In our view, however, the authority for legislating child welfare and regulating practices should rest with the Aboriginal nation. With Aboriginal jurisdiction in place, there will be greater flexibility to introduce practices in keeping with Aboriginal culture and community realities, and an increased capacity to allocate funding in a way that reinforces family health and community responsibility.

Marginal and insufficient urban services

Statistics showing projected patterns of migration between rural and urban settings indicate that by the year 2016, the urban Aboriginal population will have increased in absolute numbers from 319,997 in 1991 to 457,000, a 43 per cent rise in 25 years. (Details on current issues in urban services and demographic projections are provided in Volume 4, Chapter 7.)

Our discussion of urban issues in Volume 4, Chapter 7 highlights the policy vacuum that has impeded the development of Aboriginal-specific services in urban settings. In Chapter 3 of this volume, we analyze the threats to people's health and well-being and show how the health of urban Aboriginal people is equally, if not more, at risk.

One predominantly urban concern is the increasing involvement of Aboriginal youth in life on the street. The disadvantaged conditions that Aboriginal people experience with such frequency, and the failure of social institutions and services to respond to the resulting needs, converge in the lives of street youth. To gain some insight into this phenomenon, we commissioned a research project that worked through the staff of agencies serving street youth to locate and interview Aboriginal youth living on the street in Vancouver, Winnipeg and Montreal.[58] To provide some background to the young people's stories, the researchers also interviewed workers in these agencies as well as a few parents. Eleven young people were interviewed in all. Of these, seven were survivors of the street, two were temporarily in a detention centre, and two had left the street.

No reliable data exist on the number of youth living on the streets of Canadian cities or the proportion of them that is Aboriginal. Local studies and estimates by agency workers based on the use of services put the total number at anywhere from a few hundred to several thousand in the larger centres. There is greater agreement that Aboriginal youth make up a disproportionate number of street youth, with estimates ranging from 30 to 70 per cent of the population using needle-exchange programs for drug users and drop-in centres that provide food, clothing and shelter. Workers in the Montreal agencies serving street youth generally declined to make estimates, although one worker speculated that Aboriginal youth might constitute 10 per cent of the street population. Although there is a significant Inuit population in Montreal, Inuit youth are not visible in the street population.

Our research did not provide quantitative data on which to base pronouncements. Gilchrist and Winchester note, for example, that very young runaways, solvent sniffers, under-age prostitutes, gang members, and youth heavily addicted to alcohol and drugs were not interviewed directly in their study, although their presence on the street was often noted in interviews with others.[59] A range of characteristics and experiences is reported in the data. There is no typical profile of Aboriginal street youth. Some are as young as 11 or 12; others have been surviving on the street for close to a decade. Some have come from rural and northern reserves and settlements, others from families that have been in the city for more than a generation. Most of the youth interviewed had lost touch with their biological families following extended periods in foster or adoption care. The males in particular had experience with correctional institutions.

We found that the reasons youth take to the street can be grouped into three broad categories. Youth were

- products of the child welfare system, correctional system, and family breakdown, fleeing abusive situations or rejection because of homosexuality and, often, demeaning experiences of racism in non-Aboriginal society;[60]
- children who had failed to find meaningful relationships in the family or success in school, perhaps because of undiagnosed learning disabilities; and
- youth from rural reserves and northern communities or economically marginal urban families, seeking excitement but falling into prostitution because they had no job skills.

Children and youth who resort to the street and remain there do so because in their view it is better than what they came from. On the street they find an accepting culture – people who share and look out for one another, a family of sorts. But they also find exploitation, violence and, in some cases, early death. In an effort to mask the pain of their lives they use drugs and alcohol, which only numb their initiative, binding them in an aimless round. The following are portions of the histories of three street youth interviewed for the study.

Karen was 15 years old at the time of the interview in Vancouver and had been drifting between home and the street scene for two years. She was sexually abused by her cousin and relates her running away episodes to flashbacks she has of that prolonged and painful experience. Her mother told the interviewer that five of her 10 children suffer from fetal alcohol syndrome (described in Chapter 3 of this volume). Karen has not been diagnosed but may be one of those affected by her parents' past alcohol abuse. She described her routine on the street:

> I just kill time. I'd walk around. I'd go to Carnegie and all that. I'd go on Hastings and then I'd go to Granville and walk there…and see all my friends around Granville. That's about it.[61]

Noella and her brother Axle, interviewed in Winnipeg, were taken into foster care at an early age and placed for adoption when Noella was about four years old. Her adoptive mother died when Noella was 10 years old. Even before her mother's death, her adoptive father had been sexually abusing her. Two years later she stole her adoptive father's car. After being arrested, she was put on probation and sent home. She breached probation and ended up in custody. Her life for the eight succeeding years was spent in and out of custody, completing grade eight in school, travelling to find her biological parents, having two children, both of whom were apprehended by child welfare agencies, and moving on and off the street. At the time of the interview her partner was Travis.

Travis was adopted at the age of six months by non-Aboriginal parents. Regular disputes with his adoptive parents culminated in Travis pulling a knife on his adoptive father at the age of 14. He was forcibly removed from the home and spent two years in a correctional institution. He learned that his biological mother had died in a fire when he was seven, and he spent some time with his biological father, whose drinking was an obstacle to forming a relationship. He drifted onto the streets at the age of 16 and expresses some shame about the criminal activity he has been involved in since then.

For the seven months preceding the interview Travis and Noella had lived in a rented apartment with Noella's brother Axle. They collected social assistance, were jobless, lived in low-rent housing, used soup kitchens and free recreational services, and spent most of their time on the streets of Winnipeg or trying to get off the streets. Their motivation to achieve a different life came from their desire to regain custody of their child who was apprehended at birth, ostensibly because Travis was intoxicated when he accompanied Noella to hospital for the delivery.

The grief and bewilderment of families is captured in the account of a Winnipeg parent whose nine-year-old child became involved with child pornography:

> How she started, she met two older girls....She started bringing home things like perfume, gifts, clothing....Well, I didn't find out till she was about 11 when the police came to the house....They had a bunch of pictures of these young girls and pictures of my daughter were in there too....They caught the guy....He got seven years....She never spoke about it again. [They didn't receive counselling]...instead what they did was the family services put the children in the home and that was it. [The daughter went to a group home for two years, from which she ran away twice.] She was okay when she was locked up. She came out when she was 15. She never went back to school....She committed suicide.[62]

Gilchrist and Winchester draw on the work of Abraham Maslow in discussing human needs.[63] However, they consider a person's need for physical survival, protection, self-esteem and spiritual integrity as being of comparable importance, rather than ranked hierarchically as Maslow proposes. For youth living on the street, however, the opportunities to meet their needs are restricted at every turn.

Street youth usually lack the education and employment skills that would enable them to meet their needs for food, clothing and shelter in socially acceptable ways and are driven to panhandling, scavenging in garbage dumpsters, sleeping in stairwells and abandoned buildings, prostitution and petty crime. Children under age 16 are fearful of using street services because the law requires that they be returned to the home situation they are trying to escape. At the most basic level, street youth need safe houses, food banks and health services, including addictions treatment, and, for those who are able to make use of them, facilities to support independent living.

Street youth often need protection from the very people legally responsible for their care, be it their biological, foster or adoptive families. They also need effective protection from sexual predators and the people who profit from the sex trade. The youth themselves acknowledge the valuable assistance extended by street agencies, and Aboriginal youth look for Aboriginal faces in these agencies. At present, only a handful of services, such as the Bear Clan Patrol in Winnipeg, address the particular needs of Aboriginal children and youth on the street.[64]

Many street youth have experienced extreme trauma in their lives. Gaining or regaining the ability to hold a job and profit from counselling and education is often a long, arduous process. Aboriginal youth services, therefore, must include job skills training, alternative education options, and counselling that is relevant to their reality.

For these youth to become mature adults, they will require support to develop their identity, opportunities to learn about their cultures and traditions as Aboriginal people, and critical education that will empower them and enable them to transcend the pain of their past experience. The services needed in this area include repatriation services for adoptees and foster children, education in history and critical analysis, learning circles, access to elders, and opportunities to experience cultural practices in ceremonies and life on the land.

On reserves and in Inuit villages considerable progress has been made in recent years in developing an array of culturally relevant services, including family and children's services. The development of services in urban settings has hinged largely on volunteer efforts and unreliable and inadequate funding. In Volume 4, Chapter 7 we make a number of recommendations concerning financing of social programs for people living off Aboriginal territory. We also recommend stable support for Aboriginal service agencies and hiring Aboriginal people to design and deliver services for Aboriginal clients in mainstream agencies.

As with all children's services, remedial treatment – mending fractured lives – is necessary but not adequate in itself. We must find the means to support and heal families before they break apart.

Missy, a former street youth, made use of healing services and cultural education to begin her recovery.[65] She now works in street services, and her appeal for immediate action adds urgency to our argument for more humane and effective services on behalf of children at risk, including those who find their way onto the streets of our cities:

> If people don't start taking a look at [the street situation], we're going to see a lot more kids dying from overdoses and suicides and violent death....There are kids out there who are dying. We see that every day. But I think that government officials have to come down and take a look too.[66]

Service systems resistant to change

Despite persistent pleas from Aboriginal people that their interdependent needs be served by holistic services, the service environment continues to be fragmented between federal and provincial levels of government, between departments and ministries, and among service agencies in the community.

Rix Rogers is a former adviser to the federal government on the sexual abuse of children. Speaking at a Commission hearing, Rogers described the critical situation regarding the lack of services in Aboriginal communities, the financial constraints facing provinces, and the fragmentation of efforts to meet people's needs.

Where I think we've got a problem is in the provincial and federal mechanisms of government where we're organized on a basis of different ministries, different departments, and there's really no way of providing a sort of integration of effort.

Family violence and child abuse issues represent the first wave of very complex and multi-dimensional problems that no longer can be addressed by any one single government ministry. Governments have not caught up with that fact.

So that, if in fact we're going to get serious about meeting these needs, you'd almost have to do away with the current structures of government and create some brand new ones. And I would suggest that probably over the next 10 years that's what's going to have to happen.

Rix Rogers
Institute for the Prevention of Child Abuse
Toronto, Ontario, 3 June 1993

The Alberta commissioner of services for children is engaged in efforts to integrate children's services in Alberta. A report by the commissioner gives a summary account of what several provinces are doing to develop integrated service delivery systems that are

- responsive to all issues facing a family or child, rather than just a single problem;
- flexible enough to allow services to be tailored to the needs of the family or child – individualized approaches;
- able to provide an integrated set of services for children and families; and
- capable of assisting people with acute problems, while at the same time providing sufficient resources for early intervention.[67]

In 1994 the government of Ontario announced an Aboriginal health policy that acknowledges that Aboriginal people must play the leading role in designing health and wellness strategies in accordance with their cultures and priorities. The policy supports appropriately funded community health centres, hostels and hospices.[68]

In January 1995 the government of the Northwest Territories circulated a discussion paper, *Community Wellness: Working Together for Community Wellness*, which proposes that:

The Government of the Northwest Territories will honour the inherent ability of the community to care for itself. We will support the well-being of the people we serve by promoting healthy living, life-long learning and healing.[69]

The document outlines strategies to improve co-ordination of government services and emphasizes early childhood development.

The Alberta commissioner's research revealed, as Aboriginal people have observed, that it is extremely difficult to shift the mode of operation or priorities of complex service systems. In the recommendations in Chapter 3 in this volume, we propose practical ways to initiate a more integrated service delivery system for Aboriginal health and social needs, including child and family services.

Crisis orientation and training

Crisis orientation and inappropriate training of social work personnel are treated extensively in the discussion of service delivery in Chapter 3.

Most policy makers would agree in principle that early intervention in problem situations is most likely to be effective in preventing severe breakdown and is therefore an efficient use of resources. In practice, however, when a crisis is breaking on every front in a family, service providers cannot afford to turn their backs on urgent needs on the grounds that the children will be better off in the long term. Where children are at risk in violent situations, they may not survive, or they may not remain emotionally healthy enough to be capable of enjoying any long-term benefits.

Given the evidence that the crisis in Aboriginal family life is not subsiding, it follows that services to cope with or avert crises must continue to be provided. They include monitoring children at risk and counselling families, shelters for family members vulnerable to violence, residential treatment for addictions, anger management, respite care to relieve overburdened caregivers, opportunities to learn and improve parenting and problem-solving skills, and alternative care within the extended family or community. Longer-term yet equally essential strategies include mobilizing community support networks, providing early childhood education, and researching ways to articulate modern applications of traditional knowledge.[70]

Our human resources development strategy, set out in Chapter 3, proposes ways of dealing with the challenge of training personnel to implement new approaches to human services. Social workers typically are trained to function within mainstream agencies, which often assume the role of assessing and controlling individual and family behaviour, rather than facilitating the healing of kin networks and whole communities. There are no systematic plans or resources earmarked to train new cadres of Aboriginal workers once child and family services have been established or when service personnel change.

Information from DIAND indicates that an unspecified part of the allocation for administration can be used for staff workshops and training. Training for staff at the start-up of an agency was often built into the global budget. Now, however, agencies report that current budget constraints do not allow them to sponsor training for new staff or orientations for the volunteer committees and governing bodies essential to keeping an agency accountable to the community.

Human resource development, including training Aboriginal personnel for diverse roles in a new integrated service system, will be essential to the success of new approaches to child and family services under Aboriginal control.

2.5 Conclusion and Recommendations

Aboriginal institutions in the field of family and children's services are the way of the future. They will form part of the system for delivering integrated health and social services, described more fully in Chapter 3 in this volume.

Our recommendations here focus on affirming and implementing the authority of Aboriginal nations and their communities to act in the field of family and child welfare, and on resolving the tensions between federal, provincial, territorial and Aboriginal authority that interfere with protecting the best interests of Aboriginal children.

While we consider that protecting children's interests can be achieved best in the context of revitalized Aboriginal families, communities and nations, we do not underestimate the difficulties of turning ideals into reality.

In the recent history of Aboriginal child welfare, the best interests of the child have at times been construed as being in conflict with community goals of self-determination. One highly publicized case was the death of Lester Desjarlais, a child who committed suicide while in the care of an Aboriginal agency in Manitoba.[71]

Associate Chief Judge Dale Giesbrecht concluded from his inquiry into the death that political considerations in the local community had interfered with the agency's discharge of its responsibilities, that policies and lines of responsibility within the agency needed to be clarified and formalized, and that the provincial director of child welfare should take a more active role in monitoring the work of Aboriginal agencies. Concern about issues of political interference, organizational capacity and checks and balances in exercising of community responsibility are not confined to Manitoba.[72]

The tension between individual and group priorities surfaces in another area of child welfare. As discussed later in this chapter, judgements about guardianship and adoption placements of minor children often entail balancing a child's need for stable parental relationships with the equally compelling need to have community support in developing a mature Aboriginal identity.

Aboriginal and non-Aboriginal agencies and personnel bring different perceptions and approaches to the work of child welfare. Tensions emerge precisely because the well-being of children is such a fundamentally important issue in both Aboriginal and non-Aboriginal societies.[73]

As we reiterate often in this volume, non-Aboriginal institutions will have a continuing role in delivering services to Aboriginal people, even when Aboriginal self-government is fully operative across the country. The best interests of Aboriginal children will be served only by determined and sustained efforts on the part of Aboriginal and non-Aboriginal governments, institutions, and people to recognize and support each other's contributions to the common goal.

RECOMMENDATIONS

The Commission recommends that

Authority for Child Welfare

3.2.1
The government of Canada acknowledge a fiduciary responsibility to support Aboriginal nations and their communities in restoring Aboriginal families to a state of health and wholeness.

3.2.2
Aboriginal, provincial, territorial and federal governments promptly acknowledge that child welfare is a core area of self-government in which Aboriginal nations can undertake self-starting initiatives.

3.2.3
Aboriginal, provincial, territorial and federal governments promptly reach agreements on the authority of Aboriginal nations and their communities for child welfare, and its relation to provincial, territorial and federal laws respecting child welfare.

Funding Child Welfare Agencies

3.2.4
Block funding be provided to child welfare agencies mandated by Aboriginal governments or communities to facilitate a shift in focus from alternative child care to family support.

Voluntary Agencies

3.2.5
Until community of interest governments are established in urban and non-reserve areas, voluntary agencies endorsed by substantial numbers of Aboriginal people resident in the areas be authorized under provincial or territorial law to act in the field of child welfare
(a) where numbers warrant; and
(b) with levels of funding comparable to those of agencies providing comparable services to the general population and sufficient to meet the service needs of Aboriginal people.

3. Family Violence

Aboriginal people perceive that the family as an institution is under severe stress from internal violence, which is both a symptom of stress and a cause of further distress.[74] This message was communicated most powerfully by Aboriginal women and their organizations in our hearings, although men and young people expressed concern as well.

We observed earlier in the chapter that the well-being of children was a prominent theme in the presentations made to us. Presenters made it clear that the safety and healthy development of Aboriginal children are seriously at risk in situations where there is pervasive and unchecked violence. The assessment of many Aboriginal people is echoed in the words of a speaker at Hay River, Northwest Territories:

> Family violence is seen as the most rampant social problem of our time. It is probably the most expensive. The costs in terms of human suffering cannot be measured. The cost in dollars can only be guessed at.
>
> Our children are vastly affected by family violence even when they are not the direct victims. The cost to our children is hidden in their inability to be attentive in school, in feelings of insecurity and low-esteem, and in acting out behaviour which may manifest itself in many ways, such as vandalism, self-abuse, bullying; and often these children suffer in silence.
>
> Sharon J. Caudron
> Program Director,
> Women's Resource Centre of Hay River
> Hay River, Northwest Territories, 17 June 1993

Women spoke eloquently of the need to secure the safety and heal the spirit of all those who bear the current brunt and the past scars of family breakdown, alcoholism and violence. They pointed to the need for more effective community services; but even more important, they argued, is the need to reverse the pattern of excluding women that has taken hold in many Aboriginal communities. The experience of exclusion, powerlessness and hence vulnerability of women was especially painful when contrasted with the practice of balanced family-based decision making that traditionally prevailed in many Aboriginal nations. We highlight the perspectives of women on these and other issues in Volume 4, Chapter 2.

3.1 Naming the Problem

Family violence can be defined as a "serious abuse of power within family, trust or dependency relationships".[75] It has been brought to the fore as a public policy issue in Canada largely through the action of women's groups since the

1970s.[76] The original focus of family violence discourse was on wife-battering. It quickly expanded to include physical violence against children and, more recently, child sexual abuse. It is now widely recognized that violence against individuals in families and dependency relationships takes many forms: physical violence, including sexual abuse; psychological violence in which vulnerable people are battered by demeaning and humiliating words; and economic abuse in which women and the elderly in particular are controlled or deprived by another family member who withholds or appropriates their money.

Perpetrators of violence are found in every region, every social class and every age group. A 1993 survey by Statistics Canada used random sampling to investigate the incidence of violence against women. 'Violence' in the survey was defined as experiences of physical or sexual assault that are consistent with legal definitions of these offences and could be acted upon by a police officer. The survey was the first of its kind anywhere in the world, and the results were startling:

> The results of this survey suggest that violence against women is widespread and has serious consequences for victims. One-half (51 per cent) of Canadian women have experienced at least one incident of physical or sexual violence since the age of 16. Twenty-five per cent of all women have experienced physical or sexual violence at the hands of a marital partner (marital partners include common-law relationships throughout this report). One-in-five violent incidents reported in this survey were serious enough to result in physical injury.[77]

When only women who at some time have had a marital partner are considered, the proportion who have experienced violence rises to 29 per cent. The original concern over the vulnerability of women and children continues to be justified, but disclosures of violence inflicted on elderly people and persons with disabilities are now being made with increasing frequency.

Older people are most likely to be subjected to economic abuse, as described in a research study we commissioned. Elderly persons tend to derive their income from pensions or social assistance, and this is supplemented by food from the bush or gardens. Some children and grandchildren rely on pensioners as part of their sharing network, but others act in more aggressive ways:

> They barge in on them; they threaten them. These people [pensioners] are afraid to come out and say anything. And you can't say a thing, nobody will say anything because they don't want to go through the court. They haven't got the money. If it isn't the 'ruffians' it is the stores, because everything costs so much. The pension would be okay if it was just to provide for the pensioners themselves, it's ample. But it's the way the laws are, allows the people that are robbing to get away with it.[78]

Presentations from people with disabilities recounting the violence they had suffered were particularly disturbing:

> As far as Aboriginal people with disabilities [are concerned]...we are less recognized and the most violated against by both races, both sexes, and both communities. We are raped by disabled men; we are raped by disabled women; we are raped by Aboriginal women; we are raped by Aboriginal men; we are raped by white women; we are raped by white men. And believe you me we have been raped by our medical attendants, doctors, nurses, occupational therapists – you name it, we've had it. We know what it is like to be down low, but for God's sake, you don't have to keep us there either.
>
> Judi Johnny
> National Aboriginal Network on Disabilities
> Whitehorse, Yukon, 18 November 1992

Some Aboriginal people concerned about violence are pressing to have the definition of the problem expanded to include other situations where violence is likely to be felt personally – in employment situations where women may find it difficult to protect themselves from harassment, in communities where sharp divisions frequently flare up into confrontations, or where alienated youth are a threat to the safety of other community members.[79] Violence against gay men and lesbians and sexual abuse between siblings has received little attention in public policy to this date. The Commission heard that ritual abuse of children, which has been shielded from investigation by respect for religious freedom, is emerging as a problem in some urban settings.[80]

In the midst of devastating revelations of the violence suffered daily by Aboriginal people, frequently at the hands of the men in their families, we were urged to recognize that men are victims too. One recent study indicated that in the inner city, Aboriginal boys are generally exposed to family violence and suffer physical abuse, while girls are more likely to be subjected to sexual abuse.[81] Revelations of the extent of sexual abuse of both boys and girls in residential schools, the fact that victims of abuse often become abusers, and the shame that leads men in particular to hide these experiences are all coming to the fore. Aboriginal people in the health care field now believe that Aboriginal men have suffered more sexual abuse as children than previously believed, and they are, in all probability, as devastated by these experiences as women have been.

3.2 The Face of Aboriginal Violence

While family violence experienced by Aboriginal people shares many features with violence in mainstream society, it also has a distinctive face that is important to recognize as we search for understanding of causes and identify solutions.

First, Aboriginal family violence is distinct in that it has invaded whole communities and cannot be considered a problem of a particular couple or an individual household. Second, the failure in family functioning can be traced in many cases to interventions of the state deliberately introduced to disrupt or displace the Aboriginal family. Third, violence within Aboriginal communities is fostered and sustained by a racist social environment that promulgates demeaning stereotypes of Aboriginal women and men and seeks to diminish their value as human beings and their right to be treated with dignity.

Family violence is perceived to be widespread in Aboriginal communities, but there are few national statistics demonstrating the incidence of violence or whether the situation is improving as a result of greater public awareness and programs to combat the problem. Studies reporting on the incidence of violence are often initiated by groups providing services, raising the possibility that the study group includes a high representation of persons with service needs. Nevertheless, certain studies provide quantitative data that serve as a context for the personal statements made in the Commission's hearings.

A study by the Ontario Native Women's Association, for example, found that 8 out of 10 Aboriginal women had experienced violence. Of these women, 87 per cent had been injured physically and 57 per cent had been sexually abused.[82] According to a London, Ontario, area study, 71 per cent of the urban sample and 48 per cent of the reserve sample of Oneida women had experienced assault at the hands of current or past partners.[83]

For a study reported in 1991, 61 Aboriginal women were recruited by Aboriginal agencies in Lethbridge, Alberta. Of this non-random sample,

> 91 per cent of the respondents said they had personal experience with family violence. While these women identify psychological and verbal abuse as the most common, (ranging from blaming at 88 per cent to swearing at 82 per cent), a significant number had also been subjected to slapping (77 per cent), hitting (64 per cent), and punching (54 per cent). Sixteen per cent reported being touched unwillingly and being forced into sex with partners.[84]

Emma LaRocque, a Métis professor at the University of Manitoba, spoke at the Commission's national round table on health and social issues. She confirmed the difficulty of obtaining an accurate picture of the extent of violence affecting Métis people:

> Since it is considerably more difficult to get precise statistics on Métis people, it is virtually impossible to say with any exactness the extent of sexual violence in Métis families or communities. However, as more victims are beginning to report, there is every indication that

violence, including sexual violence, is just as problematic, just as extensive as on reserves.[85]

Pauktuutit, the Inuit women's association, published a report in 1991 entitled *No More Secrets: Acknowledging the Problem of Child Sexual Abuse in Inuit Communities*. It described the problem of child sexual abuse among Inuit in the Northwest Territories, Quebec and Labrador and promoted disclosure by explaining legal reporting requirements in provinces and territories.

An analysis of data from Statistics Canada's 1991 Aboriginal peoples survey indicated the proportion of Aboriginal people identifying certain social issues as a problem in their communities. As shown in Figure 2.2, 36 to 44 per cent of Aboriginal people saw family violence as a problem; 22 to 35 per cent of Aboriginal people saw sexual abuse as a problem in their community. Unemployment and alcohol and drug abuse were the only problems eliciting higher levels of concern among Aboriginal people in this survey.

Although it is impossible to estimate the frequency of violence in Aboriginal communities, there is clearly intense concern among Aboriginal people, especially women. The panel on violence against women, reporting in 1993, encountered similar difficulties in establishing firm data on the incidence of family violence. A survey conducted in Toronto on behalf of the panel reported that in the general population 54 per cent of women had experienced some form of unwanted or intrusive sexual experience before reaching the age of 16; 51 per cent of women had experienced rape or attempted rape; and 27 per cent of women had experienced physical assault in an intimate relationship.[86] The figures on violence at the hands of a partner are consistent with the results of Statistics Canada's more broadly based national survey conducted in 1993.

The extent of violence reported in local studies further underlines the severity of the problem and leads us to ask why violence is so pervasive in Aboriginal families and communities. In published work focusing on family violence, as well as in our hearings, Aboriginal people have consistently linked violence with situations in which individuals feel trapped in disadvantage and frustration.

Writing in *Vis-à-vis*, a national newsletter on family violence, Martha Flaherty, president of Pauktuutit, stated:

> There are many reasons for family violence. High unemployment, poor housing, child abuse, drug abuse – these have led to a loss of culture – which has in turn led to violence against ourselves and our loved ones.[87]

At public hearings in widely separated locations, Commissioners heard a similar analysis:

> I think there needs to be a tremendous stress on education which enhances the pride and abilities of our youth. A good deal is said –

FIGURE 2.2

Selected Social Problems Reported by Aboriginal Identity Population Age 15+, 1991

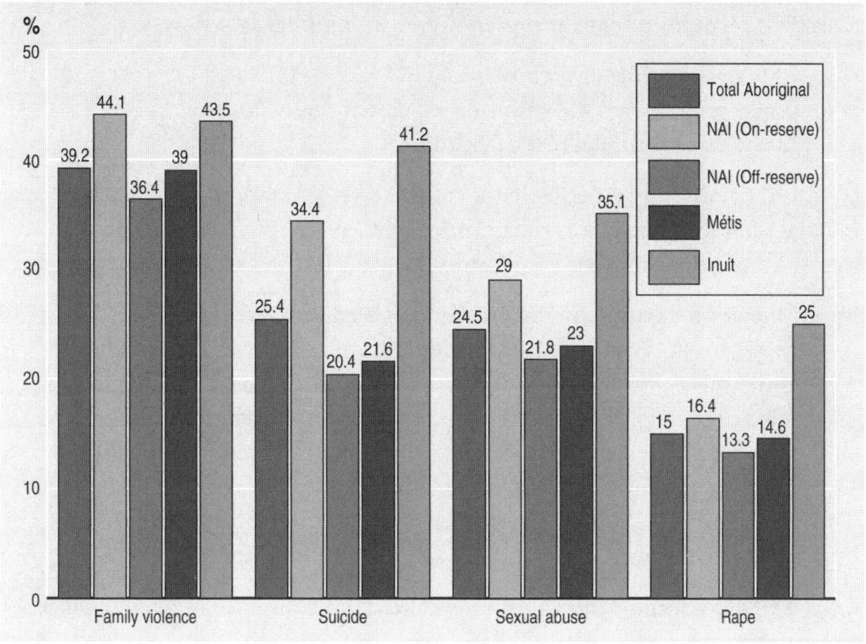

%

	Total Aboriginal
	NAI (On-reserve)
	NAI (Off-reserve)
	Métis
	Inuit

Family violence: 39.2, 44.1, 36.4, 39, 43.5
Suicide: 25.4, 34.4, 20.4, 21.6, 41.2
Sexual abuse: 24.5, 29, 21.8, 23, 35.1
Rape: 15, 16.4, 13.3, 14.6, 25

Note: NAI = North American Indian.

Source: Statistics Canada, 1991 Aboriginal Peoples Survey, catalogue no. 89-533 (1993).

and I am sure the Commission has heard this many times – about the plight of Aboriginal women. I don't want to disparage those remarks in any way. I have heard them over and over again. But my own experience is that the group within our society which is suffering the most is Aboriginal men. It is largely our men, both Indian and Métis, who are in the prisons and penitentiaries of this country.

Part of that arises out of the fact that the pride of our people has been killed in many individuals. Our young men have suffered a psychological castration complex for the last 100 years, and it is time that this was stopped so that our young men can turn to positive pursuits by way of education, so that we can break the cycle of criminality and imprisonment, so that we can break the cycle of the mistreatment of women and children in our communities.

Senator James Penton
Metis Nation of Alberta
Lethbridge, Alberta, 25 May 1993

A research study of Fort Resolution, Northwest Territories, observed that young single men lived in an environment of high unemployment, considerable dependence on social assistance, and little or no opportunity to participate in traditional subsistence activities. The researcher considered the lack of options a disastrous environment for preserving or strengthening self-esteem:

> Men in the prime of their working life may be the most dispossessed group of people in the community, which can be nothing short of a catastrophe for Dene/Métis cultures.[88]

Other Aboriginal people point to the intergenerational effects of the residential school experience as the beginning of learned patterns of violent behaviour. A respondent in a study of family violence in the Treaty 7 area stated:

> One good example is my grandpa. His education was up to grade two, I think. From what my father tells me, there was a lot of abuse going on. A lot of name-calling, a lot of put-downs with the priest towards the kids. For every little thing they got the whip. My grandpa grew up with that and he learned that, then he used it on his kids. Then my father used it on us. If I don't try to do something about it, I'm going to use it on my kids. So that's the pattern, where we picked it up from, the boarding school.[89]

The self-rejection and anger, internalized as a consequence of colonial experiences that devalued Aboriginal cultures and languages, were described by another presenter:

> When you are talking about oppression, there is a process that goes on. [First] there is a process that demeans us, that belittles us and makes us believe that we are not worthy, and the oppressed begin to develop what they call cultural self-shame and cultural self-hate, which results in a lot of frustration and a lot of anger. At the same time this is going on, because our ways are put down as Native people, because our cultural values and things are put down, we begin to adopt our oppressors' values and, in a way, we become oppressors ourselves....Because of the resulting self-hate and self-shame we begin to start hurting our own people.
>
> When you talk about things like addiction and family abuse, elder abuse, sexual abuse, jealousy, gossip, suicide and all the different forms of abuses we seem to be experiencing, it's all based on [the original] violence. It's all a form of [internalized] violence....[Churches and governments] made us believe that the way we are today is the Dene way. It isn't. That is not Dene culture.

> Roy Fabian
> Hay River, Northwest Territories
> 17 June 1993

Other respondents in the study of family violence and community stress in Treaty 7 communities thought that the values that guided Aboriginal society in former times had undergone significant change:

> It seems like it's more like me, myself, the environment. You don't share with each other. You survive for yourself. You don't share or help people anymore. Not like before. Everything was shared. It's like the 'I' generation and you don't care about the next person. So I think that's all due to residential school and getting brainwashed. Like two generations before me. They lacked nurturing and never nurtured their children....

> It's an absence of values. Before the values were so strong, so stringent that to step over those boundaries would mean severe, maybe, ostracization or the family would do something. Because the values were so strong then, individuals would have to think quite hard before they did something. Because they had so much strength and spirited value that such thoughts never entered their mind. But now there are so many things that are eroding our culture.[90]

A resident of Sheshatshiu, Labrador, who spoke at our hearings of the changes introduced to the Innu from outside their culture, speculated that their lives would have been better without the innovations often imposed by external authority.

> The Innu didn't change the way they live, or haven't changed. It is the government that [is] changing us, that wants us to live the way they live, but we can't do that, we have to maintain our way of living as well. If they hadn't bothered with the people in our communities in the early days, we would still have what we had in the past. And now it's different. We can't live the way we used to live, and a lot has been taken away, a lot has been destroyed through the governments. There have been a lot of changes, a lot of things brought in by the white man, such as alcohol and other stuff that is destroying us very slowly. In the early days, there was no such thing as alcohol, and there was no such thing as houses being burnt down. There was no such thing as the problems that we are encountering now in our communities. You wouldn't have heard or seen what happened in February when we lost six children in the community of Davis Inlet because of alcohol. There was no such thing as people going to jail, people taking pills and other substances, as are in Canada now, there was no such thing in the early days when we lived in the past, but now it's changed. Now there are courts, people taking pills and abusing alcohol. [translation]

> Elizabeth Penashue
> Sheshatshiu, Newfoundland and Labrador
> 17 June 1992

Alcohol abuse, often associated with violent episodes, is seen not as a cause of violence but as a parallel means of dealing with deep distress:

> It has been identified that alcohol and violence of different kinds have replaced traditional ways of coping in a time when peace, self-value and harmony for the individual and the community were honoured. These problems represent, for me, the grief suffered from losing that structured way of life.
>
> Harold Orton
> Community Care Centre for Substance Abuse
> Orillia, Ontario, 13 May 1993

We were reminded by the young people who spoke to us that recovering that structured way of life will not happen of its own accord. Young people need and want to be trained in the ways of their culture if they are to break the destructive patterns of social life now evident in many communities:

> All the things that I've mentioned and a few that I haven't mentioned are things like suicide, AIDS, sex abuse, cultural development, psychological training, self-image, self-esteem, recreation, et cetera. Whenever we talk about youth everybody says, 'Give them some recreation programs. You will pacify them and you'll get them out of your hair. They'll go and play'....
>
> We are the future leaders. Leaders are not born automatically to become leaders. They are trained. It's a long, drawn out process, so the adult population has to respect the fact that we require training and they have to put us under their wing and they've got to protect us until we become leaders and are prepared to go out into the mainstream society to make some political statement or to become future leaders in economic development or social development.
>
> Raymond Laliberté
> Métis Addictions Council
> La Ronge, Saskatchewan, 28 May 1992

As we discussed in *Choosing Life*, our special report on suicide, many factors contribute to weakening the fabric of a society and loosening the bonds of relationships and self-regulated behaviour: social change that is rapid or beyond the control of a society; family breakdown, which interferes with the nurturing and socialization of children; poverty and economic marginalization, which restrict opportunities for youth and contribute to a loss of hope; loss of respect for the wisdom of Aboriginal people's culture; and learned patterns of self-defeating or self-destructive behaviour passed on from one generation to another.

We pointed out in *Choosing Life* that these depressing conditions afflict Aboriginal people more frequently than others in Canada, and this is no accident. Aboriginal people were not simply caught in an onslaught of development.

In fact, they were subjected persistently and systematically to interventions that sought to eliminate or replace Aboriginal institutions with the allegedly better institutions of colonial society. In Volume 1 of our report, particularly chapters 8 to 13, we documented the historical policies that had a devastating effect on the culture and cohesion of Aboriginal nations and communities and lasting intergenerational consequences in the lives of families and individuals.

In our hearings and commissioned research we found further evidence that assaults on Aboriginal identity, culture and community institutions continue today. Aboriginal people recounted racially motivated incidents experienced in their daily lives. The stereotyping and devaluing of Aboriginal women, a combination of racism and sexism, are among the most damaging of attitudes that find expression in Canadian society. These attitudes are not held exclusively by non-Aboriginal people either. Indeed, as Roy Fabian pointed out earlier, members of powerless groups who are subjected to demeaning treatment tend to internalize negative attitudes toward their own group. They then act on those attitudes in ways that confirm the original negative judgement. Donna Sears, speaking to us at London, described the process as she saw it:

> The portrayal of the squaw is one of the most degrading, most despised and most dehumanizing anywhere in the world. The squaw is the female counterpart of the Indian male savage and, as such, she has no human face. She is lustful, immoral, unfeeling and dirty. It is this grotesque dehumanization that has rendered all Native women and girls vulnerable to gross physical, psychological and sexual violence.
>
> I believe there is a direct relationship between these horrible racist, sexist stereotypes and violence against Native women and girls.
>
> I believe, for example, that Helen Betty Osborne was murdered in 1972 by four young men because these youths grew up with twisted notions of Indian girls as squaws. Racist and sexist stereotypes not only hurt Aboriginal women and their sense of self-esteem, but actually encourage abuse, both by Aboriginal men and others. Our family violence programs attempt to help both victims and offenders to see beyond the stereotypes.
>
> Donna Sears
> Atenlos Native Family Violence Services
> London, Ontario, 12 May 1993

Not all Aboriginal communities are racked by violence, nor are all Aboriginal people whose lives have been touched by violence necessarily at risk all the time. It can be said, however, that the people who find themselves in high-risk situations are, with shocking frequency, Aboriginal people: pregnant women; children in their formative years; teenaged girls; wives who feel they have no exit from a violent home; and seniors who lack the protection of a functional family. Poverty and all its ills also have an insidious, demoralizing impact on the lives of too many Aboriginal people.

Aboriginal people who asked Commissioners for help in putting an end to violence laid out the ground rules for action: Don't stereotype all Aboriginal people as violent, but make sure that interventions are targeted to those at risk. Don't make social or cultural excuses for violent actions, but attend to the safety and human rights of the vulnerable. Don't imagine that family violence can be addressed as a single problem; rather, root out the inequality and racism that feed violence in its many forms.

3.3 Barriers to Change

Denial

Until the persistent efforts of women in mainstream and Aboriginal society brought the secret of violence into the open, the greatest barrier to correcting the problem was denial. While many still feel shame in acknowledging violence in the family, there is a growing awareness of what constitutes healthy and unhealthy behaviours, as the following presenters explained:

> [People] are becoming accountable and responsible to self, family and community. There is also a negative side to the journey to wellness, and that is that there is a lot of denial and fear out there. Communities are saying: "No, we don't have sexual abuse. We don't have an alcohol problem. We don't have child neglect here." But yet there are tragic stories to be told in our communities.
>
> Marcia Mirasty
> Health Promotion Co-ordinator
> Health and Social Development,
> Meadow Lake Tribal Council
> Ottawa, Ontario, 18 November 1993

> Aboriginal women experiencing family violence are reluctant to seek medical attention for their mental and physical injuries. The severity of injury suffered as the result of family violence is dangerously high.
>
> Twenty-four per cent of the respondents to our questionnaire indicated that they knew of deaths as a result of Aboriginal family violence. And 54 per cent of the respondents suggested that they knew of cases where a woman sustained injury which required medical treatment as a result of family violence but did not seek medical attention, out of fear and shame.
>
> Catherine Brooks
> Executive Director, Anduhyaun Community School
> Toronto, Ontario, 26 June 1992

There are many reasons why family violence is consistently under-reported:

- the attitude of the family or community that family violence is normal;
- poor self-esteem, shame and acceptance on the part of the abused spouse;
- the fear that children will be taken away by child welfare authorities;
- reluctance to have the abusive spouse charged under the mandatory charging procedures now in place in some provinces;
- fear of loss of income if the bread-winner is incarcerated; and
- a lack of faith in the system to respond or intervene effectively.[91]

In some cases, women who received inadequate or no protection as children have met violence with violence as adults, with more tragedy ensuing.

> We need to pay some attention to the security of our female population. Today in this country [Aboriginal] women make up 25 per cent of the federal prison system. Their crimes have been violent crimes. I mean murder and violent assault. And they have told us why they committed these crimes. Many were victims of incest. Many were victims of sexual assault. Many were physically abused as children.
>
> They were pushed to the wall and they responded with violence. Do you hear our men talking of violence against our women? Do you hear our men talking about incest? What is being done in our community about gang rapes? We are suffering in silence.
>
> Sharon McIvor
> Spokesperson, Native Women's Association of Canada
> Toronto, Ontario, 26 June 1992

As is the case with women in the general population, when Aboriginal women overcame their reluctance to speak about their situation they were often met with indifference from police and social agencies, or with advice from family and community to keep silent. First Nations, Inuit and Métis women reported to Commissioners that if they spoke out against abuse they had good reason to fear retaliation, even from those charged with public trust to lead and protect Aboriginal citizens.

> Documentation which substantiates these incidents is included in our submission. All these acts of retaliation are forms of violence against Métis women, emotional, financial and political abuse.
>
> Marge Friedel
> Women of the Metis Nation
> Edmonton, Alberta, 11 June 1992

> There is abuse in our communities. Women are laid off from work if they speak about their rights or talk about sexual harassment in the workplace. We have to live in those communities. We have families to support....

If we go out and speak publicly, we are threatened over the telephone....Our president in the Indigenous Women's Collective had threatening telephone calls. There are all kinds of ways of trying to silence us.

Joyce Courchene
Indigenous Women's Collective
Winnipeg, Manitoba, 3 June 1993

Women endorsed the challenge addressed to male leaders by the Aboriginal justice inquiry of Manitoba:

Most chiefs and council members are male and often exhibit bias in favour of the male partner in a domestic abuse situation. This can effectively chase the woman from her home and community.

The unwillingness of chiefs and councils to address the plight of women and children suffering abuse at the hand of husband and father is quite alarming. We are concerned enough about it to state that we believe that the failure of Aboriginal government leaders to deal at all with the problem of domestic abuse is unconscionable. We believe that there is a heavy responsibility on Aboriginal leaders to recognize the significance of the problem within their own communities. They must begin to recognize, as well, how much their silence and failure to act actually contribute to the problem.[92]

Since 1971, when Jeannette Lavell challenged discrimination against women in the *Indian Act*, the actions of women in asserting their rights and expressing their views in organizations of their own choosing have been viewed by some leaders as a betrayal of the larger mission to exercise and gain recognition of the right of Aboriginal self-government. Aboriginal women appearing before us reported that efforts to isolate them from their nations and silence their voices persist today. These women reject the notion that speaking out as women on behalf of their human and Aboriginal rights is incompatible with being a loyal member in the nation. They are also sceptical of appeals to tradition to support the privileges of insensitive leaders:

Tradition is invoked by most politicians in defence of certain choices. Women must always ask, Whose tradition? Is 'tradition' beyond critique? How often is tradition cited to advance or deny our women's positions?...Some Aboriginal men put forward the proposition that a return to traditional government would remedy the abusive and inequitable conditions of women's lives. We have no reason to put our trust in a return to 'tradition', especially tradition defined, structured and implemented by the same men who now routinely marginalize and victimize us for political activism.[93]

The Coalition is prepared to support the leadership, however, not at the expense of silencing the reality that women, children and men are being abused and killed.

Marilyn Fontaine
President, Aboriginal Women's Unity Coalition
Winnipeg, Manitoba, 23 April 1992

Nor do women want to be considered a special interest group:

Quite often, our association is regarded as a special interest group. That bothers me because we are not a special interest group. We are members of nation[s].

Marlene Pierre
Ontario Native Women's Association
Thunder Bay, Ontario, 27 October 1992

Not all Aboriginal women are able to participate in organized protests. Many are unfamiliar with formal organizational procedures and strategy, even though many women's organizations consciously attempt to reach out and reflect the values and practices of their cultures. There are also practical reasons why many women do not take part in advocacy organizations. Like the Métis women's council, they may prefer to work within the structures of organizations that aim to represent the interests of all their constituents, regardless of age or sex. All too often, women who would wish to participate in women's groups are prevented from doing so by lack of resources, time and transportation. Also, people subjected to violence generally speak out only when they feel safe. Silence perpetuates the problem, however, as each victim – whether wife, child, senior or person with a disability – remains isolated and vulnerable. It is especially important for leaders to break the silence when they become aware of violence in the community, and they must foster a safer climate by supporting groups, including women's organizations, advocating on behalf of individuals being harmed.

Shift in sex roles

Male partners, already shaken by shifts in sex roles, may deliberately try to keep their partners isolated, close to home and work.[94] The impact of changing roles on male-female relationships can be discerned in the comments of a respondent in the Treaty 7 study:

Since I've been here [in the city] my role has been the breadwinner. I worked and he didn't have a job. I went to school and he didn't go to school. There was a lot of pressure on me. He never supported me through my job – you know, moral support. He was always trying to stop me from going to work. In my community, the women have the jobs. Men are unemployed. So it's us women who are the bread-winners. That role has changed.[95]

Jeannette Lavell, one of the earliest and most prominent advocates of women's right to fair and equal treatment, has an analysis of how the stress of social change affects men and women differently, apparently placing greater stress on Aboriginal men:

> Even as people leave the communities to go outside to work it is often the women who find it easier to get into the non-Native work environment, in business or government. But it doesn't have anything to do with us as Native people and our own expectations of each other. It's how the system was set up, how people have been able to adjust or adapt. Maybe this is where, as Native women, we have that sense of being more flexible, where we can adapt just for survival. Perhaps Native men bump up against things and it's not in their character to bend. They will confront it more and if there is a confrontation they will back off. The value that Native men have, that they should be protectors, perhaps makes it more difficult for them to be flexible because it may be seen as being weak. And maybe this is why there are a lot of Native men who get into alcohol abuse and other abuses, just because of the frustration of events.[96]

Aboriginal women have identified two other barriers to change that relate, paradoxically, to aspects of culture that Aboriginal people have tended to consider their greatest strengths: the extended family and the resurgence of spirituality.

The extended family

Because almost everyone is related to each other in small communities that have existed over generations, incidents of abuse, particularly those of a sexual nature, are likely to reverberate through the whole kinship network. If the perpetrator is someone of an older generation, there is strong resistance to acknowledging the reality or confronting that person, and the abuse may continue unabated. Maggie Hodgson, executive director of Nechi Institute, wrote a manual on treatment for survivors of child sexual abuse:

> On the one hand, the cultural norm is to respect older people and to protect them. But on the other, the caregiver must protect the innocent victims of the abuse. Due to [the] sense of powerlessness [they experienced] as a child, untreated Native caregivers/victims may not see the alternatives open to deal with the disclosure about the family abuse in a legally correct manner. It is important to assist them in identifying the possibilities of treatment, not only for the victim, but also for the offender.[97]

Even in cases where evidence of abuse is undeniable, the whole family may be so fearful of the shame associated with divulging the abuse that they collude with the perpetrator to deny and cover up the situation. This puts intense pressure on the abused person to maintain silence. On occasion, where children are being sexually abused, assaults have been allowed to continue over time, eventually involving multiple victims. When multiple charges are subsequently laid, grief and anger become treatment issues for the whole community.[98] The fact that disclosure of sexual abuse of boys, usually perpetrated by men, has been slow to surface indicates the degree of discomfort with the whole issue of homosexuality. Shame about such experiences continues to be a factor inhibiting disclosure and recovery.

While the silencing influence of close-knit kin networks is particularly relevant in instances of sexual abuse, including those of a homosexual nature, the analysis applies to other situations of abuse as well. For example, a woman who marries into a close-knit kin network but has no relatives of her own nearby may be less able to defend herself than a woman with many relatives. She may also be more vulnerable to pressure to remain silent about the abuse. Furthermore, if many members of a close-knit family have been subjected to abuse, the extended family may come to see violence as a way of life rather than an aberration. The distorted view held by some non-Aboriginal people, including judges ruling on cases of violence, that family violence has a cultural explanation or justification, must be vigorously denounced.

> At one time, many white people accepted the myth that abuse was part of the Native cultures. As a woman and a child who grew up in the North, I say 'Hogwash!' It was only accepted because men, Native and white, who controlled the system did not want it changed or did not care. It is totally unacceptable in today's society and all judges should have mandatory training in this, as well as, cross-cultural [training].
>
> Mayor Pat McMahon
> Yellowknife, Northwest Territories
> 9 December 1992

Religion and spirituality

The problem posed by Aboriginal spirituality has two dimensions: the role of Christian churches, and the resurgence of interest in traditional practices and spiritual ceremonies. Both dimensions involve power relationships.

The lives of many Aboriginal people have been stunted and distorted by their experiences in residential schools operated by the Christian churches in concert with the federal government. The multiple dimensions of violence inflicted on children, families and Aboriginal people as a whole are examined through a historical lens in Volume 1, Chapter 10. The lingering, intergenerational effects of those experiences are seen by Aboriginal people as contributing to a cycle of violence in contemporary communities. The nature of that connection is articulated in documents cited in that chapter:

> Social maladjustment, abuse of self and others and family breakdown are some of the symptoms prevalent among First Nation baby boomers. The 'Graduates' of the 'St. Anne's Residential School' era are now trying and often failing to come to grips with life as adults after being raised as children in an atmosphere of fear, loneliness and loathing.
>
> Fear of care takers. Loneliness, knowing that elders and family were far away. Loathing from learning to hate oneself, because of the repeated physical, verbal or sexual abuse suffered at the hands of various care takers. This is only a small part of the story.[99]

> The residential school led to a disruption in the transference of parenting skills from one generation to the next. Without these skills, many survivors had difficulty in raising their own children. In residential schools, they learned that adults often exert power and control through abuse. The lessons learned in childhood are often repeated in adulthood with the result that many survivors of the residential school system often inflict abuse on their own children. These children in turn use the same tools on their children.[100]

Despite this painful history, Christian churches continue to play a significant role in Aboriginal community life. Some Aboriginal people would concur with the analysis of the Canadian panel on violence against women that religious institutions in Canada tend to support and reinforce the dominance of men over women and therefore perpetuate the cultural attitudes that tolerate violence against women.[101] Others look tentatively to the churches for assistance in dealing with the problem:

> On the subject of the church, we can say that the church has played an important role in bringing us to the situation in which we find ourselves today. Because of the church, we have lost many of our values. I think that if the church wanted to help repair the damage that has been done to us, it could apologize to us. However, that is not really sufficient, because too many people have been traumatized. Many have had their lives ruined. [translation]
>
> Delima Niquay
> Manawan Council of Women
> Manouane, Quebec, 3 December 1992

When speaking of church involvement in dealing with family violence, Aboriginal people appear to be of two minds, or perhaps what we are hearing are different attitudes from different constituencies. In some communities there is a long history of attachment to the church and, by all accounts, mutually respectful relations. In other communities there is a visible tension between institutions of the Christian faith and proponents of cultural renewal. Speaking about the possibilities of respectful collaboration, a Moravian minister in Labrador offered the following:

> And as we find ourselves in a period of transition, in a period of relationship that is mostly political and social, I think it becomes more and more important for us to recognize that at least one of the answers to the problems that we face as a people, whether they be substance and alcohol abuse, or family violence, or whatever, rests with our spirituality. And I would hope that in recognizing ourselves as members of part of the Christian church, particularly as members of the Moravian church, that we will find in that relationship and that membership some of the answers that we so desperately seek to turn our society around in many ways.
>
> Reverend Walter Edmunds
> Happy Valley-Goose Bay
> Newfoundland and Labrador, 16 June 1992

We explored the affirmation and revitalization of traditional Aboriginal cultures and the spirituality at the core of Aboriginal practices in Volume 1, Chapter 15. With the renewal of confidence in traditional wisdom and the recognition of elders and their special gifts, a new threat has emerged for vulnerable women and children. Many women cautioned us that 'traditions' and 'traditional healers' must not be accepted uncritically, because not all traditions are respectful of women and not all who present themselves as healers are healthy.

Martha Flaherty, president of Pauktuutit, cites the fact that in Inuit society, boys traditionally were valued more highly than girls.[102] Such attitudes, fostered in a hunting society where the group's survival depended on the skills of male hunters, clearly are prejudicial to women. Similarly, the revival of respect for elders must be approached with discretion. Elders who now occupy positions of respect may themselves have been victims of abuse and may still harbour unhealthy attitudes. There are also reports of persons who wilfully abuse the power accorded to them:

> We have also come across many self-proclaimed healers who have abused and exploited traditional spirituality in their own Aboriginal people....For controlling the spiritual malpractice, I guess it would

be through all the Elders in each community. They would know the ones who are abusing the sweat lodge and abusing the medicines.

Lillian Sanderson
Aboriginal Women's Council
Saskatoon, Saskatchewan, 13 May 1993

Brenda Daily gives several examples of the difficulties of confronting the abusive behaviour of someone recognized as a spiritual teacher or leader.[103] She clarifies that denial of abuse in such cases is rooted in fear, and the challenge required is not a challenge to spiritual beliefs but to the offence and the offender. Daily also describes a situation where the behaviour of an abused child – crying, clinging to the non-offending parent, having nightmares, and acting out – was attributed to 'bad medicine' directed against the family. Daily attributed the mother's denial and rationalization of her daughter's symptoms to her own sense of powerlessness at having been abused as a child by the same family member.

Some women report that in healing circles or community justice projects, where the focus is on restoring peace and harmony, they feel uneasy about confronting their abusers. They do not wish to appear to be violating traditional norms of peacemaking, and they feel the added pressure of having to consider the consequences of disrupting these initiatives, whose goal is to regain control of important dimensions of community life.

The lesson is that Aboriginal people themselves need to temper their faith in tradition with clear-minded judgement to ensure that trust in traditional ways and spiritual leaders does not open the door to abuses of power.

3.4 Solutions from the People

Addressing the structural roots of violence

Family violence in Aboriginal communities shares many characteristics with violence in Canadian society at large: it is widespread and takes many forms; it has been denied in public discourse until recently; it is suffered predominantly by women, children and those in dependency relationships; it is tolerated and even condoned by social institutions; and, rooted as it is in the values of our society, it can be eradicated only by changing the landscape of our whole society.

The statement by the panel on violence against women holds true for violence in Aboriginal communities as well:

Any analysis of violence against women must include recognition of the complex ways in which inequality and power imbalances structure the lives of Canadian women. Only such an understanding can lead to ways of ending violence against women.[104]

Family violence in Aboriginal communities is distinct, however, in that the unbalanced power relationships that structure the lives of Aboriginal people are not found primarily in the relationships between men and women. The imbalance lies in the powerlessness of Aboriginal people relative to society as a whole, including the social institutions that dominate every aspect of their lives, from the way they are educated and the way they can earn a living to the way they are governed.

Aboriginal people have been politically disempowered and economically marginalized. As their ways of ordering social relationships have been systematically ignored or devalued, they have had few opportunities to express themselves or apply their energies in rewarding, self-affirming ways. As a result, they experience extraordinary levels of frustration and anger.

Human beings feel anger and our self-esteem suffers when we are unable to meet our basic needs. In fact, we are biologically equipped with surges of adrenalin to respond forcefully to such threats to our survival. All cultures have generally found ways to control aggressive behaviour and channel energy into problem solving. But when cultural pathways are undermined, as they have been through Aboriginal people's experience of colonization, then the culture loses its control over individual behaviour and eventually violence may erupt. Harvey Armstrong, a psychiatrist with long experience in mental health services among Aboriginal people, describes the dynamic this way:

> Nature's way of solving problems are many, but when her creatures were threatened with the frustration of their needs, their survival, their territory, their food, their mates, water, shelter, or other things needed for survival, aggression and violence has always been one of the last and most desperate solutions. Violence is different from predation in which prey and predator, usually of different species, supply food for one another. Violence is really a phenomenon that occurs within a species....
>
> The capacity for violence is in all of us and really does require external and internal structures to prevent it from erupting....
>
> Oppressed and disadvantaged groups in society have no security that their needs will be met and meet constant frustration in fulfilling their basic needs. They have more stresses and frustrations, and are more likely to turn these frustrations, at either themselves, or those who are nearest and dearest to them, resulting in violence against spouses, children, and elders.[105]

Armstrong goes on to say that acting out violence is easier for the perpetrator if he can convince himself that the victim is less than human. Most Aboriginal violence is directed at other Aboriginal people, particularly family members – not at the administrators, employers and merchants who are the direct source of frustration. Social scientists' explanation of this phenomenon, which is observed in other colonized peoples and disadvantaged social groups as well, is that not only the self but the whole group with which the individual identifies – in this case Aboriginal people – is held in low esteem.[106]

Clare Brant, a Mohawk psychiatrist, has elaborated further on social factors precipitating violence:

> There is an erosion of the self-esteem in Native men by chronic unemployment, [which contributes to] poverty, powerlessness and anomie. Any threat to this fragile self-esteem will be vigorously defended against, usually by aggression....Indian men...unemployed and idle, are constantly humiliated by having their families being supported by the welfare system. The little work which does exist on many Native reserves, such as community health representatives, child protection workers, cleaning staff, and secretarial staff, is often awarded to women. A power struggle ensues when the Native woman is the breadwinner and the exercise of intimidation and violence may be the last resort of the down-trodden warrior.[107]

To say that family violence has its origins in imbalances of power is not to excuse it. Roy Fabian, of Hay River, Northwest Territories, presented an analysis of the origin and expression of cultural self-shame and cultural self-hate that echoes the psychiatric explanation. Fabian went on to state categorically that men who abuse women have to take responsibility for their behaviour and that, by the same token, government and churches that have abused Aboriginal people have to take responsibility for their actions.[108]

In looking for solutions, we begin by drawing attention to the structural origins of violence in relations between Aboriginal and non-Aboriginal societies. We do so because without changing these power relationships and without alleviating poverty and powerlessness, measures to reduce family violence will be patchwork solutions at best. Solutions based on individual therapy may even be destructive in an unrelentingly oppressive political, economic and social environment, because they can reinforce the perception Aboriginal people have of themselves as being weak and morally inadequate.[109]

Anomie, the third factor in Brant's trilogy of causation, is likewise more than a symptom of personal or family dysfunction. As we explained in *Choosing Life*, our special report on suicide, the rules governing individual and group behaviour have weakened as a result of deliberate interventions by Canadian governments aimed at replacing Aboriginal cultures and norms of behaviour with more 'civilized' ways. The policy agenda of assimilation, as implemented through the *Indian Act*, residential schools and community relocations, is documented in Volume 1 of our report. Among the tragic consequences of this failed policy are the scores of Aboriginal youth and young adults with no attachment to

Aboriginal ways – they may even distrust them; yet they do not have a foothold in non-Aboriginal society either, or any sort of commitment to its rules.[110]

In too many Aboriginal communities, or among subgroups within Aboriginal communities, violence has become so pervasive that there is a danger of it coming to be seen as normal. This is another reason why Aboriginal family violence must be addressed as a distinctive phenomenon, with Aboriginal-specific strategies: Aboriginal people are challenged with rebuilding nations and whole communities, as well as restoring the capacity of Aboriginal families to nurture caring, respectful, law-abiding human beings.

As emphasized in the opening chapter of this volume, initiatives to restore the healthy functioning of Aboriginal individuals, families and communities must be undertaken with full awareness of the collective experience of Aboriginal people in Canadian society, the context in which individual problems are generated and in which they must be solved. Poverty, powerlessness and anomie have invaded the homes and hearts of Aboriginal individuals. Poverty prevails because the economic vitality of nations has been undermined through the alienation of traditional lands and their wealth. Powerlessness is rampant because the institutions of leadership and decision making have been displaced, leaving no defence against intrusion and exploitation. Anomie, the breakdown of ethical order, is a direct result of deliberate interventions that undermined the authority and cohesiveness of the family as well as other institutions pivotal to Aboriginal life.

In Volume 2 of our report, we make recommendations for changes in the structure of political and economic relationships between Aboriginal people and Canadian society to dismantle the last vestiges of colonial relationships and give impetus to social, cultural, political and economic revitalization. We are confident that as these structural changes take effect the conditions that spawn violence will recede. Structural change will take time to implement, however.

Restoring community standards

At the same time as the larger changes are being implemented, it is urgent that community standards be re-established in the villages, territories and neighbourhoods where women, children, seniors and persons with disabilities are at risk. Elected and appointed leaders, as well as other individuals with perhaps less formal influence in the community, have a critical role in asserting standards. It is now widely accepted that violence is condoned by passivity and other attitudes that may not even be recognized as expressions of hostility toward women and vulnerable persons. At present, women are the most vocal about the need to break the silence. Very few leaders are speaking out on these issues. We hope our report will encourage more people to join the ranks of those speaking out.

'Zero tolerance' is a problem-specific strategy based on the notion that no level of violence should go unnoticed or uncensured. Endorsed by women, it has had beneficial effects where it has been invoked. Male leaders who are speaking out about violence concur with women who say that in addition to controlling expressions of violence, a broader change in the attitudes of leaders and community members is also required:

> We hear of some judges up North and read about it in the paper where they say, "Well, it's normal for child abuse; it's normal to batter women" and sometimes they are very lenient. We don't agree with that. We think it is not normal to batter women. It is not normal to sexually molest children. Our society has been influenced by alcohol and drugs and we think that judges have to be aware that it is no different for us and it is just as wrong for us to do those kinds of things....
>
> People have rights, women have rights, children have rights....When it comes to abuse of women and children we feel that the law should be fairly firm and it should apply. There should be some discussions on how we are going to deal with it....I think if somebody abuses a child, there is a problem often underlying it. He may need therapy or he may need shock treatment or whatever it is he needs, but *it is not acceptable to us.*
>
> We think that we can be more involved in the justice system. We can have more say and we can make it more adapted to the needs of our people.
>
> Chief Jean-Guy Whiteduck
Kitigan-Zibi Anishinabek Council
Maniwaki, Quebec, 2 December 1992

We have been told before, and I am sure that our Elders will continue to tell us all the time, that when we are talking about the regeneration and re-establishment of our nationhood, there is a specific role for the women to play that is very much a direct, powerful role that has to be acknowledged.

This summer, when we were talking with some of the traditional Chiefs of the Iroquois Confederacy, they said: 'If we are serious about going back to our original structures, then we had better be seriously prepared to change the way we think, the way we act, the way we treat our women, and the way we deal with all those matters surrounding our relationships between men and women.' I think that is something we have to deal with.

Chief Gordon Peters
Chiefs of Ontario
Toronto, Ontario, 18 November 1993

We are convinced that where community standards have been eroded it is possible to re-establish norms of respect for women and protection for vulnerable community members through the advocacy work of community leaders.

RECOMMENDATION

The Commission recommends that

Leadership Stance **3.2.6**

Aboriginal leaders take a firm, public stance in support of the right to freedom from violence of all members in the community, but particularly of women, children, elders, persons with disabilities and others who may be vulnerable, as well as in support of a policy of zero tolerance of actions that violate the physical or emotional safety of Aboriginal persons.

Inclusive forms of representation in decision making

Earlier in this chapter we looked briefly at the role of women in traditional Aboriginal societies (see also Volume 4, Chapter 2). We also observed how discriminatory treatment of women under the *Indian Act* has fostered prejudicial treatment of women in Aboriginal communities. This imbalance in relations between the sexes remains prevalent in many communities and has no doubt contributed to the victimization of women, as reported in our hearings from one end of the country to the other. The fear that self-government will reinforce the unjust treatment of women and deny them access to redress is founded in bitter experience:

> Presently the women in our communities are suffering from dictatorship governments that have been imposed on us by the *Indian Act*. We are oppressed in our communities. Our women have no voice, nowhere to go for appeal processes. If we are being discriminated against within our community, or when we are being abused in our communities, where do the women go?
>
> Joyce Courchene
> Winnipeg, Manitoba
> 3 June 1993

The solution proposed consistently by Aboriginal women to correct current injustices and prevent future ones, is the full, fair representation of women in institutions of self-government and community decision making.

Unfortunately, the imposition of southern values, laws and institutions on Inuit society has resulted in social, political and economic chaos in our communities. Women have suffered doubly for we lost status in our own society and were subjected to the patriarchal institutions born in the south. Until a proper balance is achieved among Inuit men and women, mechanisms must be put into place to ensure that women are equally represented in all decision-making processes and on all decision-making bodies.

Martha Flaherty
President, Pauktuutit
Ottawa, Ontario, 2 November 1993

I would say that there is a real need for the entrenchment of women's rights within self-government. The one thing I hear from women in the communities as well is that there is a real lack of enough advocates. There are advocates, but a lack of enough advocates for their concerns. Often times, things are brought forward to band councils at the community band or regional level and their concerns don't go any farther than that.

Sarah Calaher
Yellowknife, Northwest Territories
7 December 1992

Aboriginal women say that they and their organizations should be recognized as legitimate voices of the nation and not be regarded as upstarts threatening the status quo:

[Our] initiatives, for whatever reasons, are found to be intimidating and threatening to the male-dominated organizations that claim to represent us. In many situations, these organizations have come to oppose the initiatives of the community-based Métis women. They are in the process of negotiating self-governance while they actively try to exclude their female counterparts.

Melanie Omeniho
Women of the Metis Nation
Edmonton, Alberta, 15 June 1993

Instead, said another Métis presenter, Aboriginal leadership and governments should recognize the validity of women's voices and

accept and welcome women's views as not just a particular lobby group's views, but as a view of part of the nation, as part of the people, [acknowledging] that women have real needs and have real answers to problems.

Sandra DeLaronde
The Pas, Manitoba, 19 May 1992

Women are seeking to be included in decision making, to be represented in institutions of self-government, and to have their organizations recognized as legitimate voices in Aboriginal nations. Their full participation in shaping the institutions of self-government holds promise for healing ruptures in relations between the sexes and putting an end to situations in which women are vulnerable to abuse. As well as representing themselves in institutions of self-government, women will help to secure the well-being of the nation. Traditionally, women assumed most of the responsibility of caring for and protecting children, elders and persons with disabilities in Aboriginal communities, and they continue to carry these responsibilities. Their representation in decision making, therefore, will ensure that social needs have equitable recognition on the political agenda, along with legal and constitutional concerns.

> Unless Aboriginal women are guaranteed the right to share equally with men the powers to develop the forms of self-government and the instruments required for dealing with poverty, conjugal violence, incest, the consequences of unemployment, the exclusion of C-31 women and their children from their communities, there will be no significant improvement in living and social conditions. Since women are the main caregivers for the children, the ailing, the disabled and the very old, the organization of educational, health and other social and community services can only be successful where women share in the powers of planning and carrying out those services.
>
> Madeleine Parent
> Montreal, Quebec
> 27 May 1993

It must be emphasized, however, that women's participation in decision making is not a substitute for the direct involvement of others whose voices are now muted in decision-making councils. Just as women have asserted that men cannot assume the right to speak for them without their consent, elders, youth and persons with disabilities must also participate in decision making if they are to shed the vulnerability that is reinforced by silence.

Assumptions about proper modes of representation may be redefined as the constraints of the *Indian Act* are lifted and its influence on community life and attitudes recedes. In the past the family was the all-purpose institution mediating connections between individuals and the larger community. The form of the Aboriginal family has changed, however, taking on more of the characteristics of the nuclear family. It seems clear, therefore, that new institutions will be required to mediate between Aboriginal individuals and the body politic. Perhaps family-like or clan-like institutions will emerge to ensure that those who are now voiceless can be heard. We urge that the healing centres and lodges, proposed in Chapter 3 of this volume, seek out new avenues of healing and new forms of organization and participation that unite the wisdom of tradition with the experience of today.

Women's organizations, healing circles, ceremonial lodges, urban housing projects and friendship centres all have structures designed to bring people together to express their needs and provide mutual aid. These may become the cells or models for the cells required to constitute more inclusive, organic forms of representation and governance.

RECOMMENDATIONS

The Commission recommends that

Breadth of Representation
3.2.7
Aboriginal governments adopt the principle of including women, youth, elders and persons with disabilities in governing councils and decision-making bodies, the modes of representation and participation of these persons being whatever they find most agreeable.

Participation of Women
3.2.8
The full and equal participation of women be ensured in decision-making bodies responsible for ensuring people's physical and emotional security, including justice committees and boards of directors of healing centres and lodges.

Enforcing safety

Caring, respectful, law-abiding behaviour is the result of nurturing in a family or family-like setting where the individual has been able to form stable, trusting relationships with persons who model pro-social behaviour and attitudes. In the normal course of development, children internalize the behaviour and attitudes of their parents or trusted caregivers and in time they go out into the wider world equipped with ethics they can use to evaluate new information and make choices about how to live. Pro-social behaviour is enforced by individuals' internalized sense of right and wrong, reinforced by the expectations of people whose good opinion matters. Law enforcement agencies do not sustain peace and harmony in a community. They discipline the relatively few persons who step outside the rules endorsed and observed by the majority.

In the recollections of Thelma Chalifoux, quoted earlier in this chapter, her male relatives took it upon themselves to discipline a man in the community who had abused his wife. Given her description of the sharing, interdependent relationships that characterized the Métis social network, it is almost certain that it was the vigorous disapproval of his peers that caused the offender to change his behaviour. Community standards of behaviour have been eroded in many places. It is essential that these standards be reinstated so as to secure a safe environment for women, children, elders and persons with disabilities.

Even in a healthy community, rules must be enforced. In some contemporary Aboriginal communities where violence has come to be seen as normal, institutions to enforce the peace are essential. In our report on justice, we documented the failure of mainstream institutions to maintain the peace effectively in Aboriginal communities, to modify the behaviour of offenders and prepare them to assume their place as contributors to community well-being.

Aboriginal people have a right to enjoy security from violence, and individuals who violate that security should face the consequences of their behaviour, as Chief Gordon Peters and others have made clear. Perpetrators of violence also have needs and should have access to culturally appropriate treatment, but the perpetrator's need for rehabilitation should not override the victim's need for safety.

Police and justice institutions in geographically distinct Aboriginal communities should be attentive to the safety needs of women and vulnerable groups.[111] Aboriginal governments should ensure that this becomes the reality in every community. At present, Aboriginal people living in urban centres and non-reserve communities under provincial or territorial jurisdiction rely on public law enforcement and justice institutions for protection. For some Aboriginal communities, this will continue to be the case indefinitely. In these settings, however, as we heard at our hearings, the safety of Aboriginal people is often neglected; in addition, they are often subjected to over-zealous enforcement of control measures and racist treatment. These problems, which bear directly on the management of family violence, have been addressed by the numerous commissions and inquiries reviewed in our justice report.

In our proposals regarding recognition of and support for Aboriginal justice systems in land-based Aboriginal communities, we recommended that Aboriginal women and their organizations be involved in the planning and implementation of community-based justice systems. Further, we recommended that federal, provincial and territorial governments submit annual reports to their legislatures on progress in implementing recommendations made by previous justice commissions and inquiries. Implementing these recommendations will respond to the concerns of women about the need for greater responsiveness on the part of law enforcement and justice institutions.

The authority of Aboriginal governments to establish justice systems must be a core element in their inherent right of self-government, because it is in the community that personal ethics and community standards will be restored. The Aboriginal community is best equipped to make the delicate choices required to balance the victim's needs for protection with the perpetrator's need for rehabilitation. Moreover, the community may be the only forum in which it will be possible to bring alienated youth back into the circle of relations where ethical behaviour brings valued rewards.[112] In view of the time it will take to implement alternative justice measures in many settings, communities should be encouraged to undertake interim measures with the full participation of women to reduce violence within families. For example, communities could endorse and promote observance of codes of conduct that would support law enforcement personnel and guide ordinary citizens in creating safe communities and neighbourhoods. Codes of behaviour endorsed and enforced by popular consent are not meant to replace law enforcement as a means of restraining violence. It seems clear, however, that children and youth who are prone to developing anti-social attitudes and behaviour must be drawn back into the circle of community responsibility. As well, leaders and agencies developing alternative justice measures will benefit greatly from community initiatives to articulate and enforce acceptable standards of behaviour.

The success of the Alkali Lake community in changing behaviour by voluntary community action is well documented.[113] The work of the Bear Clan Patrol in confronting the sexual exploitation of Aboriginal children and youth on the streets of Winnipeg is another example of voluntary action that has changed the moral climate of a community.

Pauktuutit, the Inuit women's association, has taken a more wide-ranging approach to promoting community standards by formulating a set of expectations for Inuit leaders. The "Code of Conduct for Inuit Leaders", adopted at the association's annual general meeting in 1994, encouraged other Inuit organizations to adopt Pauktuutit's or a similar code. The background text called for the full participation of women in decision making and the removal of barriers to their participation. The code itself listed the responsibilities of leaders, among them the following:

> Inuit leaders have additional responsibilities as public figures and role models. These include not engaging in conduct which hurts other people, breaking laws, or is harmful to Inuit society....Acts of violence against women and children, including sexual assault, child abuse, child sexual abuse, and wife battering are absolutely unacceptable, and any leader who engages in such conduct should immediately step aside.[114]

Pauktuutit's code of conduct has moral rather than legal authority; however, as noted earlier in this report, when codes of conduct have been endorsed by a nation and its communities in assemblies and promulgated orally, they have tended to carry the moral force of law in many traditional Aboriginal societies (see Volume 1, Chapters 6 and 15).

RECOMMENDATION

The Commission recommends that

Community Codes   **3.2.9**
of Behaviour   Aboriginal leaders and agencies serving vulnerable people
encourage communities, with the full participation of women,
to formulate, promote and enforce community codes of behaviour that reflect ethical standards endorsed by the community
and that state and reinforce the responsibility of all citizens to
create and maintain safe communities and neighbourhoods.

Community healing and structural change

The foregoing proposal for self-directed community action builds on a widely
held traditional ethic of personal responsibility that derives from the world
view described in Volume 1, Chapter 15. This tradition holds that each human
being must discover his or her own unique gifts, which originate from a spiritual source. Spirit helpers protect these individuals and lend them power, or 'medicine', in their journey through life. The shared acceptance of and adherence to
natural law, sustained by unseen forces, allows human beings to live in harmony
with each other and all their relations on the land and without interference at
the level of personal relationships. Traditionally, this ethic of personal responsibility was sufficiently effective that Aboriginal societies were able to maintain
peace and order without police or jails.

The integrity of this world view and its effectiveness in maintaining order
in Aboriginal societies remain dependent on effective moral education within the
culture. The family is the principal agency or institution charged with instilling
this education. Deliberate interventions by colonial and later Canadian governments, in concert with Christian churches, sought to undermine the authority of Aboriginal families to educate their children in the values and beliefs of
their culture. The extent to which the integrity of Aboriginal families has been
compromised is evident in the statistics on family violence, in the number of
neglected and damaged children coming to the attention of child welfare agencies, and in the observation we heard across Canada that Aboriginal people have
lost their parenting skills.

In traditional Aboriginal societies, when community members were in
mourning, hungry, or infirm with age, the stronger members rallied to support
them. During the condolence ceremony of the Iroquois, described in Volume
1, Chapter 4, the 'clear-minded' members of a community offer solace to those

who have suffered loss: they acknowledge the distorted feelings and perceptions that have overtaken the mourners; they mingle their tears with the afflicted; they wipe away any obstructions preventing the mourners from communicating; they point to the sun that still rises to shed warmth and light on the living; and they remind the grieving ones that it is not good to dwell too long on loss and that there is work to be done.

When whole communities and nations have been traumatized by repeated losses, inflicted on them by unrelenting forces beyond their control, it may seem that there are no 'clear-minded ones' left to raise up the grief-stricken or remind new generations of the work to be done. Kai Erikson, an American social scientist who has studied the phenomenon of collective trauma in the context of earthquakes, has written about the consequences of overwhelming stress experienced by communities:

> By "collective trauma"...I mean to include those kinds of injury that are inflicted not on individuals directly but on the tissues of community life themselves – injuries that act to damage the bonds attaching people to one another, to impair the prevailing sense of group cohesion. Collective trauma works its way slowly into the awareness of those who come to suffer from it, so it may not be visible in the days or even months following discrete moments of disaster. But it is a form of shock all the same, a gradual realization on the part of an already numbed people that their community no longer exists as an effective source of support and that an important part of their world has disappeared without so much as a sound. As people begin to emerge hesitantly from the protective shells into which they had reflexively shrunk at the time of the assault, they learn that they are isolated and alone, living in a kind of social wasteland with no one to turn to. They have lost the solace that comes from being in fellowship with one's kind. They have lost both the physical and the spiritual health that comes from being in communion with kinsmen and neighbours who can be counted on to care....
>
> Human relations in a true community take their shape, at least in part, from expectations pressing in on them from all sides like a firm but invisible mould. They are governed by the ways of the tribe, the habits of the neighbourhood, the customs of the community. When the mould is stripped away, so to speak, something happens to those relationships. It is as if they existed in a kind of gravitational field. The human particles that make up the field are held in place by interpersonal charges passing between them, but they are also held in place by all the other magnetic forces – cultural, societal, communal – that constitute the larger field. And when those

outer currents lose their force, as can happen when the assault is serious enough, the particles begin to separate because the interpersonal charge, by itself, turns out to be less than sufficient. So
marriages break up, friendships dissolve, the bonds of kinship
weaken, and, at the outer edges of human despair, parents lose the
ability to care for their own children. Whole networks of ties begin
to snap noiselessly as the particles, drifting now in a dead gravitational
field, move farther and farther apart. And the pity of it is that people
do not know why this is happening. They never realized the extent
to which the old community validated those bonds and gave them
strength, and, partly for that reason, they do not know how to
breathe new life and meaning into them by deliberate expressions of
affection or by deliberate offers of support.[115]

Some but not all Aboriginal communities have lost the sense of cohesion
to an extent that can be described as collective trauma. Some but not all families have lost confidence in their capacity to parent their children. In urban settings, the challenge is not so much one of restoring community bonds as it is
of building them for the first time, bringing together people of diverse Aboriginal
nations with varied cultural and community experiences.

Forging bonds of community and restoring the capacity of families to care
for their members is a work of spiritual healing that can be accomplished only
from the inside and with the help of relations who are standing on firm ground
and who know the terrain that has to be traversed. A policy document cannot
prescribe where the work is most desperately needed, or when and how it should
proceed. We can recommend that self-directed community healing initiatives be
affirmed and supported and that the vestiges of colonial domination and external control that impede community initiative be dismantled immediately. We
present our recommendations for restructuring systems to affirm and support
the capacity of Aboriginal communities to care for their own members in the next
chapter, on health and healing.

Community healing is proceeding and will proceed on the initiative of
countless individuals, leaders, institutions and governments. But particular initiatives, to have their fullest effect, require complementary change in social
conditions and political and economic life. Although we have tended to emphasize the need for structural change in political and economic relations to remove
the conditions conducive to violence, it is not our intent to ignore or devalue
the important work being done at present to heal the injured and protect those
at risk. On the contrary, it will be required for some time to come. In Volume
4, Chapter 2, we elaborate on the need for places of refuge for women. In
Chapter 3 of this volume, we probe the nature and extent of ill health plaguing
Aboriginal people. As we record in those chapters, many creative and success-

ful initiatives are now being denied stable funding and professional legitimacy. Our recommendations for compiling an inventory and building on existing community service initiatives, which more often than not are the result of the work of women, are detailed in those chapters. We also make recommendations to shift services to the jurisdiction and practical control of Aboriginal people, agencies and communities.

As we propose elsewhere in this volume, we see family violence being addressed effectively through an integrated strategy to achieve whole health. Whole health refers to the ideal of harmony and balance at an individual level, involving body, mind, emotions and spirit; at a social level, implying peaceful, caring, mutually supportive relationships; and at an environmental level, enjoying safety and practising respect for the natural world. The elements of the strategy include changing the political and economic conditions that now have negative effects on Aboriginal nations, communities, families and individuals; restructuring service delivery through healing centres and lodges under Aboriginal control; adopting measures to develop Aboriginal human resources to support community planning and self-care; and making the social and institutional environment of Canadian society more hospitable to Aboriginal cultures and identities. The fundamental work of unlocking the wellsprings of health within themselves belongs to Aboriginal people. The role of Canadian governments and public policy is to remove the obstacles under their control and ensure that resources to support whole health are distributed equitably between Aboriginal nations and communities and the rest of Canadian society.

4. Aspects of Family Law

Family matters, including marriage and divorce, adoption, custody of children, and protection of children's welfare will undoubtedly be among the first areas over which self-governing Aboriginal nations will assume jurisdiction. In the commentary and recommendations that follow, we address aspects of family law that are contentious and could be clarified and made more consistent with present laws. Problems arise in a number of areas:

- recognizing Aboriginal custom in adoption and custody matters;
- dividing property on marriage breakdown; and
- protecting the victim's civil interests in cases of family violence.

4.1 Continuity of Customary Law

Section 35(1) of the *Constitution Act, 1982* states that "the existing Aboriginal and treaty rights of the Aboriginal peoples of Canada are hereby recognized and affirmed", and section 35(2) provides that the "Aboriginal peoples of Canada" include the Indian, Inuit and Métis peoples of Canada. Elsewhere in this report we discussed the significance of the word 'existing' and, in particular, the statement of the Supreme Court of Canada in *R. v. Sparrow* that the word 'existing' makes it clear that the rights to which section 35(1) applies are those in existence when the *Constitution Act, 1982* came into effect; rights that had already been extinguished by that time were not revived by the section.

The court said, moreover, that an existing Aboriginal right could not be read so as to incorporate the way it was regulated before 1982, as this would inject into the constitution, as far as the rights of Aboriginal peoples were concerned, "a crazy patchwork of regulations". Moreover, because a "frozen rights" approach to constitutional interpretation was unacceptable, the rights recognized and affirmed in section 35(1) of the constitution were affirmed in a contemporary form and had to be interpreted flexibly to permit their evolution over time.

Constitutional scholars have concluded that the affirmation of Aboriginal rights in section 35(1) incorporates into Canadian law the common law principle of continuity. Under this principle the customary laws of Aboriginal peoples were deemed to have survived the Crown's acquisition of their territories, provided that this result was not incompatible with the sovereignty of the Crown.

As discussed in Volume 2, Chapter 3, two leading decisions of the United States Supreme Court, *Johnson* v. *M'Intosh* and *Worcester* v. *Georgia,* held that Indian tribes in the United States had the status of domestic dependent nations united by special ties to the Crown as ultimate sovereign. In *Sioui,* Justice Lamer of the Supreme Court of Canada used the words of the chief justice of the United States to describe British policy toward the Indians in the mid-eighteenth century:

> [S]he considered them as nations capable of maintaining the relations of peace and war; of governing themselves, under her protection, and she made treaties with them, the obligation of which she acknowledged.[116]

It would appear, therefore, that at least to some extent Aboriginal customary laws survived the advent of the colonizers. Constitutional scholars seem to be in agreement that certain aspects of customary law pertaining to the family have survived. Customary laws on marriage and adoption have been upheld even in the face of legislation that might be taken to have abridged such laws.[117] We referred earlier to the Quebec case, *Connolly* v. *Woolrich,* which upheld the validity of a marriage contracted under Cree customary law between a non-Aboriginal man and a First Nations woman in the Canadian northwest.[118]

In *Re Katie's Adoption Petition,* Justice Sissons held that adoptions "made according to the laws of the Territories" within the meaning of section 103 of the *Child Welfare Act* included adoptions in accordance with Indian and Inuit custom.[119] In *J.T.K.* v. *Kenora-Patricia Child and Family Services,* the court issued a custody order in favour of relatives of the child's parents over the objections of the Crown.[120] The court found that such an order was in accordance with the tribal tradition of customary adoption among the Ojibwa people.

In *Michell* v. *Dennis*, however, it was held, in a case brought under the *Family Compensation Act*, that under the common law a customary adoption confers no legal rights on either the adoptive parents or the adopted children, only moral obligations.[121] Neither the adoptive parent nor the child adopted by Indian custom had any right of action under that legislation.

One of the important issues facing courts dealing with the custody and adoption of Aboriginal children is the significance of the children's Aboriginal culture and heritage. How much weight should be given to this factor in applying the 'best interests of the child' test? In 1983 the Supreme Court of Canada faced this issue in *Racine* v. *Woods*, involving an Ojibwa girl named Letitia.[122] At birth, Letitia had been placed voluntarily in the care of a children's aid society (CAS) by her mother. When her mother wanted her six-year-old daughter back (she had overcome poverty and alcoholism to regain control of her life), she encountered resistance from CAS officials and from Letitia's foster parents, who had cared for Letitia for five-and-a-half years and had applied to adopt her. The court rejected the birth mother's argument that the adoption would interfere with the child's continuing link to her Aboriginal heritage. The evidence showed that the foster father was a Métis person, that both foster parents were active in the Métis association, and that they had been conscientious in instructing Letitia on her background and culture. While the court acknowledged the importance of the child's cultural background and heritage in applying the best interests test, it found that this factor diminished in significance over time as the child bonded with her adoptive parents.

Courts face the issue of cultural diversity in a variety of situations. They may be asked, for example, to determine whether an Aboriginal child is in need of protection and should be removed from its parents. But should judges apply criteria for determining removal that reflect the values of their own culture or those of the Aboriginal community? While the answer may seem obvious, in most cases judges are not familiar with values outside their own culture.

A good example of this type of case is *Re E.*, in which application was made by a child welfare agency for permanent wardship of the two-year-old child of a 24-year-old Cree mother.[123] The judge began by developing a threshold test for intervention. He said:

> In my view, in order for a child to be found in need of protection there must be a significant departure from a standard of child care that one would generally expect for a child of the age of the child in question. Furthermore, while there is a minimum parental standard for all society, a secondary standard must be established for parents

of the age of the parent in question and for the type of community in which the parent resides. A teen-aged parent cannot live up to the standard expected for a middle-aged parent. Similarly, different standards of parenting apply to parents of Cree ancestry who reside in a small rural community in northern Saskatchewan than would apply to white middle-class parents living, for example, in Regina. What is an acceptable standard for the former might be unacceptable for the latter.

He then proceeded to develop a detailed list of the differences between a northern Saskatchewan Cree community and that of a non-Aboriginal middle-class family living in Regina. The standards of the Cree community were those against which the mother's conduct would be compared to determine whether there had been a "significant departure". The court proceeded on the assumption that a significant departure was necessary before the child could be found to be in need of protection. The standards included cultural differences, acquired community habits, and conditions forced on the community such as dependence on government assistance. In applying these community standards to the facts of the case, the judge found that a single parent in Pelican Narrows, Saskatchewan, might be expected to live in crowded conditions in a house owned by a relative, to be unemployed (lacking in job skills and employment opportunities), and to have problems with alcohol. He ultimately concluded that a permanent wardship order was indeed required, since the mother had departed significantly from community standards and her situation would not likely improve with time or counselling. The approach taken in *Re E.* marked an important step forward in child protection case law dealing with cultural minorities.

In other cases judges may have to determine custody and access where each parent offers a different cultural environment for the child. How can judges decide what will be best for the child without injecting their own cultural values? Moreover, it is difficult to formulate guiding principles that would enable judges to make consistent and predictable decisions in cases where diverse cultural values come into conflict. Indeed, it may even be impossible, given the diversity in cultural concepts of family. In one culture the family may signify a small nuclear unit, while in other cultures it may encompass grandparents, aunts and uncles, other relatives – perhaps the entire community. Clearly, then, guiding principles cannot be premised on the values of a single culture; hence the maxim, "a prime function of law is to prevent one person's truth...from becoming another person's tyranny".[124]

With the advent of self-government, Aboriginal nations will be in a position to make their own family law. Indeed, they can proceed with initiatives in this area now, since family law falls within the core of Aboriginal self-governing jurisdiction. While their customary laws in some areas have continuing validity under section 35(1) of the constitution, in other areas they have been pre-empted by federal or provincial laws. It seems likely, therefore, in view of the fundamental importance of family and family relationships, that Aboriginal people will wish to have their own laws in place as soon as possible. There would seem to be particular urgency in this regard concerning laws and policies affecting children – laws on apprehension, custody and adoption, for example – as well as other areas with an impact on children, including their quality of life and personal security, parental responsibilities with regard to support and maintenance, protection from violence, and property and inheritance. As Aboriginal people have told us, their children are their future.

4.2 Division of Property on Marriage Breakdown

> In marriage, a wife who was abused, who was inadequately provided for by her husband, or who was otherwise unhappy could terminate her marriage simply by announcing that she was leaving. In nations in which a woman was proprietress of the home and its contents, she could dismiss an unsatisfactory spouse with a demand that he vacate the premises or by simply placing his personal effects outside the door. The ousted husband had no alternative but to comply.[125]

There is obviously a vast gulf between the traditional rights of Aboriginal women to hold property and the way those rights have shrunk over the past century. At present, family law, including the division of family assets on marriage breakdown, is governed by provincial law. Two decisions of the Supreme Court of Canada bear witness to the discriminatory impact of the *Indian Act* on Aboriginal women's property rights.[126]

In *Paul* v. *Paul*, two members of the Tsartlip Indian Band, located near Sidney, British Columbia, had been married for 19 years and had three children, ranging in age from eight to 18. The husband held a certificate of possession for reserve property under section 20 of the *Indian Act*. The couple had built their matrimonial home on the reserve property and had lived there for 16 years. In July 1982, the parties separated and the wife was awarded interim possession of the matrimonial home for herself and the children under British Columbia's *Family Relations Act*. When this order was overturned by the British Columbia Court of Appeal, Mrs. Paul appealed to the Supreme Court of Canada. Two provincial attorneys general intervened on behalf of Mrs. Paul, while the attorney general of Canada intervened on behalf of her husband. The wife sought interim possession of the marital home, not a division of family assets. The Supreme Court held that it had no authority to make such an order, since section 77 of the act had no application to a marital home located on a reserve.

In *Derrickson* v. *Derrickson*, another case involving a separated husband and wife, the Supreme Court also rejected the wife's appeal of a B.C. appeal court decision, denying that she had any interest in property for which her husband held a certificate of possession under the *Indian Act*. It confirmed that British Columbia's *Family Relations Act* had no application to land on a reserve held by an Indian person. The provincial legislation, however, did apply to the extent of allowing the provincial court to make an order for compensation to the wife for the financial share of the property to which she was entitled under the relevant law of general application.

However, as noted in the report of the Westbank inquiry, the order for compensation may in reality be hollow:

> Although some spouses may benefit in future from that aspect of the [Derrickson] decision, it was not of great practical assistance to Rose Derrickson. In order to obtain a compensation order in lieu of division of lands, she would have had to return to the Supreme Court of British Columbia. This would entail further expenditure. Furthermore, it would have to be established that her husband had sufficient liquid resources to comply with any order....If the only substantial asset is real property on a reserve, any enforcement of a compensation order may be practically impossible.[127]

In Volume 4, Chapter 2, with regard to child support, we noted similar difficulties in gaining access to the assets of Indian people, generally men, living on-reserve. Women have reported difficulties with the enforcement of child support and wage garnishee orders directed to men living on-reserve, even when the child for whom support has been ordered or the support recipient is an Indian person. In cases where neither the support recipient nor the child is an 'Indian' as defined by of the *Indian Act*, the income earned on a reserve by an 'Indian' cannot be garnisheed or subject to a support order, nor can property on a reserve be seized.[128]

We believe that it is entirely possible to protect the integrity of a nation's lands while recognizing the interest accumulated by individuals in improvements on designated properties. In Chapter 4, later in this volume, we indicate that a combination of public investment and private contributions by householders is necessary to raise the health and safety standards of the on-reserve housing stock. Policies to support shared investment should clarify ambiguities concerning ownership of houses and private interests acquired in reserve lands held in common by First Nations communities.

Acknowledging that it may be some time before full self-government and a new land tenure system for Aboriginal lands are in place, we recommended in Volume 2, Chapter 3 that, in the transition phase, Parliament pass an Aboriginal Nations Recognition and Governance Act to make explicit what is implicit in section 35 of the *Constitution Act, 1982* – namely, that Aboriginal nations constitute an order of government within the Canadian federation and can exercise law-making authority in areas they deem to be core areas of their jurisdiction. Such legislation would make resources available to proceed with rebuilding Aboriginal nations in anticipation of nation-to-nation negotiations for the full implementation of a new relationship. Legislation recognizing this relationship would also facilitate an early start on resolving the anomalies in the field of civil law that we have begun to describe here.

Aboriginal people and legal scholars agree on the broad objectives required. In a commentary on Aboriginal families and the law, Rita Dagenais sums up the situation this way:

> We therefore face a significant legal vacuum. Provincial law does not apply to a matrimonial home located on a reserve. There is no federal legislation governing family residences or other matrimonial matters for Indian persons living on-reserve. The *Indian Act* does not recognize the legislative authority of a band council in the area...
>
> The solution is obvious. Aboriginal communities should be able to legislate in this area. Federal and provincial governments should acknowledge the authority of Aboriginal governments to adopt laws with regard to the matrimonial home and to establish their family law regimes compatible with their cultures and traditions.[129] [translation]

4.3 Civil Law and Violence Within the Family

Aboriginal women have been instrumental in bringing to light the pervasiveness and severity of the violence that has invaded many Aboriginal homes and communities. Like women in Canada generally, Aboriginal women want police protection and recognition from the courts that assaults on women and children are serious crimes. Although women recognize that many abusers are themselves victims, they want the abusers censured for their unacceptable behaviour by the courts, community leaders, family members and peers. Instead, women often discover that reporting abuse causes them more trouble than it appears to bring the abuser. We noted that many women are reluctant to report assaults because experience has led them to believe that no action – or no effective action – will be taken; because of fear that the violence will escalate; for fear of losing their children; for fear they will lose financial support for the family; and for fear that they might have to relive the violence in adversarial court proceedings. In many cases, they remain trapped in violent situations because they simply have nowhere to go for refuge.

The fact that spousal assault is a criminal offence, while decisions on occupancy of a marital home and child custody are civil matters, creates problems. On reserves, for generations dwellings allocated to individuals were registered by means of certificates of possession (CP). The strong patriarchal bent of policy has meant that most CPs were issued in the name of the eldest male in the household.

The male partner's control of the residence becomes problematic if a woman is assaulted and calls for protection in the form of a restraining order restricting the man's access to the marital home. The assault charge will be dealt with as a criminal matter, but if she wishes to have sole occupancy of the marital home, the woman must also launch a civil action in another court. If the marital home is on a reserve, the provincial court is unable to handle the case because it falls within federal jurisdiction over "Lands reserved for the Indians", yet federal legislation to deal with the matter does not exist. Consequently, women often have no alternative but to leave the marital home. Given the shortage of housing on most reserves, women in these circumstances usually have to choose between moving in with relatives already living in overcrowded homes, or leaving the community. The trauma of abuse is thus compounded by the loss of the woman's home, extended family and familiar surroundings.

Particularly for Aboriginal women in urban centres without an Aboriginal family service agency to advocate on their behalf, to report violence in the home that was witnessed by their children or that they have suffered directly is to face the possibility of losing the children to child welfare authorities. In a 1995 report, the law reform commission of Nova Scotia addressed domestic violence. It recommended that an abused spouse not lose custody of her children solely on the grounds that she did not report she was being abused. The harmful effect of exposing children to violence is not to be dismissed, however. The law reform commission recommended that child protection authorities retain responsibility for intervening to protect a child where circumstances require. The commission also recommended that domestic violence be a determining factor in custody and access decisions under Nova Scotia's *Family Maintenance Act*.[130]

The Nova Scotia commission considered but chose not to recommend that family violence be handled in a unified family court with a mandate to hear all family-related matters. It took the view that enlarging the jurisdiction of a family court to hear criminal charges might detract from the seriousness of violence within families, a point that commissioners thought it essential to reinforce. It did recommend that domestic violence be a consideration in granting an order for exclusive possession of a matrimonial home, that such an order be available to common-law and same-sex couples, and that rented residences be included in such orders.

Recognizing the jurisdiction of Aboriginal nations to legislate, administer and adjudicate civil and criminal matters will presumably resolve problems related to gaps between federal and provincial systems and lack of co-ordination between civil and criminal court processes. Similarly, the problem of applying culturally appropriate standards in decisions about neglect of children or the capacity of parents can give way to community standards applied by Aboriginal

adjudicators. As well, the development of new institutions and the full participation of women will help correct the sexist bias now found in some regulations
and practices under the *Indian Act.*

5. CONCLUSION AND RECOMMENDATIONS

At our public hearings, Aboriginal women spoke at length about their responsibilities, particularly in relation to the family, but they said very little about their
rights. Yet it seems inconceivable that Aboriginal women's civil, political and
property rights would not be included in the Aboriginal rights recognized and
affirmed in section 35 of the constitution. Although women's ability to exercise
their rights was subject to extensive regulation under the *Indian Act*, there is no
convincing argument that the rights were extinguished before 1982. They were
therefore "existing" Aboriginal rights within the meaning of *Sparrow* and protected by the equality guarantee (Aboriginal and treaty rights "are guaranteed
equally to male and female persons") in section 35(4).

One of the challenges facing Aboriginal nations will be to give full effect
and recognition to these rights by according Aboriginal women equal participation in designing and implementing Aboriginal self-governing structures and
in creating Aboriginal law and policy. In Volume 4, Chapter 2, we made recommendations concerning this challenge.

Aboriginal nations have an opportunity to start from first principles in creating a family law regime that reflects their cultures, and we believe that they
should be encouraged to do so. The courtroom is not a therapeutic institution,
nor is law a sufficiently refined tool to define family relationships in culturally
appropriate ways. Indeed, law and family do not walk easily hand in hand. As
law professor Harry Arthurs has written:

> "Law", at least in the formal sense, implies authority, conflict, and
> if necessary, coercion. "Family" implies partnership, compromise
> and ultimately, love. "Law" is general, applying to all citizens within
> a state. "Family" is particular, and is shaped for each of us by our own
> individual personalities, and by the very different and complex inter-
> play of religion, ethnicity, class and culture. "Law" is form: due
> process, precision, predictability. "Family" is substance: traditionally
> home, children and loyalty, or in a more modern idiom, sharing and
> caring.[131]

It will require a great deal of planning and deliberation to devise laws that
reflect the non-coercive cultures that Aboriginal people are determined to preserve and at the same time protect vulnerable people in an often troubled envi-

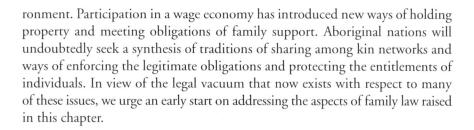

ronment. Participation in a wage economy has introduced new ways of holding property and meeting obligations of family support. Aboriginal nations will undoubtedly seek a synthesis of traditions of sharing among kin networks and ways of enforcing the legitimate obligations and protecting the entitlements of individuals. In view of the legal vacuum that now exists with respect to many of these issues, we urge an early start on addressing the aspects of family law raised in this chapter.

RECOMMENDATIONS

The Commission recommends that

Core Area of Self-
Government

3.2.10

Federal, provincial and territorial governments promptly acknowledge that the field of family law is generally a core area of Aboriginal self-governing jurisdiction, in which Aboriginal nations can undertake self-starting initiatives without prior federal, provincial or territorial agreements.

Validity of
Customary Law

3.2.11

Federal, provincial and territorial governments acknowledge the validity of Aboriginal customary law in areas of family law, such as marriage, divorce, child custody and adoption, and amend their legislation accordingly.

Consultation on
Family Law

3.2.12

Aboriginal nations or organizations consult with federal, provincial and territorial governments on areas of family law with a view to

(a) making possible legislative amendments to resolve anomalies in the application of family law to Aboriginal people and to fill current gaps;

(b) working out appropriate mechanisms of transition to Aboriginal control under self-government; and

(c) settling issues of mutual interest on the recognition and enforcement of the decisions of their respective adjudicative bodies.

Family Law
Committees

3.2.13

With a view to self-starting initiatives in the family law area or to self-government, Aboriginal nations or communities estab-

lish committees, with women as full participants, to study
issues such as

(a) the interests of family members in family assets;

(b) the division of family assets on marriage breakdown;

(c) factors to be considered in relation to the best interests of
the child, as the principle is applicable to Aboriginal custody and adoption;

(d) rights of inheritance pertaining to wills, estates or intestacy;
and

(e) obligations of spousal and child support.

In this chapter we have attempted to convey our understanding of what
Aboriginal people mean when they talk about the family and to emphasize the
critical importance of the family in rebuilding the strength of individuals, communities and nations. We have also examined threats to the health of family life.

It is clear that 'the family' in Aboriginal discourse signifies not only the
household and smaller circle of immediate kin, but also, as it did in traditional
times, a broader caring community that acts as a bridge or mediator between
individuals and the world at large. In traditional times the family ensured recognition by society of the particular gifts and needs of its members; it instilled
respect for self and other beings and for the forces that sustain life; it practised
sharing, thereby building durable networks of mutual aid; and it passed on the
knowledge and skills necessary for members to fulfil their responsibilities in the
natural order.

In some situations, restoring the family to a healthy state will mean making
it possible for extended kin networks to make a living from the land and practise sharing and self-reliance in very traditional ways. In many more situations
it will mean articulating traditional values and applying them in circumstances
that differ radically from the past. In some situations, where Aboriginal people
have become alienated and distrustful of any kind of family, recreating a sense
of family may entail devising entirely new ways of forging personal connections
and community ties.

It is evident that while Aboriginal nations are being rebuilt and the ethical systems that maintain the integrity of community life are being restored to
efficacy, public institutions such as child welfare agencies and police will be necessary to enforce responsibility and restrain aggression. Aboriginal people are wary
of replicating the institutions of colonial control that have been so intrusive and
destructive of family life. It is possible to respect the autonomy of families and
communities while protecting the interests of individual members; it is a matter
of striking a balance.

In addressing child welfare, family violence and family law in this chapter, we have endorsed early recognition of the authority of Aboriginal nations to act in these areas. Their capacity to achieve a balance between protecting individuals and respecting family autonomy, and their effectiveness in promoting family healing, will be critical tests of the success of self-government.

NOTES

1. Items in the Commission's mandate related specifically to family life include social issues of concern to Aboriginal peoples; quality of life concerns, including child care, child welfare and family violence; and cultural issues of concern to Aboriginal peoples, including recognition by Canadian society and institutions of the intrinsic value of Aboriginal family structures and child care patterns. See Volume 1, Appendix A for the full terms of reference.

2. Ernest S. Burch, Jr., "The Caribou Inuit", in *Native Peoples, The Canadian Experience*, ed. R. Bruce Morrison and C. Roderick Wilson (Toronto: McClelland & Stewart, 1986), p. 116.

3. For a look at Innu practices, see José Mailhot, *Au pays des Innus, Les gens de Sheshatshit* (Montreal: Recherches amérindiennes au Québec, 1993).

4. Burch, "The Caribou Inuit" (cited in note 2), p. 118.

5. Marlene Brant Castellano, "Women in Huron and Ojibwa Societies", *Canadian Woman Studies* 10/2&3 (Summer/Fall 1989), p. 47.

6. Obituary of Clemence Gourneau Berger, *Democrat-News*, Lewistown, Montana, 31 December 1943, quoted in Verne Dusenberry, "Waiting for a Day that Never Comes: The Dispossessed Métis of Montana", in *The New Peoples: Being and Becoming Métis in North America*, ed. Jacqueline Peterson and Jennifer S.H. Brown (Winnipeg: University of Manitoba Press, 1985), p. 125.

7. For a description of Métis family and community in recent history, see Maria Campbell, *Halfbreed* (Toronto: McClelland & Stewart, 1973).

8. Paulus Maggo, "Remembering the Years of My Life", in Carol Brice-Bennett, "Labrador Inuit Life Histories", research study prepared for the Royal Commission on Aboriginal Peoples [RCAP] (1994). For more information about RCAP research studies, see *A Note About Sources* at the beginning of this volume.

9. See Alexander Ross, *The Red River Settlement: Its Rise, Progress, and Present State, With Some Account of the Native Races and its General History to the Present Day* (Edmonton: Hurtig Publishers, 1972), p. 249.

10. For a fuller discussion of mediating institutions, see Peter L. Berger and Richard John Neuhaus, "To Empower People", in *People-Centred Development: Contributions Toward Theory and Planning Frameworks*, ed. David C. Korten and Rudi Klauss (West Hartford: Kumarian Press, 1984), pp. 250-261; and Lorna

Williams, Sharon Wilson, Adeline Saunders and Patrick Maxcy, "Elementary Education Study: Vancouver Inner City Project, Feuerstein's Instrumental Enrichment and Related Applied Systems: Case Study Plan", research study prepared for RCAP (1993).

11. For testimony on the effects of residential schooling see the section on current issues in this chapter. See also Assembly of First Nations, *Breaking the Silence: An Interpretive Study of Residential School Impact and Healing as Illustrated by the Stories of First Nation Individuals* (Ottawa: Assembly of First Nations, 1994).

12. John S. Murdoch, "Education for Cree Children in the James Bay Territory of Northern Quebec: A Retrospective View of Foundations and Processes", research study prepared for RCAP (1994).

13. See Donald McCaskill, "The Urbanization of Canadian Indians in Winnipeg, Toronto, Edmonton and Vancouver: A Comparative Analysis", PH.D dissertation, York University, 1979, pp. 82-89.

14. Tony Snowsill, producer and director, *Our Children Are Our Future* (Scarborough, Ontario: Direction Films, 1991). The film is available through Canadian Learning Company, 1-800-267-2977.

15. A discussion of the Spallumcheen child welfare by-law is presented in RCAP, *Bridging the Cultural Divide: A Report on Aboriginal People and Criminal Justice in Canada* (Ottawa: Supply and Services, 1996), p. 100. Community experience in implementing the by-law is reported in Monique Godin-Beers and Cinderina Williams, "Report of the Spallumcheen Child Welfare Program", research study prepared for RCAP (1994).

16. Patrick Johnston, *Native Children and the Child Welfare System* (Toronto: Canadian Council on Social Development in association with James Lorimer & Company, 1983).

17. Johnston, *Native Children*, p. 23.

18. As with many statistics relating to First Nations, Inuit and Métis populations, for the most part only statistics for First Nations people ordinarily resident on reserves are available, because funding for services to Indian people on-reserve – the costs of maintenance and supervision of children in care – flow from the federal government, which maintains statistics on these expenditures. Statistics on services rendered to off-reserve registered Indians, non-status Aboriginal persons, Métis people and Inuit outside the Northwest Territories and territories covered by land claims settlements are not gathered separately from data on the general population. There is no means, therefore, of obtaining figures for Canada-wide comparisons.

Comparisons are also difficult because of the different methods used for collecting data. For example, agencies may gather statistics on the basis of admissions. One family with several members admitted to care several times for short periods will inflate the numbers. Similarly, children in long-term care may not be distinguished from short-term placements in counting numbers of children in care at a particular point in time. Days of care provided may be a clearer quantitative measure but the numbers do not shed light on patterns of care and duration of placements. Johnston uses the term "Native children" to include status and non-status Indians and Métis people and Inuit, although statistics on non-registered "Native children" are often based on estimates made by service agencies.

See Volume 1, Chapter 2 (particularly the endnotes) for a general discussion of the sources of data used by the Commission in this report.

19. Johnston, *Native Children* (cited in note 16). These figures are summarized from tables appearing on pp. 24-54.

20. Johnston, *Native Children*, p. 56. The higher figure of 7.3 per cent reported for Alberta is inflated by the inclusion of children in conflict with the law and children with disabilities.

21. Johnston, *Native Children*, p. 57.

22. See Volume 1, Chapter 10 of this report; and John S. Milloy, "Suffer the Little Children: The Aboriginal Residential School System, 1830-1992", research study prepared for RCAP (1996). See also George Caldwell, *Indian Residential Schools* (Ottawa: Canadian Welfare Council, 1967).

23. 'Apprehension' is the term used when a government agency authorized under child welfare law removes a child from parental care to agency control.

24. Johnston, *Native Children* (cited in note 16), pp. 60-61.

25. See Peter Hudson, "Une évaluation des services d'aide à l'enfance indienne : le cas du Manitoba", *Recherches amérindiennes au Québec* 16/1, pp. 29-40. Brad McKenzie and Pete Hudson, "Native Children, Child Welfare, and the Colonization of Native People", in *The Challenge of Child Welfare*, ed. Kenneth L. Levitt and Brian Wharf (Vancouver: University of British Columbia Press, 1985), pp. 125-141; House of Commons, Special Committee on Indian Self-Government, *Report of the Special Committee* (Ottawa: Queen's Printer, 1983); and Bradford Morse, "Native Indian and Métis Children in Canada: Victims of the Child Welfare System", in *Race Relations and Cultural Differences: Educational and Institutional Perspectives*, ed. Gajendra K. Verma and Christopher Bagley (New York: St. Martin's Press, 1984), pp. 259-277.

26. McKenzie and Hudson, "Native Children, Child Welfare".

27. Joyce Timpson, "Aboriginal Peoples, Child Welfare Policy and the Canadian State: Historical Context and Contemporary Consideration for First Nations' Controlled Service", research study prepared for RCAP (1993).

28. Review Committee on Indian and Metis Adoptions and Placements, *No Quiet Place: Final Report to the Honourable Muriel Smith, Minister of Community Services* (Winnipeg: Manitoba Community Services, 1985), pp. 268, 272-276.

29. Department of Indian Affairs and Northern Development [DIAND], "Growth in Federal Expenditures on Aboriginal Peoples", background paper prepared for RCAP (1993).

30. Brad McKenzie, "Aboriginal Foster Family Care in Canada: A Policy Review", research study prepared for RCAP (1995).

31. McKenzie, "Aboriginal Foster Family Care".

32. McKenzie, "Aboriginal Foster Family Care".

33. *Child Welfare Amendment Act, 1985*, S.A., c. C-8.1, s. 73.

34. *Child Welfare Act*, R.S.N. 1990, c. C-12, s. 4(2)(g).

35. *Aboriginal Custom Adoption Recognition Act*, S.N.W.T. 1994, c. 26.

36. Summary based on *Aboriginal Custom Adoption Recognition Act*, S.N.W.T. 1994, c. 26, ss. 2, 3, 5.

37. *Children's Act*, S.Y. 1986, c. 22, s. 107.

38. R.S.Q., c. P-34.1, s.2.4, (5°)(c).

39. *Child and Family Services Act*, R.S.O. 1990, c. C-11, ss. 1, 13, 37, 53, 57, 130, 191, 195, Part X, O. Reg. 206/90.

40. *An Act respecting the Commission des droits de la personne et des droits de la jeunesse*, S.Q. 1995, c. 27, s. 2.

41. DIAND, "Growth in Federal Expenditures" (cited in note 29).

42. For a graph representing these statistics and citing sources, see Figure 3.2 in Chapter 3 in this volume.

43. In *Native Children* (cited in note 16), Patrick Johnston cites the 1981 figures for Aboriginal children in care as 4.6 per cent, compared to nearly one per cent of children in care from the general population. Variations result from differences in 'Native' as compared to registered Indian on-reserve population counts and varied reporting categories for children in care. Data are not strictly comparable and should be read as estimates only.

44. Alberta Commissioner of Services for Children, *Finding a Better Way: The Consultations and Research Leading to the Redesign of Children's Services in Alberta* (Edmonton: 1994), p. 28.

45. Pete Hudson, "Politics and Program: A Case Study of a First Nations Child and Family Service Agency", research study prepared for RCAP (1994).

46. See Suzanne Manomie, "A Second Look at Custom Adoption. Is an Age-old Tradition Endangering Some Children?", *Arctic Forum* (Fall 1994), pp. 7-8. Brad McKenzie suggests families providing customary care require training and support if they are to deal with the special needs arising from trauma and neglect suffered by many children needing alternative care. The move toward developing minimum standards for customary care reflects "the growing realization that abuse and poor quality care can occur within alternative care arrangements and that there is a need to protect children in care from these situations". McKenzie, "Aboriginal Foster Family Care" (cited in note 30).

47. In 1991, Pauktuutit, the national Inuit women's organization, published *No More Secrets*, a report acknowledging the problem of child sexual abuse in Inuit communities and promoting community responsiveness to disclosure and the need for healing of all those affected. See Rosemarie Kuptana, *No More Secrets: Acknowledging the Problem of Child Sexual Abuse in Inuit Communities: The First Step Towards Healing* (Ottawa: Pauktuutit, 1991).

48. RCAP, *Choosing Life: Special Report on Suicide Among Aboriginal People* (Ottawa: Supply and Services, 1994), p. 56 and following.

49. Joan Glode, quoted in Patricia E. Doyle-Bedwell, "Reclaiming Our Children: Mi'kmaq Family and Children Services", research study prepared for RCAP (1994).

50. *No Quiet Place* (cited in note 28), pp. 272-276.

51. Godin-Beers and Williams, "Spallumcheen Child Welfare Program" (cited in note 15).

52. H.B. Hawthorn, ed., *A Survey of Contemporary Indians of Canada: A Report on Economic, Political, Educational Needs and Policies* (Ottawa: DIAND, 1966).

53. See Allan Moscovitch and Andrew Webster, "Social Assistance and Aboriginal People", research study prepared for RCAP (1993).

54. On 1 April 1996, under the *Budget Implementation Act, 1995,* S.C. 1995, c. 17, Parts IV and V, the Canada Assistance Plan was replaced by the Canada Health and Social Transfer, a system of block grants from the federal government to the provinces.

55. H. Philip Hepworth, *Foster Care and Adoption in Canada* (Ottawa: Canadian Council on Social Development, 1980), pp. 111-122; and Johnston, *Native Children* (cited in note 16).

56. Hudson, *Politics and Program* (cited in note 45).

57. Connie H. Nelson, Mary Lou Kelley and Dennis H. McPherson, "Rediscovering Support in Social Work Practice: Lessons from Indian Indigenous Human Service Workers", *Canadian Social Work Review* (1985), pp. 233-235.

58. Lauri Gilchrist and R. Anthony Winchester, "Kāptītipis, ē-pimohteyahk: Aboriginal Street Youth; Vancouver, Winnipeg and Montreal", research study prepared for RCAP (1995).

59. Gilchrist and Winchester, "Kāptītipis, ē-pimohteyahk".

60. Gilchrist and Winchester quote an estimate by an agency worker in Vancouver that 70 per cent of the male prostitutes in a district known as 'Boystown' are Aboriginal. Gay males experience double discrimination: from Aboriginal people because of their homosexuality and from non-Aboriginal people because of their Aboriginal identity.

61. Gilchrist and Winchester, "Kāptītipis, ē-pimohteyahk".

62. Gilchrist and Winchester, "Kāptītipis, ē-pimohteyahk".

63. The following analysis of needs and services is drawn from Gilchrist and Winchester, "Kāptītipis, ē-pimohteyahk".

64. See RCAP, *Choosing Life* (cited in note 48), pp. 54-55, for a description of the work of the Bear Clan Patrol.

65. A summary account of Missy's story can be found in RCAP, *Choosing Life*, pp. 31-36.

66. Gilchrist and Winchester, "Kāptītipis, ē-pimohteyahk" (cited in note 58).

67. Alberta Commissioner of Services for Children, "Focus on Children" (November 1994).

68. Ontario Ministry of Health, *New Directions, Aboriginal Health Policy for Ontario* (Toronto: 1994), pp. 15 and 31.

69. Government of the Northwest Territories, *Community Wellness: Working Together for Community Wellness, A Directions Document* (Yellowknife: 1995), p. 2.

70. In our special report on suicide, *Choosing Life* (cited in note 48), p. 90, we articulate a three-pronged strategy of local prevention and crisis intervention services to offset risk, community development to address the most pressing local causes of suicidal hopelessness and helplessness, and the opportunity to achieve autonomy and self-determination as Aboriginal peoples. The approach is applicable to family support and child protective services as well.

71. Associate Chief Judge Dale Giesbrecht, *Fatality Inquiries Act: Respecting the Death of Lester Norman Desjarlais* (Brandon, Manitoba: 1992).

72. Women appearing at our hearings were particularly concerned about abuses of political power that affect their well-being. For our position on the protection of human rights in the context of justice systems under Aboriginal nation authority, see RCAP, *Bridging the Cultural Divide* (cited in note 15), in particular Chapter 4, "Application of the *Canadian Charter of Rights and Freedoms* to Aboriginal Justice Systems" and "Ensuring the Safety of Women and Children in Aboriginal Justice Systems". On the development of local capacity to deal with child abuse and organizational effectiveness, see presentations on the Grand Lac Victoria Community and Atikamekw Health and Social Services, reported in RCAP, *The Path to Healing: Report of the National Round Table on Aboriginal Health and Social Issues* (Ottawa: Supply and Services, 1993).

73. The commitment of Canadian governments to the well-being of children gained prominence with Canada's participation in the United Nations World Summit for Children in September 1990, its involvement in developing the UN *Convention on the Rights of the Child*, and its subsequent ratification of the convention in December 1991. The rights of Aboriginal children are given specific attention by the Canadian government in monitoring actions to implement the convention. See Department of Canadian Heritage, *Convention on the Rights of the Child: First Report of Canada* (Ottawa: 1994).

74. Madeleine Dion Stout, "The Missing Peace: Family Violence in Aboriginal Communities", policy paper prepared for RCAP (1995).

75. Government of Canada, *Family Violence: Situation Paper* (Ottawa: Supply and Services, 1992), p.1.

76. For a discussion of women's action to promote non-violence in Aboriginal communities in Quebec, see Clotilde Pelletier, "Un premier colloque autochtone sur la violence", *Recherches amérindiennes au Québec* 25/1 (1995), pp. 97-98.

77. Statistics Canada, "The Violence Against Women Survey: Highlights", *The Daily*, 18 November 1993, catalogue no. 11-001E, p. 2.

78. Peter Kulchyski, "Community Study: Solutions from Fort Simpson", research study prepared for RCAP (1994).

79. Freda Lundmark, Metis Women of Manitoba, RCAP transcripts, Thompson, Manitoba, 31 May 1993; and Tom Lindley, Westbank Indian Band, Kelowna, British Columbia, 17 June 1993.

80. See presentation by Marilyn Fontaine, President, Aboriginal Women's Unity Coalition, RCAP transcripts, Winnipeg, Manitoba, 23 April 1992.

81. Carol La Prairie, *Seen But Not Heard: Native People in the Inner City* (Ottawa: Public Works and Government Services, 1994).

82. Ontario Native Women's Association, *Breaking Free: A Proposal for Change to Aboriginal Family Violence* (Thunder Bay, Ontario: 1989).

83. Women's Education and Research Foundation, *Native Women's Needs Assessment Survey (Urban and Oneida Reserve Population): Final Report* (London, Ontario: 1986).

84. Joan Wierzba, Betty Bastien and Elsie Bastien, "Native Family Violence in Lethbridge", *Native Studies Review* 7/1 (1991), p. 136.

85. Emma D. LaRocque, "Violence in Aboriginal Communities", in RCAP, *The Path to Healing* (cited in note 72), p. 73.

86. Canadian Panel on Violence Against Women, *Changing the Landscape: Ending Violence – Achieving Equality* (Ottawa: Supply and Services, 1993).

87. Martha Flaherty, "Family Violence – An Inuit Perspective", *Vis-à-vis: A National Newsletter on Family Violence* 10/4 (Spring 1993), p. 11.

88. Lynda Lange, "Fractured Vision: Frustration and Hope in Fort Resolution, N.W.T.", research study prepared for RCAP (1994).

89. Unidentified male respondent, quoted in Brenda ManyFingers, "Treaty 7 Community Study: Family Violence and Community Stress", research study prepared for RCAP (1994).

90. ManyFingers, "Treaty 7 Community Study".

91. Dion Stout, "The Missing Peace" (cited in note 74).

92. Public Inquiry into the Administration of Justice and Aboriginal People, *Report of the Aboriginal Justice Inquiry of Manitoba, The Justice System and Aboriginal People* (Winnipeg: Queen's Printer 1991), p. 485.

93. Women of the Metis Nation, "Women Who Own Themselves: Final Report on the Conference on Métis Women and Governance", brief submitted to RCAP (1993), pp. 25-27. For more information about briefs submitted to RCAP, see *A Note About Sources* at the beginning of this volume.

94. See Jacques Leroux, "Les métamorphoses du pacte dans une communauté algonquine", *Recherches amérindiennes au Québec* 25/1 (1995), p. 58.

95. Quoted in ManyFingers, "Treaty 7 Community Study" (cited in note 89).

96. Jeannette Lavell, quoted in Marlene Brant Castellano and Janice Hill, "First Nations Women: Reclaiming Our Responsibilities", in *A Diversity of Women: Ontario, 1945-1980*, ed. Joy Parr (Toronto: University of Toronto Press, 1995), p. 244.

97. Maggie Hodgson, "Where to From Here? Developing Effective Treatment Programs for Sexual Abuse in Native Communities", in Tony Martens, ed., *The Spirit Weeps: Characteristics and Dynamics of Incest and Child Sexual Abuse* (Edmonton: Nechi Institute, 1988), p. 130.

98. Hodgson, "Where to From Here?", p. 127.

99. Letter from Chief Ed Metatawabin to Tom Siddon, minister of Indian affairs, 15 November 1990.

100. DIAND File E6757-18, Vol. 13, Memorandum for the Deputy Minister from J. Cochrane, 6 June 1992 and the attached First Nations Health Commission Proposal, May 1992.

101. Canadian Panel on Violence Against Women, *Changing the Landscape: Ending Violence – Achieving Equality*, Executive Summary/National Action Plan (Ottawa: Supply and Services, 1993), Part V, p. 88.

102. Martha Flaherty, RCAP transcripts, Ottawa, Ontario, 2 November 1993.

103. Brenda Daily, in *The Spirit Weeps* (cited in note 97), p. 117.

104. Canadian Panel on Violence Against Women, *Final Report of the Canadian Panel on Violence Against Women* (Ottawa: Supply and Services, 1993), p. 4.

105. Harvey Armstrong, "An Overview on Family Violence", in *Family Violence, A Native Perspective*, Transcribed and Edited Proceedings of the 1987 Meeting of the Canadian Psychiatric Association, Section on Native Mental Health, London, Ontario, 1987, pp. 9 and 11.

106. See Frantz Fanon, *The Wretched of the Earth* (New York: Grove Press, 1965) for a widely recognized analysis of the effects of colonial experience on collective self-esteem.

107. Clare Brant, "Violence in the Native Community", in *Proceedings of the Third Symposium on Violence and Aggression* (Saskatoon: University of Saskatchewan and Regional Psychiatric Centre (Prairies), 1990), p. 63.

108. Roy Fabian, RCAP transcripts, Hay River, Northwest Territories, 17 June 1993.

109. For a discussion of the dangers of individual therapies for personal dislocation resulting from powerlessness and exploitation, see Roland D. Chrisjohn and Sherri L. Young, "The Circle Game: Shadows and Substance in the Indian Residential School Experience in Canada", research study prepared for RCAP (1994), Chapter 6: The Forest and the Trees.

110. The over-representation of Aboriginal youth in the justice systems across Canada is another manifestation of the problem of alienation from the cultural norms of both Aboriginal and non-Aboriginal society. For a fuller discussion of this issue see Chapter 2, "Current Realities", in RCAP, *Bridging the Cultural Divide* (cited in note 15).

111. See RCAP, *Bridging the Cultural Divide,* in particular, "Ensuring the Safety of Women and Children in Aboriginal Justice Systems" in Chapter 4, and recommendations 7, 8 and 10. For an example of a regional effort to change the way conflicts and violence in the family and community are dealt with, see Makivik Corporation/Kativik Regional Government Task Force, *Blazing the Trail to a Better Future* (1993). The task force was established by Inuit of Nunavik to examine all aspects of the justice system as it operates in their territory. It consisted of six people and consulted extensively in all member communities. It made specific recommendations to incorporate Inuit values and customs in the adjudicative, sentencing and detention phases of the existing justice system, pending development of a more complete Inuit system of justice.

112. For examples of culture-based community experience in rehabilitation, see Volume 1, Chapter 15, as well as the case studies of Aboriginal Legal Services of Toronto and Hollow Water First Nation's holistic circle healing project in RCAP, *Bridging the Cultural Divide*, Chapter 3.

113. See *The Honour of All: The Story of Alkali Lake* (Phil Lucas Productions, 1985, video, 56:48 min.)

114. Pauktuutit, "Code of Conduct for Inuit Leaders", annual general meeting, Cambridge Bay, Northwest Territories, 1994.

115. Kai Erikson, foreword, in Anastasia M. Shkilnyk, *A Poison Stronger than Love: The Destruction of an Ojibwa Community* (New Haven: Yale University Press, 1985), pp. xvi-xvii.

116. *R. v. Sioui*, [1990] 1 S.C.R. 1025 at 1054.

117. *Re Noah Estate*, [1961-62] 36 W.W.R. 577 (N.W.T. Terr. Ct.) dealt with the application of the *Northwest Territories Act* to Inuit living in the Territories. Section 22(2) of that act provides: "All laws of general application in force in the territories are, except where otherwise provided, applicable to and in respect of Inuit in the Territories."

It was held in *Re Noah Estate*, at 600, that this section did not succeed in providing blanket application of territorial ordinances to Inuit. In a line of cases starting with *Re Noah Estate* and dealing with customary marriage and adoption, the courts have not felt compelled to apply the section strictly in accordance with its terms. In the words of Justice Sissons: "Vested rights are not to be taken away without express words of necessary intendment or implication". It was held in this line of cases, therefore, that rights created through customary law were unaffected by section 22(2) and other similar legislation.

118. *Connolly* v. *Woolrich* (1867), 17 Rapports judiciaires revisés de la Province de Québec 75 (Que. Sup. Ct.). See Volume 2, Chapter 3, in particular the section on an Aboriginal order of government.

119. *Re Katie's Adoption Petition*, [1962] 38 W.W.R. 100 (N.W.T. Terr. Ct.).

120. *J.T.K.* v. *Kenora-Patricia Child and Family Services*, [1985] 4 C.N.L.R. 76 (Ont. Prov. Ct.).

121. *Michell* v. *Dennis*, [1984] 2 W.W.R. 449 (B.C.S.C.).

122. *Racine* v. *Woods*, [1983] 2 S.C.R. 173 at 174.

123. *Re E.*, [1980] 4 W.W.R. 296 at 296-297.

124. Joseph Goldstein, Anna Freud and Albert J. Solnit, *Before the Best Interests of the Child* (New York: The Free Press, 1979), p. 93.

125. Verna Kirkness, "Emerging Native Woman" (1987-1988) 2 C.J.W.L. 408 at 411 [note omitted].

126. *Derrickson* v. *Derrickson*, [1986] 1 S.C.R. 285; and *Paul* v. *Paul*, [1986] 1 S.C.R. 306.

127. *Report of the Commission of Inquiry Concerning Certain Matters Associated with the Westbank Indian Band* (Ottawa: Supply and Services, 1988), pp. 524-525.

128. Correspondence to RCAP Commissioner Mary Sillett from the Ontario Ministry of the Attorney General, 9 September 1993, concerning the enforcement of support orders.

129. Rita Dagenais, "Le droit de la famille autochtone", in *Droit civil et droits autochtones: confrontation ou complémentarité* (Association Henri-Capitant, 1992), pp. 32-33.

130. Law Reform Commission of Nova Scotia, *Final Report: From Rhetoric to Reality, Ending Domestic Violence in Nova Scotia* (Halifax: February 1995) pp. 90, 102.

131. H.W. Arthurs, "The Future of Family Law", in *Family Law: Dimensions of Justice*, selected papers presented at the Judicial Conference on Family Law, 1981, ed. Rosalie S. Abella and Claire L'Heureux-Dubé (Toronto: Butterworths & Co., 1983), p. 295.

3

HEALTH AND HEALING

The wellness of our people, including their social, economic and spiritual well-being, crosses the boundaries of the separate terms [of reference of the Royal Commission]. Wellness is a community issue, a national issue, a women's issue. It touches youth concerns, family considerations, even self-government and historical concerns. I firmly believe that no other [issue] so fundamentally relates to the survival of our people as that of health.

Tom Iron
Fourth Vice-Chief
Federation of Saskatchewan Indian Nations
Wahpeton, Saskatchewan, 26 May 1992*

CANADA IS WIDELY THOUGHT to be one of the best countries in which to live. In 1994, the United Nations Development Programme measured the quality of life around the world, using a variety of social and economic indicators. Canada placed first.[1]

Yet, within Canada's borders, there are two realities. Most Canadians enjoy adequate food and shelter, clean water, public safety, protection from abject poverty, access to responsive medical and social services, and the good health that results from these things. Aboriginal people are more likely to face inadequate nutrition, substandard housing and sanitation, unemployment and poverty, discrimination and racism, violence, inappropriate or absent services, and subsequent high rates of physical, social and emotional illness, injury, disability and premature death. The gap separating Aboriginal from non-Aboriginal

---

* Transcripts of the Commission's hearings are cited with the speaker's name and affiliation, if any, and the location and date of the hearing. See *A Note About Sources* at the beginning of this volume for information about transcripts and other Commission publications.

people in terms of quality of life as defined by the World Health Organization remains stubbornly wide:

- Life expectancy at birth is about seven to eight years less for registered Indians than for Canadians generally.[2]
- Part of this difference in life expectancy is explained by high rates of infant mortality among registered Indians. For infants, the death rate is about twice as high as the national average.[3] There are also high rates of injury and accidental death among Aboriginal children and adolescents. Mortality in all age groups is higher for registered Indians than for Canadians generally.
- Infectious diseases of all kinds are more common among Aboriginal people than others.
- The incidence of life-threatening degenerative conditions such as cancer, heart, liver and lung disease – previously uncommon in the Aboriginal population – is rising.
- Overall rates of injury, violence and self-destructive behaviour are disturbingly high.
- Rates of overcrowding, educational failure, unemployment, welfare dependency, conflict with the law and incarceration all point to major imbalances in the social conditions that shape the well-being of Aboriginal people.

We believe that most Canadians are disturbed by these facts. Non-Aboriginal people are baffled and feel helpless. The stories they hear about ill health in Aboriginal communities do not sound like *their* Canada. They do not understand why so much ill health persists among people living in such a great country, or what should be done about it. Aboriginal people feel ashamed or angry. They see that some communities have made great strides toward the dynamic state of health and harmony to which all aspire, but they also see that many health and social problems go unchecked and that some are getting worse. They know they did not live with such high levels of illness and unhappiness in the past, and they do not understand why they must do so now. In this chapter, we hope to answer the questions posed by Aboriginal and non-Aboriginal people alike.

The mandate of the Commission directed our attention to social issues of concern to Aboriginal peoples in these words:

> The Commission may study and make concrete recommendations to improve the quality of life for aboriginal peoples living on-reserve, in native settlements and communities, and in rural areas and cities. Issues of concern include, but are not limited to: poverty, unemployment and underemployment, access to health care and health concerns generally, alcohol and substance abuse, sub-standard housing, high suicide rates, child care, child welfare and family violence.

These and other indicators of continuing ill health in Aboriginal communities are a source of pain, suffering, anger and feelings of betrayal and despondency.

We believe that one of the most significant contributions the Commission can make to Aboriginal life in Canada is to highlight reasons for these unacceptable conditions and to identify priorities for action that will, in Aboriginal terms, restore balance in the life support systems that promote mental, emotional, physical and spiritual well-being – in other words, health.

During our public hearings, Aboriginal people – particularly women – accorded enormous significance to the Commission's work on health and healing. Many named 'healing' as the first priority among the four 'touchstones for change' put forward in the Commission's discussion paper, *Focusing the Dialogue.*[4] Many more identified healing as a prerequisite for progress toward self-government and economic self-reliance.

The word 'healing' is familiar to non-Aboriginal people, of course, but the idea that Aboriginal people have in mind when they use it is likely not. Healing, in Aboriginal terms, refers to personal and societal recovery from the lasting effects of oppression and systemic racism experienced over generations. Many Aboriginal people are suffering not simply from specific diseases and social problems, but also from a depression of spirit resulting from 200 or more years of damage to their cultures, languages, identities and self-respect. The idea of healing suggests that to reach 'whole health', Aboriginal people must confront the crippling injuries of the past.[5] Yet, doing so is not their job alone. Only when the deep causes of Aboriginal ill health are remedied by Aboriginal and non-Aboriginal people working together will balance and harmony – or health and well-being – be restored.

At least in part, it is to achieve whole health that Aboriginal peoples so vigorously seek self-determination. The relationship between self-determination and health is a circle, however; thus, only when whole health is achieved will successful and mature self-determination be possible:

> With the healing in place we can have self-government, but without that healing we will have dysfunctional self-government.
>
> Jeanette Costello
> Counsellor, Kitselas Drug and Alcohol Program
> Terrace, British Columbia, 25 May 1993

> Without healthy, socially developed youth, we have no leaders for the future. Without available, high-quality care for the elderly, we have no guidance or wisdom from the past. Without strong, committed people acting today to champion our rights and to further our nations' interests, we have no guarantees for anyone beyond today....If we are to survive as a vibrant culture, and as strong and independent nations, we must attend to the health of our people.
>
> Tom Iron
> Fourth Vice-Chief
> Federation of Saskatchewan Indian Nations
> Wahpeton, Saskatchewan, 26 May 1992

Health and social services are important because they enhance people's comfort and attachment to life. But whole health is not a product that can be delivered by external agents; it requires the full engagement of persons interacting with their environment to create and sustain life. Because health services touch people's lives so intimately, they can encourage action in the broader community where conditions essential to health are determined.

With these considerations in mind, the objectives we set for our work on health and healing are

- to further the work of restoring whole health to all Aboriginal people in Canada, both for its own sake and as a requisite for social, political and economic development;
- to place health and healing concerns in the context of history, culture and the imperatives for change in the relationship between Aboriginal people and Canadian institutions; and
- to change the way Aboriginal health is understood and promoted and, by extension, to transform the system of medical and social services delivery.

Statistics on indicators of physical ill health and social distress among Aboriginal people have been repeated so often in the media that they can easily be seen as old news. Still, we consider it necessary to re-examine the burden of ill health borne by Aboriginal people in physical, social, emotional and community terms. Our intention is not to shock, although it is shocking to realize that in a number of health-related areas we may be losing ground. Instead, we intend to demonstrate that in the face of continuing threats to well-being, effective action is possible – and already under way – by drawing on community strengths, traditional knowledge and creative use of professional services.

We have observed that Aboriginal people have well-articulated insights into their individual and collective poor health and that these insights converge with recent scientific research on determinants of health. We conclude that the convergence between Aboriginal perspectives and health sciences research provides a powerful argument for adopting a health strategy based on

- equitable access to health services and equitable outcomes in health status;
- holistic approaches to treatment and preventive services;
- Aboriginal control of services; and
- diversity of approaches that respond to cultural priorities and community needs.

Several fundamental changes are necessary to implement our proposed health and healing strategy. The first element – and the core of the strategy – is to develop a system of healing centres for front-line services and healing lodges for residential treatment. Healing centres and lodges would be accessible in urban, rural and reserve settings to First Nations and Métis people and to Inuit. They would operate under Aboriginal control to deliver integrated health and social services.

The second element is a human resource strategy, incorporating traditional knowledge and training of Aboriginal people to transform Aboriginal health and social services. We present detailed proposals on what should be done in health and social services to achieve the education goals described more generally in our chapters on education in this volume and on economic development in Volume 2.

The third element of the strategy is to adapt mainstream service systems to complement Aboriginal institutions. The fourth element of our proposed strategy, bringing housing and community infrastructure up to prevailing Canadian standards, is summarized here and discussed in detail in Chapter 4 in this volume.

Finally, we place our proposals in the context of the political and economic restructuring needed for Aboriginal communities to achieve whole health.

1. THE BURDEN OF ILL HEALTH

1.1 From the Past to the Present

There is considerable evidence to show Aboriginal people enjoyed good health at the time of first contact with Europeans. Historical records and the findings of modern paleo-biology suggest that many of the illnesses common today were once rare, and that mental and physical vigour once prevailed among Aboriginal people:

> [Aboriginal people] were not subject to disease, and knew nothing of fevers....They were not subject to the gout, gravel, fevers or rheumatism. The general remedy was to make themselves sweat, which they did every month and even oftener.[6]

> Before the Indian began to use the white man's foods, he was perforce compelled to live on a comparatively simple diet. His choice was limited, his cooking simple. Yet he lived in perfect health and strength...and attained a vigour, a robustness, that puts to shame the strength and power of civilized man.[7]

> Skeletal remains of unquestionably precolumbian date...are, barring a few exceptions, remarkably free from disease. Whole important scourges [affecting Europeans during the colonial period] were wholly unknown....There was no plague, cholera, typhus, smallpox or measles. Cancer was rare, and even fractures were infrequent....There were, apparently, no nevi [skin tumours]. There were no troubles with the feet, such as fallen arches. And judging from later acquired knowledge, there was a much greater scarcity than in the white population of...most mental disorders, and of other serious conditions.[8]

Canadian historian Olive Dickason quotes from the Jesuit *New Relation of Gaspesia*, then adds her own commentary:

> "Amerindians are all by nature physicians, apothecaries and doctors, by virtue of the knowledge and experience they have of certain herbs, which they use successfully to cure ills that seem to us incurable"....The process by which the Amerindians acquired their herbal lore is not clearly understood, but there is no doubt about the results. More than 500 drugs used in the medical pharmacopoeia today were originally used by Amerindians.[9]

Some analysts argue that disease agents themselves were rare in pre-contact America until the tall ships began to arrive with their invisible cargo of bacteria and viruses.[10] What is more likely is that Aboriginal people had adapted well to their home environments: they had developed effective resistance to the micro-organisms living alongside them and had knowledge of herbs and other therapies for treating injury and disease. Of course, some Aboriginal people died prematurely. But more stayed well, or recovered from illness, and thus lived to raise their children and continue the clans and the nations. Aboriginal populations fluctuated largely in relation to food supply.

It was the European explorers and settlers who were more likely to be weak and sick when they first met Aboriginal people.[11] Many arrived suffering from illnesses they brought with them or from the effects of conditions they endured on the voyage: crowded quarters with primitive sanitary facilities, limited and sometimes contaminated drinking water, and limited and sometimes diseased food. Those who accepted the herbal remedies and unfamiliar cures prescribed by Aboriginal healers – bathing, fasting and sweating among them – were the most likely to recover.

In his classic study of Native American health during the colonial period, Virgil Vogel shows how the tone of contemporary observations changed from admiration to disgust after Aboriginal people began to show the effects of contact with Europeans. Written accounts increasingly describe epidemic disease, violence and death in Aboriginal communities.[12] Many writers stated or implied, with blithe disregard for the facts, that Aboriginal people themselves were responsible for the misery they were enduring.

Hundreds of thousands sickened and died as a result of their encounters with Europeans. (For a full discussion of the population dynamics of Aboriginal peoples before and after European contact, see Volume 1, Chapter 2.[13]) Famine and warfare contributed, but infectious diseases were the great killer. Influenza, measles, polio, diphtheria, smallpox and other diseases were transported from the slums of Europe to the unprotected villages of the Americas. The subsequent decline of the indigenous population is often described as genocide or a holocaust. Estimates of the Aboriginal population before contact in the area that was to become Canada range from 220,000 to two million, with a figure of 500,000 now being widely accepted. An 1871 census estimate of the Aboriginal population in Canada was 102,000 (see Volume 1, Chapter 2).

Aboriginal people were well aware of the link between the newcomers and the epidemics that raced through their camps and villages.[14] During the eighteenth and nineteenth centuries, their leaders sought agreements or treaties with representatives of the British Crown aimed at ensuring their survival in the face of spreading disease and impoverishment. In the expectation of fair compensation for the use of their lands and resources, and in mounting fear of the social and health effects of Euro-Canadian settlement, many Aboriginal nations, clans and families agreed to relocate to camps, farms, villages or reserves distant from sites of colonial settlement. Many did so in the belief that the Crown would guarantee their well-being for all time.[15] Given the gulf that separated Aboriginal and non-Aboriginal cultures, it is not surprising that the meaning of those oral and written agreements has been a matter of conflicting interpretation ever since.[16]

The transformation of Aboriginal people from the state of good health that had impressed travellers from Europe to one of ill health, for which Aboriginal people were (and still are) often held responsible, grew worse as sources of food and clothing from the land declined and traditional economies collapsed. It grew worse still as once-mobile peoples were confined to small plots of land where resources and opportunities for natural sanitation were limited. It worsened yet again as long-standing norms, values, social systems and spiritual practices were undermined or outlawed.

Traditional healing methods were decried as witchcraft and idolatry by Christian missionaries and ridiculed by most others. Ceremonial activity was banned in an effort to turn hunters and trappers into agricultural labourers with a commitment to wage work. Eventually, the *Indian Act* prohibited those ceremonies that had survived most defiantly, the potlatch and the sun dance.[17] Many elders and healers were prosecuted. In these ways, Aboriginal people were stripped of self-respect and respect for one another.

The low point for Aboriginal health and social conditions in Canada came in the early years of the twentieth century. Newspaper stories and official reports on the destitution and continuing epidemics of disease on reserves and in isolated Inuit, First Nations and Métis settlements were a source of shame to many. The first person assigned a position of responsibility for improving Indian health was Dr. Peter Bryce, who was appointed general medical superintendent in the department of Indian affairs in 1904. Despite the lack of interest and sometimes outright racist attitudes of his colleagues toward his work, Dr. Bryce fought tirelessly (although not always successfully) to raise the standards of health and welfare among the Aboriginal population until leaving office in 1910.[18] Many of his successors have done likewise.

From the end of the nineteenth century to the middle of the twentieth, health care was provided, first by an assortment of semi-trained RCMP agents, missionaries and officers, and later by a growing number of nurses and doctors in the full- or part-time employ of the federal government. In 1930, the first on-reserve nursing station was opened in Fisher River, Manitoba. By the 1950s, the department of national health and welfare was operating a network of 33 nursing stations, 65 health centres, and 18 small regional hospitals for registered Indians and Inuit.[19] This undertaking was motivated by the post-war spirit of humanitarianism that propelled the emerging Canadian welfare state and by fear of the threat posed to Canadians by sky-high rates of tuberculosis in Aboriginal communities.

The new health system operated on the assumption that Aboriginal people would welcome western-style health care services, and for the most part they did.[20] Where infectious diseases were still a major killer, the impact of medical treatment was immediate. In the longer term, infant mortality began to decline and life expectancy began to increase. But these benefits did not come without a price:

- Aboriginal people with serious illnesses were often sent, unaccompanied, to distant medical facilities for treatment in strange and sometimes hostile environments.
- In their own communities, Aboriginal people were offered health care services that had no foundation in local values, traditions or conditions. At worst, a few were forced (or convinced) to suffer invasive medical procedures, including sterilization.[21]
- Virtually all providers of health and social services were non-Aboriginal, many with little interest in the cultural practices or values of their Aboriginal clients. Encounters were often clouded by suspicion, misunderstanding, resentment and racism.[22]
- Indigenous healing skills and knowledge of herbal medicines and other traditional treatments were devalued by medical personnel and hidden by those who still practised or even remembered them. Much knowledge was eventually lost.
- Aboriginal people learned that they were not in charge; non-Aboriginal people learned that they were. This legacy is difficult for both sides to put behind them.

Aboriginal health came to national attention again in 1978 when the federal government attempted to reduce its financial responsibility for First Nations and Inuit health care. The specific issue was the provision of non-insured health benefits (that is, benefits such as prescription drugs and eye glasses not universally available through medicare) to registered Indian people and Inuit. This action provoked a forceful protest from the major Aboriginal organizations, whose leaders claimed that services to which their members had a right were being cut off without negotiation. The ensuing debate gradually widened to include all aspects of federal policy on health care for Aboriginal people. Ultimately, it led to a new federal policy statement on Aboriginal health, commonly called the 'three pillars' policy.[23] The pillars of Aboriginal health it identified were community development (promoted as the key strategy for improving Aboriginal health), the continuing special responsibility of the federal government for the health and well-being of First Nations people and Inuit, and the essential contributions of all elements of the Canadian health system, whether federal, provincial, territorial or municipal, Aboriginal or non-Aboriginal, public or private.

Although not listed as a pillar, the federal government's commitment to greater participation by Aboriginal people in planning and delivering their own health services was also stated in the new policy. This commitment was given greater weight and specifics by the 1980 *Report of the Advisory Commission on Indian and Inuit Health Consultation*, written by Justice Thomas Berger. The object of this report was to propose "methods of consultation that would ensure substantive participation by the Indian people and the Inuit people in decisions affecting the provision of health care to them".[24] The language was conservative, but the report was radical, giving support to the concept of community control by Aboriginal people. Thus, it gave credence to the then-startling idea that Aboriginal people could manage their own affairs. In fact, Berger imagined a complete end to the institutional dependency long fostered by the Canadian state.

Community control was understood by those who supported the report as a means of empowerment, but it was interpreted in a much more restrictive way by most federal officials. They understood it as a transfer of administrative responsibility for certain existing health-related programs, starting with the National Native Alcohol and Drug Abuse Program and the Community Health Representative program in 1980-1981. (We discuss these important programs in more detail later in this chapter.) The idea of transfer of administrative authority for community health services more generally was to be tested in a five-year Community Health Demonstration Program, which got under way in 1982.[25]

Perhaps even more significant during this period was the case-by-case success of some Aboriginal nations and communities in gaining control over their health services. These successes were achieved not as a result of progressive federal policies, but independently of one another as a result of particular local struggles. Some involved non-status, urban, Métis, and Inuit communities to whom the federal transfer initiative did not even apply. We describe only a few here:[26]

- The Kateri Memorial Hospital Centre is the oldest such case. It came into being in 1955, when a local Mohawk woman broke new ground by securing joint funding from the Quebec government and the Mohawk Council of Kahnawake to keep open the local hospital, which had been in the community since 1905. Through 35 years of tumultuous relations with federal, provincial and university (McGill) agencies, the hospital now provides treatment and prevention services to residents of the Kahnawake reserve and to Aboriginal people from nearby Montreal.[27]

- Hailed by some as a model of self-government, the James Bay and Northern Quebec Agreement (JBNQA) of 1975 created the first independent Aboriginal health and social service boards in Canada. Debate continues regarding the strengths and weaknesses of JBNQA. Participating communities have continually charged that the control they were promised has never, in practice, been realized.[28] But within some significant limits, community control has been greatly extended.

- In Labrador, where communities were dependent on the International Grenfell Association for health care, Inuit created the Labrador Independent Health Commission (LIHC) in 1979. LIHC concentrates primarily on health education and promotion and public health needs.[29]

- The Alberta Indian Health Commission (AIHCC) was established in 1981 to address First Nations' concerns about health in the province. In addition to consulting and being a liaison with Aboriginal and provincial agencies, AIHCC provides urban community health representatives in Edmonton and Calgary.[30]

- Anishnawbe Health Toronto was first funded by the provincial government in 1988 as a multi-service urban community health centre. It is grounded in the principles of the Medicine Wheel and has a mandate to provide services to off-reserve, non-status, and Métis people living in Toronto.[31]

By 1986, the federal government's Community Health Demonstration Program (CHDP) for First Nations communities had funded 31 projects and attracted a volley of criticism. Only seven of the projects funded actually focused on transfer-related issues, yet other initiatives toward greater Aboriginal control of health and social services had been put on hold in favour of CHDP. Many First Nations objected to the very idea of demonstration projects, arguing that they should not have to prove to the federal government's medical services branch (MSB) or any other authority that they could manage their own affairs. Some objected to the MSB policy of working only with individual bands, which discouraged the development of regional and nation institutions. Few were aware that MSB intended (at first) to restrict the health transfer program to First Nations communities participating in CHDP.[32]

By 1987, the demonstration phase, with all its faults, was over. Health transfer itself had begun. Some of the shortcomings of CHDP had been corrected, but transfer remained (and remains) controversial. The Assembly of First Nations, along with several communities and tribal councils, continued to argue that self-determination in health should be part of comprehensive self-government and that the federal government had a hidden agenda of divesting itself of responsibility for Aboriginal health and welfare long before Aboriginal people had achieved good health. Certainly there were yawning gaps in the scope of transfer. For example, major components of care, notably the services covered under the non-insured health benefits program, were excluded from transfer agreements, except in the case of Inuit in Labrador.[33] Budgets transferred to First Nations' control took no account of members living off-reserve, many of whom come home for health care or need culturally appropriate programs wherever they are. It also appeared that transferred funds were to be frozen at pre-transfer levels, thus preventing the development of new programs except at the expense of old ones.[34]

Yet the offer of increased responsibility was irresistible to many First Nations communities. Band and tribal councils weighed the pros and cons of the transfer program and made their decision. By 1989, 58 pre-transfer initiatives involving 212 First Nations communities were under way.[35] Those that chose to participate did so with the full understanding that they were co-operating in a less than perfect process, as one leader of the Swampy Cree Tribal Council made clear a few years later:

> This policy direction had been criticized as an attempt to abrogate treaty rights and have Indian people administer their own misery. Nevertheless, we entered the transfer process – but with our eyes wide open. We saw transfer as a way to achieve some of our objectives, and we felt we could look after ourselves in dealing with government.[36]

By March 1996, 141 First Nations communities had assumed administrative responsibility for health care services, either individually or collectively through multi-community agencies or tribal associations; 237 First Nations communities were involved in the pre-transfer process.[37] As the program has evolved (and as clever negotiators have pushed back the edges), the benefits of transfer have been significant. Gains include flexibility in the use of program funds, more freedom to adapt services to local needs and priorities, reduced paperwork in accounting to MSB, and a greater sense of community ownership of services.[38] But there are significant disadvantages, too, as we heard in public testimony. The drawbacks remain much as they were when the program began: the restricted nature of the programs and services that can be transferred, the brief time available for planning and community education for program responsibility, the cap on funds regardless of need, and the possible failure of the federal government to live up to its fiduciary obligations to Aboriginal people.[39]

> When we talk about health planning [for transfer] in First Nations, the first thing the government does immediately is to slot your concerns into 15 budget line items. They are asking us to do the health

plan based on only these 15 items, and by no means does that help us to build a comprehensive health system. All they are interested in is their budget items and "how does your planning fit into our planning?"....We can do all the planning in the world, but Medical Services Branch has no money for enrichment of services. So no matter what kind of health plan we come up with, if we don't put it within the 15 budget line items, then it's up to us to come up with our own resources, or to handle those as best we can.

> Gloria Thomas
> Six Nations Community Health Review
> Brantford, Ontario, 13 May 1993

The "no enrichment" policy of transfer creates the question: is this a set-up for failure? Is the consequence to this policy that we have administrative responsibility for an already underfunded system? Can we really deliver [creative new] programs under transfer? Can we expand and develop new facilities and additional services in response to new health needs and challenges? Would the transfer of funding to our control be a true [instance of Aboriginal control] since the multi-tiered structure of Medical Services Branch makes it difficult to determine an individual community's share of programs and services?

> Claire Campbell
> Community Health Nurse, Nipissing First Nation
> North Bay, Ontario, 11 May 1993

[Even after transfer], there remain a number of issues which are barriers to providing comprehensive health care services for the Tribal Council membership. Some of these are that we have inadequate community-based mental health programs; we lack adult care; we lack services for the disabled; we have poor, inadequate emergency medical transportation services. Transportation is a non-insured health benefit, and we protest that those benefits are not on the table for transfer of control.

> Glen Ross
> Cree Nation Tribal Health Centre
> The Pas, Manitoba, 20 May 1992

The federal government must not interpret Aboriginal participation in its Federal Health Transfer Program as an abrogation of its fiduciary responsibility to provide health care to Aboriginal peoples on Indian reserves. The federal transfer of health should not be limited to nurses, community health representatives, NNADAP [alcohol and drug addiction] and janitors. Services must be expanded beyond para-professional services, and beyond the ad hoc mentality. Transfer does not mean that Aboriginal people automatically become provincial responsibility. Federal responsibility must remain intact and must be identified as a responsibility within the Canada Assistance Plan as a cost sharing arrangement....

The federal transfer of health must now move into a self-government model....Local control and local development must be encouraged, not discouraged with a narrow interpretation of federal and provincial responsibilities. Federal transfer of federal finances to First Nations, such as the Nisga'a, should be viewed by Canada as assistance to a developing nation with sovereignty and dignity remaining as an ideal sought by both partners.

Peter Squires
Chairman, Nisga'a Valley Health Board
Terrace, British Columbia, 25 May 1993

Governments are quick to point out that since their first, reluctant acceptance of a major role in ensuring the health and well-being of Aboriginal people, improvements in Aboriginal health status have been dramatic. The greatest strides have been in controlling once-rampant infectious diseases and in reducing infant and child mortality rates that rivalled those of developing countries. Commissioners do not dispute these achievements. However, we believe that their contemporary significance can be – and often is – overstated.[40]

We are deeply troubled by the evidence of continuing physical, mental and emotional ill health and social breakdown among Aboriginal people. Trends in the data on health and social conditions lead us to a stark conclusion: despite the extension of medical and social services (in some form) to every Aboriginal community, and despite the large sums spent by Canadian governments to provide these services, Aboriginal people still suffer from unacceptable rates of illness and distress.[41] The term 'crisis' is not an exaggeration here.

The statistical data in this chapter present only a snapshot of the crisis; our tables and figures are key indicators of health and social well-being – or, in this case, of ill health and social malaise. Although the life expectancy of Aboriginal people throughout North America as measured from birth is significantly lower than for non-Aboriginal people, it has improved since the Second World War. In the United States, Native American males have gained about 15 years of life expectancy, females, more than 20 years.[42] In Canada, comparable figures are difficult to come by, but the trend is the same: life expectancy for registered Indians rose by about four to five years between 1976 and 1986.[43] Life expectancy for Inuit in the Northwest Territories more than doubled between 1940 and 1980,[44] although it has remained well below that of other Aboriginal peoples.[45] Registered Indians have made smaller gains since 1978, as illustrated in Table 3.1.[46]

TABLE 3.1

Life Expectancy at Birth, Age 30 and Age 60, Registered Indian and Total Populations, 1978-1981, 1982-85, and 1990

	At Birth		At Age 30		At Age 60	
	Registered Indians	Total Population[1]	Registered Indians[2]	Total Population[1]	Registered Indians	Total Population[1]
	Years					
Male						
1978-1981	61.6	71.0	39.5	43.4	18.4	17.5
1982-85	64.0	72.4	40.8	44.4	17.9	18.0
1990	66.9	73.9	41.1	45.7	16.9	19.0
Female						
1978-1981	69.0	79.2	44.1	50.7	21.4	23.4
1982-85	72.8	80.1	46.8	51.4	22.5	23.8
1990	74.0	80.5	46.7	51.6	20.5	23.7

Notes:
1. Total population is the total population of Canada, including Aboriginal persons.
2. Life expectancies at age 30 and 60 for registered Indians in 1990 are the average life expectancies for ages 30-34 and 60-64 respectively.

Source: Health and Welfare Canada, "Health Indicators Derived from Vital Statistics for Status Indian and Canadian Populations, 1978-1986" (September 1988); DIAND, "Life Tables for Registered Indians, 1985 and 1990", Information Quality and Research Division, unpublished tables (May 1995); Statistics Canada, *Report on the Demographic Situation in Canada*, catalogue no. 91-209E (Ottawa: 1993).

Table 3.1 also shows that the gap in life expectancy between Aboriginal and non-Aboriginal people is narrowing. Yet Indian women born in 1990 can expect to die 6.5 years earlier than other women in Canada, and Indian men seven years before other men. The greatest discrepancies occur among the young. By age 30 the difference in life expectancy has been halved; by age 60 it has declined by half again.

Inuit continue to have the lowest life expectancy of all Aboriginal people, among both women and men, followed by Indian people living on-reserve (see Table 3.2).[47] Indian people in urban settings, whether registered or not, have the highest life expectancy of Aboriginal people, exceeding that of urban Métis people by about one year for both women and men.

Figure 3.1 shows that the pattern of illness and injury leading to death was quite different for registered Indian people than for other Canadians in 1992. The two leading causes of death in the general population were circulatory diseases and neoplasms (cancers). Among registered Indian males, injuries, including accidents, suicides and homicides, are the leading cause of death. While

TABLE 3.2
Estimated Life Expectancy at Birth, Total and Aboriginal
Populations, 1991

	Male	Female
	Years	
Total population	74.6	80.9
Total Aboriginal population	67.9	75.0
Total, North American Indians*	68.0	74.9
Registered North American Indians	66.9	74.0
On-reserve	62.0	69.6
Non-reserve, rural	68.5	75.0
Non-reserve, urban	72.5	79.0
Non-Registered North American Indians	71.4	77.9
Rural	69.0	75.5
Urban	72.5	79.0
Métis	70.4	76.9
Rural	68.5	75.0
Urban	71.5	78.0
Inuit	57.6	68.8

Note:
* North American Indians includes all who self-identified as North American Indian on the 1991 Aboriginal Peoples Survey, whether or not they are registered under the *Indian Act*.

Source: M.J. Norris et al., "Projections of the Aboriginal Identity Population in Canada, 1991-2016", research study prepared by Statistics Canada for RCAP (February 1995).

injuries play a lesser role among registered Indian women, they still account for three times the proportion of deaths among women in the general population.

Table 3.3 shows rates of hospital admission and reasons for admission in Manitoba in 1990-91. At least in Manitoba, Aboriginal people continue to be adversely affected by many causes of illness and death that are better controlled in the non-Aboriginal population. Table 3.4 shows that, in one province, Aboriginal people in all age groups (except 65 and older) used two to three times more hospital days than a comparable number of people in the general population, indicating their lower general health and the severity of their illnesses upon admission.

Table 3.5 and Figure 3.2 provide some indicators of the social conditions prevalent among Aboriginal people in Canada. Table 3.5 shows that Aboriginal

122 GATHERING STRENGTH

FIGURE 3.1
Selected Causes of Death as a Percentage of all Deaths, 1992

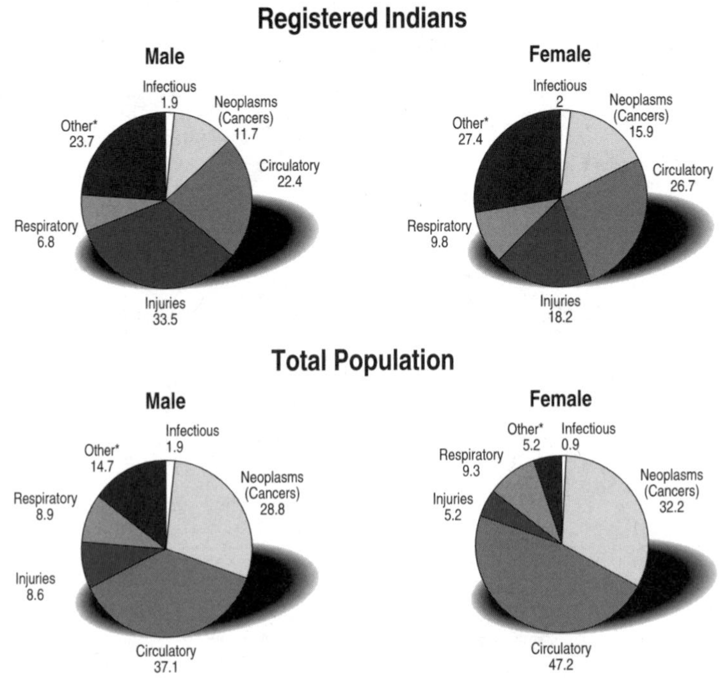

Registered Indians

Male

- Infectious 1.9
- Neoplasms (Cancers) 11.7
- Other* 23.7
- Circulatory 22.4
- Respiratory 6.8
- Injuries 33.5

Female

- Infectious 2
- Neoplasms (Cancers) 15.9
- Other* 27.4
- Circulatory 26.7
- Respiratory 9.8
- Injuries 18.2

Total Population

Male

- Infectious 1.9
- Other* 14.7
- Neoplasms (Cancers) 28.8
- Respiratory 8.9
- Injuries 8.6
- Circulatory 37.1

Female

- Other* 5.2
- Infectious 0.9
- Respiratory 9.3
- Neoplasms (Cancers) 32.2
- Injuries 5.2
- Circulatory 47.2

Note: * Includes endocrine/metabolic/immunity disorders, blood/blood-forming organs, mental disorders, nervous system and sense organs, digestive system, genito-urinary system, complications of pregnancy/childbirth, skin and subcutaneous tissues, musculoskeletal system, congenital anomalies, conditions from perinatal period, symptoms/signs and ill-defined conditions, and others.

Source: Health Canada, Medical Services Branch, unpublished tables, May 1995.

people derive a greater portion of their income from government transfers than do members of the general population. Figure 3.2 provides data on registered Indian children 'in care' (children under the supervision of child welfare authorities) over time. It shows a high rate of child apprehensions among registered Indian people, a rate that has fallen rapidly since 1980 but that continues to be problematic. (The complexities of child welfare are discussed in Chapter 2.)

Many studies have attempted to measure or estimate rates of social dysfunction among Aboriginal people. Because these conditions are difficult to define, let alone measure, the conclusions of such studies are often disputed.[48] The majority of studies, however, point to disproportionate rates of social and community ill health among Aboriginal people. Moreover, we are convinced that

TABLE 3.3
Hospital Utilization Rates by Diagnostic Category, Registered Indian and Provincial Populations, Manitoba, 1990-91

	Registered Indians[1]	Provincial Population[2]
	In-patient cases per 1,000 population	
Infectious/parasites	33	18
Neoplasms (cancers)	24	133
Endocrine/nutritional/metabolic	59	31
Blood and blood-forming organs	15	8
Mental disorders	80	176
Nervous system and sense organs	42	81
Circulatory	98	228
Respiratory	221	110
Digestive	134	103
Genito-urinary	71	53
Pregnancy/childbirth	220	75
Skin and subcutaneous tissue	54	19
Musculoskeletal	48	64
Congenital anomalies	17	6
Perinatal	8	3
Symptoms/signs ill-defined	63	50
Injury/poisoning	181	142
Other	88	156

Notes:
1. On- and off-reserve population.
2. All Manitoba residents.

Source: MHSC Hospital, Table 25, 1989-90, in Postl et. al, 1992.

the social problems facing Aboriginal people today are proving more resistant to change than are their physical health problems.

Table 3.6 shows expenditures on health and social services delivered to Aboriginal people by federal, provincial and territorial governments, comparing them with the amounts spent on services delivered to Canadians generally. The difference in per capita expenditures is not what concerns us here. What concerns us is that rates of ill health and social dysfunction among Aboriginal

TABLE 3.4
Hospital Utilization Rates by Age, Registered Indian and
Provincial Populations, Manitoba, 1990-91

	Registered Indians[1]	Manitoba[2]
	days per 1,000 population	
under 10 years	1105	338
10-17	622	272
18-34	1318	600
35-64	1983	941
65+	7200	7022

Notes:
1. On- and off-reserve population.
2. All Manitoba residents.
Source: MHSC Hospital, Table 25, 1989-90, in Postl et al., 1992.

people living in Canada – a country that prides itself on high standards of good health and social well-being – remain shockingly high *despite* the money being spent. On 17 November 1993, when its representatives addressed the Commission, the Canadian Medical Association issued a press release urging the federal government to "acknowledge that the degree of ill health among Canada's Aboriginal population is unacceptable and take immediate and specific measures to improve it".[49]

It could be that the amounts being spent, however great, are still too small to solve outstanding problems. Certainly, for some health problems and for some Aboriginal people, we will argue that this is the case and that greater investment is required. But Commissioners believe that the main impediment to restoring good health to Aboriginal people is not the amount of money spent but *how* it is spent. As we will show in this chapter, the causes and dynamics of ill health among Aboriginal people are not the same as among non-Aboriginal people – and because illness is not the same, prevention, cure and care cannot be the same either.

In the next few pages we examine the causes and dynamics of ill health among Aboriginal people. Our purpose is threefold:

- to show the extent and seriousness of the conditions summarized by the statistics presented in our research;
- to examine representative illnesses to discover themes and commonalities regarding ill health in Aboriginal communities; and
- to lay the groundwork for a strategy to transform the health conditions of Aboriginal people.

TABLE 3.5
Percentage Distribution of Income by Source, Aboriginal Identity and Non-Aboriginal Populations, 1991

	Employment Income	Government Transfer Payments	Other Income
	%	%	%
Non-Aboriginal	77.8	11.4	10.8
Total Aboriginal	73.5	23.3	3.1
North American Indians			
Registered	68.5	28.5	2.8
Non-registered	80.2	14.8	4.8
Métis	77.1	19.8	3.0
Inuit	77.8	20.9	1.2

Note: Aboriginal identity population age 15 and older not attending school.

Source: Statistics Canada, 1991 Aboriginal Peoples Survey, custom tabulations; Statistics Canada, 1991 Census, Profile of Urban and Rural Areas, Part B, catalogue no. 93-340 (Ottawa: February 1994).

1.2 Physical Health

Over time, all peoples of the world tend to experience three stages of health and illness patterns as they become more urbanized and industrialized.[50] The first stage is marked by famine, high rates of infectious disease and high death rates, especially among infants and children. The second is marked by declining rates of infectious disease and rapid population growth. The final stage is marked by the rise of chronic and degenerative diseases.

Aboriginal peoples in North America appear to be in transition from the second to the third stage. The birth rate is high. Infectious diseases, although far from controlled, are declining from the peak of devastation reached in the nineteenth century. Degenerative conditions such as heart disease, cancer and diabetes are on the rise.[51] Social pathologies – particularly alcohol and drug abuse – continue to cause widespread concern, while interpersonal violence and suicide contribute to high rates of injury and death.

The issues of physical ill health facing Aboriginal people demonstrate intractable problems in four major categories: infant and child health, infectious disease, chronic disease, and disability.

Infant, child and maternal health

Infant mortality (death among children in the first year of their lives) is an important measure of population health the world over. Although the infant mor-

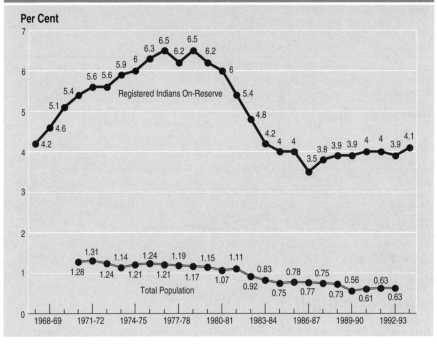

FIGURE 3.2

Children in Care as a Percentage of Registered Indian (On-Reserve) and Total Populations

Notes:
1. Programs, definitions and reporting systems vary considerably between provinces and within a given province over time. As a result, data are not comparable and should be used as estimates only.
2. Before March 1983, Quebec data include all child welfare services as well as children in care. Data from March 1983 to March 1990 include the number of interventions made on behalf of children in foster homes, institutions, protection cases and children with disabilities. Therefore, the data are not comparable over time. Quebec data from March 1990 on are not available.
3. Yukon data for 1975-76 to 1977-78 are included in Northwest Territories data.
4. March 1987 data for Ontario and Alberta are estimates.
5. From 1987 to 1988, Ontario data are for June or December, depending on the availability of the data.
6. Recent data are subject to revision.

Source: DIAND, Basic Departmental Data, 1994, Information Quality and Research Directorate (Ottawa: January 1995); Human Resources Development Canada, Cost-Shared Programs Branch, Social Development and Education, Table 421 (March 1994); and Statistics Canada, Population Estimates Division, Population Estimates for Canada and Selected Provinces and Territories, 1971-93.

tality rate (IMR) among Aboriginal people in Canada has declined steeply, a significant difference in the rates for Aboriginal and non-Aboriginal people remains (see Figure 3.3). From a high of more than 200 deaths per 1,000 live births in the 1920s and 1930s, the IMR among Aboriginal people has fallen to about 14

TABLE 3.6
Selected Government Expenditures on Aboriginal and Total Populations, 1992-93

	Health	Social Development	Housing
Federal expenditures on Aboriginal population ($ millions)	798	1,450	410
Provincial/territorial expenditures on Aboriginal population ($ millions)	1,215	1,313	133
Total expenditures on Aboriginal population ($ millions)	2,013	2,763	542
Expenditures per person, Aboriginal identity population ($)	2,720	3,733	732
Expenditures per person, total population ($)	1,652	2,946	130
Ratio of Aboriginal to total per capita expenditures	1.6	1.3	5.5

Notes: Expenditures include those on programs intended specifically for Aboriginal people as well as a share of expenditures on general programs. The relevant shares were calculated by program area based on the Aboriginal share of the client population and information about the rate of use by Aboriginal people. Thus, for example, health care expenditures include a share of provincial hospital, preventive and other health care expenditures. Social development expenditures include a share of old age security, employment insurance and workers compensation as well as social assistance and transfer payments to Indian bands, Inuit settlements and agencies delivering services. The amounts pertain to all Aboriginal peoples, including First Nations, Métis and Inuit.

Source: RCAP estimates. See Volume 5, Chapter 3.

among registered Indian people and about 20 among Inuit.[52] The IMR for Canadians generally, however, is about seven per 1,000 live births. Thus, the ratio of Aboriginal to non-Aboriginal infant deaths is just about the same today as it has been for 100 years – about twice as high for Indian people and three times as high for Inuit in the Northwest Territories as for other Canadians. These ratios hold true for stillbirths (deaths of fetuses of less than 28 weeks' gestation) and perinatal mortality (deaths of fetuses after 28 weeks' gestation and of infants until the end of the first week of life).[53] The stillbirth and perinatal death rates among Indians are about double the Canadian average. Among Inuit living in the Northwest Territories, they are about two and a half times the Canadian average.

Beyond the risk of premature mortality, long-term human health is influenced by what happens in the womb and in the first months and years of life. Health researchers are only beginning to understand how subtle and far-reaching the effects of pre- and postnatal health can be. It is now well established that

FIGURE 3.3
Infant Mortality Rates, Registered Indian, Inuit and Total Populations

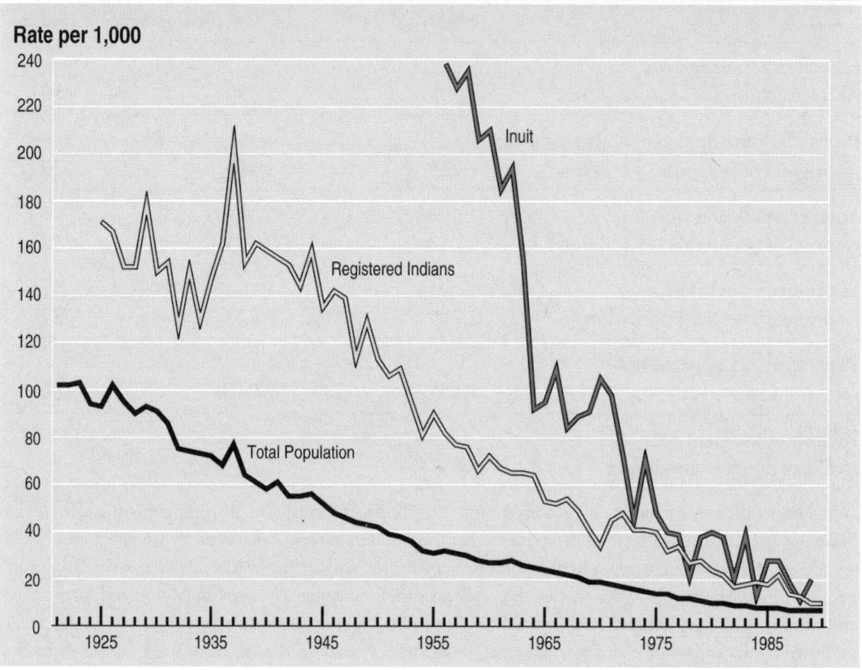

Rate per 1,000

Source: Kue Young, "Measuring the Health Status of Canada's Aboriginal Population: a statistical review and methodological commentary", research study prepared for RCAP (1994).

fetal and perinatal distress can impair the full physical and mental development of children. Research on programs similar to Head Start suggests that early stimulation can lead to gains in health status as well as educational achievement.[54] One leading health analyst writes:

> The search for causes of Western diseases has concentrated on the adult environment. The importance of the childhood environment in determining responses in later life [appears to] have been underestimated.[55]

Neonatal and infant health is largely the result of the living conditions and health care choices of pregnant women and new mothers. The Commission looked at three key factors in infant and child health: abnormal birth weight, the use of alcohol during pregnancy, and childbirth practices and policies.

Abnormal birth weight, particularly low birth weight, is a known risk factor for ill health in childhood and later life. It contributes to many of the common problems of infancy, from the stresses of prematurity generally and colic specif-

TABLE 3.7
Percentage of Low and High Birthweight Babies,
Registered Indian and Total Populations, 1979-1992

	% Low Birth Weight[1]		% High Birth Weight[2]	
	Total Population	Registered Indians	Total Population	Registered Indians
1979	6	5	10	—
1980	6	5	10	—
1981	6	5	10	—
1982	6	5	11	—
1983	6	4	11	—
1984	6	4	11	—
1985	6	4	11	—
1986	6	4	11	—
1987	5	4	12	—
1988	6	3	12	—
1989	5	4	12	14
1990	5	3	12	14
1991	6	5	12	9
1992	5	4	13	16

Notes:
1. Less than 2.5 kilograms.
2. More than 4 kilograms.
— = data not available.
Figures have been rounded to the nearest per cent.

Source: For registered Indian population, Health Canada, Medical Services Branch, unpublished data; for total population, Statistics Canada, catalogue nos. 84-204 and 84-210.

ically, which interfere with family bonding, to the risk of death itself. The Canadian Institute of Child Health has cited low birth weight as being a major health concern in Canada.[56]

Alcohol consumption during pregnancy is another leading cause of ill health in infancy. Fetal alcohol syndrome and fetal alcohol effect (FAS and FAE) are matters of extreme concern in Aboriginal communities where there is or has been alcohol abuse.

Childbirth practices and policies have been the subject of extensive debate in recent years, and they are seen increasingly as an issue by Aboriginal people. Many have argued that normal birth, where health and safety are not threatened, should once again become a non-medical, family and community event.[57]

Abnormal birth weight

The birth weight of infants is defined as low when it is below 2.5 kilograms (5.5 pounds). In 1990, almost 22,000 low birth weight (LBW) babies were born in Canada, most often to teenage girls or women over 40. About 15 per cent died in the first month of life. At present, Aboriginal women appear to run about the same or a slightly lower risk of giving birth to an LBW baby as non-Aboriginal women (see Table 3.7). Aboriginal women have a higher than average risk of giving birth to a high birth weight (overweight) baby, a condition that also carries ill health effects, although these are not so well understood.

Low birth weight increases the chance of death in infancy and of life-long health and social problems. LBW babies are likely to have underdeveloped respiratory and other systems. They are also likely to have weakened immune systems. On both counts, they are at risk for serious and/or chronic ill health. LBW babies are also likely to be 'difficult' babies – often because they are in pain. They may fuss and cry more than other babies, which increases their risk of parental neglect and abuse. Their care and nurture is costly (ranging from $500 to $1,000 per day in Canada), both to families and to the publicly funded health system.[58]

The factors that put a woman at risk of delivering an LBW baby are complex. Those that are considered preventable include

- inadequate nutrition during pregnancy;
- smoking and drinking during pregnancy;
- poverty and stress;
- pregnancy during adolescence;
- physical inactivity during pregnancy; and
- general self-neglect by pregnant women.[59]

The co-ordinator of the Healthiest Babies Possible Pregnancy Outreach Program of the Native Friendship Centre in Prince George, British Columbia, gave Commissioners some insights into the sources and dynamics of the risks faced by Aboriginal women:

> Many Aboriginal women are isolated, impoverished and suffering from low self-esteem and sometimes emotional pain. Frequent barriers these women encounter in accessing health care [include] lack of medical coverage. Often women are transient and come here from other provinces, and there's a lapse in their care. Sometimes [such a lapse] occurs when teens are away from their families [when pregnant] and don't have communication with them and they don't have their [health] card numbers, and it takes us days and days to get them to a physician....
>
> Transportation is an issue. [Many of our clients have] no bus fare....Lack of child care is also an issue. Respite care is needed for

many of these women to attend their appointments. And often this ties into transportation, juggling around strollers and babies who are ill, to get them to the doctor.

Shortages of food [are an issue]. The pregnancy outreach programs across B.C. are currently lobbying for an increased natal allowance from social services. The $25 a month has not been increased for many, many years....

Lack of appropriate and affordable housing leads to frequent changes of address and the stresses of finding housing. Low literacy often leads to the inability to seek appropriate [help]. They are unable to read bus schedules, posters, et cetera.

Low self-esteem and loss of identity [is an issue]. Many are grieving individual and/or collective Aboriginal spiritual and cultural losses and, therefore, feel powerless [to help themselves].

> Marlene Thio-Watts, RN
> Co-ordinator, Healthiest Babies Possible
> Pregnancy Outreach Program
> Executive Director, Northern Family Health Society
> Prince George, British Columbia, 1 June 1993

Thio-Watts told Commissioners that she and the caregivers working with her are attempting to help pregnant women and new mothers with needs that go well beyond the mandate (and funding capacity) of her program. The problems they dealt with include, for example,

- providing support and counselling for the victims of rape, assault and abandonment;
- investigating child neglect and abuse allegations;
- providing child welfare and family strengthening services (for example, parenting education); and
- providing addictions counselling and support for children with fetal alcohol syndrome or effect (discussed in more detail later).

Clearly, many of the risk factors for abnormal birth weight are social and economic and do not fall within the scope of medical services. Aboriginal health authorities cannot address the full range of risk factors unless they are treated as 'health' issues and become priority targets for health program funds. The Child Development Initiative (formerly Brighter Futures) of Health Canada's medical services branch has taken a significant step in this direction with its community-controlled 'healthy babies' program. Yet its reach is limited, because its funding is modest and because only reserve communities are eligible.

Thio-Watts recommended a storefront-style health centre with 'one-stop shopping' services to meet the needs of Aboriginal women who are pregnant or already struggling with infants and young children. Under the current care system, however, only a minority of Aboriginal communities have that possibility open to them: on-reserve communities where authority transferred from the federal government enables them to set their own priorities, and off-reserve communities fortunate enough to have access to relevant provincial or territorial programs. Thus, the way forward for pregnant Aboriginal women is stymied by both program and jurisdiction rigidities.[60]

Fetal alcohol syndrome and effect

Fetal alcohol syndrome (FAS) is the term used to describe a continuum of disabling effects on a child brought about by a mother's heavy drinking during pregnancy (two or more drinks per day). FAS and its milder form, FAE (fetal alcohol effect), can cause low birth weight, growth retardation and small body size, facial anomalies (such as close placement of the nose to the lips and of the eyes to one another), skeletal abnormalities, and cardio-vascular problems. Equally problematic and more difficult to diagnose are the effects of FAS and FAE on the brain and nervous system. These range from difficulty understanding cause-and-effect relationships, impulsiveness and impaired judgement, to severe mental disability. Researchers now recognize that prenatal alcohol exposure may cause subtle deficits in judgement and reasoning in people with apparently normal intelligence.[61] The degree of brain and neural damage varies with the amount of alcohol consumed and perhaps with the timing and concentration of consumption.

No one knows how many people are affected by FAS or FAE, as the syndrome was identified only about 20 years ago and reliable studies are few.[62] Studies of FAS among Aboriginal people are fewer still, but some conducted in Canada have indicated an alarmingly high prevalence.[63] The experience of local health and social service workers supports the idea that FAS is a serious problem in at least a few Aboriginal communities where alcohol abuse has been a long-standing health problem, and a lesser but still troubling problem in others.[64] FAS causes particularly acute pain among Aboriginal people – the pain of accepting responsibility for having caused harm. This is the dilemma facing a woman whose drinking has damaged her children and the community that allowed it to happen. FAS and FAE are entirely preventable, but there is no known way to cure their effects, which are permanent. The estimated cost of meeting the needs of someone who is severely affected by FAS over a lifetime is $1 to $1.5 million.[65] The social and emotional cost to families and communities is also great, as Commissioners heard in testimony:

> Children with FAS or FAE are often difficult babies, especially if they are withdrawing from the alcohol that surrounded them in the [womb]. If the mothers are still actively abusing alcohol, these children often are subject to attachment breaks, abuse, and/or neglect,

and they often become involved with the child welfare system as foster or adopted children.

Betsy Jackson
Alcohol-Related Birth Defects Committee
Whitehorse, Yukon, 18 November 1992

They are hard to care for, their disability is not understood, there are many peer and social pressures, no skills to fall back on....Currently we believe many adults [who were born] with FAS/FAE are either on the street or in jail.

Lorraine Stick
Alcohol-Related Birth Defects Committee
Whitehorse, Yukon, 18 November 1992

FAS in its extreme forms is a severely disabling condition. In its milder forms, it is a probable cause of the behavioural problems of many children, both Aboriginal and non-Aboriginal. Support for its victims and public education for the prevention of new cases are needed.

Prevention depends on just one thing: the reduction of alcohol consumption during pregnancy. Aboriginal women who are pregnant need clear and accessible information about the potential effects of alcohol. The desire for a healthy child gives all pregnant women a powerful motivation to stop using alcohol and drugs. Indeed, they are likely to be more open to reducing their drinking during pregnancy than at any other time in their lives. This suggests to us that priority be given to alcohol and drug programs for pregnant Aboriginal women. Yet we have been told that treatment services are unprepared to deal with pregnant women, or with women who already have children.[66] As well, Aboriginal women who are pregnant need culture-based prenatal outreach and support programs, designed to address their particular situation and vulnerabilities, such as the Healthiest Babies Possible program in Prince George, described earlier.

Support issues are more complex:

- Family caregivers in Aboriginal communities are often forced, by lack of private means or public programs suitable for their children as they grow up, to place their children in provincial care facilities.
- Schools may treat FAS and FAE children as having incorrigible behaviour problems without recognizing their capacity for skills development by means of a hands-on learning style. Some FAS and FAE children have super-abundant physical energy, which could be directed to athletics. Some have an active fantasy life, which could be channelled into artistic activities.
- Many FAS and FAE children have social and emotional problems related to their condition and can be at increased risk of suicide in adolescence.

- Some with FAS and FAE are seriously disabled and need extensive supervision. Others need a sensitive assessment of their limits and strengths and assistance in reaching their potential.
- Once FAS and FAE children become adults, their needs change. Although some can be capable of independent living, others need access to supervised shelter operated by people who understand the nature of their impairment.

In 1992, the government of Canada rejected the recommendations of a House of Commons standing committee for "aggressive public information campaigns" among Aboriginal people and "more effective and appropriate community-based ways of dealing with learning disabilities, of which FAS is the major portion of demand" in Aboriginal communities.[67] According to the minister of health at the time, current health programs provide ample opportunity for Aboriginal communities to undertake prevention and support for families coping with FAS and FAE.[68] The minister argued as well that no group in Canadian society is at greater risk of FAS or FAE than any other and that programs targeted to Aboriginal people would have the effect of stigmatizing them.

The Commission takes a different view. The extent of FAS and FAE in Aboriginal communities is unknown. Aboriginal communities with high rates of alcohol abuse in the past may have a high incidence of FAS and FAE effects today. Until the facts are established, no one can say whether special provisions are needed. Ministerial pronouncements of this sort simply underline the powerlessness of Aboriginal nations and their communities to determine their own health and social service needs and set their own priorities.

Control over Aboriginal health research and over special health education campaigns is still denied to Aboriginal people. Within the limits of what is now possible, a number of proposals to prevent FAS and FAE and to support its victims were made to the Commission.[69]

Family-centred birthing

At our hearings in the provincial and territorial north, Aboriginal women raised an issue of special concern in the north: the mandatory transportation of birthing women to distant hospitals, regardless of their medical risk. Since the early 1960s, medical services branch and almost every health jurisdiction in Canada has had a policy of transporting all Aboriginal women who are pregnant to secondary or tertiary care hospitals for childbirth.[70] No doubt lives have been saved by this policy. However, for women with no apparent risk of medical complication, enforced transportation has meant an end to family-centred birth, community-based care and the possibility of culture-based choice. Aboriginal people have objected to the interruptions and strains this causes to family life, the isolation and stress for mother and infant, and the fact that it interferes with indigenous birthing knowledge, local midwifery skills and tra-ditional family-centred ceremonies.[71]

In a minority of pregnancies, where there are risks to the health of the preg-nant woman or the newborn, transporting the woman to hospital is appropri-ate. But for healthy Aboriginal women, enforced evacuation has profoundly negative consequences. A woman must leave her family behind and live in a hostel for a two-week waiting period, then enter a hospital for delivery. She may find that no one speaks her language or understands her background. She may give birth attended by strangers. What was traditionally a joyous, even sacred event can be frightening and alienating. Her family and community are denied the life-affirming experience of sharing in the miracle of new life. The father, sib-lings, grandparents and other relatives are excluded from the birth and from the all-important first days or weeks of the infant's life when the bonds of love and responsibility are forged. In the Innuulisivik (Povungnituk) case study, some informants speculated that excluding fathers (and others) from pregnancy and birth contributes to the abuse of women and the neglect of children by distancing family members from the newborn.[72]

In addition, when the birth occurs away from the community, traditional rituals to name and welcome the child are delayed or abandoned. The vital con-tributions of the traditional Aboriginal midwife to health promotion and family solidarity are lost as well.

The idea that midwives can provide safe, supportive and cost-effective care for pregnant women in low-risk childbirth situations has become more widely accepted in Canada in the last 10 to 15 years. Ontario passed legislation to rec-ognize and regulate the practice of midwifery in 1991. Most other provinces are moving in a similar direction. In the Northwest Territories, where traditional midwifery has survived the longest, all pregnant women are the object of trans-portation policies, and authorities have so far expressed little interest in change. A pilot project is under way in Rankin Inlet to explore possibilities for birthing in facilities close to the pregnant woman's community.

Most expert evidence suggests that when the pregnancy is normal, mid-wifery services decrease the risks of complications in childbirth – or at the very least, do nothing to increase complications.[73] (No kind of care can guarantee problem-free birth.) As Martha Greig of Pauktuutit argued, the barriers to cre-ating community-based maternity services staffed primarily by Aboriginal mid-wives are political, the result of ignorance of Aboriginal ways:

[Inuit women] would like to find alternatives to the present system of removing pregnant women from their families at the time of birth. We seek alternatives which benefit the entire family and which do not expose women and newborn infants to unnecessary risk;

alternatives which allow us to feel pride and respect in ourselves and our culture. To us, healthy children are born into their family and their community; they are not born thousands of miles from home to an unhappy, frightened mother.

Unfortunately, the debate we often find ourselves engaged in is premised on a disrespect for our history and for the knowledge and skills which many of our elders still possess. We often find ourselves on the defensive, endlessly declaring that, of course, we too are concerned about maternal and infant mortality rates. We have not been allowed to engage in this debate as equals. Recognition of our traditional skills, knowledge, values and approaches to life is necessary, not just around issues of childbirth but in all spheres.

Martha Greig
Vice-President, Pauktuutit
Ottawa, Ontario, 2 November 1993

The example often mentioned to us of a new midwifery service that has returned control of the birth experience to Aboriginal women and their families, in a safe and meaningful form, was the Innuulisivik Maternity Centre in Povungnituk, northern Quebec. There, planning for a small, regional hospital built in the early 1980s provided the occasion for Inuit women to ask for an end to the policy of routine travel to Moose Factory or Montreal for childbirth. Following community consultation, the planning committee undertook to develop a regional maternity service, staffed primarily by midwives and Aboriginal birth attendants in training to become midwives, with support from other hospital personnel.

'The Maternity', as it is known in the region, has been a great success. Since opening in September 1986, it has responded to the birthing preferences of Inuit women in a socially and culturally appropriate manner, and its record in maintaining or improving the health outcomes of its clientele has been confirmed by independent evaluation.[74] In its first two years, staff managed 84 per cent of the births (a total of 350) in the eight Hudson Bay communities it serves and achieved perinatal mortality rates comparable to or lower than the rates for Quebec as a whole.[75] Staff were able to help new mothers with post-natal care and advise on crucial issues such as infant nutrition. The positive psycho-social and cultural effects are less quantifiable, but were often cited by residents of northern communities.[76]

The pressure for community-based, culturally sensitive birthing services in the north demonstrates the problems that have accumulated over the past 50 years as a result of imposing 'illness care' protocols on Aboriginal communities. Such protocols are not necessarily the best approach, are not necessarily wanted, and often interfere with creative, culture-based solutions. This is not to suggest that modern medical care is devalued by Aboriginal people – far from it. Rather, the wholesale replacement of traditional health and healing systems with western systems has had negative and positive results. In the case of childbirth, many Aboriginal women (in the south as well as in the north) are arguing for a combination of traditional and modern practices. To us, this approach makes sense – not only with respect to birthing but for other health objectives as well.

The persistence of infectious disease

The decline of infectious diseases in developed societies since the late nineteenth century is often thought to be the result of modern medical care. In fact, it is largely the result of improved standards of living, higher real wages, higher quality housing and sanitation, and access to more and better food.[77] To the extent that Aboriginal people have shared in Canada's rising standard of living, their health has improved as well. To the extent that they have continued to experience lower incomes, inferior housing conditions and more contaminated water, they continue to suffer from infectious diseases in like measure.

Epidemics of smallpox, diphtheria, polio, measles, mumps and rubella wreaked havoc among Aboriginal peoples in the past. Infectious diseases killed or disabled infants, children and elders, as well as adults in the prime of their lives, the people who hunted and trapped for food, cooked the meals and cared for the children, led the councils of government and communicated with the spirit world. It is difficult for us to imagine the misery and chaos; entire clans all but disappeared, leaving only a few orphans to tell the stories of what once was.

The far-reaching effects of infectious diseases on the social stability of First Peoples is illustrated by a story told by Chief Frank Beardy at our public hearings in Big Trout Lake:

> I would like to take you back in time. I would like to take you back to the days and years before 1929 [when the adhesion to Treaty 9 was signed]....What happened in the 1800s and early 1900s, I am told by the elders, is that certain diseases swept across our lands and the lands of the Big Trout Lake people. Smallpox, chicken pox, tuberculosis, mumps, measles. Diseases that [our healers] didn't know how to heal or how to counter with their herbal medicines. [These diseases] totally decimated our villages. [They] totally decimated the clan structure that we knew, the clan system that governed our lives.
>
> What also happened was that, at the same time as these diseases were sweeping across the north...Ontario's conservation officers...were already implementing game laws that were made up in the halls of Queen's Park and on Parliament Hill....[T]hese conservation officers were confiscating fish nets, they were confiscating guns, they were

confiscating the animals that were [used] by our people for food, because they were saying that the Indian people were breaking their conservation laws....

My grandfather, who was a headman in Bearskin Lake at that time, heard about the treaties that had happened in Northern Manitoba in the Island Lake area. Through the missionaries or the Hudson Bay managers that were already in the area, he wrote a letter to the Queen, requesting that they be allowed to sign treaty with the Queen of England or the King of England. It was only because of these illnesses that plagued our people, and because the conservation officers were really hard on our people and confiscated their livelihood, that...my grandfather was, in a way, forced to request for the treaty to be signed in Big Trout Lake.

Chief Frank Beardy
Muskrat Dam First Nation community
Big Trout Lake, Ontario, 3 December 1992

Epidemics were not confined to the distant past. Aboriginal people in the Yukon were stricken many times during the construction of the Alaska Highway in the 1940s.[78] In 1952, Inuit on Baffin Island and the Ungava peninsula of Quebec suffered an epidemic of measles that infected nearly everyone and killed between two and seven per cent of the population.[79]

We have chosen to discuss tuberculosis as an example of the persistence of infectious diseases among Aboriginal people. We have also examined the preliminary evidence on the rise of HIV/AIDS, a new threat. If unattended, HIV/AIDS could devastate Aboriginal people as much as other infectious diseases have in the past.

Tuberculosis

Tuberculosis was one of the first epidemic diseases noted in Jesuit accounts of Aboriginal life in the new world. It spread steadily and disastrously until, by the early 1900s, some observers thought TB might completely eliminate the indigenous nations of Canada.[80]

The spread of TB was exacerbated by the crowded and often unsanitary conditions created by reserve and settlement living – and by gathering Aboriginal children into boarding schools. Many arrived at school in good health, only to test positive for TB within two years.[81] Many TB survivors carried the disease back home.[82]

After denying responsibility for several decades, the federal government began aggressive control measures in the mid-1930s. In 1936, the budget for TB treatment was already $50,000, ballooning to $4 million by 1946. From 1950 to 1952, nearly 14,000 Aboriginal people were hospitalized. Most were sent to facilities far from home, cut off from family and culture, sometimes lost to both forever. It took 20 more years for TB infection rates to fall below crisis levels. The

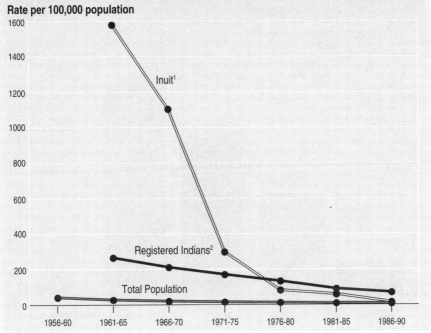

FIGURE 3.4
Incidence of Active Tuberculosis, Registered Indian, Inuit and Total
Populations, 1956-1990

Rate per 100,000 population

Notes:
1. Inuit living in the Northwest Territories.
2. Data on registered Indians for the years 1965, 1970, and 1975 are single-year figures; all other rates shown based on five-year averages.

Source: Kue Young, "Measuring the Health Status of Canada's Aboriginal Population: a statistical review and methodological commentary", research study prepared for RCAP (1994).

data on rates of infection available to the Commission begin in 1956-1960 (see Figure 3.4).

Part of the reason for a decline in TB infection was that Aboriginal people were at last developing their own immunity. Given sufficient time, natural selection (by which some individuals in an epidemic survive and gain immunity, or are naturally immune and pass their immunity on to their children) enables any people to acquire increased immunity to a new bacillus. This is an aspect of the natural history of infections, independent of medical intervention.

The decline of TB now appears to have stalled. It is still more common among Aboriginal families and communities than among other Canadians. Based on 1992 figures, rates of infection are 43 times higher among registered Indians than among non-Aboriginal Canadians born in this country. The rate

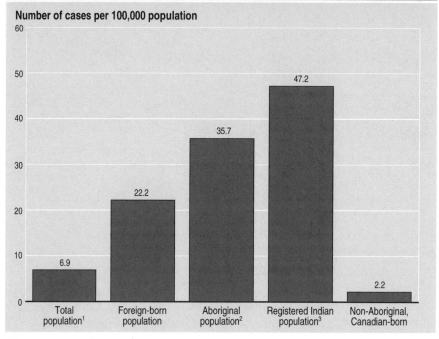

FIGURE 3.5
Tuberculosis Rates, Aboriginal and Total Populations, 1993

Number of cases per 100,000 population

Total population[1]	6.9
Foreign-born population	22.2
Aboriginal population[2]	35.7
Registered Indian population[3]	47.2
Non-Aboriginal, Canadian-born	2.2

Notes:

1. Includes new and reactivated cases.
2. Includes registered and non-registered Indian persons, Métis persons and Inuit.
3. Calculated using population counts from DIAND registry.

Source: Statistics Canada, Health Statistics Division, unpublished tabulations.

is about the same for Aboriginal people living in Canada as for people living in Africa[83] (see Figure 3.5). In Sioux Lookout, we were told

> Tuberculosis has become, once again, a significant health concern in the First Nations of our area. We have about 100 cases per 100,000 compared to 8 cases per 100,000, which is the national average. The federal government has initially responded to the TB epidemic by providing personnel to contain the outbreak in a few identified communities, and is now in the process of considering the possibility of a much needed long-term commitment to delivering a preventative TB program.
>
> Nellie Beardy
> Executive Director,
> Sioux Lookout First Nations Health Authority
> Sioux Lookout, Ontario, 1 December 1992

Controlling TB requires two approaches: improvements in housing, sanitation and nutrition; and case identification of those now infected, followed by medically supervised, self-administered antibiotic treatment. The health implications of housing, water quality and nutrition are discussed later in this chapter. (Housing is discussed further in Chapter 4 of this volume.) Self-administered treatment is a problem because Aboriginal people show poor compliance with medical instructions, including drug-taking orders.[84] This means, in short, that they do not always do as they are told, especially by non-Aboriginal medical personnel. In the case of active TB, compliance is critical: failure to follow through with medication means failure of the cure. Thus, preventive public health education designed for and by Aboriginal people is essential for successful control of this continuing obstacle to improved Aboriginal health.

In the Commission's view, control of TB is an urgent priority, at least in some regions of Canada; it is, however, only one of many contagious diseases to occur more often in Aboriginal than non-Aboriginal communities. In almost all categories of infectious disease identified by the international classification of diseases, registered Indians run a greater risk of illness than other Canadians.[85] In some cases, the ratio of Aboriginal to total Canadian disadvantage is four to one. We are especially concerned that HIV/AIDS poses a growing threat to Aboriginal people.

HIV/AIDS

There are no adequate national data on the incidence of sexually transmitted diseases among Aboriginal people.[86] With regard to AIDS (acquired immune deficiency syndrome), 97 of the 9,511 Canadians diagnosed (and surviving) as of April 1994 were Aboriginal, based on self-definition or physicians' records. Although the number of diagnosed AIDS cases (97) is relatively small, it is four times the number given in the first report of the Joint National Committee on Aboriginal AIDS Education and Prevention just four years earlier. Figures on the rate of HIV infection among Aboriginal people are even more difficult to come by. In Canada as a whole, the ratio of persons infected with HIV to those with AIDS is thought to be about four to one.[87]

Risk factors identified among Aboriginal people suggest that a serious AIDS problem may be in the making:[88]

- The overall health of Aboriginal people is poorer than that of non-Aboriginal people in Canada, suggesting that Aboriginal people may have weaker immune systems in general.
- Aboriginal people have higher rates of several illnesses associated with HIV/AIDS.[89]
- Anecdotal evidence and some limited survey data would seem to indicate that unprotected sexual activity is the norm among Aboriginal people.[90]

- Excessive use of alcohol, which increases the chance of unprotected sexual activity, is also a risk factor in some communities.
- Groups in which the rate of HIV/AIDS is already high – such as street youth, prostitutes and the prison population – include a significant number of Aboriginal people.

Even more troubling is that many Aboriginal people apparently do not think of AIDS as a disease that affects Aboriginal people. We were told that some think of it as a gay disease, imagining that homosexuality is rare among Aboriginal people; as a city disease, imagining that it will not follow them into small or isolated communities; or as a white man's disease, imagining that it can somehow be restricted to non-Aboriginal people.[91]

These are false hopes. Although the Commission has no data on the incidence of homosexuality and bisexuality, we have no reason to believe it is less common among Aboriginal people than among non-Aboriginal people.[92] The fact that many – and perhaps most – Aboriginal people who are gay choose to hide their sexuality increases their risk.[93] Further, the tendency of Aboriginal people to migrate freely between their home communities and urban centres makes it inevitable that transmission of the virus from city to country will occur. As for cultural or group distinctions, HIV/AIDS spares no one. In other words, Aboriginal people are vulnerable – all the more so if they do not think they are and therefore take no precautions. Aboriginal youth are at particular risk.[94]

At present, there is no continuing mechanism through which information on HIV/AIDS can be exchanged by Aboriginal people, no monitoring being done on HIV/AIDS in Aboriginal communities, no research being undertaken on the risks to Aboriginal people, and no Aboriginal-specific policy being developed.[95] Given the lessons history has taught about the impacts of infectious diseases on unprotected peoples, this seems to us an irresponsible omission by health and social service agencies, both Aboriginal and non-Aboriginal.

We are also disturbed to hear that some Aboriginal communities are rejecting their own members who are HIV-positive or who have AIDS:

> People are dying in cities and in rural communities. They are our brothers, sisters, aunties, mothers, fathers, nieces and nephews. They are human beings. But often they are not treated like human beings, and die alone because nobody wants them in their own communities. Why? Because of fear and ignorance based on lack of education about the transmission of HIV....
>
> One of [our] concerns is the lack of education on the virus and the lack of support, care and treatment for those individuals who are living with AIDS. Often entire families are shunned, rejected, and even attacked in communities when other members learn a family has

AIDS. At a time when the individual and their families most need support and compassion, the individual cannot even return home to receive proper care and treatment. This is also often due to a combination of a lack of resources, both financial and medical, or because they are not wanted or welcome in their own communities. Fear based on ignorance has meant that people who are living with AIDS are denied the right to live and die with dignity in their own communities.

Linda Day
Executive Director, Healing Our Spirit
B.C. First Nations AIDS Society
Vancouver, British Columbia, 2 June 1993

This issue needs to be addressed with care and compassion and, most of all, with speed. Further, proposals for action to support people with HIV/AIDS and for appropriate public education measures to prevent the spread of the infection among high-risk groups must come from within Aboriginal nations and their communities. If the ideas originate elsewhere, they will fail to take into account Aboriginal sensibilities and social realities.[96] This is true of all health and social welfare issues, but particularly issues that are culturally or socially sensitive.

The inroads of chronic disease

Although still serious, rates of infectious disease have declined among Aboriginal people since the turn of the century. Cardiovascular diseases and cancer, the leading killers of Canadians generally, are found at lower rates in the Aboriginal population, though they remain significant causes of death. Metabolic disorders, particularly diabetes, and respiratory and digestive disorders are also significant factors in Aboriginal illness and death, as shown in Figures 3.1 and 3.6. Chronic conditions are sometimes called the diseases of modernization, or western diseases because they attend the lifestyles typical of western industrial nations: reduced physical exercise; diets overloaded with fat and sugar; high levels of stress; and increased exposure to a wide range of pollutants in the air, water and food supply. These risk factors set the stage for a wide range of diseases, including cancer, heart disease, obesity, gall bladder disease and diabetes.

The Commission has chosen to discuss diabetes as an example of a serious chronic disease with specific dynamics of cause and effect among Aboriginal people. Diabetes affects Aboriginal people disproportionately (see Figure 3.7), and the cost of that prevalence is great. As well as leading to premature death, diabetes causes medical complications and disability, including kidney disease, heart and circulatory disease, blindness, amputations, nervous system disease, and birth defects among infants born to diabetic mothers. In Canada, diabetes is the cause of 30 per cent of new cases of kidney disease and is the leading cause of

FIGURE 3.6
Mortality Rates by Selected Causes, Registered Indian Population,
1982-1992

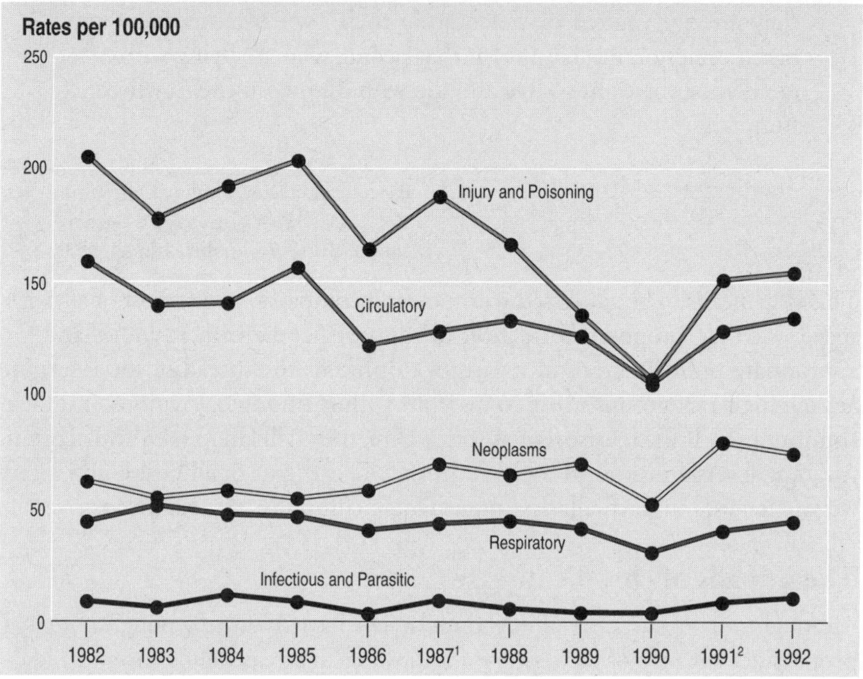

Rates per 100,000

Notes:
1. Rates since 1987 no longer include Indian persons in the Northwest Territories because of the transfer of health services to the government of the Northwest Territories.
2. British Columbia data were not included in counts and rates for 1985 to 1990, but are included beginning in 1991.

Source: DIAND, Information Quality and Research Directorate, *Basic Departmental Data, 1994* (Ottawa: January 1995).

new cases of adult blindness. It causes 50 per cent of all non-traumatic amputations and doubles the rate of heart disease (for women, it multiplies this rate by five). It triples the rate of birth defects and increases the risk of neonatal complications requiring intensive medical intervention by a factor of five.[97]

Dialysis for kidney disease costs about $40,000 per patient per year in Canada. The total cost to Canadians of all treatment (for both direct and indirect ill health effects of diabetes) in 1994-95 has been estimated at $4 billion.[98]

In our public hearings, several community health caregivers told us they are alarmed about the growing number of people with diabetes in Aboriginal populations.[99]

FIGURE 3.7
Prevalence of Diagnosed Diabetes, Registered Indian, Inuit and Total
Populations, 1987

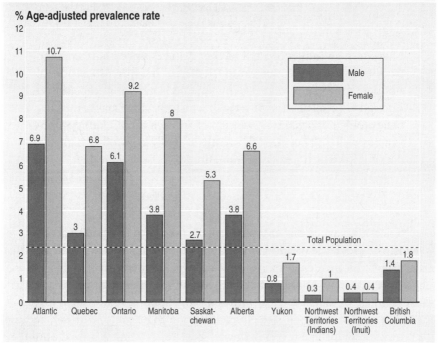

Source: T.K. Young, E.J.E. Szathmary, S. Evers and B. Wheatly, "Geographical distribution of diabetes among the Native population of Canada: A national survey", *Social Science and Medicine* 31 (1990), pp. 129-139.

Our health status report gives a representative view of the health status of Inuit people. We know the bleak statistics with regard to Aboriginal health status [elsewhere] in Canada, and our health status assessment shows no differing results here in this region. Diabetes, hypertension, overweight, poor nutritional status are epidemic amongst Native people in Canada today.

Bette Palfrey
Keewatin Regional Health Board
Rankin Inlet, Northwest Territories, 19 November 1992

Over the last decade...diabetes mellitus has been recognized as a major disease among Aboriginal communities across North America. In the Sioux Lookout zone [population approximately 15,000], approximately 1,095 people of the population over 25 years of age...are known to be diabetic. It is significant that 50 per cent of the cases have been diagnosed within the last five to ten years.

Nellie Beardy
Executive Director,
Sioux Lookout First Nations Health Authority
Sioux Lookout, Ontario, 1 December 1992

I have seen an unprecedented level of diabetes since I have come to work with the Native community. There is a predisposition in Aboriginal people to diabetes, but the poor nutrition imposed on Aboriginal people by the poverty in which they live makes this diabetic problem much, much worse....I have seen a lot of kidney problems as well....[They are] the result of badly controlled diabetes, diabetes for which people cannot afford to eat the right diet.

Dr. Timothy Sheehan
Sagkeeng Health Care Centre
Fort Alexander, Manitoba, 30 October 1992

Since 1940, when diabetes was virtually unknown in Aboriginal people in Canada, the incidence of and complications from diabetes have increased significantly.[100] Its incidence rate is at least two to three times higher among Aboriginal than non-Aboriginal people. Kewayosh argues that this is a conservative estimate of the difference, with Aboriginal rates actually much higher.[101] Rates also vary from region to region and nation to nation.[102] Further, because the symptoms of diabetes develop slowly, they often go unrecognized until they are well advanced. Thus it has been said that for every known case of diabetes, at least one goes undiagnosed.[103]

There appears to be an inherited tendency among Aboriginal people to diabetes;[104] nevertheless, the disease was rare in pre-contact times. What, then, has changed in Aboriginal lives to stimulate its occurrence? The main risk factors for diabetes are obesity, poor eating habits and physical inactivity. Obesity is thought to be a growing problem in Aboriginal communities.[105] Physical activity has decreased, as a result of the historical confinement of some Aboriginal people to reserves and settlements and the adoption of a sedentary lifestyle by urban migrants. Another factor is the consumption of alcohol. Perhaps most serious of all has been a change in diet from high quality country foods to processed foods with high levels of fat and sugar. We discuss the nutritional value of country food (fish, game and vegetables available directly from surrounding lands) in more detail later in this chapter and in Volume 4, Chapter 6.

At a recent international conference on diabetes and Aboriginal people, Elder Simon Lucas of the Hesquiaht First Nation community at Tofino, British Columbia (himself a diabetic) described the changes in his people's lifestyle and diet:

The traditions of our forefathers were amazing. Our people were so busy they didn't have time to be sick. My father built his last canoe when I was 8 years old, and [thinking about] this has made me remember how busy I was as a young boy. It was nothing for me to row 10 to 15 miles in one day. Because of the teachings of my mother and father, I never had to take a lunch with me on those trips. I knew the kinds of berries and leaves or herbs to eat as a young boy....I could hunt, I could fish....

Now, many of our beaches in British Columbia are closed because of contamination. Many of our inlets are closed because of...toxins....[T]he foods we survived on for thousands of years are sicker than we are. Every resource in British Columbia has been commercialized [and depleted]....My forefathers say...you must not [destroy] those things that keep you alive.[106]

Health caregivers and researchers have observed that failure to comply with a doctor's orders on medications, diet and exercise is common among Aboriginal diabetics. It has also been observed that standard prevention and treatment programs are "simply not successful" among Aboriginal populations.[107] The lifestyle changes necessary to prevent or control diabetes are difficult for everyone, but Aboriginal people approach diet and weight control from the point of view of their culture, values and experience. They require culture-based prevention programs. Alethea Kewayosh put it this way:

Low compliance rates with treatment protocols can in part be attributed to non-culturally relevant educational and prevention materials. This is best illustrated by the problems of dietary compliance. Native people with diabetes often fail to comply with [prescribed] dietary changes due to: (a) their perception of the role of food; (b) strong cultural beliefs that equate health and prosperity with being overweight; (c) the lack of familiarity with many of the food items recommended on the diet, and (d) the high cost of many of the recommended dietary items that are not only difficult to obtain, but may require special preparation.[108]

Dr. Jennie Joe, director of the Native American Research and Training Center in Tucson, Arizona, has also concluded that non-compliance stems from the use of health programs and materials developed for use in non-Aboriginal cultures. For greater success in Aboriginal communities, she recommends such strategies as

- showing (with slides, videos and other visual aids) what can happen as a result of diabetes, instead of describing it in writing;
- involving families in treatment and whole communities in prevention;

- recognizing the cultural significance of food among peoples for whom it was often scarce, even in recent memory; and
- acknowledging that chronic disease is a new concept for Aboriginal people and that they may have difficulty accepting that preventive measures to forestall or control diabetes must last a lifetime.[109]

The Commission is aware of a number of promising initiatives to develop culture-based diabetes prevention programs for Aboriginal people in Canada. One of them is the Diabetic Outreach Program in the High Prairie region of northern Alberta. Another is the Walking in Balance Program developed at the Anishnabe Spiritual Centre on Manitoulin Island.[110] The most comprehensive is the four-part initiative undertaken at the Kateri Memorial Hospital Centre at Kahnawake, Quebec. Commissioners believe that the Kateri Centre could, and should, serve as a base for training caregivers from other Aboriginal communities in preventing and managing diabetes.[111]

The stresses of disability

Disability among Aboriginal people was raised in a number of presentations to the Commission, pointing out the long-time neglect of people with disabilities.[112]

According to Statistics Canada's 1991 Aboriginal peoples survey (APS), 31 per cent of Aboriginal people have some form of disability – more than twice the national average. For young adults, the rate is almost three times as high.[113] Disabilities affecting mobility and agility are most common, but hearing and visual disabilities affect a large portion of the Aboriginal population. About one in three of the APS sample reported a hearing impediment, compared with one in four in the general population. About one in four reported a problem with sight, compared with one in 10 in the general population. Problems with sight are most common among Indian people on-reserve; problems with hearing are most common among Inuit (see Table 3.8).

The disparity between Aboriginal and non-Aboriginal rates of disability corresponds to disparities in rates of injury, accident, violence, self-destructive or suicidal behaviour, and illnesses (such as diabetes) that can result in permanent impairment. But why do Aboriginal people suffer disability more often than others? A special committee of the House of Commons summed up the answer this way:

> Native communities, and Native people living in non-Native communities, suffer on a daily basis from living conditions which other Canadians experience only rarely. These adversities – economic, political, social and cultural in nature – greatly increase the probability of being disabled at some time in a person's lifetime.[114]

Reversing these adversities is the objective of primary prevention, which involves programs to improve health and safety conditions in Aboriginal homes

TABLE 3.8
Persons with Physical Disabilities, Total and
Aboriginal Populations, 1991

| | Total Population | Total Aboriginal | North American Indians | | Métis | Inuit |
			On-reserve	Non-reserve		
Mobility disability	45	45	47	45	44	36
Hearing disability	23	35	39	33	34	44
Seeing disability	9	24	32	21	22	24
Agility	44	35	34	36	38	26
Speaking disability	10	13	14	13	13	10
Other disability	37	36	37	37	35	36

Notes: Population is those 15 years of age and older.

Source: Statistics Canada, "The Daily", 25 March 1994, catalogue no. 11-001E.

and communities so that injury and accident are reduced, efforts to improve social and economic conditions so that violence and self-destruction are reduced, and programs in health promotion and disease prevention so that illness-based disability is reduced. However, the testimony before Commissioners was aimed almost exclusively at providing support for Aboriginal people who already have disabilities:

> [After my accident] I was in the hospital for 14 months. Ever since I ended up in this wheelchair, I had no place to go....Right now I am living in [name of institution]. I don't call that home. What I call home is my own house....I was wondering if disabled [Aboriginal] people could get their own places, and if they could...pay somebody to help take care of a disabled person in his own house....I am not just talking for myself; I am talking for other disabled Native people.
>
> Victor Cody
> Native Disabled Group
> Saskatoon, Saskatchewan, 27 October 1992

The kinds of disabilities I am working with are quadraplegics, para-plegics, heart and stroke victims, vision (partially and totally impaired), hearing (partially and totally impaired), head and brain injuries, and also people on dialysis. Each one of these people has a very unique type of disability, and it takes a lot time dealing with each and every one of them because of the individual problems they have....

Also, there is a lot of racism in institutions such as private home care institutions, larger institutions too. It makes it more difficult for Native people who are disabled living in these institutions. I strongly believe that an all-Native home should be provided....

There is a lot of abuse taking place also with Native disabled people....And without somebody like me who can go out there and investigate this [a resource which most disabled Aboriginal people certainly do not have], there is nothing that can be done for those people to get help.

Isabelle Smith
Disability Counsellor
Saskatoon Indian and Metis Friendship Centre
Saskatoon, Saskatchewan, 27 October 1992

Aboriginal people with disabilities who live on reserves and in rural settlements face such problems as inaccessible buildings, including band offices, schools, churches and homes; inaccessible places of community activity, including community centres, arenas and meeting halls; lack of appropriate recreation opportunities; the difficult choice between staying on under-serviced reserves and settlements or leaving home to seek services away from relatives, friends and familiar surroundings.[115]

The Commission has selected the example of hearing impairment to illustrate some of the origins and consequences of disability specific to Aboriginal people. Most premature hearing loss results from excessive noise or from otitis media (OM). OM is an acute or chronic inflammation of the middle ear, to which children are highly susceptible. It occurs when an infection of the nose or throat – including an infection caused by a cold or flu – blocks the passageway connecting the back of the throat to the middle ear (the eustachian tube). Some children have recurrent attacks, sometimes every few weeks over a period of years, especially in the winter.[116] Children who are otitis-prone are likely to have temporary or permanent hearing problems that interfere with language learning, school success and social development generally.[117] Most of this hearing loss is preventable.[118]

As with all infectious diseases, inadequate housing conditions – overcrowding and less than ideal sanitation facilities – are major risk factors. For OM in particular, anything that increases the child's exposure to colds and flu or weakens the immune system adds to the risk. Bottle feeding increases risk, especially if the child is fed while lying flat. (This position allows milk to pool in the pharynx and puts pressure on the ear. Breast feeding offers protection through better positioning of the child and through the transfer of antibodies from mother to child.)[119] Exposure to second-hand cigarette smoke is also a risk factor.

Inuit children have especially high rates of OM. As many as 80 per cent show evidence of current infection or scarring from past episodes.[120] In one community, research showed found that one child in 10 had suffered permanent hearing loss as a result of past infections.[121] In another, one child in five was found to be at least partly deaf.[122]

Dr. James Baxter, an expert in this field, has indicated that OM went from a rarity among Inuit to a serious health problem in only a few years, starting in the 1950s.[123] Lifestyle changes were responsible. Once-migratory Inuit began to live in close quarters year-round; colds and flus were thus in greater circulation. Inuit moved into government-built houses that were often inadequate for the climate, and their immune systems were compromised by inferior store-bought food, alcohol consumption and cigarette smoke. Bottle-feeding replaced breast-feeding in many households. All the conditions needed to promote OM at high rates were in place, and indeed the condition was epidemic until very recently. Improvements are primarily the result of outreach to parents, aggressive case finding by medical and school personnel, and treatment by specialized personnel from southern hospitals and university medical faculties.[124]

Such strategies can be applied to other Aboriginal health and social services. Outreach and case finding are feasible for most Inuit and reserve communities now. Access to specialized personnel is notoriously difficult to come by, however, especially in northern and isolated communities.[125] Yet, as Commissioners heard many times in testimony, fly-out patient programs are expensive and disruptive to patients and their families, and they work only when accurate local diagnosis can be depended on. Fly-in expertise is irregular, unreliable, and sometimes insensitive to local cultures and conditions. The magnitude of the issue of access to trained personnel suggests the need for a comprehensive human resources strategy. We return to this matter later in the chapter.

The problems of Aboriginal disability raise a broader issue: the difficulty of providing equitable programs and services for all Aboriginal people when responsibility is divided between federal and provincial/territorial governments. In 1981, a special committee of the House of Commons urged all governments to develop programs for Aboriginal people with disabilities.[126] Little was done for a decade. Then, in September 1991, the federal government announced a national strategy for the integration of persons with disabilities. The program has been funded to a maximum of $158 million over five years and has a long list of commendable objectives, including some that apply to Indian people on-reserve and to Inuit in the Northwest Territories. As part of the national strategy, the department of Indian affairs is spending $5 million to improve co-ordination and accessibility and to promote sensitive design and delivery of existing programs and services to people with disabilities living on-reserve. Health Canada has conducted a major consultation on key issues regarding the care of elderly people and persons with disabilities on-reserve, with the promise of action to come. Medical services branch has allocated $2 million over five years to retrofitting existing health facilities. (It estimates that retrofitting all the health facilities it operates in Aboriginal communities would cost $7.5 million.) Even so, these initiatives leave untouched the major problem areas identified in 1981: housing, employment and economic security, education, emotional support and service delivery.

In March 1993, however, a House of Commons committee released another report on Aboriginal people with disabilities.[127] It pointed out that no comprehensive plan of action covering all Aboriginal people with disabilities exists even now, and that no single agency is charged with developing one. It identified fragmented efforts within the federal government and jurisdictional murkiness between federal and provincial/territorial governments as the two main barriers to relieving unacceptable human suffering.

The problem of inequities in services and community self-development is rooted in the distinctions of responsibility of different levels of government. It is a pervasive problem that requires complex solutions. Our proposals for reorganizing the delivery of health and social services are designed to overcome problems of unequal access to culturally appropriate services. A complementary action to fill the policy vacuum affecting urban, Métis and other Aboriginal people is discussed in Volume 4, Chapter 7.

1.3 Social and Emotional Health

Commissioners agree with health analysts all over the world and with scores of Aboriginal people who addressed us during our public hearings that health involves much more than the physical. In the imagery common to many Aboriginal cultures, good health is a state of balance and harmony involving body, mind, emotions and spirit. It links each person to family, community and the earth in a circle of dependence and interdependence, described by some in the language of the Medicine Wheel.[128] In non-Aboriginal terms, health has been seen primarily as an outcome of medical care. But we are quickly learning that any care system that reduces its definition of health to the absence of disease and disability is deeply flawed.

Testimony and research show that many Aboriginal people suffer from social and emotional ill health. The Commission heard accounts of the years lost by Aboriginal people in jails and prisons, in struggles with alcohol and drugs, and in violence and suicide, and of the breakdown in community and family order that underlies these social and emotional ills. Social disorder contributes to accidents, injuries and lack of self-care. Further, social ills undermine the collective self-esteem of Aboriginal people; many are ashamed and afraid of the self-destructive and antisocial behaviour they see around them. As well, the images of social and emotional distress in circulation in the wider population carry a distorted message to Aboriginal and non-Aboriginal people alike about what it means to be Aboriginal.

TABLE 3.9
Rates of Death for Selected Types of Injury, Registered Indian
and Total Populations, 1989-1992

	Registered Indians		Total Population	
	Male	Female	Male	Female
Motor vehicle accidents	59.7	24.7	20.0	8.3
Accidental falls	9.9	7.1	6.1	6.3
Fire	12.1	6.6	1.6	0.8
Drowning	20.8	3.1	3.0	0.6
Suicide	51.5	15.1	19.2	4.9
Homicide	18.2	6.8	2.7	1.5
Poisoning	21.1	11.7	3.0	1.2

Note: Death rates per 100,000 population.

Source: Health Canada, Medical Services Branch, unpublished tables, 1995.

We have discussed some of these matters in other publications and in other parts of this report.[129] To illustrate the complexity of the problems and possible solutions, we examine three additional aspects of social and emotional ill health: injury and accidents, alcohol abuse and child protection.

Injury and accidents

In 1992, fatal injuries were the leading cause of death among registered Indian males and the second most frequent cause of death among registered Indian females in regions for which Health Canada collects data (see Figure 3.1, Figure 3.6, Table 3.9 and Figure 3.8). 'Injury' includes all forms of accidental death (unintentional injury) and homicide and suicide (intentional injury). For young people aged 15 to 24, fully 85.5 per cent of all deaths were the result of injury.[130] Even among those aged 25 to 44, 59 per cent of all deaths resulted from injury. We discussed suicide and violence among Aboriginal people in *Choosing Life*; here we are concerned primarily with accidental death and wounding.

The majority of Aboriginal deaths from injury are the result of motor vehicle accidents (with alcohol as a major contributing factor), drownings, house fires and gunshot wounds.[131] Such injuries are considered preventable in about nine cases out of 10.

The rate of death by injury among Aboriginal people has decreased substantially in the last 20 years. However, it is still almost twice as common among Aboriginal people as among Canadians generally. In some age groups, it is more than four times as common. Furthermore, injury is responsible for a large number of non-lethal ill health effects among Aboriginal people (temporary wounds and long-term

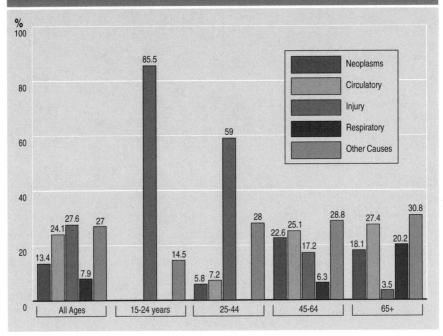

FIGURE 3.8
Selected Major Causes of Death, Registered Indian Population, 1992

Note: If a cause of death is not a major one for a given age group, it is counted in the 'other causes' category for that age group. For example, neoplasms (cancers) and circulatory and respiratory diseases are grouped in the 'other' category for the age group 15-24 years.
Source: Health Canada, Medical Services Branch, unpublished data, 1992.

disabilities that require hospitalization and other treatment). Thus, in terms of human suffering and days of life and labour lost to Aboriginal nations and their communities and to the country as a whole – plus the cost to the health care system – injury among Aboriginal people is an extremely serious social health problem.

High rates of injury when war is not a factor arise primarily from adverse psycho-social and economic factors. In the case of Indigenous people in Canada, the cultural and material losses they have suffered and their place of relative powerlessness in Canadian society have contributed to anger that has no harmless outlet, grief that does not ease, damaged self-esteem, and a profound sense of hopelessness about the future of Aboriginal people in general and themselves in particular. These contribute in many subtle and not so subtle ways to the incidence of injury:

- Reckless and potentially self-destructive behaviour, such as operating a motor vehicle (car, truck, snowmobile or boat) while under the influence of alcohol, may be caused or triggered by the powerful emotions of grief, anger and hopelessness. Other forms of violent and self-destructive behaviour, including homicide and suicide, can be triggered in the same way.

- The correlates of poverty, especially substandard housing and community infrastructure, increase the incidence of fires and other household accidents.
- In a somewhat different vein, the casual storage and occasional misuse of firearms (which are a necessary part of everyday life in hunting cultures) may also contribute to high rates of lethal or wounding injury.

Until recently, accident and injury have received little attention in government-sponsored health promotion programs for Aboriginal people. High rates of injury, to some degree, result from injustices to Aboriginal people in Canada and will not be reduced simply through education and prevention measures. Nevertheless, such approaches must be tried and assessed.

Mainstream public health offers models for successful prevention and control of injuries. Some of these have been considered – but apparently not tested – in Aboriginal communities.[132] By and large, culturally appropriate prevention strategies for Aboriginal people are underdeveloped, and we believe they are very much needed.

Brighter Futures, a child health initiative of Health Canada, now includes a component aimed at preventing injury among First Nations children. It has been funded for five years, from fiscal year 1992-93 to fiscal year 1996-97. About 80 per cent of the program budget is available for community-based programming. The remainder is reserved for national projects in support of local activity. These include materials development, training and the development of a culturally appropriate data collection system. Medical services branch data suggest that few First Nations have made use of the injury prevention component of the program so far.[133]

Strategies should be directed to the three phases of prevention. The preevent phase could include developing programs to encourage the safe use of wood stoves and fires, the safe storage of guns and other lethal weapons, the safe use and storage of poisonous household products, and so on. The event phase could include forming a volunteer fire brigade or an after-hours safety patrol, providing training in cardio-pulmonary resuscitation and other first aid techniques, developing a well-advertised electronic link with an urban poison control centre for isolated communities, and training crisis intervention specialists. The postevent phase could include developing advanced first aid skills among community members, and implementing special emergency response education for community health representatives and other community caregivers for such common injuries as burns, poisonings and overdoses. For example, the Indian Health Service in the United States conducts an injury control fellowship program to assist junior-level health workers in upgrading their knowledge of injuries, including their prevention.

It is clear from the social nature of the causes of injury among Aboriginal people, however, that prevention cannot be limited to education and behaviour modification. Long-term strategies must address community norms for safe and careful activity and, more important, the broad social conditions that provoke recklessness and lack of self-care. They must also address the possibility of dangerous products and hazards in the environment, which may require modification or regulation.

The Canada Safety Council has offered its expertise to Aboriginal people to increase preventive education about the leading causes of accidental death. In particular, representatives discussed with us the possibility of adapting its courses on driver safety awareness to suit Aboriginal audiences. (In the Commission's view, this program must extend to snowmobile and all-terrain vehicle safety, as well as the more common car and truck driver education.) We have also discussed the possibility of assessing the potential of the Council's new aggression control workshop program for use by Aboriginal communities and of working in partnership to develop culturally appropriate awareness programs about the other causes of death by injury that are at issue in Aboriginal communities: the misuse of firearms, drowning, fire, and drug overdose. We encourage Aboriginal health authorities to take the Council up on its offer. We will have more to say about such offers of positive support from non-Aboriginal health organizations later in this chapter.

As an example of co-operation already under way, we note that St. John Ambulance, a nation-wide voluntary organization that focuses on first aid and general health promotion, has entered into a partnership with the Meadow Lake Tribal Council (MLTC) of northern Saskatchewan to address the problem of injuries in the MLTC region. Members of St. John Ambulance are working with the tribal council's health and social development unit on three initiatives:

- adapting general training programs, such as the Northern Wilderness First Aid course, to Meadow Lake's needs;
- modifying special training programs on child care, babysitting and elder care to reflect Aboriginal norms and values; and
- assisting MLTC in developing other strategies for injury prevention.

We received few presentations in testimony on the problems of injury. We urge those in leadership positions to place greater priority on the prevention of injury among Aboriginal people of all ages and, where it cannot be prevented, on harm reduction. 'Harm reduction' is a phrase commonly used in the addictions field to describe a treatment goal of reducing the intake of alcohol or drugs to reduce harmful consequences; it is an alternative to total abstinence. In the field of accident and injury, if outright prevention is impossible or unlikely, harm reduction may be feasible. For example, since wood stoves cannot realistically be eliminated in Aboriginal communities, those who use them can be informed about safe use and emergency procedures in case of fire. More important, strategies can be developed to reduce alcohol abuse and encourage adult supervision of children in households with wood stoves.

The general approaches sketched here must be made specific to the patterns of injury experienced by particular Aboriginal cultures, communities and age groups. This requires a serious initiative to gather and interpret information. Medical services branch has promoted such an initiative (for First Nations only) with its 'injury surveillance project'.[134] Some other jurisdictions have small projects under way, but these lack co-ordination. Aboriginal nations and their communities across the country would benefit with help from an intergovernmental and inter-agency planning mechanism to facilitate the sharing of ideas, materials and resources.

Alcohol abuse

Alcohol was introduced to Aboriginal people in the course of trade and social interaction with European explorers, fur traders and merchants.[135] It became a part of business and a part of pleasure. The effects were somewhat similar to those of introducing smallpox and other infectious diseases: Aboriginal people had no 'immunity' to alcohol, in the sense that social norms and personal experience can 'protect' against over-consumption. Stereotypes of drunkenness among Aboriginal people have been greatly exaggerated, but there can be no doubt that the problem of abuse was – and is – real.

Excessive consumption of alcohol has serious physical health consequences; it increases the risk of heart disease, cirrhosis and liver disease, gastritis and gastro-intestinal cancers, hepatitis and fetal alcohol syndrome. Its social and emotional correlates include accidents, suicides, family violence and breakdown, unemployment, criminal behaviour and, to apply a concept from pediatrics, 'failure to thrive'.[136] Commissioners heard contradictory evidence regarding the current extent of alcohol abuse. Many Aboriginal people told us, often in graphic terms, that the effects of alcohol abuse still run wide and deep:

> Twenty-three years ago, I woke up one morning and knew I was going to die unless I quit drinking, so I quit....Of the men of my generation who were my working and drinking companions, most are dead in violence, in accidents or from alcohol-related diseases.
>
> Winston McKay
> Métis Addictions Corporation of Saskatchewan
> La Ronge, Saskatchewan, 28 May 1992

> In Canada they say there's about 80 per cent of the Native people that are directly or indirectly affected by the alcohol and drug abuse. Let me explain that. What I mean by 'directly or indirectly', it doesn't

mean that 80 per cent of Native people are addicted and should be in a treatment centre, but that somebody in their family is addicted, and that one causes [many other problems].

Robin Dupuis
Executive Director,
Labrador Inuit Alcohol and Drug Abuse Program
Happy Valley-Goose Bay, Newfoundland and Labrador
16 June 1992

I became a drinker as well, and it was to hide the pain and the hurt I suffered [from abuse] in my childhood. And because I married a violent person as well, I continued drinking to mask all that fear and hurt....I didn't become aware of that cycle of violence until I was much older. I had raised my children already, and they in turn [had become] its victims.

Edith Young
Swampy Cree Tribal Council
Thompson, Manitoba, 31 May 1993

The chain reaction of addiction hurts many people....It can cripple individuals, families in our society, and even make [a whole] region dysfunctional....Myself, I am a sober alcoholic and drug addict. My sister perished when she was drunk. My nephew killed himself and his own father and mother while they were drunk. My older brother shot himself when he was drunk.

Henoch Obed
Addictions Counsellor
Labrador Inuit Alcohol and Drug Abuse Program
Nain, Newfoundland and Labrador, 30 November 1992

We also heard testimony suggesting that for many individuals and communities the curtain is beginning to lift:

I am sure you hear a lot of bad news in your Commission. I am here to bring you good news. Things are moving ahead [in relation to addictions]....Seventy-six per cent of the [former drinkers] that we have surveyed had two to 10 years of sobriety....The Native Addictions programs, the Health and Welfare program, they are working. Things are changing....I believe that in the area of substance abuse, we are finally making progress. I believe that we have assumed responsibility [for our own recovery].

Maggie Hodgson
Nechi Institute on Alcohol and Drug Education
Edmonton, Alberta, 11 June 1992

As a collective, [the National Native Association of Treatment Directors has] identified our successes as deriving from: [doing our own] program development and delivery; cultural programming to increase awareness and self-esteem; the use of Native counsellors as role models; introducing or strengthening traditional spirituality; and helping our clients learn to help themselves.

We cannot say that 40, 60, 70 or 80 per cent of the 7,500 people we treat annually have remained sober or drug-free, because we do not have access to tracking. We do know, however, that every client who completes our treatment programs...[has] begun the healing journey.

Patrick Shirt
President, National Native Association
of Treatment Directors
Calgary, Alberta, 27 May 1993

The evidence put forward by researchers in the field is contradictory. The Canadian Centre on Substance Abuse reported in their presentation to the Commission that one in five hospital admissions for alcohol-related illness in Canada is an Aboriginal admission, that alcohol psychosis occurs among Aboriginal people at four times the national average rate, and that the rate of liver disease among Aboriginal people is three-and-a-half times the national average.[137]

However, survey data from a number of sources indicate that alcohol consumption rates among Aboriginal people are in fact lower in some measurement categories than among non-Aboriginal people. The primary source of national data is the Aboriginal peoples survey (APS). The picture it presents is based on self-reports, and as such must be regarded with some caution, though it is regarded as reasonably reliable by experts in the field.[138] The APS found that a lower proportion of Aboriginal people than Canadians generally drink daily or weekly. Abstinence is almost twice as common among Aboriginal people (see Table 3.10). Additional findings of the APS are that of those in the Aboriginal population who do use alcohol, consumption rates are higher among those with the most education and income, higher among men than women, and lowest among those aged 55 and over.

The findings of the APS are supported by those of the *Yukon Alcohol and Drug Survey*, also based on self-reports.[139] The Yukon survey found that abstinence is about twice as common among Aboriginal people as among other Canadians. It also found that, of those who do report drinking, more Aboriginal people are heavy drinkers, both in the frequent ('regular') and infrequent ('binge') patterns. A third survey, conducted in nine Cree communities in northern Quebec, found a similar pattern of self-reported drinking behaviour in which both abstinence and heavy drinking are more common than moderate consumption.[140]

TABLE 3.10
Percentage of Persons Who Reported Drinking Alcohol in the Past Year, Total and Aboriginal Identity Populations, 1991

	North American Indians			Métis	Inuit	Total Aboriginal	Total Population
	On-reserve	Non-reserve	Total				
Use of alcohol in the past year (%)							
Never	22	13	16	11	22	15	8
None	18	14	15	14	11	15	11
Some	60	73	69	75	67	70	81
Frequency of drinking among drinkers (%)							
Daily	1	2	2	2	1	2	7
Weekly	31	37	35	34	30	35	46
Monthly	38	31	33	32	32	33	24
Less than once a month	30	30	30	32	37	31	24

Notes:
Population aged 15 and over.
Never = persons reporting lifetime abstention.
None = persons reporting drinking no alcohol in the past year.

Source: Statistics Canada, Language, Health, Lifestyle and Social Issues: 1991 Aboriginal Peoples Survey, catalogue no. 89-533 (June 1993); Thomas Stephens and Dawn Fowler Graham, eds., Canada's Health Promotion Survey 1990: Technical Report, catalogue no. H39-263/2-1990E (Ottawa: 1993).

The explanation for these discrepancies is a matter of conjecture. The most optimistic interpretation is that Aboriginal people are now beginning to achieve higher levels of sobriety, thus breaking patterns recorded by earlier studies that continue to be reflected in mortality and morbidity data. This possibility is given weight by the follow-up study by Kinzie and colleagues in 1988 of mental health issues in a northwest coast village previously studied by Shore and colleagues in 1969. Alcohol use and abuse rates in 1988 were still high, but were lower than those reported in 1969. The success of drug education and treatment programs were thought to offer one possible explanation for the change.[141]

A less encouraging possibility is that Aboriginal people may under-report alcohol consumption, despite assurances of anonymity and confidentiality. Or, it could be that the small number of heavy drinkers in the Aboriginal population skews the social and medical effects data toward an unrepresentative extreme. In any case, the widely held belief that most Aboriginal people consume excessive amounts of alcohol on a regular basis appears to be incorrect.

Canadian governments have been slow to expand their services to include social and emotional ill health, or what is sometimes gathered together under the term 'mental health'.[142] Yet, fully 20 years ago, the federal government funded a demonstration program, the National Native Alcohol and Drug Abuse Program (NNADAP), to find ways to reduce the incidence and effects of alcohol use in Aboriginal communities.[143] Today, NNADAP provides funds for about 400 community-based prevention and treatment programs, 51 regional residential treatment centres, and basic training to prepare Aboriginal staff to deliver most of these services.[144] Budget estimates for 1994-95 show about $59 million allocated to NNADAP. Thus, alcohol and drug addiction is the only one of the interlinked social and emotional problems facing Aboriginal people to have received long-term funding from government for services that are designed and delivered by Aboriginal people.

NNADAP has both supporters and critics. Both sides have argued the need for a full program review. The Commission believes this would be a useful way to identify the strengths and weaknesses of the many approaches to treatment funded by the program. We believe there are many worthwhile insights to be built upon.[145] Indeed, we would like to see the insights of Aboriginal addictions workers applied to social and emotional health problems more broadly.

In our view, the failure to do so reflects the half-hearted approach taken by Canadian governments to Aboriginal mental health issues generally. Alcohol addiction is seen by most health authorities – and by many of those who work in the treatment field – as a stand-alone problem with treatable causes. Some see it as a disease. Moreover, it is funded as a stand-alone problem with treatable causes. The most successful alcohol treatment programs developed by and for Aboriginal people have gone far beyond this restricted understanding of addictions; they have tackled related problems of physical and sexual abuse, loss of self-esteem and cultural identity, lack of personal opportunity and exclusion from mainstream Canadian society. Counsellors have found that Aboriginal addictions are part of a circle of oppression, despair, violence and self-destructive behaviour that must be addressed as a whole. For most of their clients, tackling addictions is like grabbing the tail of the tiger – family violence, suicide, self-injury, accidental injuries and deaths all being stripes on the same animal:

> In a Native-run [alcohol and drug] treatment centre, we get clients that come in, and they have multiple problems. We have only a limited three weeks to work with clients, and they have so many problems. It is really overwhelming what to do with these people that come in. For example, I myself have had to deal with an individual who had five family members die in one year, and she was contemplating suicide. I had to try to deal with her prescription drug problem and also her grieving. It was really overwhelming....We need workers that can practise a generalist approach, where they would be able to deal with all problems, with the many issues of the clients.
>
> Harold Fontaine
> Social Worker, Sagkeeng Al-Care Centre
> Fort Alexander, Manitoba, 30 October 1992

Staff at treatment centres have sometimes broadened the scope of their programs hesitantly, fearing that they were being diverted from the 'real' issue of alcohol abuse by the multi-dimensional social and emotional needs of their clients.[146] But, as they moved toward a model of holistic treatment, most have come to see such treatment as the most powerful tool at their disposal. They have found that truly effective treatment involves

- not just the mind and body of the addicted person, but his or her emotions, spirit, relationships and identity;
- not just the individual, but his or her family, friends and community; and
- not just change in the use of addictive substances, but change in fundamental patterns of living.

For Aboriginal youth who are abusing alcohol and drugs, programs such as Rediscovery (which teaches traditional skills and values and pride in Aboriginal culture) and sustained pursuit of challenging sports and recreational activities might provide the change of focus that is needed. (See Volume 4, Chapter 4 for a more detailed discussion of the role of sports and recreation in a balanced life.)

A number of people who spoke before us proposed the establishment of comprehensive mental health services encompassing the full range of psychosocial distress presented by the clients of addictions services, with flexible funding to match. It is an important proposal, and one that we will address in the discussion of services reorganization later in this chapter.

One recommendation I would suggest is [holistic] Native treatment centres that not only cover alcohol treatment but the other issues we face, such as being ACOA [adult children of alcoholics], co-dependency, the [impacts of the] mission schools, the sexual abuse and all that. I went to a treatment centre...in 1990. I dealt with my alcoholism, but when I came back [to my community] I had a lot of other issues to face, because everything else [surfaced] for me. It was quite a struggle. We badly need treatment centres to deal with these other issues, not just alcohol. You are not better just because you deal with your alcohol abuse.

Ann Bayne
Watson Lake, Yukon
28 May 1992

One thing we [object to] in government funding, both federal and provincial, is this: the government funds programs on an individual basis. They break everything up. For instance, drugs and alcohol is one funding. Sexual abuse is another category. Family violence [is another]. And what we are saying is we want...to be funded for a holistic approach.

The holistic approach tells us [that] we cannot separate the issues in our community. If somebody comes to our drug and alcohol counsellors for counselling in the area of alcohol, and the root cause of that person's drinking in the end we find is sexual abuse, what do we do? In treatment programs, we have seen also a pattern why people drink. Some of the main reasons they give, a lot of the root cause we are finding is deeper, and the ones that are being treated for drugs [need to be treated] not for just sexual abuse but also for the loss of culture, loss of identity. The shame they feel is another area they have identified....

We are talking about one global treatment centre, dealing with all the different areas people need.

Lynda Prince
Northern Native Family Services
Carrier Sekani Tribal Council
Stoney Creek, British Columbia, 18 June 1992

We have found support for the idea of approaching social and emotional ill health from a holistic perspective in research and health policy analysis. In a major literature review prepared for the Commission, Laurence Kirmayer and colleagues concluded that

The fragmentation of mental health programs into substance abuse, violence, psychiatric disorders and suicide prevention...does not reflect the reality of great overlap among the affected individuals, the professional expertise needed...and the appropriate interventions. In many cases, it is not helpful to single out a specific problem as...a focus...because focusing attention exclusively on the problem without attending to its larger social context can do more harm than good. A comprehensive approach to mental health and illness should therefore be integrated within larger programs....[147]

The government of Canada has made the same case. In 1991, the Agenda for First Nations and Inuit Mental Health demonstrated that there was a critical lack of mental health services in Aboriginal communities and put forward a detailed plan for developing them.[148] It offered the following definition of mental health:

Among the First Nations and Inuit communities, the term mental health is used in a broad sense, describing behaviours which make for a harmonious and cohesive community and the relative absence of multiple problem behaviours in the community, such as family violence, substance abuse, juvenile delinquency and self-destructive behaviour. It is more than the absence of illness, disease or dysfunction – it is the presence of a holistic, psychological wellness which is part of the full circle of mind, body, emotions and spirit, with respect for tradition, culture and language. This gives rise to creativity, imagination and growth, and enhances the capacity of the community, family group or individual to interact harmoniously and respond to illness and adversity in healing ways.[149]

In many cases, the concept of mental illness is foreign to Aboriginal understandings of health. Physical, emotional, spiritual and environmental health are all essential aspects of well-being. When they are in balance, health and wellness prevail. When they are out of balance, ill health and social discord predominate. There is no expression for mental health in Inuktitut as spoken in northern Quebec. When local caregivers decided to get together to address psycho-social problems in the community, they called their group the Peace of Mind Committee.[150]

The Agenda for First Nations and Inuit Mental Health proposed 'healing' as the overriding goal of Aboriginal mental health services, and recommended that training needs be met, and intergovernmental jurisdiction and mandate issues be sorted out, to permit culturally appropriate and community-controlled and -delivered services to become a reality. The decisive action proposed in the agenda has still not been taken. As a kind of compromise, the multi-purpose Brighter Futures program has joined the National Native Alcohol and Drug Abuse Program, the Family Violence and Child Sexual Abuse Program, and the Non-Insured Health Benefits Program (which pays for some private psychiatric and counselling services) to make up the family of federally funded programs to promote social and emotional health among the minority of Aboriginal people to whom federal services apply. Programs are loosely co-ordinated through an administrative unit of the medical services branch called Addictions and Community Funded Programs. The situation is a far cry, however, from the Aboriginal-designed and comprehensive services envisaged by the consultative process of the Steering Committee on Native Mental Health in 1991, whose agenda we heartily endorse.

As well, we are aware of evidence to suggest that the government has adopted a stance of offloading responsibility for 'social problems' in Aboriginal communities without ensuring that communities are able to pick up the load. As an example, in the spring of 1993, the community of Povungnituk, in northern Quebec, revealed to the media and its own citizens that two community members (one non-Aboriginal, one Inuk) had sexually assaulted more than 80 of the community's children. The government's initial response when asked for help was that, although some aid would be forthcoming, solutions must come from within.[151] Such encouragement to take charge is attractive to people who have long been treated as if they are incapable of running their own affairs. In our view, however, such encouragement amounts to abandonment in the guise of empowerment unless it is accompanied by the institution building and human resource development needed to equip Aboriginal people to do the job. We discuss the need to build such capacity later in the chapter.

Child protection

One aspect of social and emotional distress in Aboriginal societies that causes most concern to Aboriginal people and service providers is the evidence of widespread family dysfunction and the resulting neglect and abuse of children. The evidence derives from high rates of children requiring placement in alternative care, the frequency of violence against women and children, and the phenomenon of homeless and vulnerable Aboriginal children on the streets of Canadian cities. Institutions for young offenders, provincial correctional institutions and federal prisons house scores of Aboriginal youth and young adults, a very large proportion of them casualties of dysfunctional families and failed efforts by child welfare agencies to protect them.

In Chapter 2 of this volume and in our special report on justice, we examined family and justice issues in detail and presented proposals for new approaches to support family life and deal with antisocial behaviour. In Chapter 5 we propose that all Aboriginal children have access to early childhood education services that reflect the priorities and complement the strengths of Aboriginal families. Here we wish to underline that issues of family, children and justice must be addressed in concert with the other symptoms of malaise that plague Aboriginal people.

1.4 Community Health

It is a cherished belief of Aboriginal cultures that human beings are profoundly interdependent and have their greatest potential to live in health, happiness and prosperity when they congregate and co-operate in communities, large or small. (See Volume 1, Chapter 15 for a discussion of Aboriginal cultures and their norms, values and beliefs.) 'Community' is an old and honoured notion in western cultures as well, although it generally takes second place to 'individual' as a core value.

According to Aboriginal tradition, the health and well-being of individuals depend in part on community health and social dynamics. Much of the most convincing recent health policy literature agrees. Both sources provide evidence that some aspects of ill health cannot be understood except in terms of social behaviour, and they cannot be alleviated except through collective action. Examples range from the transmission of infectious diseases to the norms that tolerate family violence.

We have identified three dimensions of community health as particularly important to the health status and well-being of Aboriginal people:

- poverty and social assistance;
- adequacy of the built environment, primarily in reference to shelter, water and sanitation facilities, but extending to community infrastructure more broadly; and
- environmental conditions, including all forms of pollution and land and habitat degradation.

Poverty and social assistance

The research literature that asks "What makes people healthy?" consistently concludes that economic status – personal income and the general prosperity of communities and nations – is of great significance.[152] For example, in every industrial nation where the relationship between income and life expectancy has been evaluated, people with higher incomes are found to live longer.[153] In one classic Canadian study, men whose income placed them in the top 20 per cent of earners were found to live about six years longer than those in the bottom 20 per cent. They were also free of major illness and disability for 14 years longer than the most disadvantaged group. The comparable figures for women are three years more life expectancy and eight years longer without major illness or disability for those in the top quintile.[154] A recent annual report of the provincial health officer of British Columbia shows that in Vancouver and Victoria there are twice as many infant deaths in the poorest neighbourhoods as in the richest.[155] In Winnipeg, premature death (defined as death before age 65) occurs at an increasing rate the lower the income level of the neighbourhood.[156]

The ill health effects of poverty on children are well documented and particularly disturbing. Poor mothers are more likely to have low birth weight babies. Poor children are more likely to have chronic health problems and to be admitted to health care facilities. Poor children are more likely to die of injuries. Poor children are more likely to have psychiatric and emotional disorders. Poor children are more likely to do badly in school and drop out.[157] It has been estimated that 50 per cent of Aboriginal children, whether living on- or off-reserve, are living in poverty.[158]

Part of the explanation for the link between poverty and ill health is that people who are poor experience the major risk factors for illness with greatest frequency: low birth weight, inferior nutrition (especially in childhood), exposure to various pathogens and toxins, unsafe houses and neighbourhoods, dangerous jobs (or alternatively, no job, which also constitutes a health risk[159]), stress, smoking and drinking behaviour, lack of familiarity with the concepts of health education, and so on. Further, the knowledge, resources, confidence and mobility to obtain superior treatment and remediation services are less common among the poor.

The Canadian Institute for Advanced Research has emphasized the significant improvements in public health that could be achieved by measures directed to improving the social and physical environment, for example, reductions in poverty and unemployment and support of mothers and children.[160]

Aboriginal people are among the poorest in Canada (see Volume 2, Chapter 5). Based on the evidence we have reviewed, we are in little doubt that the stark economic facts of Aboriginal life are causally related to the stark facts on ill health. We are deeply concerned, therefore, about the standard of living that can be achieved by Aboriginal people – not just for its own sake, but also *as a health issue.*

Poverty among Aboriginal people is, for some, the result of low-paying or part-time work. For others, it is the result of continued participation in the hunting and trapping sector of the economy. (In Volume 4, Chapter 6 we discuss the need to give additional support to this sector.) For most, however, the principal cause is unemployment.

In our cash-based economy, those without wages are forced to look elsewhere for money to live. In our individualistic society, they have learned to turn, not to the extended family or local community, but to the collection of government programs known as the social safety net. The safety net was designed to protect people from extreme poverty through a mix of income security, social insurance and social adjustment services. Its main mechanisms are

- provincial and municipal social assistance (welfare);[161]
- unemployment insurance (now termed employment insurance);
- the Canada and Quebec pension plans;
- Old Age Security and the guaranteed annual income supplement for low-income seniors; and
- other, lesser (and sometimes temporary) mechanisms such as education and training subsidies, disability allowances and tax adjustments.

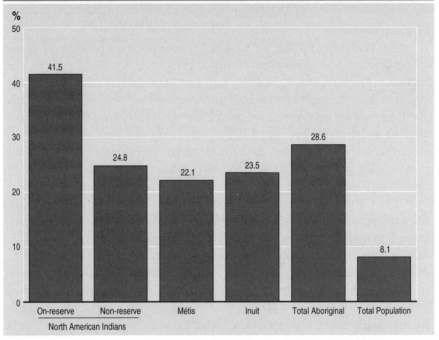

FIGURE 3.9
Percentage Receiving Social Assistance, Aboriginal Identity and Total Populations, 1991

Note: The question on the 1991 APS about the receipt of social assistance was asked of persons age 15 and older. This figure is not intended to imply that eligibility for social assistance begins at age 15.

Source: Statistics Canada, Aboriginal Peoples Survey, catalogue no. 89-534 (1993); Statistics Canada, "Quarterly Demographic Statistics", catalogue no. 91-002; Social Program Information and Analysis Directorate, Strategic Policy Group, Human Resources Development Canada.

For Aboriginal people, by far the most important of these is social assistance – welfare. (See Volume 2, Chapter 5 for a detailed discussion of income support and alternatives to the present system.) As shown in Figure 3.9, based on data from the Aboriginal peoples survey, the percentage of all Aboriginal people over the age of 15 years who relied on social assistance for at least part of the year in 1990 was 28.6, compared to 8.1 per cent of the general Canadian population. Indian people on-reserve had the highest rates of dependence at 41.5 per cent, while the rates were 24.8 per cent for Indian people off-reserve, 22.1 per cent for Métis people and 23.5 per cent for Inuit.

According to DIAND information using other data sources, dependence on welfare by Indian people living on-reserve remained fairly constant at around 38 per cent through the 1980s, then increased to 43 per cent by 1992. The rate for the non-Aboriginal population shows a similar pattern of change during this period, increasing from 5.7 to 9.7 per cent, but still at much lower levels than for Aboriginal people.[162]

The cost of dependency is reflected in government spending on 'social development', which includes other social services as well but is driven largely by social assistance expenditures. Federal government expenditures on social development grew from $221 million in fiscal year 1981-82 to $731 million in 1991-92, somewhat faster than the threefold growth rate of most government programs. (See Volume 5, Chapter 2 for an analysis of federal government spending on Aboriginal people. The figures quoted here are not adjusted for inflation.) Allocations for social development in federal estimates for 1995-96, at $1,108 million, show a continuation of this trend. When provincial government expenditures on Aboriginal social development are added to federal expenditures and calculated for 1992-93, the total is more than $2.2 billion per year.

Labour market data for Aboriginal people over the decade 1981-1991 show a similar disturbing trend. As shown in Table 3.11, using 1981 census and 1991 APS data, the unemployment rate (that is, the percentage of the total Aboriginal population that was available and looking for work) increased from 15.8 per cent in 1981 to 24.6 per cent in 1991. During the same period the Canadian unemployment rate rose from 7.2 to 9.9 per cent.

The increase in the unemployment rate reflects not only workers falling out of work; it also reflects new workers joining the labour force but not being able to find steady work. The number of Aboriginal people over the age of 15 is growing rapidly as a result of high birth rates and decreasing rates of mortality. In addition, a larger percentage of Aboriginal adults is in the labour market, as reflected in the rise in the participation rate shown in Table 3.11. In 1981, 51.8 per cent of Aboriginal people over the age of 15 participated in the labour market; in 1991, 57 per cent of them were employed or looking for work. These figures compare to 65 per cent and 68.1 per cent of non-Aboriginal people participating in the labour force in 1981 and 1991 respectively. The indications are that even when some progress in employment development is being made on an absolute basis, the gains are overtaken by population growth, which adds to the Aboriginal labour pool and drives up the unemployment rate.

The sum of our analysis is that unemployment and dependency on welfare are high and likely to get higher and that rising investment in social assistance, while necessary to provide a minimal income flow, is not an adequate response to the situation.

We now turn to our hearings for Aboriginal perspectives on poverty and to research on its health effects. In public testimony and research studies, many Aboriginal people say they detest and feel diminished by the atmosphere of passivity that has settled upon some of their communities as a result of the welfare economy and that they are anxious to replace dependency with productivity:

TABLE 3.11

Participation and Unemployment Rates, Aboriginal and Non-Aboriginal Populations, 1981 and 1991

	Participation Rate[1]		Unemployment Rate	
	%	%	%	%
	1981[2]	1991	1981[2]	1991
Non-Aboriginal	65.0	68.1	7.2	9.9
Total Aboriginal	51.8	57.0	15.8	24.6
North American Indians				
Registered[3]				
On-reserve	37.4	45.3	19.3	30.1
Non-reserve	55.9	56.0	15.6	29.4
Non-registered	62.7	67.5	14.3	21.1
Métis	57.0	63.7	14.5	21.3
Inuit	48.2	57.2	15.2	24.1

Notes:

1. Participation rate is the percentage of all persons aged 15 and older who are employed and unemployed, i.e., active in the labour force.

2. For comparison purposes, the Aboriginal rates for 1981 exclude reserves that were enumerated incompletely in the Aboriginal peoples survey.

3. Data for registered North American Indians in 1991 exclude persons who regained Indian status after 1985 as a result of Bill C-31, which amended the *Indian Act* with regard to eligibility for Indian status. Such persons were added to the 1991 North American Indian non-registered population for purposes of comparing 1991 and 1981 data.

Source: D. Kerr, A. Siggner and J.P. Bourdeau, "Canada's Aboriginal Population, 1981-1991", research study prepared for RCAP (1995).

Social financial assistance is the single most destructive force on our heritage. Our people do not want to be part of a welfare state that looks after them from cradle to grave. If the social financial assistance can be transferred to First Nations, we can begin to develop our people, or at least provide employment which will make each individual feel like they are a productive member of the community.

Elizabeth Hansen
Councillor, Inuvik Native Band
Inuvik, Northwest Territories, 5 May 1992

Welfare is a number one problem of [Inuit] society today, although it might be seen as a solution to the need of those that are unemployable....My father-in-law, when he first heard that welfare was to be introduced in the North, he shuddered that this solution will not create a long-term solution that is acceptable, but it will create a great dependency where no one will get out of it. He has been right ever since. Social programs that work are good, but these social programs should not be used to create dependency.

Charlie Evalik
Economic Development Facilitator
Cambridge Bay, Northwest Territories, 17 November 1992

In our community, a significant number of residents contribute economically through trapping, fishing and hunting. All these economic activities are potentially productive and renewable but only if the ecology is not disrupted and is properly managed. The damming and flooding required by hydroelectric projects in Saskatchewan has caused severe impacts on the ecology. In fact, as time passes, these harsh effects have intensified to the point where 90 per cent of the main income earners in our First Nation communities have lost their employment, and are required to rely on social assistance.

Peter Sinclair
Mathias Colomb First Nation
Thompson, Manitoba, 1 June 1993

There are many Indian people who get up in the morning and look for jobs. The first stop is usually at the Band Office, but there are no jobs, or limited jobs. The next stop is at the local employment office. Once there, they are reminded that they do not have the training or education to apply for these jobs. The last stop will be at the social assistance office. Without much hope for becoming financially independent, they become part of the forgotten Indian people. They are lost in the process.

Linda Chipesia
Whitehorse, Yukon
18 November 1992

Aboriginal people living in urban centres fare somewhat better than reserve residents in gaining employment, but their unemployment rate is still two and a half times the unemployment rate of non-Aboriginal people, and their total annual income from all sources lags behind by 33 per cent. The situation varies by region. On the basis of 1991 census data on household incomes, more than 60 per cent of Aboriginal households in Winnipeg, Regina and Saskatoon were below the low-income cut-off or poverty line established by Statistics Canada. The situation was even more disastrous for female single-parent households in these cities, where 80 to 90 per cent were below the poverty line, many of them undoubtedly maintained at this level by social assistance.

The effects on physical health and morale of living in hopeless poverty are a concern to health advocates as well as to Aboriginal people. Yet social assistance itself is a legislated form of poverty. No jurisdiction provides a level of income support through social assistance that comes close to the low-income cut-off established by Statistics Canada. In most cases, the level of support is 30 to 50 per cent below the poverty line.[163]

Moreover, there is no indication that levels of assistance are becoming more adequate with the passage of time. On the contrary, increases in benefit levels in the past decade have not kept pace with increases in the cost of living.[164] Real rates of social assistance declined between 1986 and 1993 for most categories of recipients in nine of the 12 jurisdictions surveyed by the National Council of Welfare in 1993, and only one jurisdiction provides automatic adjustment of entitlements to take into account increases in the cost of living. (In Quebec, benefits are indexed to the cost of living for those served by the Financial Support Program.) As a result of these trends, poverty has been increasing in Canada generally. There are half a million more children living in poor families today than there were 10 years ago.[165]

The low levels of income support available through social assistance programs have negative health and social effects on all recipients. The National Council of Welfare has said:

> Many thousands of children from welfare families go to school hungry. Many thousands of people with disabilities face disproportionately larger problems because of the additional expenses related to their disability. Many thousands of single people and families live in substandard housing. The only "choice" many people on welfare have is deciding how to cut back on food as the end of the month approaches and the money starts to run out.[166]

The Canadian Institute of Child Health has said:

> [Not having enough money] means not having enough food to eat. It means living in houses in ill-repair. It means not having warm clothes in the winter. It means not having the kinds of play and recreation facilities that children need to grow and develop. It means being less likely to finish high school and even less likely to go to college or university, which means being less likely to find a job.[167]

In testimony to Commissioners, Aboriginal people also expressed their concerns about the inadequacy of welfare:

> A man came to me one time when I was a Deputy Grand Chief and he said, you know, Lindy, I had a trap line out here, and for 30 years I provided for my family. I raised my family. He said, I still have a

couple of kids at home. I have eight children and, he said, now I have nothing. How am I going to provide for my children? He said, I have no bush left on my reserve. There is no marten, there is no beaver, there is nothing there. He said, welfare doesn't cover what I used to make with the trapline and they have no other trap line to give me....He said, all I get now is social assistance.

I want to tell you, social assistance in this country does not meet the needs of the Native people....For example, Attawapiskat. You get $50 per person, but little do [authorities] know that we have to pay $5 for a pound of butter. Here [in Timmins] you pay $3, but over there [in Attawapiskat] you have to pay $5 because you have to pay the air freight. That is not compensated. [In Attawapiskat] you can't buy a file unless you pay $10 for a file to sharpen your axe to go and catch a rabbit. They need to trap in order to fill in for the welfare that is not provided....[They] only get so much a head, and it is not enough to fill the grocery basket.

Lindberg Louttit
Wabun Tribal Council
Timmins, Ontario, 5 November 1992

The single, unemployed person [with no children] can only get assistance for two months. If they have not successfully gained employment, then they have nothing to live on. It is either stealing to feed themselves again, or go back home to the senior parents....The senior parents are not the welfare office. Some of them can barely make ends meet. They get debt-ridden because they have to support their grown children.

The single parent with one child has to work. Yes, they put their child in a subsidized daycare home and the parent pays a certain amount and the government pays a certain amount. In the long run, this is causing more problems, wasted money, and the child suffers. It rarely sees its parent, and when it does see its parent, the parent is usually too tired [to] fulfil the role of a loving, caring parent. What have we caused here? A possible child neglect and/or abuse [case], and the child may become a behaviour problem later on.

Frances Ebersbach
Lac La Biche, Alberta
9 June 1992

Two per cent [of the local social assistance budget] is designated [by the federal government] for preventative social services, family violence, community-based programs and family support. We are only given enough money to become dependent on the government. We are not given enough to develop the programs and the services that are really needed, such as life skills counselling services, job readiness, healing centres, daycare centres, group homes, youth treatment programs, et cetera – all of which is readily available to non-Natives and other groups that do not reside on reserves.

Linda Hill George
Social Development Officer
Gitksan and Wet'suwet'en First Nations
Kispiox, British Columbia, 16 June 1992

The adequacy of social assistance benefits is of particular concern to the Commission because of the ill effects of poverty on the health of children. The move in several jurisdictions to reduce welfare rates across the board, without regard to the long-term effects on children, seems particularly short-sighted. Tying Aboriginal welfare rates to provincial rates despite radically different community circumstances compounds the problem.

In seeking to replace welfare with productive work, Aboriginal people face a forbidding set of circumstances in relation to economic opportunity. They report that the greatest barrier to gaining employment is the absence of jobs. They lack a land and resource base as a foundation for local economic development. When they migrate to urban centres, their education and skills often prove insufficient to compete successfully in the job market. They encounter discrimination in the labour market. The restructuring of national and international economies is substituting technology for human labour, reducing demand and raising the skill levels required for employment.[168]

The solution to the problem of economic dependency ultimately lies in

- recognizing Aboriginal rights, honouring historical treaties and concluding new ones to establish an adequate land and resource base for Aboriginal nations;
- revitalizing Aboriginal economies by extending Aboriginal jurisdiction over economic development, improving access to capital and business development, and encouraging a mix of harvesting and wage-based activities on traditional lands;
- implementing more effective education and training so that Aboriginal people are equipped to lead the renewal of their own economies and participate equitably in the Canadian market and wage economy; and
- removing the barriers that operate to exclude or disadvantage Aboriginal workers in the labour market.

The steps necessary to effect fundamental change in Aboriginal economic life are set out in Volume 2, Chapters 4 and 5. In addition, the substantial resources now directed to social assistance can be applied more effectively.

In Volume 2, Chapter 5 we propose that social assistance policy should conform to three criteria. Social assistance should

- actively support individuals' social and economic development, including acquisition of life skills, education and employment;
- contribute to integrated social and economic development in the community, involving employment, health, housing, social services, education, training, recreation and infrastructure, as well as income support; and
- be directed by Aboriginal people so that adaptations to the cultures and conditions of the people served can be made.

As part of our economic development strategy we developed two models of social assistance reform. One retains current characteristics of individual entitlement to assistance, modified to support employment and economic development initiatives and to strengthen traditional mixed economies. The other introduces the concept of community entitlement to a budget roughly equivalent to current social assistance allocations, for initiatives that advance the community's social and economic objectives. In both cases, flexibility to opt for different models at different times and measures to ensure accountability to the people whose current entitlements would be re-directed are built into the models. In addition, the interests of those who are unable or unwilling to participate in personal or community development projects are protected in the proposed models.

We conclude that poverty among Aboriginal people is a serious health issue. Its negative health effects will persist if social assistance is maintained at its present levels and in its present form. They will increase if social assistance is reduced without realistic alternatives.

Living conditions

The issues discussed here are part of a broader concern, namely community infrastructure. 'Infrastructure' in the broadest sense refers to a wide range of facilities and services, including power and energy, communications, roads and transportation, public services and recreation, fire and emergency services, services to business and industry, and so on. Here, we are concerned with the aspects of infrastructure tied most closely to health and well-being – water, sanitation and housing. Further discussion of Aboriginal housing conditions and supply, and the Commission's recommendations for increasing the supply and for upgrading infrastructure generally, are in Chapter 4 of this volume.

The health effects of water quality, sanitation and housing conditions have been acknowledged at least since the era of the early Greeks and the writers of the Old Testament. More recently, in the nineteenth century, the leaders of the public health movement in Europe fought long and hard for their belief that the deplorable living and working conditions of their times were largely responsible for the epidemics of infectious disease that were killing thousands in the new and rapidly growing cities.

After years of resistance, governments in the industrial countries began to address conditions that were beyond the control of individual citizens: over-crowded and unsafe housing, unclean food and water, open sewers, inhumane and unsafe conditions in the workplace. The impact on population health status was dramatic. In France, for example, life expectancy in major cities increased from 32 years in 1850 to 45 years in 1900 as the supply of clean water and waste water disposal facilities grew.[169] Similarly, in North America, water-borne infectious diseases (a leading cause of death in the nineteenth and early twentieth centuries) declined as public water supplies and sewage systems expanded.[170] Even so, because infectious diseases have remained a threat to health in so much of the world, the United Nations proclaimed the 1980s the International Drinking Water Supply and Sanitation Decade.[171]

Access to potable water, adequate sanitation and waste disposal services has been routine for so long in this country that most Canadians take them for granted. The same access is not guaranteed for Aboriginal people, however, and their health suffers as a result. Inadequate housing is a problem for Canadian society generally, but it is a greater problem for Aboriginal people (see Table 3.12).

In testimony and in briefs submitted to the Commission, we heard evidence that water, sanitation and housing conditions in many Aboriginal communities compare with those of developing countries:

> We have a huge backlog in housing for our members which consists of families, single parents, bachelors, seniors and the disabled, for people who require medical attention and other special needs. Some cases we have 12 to 17 people sharing a 24 [-foot] by 36 [-foot] bungalow without indoor plumbing. And we are forced to dump our sewage in open pits and use our outdoor privies at 30 to 40 [degrees] below winter temperatures. This practice causes people of all age groups to get sick....
>
> Water and sewer. This is the other major obstacle in providing the basic needs to improve the quality of life on our reserve. We have water lines...of which half are frozen due to the way they were installed, and due to the lack of funding to maintain the system. We can't provide...adequate fire protection – which we feel is a priority service to the community [because] to lose someone's home is a very devastating experience, and to lose a human being is even more tragic.
>
> Chief Ignace Gull
> Attawapiskat First Nation
> Moose Factory, Ontario, 9 June 1992

TABLE 3.12
Selected Housing Indicators, Aboriginal and Total Populations, 1981 and 1991

	Total Aboriginal*		Total Population	
	1981	1991	1981	1991
Dwellings with no central heating (%)	26.0	12.5	9.0	3.6
Dwellings in need of major repairs (%)	16.2	19.6	6.5	9.8
Dwellings without bathroom facilities (%)	13.1	3.2	1.1	0.6
Dwellings without piped water (%)	—	9.4	—	0.1
Average number of persons per dwelling	—	3.5	—	2.7
Tenant-occupied dwellings (%)	—	48.7	—	37.1

Notes:
— = not available.
* Total Aboriginal in 1981 refers to persons reporting Aboriginal origins on their census forms. Total Aboriginal in 1991 refers to persons who self-identified as Aboriginal on the 1991 Aboriginal peoples survey.
Source: Statistics Canada, Canada's Native People, catalogue no. 99-937 (Ottawa: 1984), Table 7; Statistics Canada, Disability and Housing: 1991 Aboriginal Peoples Survey, catalogue no. 89-535 (Ottawa: 1993).

It is the year 1993, and many of our communities still do not have running water or sewer lines. We need water and sewer for our children, for the health of our people. There are many children in our communities that require those very services. Certainly today governments cannot refuse that very service. The elders and other [vulnerable] users should not be without that running water. It's a health hazard. And today the present use of outhouses in many communities [is also a] health hazard.

The only facilities that seem to have the running water in northern communities are the stores, [and] of course the Royal Canadian Mounted Police, the fire halls, the nursing stations, the teachers. So what about the people that live [permanently] in that very community?....The Métis people feel they are excluded.

Sydney J. McKay
Manitoba Metis Federation
Thompson, Manitoba, 31 May 1993

Our homes [in Davis Inlet, Labrador] were built very poorly. Growing up in our large family of 11 and living in these houses proved to be very hard for us: no heating, no water and no sewer. Our

Unsafe Drinking Water at Pukatawagan

In November 1993, the environmental health officer for the Cree Nation Tribal Health Centre in The Pas, Manitoba, issued an official 'boil order' to the people of Pukatawagan. The water system, he said, could not be relied on to provide safe drinking water. Samples collected over several months had indicated the presence of coliform bacteria, meaning that the water was unfit for human consumption.

By May 1994, the health officer was still unable to rescind the order to boil water before drinking and bathing. In correspondence with federal authorities, he listed the problems: the water treatment plant was much too small for the population; it had no filtration capacity; chlorination capacity was insufficient; and in winter, freezing threatened to rupture the intake lines. Moreover, there were contributing problems with the sanitation system: both the sewage treatment plant and lagoon had been constructed *upstream* from the water treatment plant, and from the most popular swimming spots on the Churchill River. The overflow was contaminating water and soil. Children were ill. Nursing station statistics indicated high levels of gastro-intestinal and skin disorders. He feared something worse, such as an outbreak of hepatitis A.

By June, illness and fear of illness were at such a pitch in the community that the chief of the Mathias Colomb Cree Nation escalated his attempts to generate a response. He wrote to Member of Parliament Elijah

home had only 2 rooms and 1 small room that was supposed to be a bathroom but [there was] no bathtub, toilet or even a sink, just an empty little room that we eventually used as an extra bedroom. As of today, our houses are still built that way....

In summer, we'd fetch water from the nearest brook, and [my mother] would heat it up on a wood stove, and that's where our hot water came from. In winter, she'd have to dig through 8-10 feet of snow and then through the ice [to get water] from the same brook with a small dipper. As of today, she still gets water the same way, and I do exactly the same....

As of today, we still don't have any heating, nor water or sewer in our homes. [Last year] five children died [in one house fire] because they were trying to keep warm by an electric hotplate because there was no heating in their house. And there are still fire accidents happening, and more fire accidents will continue to happen if no improvement is made.[172]

Harper and to the press. In responding to the subsequent *Winnipeg Free Press* story, provincial authorities said that the problem was the responsibility of the federal government; a spokesperson for the federal health department said that public health was now the responsibility of the band. The Chief pointed out that the faulty water and sanitation systems had been built by DIAND in the first place, and no monies for their improvement had been included in the budget drawn up when medical services were transferred to the Cree health board.

At the end of June, the chief medical officer of health for Manitoba wrote to the minister confirming that an emergency situation existed in the community of Pukatawagan. He reported that the community had produced a plan to rectify its problems, but lacked money and skills to carry it out. He suggested that funds should be supplied by the federal government.

The women of Pukatawagan began to organize 'Walk for Life' – a 600-kilometre trek...from The Pas to Winnipeg – to dramatize their fears of continuing illness, especially among children and elders. Media coverage of the issues continued to be intense. In July, the federal minister of Indian affairs visited the community, promising short- and long-term assistance. By the summer of 1995, the sewage discharge pipe had been moved to a point downstream from the drinking water source, but no action had been taken to upgrade the sewage treatment plant.

Research studies confirm these descriptions, as discussed in Chapter 4 of this volume. In early 1995, a preliminary internal government report on community water and sanitation services in First Nations reserve communities concluded that 25 per cent of the water systems and 20 per cent of the sanitation systems are substandard. They either pose a danger to health and safety or they are in need of repairs to meet basic government standards.[173] Problems identified in the report include

- operational factors such as poor operation and maintenance procedures, chlorinators not working properly, lack of chlorine contact time, or contamination of buckets or barrels, which can result in high bacteria counts;
- contamination caused by agents such as trihalomethanes, fluoride, aluminum or lead;
- insufficient quantity of water to meet domestic and/or fire protection requirements;
- sewage effluent that does not meet discharge criteria after treatment; and

- deterioration of assets resulting from poor maintenance, equipment under-sized for present use, and poor construction techniques.

At the time of the survey, conducted by environmental health officers from Health Canada, 10 communities were under 'boil orders' or 'do-not-use orders' with respect to their water systems.[174] Thirty-eight communities (nine per cent of those assessed) were judged to have sewage systems that posed an immediate risk to public health.[175]

In Chapter 4 of this volume, we document the extent of the housing crisis facing Aboriginal people:

- Standards of Aboriginal housing are measurably below what is required for basic comfort, health and safety.
- Problems include the need for major and minor repairs and new units for households occupying unfit or overcrowded dwellings.
- The major obstacle to meeting housing needs is the gap between incomes and costs, that is, affordability.
- On reserves, an estimated 84 per cent of 74,000 households have insufficient income to cover the full cost of housing. In housing policy terms, they are in 'core need'. Half of this 84 per cent are able to contribute to the cost of housing.
- Among all Aboriginal households (owners and renters), an estimated one-third are in 'core need', compared to between 11 and 12 per cent of all Canadian households.
- Substantial government contributions to housing construction on-reserve over the past decade have had minimal effect because of the rapid deterioration of relatively new housing stock.
- Urban and rural housing programs targeted to Aboriginal people have made significant contributions to quality of life and community relations. They are in jeopardy because of the termination of new investment by governments.

The ill health effects of unclean or insufficient water supplies, of inadequate sanitary facilities and of overcrowded or unsafe housing are well established in the international health literature. For example, a recent CIDA development issues paper said, "The provision of clean drinking water and safe waste disposal, combined with improved personal hygiene, leads to a reduction in sickness and death and in the percentage of people rendered less productive by disease. The International Institute for Environment and Development quotes World Health Organization estimates that 80 per cent of all sickness and disease in the world is attributable to inadequate water or sanitation".[176]

Contaminated water is one of the most significant factors in the spread of infectious disease, especially where the source of contamination is human waste. Although it is sometimes said that the safe disposal of human waste matters less when a society can afford to treat its water supplies, the growing cost of such services, even in 'rich' societies, makes prevention preferable to treatment.

Water quantity is at least as important as water quality, and perhaps more so. Critical hygienic practices depend on easy access to water. People are much less likely to wash their hands after defecating or before handling food if they have to haul their water from outside the house or wait for the water delivery truck. There is a positive correlation between the greater use of water for personal hygiene and improved levels of health, even when the quality of the water is poor.[177]

Poor housing has been linked to a number of ill health conditions, including infectious diseases, non-infectious respiratory diseases such as asthma, chronic congestive diseases, and injuries. Crowding is a critical factor in the transmission of infectious diseases, both airborne and water-borne. The majority of the inter-human contacts that determine the incidence of communicable disease occur in the home or yard.

Poor quality construction of houses is also associated with health risks arising from cold, noise, airborne pollution, insects and rodents. Lack of central heating increases the risk of respiratory illness. Poor quality heating and cooking equipment and the absence of smoke detectors and other safety devices increase the risk of fire.[178]

Indoor air quality can be compromised by wood stoves, which are common in rural Aboriginal communities and emit a number of pollutants linked to respiratory disease. These include particulates, oxides of sulphur and nitrogen, hydrocarbons, carbon monoxide, organic hydrocarbons, formaldehyde, and others. The Commission notes, however, that a much greater risk to health from indoor air quality is posed by cigarette smoke.

Water, sanitation and housing quality have effects on mental and spiritual health as well. Crowding is an important contributing factor in mental illness, especially in relation to personal violence.[179] Design and construction can depress individual and collective self-esteem by ignoring cultural traditions. The location of individual units and the overall community layout can affect social interaction patterns and psycho-social comfort levels.

Studies of the ill health effects of substandard water supplies, sanitation facilities and housing stock in Aboriginal communities in Canada are few and far between. Many have been judged by at least one team of reviewers to be methodologically flawed.[180] Even so, it would fly in the face of experience in countries around the world to imagine that the ill effects are anything other than serious. We know that illness and death from infectious diseases are higher among Aboriginal than non-Aboriginal people. As well, particular water- and airborne infections (tuberculosis and otitis media, for example) are more common among Aboriginal than non-Aboriginal people. These conditions are typical of the effects of poor water quality, inadequate sanitation and overcrowded housing. The case of a recent epidemic of shigellosis in Manitoba is instructive.

Shigellosis is a highly contagious diarrheal disease that can require hospitalization and, in severe cases, cause death. In developed countries, including

Canada, shigellosis has largely been eliminated as a result of high quality public water supplies and sanitation services. Nevertheless, a recent and serious epidemic occurred in Manitoba, lasting from 1 September 1992 to 31 August 1994. Although only about eight per cent of the population of Manitoba are registered Indians, 69 per cent of those who became infected with shigellosis were First Nations people. A study that looked at the relationship between cases of shigellosis and living conditions (water, sanitation and housing) found that the disease was most likely to occur in circumstances where

- there were no public sewage disposal services (so that families have to use outdoor privies or indoor pails for human waste) and where there was no safe and easy way to dispose of soiled diapers;
- there was crowding; and
- there were no public water services of any kind, or where there was a truck delivery and barrel storage system.[181]

The study concluded that fully 90 per cent of shigellosis infections – as well as several other common intestinal, droplet and skin infections – could be prevented by supplying adequate water, sanitation and housing facilities to Aboriginal communities.

Aboriginal service providers are well aware of the gains in health and well-being that can come from improvements to water, sewage and housing facilities. In some places, such as Grand Lac Victoria in Quebec, pleas for government assistance have produced new services. In other places, similar pleas have produced only frustration:

> At Grand Lac Victoria...the medical team observed very high sickness and mortality rates, infectious diseases – ear infections, pneumonia, nutritional diseases, accidents, et cetera. These pathologies were very prevalent....
>
> In a very short time, we identified major sanitation problems: contaminated drinking water, accumulation of garbage around the houses, rudimentary toilet facilities, et cetera. To promote basic hygiene, we obtained the co-operation of other [government] departments for digging wells, developing a garbage collection system, improving access roads to camp sites, et cetera. Our program evolved into a classic public health program centred on prevention and sanitation. [translation]
>
> Ghislain Beaulé
> Research Officer
> Quebec regional health and social services board
> of Abitibi-Témiscamingue
> Val d'Or, Quebec, 30 November 1992

Council supplies 20 gallons of water to each family in Rigolet each day. The water is given in buckets and is trucked in summer and delivered by skidoo in winter. Sewage disposal is on the frozen harbour ice in the winter and dumped anywhere in the summer. This is very bad for the spread of germs and disease....

There are many benefits of having a good water and sewer system.... Health risks would be lowered, the quality of water would be improved. There would be more opportunity for residents to enter into business ventures. The community council would save money. The number of dumps in our community would be less. Food costs would be lowered. These are some of the benefits we could and should be enjoying. Having no water and sewer system is degrading, and holds communities back.

Henry Broomfield
Mayor, Rigolet
Makkovik, Newfoundland and Labrador, 15 June 1992

The solution to these problems is clear. What is needed is a capital construction program such that Aboriginal people can have what most Canadians take for granted: safe and adequate supplies of water, effective sanitation systems, and safe and adequate housing.

We have concluded that some extraordinary expenditure *is* indeed justified, given the crisis in Aboriginal health and the benefits to health and well-being that could be gained from such public works. Our proposals are detailed in Chapter 4 of this volume. Because of the cost implications, however, we advise that much more serious attention be paid to adapting or developing cost-effective technologies suitable for rural and isolated Aboriginal communities where the need is greatest. In this, inspiration could be taken from projects launched in developing countries, where cost is also a factor. Indeed, the Aboriginal community of Split Lake, Manitoba, has already benefited from an initiative to develop appropriate technology for water-quality testing (see box).

The health issues raised in this section are a small part of the 'healthy cities, healthy communities' concept, which has served as an organizing concept for the World Health Organization and other international health agencies. It is an updated version of an old and honoured approach to health promotion – community development. Community development situates individual health in a web of determining factors that are social and collective. Its starting points are that broad-based community participation in public life is essential to social and individual health and that a strong, active community, with effective public support systems and informal mutual aid and self-help networks, offers the best chance to achieve the World Health Organization's goal of "health for all by the year 2000".[182]

Strategies to build the capacity of Aboriginal nations and their communities for self-government, as described in Volume 2, Chapter 3, together with the social development proposals made in this volume, build on these concepts. The plan for bringing housing and infrastructure in Aboriginal communities to basic standards

Using Appropriate Technology

The community of Split Lake is located on a peninsula on the north shore of Split Lake in northern Manitoba. It has a population of about 1,600, almost all of whom are members of the Cree Nation. The community is one of five which are seriously affected by the Churchill-Nelson hydro-electric project. The project has caused water levels in the lake to fluctuate widely as a reflection of fluctuating demands for power elsewhere. Changes in water levels in the lake in turn affect the quality of the communities' drinking water.

Water-quality monitoring in the region has been difficult. The required laboratory facilities are located hundreds of kilometres to the south. Current monitoring procedures, administered by Health Canada, require that a Community Health Representative (CHR) collect water samples at predetermined sites. The samples are brought together, packaged, and delivered over land or by air to the laboratory. It takes 4-6 weeks for results to reach the communities, during which time conditions may change. Communities have alleged that the health implications of test results are not always made clear.

The need for local means of monitoring water quality is a world-wide issue. An international research team, working with the health services staff of Split Lake, came up with three simple, reliable, and inexpensive methods of testing water quality that can be performed in the field, on site. They are now successfully in use locally, and the Split Lake First Nation community is investigating the possibility of operating a test service for other settlements in the area.

Source: Gilles Forget, *Health and the Environment: A People-Centred Research Strategy* (Ottawa: International Development Research Centre, 1992), pp. 23-25.

that support health and self-esteem is particularly suited to the task of building local economies and skills and stimulating broad community participation.

The environmental envelope

Aboriginal people from almost every culture believe that health is a matter of balance and harmony within the self and with others, sustained and ordered by spiritual law and the bounty of Mother Earth. They have long understood that the well-being of people depends on the well-being of the air, water, land and other life forms. This belief has been confirmed by the findings of countless scientific studies of poor health in a compromised environment.[183] Although the details of cause and effect have not been fully established, the general scientific conclusion is clear: human health depends largely on the condition of the natural environment and of the built environment.

Despite this dependence, human activity is the main source of damage to the environment. The willingness of our society to protect the ecosystems around us has not kept pace with our capacity to do harm. Thus, chemical pollution, toxic waste mismanagement, depletion of the ozone layer and other environmental problems have created serious hazards for human health. Exposure to toxic substances in contaminated air, water and soil has been linked to many ill health conditions, including cancer, respiratory illness, birth defects and reproductive problems, allergic reactions and chemical hypersensitivity, immune system suppression, and decreased resistance to disease agents of all sorts.[184]

Environmental degradation may have an especially damaging impact on Aboriginal people whose lives remain closely tied to the land. Many who live on-reserve or in rural settings depend for daily life on the resources at their front doors. Ojibwa families in northern Ontario, for example, pull their drinking water by pail from a lake or river year round, eat an average of two freshly caught fish per person every day in summer and an equivalent amount of moose, beaver and other wild meats in winter, spend almost all their waking hours working (or playing) on land and water, and derive their greatest peace of mind in natural settings.[185] Some Aboriginal people who live in towns and cities still escape to the bush as often as they can and retain strong practical and spiritual bonds with Mother Earth.

When treaties were negotiated, a number of First Nations bargained for territory at or near the mouths of major rivers to be close to traditional food sources and to have access to the natural transportation corridor into the interior where their traplines were located. Pulp mills, mining operations and other industrial complexes were attracted to these same rivers, placing those Aboriginal communities at particular risk for negative impacts.[186]

Environmental degradation affects the health and well-being of Aboriginal people in three ways. First, pollutants and contaminants, especially those originating from industrial development, have negative consequences for human health. Second, industrial contamination and disruption of wildlife habitat combine to reduce the supply and purity of traditional foods and herbal medicines. Finally, erosion of ways of life dependent on the purity of the land, water, flora and fauna constitutes an assault on Aboriginal mental and spiritual health. Urban Canadians, who are separated by generations from their roots in the land, may not fully appreciate this.

What we heard in public hearings regarding environmental degradation was like an extended lament, a refrain of loss and fear:[187]

> There was a time when our people depended on the land for food,
> medicines and trade. The land was regarded as sacred, and because

the people were very dependent on it, the land was referred to as their mother. The newcomers [from Europe] brought with them their different languages, cultures, religions and values, along with their diseases, weeds and insects that neither Mother Earth nor the [Indigenous] people could cope with. Today we see the evidence of these tragedies in clear-cut forests, insect-infested forests, knapweed invasions, water pollution, air pollution, and also in the suicides, alcohol and sexual abuse, incarcerations, unemployment and welfare.

Paul Scotchman
President, Western Indian Agricultural
Producers Association
Kamloops, British Columbia, 15 June 1993

Dams have created mercury [pollution]. Dams have polluted our fish, polluted our animals. Towns are dumping their [garbage] into the creeks, into the rivers....Timmins – and many other towns – has mining tailings which are not watched, are not monitored....When we go trapping now, we are afraid to dip the water out of the creeks to make a cup of tea because we are afraid it is polluted.

Lindberg Louttit
Wabun Tribal Council
Timmins, Ontario, 5 November 1992

You can't even catch a rabbit. You shoot a rabbit now, you open it up, you'll see nothing but sores on them, and the same with beavers. Any kind of animal that's living out there around [the tar sands developments], you cannot eat them.

Nancy Scanie
Fort McMurray, Alberta
16 June 1992

Many people now go to town to buy their groceries because our traditional food is not there to survive on. With the disappearance of the forests, the animals don't number as many. As the tree line fades, the animals fade with it. When the land is flooded, it drowns, it cannot survive. Why is it so difficult for the non-Aboriginal people to understand the devastating effect that pollution, flooding and logging has on [us]?

Chief Allan Happyjack
Waswanipi First Nation Council
Waswanipi, Quebec, 9 June 1992

The federal government has issued a directive to their employees at Walpole Island not to drink the water on Walpole Island. The federal government supplies them bottled water....[But] we are drinking the water....We have a high incidence of respiratory disorders. Many [families] have machines for their kids to breathe, breathing apparatuses, on our island. There is a high incidence of cancer, a high rate of miscarriages....All the different diseases that are plaguing our people now, we cannot prove [they] come from pollution. [The authorities require] us to prove it ourselves. Meanwhile, our people, and our children are dying with cystic fibrosis, spina bifida, and some other diseases....

> Ed Isaac
> Walpole Island First Nation Community
> Sarnia, Ontario, 10 May 1993

Whether the speakers were talking about damage to lands, seas, rivers, air, forests, wildlife, or other living things, their sense of ongoing violation was palpable. Of course, some non-Aboriginal people are equally critical of those who exploit the environment and its sources of life for short-term gain. But for Aboriginal people who retain a grounding in traditional cultures and spirituality, their distress comes from a deeper place: a connection with the forces of the natural world.[188]

In traditional Aboriginal cosmologies, all life forms are seen as aspects of a single reality in which none is superior. The elements of nature – from muskrat to maple to mountain – are like parts of the self. Thus, loss of land and damage to lands, waterways and so on are experienced as assaults on one's own body and on the personal and collective spirit.[189] In contrast, the non-Aboriginal world view portrays nature as something apart from human beings – indeed, as something created (or fortuitously available) for human use.

To be sure, all peoples 'use' the resources of the earth in order to live, but their patterns of use are conditioned by cultural values they may scarcely perceive. In public testimony, many Aboriginal speakers commented on differences in values between Aboriginal and non-Aboriginal people, expressing the hope that one day, all people will acknowledge and learn from the respectful, Aboriginal approach to Mother Earth and the sacred circle of life:

> Our experience from what we witness between governments and businesses [is] that exploitation of the land continues for the benefit of the almighty dollar....We promised our ancestors that we would preserve and protect the land and its natural resources for our children of today and tomorrow.

> Peter Stevens
> Eskasoni First Nation Council
> Eskasoni, Nova Scotia, 7 May 1992

What happens on Mother Earth is important for Aboriginal people. We don't put ourselves on an island and isolate ourselves, because we know [nature] is all one network, it all works together....We have always known that there are ways you treat the things you love that make them last for generation after generation. [translation]

Ethel Blondin
Member of Parliament for the Western Arctic
Fort Simpson, Northwest Territories, 26 May 1992

How then do we create harmonious relations between, on the one hand, the Amerindian who respects life and, on the other, the dominating white man who thinks always about industrial and economic development since he imagines that it is acceptable to dominate nature, and who has not yet understood that before you can order nature around, you must first obey? [translation]

Roger Julien
Montreal, Quebec
2 December 1993

There is going to come a time where the non-Indian people are going to come to us and ask us, what do we do? [They are going to say] we have abused our Mother [Earth] so much that we are now beginning to kill ourselves because we have polluted the life blood – the water, the air and all...that is around us. They're going to ask us, what we do? We have the answer whenever they come and ask us that question.

Roger Jones
Councillor and Elder
Shawanaga First Nation
Sudbury, Ontario, 1 June 1993

Aboriginal speakers made it clear to us (as they have told previous inquiries) that they are not naively opposed to development or modernity, as is sometimes alleged. They do not want to give up telephones, snowmobiles, or video games. They accept that industrial development is a necessary part of the economic fabric of every country. Indeed, many pointed to their need and desire for greater participation in Canada's industrial economy. But few Aboriginal people would choose to participate at the expense of the land and life forms that anchor them in their past and link them to the future.

We also recognize that the traditional ways that once served to limit Aboriginal use of land and conserve resources are changing. Some Aboriginal people, especially among the young, have lost their sense of connectedness with the environment and their responsibility to it. Even those who retain this sense have access to technology designed to make exploitation attractive and easy – snowmobiles, high-powered rifles, electronic fishing gear, and so on. We were warned by a few speakers in public testimony that Aboriginal people are just as capable of destructive behaviour as anyone else.[190] We were urged by others to recommend that federal, provincial and territorial governments retain control over all land and its use:

> There are some Natives who choose not to use [their hunting and fishing] rights in a responsible manner, and have little or no regard in the taking of wildlife. Some of them practise methods that can be best termed as unethical, and are often excessively detrimental to wildlife. There are many documented instances of night hunting, excessive netting at spawning times, the hunting of wildlife in the spring just before a new generation is being born, commercial-type hunting where refrigerated semi-trailers are brought into an area, often by status Natives that aren't residents of this province. There are many other types of these abuses....
>
> Natives are one of the fastest growing groups in Canada. Their numbers in many areas now exceed that [which] existed at the time the treaties were signed and it appears that that trend will continue. We feel wildlife couldn't cope with that pressure even if primitive conditions and methods were used, but with modern technology such as four-by-fours, rifles, off-road vehicles, quads, it can very negatively affect and quickly negatively affect game populations.
>
> Andy von Busse
> Alberta Fish and Game Association
> Edmonton, Alberta, 11 June 1992

> Another aspect of the problem concerns the loss of income among outfitters as a result of overlapping activities with Aboriginal people....Non-Aboriginal big-game hunters are very reluctant to hunt in areas frequented by Aboriginal hunters because they know full well that Aboriginal hunters take their prey before hunting season begins....In our opinion, the Wildlife Conservation Act [of Quebec] should apply to everyone in the same way. [translation]
>
> Thérèse Farar
> Quebec Federation of Outfitters
> Montreal, Quebec, 30 November 1993

> The [Canadian Wildlife] Federation recommends that Canadian governments – federal, provincial or territorial – should maintain the authority to regulate and restrict harvests and harvesting methods. Any splintering of this authority would be detrimental to the health of wildlife resources.[191]

Issues of conservation, regulation and fair use are discussed in Volume 2, Chapter 4. Environmental stewardship, protection of country food and application of traditional Aboriginal knowledge in management regimes and international accords are considered in Volume 4, Chapter 6. Here, we are concerned with the ill-health effects of mistreatment of the land and its resources.

Pollution

Contamination of water, soil, air and food supplies by industrial and domestic wastes poses serious health hazards. The tailings from mining operations contain toxins that wash into streams or seep into ground water. The effluent from pulp and paper mills contributes hazards to health such as chlorine, dioxins and furans. Smelters and other processing operations release sulphur dioxide and a variety of airborne pollutants. Tankers and pipelines leak oil. Dams flood acres of bush and forested land, releasing poisonous methylmercury into the water. Within communities, crowded and inadequate housing encourages infectious diseases. Unsafe heating and wiring contribute to high rates of accident and injury. Untreated sewage is host to the bacteria responsible for various infectious diseases, most of them more common among Aboriginal than non-Aboriginal people in Canada.

Regulations to protect land and people from these contaminants are now more strict than they once were, but staggering problems remain: years of accumulated pollutants to be cleaned up, continuing denial and non-compliance from some polluters, the ever-present threat of accidental spillage, and always the fear that unseen agents are inflicting invisible damage to the delicate balance of life on earth.

The health hazards of environmental pollution became a contentious issue between Aboriginal people and Canadian governments in the 1960s, when it was first realized that methylmercury had entered the aquatic food chain and rendered fish, a dietary staple of many First Nations communities, unfit for human consumption.[192] Perhaps the best known case is that of the Grassy Narrows and White Dog First Nation communities in northwestern Ontario (see box).

This case is significant in reconsidering public health policy for Aboriginal people because contamination of aquatic environments is so prevalent. Mercury contamination in particular is a problem because it is an unintended consequence of the construction of dams for generating hydroelectric power, many of which have been built on lands used primarily by Aboriginal people. The reservoirs created by damming major rivers necessarily cover large tracts of land with water: 7,500 square miles in the case of the James Bay hydroelectric project in northern Quebec, for example. A great tonnage of submerged vegetation begins to rot. As part of the decomposition process, methylmercury is released into the water system, where it accumulates in the food chain over a period of decades.

The story of the Grassy Narrows and White Dog communities is also significant because it had characteristics that continue to hamper effective monitoring and control of environmental health hazards. In addition, compensating Aboriginal communities for hazards that remain uncontrolled has proved difficult. The continuing impediments are as follows:

- The communities involved were small, isolated, highly dependent on the river and its ecosystem, and did not have the political power or technical skills needed to overcome the inertia of governments and industry.
- The combination of federal responsibility for public health on-reserve and provincial responsibility for environmental protection and the regulation of industry off-reserve (where the problem originated) left the communities with no defined authority to appeal to or work with.
- The effects of industrial pollutants on the river system were difficult to prove; causal effects on community health were more difficult still.[193]
- The companies producing the contamination resisted the idea of pollution controls and continued to discharge suspect chemicals into the river until forced to stop by government order after more than 10 years of investigation.
- Contamination will stay in the food chain for several generations of Ojibwa. The people of Grassy Narrows and White Dog will not be able to use their most valued waterways and aquatic resources, no matter what future land settlements or economic development plans they may negotiate.

Decline of traditional food sources

An equally important health effect of environmental degradation is its impact on the traditional diet of rural Aboriginal people, many of whom depend largely on country food.[194] Two processes of change are usually at work simultaneously:

- Habitat destruction and related impacts of large-scale industrial development (manufacturing, mining, oil and gas extraction, hydroelectric power production and so on) reduce the supply of game and other country foods.
- The newly required labour force immigrates to the region from non-Aboriginal communities, stimulating an increase in the availability and attractiveness of store-bought food.

The items most often bought are low-cost, quick-energy, low-nutrient foods – in part because the cost of importing more nutritious foods, especially fresh vegetables and fruits, to remote locations is high, and in part because preparation and cooking methods for imported foods are unfamiliar to many Aboriginal people.

Despite its significance, the impact of industrial development on traditional food sources has received only limited attention in official project impact assessment statements.[195] What studies have been done show a significant decrease in the use of country foods and an increase in the consumption of starches, fats, sugar and alcohol where industrial development takes place.[196] Thus, the foods eaten to replace the country food lost or no longer harvested are nutritionally inferior:

> Although more work needs to be done, the general indication is that the traditional diet of the northern Native peoples was far superior to the diet presently available to them. [A variety of studies] have all

The White Dog and Grassy Narrows Story

The English-Wabigoon River system is the source from which the Ojibwa people of Grassy Narrows and White Dog have taken most of their food and all of their drinking water since time immemorial. By 1970, it was so badly polluted with mercury-laden effluent from the pulp and paper operations of nearby Dryden, that the government of Ontario was forced to close commercial and sports fishing completely and for an indefinite period. In a single stroke, the people of Grassy Narrows and White Dog lost their two main sources of employment (guiding and commercial fishing), and their confidence in the safety of their food and water. Over 300 miles of a productive river ecosystem are expected to remain contaminated for 50-100 years.

Significant amounts of mercury had been dumped into the river system since 1962. The risks from its ill health effects had been on record at least since 1968.[1] No one had discussed them with the Ojibwa. Nor did the Ojibwa have any one to tell about the diseased fish and animals they were finding in and around the river, nor any means of interpreting the unnatural animal behaviour they were seeing – especially in birds and cats, the fish-eating species.[2]

By 1975, the Ojibwa (with help from the environmental office of the National Indian Brotherhood) had learned a lot about the ill health effects of mercury, and about the early symptoms of Minamata Disease: loss of vision, loss of feeling in hands and feet, loss of coordination and concentration, tremors, nervous disorders. To their distress, they could see these very symptoms in the other fish-eating species living by the English and Wabigoon rivers: themselves. But they have never been able to prove a link between their ill health and the mercury in their food and water, at least not to the satisfaction of federal and provincial authorities.[3]

discussed the relative merits of wild game and store meats, and have concluded that the wild game is generally higher in protein, ascorbic acid and iron, and lower in fat content.[197]

Dietary change from wild meat and other country foods to less nutritious commercial products can have measurable health consequences. In particular, it increases the incidence of obesity, diabetes, high blood pressure and dental caries.[198] Commissioners heard testimony to this effect from front-line health care workers and researchers alike:

Not only is [the use of country foods] an important part of cultural expression, but it can be a helpful kind of a diet. In particular, for

Federal authorities attempted to assist the suffering communities by importing clean fish from Lake Winnipeg, by promoting alternative economic activity, and finally, in 1990, by compensating the families who had lost the most in potential income and family sustenance. Yet, neither the food and water nor the economic base could be brought back. Nor could the people's faith in the land, in the "river of life" that was now poisoned, or in their place in the circle of life. The two communities have struggled with serious health and social problems for 25 years.[4]

1. Mercury poisoning had been established as the cause of Minamata disease in 1962. Canadian health authorities had been warned several times during the 1960s about the dangers of mercury consumption, but showed no signs of alarm despite heavy use of the substance in several industrial processes. In 1967 and 1968, a graduate student from the University of Western Ontario, Norvald Fimreite, conducted doctoral studies that established a high mercury content in fish and fowl from mercury-contaminated waterways in Alberta, Saskatchewan and Ontario. (Norvald Fimreite, "Mercury Contamination in Canada and its Effects on Wildlife", PH.D. dissertation, University of Western Ontario, 1970.) Despite his urging, the government of Ontario took no action.

2. In Minamata, the people had dubbed the strange disease affecting them 'cat dancing disease' because, as the mercury destroyed the brains of the cats that lived on mercury-contaminated fish, they passed through a stage of spinning and whirling in madness. See W. Eugene Smith and Aileen M. Smith, *Minamata* (New York: Holt, Rinehart and Winston, 1975).

3. The extraordinary saga of their attempts, which included extensive testing by Japanese medical experts, is detailed in Warner Troyer, *No Safe Place* (Toronto: Clarke, Irwin & Co., 1977), especially chapters 13-16.

4. See Anastasia M. Shkilnyk, *A Poison Stronger Than Love: The Destruction of an Ojibwa Community* (New Haven and London: Yale University Press, 1985).

example, the person with diabetes. Use of wild game and use of fish, both of which are lower in fat than the beef and pork that you buy in the store, is a much better choice for people with diabetes.

Rhea Joseph
Health Policy Adviser, Native Brotherhood of B.C.
Vancouver, British Columbia, 3 June 1993

The diseases of the so-called "western diet" are striking [all indigenous peoples] – rural and urban, rich and poor alike. Chronic diseases that were unknown...are now on the increase among them, and building into an impressive list: obesity and diabetes, the cardio-vas-

cular diseases, cancer, infant morbidity and mortality in higher fre-
quencies are all part of this diet and [ill] health picture that has
been emerging for indigenous people for the last 100 years.[199]

The trend toward higher rates of chronic disease is deepened by changes in
local ecosystems that reduce the level of physical activity in Aboriginal people. Where
self-sufficiency through trapping or the commercial sale of traditional fish stocks
becomes impossible because of dwindling numbers or product contamination,
unemployment and the tendency to adopt a low-activity lifestyle increase. Physical
fitness, with its positive impact on health, declines proportionately.

Traditional foods, and traditional means of obtaining and preparing them,
are part of a cultural heritage. Thus, food is holistically entwined with culture
and personal identity, as well as with physical health. Dietary change is not often
mentioned in analyses of the loss of identity that is at the heart of the social dysfunction affecting Aboriginal communities. Yet many of the Aboriginal people
who spoke to us expressed sadness and bitterness about the disappearance of fish,
game and plants such as wild rice that their ancestors had long depended on.
Where those foods have been contaminated, people can no longer trust the
sources of life that were central to their cultures. Despite their increasing urbanization, this remains important to Aboriginal people:

Our rivers and our lakes, we can't even trust any more.

Nancy Scanie
Cold Lake First Nation
Fort McMurray, Alberta, 16 June 1992

Since I was younger, the urban population of Natives has almost
tripled. One of the reasons [they move to the cities] is that the water
is so polluted on Ohsweken. Down river, they can't even bathe their
children in it, they get blisters. So the mothers are moving off-
reserve just for their own protection, to raise the children.

Peter Cooke
Toronto, Ontario, 3 November 1992

Because of the focus on the contaminants, our community is going
through a lot of fear right now, fear of the unknown....When we see
these [water importation] trucks rumbling down our roads, we know
that something is wrong [with the river], and it puts...fear into our
community.

Dean M. Jacobs
Walpole Island Heritage Centre
Sarnia, Ontario, 10 May 1993

A case example that combines the problems of industrial contamination
and the decline of a traditional food supply is that of fluoride contamination in

Akwesasne, a Mohawk community located on the banks of the St. Lawrence River, near Cornwall, Ontario (see box).

Airborne contamination is a problem in many communities, but particularly in the Arctic. In winter, a layer of pollution haze from Eurasian industrial sites lies over a region the size of Africa.[200] In both Akwesasne and the Canadian North, the transborder origins of contaminants add enormously to the problems of hazard identification, mitigation of effects and compensation for damages.

Mental and spiritual ill health

Among researchers studying addictions, depressive and suicidal behaviour, family violence and other social pathologies, there is endless argument about their causes. In our experience, Aboriginal people have no doubt whatsoever that the destruction of their ways of life, including the multi-faceted rupture of their spiritual ties to the land, is a major factor. The words of Paul Scotchman, quoted a few pages earlier, are one expression of a common conviction that damage to the land and its inhabitants is reflected in social disorganization in Aboriginal lives and spiritual emptiness in Aboriginal souls. Others have expressed the same theme:

> Forests provide more than fuel, shelter and food to Native people. They are an essential ingredient in the cultural and spiritual well-being of the Indian population....Preservation of the natural habitat is a vitally important factor in the agricultural, cultural and spiritual practices of Indian bands.
>
> Robert Moore
> Program Manager, Six Nations of the
> Grand River Forestry Program
> Brantford, Ontario, 13 May 1993

> We have listened to endless excuses, and sometimes, Mr. Chairman, to shameful deceptions. Meanwhile we have suffered, and continue to suffer...from a numberless list of specific impacts which combine as an ecological disaster and a social disaster.
>
> Chief Allan Ross
> Norway House First Nation
> Manitoba Northern Flood Committee
> Winnipeg, Manitoba, 17 November 1993

> [The people promoting hydroelectric development in northern Quebec] live in the south. Their lives do not depend on the continued health of the land which they are presently destroying. Rather, they are proud of the fact that electricity is being taken from the area. They do not have to live on a day to day basis with the degradation of the environment which they have caused. My people live with this

Fluoride Contamination at Akwesasne

Akwesasne is a Mohawk community straddling two borders, one between Ontario and Quebec, the other between Canada and the United States. According to local records, the community has been subject to damaging effects of environmental change since 1834, when British engineers began to modify the water levels of the river for navigation purposes. One hundred and twenty years later, the building of the St. Lawrence Seaway drew heavy industry to the area, particularly on the U.S. side of the border. By the 1970s, as a result of contaminants in the air and water, Akwesasne was widely thought to be the most polluted reserve in Canada.

By long tradition, Akwesasne was a farming community, raising and selling vegetables and cattle. In 1963, four years after a new aluminium smelting plant began operations a mile from the reserve, cattle began to sicken and die. It took almost a decade to identify the problem: airborne fluoride from the Reynolds Metals Company and, to a lesser extent, the General Motors Central Foundry, both on the New York state side of the reserve. Excessive fluoride was found in the air, in the water and on the surfaces of plants:

> By 1972, we had effectively identified fluoride as being the problem, and it was coming from the [aluminium] plant in gaseous and particulate form, landing on vegetation on Cornwall Island and being consumed by the cattle. And the teeth would rot in the mouths of these animals. Some of our farmers...used to take porridge out to the cattle in buckets in order that they could eat, that's how close they were with their animals. But still they saw the whole cattle industry begin to disappear.
>
> Henry Lickers
> Director, Department of the Environment
> Mohawk Council of Akwesasne
> Akwesasne, Ontario, 4 May 1993

degradation. We are not proud of the La Grande project....It eats away daily at the soul of my people.[201]

When the bond between Aboriginal people and their lands is ruptured, it is as if they have lost their place in creation. Many have lost that place quite literally, in that they can no longer hunt and trap for sustenance or trade; at the same time they face great obstacles in developing what resources they possess in other ways. More important, they lose their symbolic place in the order of things, as stewards

As in the case of Grassy Narrows and White Dog, the cause and effect relationships between pollutants and patterns of ill health found on the Akwesasne reserve have been difficult to prove.[1] In 1972, under public pressure but not under government order, the offending plant installed pollution control devices, which reduced fluoride emissions by more than 75 per cent. Yet, even today, the people of Akwesasne contend that the damage continues; they say it merely takes longer for the cattle to become ill.

The consequences for human beings of long-term exposure to airborne fluoride are unknown. Whether or not residents are accumulating physical ill health effects from breathing and ingesting fluoride, they have already suffered indirect effects. Their diet now depends on imported, processed food rather than fresh, locally grown produce. In addition, as farming went into decline, so did fishing – a casualty of unrelated industrial pollution. Dependence on welfare has grown as ways to earn a living have shrunk. Social bonds forged by barter and support relations between farmers and fishers, which once gave the community its great solidarity, have weakened.[2]

---

1. According to a study published in the veterinary sciences journal of Cornell University, "Chronic fluoride poisoning in Cornwall Island cattle was manifested clinically by stunted growth and dental fluorosis to a degree of severe interference with drinking and mastication [chewing]. Cows died or were slaughtered after the third pregnancy. Their deterioration did not allow further [productivity]. Studies by Dr. C.C. Gordon of the University of Montana Environmental Studies Laboratory indicated high levels of fluoride in hay and other plant life, suggesting that the emissions [of fluoride] may be responsible for declines in farm vegetable production as well." Doug Brown, "Akwesasne Pollution Project Report", *Indian Studies* (March/April 1984), p. 8.

2. James Ransom and Henry Lickers, "Akwesasne Environment: Appraisals of Toxic Contamination at the St. Regis Mohawk Reservation", *Northeast Indian Quarterly* (Fall 1988), pp. 24-25.

of a particular homeland, as skilled managers and survivors of its rigours. They may lose the very sense of their traditional names for themselves: 'people of the caribou', or of a particular river or island in the sea. They may see fewer and fewer reasons to stay on diminished homelands, yet find little welcome in the cities. Even urbanized Aboriginal people retain fragments of a land-based identity.

When the dynamics of a culture change in profound ways, a sense of disorientation and anxiety pervades the inner reaches of the human spirit.[202] Peace of mind and purpose in life are jeopardized. Dr. Brian Wheatley has suggested that environmental contamination and dietary change have a tip-of-the-iceberg relationship to the major social, economic and cultural transformations in Aboriginal life – which in turn contribute substantially to drug and alcohol use and high rates of injury, accidents and violence.[203] As traditional Aboriginal ways of life lose value and sustaining capacity, a kind of 'care-less-ness' takes hold: carelessness of one's own safety and the safety of others, carelessness of other life forms.

Nearly 20 years ago, the Berger commission (the Mackenzie Valley pipeline inquiry), argued that the profound social changes linked with the construction of a northern pipeline would aggravate already serious problems of alcohol abuse and other social pathologies among Aboriginal people in the North.[204] Studies of Grassy Narrows and White Dog, where rates of alcoholism and violence increased relative to neighbouring communities unaffected by mercury contamination, are consistent with this view.[205] So are the observations of Geoffrey York, who linked social dysfunction in Aboriginal communities in northern Manitoba with the decline of traditional hunting and trapping economies following major hydroelectric development.[206] Such economic decline is the most visible link in the chain of disruptions leading from environmental change to mental imbalance and social ill health in Aboriginal communities.

The difficulty of generating action

The precise relationship between environmental degradation and human health effects is, for technical reasons, often difficult to prove.[207] Most western nations thus have mechanisms for assessing the *probable* impacts of planned development, for monitoring the continuing effects of existing developments, and for adjudicating charges of damage. Although several agencies to protect people from environmental hazards exist in Canada, a number of Aboriginal people told the Commission they have difficulty persuading such authorities to act on what they perceive as a health hazard:

> Fort McKay is [at] the epicentre of the tar sands development....The government tells us that there is no pollution. They have done studies that say there is no pollution. But we say they are wrong, because we have seen the changes that have taken place in the environment. The pollution has not only damaged the environment, it has made the people of Fort McKay sick. For a small community of 300, we have high rates of cancer and other illnesses....When we approach the government for funding to correct these problems, they tell us, you go see the next department, and then they give us the run-around. They tell us to set up a committee. So we set up a committee, and we sit around the table and we talk and we talk and we talk, but that's as far as it gets.
>
> Chief Dorothy McDonald
> Fort McKay
> Fort McMurray, Alberta, 16 June 1992

[Walpole Island is] in the middle of the Great Lakes, [at the intersection of] three upper connecting channels and three lower connecting channels. That puts us in...the gut or the stomach of the Great
Lakes. We are one of the real indicators of the health of the Great
Lakes, because [whatever flows through those channels] goes through
our community....We can't prove a direct connection [between our
health problems and] the contaminants in the water. All the governments and agencies are always looking for the dead bodies or the two-
headed babies, and that is unfortunate because we can't produce that
right now. But our community knows there is a direct connection
[between our health] and the pollution in the river.

Dean M. Jacobs
Walpole Island Heritage Centre
Sarnia, Ontario, 10 May 1993

The problem of stimulating action to protect the environment surrounding Aboriginal communities, whether for health or other reasons, begins with
the issue of control. Aboriginal people have very little say in the management
of lands and resources that affect their health and well-being. Not only are they
prevented from exercising responsibility for the environment on their own
behalf, they must struggle to make sense of a confusing map of governmental
departments and agencies that might (or might not) have that responsibility. Such
confusion is common with regard to issues affecting Aboriginal people. With
responsibility divided between governments and among government departments, there is ample opportunity for buck-passing and failure to act. In the case
of environmental health issues, the general problem of defining the segments of
the Aboriginal population to whom government support and intervention programs apply is compounded by the fact that responsibility for the environment
is itself divided among federal, provincial and territorial governments.

Environmental problems that are fully contained within reserve boundaries
are generally taken to be the responsibility of the federal government. Since the
early 1960s, medical services branch has funded a corps of environmental health
officers responsible for inspecting buildings and infrastructure facilities on
reserves (for example, water and sanitation systems) and reporting any related
adverse health and environmental effects. Unfortunately, however, there is no legislative or program mechanism to remedy such adverse effects. Each issue that
comes up requires ad hoc action to investigate the problem, decide what can be
done about it, and take remedial or compensatory steps. Since there is no established program, there is no budget line to cover such costs. Each case requires a
special submission to Treasury Board and faces an uphill battle for approval.[208]

If an environmental problem on-reserve is sufficiently serious, or if its
causes or consequences involve lands and people off-reserve (as in the cases of
Grassy Narrows and White Dog and Akwesasne), provincial or territorial author-

ities must become involved. This further complicates the route to solutions. All provincial and territorial governments have monitoring, investigation and enforcement capacities designed to protect their citizens from the effects of environmental hazards, but not all recognize reserve communities as eligible for the protection provided by their legislation. Sometimes, an intergovernmental or inter-ministerial committee investigates. Such bodies generally lack the authority or mandate to make judgements and prompt remedial action. At other times, no such co-operation takes place, and those affected by the problem bounce between competing agencies, none of whom have authority to act.

To prevent or limit negative impacts from proposed new land uses, including those on health, all Canadian governments have discretionary mechanisms for environmental assessment and review in advance of development. No equivalent mechanism exists at present within the terms of self-government agreements to enable First Nations, Inuit and Métis people to control environmental impacts on their lands. Nor are the avenues for their participation in federal, provincial and territorial review processes either clear or satisfactory. The situation as it stands offers Aboriginal people no reliable means of protecting themselves from existing or potential health hazards. Clarity requires that all governments, in consultation with Aboriginal peoples and their organizations, develop written policies to

- specify the responsibilities of each level of government to provide environmental protection to Aboriginal people on and off reserves;
- establish guidelines for investigating problems that affect the health of Aboriginal lands and people, for rectifying those problems and for compensating victims; and
- define the extent of Aboriginal participation in preventive, investigatory and compensatory hazard assessment procedures at the provincial, territorial and federal levels.

Detailed discussion of jurisdiction and management regimes governing land appears in Volume 2, Chapters 3 and 4.[209] In Volume 4, Chapter 6 we propose a model of environmental stewardship that, although especially relevant to the territories, is a useful model for land management everywhere. In this chapter, we wish to make the point as strongly as possible that the regulation of environmental impacts is as much a health issue as it is an economic issue.

Without a clear and dependable regulatory framework to help Aboriginal nations protect the environment, some communities have taken their own initiatives to protect the natural resources on which they depend. The Six Nations of the Grand River (Ontario), for example, have established a multi-disciplinary natural resources department to develop a sustainable natural resource base according to Aboriginal needs and values and to protect it for all time.[210] The Mohawk Council of Akwesasne has had an active environmental department for almost 20 years.[211] The First Nations of British Columbia are establishing an Indian water rights commission to provide support and expertise to communities that identify clean and productive water issues as important to them.[212] The Eskasoni First Nation in Nova Scotia is developing a plan to take control of its resources and environment.[213] We take the position that, for Aboriginal people to develop and exercise responsibility for the health effects of the use and misuse of lands and resources, they must gain greater authority over their own lands and be included routinely as an interested party in land use planning for the territory that affects them.

1.5 Conclusion

In this brief investigation of the burden of ill health borne by Aboriginal people, we have seen that the problems are many, serious and persistent. Notwithstanding that medical services are now delivered to Aboriginal people even in the remotest parts of the country and that some causes of morbidity and mortality have been brought under control, the gap in health and well-being between Aboriginal and non-Aboriginal people remains. It extends from physical ill health to social, emotional and community ill health. When we examine its patterns and dynamics over time, we are forced to conclude that, no matter which diseases and problems of social dysfunction are plaguing Canadians generally, they are likely to be more severe among Aboriginal people.

We have no doubt that Canadian governments have made and are continuing to make genuine efforts to improve the health and well-being of Aboriginal people. However, as we have shown here, the current system of services does not adequately address the causes of disproportionate rates of illness and dysfunction. The system's assumptions about Aboriginal health and well-being and how to promote them are wrong for the job.

Next, we examine the assumptions about health and wellness held by Aboriginal people themselves and establish their congruence with emerging insights from the field of population health (epidemiology). From this analysis we derive a new set of guidelines for health policy and action that *are* right for the job of restoring well-being to Aboriginal people, their nations and communities.

2. TOWARD A NEW ABORIGINAL HEALTH AND HEALING STRATEGY

The preceding analysis showed that the factors contributing to ill health of Aboriginal people stem not from bio-medical factors, but from social, economic and political factors. Given the many causes of Aboriginal ill health, Commissioners are convinced that the problem-by-problem approach of Canada's health care system is not adequate; it does not address underlying causes and cannot trigger the fundamental improvements in life circumstances that Aboriginal people need. Nor can very much difference be made simply by providing 'more of the same' –

more money, more services, more programs. Such responses would indeed help some individuals in poor health, but this will not stem the flow of ill and dysfunctional Aboriginal people to fill up the spaces left by the newly cured.

Although we were greatly disturbed by the evidence of continuing ill health in Aboriginal communities, we were also encouraged by the energy and imagination with which many Aboriginal people are tackling their health and social problems. They know what ails them. In testimony and consultation, they offered a critique of existing health and social services and proposed alternative ways of making progress toward health and well-being. They are already acting on those ideas in some communities.

Commissioners were struck by the fact that many of the insights of traditional values and practices echo those at the leading edge of new scientific ideas on the determinants of health and well-being. We believe that there is, at the meeting point of these two great traditions – the Aboriginal and the bio-medical – real hope for enhanced health among Aboriginal people and, indeed, enhanced health for the human race. For Aboriginal people, the conviction that they have a contribution to make is deeply held and a source of strength. In the analysis that follows we show the solid ground on which this belief stands.

2.1 Aboriginal Perspectives on Health and Healing

Aboriginal people have not been passive in their dealings with Canada's system of health and social services. They have struggled to make it work and in doing so have developed a critical analysis of its failings. Many Aboriginal people say they have never had access to enough services that are sensitive to their unique history and needs. At a deeper level, they say the system is incapable of delivering health and well-being to Aboriginal people and that more of the same will not alter this fact. Many who spoke to us argued that strategies for health that originate from within Aboriginal cultures are the key to restoring well-being among Aboriginal people. The critique of existing service systems and the affirmation of the relevance of Aboriginal traditions of health and healing were consistent refrains in our hearings and research. We highlight here five main themes, often intertwined, in the scores of presentations we heard.

The demand for equal outcomes

The starting point for many presentations was that there is no equality of health status and social outcomes between Aboriginal and non-Aboriginal people. The findings reported earlier in this chapter amply demonstrate the truth of this contention. This is not just an abstract finding; Aboriginal people see the human consequences of unequal risk, unequal rates of illness, social dysfunction and inadequate services, and they measure the cost in the ill health and unhappiness of their neighbours, families and themselves.

The fact that Aboriginal people suffer an unequal burden of ill health in a country that espouses 'equality for all' is an outrage to many Aboriginal people. We believe it should be equally unacceptable to all Canadians and their governments.

The last two decades have witnessed the emergence of overwhelming health problems [among our people], such as cardiovascular disease, respiratory disease, renal disease, poor nutrition, cancers, dental caries, ear-nose-and-throat infections, high risk pregnancies, birth anomalies, multiple mental illnesses, poisonings and injuries, communicable diseases, and the re-emergence of tuberculosis. Any disease category related to the First Nations is two to three times higher than the national figures....

The federal government has had [years] to provide hospital and health services to the First Nations communities. Unfortunately, we are still facing Third World health conditions.

Nellie Beardy
Executive Director, Sioux Lookout Aboriginal Health Authority
Sioux Lookout, Ontario, 1 December 1992

The average Canadian...is unaware of the degree of ill health in the Aboriginal population in Canada. It is a fact that in many areas of this country, the health of Aboriginal peoples is equivalent to poor Third World standards.

Dr. Chris Durocher
Yukon Medical Association
Teslin, Yukon, 27 May 1992

[There is an] epidemic of substance abuse and hopelessness that envelops our young people and results in the highest suicide rates among [youth] in the nation today. Of the 200 to 275 deaths by injury and poisoning that have occurred among First Nations in the last decade, fully three-quarters were in the 10-year to 20-year age group. Those deaths compare to the 65 to 70 deaths that occurred in the same category nationally....

Fetal and infant death among First Nations babies was nearly twice the national average reported since 1987. Once again the social and economic factors of poor housing, lack of sewage disposal and potable water, and poor access to health services were considered factors in the higher rate. As well, the poor health of the mother, inadequate nutrition and lack of pre-natal care, as well as the adverse effects of drugs and alcohol, also contributed.

Tom Iron, Fourth Vice-Chief
Federation of Saskatchewan Indian Nations
Wahpeton, Saskatchewan, 26 May 1992

Canadians enjoy homes with a lot of rooms, [complete] with full finished basements, water and sewer facilities, central heating, infrastructure to support the community. In Fort Albany, I have 80-year-old elders that struggle to get water from [outside] sources of water, standpipes as we call them. I have them struggling in 40-below weather to empty sewage pails in the places where they can empty them. I have them sitting in houses that are sitting on the ground without a proper foundation, subjected to frost, cold, wind, made of plywood substandard housing....They are not living like Canadians. We can only ask that we be allowed to live like Canadians.

Chief Edmund Metatawabin
Fort Albany First Nation
Timmins, Ontario, 5 November 1992

In addition to the gap in health and social outcomes that separates Aboriginal and non-Aboriginal people, a number of speakers pointed to inequalities between groups of Aboriginal people. Registered (or status) Indians living on-reserve (sometimes also those living off-reserve) and Inuit living in the Northwest Territories have access to federal health and social programs that are unavailable to others. Since federal programs and services, with all their faults, typically are the only ones adapted to Aboriginal needs, they have long been a source of envy to non-status and urban Indians, to Inuit outside their northern communities, and to Métis people. Further, as we discuss at greater length in Volume 4, some Aboriginal women told us that health and social issues are given a back seat to the 'hard issues' of politics and economics by local (male) leadership – to the detriment of all, particularly women and children:

Women [have been] doing a lot in their communities...but they have been meeting a number of obstacles year after year after year, and it comes from the top. In the communities, who are the leaders? Well, mostly men. They do not have the political will [to address our concerns]....Our concerns are with the social problems of this society, and it doesn't [stop] with Aboriginals. It covers the whole society in Canada. They are just not a priority for the governments, the different governments or the different representative groups out there. I think women now have to...hold their politicians...a little more responsive to the social needs.

Margaret Eagle
Native Women's Association
Yellowknife, Northwest Territories, 7 December 1992

Pauktuutit's role in publicly addressing such issues as family violence, child sexual abuse, sexual assault, AIDS and numerous other health and social issues has reinforced the perception that these things fall into the female sphere of influence. This is not bad in itself, but it means that there is incredible pressure on individual women and the organizations which represent them to right the wrongs and heal the wounds that three decades of change have brought to the North....In spite of this, Inuit women are still under-represented in leadership positions. This is particularly true in relation to issues which are seen as falling more naturally into the male sphere of influence – that is, land claims, economic development, self-government, renewable resource management.

> Martha Flaherty
> President, Pauktuutit
> Ottawa, Ontario, 2 November 1993

Our voices as women for the most part are not valued in the male-dominated political structures....The Aboriginal leadership is fond of saying that our children are our future. Is there an understanding of what is demanded by that belief? If our children are to have a future, the time is now to reshape the political agenda. We say this to the leaders of First Nations: Assess the status of children in our society, what are their real needs. For the first time in the history of the *Indian Act* leadership, define an agenda that will address the real conditions of our children and families in our society.

> Marilyn Fontaine
> Spokesperson, Aboriginal Women's Unity Coalition
> Winnipeg, Manitoba, 23 April 1992

The belief in interconnectedness

Other presentations focused on solutions. The idea brought forward perhaps most often was that health and welfare systems should reflect the interconnectedness of body, mind, emotions and spirit – and of person, family, community and all life – which is essential to good health from an Aboriginal point of view. Further, this reflection should be substantial, not simply rhetorical.

Classic Aboriginal concepts of health and healing take the view that all the elements of life and living are interdependent and, by extension, well-being flows from balance and harmony among the elements of personal and collective life:

> The Native concept of health...is said to be holistic because it integrates and gives equal emphasis to the physical, spiritual, mental and emotional aspects of the person. The circle is used to represent the inseparability of the individual, family, community and world....The circle (or wheel) embodies the notion of health as harmony or balance in all aspects of one's life....[Human beings] must be in balance with [their] physical and social environments...in order to live and

grow. Imbalance can threaten the conditions that enable the person...to reach his or her full potential as a human being.[214]

The Aboriginal concept goes beyond the conventional wisdom of bio-medicine, which focuses on the human organism and its symptoms of dysfunction.

For a person to be healthy, [he or she] must be adequately fed, be educated, have access to medical facilities, have access to spiritual comfort, live in a warm and comfortable house with clean water and safe sewage disposal, be secure in their cultural identity, have an opportunity to excel in a meaningful endeavour, and so on. These are not separate needs; they are all aspects of a whole.

Henry Zoe
Dogrib Treaty 11 Council
Member of the Legislative Assembly
Yellowknife, Northwest Territories, 9 December 1992

Being alcohol-free is just the first stage [in becoming healthy]. The next level is healing the mind and then the soul....If we begin with ourselves, then we can begin to help our families...and our communities.

Eric Morriss
Teslin Tlingit Council
Teslin, Yukon, 26 May 1992

The western notion the body is expressed in a metaphor [that] holds that the body is a machine....Scientific thought distinguishes the body from the person, establishes a dichotomy between the body and the spirit, and separates the individual from the human and physical environment....

The Inuit vision of the body offers a holistic vision of the individual and his or her unity with his/her surroundings, a part of a whole that draws its meaning from the relationships that the human being entertains with whatever is living and whatever surrounds him or her....It is a model that is characterized by its continuity with the environment....

From the different representations of the body follow certain notions of health and illness, certain practices and behaviour, certain customs and conduct in restoring and maintaining health. [translation]

Rose Dufour
Laval University Hospital Centre
Wendake, Quebec, 18 November 1992

As these speakers described it, interconnectedness is a philosophical concept. But others described it as a practical idea with concrete implications for the design and delivery of medical and social services:

For a number of years, we had been receiving more and more specialists trained in medicine, in nursing, in mental health. But even though more and more health and social services were being put into place, we had more and more sick people. New specialists arrived, and they kept finding that we had new illnesses....Self-help groups are now beginning to emerge and share their knowledge of traditional healing, because modern medicine does not heal the whole person. [translation]

Danielle Descent
Director, health and social services
Innu Takuaikan Council
Sept-Îles/Mani-Utenam, Quebec, 20 November 1992

Government funding systems are presently administered by specialized departments...which address very narrowly defined social problems. Examples of this would be programs for violence against women as opposed to family violence. Or alcohol and drug abuse programs as opposed to a more overall program designed to address all of the related problems that accompany alcohol and drug abuse....

This means that there is no [long-term program for] solving the social problems, and [short-term programs] are vulnerable to political bandwagons. It is our recommendation that the Royal Commission on Aboriginal Peoples recommend programs and program funding sources that are more generic and can deal with the social problems in a more holistic, rather than specialized way.

Bill Riddell
Baffin Regional Council
Tuvvik Committee on Social Issues
Iqaluit, Northwest Territories, 25 May 1992

I don't believe that education, economic development, recreation, health, job creation and all of these programs can work in isolation of one another, and yet sometimes that happens in our Native communities.

Tom Erasmus
Alberta Mental Health Association
Lac La Biche, Alberta, 9 June 1992

These speakers and many others articulated a vision of health care in which each person is considered as a whole, with health and social problems that cannot be cured in isolation from one another, and with resources for achieving health that come not just from expert services but also from the understanding and strength of family, community, culture and spiritual beliefs. It is a vision quite different from that of mainstream health and social services, which tend to isolate problems and treat them separately. To operate on the basis of their vision, Aboriginal people told us they would have to take control of programs and services more completely than has been possible to date.

The transition from dependency to autonomy

The legacy of enforced dependence on (or, in the case of Métis people and non-status Indian people, neglect by) the Canadian state has left most Aboriginal nations without the levers of authority and control over health and social services that Canadian provinces and communities take for granted. (The issue of a transition from dependency to self-control is discussed with particular reference to the North in Volume 4.) Health transfer agreements (and the terms of the few existing self-government agreements) have begun to change the picture for some, but for the most part they work within systems that do not comprehend their deepest needs and within programs that they did not design and that do not reflect their priorities. Many believe that the consequences of dependency and lack of control have been disastrous:

> During the inquiry [into the accidental death of six Innu children in a house fire], we listened to each other speak about the impact that the government, the church, the school, the [health and social services] clinic and the police have had on our lives. Many of the people expressed the belief that we have lost too much by giving over power to these non-Innu organizations. If we are to have a future, we feel that we must be the ones who begin to take responsibility for such things in our lives once again.
>
> As one of the couples in our village said during the inquiry, in the past, we were like we were asleep. White people were doing everything for us. We thought white people knew everything, but we were wrong. The advice they gave us never worked.
>
> Chief Katie Rich
> Innu Nation
> Sheshatshiu, Newfoundland and Labrador, 17 June 1992

Often programs set up by Health and Welfare Canada to serve Aboriginal communities cause more harm than relief. Typically, these programs are imposed on Aboriginal communities without consultation and research to best address Aboriginal needs and values. In addition, the large overhead bureaucracy in Ottawa and...in the province[s] consume a major share of the resources available, leaving Aboriginal communities the task of managing foreign programs with inadequate funding. The design of health services for Aboriginal communities [should be done by] Aboriginal people.

Sophie Pierre
Ktunaxa/Kinbasket Tribal Council
Cranbrook, British Columbia, 3 November 1992

In our treatment centre we cannot say what [our money] can be spent on. The government tells us what it should be spent on....For instance, the government would probably not respect us for using our own traditional medicines within the treatment setting, but those kinds of things [are what work]....It would be nice to see some flexibility in some of these funding schemes. I think we are capable of designing the programs that we feel suit our clients.

Paul Nadjiwan
Weendahmagen Treatment Centre
Thunder Bay, Ontario, 27 October 1992

There are many examples we see in small communities where Native-run community health groups are very successful. That is because they are Native-run....There is no way we can cross that. It is unrealistic for us, no matter how good-hearted we [non-Aboriginal caregivers] are, to think we can cross it.

Dr. David Skinner
Yukon Medical Association
Teslin, Yukon, 27 May 1992

Aboriginal people told us that control will permit them to redesign health and social programs to more fully reflect their values and diverse cultures. Earlier in this chapter, in relation to the problem of compliance, we indicated how effective culture-based programming can be.

The need for culture-based programming

It is often pointed out that much of the content of Aboriginal cultures has been lost and that the dominant non-Aboriginal culture has been absorbed by Aboriginal people. This is true, but to exaggerate this point is to miss one of the central facts of Aboriginal existence: Inuit and the First Nations and Métis peoples of Canada are unique peoples, and they are determined to remain so. Traditional norms and values, though changed and constantly changing, retain much of their power. Often, the ideas and practices of the dominant culture – in health and social services and in all fields – simply fail to connect with Aboriginal feelings, Aboriginal experience and Aboriginal good sense. Better connections come from within. In fact, as several speakers told us, it is often the most distressed and alienated Aboriginal people who find the greatest healing power in the reaffirmation (or rediscovery) of their cultures and spirituality.

Even if the insights and practices of Aboriginal cultures were to add nothing to the health of Aboriginal people (which we think highly unlikely), they claim the right to find out for themselves:

> I want the rest of the country to recognize that there is more than one way to heal. Social workers and medical people have to realize the validity of our ways. Your way is not always the right way.
>
> Sherry Lawson
> Native Education Liaison Worker, Twin Lakes Secondary School
> Chippewas of Rama First Nation
> Orillia, Ontario, 13 May 1993

> The only way for our people to heal is to go back to those original instructions that were given to us, go back to the sacred fires, go back to the wisdom and knowledge that was given to us, and apply that to our lives today.
>
> Alma Brooks
> Wabanaki Medicine Lodge
> Kingsclear, New Brunswick, 19 May 1992

> It must be clearly understood that, when dealing with First Nations people, whether it be in education or with health, it must be in the context of the culture, whatever that culture may be, or it is just another form of assimilation.
>
> Jeanette Costello
> Counsellor, Kitselas Village Drug and Alcohol Program
> Terrace, British Columbia, 25 May 1993

Aboriginal people told us that the choice and flexibility inherent in the idea of cultural appropriateness should recognize the diversity among Aboriginal peoples as well. Just as non-Aboriginal approaches to health and healing are not necessarily right for all others, so too the programs and services developed by one Aboriginal nation may not necessarily be right for others. Métis people and Inuit, for example, strongly object to the imposition of programs designed for or by First Nations:[215]

> The Métis Addictions Corporation of Saskatchewan exists because we are recognized as a separate people, culturally different from both the dominant society and the Indian people, but we have been denied the resources we need for our own research and development, so we have used models of treatment borrowed from the dominant society [and] of those developed by and for Indian people. Neither are culturally appropriate for us.

A clinical one-to-one approach does not work well for us, [because] we cannot divorce the healing of individuals from the healing of families and communities. Indian people often find spiritual wholeness in a return to their traditional ceremonies. That rarely works for us. Traditionally, our people were Roman Catholic or Anglican....We desperately need the resources, money and manpower to develop our own culturally appropriate programs.

Winston McKay
Métis Addictions Corporation of Saskatchewan
La Ronge, Saskatchewan, 28 May 1992

We found that Inuit women or Inuit communities need different solutions [to problems of violence] because of culture, different beliefs and isolation, and [because] there are hardly any programs or facilities in Inuit communities. That's why we decided to have different solutions, a different section for Inuit [in the report of the Canadian Panel on Violence Against Women]. But it was very hard for me to try to get the Inuit section, because I was lumped with other Aboriginal groups all the time. I fought and fought and fought. I kept saying..."I am not like other Aboriginal people...I am not white, I am not Indian, but I am Inuk." I had to tell [the other members of the Panel], it is like lumping Japanese and Chinese together [to put all Aboriginal people in a single category].

Martha Flaherty
President, Pauktuutit
Ottawa, Ontario, 2 November 1993

Culture-based programming has become more widely accepted in the human services field because of its effectiveness (and the welcome it has received). More controversial is the idea that the physical, psycho-social and spiritual healing methods of traditional practitioners might have direct applicability to today's health issues.

A new role for traditional healing

We believe that traditional cultures can – and should – act as a kind of source book of ideas for reconceptualizing and reorganizing Aboriginal health and social services. It is not a very big step from there to recognizing that traditional healers can (and should) play a significant part in redesigned care systems.

A number of thoughtful speakers argued that traditional healing methods and therapies can make two sorts of contribution: they are valuable in their own right for their direct efficacy in treatment, and they contain ideas that can be adapted to solve difficult problems in restoring whole health to Aboriginal people. The attitude of these speakers was not revivalism but inquiry into the past. They spoke of applying old practices to new problems, of combining them with western therapies in a spirit of experimentation and learning.

The majority of traditional healers were forced long ago to renounce their practices (or to practise covertly) because of persecution by Canadian governments and Christian churches and contempt on the part of bio-medical practitioners for their ceremonies, herbal treatments and other therapies. Newcomers' disrespect was eventually mirrored in the feelings of most Aboriginal people themselves. Yet, traditional practices never faded away completely. In the Peguis First Nation, they are playing an increasingly important part in medical services (see box).

Only a few healers came forward to speak to the Commission. They told us of the ancient power of their traditions and of the interest in their work that is growing all over the country:

> It is with great concern that I present this brief for the protection and preservation of our traditional and spiritual beliefs and culture. The inherent right to practise our traditional beliefs was given to us when the Creator first put the red man here on earth....In times of great difficulty, the Creator sent sacred gifts to the people from the spirit world to help them survive. This is how we got our sacred pipe, songs, ceremonies and different forms of government. These were used for the good health, happiness, help and understanding for the red nation....[Each tribe] had our own sacred traditions of how to look after and use medicines from the plant, winged and animal kingdoms. The law of use is sacred to traditional people today....
>
> By the 1960s, traditional spiritual people were almost extinct except for those who went underground. A lot of our traditional spiritual elders went to their graves with much knowledge. Since then there has been a rebirth....[Even non-Aboriginal people] are coming to traditional spiritual people for help....The present health care system is in a crisis and heading for financial collapse unless there are alternatives. Traditional spiritual people want to create alternatives for all people to get help.
>
> Elder Dennis Thorne
> Edmonton, Alberta
> 11 June 1992

David Newhouse told the Commission that rekindled interest in traditional healing and its modern potential is part of a general restoration of respect for Aboriginal ways:

> Within the Aboriginal community, over the past decade particularly, there has been a move to relearn the traditional ways and to move these ways back to the centre of Aboriginal life....What is occurring

Peguis Explores Cultural Roots

It was in the 1980s, after a period of intense social turmoil, that some members of the Peguis First Nation community in Manitoba began exploration of their fading cultural roots. Resulting interest in traditional medicine encouraged a new openness among the few who sought to rediscover and follow its practices. It also aroused fierce opposition from those who did not want to be branded 'ignorant' or reactionary – opposition that is only now beginning to subside.

As awareness spread, more and more people began to ask for access to traditional healers as part of the range of services provided by the local Health Centre. The Aboriginal nurse in charge of the centre agreed and sought financial help from Medical Services Branch to bring experienced healers to Peguis (and to send clients to healers elsewhere). Travel costs and related expenses became a special category within the Non-Insured Health Benefits Program.

Now, demand for a referral to the traditional healers who visit Peguis is as high as 30 to 40 per month. Interest is particularly high among those who suffer from emotional problems, including those related to alcohol and drug abuse, violence and suicide. Their positive experiences have influenced the community mental health program, which is experimenting with a blend of traditional and western approaches to healing.

Source: Benita Cohen, "Health Services Development in an Aboriginal Community: The Case of Peguis First Nation", research study prepared for RCAP (1994).

is that today's Aboriginal identity [is being] examined and deliberately reconstructed to be as Aboriginal as possible....These reconstructed identities will provide a solid foundation for experimentation and perhaps change.

David Newhouse
Native Management Program, Trent University
Toronto, Ontario, 3 November 1992

Many speakers thought it possible that Aboriginal and western healing methods might enrich each other, inspiring improved services and outcomes. The precise relationship between the two systems is a matter of continuing debate among Aboriginal people. Some see traditional healing as an adjunct treatment service; others see it as a full partner with bio-medical and psychological therapies; still others insist on it remaining an alternative service, completely separate from western-style medicine and social services:

How can effective health care be delivered to the Aboriginal nations? I think what has to happen here is a common ground must be reached by Aboriginal people and the western medical profession to combine Aboriginal medical teachings and Western medicine in the delivery of health care services to Aboriginal people.

Traditional healers must be recognized by the college of physicians and surgeons in each respective province....Aboriginal people talking to doctors, and taking a look at traditional healing methods, traditional medicine, and putting it all together so that [we] can deliver an integrated service to Aboriginal people that has the Aboriginal component built in.

Harold Morin
Executive Director, Central Interior Native Health Society
Prince George, British Columbia, 1 June 1993

I want to be very clear that there are significant political differences [about]...the issues of establishing a comprehensive health care delivery system which seeks to bring traditional medicine into the fold, so to speak, as opposed to the view of bringing western medical know-how into the healing circle....I believe that the ideal model is one which aims to bring western medicine into the circle versus one that aims to bring traditional healing into the western medical framework. I believe that in choosing the latter we choose to give away our power.

Yvon Lamarche, RN
Treatment Co-ordinator, Georgian Bay Friendship Centre
Orillia, Ontario, 13 May 1993

What is clear is the interest of many in exploring the possibilities of the old ways and co-operation between Aboriginal and non-Aboriginal healing traditions. We heard evidence that the application of traditional approaches has already begun with statements of principles to guide Aboriginally controlled health and healing services and the design of programs to promote psycho-social healing from the effects of discrimination and oppression:

[We] believe it is important [for you] to have an understanding of the values and principles that guide health and social services in Kahnawake. These principles are based on the traditions of our people and are supposed to govern all our relationships with the world around us. They are the principles of peace, respect and a good mind.

We also operate and advocate the traditional ethic of responsibility. As I mentioned earlier, health is a responsibility given to us by the Creator....It is up to us to ensure that we take care of what He has given us. It is important for us to deal with others in an honest and forthright manner, always keeping in mind our responsibility to our community. We believe health is one of those responsibilities.

Rheena Diabo
Health Consultation Committee
Kahnawake Shakotii'takehnhas Community Services
Kahnawake, Quebec, 5 May 1993

One solution that we in the Prince George Native Friendship Centre have come up with is, we developed a Sexual Abuse Treatment Services Program, otherwise known as the SATS program. What makes this such a unique program is that we have taken the holistic approach to healing. We will be providing treatment to [the whole family]....We have incorporated traditional and contemporary healing methods. For example, sweats, smudging, healing/talking circles, ceremonial rites versus art and play therapy, psychodrama, gestalt and psychotherapy. Our traditional healing methods were very effective before European contact. If they worked then, why can't they work now?

Lillian George
Director, Sexual Abuse Treatment Services Program
Wet'suwet'en First Nation
Prince George, British Columbia, 31 May 1993

Defining the place of traditional healing and healers in future health services is complex and challenging. We give it further consideration in Appendix 3A.

Conclusion

Throughout this chapter, we have referred to Aboriginal people's ideas, innovative programming and recommendations for system change, described in presentations, briefs and documents tabled at our hearings. We have seen that they are part of a comprehensive analysis of what will restore health and well-being to Aboriginal nations and their communities. It would seem reasonable to support many or most of the ideas we heard simply on the grounds that Aboriginal people are likely to know best what will work in their own communities. We have also found other reasons to support and build on the vision of health and healing presented to us by Aboriginal speakers: its concepts and understandings are affirmed by the leading edge of scientific research on the determinants of health.

2.2 The Determinants of Health

For a long time, most Canadians have equated health with medical care. Doctors, drugs, hospitals, and the research that informs them, get most of the credit for keeping us free of disease and able to enjoy our increasingly long lives. We take for granted the achievements of the public health movement of the previous century: clean water, safe food, reliable sanitation, safe houses and workplaces, and public welfare. During the 1960s, the idea that individual health behaviour choices contribute to good or ill health started to take hold. Personal decisions – whether to smoke, eat well, use alcohol and drugs, keep fit and fasten our seat belts – have been found to play a large part in preventing ill health and encouraging wellness. In fact, health policy in Canada today is concerned mostly with maximizing those two factors: access to sophisticated bio-medical treatment and healthy lifestyle choices.[216]

Now, a new idea has been gaining force – one with the potential to transform our understanding of what makes people healthy. Research indicates that several other factors are probably more significant than the public illness care system and private lifestyle choices in determining health:

- wealth, poverty and other economic conditions;
- social, psychological and spiritual well-being;
- environmental conditions; and
- genetic inheritance.

One of the main reasons to rethink the determinants of health is the research finding that, beyond a certain baseline, high levels of expenditure on illness care services do not yield corresponding levels of improved health.[217] Furthermore, the countries that spend the most money on illness care do not have the healthiest people. The United States and Canada have the highest levels of expenditure, but Japan, Sweden and Finland have lower morbidity rates and higher life expectancy.[218]

Analysis of these differences suggests that medical care, important as it is, is only one element in a complex picture of interdependent factors that determine health and well-being. Aaron Wildavsky has summarized the limits of the bio-medical model of ill health and how to treat it in this challenging way:

> According to the Great Equation, medical care equals health. But the Great Equation is wrong. More available medical care does not equal better health. The best estimates are that the medical system (doctors, drugs, hospitals) affects about 10% of the usual indices for measuring health: whether you live at all (infant mortality), how well you live (days lost to sickness), how long you live (adult mortality). The remaining 90% are determined by factors over which doctors have little or no control, from individual lifestyle (smoking, exercise, worry), to social conditions (income, eating habits, physiological inheritance), to the physical environment (air and water quality). Most of the bad things that happen to people are beyond the reach of medicine.[219]

For brevity, we will use the phrase 'the new determinants of health' to refer to the non-medical factors listed by Dr. Wildavsky. Those working on the new determinants of health point out that the old determinants – public health (sanitation, food and water quality, housing conditions) and basic medical care – must exist at a minimum standard to ensure health. In addition to this, however, another set of factors must be considered. Among the new determinants of health, four are especially significant for public policy and the reform of Aboriginal health and wellness systems: economic factors, social factors, emotional factors and environmental factors.

Economic factors

The most powerful argument for thinking differently about the determinants of health is found in economic analysis. Major studies dating back 20 years and more have shown that population health gains in the nineteenth and early twentieth centuries were attributable in large part to the expansion of the middle class and the resulting spread of such amenities as soap, window glass, fresh nutritious food, and the ability to buy them.[220] Today, the socio-economic status of individuals (their wealth or poverty and their social class position) is still a good predictor of life expectancy and the incidence of illness.[221]

The general prosperity of a nation also affects the health status of its people.[222] More important, the distribution of income within a country is associated with health status. Simply put, wealthy countries that have a relatively equitable distribution of income (for example, Japan) enjoy higher health status than countries where wealth is distributed less equitably (for example, the United States) – despite the fact that the United States spends twice as much as Japan on medical services per capita.[223] Countries where poverty abides, despite the wealth of the country as a whole, do not achieve the most favourable standards of population health. Thus, it appears that living in the just society – a society where wealth and life chances are equitably distributed and the quality of life is reasonably high for everyone – is good for your health.

The availability of jobs also contributes to health. Unemployment has been correlated with mental and physical ill health and with early death.[224] One Canadian study found that the unemployed reported more anxiety, depression, visits and phone calls to doctors, and days in hospital than did the employed.[225] The high level of stress associated with unemployment appears to be the explanation. The human 'stress response' triggers physiological imbalance, such as increases in blood pressure and blood lipids. Further, it is associated with behavioural risks to health such as increased rates of smoking, drinking, drug taking, and the consumption of so-called 'comfort foods' with their high content of fats and sugars. Stress (from any cause) is also known to depress the immune system.[226]

Social factors[227]

Those who do have jobs face risks to health as well – and not just the health and safety hazards associated with certain kinds of work. The famous Whitehall studies of the health of British civil servants found that, even among those fully employed in physically 'safe' white collar work, health status differed by rank and seniority. The closer people were to the top, the healthier they were.[228]

Upon investigating further, Dr. Leonard Syme, a professor at the University of California at Berkeley, reported that he found "a similar gradient almost everywhere in the world and for virtually every disease that has been studied".[229] Those with the most power and authority were least likely to become ill. But why? Syme was struck by the fact that people farther down in the organizational hierarchy are less able to make their own decisions about work and life demands than those higher up. They are not in control of critical factors that affect their jobs and thus, their daily lives. He concluded: "The only hypothesis that I have been able to come up with is that as one moves down the social class hierarchy, one has less control over one's own destiny." In Syme's view, the absence of control explains a portion of ill health.

In our view, the issue of control is more than a work-related issue. If powerlessness at work is a factor in individual health status, it is reasonable to suppose that powerlessness in other areas of life may also lead to illness. Indeed, in his review of studies of this issue, Gus Thompson reports that

> Personal attitudes such as optimism, assertiveness, and a belief that one
> can control one's environment are associated with lowered incidence of
> a variety of illnesses (major and minor). The reverse is true for those who
> are accepting of events, pessimistic, passive and compliant.[230]

Thompson is speaking about individual health outcomes, but we must also consider the probable effects of powerlessness on population health outcomes. Commissioners have concluded that the lack of economic and political control that Aboriginal people continue to endure, both individually and collectively, contributes significantly to their ill health.[231]

In addition to issues of control, a second set of social factors increasingly found to have significant health effects is the events of early childhood. One leading researcher put it this way:

> Rapidly accumulating evidence is revealing an impact of childhood
> experiences on subsequent health, well-being, and competence which
> is more diverse, profound and long lasting than was ever understood
> in the past.[232]

Observation throughout the ages has revealed that if animals or people are raised without adequate nurturing and affection, they do not thrive.[233] New insights from the neuro-sciences show that the stimulation people receive in childhood, when the brain is at its most 'plastic', affects behaviour, cognition, competence and the development of coping skills.[234] It appears that early childhood stimulation and complex experience actually build the biological (neural) pathways that encourage these aspects of development and thus contribute to variations in health status.[235]

Even what happens in the womb is important. As discussed earlier, babies born with low birth weight (LBW) are at risk for physical and learning disabilities, increased rates of disease and premature death. LBW babies are more commonly born to women who are young, single, poor and who have below-average education, suggesting that social rather than medical factors are at work.[236] This profile applies disproportionately to Aboriginal women, whose risk is thus more difficult to eliminate.

Emotional and spiritual factors

The Canadian health care system approaches mental health with some unease; conditions such as depression and substance abuse are often ineligible for coverage under medical insurance plans – unless they are classified as 'diseases' and treated at least in part by medication. The complex relationships linking the mind, body and spirit are barely acknowledged, even in relation to these conditions. Nevertheless, there is growing evidence that psychological factors play a complex role in determining health.

The ill health effects of major life trauma are now well established.[237] Heart attack victims, for example, are often found to be suffering from severe stress, such as the death of a loved one or an instance of personal danger. Similarly, people who have just lost spouses are more likely to die suddenly than a matched sample of the same age.[238] Other evidence suggests that people who choose to struggle against life-threatening diseases and receive the support of psychotherapy and group therapy live longer than people with similar illnesses who receive no such support.[239] Still other studies have established firm connections among stress, personality type and the onset of heart disease.[240] Conversely, the ability to cope well with stress is associated with the ability to achieve metabolic control over diabetes.[241]

The precise explanation for these findings is not known. However, what is clear is that the mind and body are in direct communication through neurobiological links involving the hormone and immune systems. In fact, whole new areas of scientific research are charting the pathways that connect mental and emotional functioning with biological functioning. Two examples are psychoneuroimmunology and psycho-neuroendocrinology. These fields are beginning to show how physical functioning and resistance to disease can be affected by feelings and perceptions – that neurological systems 'talk' to the immune systems through the endocrine system in ways that affect resistance to disease and the functioning of vital organs.[242]

In times of high stress, including periods of grief, depression or anger, changes in hormone production seem to depress the immune system, leaving a person increasingly vulnerable to invasion by disease organisms – and perhaps to careless or high-risk behaviour as well.[243] We have argued elsewhere that grief, depression and anger are endemic in Aboriginal life. On the basis of the research cited here, the restoration of whole health depends on effectively addressing their causes.

Environmental factors

For many years, the focus on high tech medicine and drug therapies to control disease masked the links between the health of the earth and that of its human inhabitants. Recently, however, that relationship has come back into focus. We have come to realize the extent of the damage borne by the natural systems essential to life on earth. We have come to understand that the health of the air, water and soil – not only in our own backyards, but in the vast world to which we are ever more closely connected by global patterns of food and commodity production – matters greatly to our own health.

In addition, the built environment of human communities and shelters has its own health hazards, just as it did in the nineteenth century when the champions of public health first fought for enforceable standards of housing quality, sanitation, and food and drinking water quality. New concerns are the effects of indoor air quality and the conditions leading to accidental injury and death. We discussed environmental health earlier in this chapter. We expect that the great sensitivity of many Aboriginal people to this dimension of well-being will lead to breakthrough ideas and programs in the coming era of Aboriginal self-management in health and wellness.

2.3 Two Great Traditions of Health and Healing

Commissioners see a powerful resonance between the findings of bio-medical researchers and Aboriginal philosophies of health and well-being. Principles of health and healing long held by indigenous cultures are now being confirmed by scientific research. Penny Ericson, speaking for the Canadian Association of University Schools of Nursing, made a similar observation:

> The current paradigm shift in health care confirms what Aboriginal
> people have always believed about health and healing. For example,
> Primary Health Care is the World Health Organization's framework
> for health care in today's society.... The principles of Primary Health
> Care are similar to those of the Circle of Life or the Medicine Wheel,

which have served as a guide for health care for generations of some of Canada's Aboriginal people.

It is powerful for Aboriginal people to realize that one of their traditional approaches to health is now viewed as progressive and crucial by health care educators and policy planners within the United Nations and in Canada. The partnership between consumer and health care worker that underlies the teachings of Primary Health Care ensures a powerful bridge between traditional values and health care initiatives. The interplay of the physical, emotional, social and spiritual for achieving well-being has long been inherent in the Aboriginal health paradigm and is now appearing as a stated value in health care teaching in Canada.

Penny Ericson
Dean of the Faculty of Nursing
University of New Brunswick
Canadian Association of University Schools of Nursing
Moncton, New Brunswick, 14 June 1993

We identified several areas of convergence between Aboriginal concepts of health and those of mainstream health sciences. The first is at the heart of both discourses: the idea that true health comes from the connectedness of human systems, not their separate dynamics.[244] We have already described the Aboriginal concept of the circle that links body, mind, emotions and spirit and each individual to the community and the land in which the human being is rooted. The cumulative research on health determinants agrees. It paints an increasingly complex picture of the impacts on physical health of disturbances in the mind, emotions or spirit. 'Health' is the total effect of vitality in and balance between all life support systems.

The second common theme is the awareness that economic factors (personal and community poverty or comfort) play a particularly important role in determining health. Community living conditions identified as critical by nineteenth-century public health advocates are a vital component of this thread. We discussed both earlier in the chapter.

A third converging theme is that of personal responsibility. In the health determinants field, this theme has taken two forms. One is the idea that personal health choices matter, and that we can all make a difference to our future health status by stopping smoking, reducing alcohol intake, eating properly, exercising regularly and so on. Added to this is the idea that medically trained experts are not the only ones with insight into health and wellness – that, in fact, the final judge of our well-being can only be ourselves. In the Aboriginal view, collective responsibility is also significant. Many speakers told us that solving health and social problems must become the responsibility of Aboriginal people taking action together, and that individual self-care must be matched by community self-care.

A fourth converging theme is the Aboriginal idea that the essence of good health is balance and harmony within the self and within the social and natural environments we inhabit. This idea is echoed in scientific studies of the role of stress in determining health and illness. Harmony and stress are opposing ends of a continuum: at one end, stress and ill health; at the other, harmony and good health.

A final converging theme is the importance of childhood. We have cited a great deal of evidence that health status, good or bad, begins in childhood – even before birth. The experiences and quality of life of Aboriginal children and youth have long-term implications for health, most dramatically in the case of abnormal birth weight, fetal alcohol syndrome and poverty, but also in relation to accident, injury and disability. Aboriginal people know the importance of a happy and healthy childhood as the foundation for life and of healthy children as the foundation of a people.

One area where convergence is still weak is in relation to the role of spirituality and the connection between people and the natural world. Non-Aboriginal definitions of health are beginning to recognize this dimension; Aboriginal people have always held that spirituality is central to health. Indeed, we were told more than once that, in terms of understanding the human spirit, Aboriginal people and their traditions have much to offer the world:

> In the last 20 years there has been an increased effort to understand the psychology of the human being....Western consciousness has now incorporated the mind, body and emotions as critical elements of what it is to be human. Less explored and least understood is the human spirit. Spirituality, the once-guiding force in the lives of indigenous people and many of the peoples of the world has become a footnote in the lives of [most] human beings....
>
> Many contemporary writers have begun to propose that global change will require transformation of the individual, or a shift of consciousness. The underlying question is: What is the process of transformation and how does it happen within an individual, a community or a nation?...
>
> We know that Indigenous people lived for tens of thousands of years in a spiritually based way of life which was harmonious with all of creation. It is imperative to begin the path of serious exploration of that aspect of ourselves, which can provide the essential transformative process, the healing and renewing of the human being and the earth. I see a day when Indigenous people will be sitting in the position where the white people and other people of the world will come to us and say, "Tell us what to do; tell us how to live on this earth. Tell us how to correct the damage that we have created on this earth."

The assumption is always that we are the problem, but the truth is that Indigenous people are the solution to what is happening in the world today.

Dave Courchene, Jr.
Mother Earth Spiritual Camp
Fort Alexander, Manitoba, 30 October 1992

Commissioners believe that the convergence of Aboriginal and science-based knowledge presents an exciting and important prospect for Aboriginal and non-Aboriginal people alike. It suggests the possibility of sharing insights and understanding, of building genuine partnerships – and, quite possibly, of transforming human health.[245]

2.4 Characteristics of a New Strategy

One aspect of the work of royal commissions such as ours is to find the root causes of troubling conditions that have defied society's efforts to improve them. To fulfil this role is to shift the terms of debate about life in Canada so that new energies for collective betterment can be released. We believe this need is nowhere greater than in relation to Aboriginal health and wellness.

According to almost every indicator we have examined, Aboriginal people are suffering rates of illness and social dysfunction that exceed Canadian norms. The practice of the present system of services is to isolate symptomatic 'problems' – teen pregnancy, diabetes, disability and suicide – and design stand-alone programs to manage each one. In our public hearings, Aboriginal people called this the 'piecemeal' approach to health care. It is not working. Indeed, we have concluded that the business-as-usual approach to services *perpetuates* ill health and social distress among Aboriginal people. However much good a particular health or social program may do in the narrow sphere it addresses, it does not shift the overall picture of Aboriginal disadvantage – the pattern of poverty, powerlessness and despair – that determines health and illness.

The weight of the evidence in this chapter is clear: substantial improvements in the health and welfare of Aboriginal people will not be accomplished by tinkering with existing programs and services. Commissioners believe that to restore well-being to Aboriginal people – and their communities and nations – a major departure from current practice is needed. We have found guidance for this departure in the insights of Aboriginal people, coupled with our analysis of the new determinants of health. We hope to give force to these two powerful strands of thought by establishing and building on their convergence.

The Commission proposes that new Aboriginal health and healing systems should embody four essential characteristics:

- pursuit of equity in access to health and healing services and in health status outcomes;

The Innu of Labrador

The terms of union under which Newfoundland joined Confederation in 1949 make no mention of Aboriginal peoples. Arrangements for service delivery to the Innu and others were made later, under a series of federal-provincial agreements. Until recently, the government of Newfoundland provided all health, education, welfare and related services, and the federal government contributed 90 per cent of the cost of programs the province chose to deliver. The federal government has now begun to provide direct funding to the Innu for some – but not all – health and social programs.

The Innu have long held that federal refusal to treat them in the same way they treat First Nations registered under the *Indian Act* for purposes of program and service delivery constitutes discrimination, an infringement of their rights as Aboriginal people, and an abrogation of fundamental federal responsibilities. In August 1993, a special investigator appointed by the Canadian Human Rights Commission (CHRC) submitted a report on those allegations to the CHRC.

The special investigator found that the federal government had failed to meet fully its responsibilities to the Innu, allowing the province to intervene in the direct, nation-to-nation relationship. Further, he found that although it is difficult to compare the services available to the Innu

- holism in approaches to problems and their treatment and prevention;
- Aboriginal authority over health systems and, where feasible, community control over services; and
- diversity in the design of systems and services to accommodate differences in culture and community realities.

Equity

Commissioners believe that, whatever health and healing system is put in place for Aboriginal people, it must deliver services equivalent to those available to other Canadians. Even more important, the system must produce health outcomes that are at least equivalent to those of other Canadians. Aboriginal people in Canada should not have to experience disproportionate levels of illness and social problems; their experience of whole health and well-being should be at least as good as that of the general population.

Our emphasis on 'outcomes' rather than 'services' is deliberate; equal services do not always deliver equal outcomes. In instances where threats to health are elevated above the norm, or where the causes or consequences of Aboriginal with those available elsewhere, past federal-provincial agreements did not provide as high a level of funding as would have been available if the Innu had been registered under the *Indian Act*. As far as today's services are concerned, the investigator compared the provisions made for the Davis Inlet Innu with those made for a First Nation reserve community in Nova Scotia of similar size and in similar circumstances. The Davis Inlet Innu were disadvantaged in a ratio of $2.4 million to $4.1 million.

On these and other grounds, the investigator concluded that the federal government had breached its fiduciary obligations to the Innu. He concluded that government actions were discriminatory, that they resulted in treatment that was inequitable relative to treatment afforded other Aboriginal people, and that the government failed to act for the benefit of the Innu as is its duty because of its special trust relationship with all Aboriginal peoples. The remedy he proposed was for the federal government to take immediate action to ensure that the Innu are "in the economic, social and spiritual situation they would have been in if government responsibilities had been properly exercised and appropriate human rights standards met".

Source: Donald M. McRae, "Report on the Complaints of the Innu of Labrador to the Canadian Human Rights Commission", 18 August 1993.

ill health are unique, enriched services are necessary. Enrichment is appropriate where a threat to health is spreading with particular rapidity among Aboriginal people (HIV/AIDS or shigellosis, for example). It is also appropriate where special measures are needed to relieve an outbreak of suicide or high rates of addiction or where a whole community needs to rebuild physically, socially and economically to restore well-being to its people. In the Commission's view, when the burden of ill health is greater than the norm, so too must be the healing response.

Equity, as we use the term, also means equity among Aboriginal peoples. The arbitrary regulations and distinctions that have created unequal health and social service provision depending on a person's status as Indian, Métis or Inuit (and among First Nations, depending on residence on- or off-reserve) must be replaced with rules of access that give an equal chance for physical and social health to all Aboriginal peoples. The Innu of Labrador, for example, have long been denied equitable health and social services (see box). Theirs is only one case of inequity among many, but it is a particularly disturbing one because of the severe health risks facing Innu communities.

The present jurisdictional tangle makes some health and social problems almost impossible to solve.[246] For example, the problems of Aboriginal people with disabilities cannot be dealt with by any one level of government in the absence of co-operation from the others. Similarly, action to stop environmental contamination usually involves two if not three levels of government – none of which has sole authority or the motivation to bring about change. In Volume 4, Chapter 7, dealing with urban perspectives, we discuss in detail the repercussions of divided and disputed jurisdiction as it affects Aboriginal people – and we recommend a solution.

Holism

Restoring health and well-being to Aboriginal people requires services and programs founded on an integrated, or holistic, view of human health.[247] In testimony, we heard a great deal about the fragmentation of services meant to solve interconnected problems. Aboriginal caregivers expressed great frustration because health and social programs are narrowly targeted to specific diseases and social problems, not to whole health. We learned that problem-specific programs may offer nutritional supplements for low birth weight babies but not vocational training for mothers who are too poor to eat properly; inoculations against infectious disease but not the means of cleaning up contaminated drinking water sources; treatment programs for alcohol addiction but not counselling for the trauma of attending residential school; wheelchairs for people with disabilities but not appropriate housing or jobs; social assistance for those who are unemployed but not life skills education or vocational upgrading.

To be truly effective, Aboriginal health and healing systems must attend to the spiritual, emotional and social aspects of physical health problems and to the physical health aspects of spiritual, emotional and social problems. This entails

- attention to health education and the promotion of self-care;
- changing the conditions in communities and in their environments that contribute to ill health; and
- addressing the social, economic and political conditions that contribute to ill health.

An effective service system will no longer split human problems into separate symptoms and assign them to separate offices to be dealt with in a segmented, disjointed manner. A holistic approach requires that problem solving be comprehensive, co-ordinated and integrated, and that services be flexible enough to respond to the complexity of human needs. Services that affect health outcomes, such as child care and child welfare, education, justice, recreation and others, must be delivered with reference to health objectives – and vice versa.

The holistic approach to health has been championed by a number of public health and population health experts in Canada and elsewhere for many years.[248] It is also featured in the systems approach to organizations. This kind of thinking has not had much influence on the illness care system, however, which continues to be dominated by specialists. In our view, integrated systems and services must have a central place in redesigned health and healing systems for Aboriginal people.

Control

The Commission believes that Aboriginal health and healing systems must be returned to the control of Aboriginal people. We base our position on three other conclusions reached in our deliberations.

First, we conclude that self-determination for Aboriginal peoples is an immediate necessity. As we discussed at length in Volume 2, the thrust of public policy historically has been to break up independent Aboriginal nations and replace their fully functional institutions (whether of government, justice, health care or any other) with those of Canada. Reclaiming control over health and social services is just one aspect of self-determination more generally.

We also believe, in light of the deep relationship between powerlessness and ill health, that Aboriginal health and healing systems must be returned to Aboriginal control. The evidence shows that people with more power over their life circumstances have better health outcomes and longer lives; we will have more to say about this extremely significant relationship.

Finally, we found overwhelming evidence that control of health and social services by outsiders simply does not produce good results – in any community. All across Canada, non-Aboriginal communities are being given more power over decision making about important services. This is happening in part because of the frequent failure of top-down approaches to community problems, that is, the failure to win support for solutions introduced from the top and failure to generate them from the bottom. Top-down approaches are not responsive to local conditions, priorities, resources and sensitivities; only local people know such things about their communities, and their knowledge is essential to implementing successful programs and services. It is now being acknowledged that centrally controlled programs and services often cost more because of the administration needed to manage them from afar.

The persistence of ill health and social dysfunction in Aboriginal communities demonstrates that existing services fail to connect with real causes. It is not just that programs and services are based on the norms and values of other cultures (although they often are), or that they are directed by caregivers from other cultures (although they usually are), but that they reflect priorities and timetables developed outside the communities. Today's governments show a greater tendency to consult and work with Aboriginal people. Nevertheless, programs come and go, expand or contract, add new rules and subtract others – all without notice to or approval from the people they are intended to help.

We saw in relation to fetal alcohol syndrome that a former minister of health denied the need for special program support to Aboriginal communities, thus overruling the recommendations of a House of Commons committee based on evidence gathered from Aboriginal people (and others with relevant experience). With regard to pollutants, we saw that Aboriginal people have difficulty proving ill health effects to outside 'experts' who control environmental review processes.

However, we also saw that local control over birthing in one northern community led to an innovative new program with excellent health outcomes for Inuit women in a particular region. We saw that control over the design of diabetes prevention elsewhere led to culture-based materials that increased their effectiveness. We saw that increased control over welfare monies allowed several northern regions to provide support for struggling hunters and trappers (see Volume 2, Chapter 5).

In the words of one leading analyst, community control means

> that the decision-making processes and organizational structures within a community are especially designed to give all members of a community the power and means to manage their own affairs. Since society is primarily organized on a top-down basis, community control will necessarily require a transformation from hierarchical to non-hierarchical structures so as to allow for the maximum participation by community members in the decision making and development process.[249]

But control does not apply only at the level of the community. It applies at the level of the individual, and in the case of Aboriginal people, at the level of the nation. In Volume 2, we discussed the nation-to-nation relationship needed between Aboriginal and non-Aboriginal governments in Canada. In practice, Aboriginal nations and their people will decide for themselves how to allocate authority and responsibility for programs and services, in keeping with their political cultures and traditions.

Diversity

We believe that health and healing systems for Aboriginal people should be free to diverge – as far as their users want them to – from the bio-medical and social welfare models that predominate in non-Aboriginal society. Aboriginal communities should also be free to diverge from one another. With this flexibility, they will be able to reflect Aboriginal cultures and traditions generally, the preferences of each Aboriginal culture specifically, and the diversity of local and regional conditions and priorities.

As we have seen, there are important differences between Aboriginal and non-Aboriginal approaches to health and healing, as well as among and within Aboriginal cultures and communities themselves. Any system that fails to recognize this diversity, or fails to offer sufficient scope for it, cannot be fully effective. Culturally appropriate program design and delivery is not a frill to be tacked on to health care and social services; it must be at the heart of generating well-being in any community. Programs must be designed and delivered by people familiar with the language and traditions of the community. It also means that a variety of health and healing strategies, including those of traditional medicine, must be made available so that the needs of everyone seeking care can be met.

We have already discussed some of the features and unique qualities of Aboriginal perspectives on health and healing. One of the means by which they will be given full expression in new health and social service systems is through the encouragement of traditional healers and healing methods. This important topic is explored more fully in Appendix 3A.

Aboriginal people must be recognized as the experts on their own health and healing needs. As they take charge of their own systems of care, and as those systems emerge and develop, they may look similar to the systems evolving in non-Aboriginal communities – or they may look very different. The differences are as worthy of respect as the similarities.

Conclusion

A new approach to Aboriginal healing that embodies the characteristics of equity, holism, Aboriginal control and diversity, has the power to do what the present system cannot: to go beyond services to focus on whole health. It will break down restrictive program boundaries to focus on healing, not just for individuals but for communities and nations. It will restore a focus on aspects of well-being that are lost in the current system: child and maternal health, health promotion and education for self-care, social and emotional health, the jurisdictional issues that block the way to health problem solving for all Aboriginal peoples. It will blend the insights of traditional and contemporary Aboriginal analysis with the emerging analysis of the determinants of health. It will honour the needs, values and traditions of those it serves.

The four characteristics of a new health policy – equity, holism, Aboriginal control, and diversity – are interdependent and mutually reinforcing. Only if taken together will they provide the basis for Aboriginal and non-Aboriginal people, working together, to construct the transformed health and healing systems that Aboriginal people have said they want and that all the evidence at our disposal says they need.

RECOMMENDATION

The Commission recommends that

Fundamental
Principles

3.3.1

Aboriginal, federal, provincial and territorial governments, in developing policy to support health, acknowledge the common understanding of the determinants of health found in

Aboriginal traditions and health sciences and endorse the fundamental importance of
- holism, that is, attention to whole persons in their total environment;
- equity, that is, equitable access to the means of achieving health and rough equality of outcomes in health status;
- control by Aboriginal people of the lifestyle choices, institutional services and environmental conditions that support health; and
- diversity, that is, accommodation of the cultures and histories of First Nations, Inuit and Métis people that make them distinctive within Canadian society and that distinguish them from one another.

The challenge is to begin now to construct new approaches to restore and sustain Aboriginal well-being on the foundation of analysis and hope laid down in the preceding pages.

3. An Aboriginal Health and Healing Strategy

3.1 Initiating Systematic Change

The essential characteristics of a new approach to enhancing and sustaining Aboriginal health are holism, equity, Aboriginal control and diversity. These concepts are goals to strive for and guidelines for action. However, concepts in the abstract are not sufficient to change reality. They must be translated into purposeful action capable of engaging the energy and commitment of those with a stake in better Aboriginal health – the Aboriginal community and Canadian society.

While health is not the outcome of services alone, the failure of services is a serious impediment to the achievement of well-being. Later in this chapter, we return to the issue of where health services fit in our proposed agenda for change. Our focus now is on strategies specific to health and social services.

Over the past two decades, many changes have extended services to Aboriginal people and made them more accessible and appropriate, especially for groups designated for federal government attention. We wish to acknowledge and applaud the efforts made to date. However, without a major reorientation of effort, the persistent problems illustrated in this chapter will continue to exact an enormous toll on the well-being of Aboriginal people, sapping the energies of Aboriginal nations and consuming the resources of the public purse. Far from abating, problems in some areas show disturbing prospects of becoming worse.

In devising an integrated health strategy, we looked to the goals and guidelines that emerged from our analysis. We considered criteria of efficiency and effectiveness that should be applied to any public program and that are especially important in times of fiscal restraint. We considered the huge and complex network of health and social institutions now in place – we are not beginning with a blank slate. We also considered that the urgency of immediate action on pressing concerns should be consistent with efforts to achieve self-government and self-reliance, which will proceed in parallel with service reorganization.

The strategy we propose has four parts that complement and support one another:

1. the reorganization of health and social service delivery through a system of healing centres and lodges under Aboriginal control;
2. an Aboriginal human resources development strategy;
3. adaptation of mainstream service, training and professional systems to affirm the participation of Aboriginal people as individuals and collectives in Canadian life and to collaborate with Aboriginal institutions; and
4. initiation of an Aboriginal infrastructure program to address the most pressing problems related to clean water, safe waste management, and adequate housing.

The first part, and the one that will require the most significant reorganization of effort, is the restructuring of health and social service delivery through healing centres under the control of Aboriginal people. The concept of healing centres was brought forward by presenters in many parts of the country, either explicitly in requests for support of particular centres or implicitly in the plea for a place where health and social needs could be addressed holistically. Local centres for integrated health and social services are not a new idea. They have been introduced in Quebec and are part of current plans for service reorganization in Alberta and the Northwest Territories. Aboriginal healing centres would build on the strengths of current programs while reorienting services to correspond to the goals and guidelines we consider essential to an Aboriginal health strategy.

They could bring together resources to support families, monitor health, devise education programs to promote healthful living, make referrals or facilitate access to specialist services, emphasize priorities specific to the nation or community, and be larger or smaller depending on the population served. With the realistic possibility of influencing the way needs are met, local ownership and involvement in health initiatives could replace the present sense of powerlessness and alienation many Aboriginal people feel. Policy, planning and administrative experience gained through direct service, local boards and regional policy-making bodies could contribute significantly to the development of institutions of self-government. Given the urgency of some of the needs we encountered in our investigation, the implementation of health and healing centres should not await the structural change in public institutions proposed in Volume 2 of our report. With the will to abandon fruitless debates about who is responsible, federal and provincial governments could begin now to co-operate with Aboriginal administrations and organizations to transform a fragmented and inefficient service delivery system, to fill gaps where localities and populations have been neglected, and to modify services to make them more appropriate to the needs of Aboriginal people.

The second part of our strategy is the mobilization and training of Aboriginal personnel through a major human resources development effort. Aboriginal control of human services is necessary because control over one's situation is a major determinant of health. In addition, only Aboriginal people can mobilize the capacity for self-care and mutual aid that is an essential complement to professional services. Only they can make effective decisions about the interventions that will make them well in body and spirit.

Preparation of personnel as planners, administrators, front-line workers and evaluators will be a significant part of the challenge of implementing self-government. The human resources development plan we set out here thus forms an important complement to our proposals for capacity building in Volume 2, Chapter 3 and our proposals for education and training in Volume 2, Chapter 5, and Chapter 5 of the present volume.

Part of the human resources requirement is to train personnel to develop distinct Aboriginal institutions and apply Aboriginal knowledge in unique ways. Another part is to involve Aboriginal people in mainstream service institutions as managers, professionals and informed consumers so that the Aboriginal presence in Canadian life becomes recognized and affirmed.

The third part of our strategy is the adaptation of Canadian institutions engaged in the delivery of health and social services. While Aboriginal institutions operating under the jurisdiction of Aboriginal governments form a significant part of the future we foresee for health and social services, they cannot occupy the whole field. They will predominate, most likely, in territories where institutions of self-government are established. Distinct institutions might also emerge to serve communities of interest in urban locations where substantial concentrations of Aboriginal people come together for recognition as self-governing entities. However, Aboriginal institutions cannot operate in isolation from the mainstream. Access to provincial medicare is just one example of an area where co-operation between Aboriginal and mainstream institutions will be necessary. Others include billing of physicians' services, referrals between healing centres and hospitals, admissions and discharges, and co-ordination of auxiliary and home care services. Aboriginal people will continue to move between their home territories and towns and cities, and they should be able to have their culture and identity recognized and affirmed in interactions with mainstream institutions. These institutions also need to aid in the development of Aboriginal institutions by providing back-up and specialist services, mentoring and support for Aboriginal personnel.

The fourth part of our proposed strategy is an infrastructure program, concentrated in the first 10 years following the release of our report, to raise housing, water supply and waste management in Aboriginal communities to generally accepted Canadian standards of health and safety. Immediate threats resulting from inadequate infrastructure are so serious and so devastating that solutions cannot await the development of new partnerships or reformed service delivery systems. Such problems undermine the ability of Aboriginal nations to organize for their own future, and they ravage the spirit of individuals and whole communities. Details of a carefully targeted and adequately funded housing and infrastructure initiative are developed in Chapter 4 of this volume.

By focusing on policy in the social sector we do not wish to imply that the health and well-being of Aboriginal people in Canada can be secured solely by changing how health and social services are organized and delivered. While reorienting existing systems is important, health and social conditions must also be understood as natural by-products of a safe and healthy environment, economic self-reliance and the empowerment of individuals and nations. They are not determined by the range and quality of services alone.

Those involved in political, economic and other fields often fail to recognize that what they do is intimately bound up with the health of individuals and peoples. We believe that a stronger recognition of the interconnections between various fields is required and that positive health outcomes should be a consideration of all those involved in Aboriginal institutional development and self-determination.

Given the present distribution of authority and responsibility for health and social services, implementation of our proposed integrated strategy will require action on the part of federal, provincial and territorial governments. Since health is central to maintaining the well-being, identity and culture of Aboriginal peoples, we believe that it falls within the core area where Aboriginal governments can exercise law-making powers on their own initiative. We anticipate that health and social services will be among the policy sectors where Aboriginal nations will wish to exercise authority at an early date. There will also be a practical need to harmonize Aboriginal service systems with those in adjacent jurisdictions.

It is essential to establish the environment within which changes can proceed, to ensure that health concerns are given appropriate attention in policy and institutional development, and to endorse the characteristics that we propose are essential to a new service system.

RECOMMENDATIONS

The Commission recommends that

Health: A Core **3.3.2**
Area of Self-
Government Governments recognize that the health of a people is a matter
of vital concern to its life, welfare, identity and culture and is
therefore a core area for the exercise of self-government by
Aboriginal nations.

Action to Agree on **3.3.3**
Jurisdiction and
Service Delivery Governments act promptly to
(a) conclude agreements recognizing their respective jurisdictions in areas touching directly on Aboriginal health;
(b) agree on appropriate arrangements for funding health services under Aboriginal jurisdiction; and
(c) establish a framework, until institutions of Aboriginal self-
government exist, whereby agencies mandated by
Aboriginal governments or identified by Aboriginal organizations or communities can deliver health and social services operating under provincial or territorial jurisdiction.

Health Effects of **3.3.4**
Policy Governments, in formulating policy in social, economic or political spheres, give foremost consideration to the impact of such
policies on the physical, social, emotional and spiritual health of
Aboriginal citizens, and on their capacity to participate in the life
of their communities and Canadian society as a whole.

Four-Part Strategy **3.3.5**
Governments and organizations collaborate in carrying out a
comprehensive action plan on Aboriginal health and social
conditions, consisting of the following components:
(a) development of a system of Aboriginal healing centres and
healing lodges under Aboriginal control as the prime units
of holistic and culture-based health and wellness services;
(b) development of Aboriginal human resources compatible
with the new system, its values and assumptions;
(c) full and active support of mainstream health and social service authorities and providers in meeting the health and
healing goals of Aboriginal people; and

(d) implementation of an Aboriginal community infrastructure development program to address the most immediate health threats in Aboriginal communities, including the provision of clean water, basic sanitation facilities, and safe housing.

3.2 Healing Centres

A snapshot of community services

It is 10 a.m. on a Monday morning in a remote First Nation of about 750 people. In one building, sometimes described as a health centre, but usually referred to by the historical term, nursing station, two non-Aboriginal nurses prepare to see the first of their clinic patients: one, a young mother with a cranky child, and the other, an elderly woman in obvious pain. The elderly woman is telling the clerk-interpreter, who is from the community, that the pain started the previous evening but she was unable to get relief because the clinic was closed. Her manner is mild, but it is clear that she sees the rigidity of the schedule as an indication of lack of concern on the part of the nurses. Although the clerk-interpreter is nodding in sympathy, she will not report this conversation to the nurses, largely because neither has been in the community for more than a month.

In another examining room down the hall, a young male non-Aboriginal physician looks through the chart of his first patient of the day, a young man injured in an accident over the weekend. The physician arrived in the community for the first time an hour ago by aircraft and will return in three days to his home in the city after seeing nearly a hundred people for problems ranging from attempted suicide to diabetes to otitis media.

Across town in the band office, the community health representative, a local woman who has done this job for 20 years, prepares her equipment to collect water samples from several buildings in town. These she will mail to the provincial testing facility several hundred miles to the south. She will wait several weeks for the results. After lunch she plans to visit the homes of several elderly people in town to check their medication and provide foot care.

Across from the band office, an Aboriginal social worker who moved here two months ago and is originally from a reserve in another province reviews the client file of a young mother who is seeking supplementary welfare benefits. Her aunt from another community has joined the household recently in preparation for the time, a few weeks hence, when the mother will have to leave her older children to have her baby in a distant city. The aunt will provide child care, but her presence over-taxes the family's budget, because the family's only income is the minimum wage that the husband earns on a temporary employment project sponsored by the band council.

Later that day, in a partially renovated house in the oldest part of town, several older women and one elderly man are gathering for a meeting of the alcohol committee. Waiting for them is a middle-aged man who returned to the community several years ago after recovering from nearly a decade of alcohol abuse. He is now the local National Native Alcohol and Drug Abuse Program (NNADAP) worker and responsible for providing counselling to individuals with alcohol abuse problems in the community. The purpose of the meeting is to discuss preparations for the upcoming visit of several Aboriginal people from a church group on a reserve in another province who have developed a healing strategy for survivors of sexual abuse. Neither the meeting nor the upcoming workshop will be reported in any of the committee's records, because the funding policy for NNADAP activities is restricted to substance abuse problems.

Several miles out of town, a middle-aged man splits wood for the ceremonial fire he will need to run his sweat lodge at sundown, while his 11-year-old son watches and helps. Later, he will collect some roots from a plant that grows near the nursing station and grind them into a poultice for a young woman suffering from a skin rash. He is thinking about two of the people who have asked for the sweat lodge: one recently returned from a provincial jail who wants to obtain a traditional name, and the other, a young man from an abusive family who recently attempted suicide after a long bout with solvent abuse.

In the history of this community, these service providers have never sat down together in one room to discuss their work or the needs of their clients. On occasion, the nurses might meet with other non-Aboriginal workers in the community, such as RCMP officers or teachers, to discuss community problems, but these meetings rarely produce integrated action plans. Furthermore, local administrators of housing, economic development and municipal services rarely discuss their responsibilities in relation to health issues.

There are many variations on the scenes described. Larger communities might have resident physicians; smaller communities might have only a community health representative supported by visiting nurses. Reserves and communities near larger towns or cities, on road systems, or in the southern parts of provinces may rely more heavily on service providers external to the community. In rural Métis communities and in many small towns with a substantial non-status Aboriginal population, there is a virtual service vacuum. Such communities often have to rely on provincial services that are geographically distant and culturally inappropriate and over which they have little influence. In cities there is a wide variety of services, but they rarely recognize the distinct social and cultural needs of Aboriginal clients.

Services in these various settings have been undergoing change, as we will discuss, but for the most part they have common characteristics that are sum-

Table 3.13
Comparison of Current and Proposed Approaches to Community Health Care

Current Approach to Community Health Care	Proposed Approach to Community Healing and Wellness
Historically grounded in infectious disease public health model	Oriented to health promotion framework encompassing spiritual, social, psychological and physical illness
Dominated by biomedical approach to treatment and care	Based on holistic, culturally appropriate understanding of illness
Hierarchical in structure with professional expertise as determining factor	Consensual in structure, applying expertise indigenous to the nation and community
Segregation of program activities by discipline and/or bureaucratic reference	Integration of program activities to reflect holistic perspective
Program-specific funding within narrow definition of health	Block funding of healing centres under federal or provincial jurisdiction; inter-governmental transfers for centres under Aboriginal jurisdiction; permits program activity based on holistic understanding of health
Programs and service providers accountable to authorities external to community	Programs and service providers function under Aboriginal jurisdiction, with accountability to the community served
Health research developed externally and divorced from community planning and priorities	Health research generated to respond to self-identified needs of the nation and community
Health care system encourages transfer of clients out of community to non-Aboriginal institutions	Health care system encourages providing services to client at home, in community or in regional Aboriginal institution

marized in Table 3.13 and that contrast with the holistic and culture-based health and wellness services we propose. Transforming the present system into an effective Aboriginal system can best be accomplished by developing a network of healing centres and healing lodges. We begin the rationale for our proposal with a description of the kind of agency we propose.

Healing centres

Community health centres or local service centres, as they are sometimes called, are designed to overcome the fragmentation of service delivery for social needs that are interrelated, whether in Aboriginal or non-Aboriginal communities. Different programs for income support, child protection, mental health and home care have evolved separately, often through different departments of government. In cities and towns, government services are often supplemented by voluntary or religious organizations supported by fundraising campaigns. Health centres operating in some provinces are intended to co-ordinate and integrate the different services, so as to avoid duplication or conflict. The range of services available, however, is determined by the agencies involved.

The holistic approach advocated by Aboriginal people goes further. It proposes that services be defined by the needs and situation of the person seeking help. For example, if the health problem presented is an infant's diaper rash, the need could be for an adequate water supply to do laundry; a holistic service would respond accordingly. A redefinition of services is needed to fill the gaps in the current system of delivery.

Aboriginal people speaking at our hearings made a distinction between a healing centre that adopts a holistic approach and a health centre dedicated to reacting to specific problems.

> What I would like to see happening is more healing centres – not treatment centres but healing centres; there are a lot of treatment centres around – established within our own community and the urban centres as well, for young people....We have a lot of treatment centres and a lot of detox centres. And yes, I am talking about a physical building, a healing centre where people can go and go through the processes. Once you take the symptom away – and by the symptom I mean alcohol, drugs – then you have to deal with the root of the problem, because all those other abuses, substance and chemicals, they are a symptom of a much larger problem.
>
> Cindy Sparvier
> Social Worker, Joe Duquette High School
> Saskatoon, Saskatchewan, 27 October 1992

> A treatment centre, [in] my version of what it means to me...is basically for treatment for addictions. A healing centre is to heal oneself and provide healing for others, I guess, on a more personal basis, instead of addictions to drugs and alcohol, that could take in sexual abuse.
>
> Della Maguire
> Drug and Alcohol Counsellor,
> MicMac Native Friendship Centre
> Halifax, Nova Scotia, 4 November 1992

We use the term healing centre in this discussion as a symbol for the approach we are recommending. Presenters used different terms, and Métis people and Inuit may choose other words to describe the resources that we have in mind. The features of such centres were elaborated in presentations made to us.

Community healing centres should be based on traditional Aboriginal concepts of holistic health. While services might differ from community to community, depending on the size and particular needs and priorities of the community, the centres should provide a comprehensive range that might include services usually associated with a medical clinic (for example, basic assessment, preventive, curative, rehabilitative and emergency services). They might also provide child and family support services, addiction and mental health services, and income support and employment services. Many of the presentations described the broad dimensions that a healing centre should encompass:

> The healing house could also be used as a gathering place for: support groups of our elders, adult day programs, social assistance recipients; Al-Anon, Alateen and Alcoholics Anonymous, alcohol and drug counsellors; [programs to end] domestic violence; teen programs, elder programs, men's and women's groups; offenders, long-term care; diabetic programs, women's clinics, AIDS education; [education programs on] fetal alcohol effect and syndrome, eating disorders; homemakers, public and long-term care nurses; general workshops on self-esteem...people returning from treatment centres; art and play therapy; positive Indian parenting programs, healthy baby programs, pre- and post-natal.
>
> Mary Anne Wilson
> Community Health Representative, Skidegate Caregivers
> Prince Rupert, British Columbia, 26 May 1993

Community healing centres would play an important role in providing traditional healing and other culture-based programs. In some cases, traditional healers might wish to use the centre as a place to meet with clients; in others, the centre might refer clients to the healers. In all cases, however, the philosophical approach of the healing centre would be based on the cultural understanding of health in a particular community. In this way, it would provide an important forum for exploring how Aboriginal and western approaches could work together to meet Aboriginal community needs.

To provide the range of services we have discussed, a team approach would be required. Traditional healers, elders, community health representatives, medical interpreters, nurses, addiction counsellors, midwives, therapists, social workers, doctors, psychologists, rehabilitation specialists and support staff might all be required, depending on the circumstances of the community. Aboriginal personnel employed currently in health and social services usually fill front-line positions defined as 'paraprofessional', for example, community health representatives and NNADAP positions. Some senior personnel are Aboriginal, but professional positions are filled predominantly by non-Aboriginal persons who come and go with unsettling frequency. Preparing Aboriginal personnel to staff healing centres is essential to provide the continuity of service and cultural sensitivity central to the strategy. The centres could play an important role in human resources development by providing training and education opportunities for community members, in collaboration with other Aboriginal and non-Aboriginal educational institutions.

In small communities, some of the more specialized service providers would not be required full-time. We foresee a regional system where more specialized staff would reside in one or two of the larger communities and be available to residents in smaller communities on a regular visiting basis. They would be responsible for developing in-service holistic training strategies for general staff such as community health representatives and community health nurses to enhance the range of skills.

We propose that healing centres deliver community-based services. We believe that a strong emphasis on community-based care would reduce the need for institution-based care. Indeed, we have learned from the example of some First Nation communities that have developed holistic, community-based healing services that this view is correct.[250] One of the main reasons for promoting community-based solutions is that most people want services to be provided in their own homes and communities.

Healing centres would provide the point of first contact for members of the community and they would be responsible for providing general care services to meet most community needs. If services could not be provided by the staff of the centre, appropriate arrangements would be made by the staff on behalf of the client. For example, this case management function might involve arranging for specialists to come to the community. In addition, staff would have a role in liaison with agencies and experts outside the community to ensure that orderly access to needed services was assured. The centre, however, would retain overall responsibility for co-ordinating and integrating services to members of the community.

The development of services under Aboriginal control will also make the revitalization of traditional modes of helping more feasible. In Chapter 2 of this volume we talked about the helping networks based on reciprocal responsibility and mutual obligation that functioned in small kin-based societies. These networks still exist in many rural and reserve communities and they hold the promise of reinstating mutual aid for many needs, including in-family or customary care to replace formal foster home placement of children in need of care outside their nuclear family. They also seem particularly suited to reintegrating into communities street youth who are angry and disillusioned with the failure of conventional authoritarian service agencies.

While community healing centres would have an important service delivery role, we see them as having other important functions. These might include

- providing public education about health and healing;
- promoting community involvement in health and healing;
- promoting healthy lifestyles in Aboriginal communities;

- assessing local health and healing needs and contributing to health research on a broader basis;
- participating in local and regional planning;
- collaborating with other programs and agencies on primary prevention strategies (for example, those related to potable water, safe sewer systems or adequate housing);
- providing education and training opportunities for community members, especially youth exploring career options; and
- liaison with Aboriginal and non-Aboriginal health and healing organizations outside the community.

The role of community healing centres in participatory research and planning is particularly important. Centres should have the capacity to monitor the health status of the community; conduct needs assessments; investigate the causes of ill health in Aboriginal communities; evaluate the effectiveness of programs and services; and develop plans and programs for addressing community priorities. In other words, they should play an important role in developing holistic health strategies. Without this capacity, centres could easily become preoccupied with treating symptoms of ill health.

While we have referred to community healing 'centres' throughout the discussion, what we have in mind does not necessarily require the construction of a new building. While the centre, or some of its programs, might be housed in a dedicated health and healing facility, some programs might not require a building at all. In some presentations made to the Commission, healing centres were envisioned in the context of community centres or urban friendship centres:

> I consider it imperative that we institute immediate action to improve on the delivery of services from community centres irrespective of the location on- or off-reserve. When I look at community centres, I see places which were once our traditional gathering places. The gathering fire was the hub of the community; from this place all other activity evolved. I believe that a significant effort needs to be put into making our community centres into living community centres again, community centres which are a continuous beehive of activity, day and night. That whenever people desire to, or need to gather by the fire it will be there. No one need ever be alone and helpless again.
>
> I realize that some people might scoff at this notion and ask where all the money will come from to run such a facility. Money is only a part of the solution. I say that it takes more than wood to build a strong fire, it must also have great spirit. Great leadership is also necessary to keep the fires burning brightly.
>
> In conclusion, it is my opinion that some of the solutions to the process of healing lie in building strong, purposeful gathering places.

That community centres, where they exist, can be strengthened to provide comprehensive health care services which stem from traditional practices and which incorporate western medical know-how. We can best address the issues of healing from those places in the centre of our communities.

Yvon Lamarche, RN
Treatment Co-ordinator,
Georgian Bay Friendship Centre
Orillia, Ontario, 13 May 1993

I am proud to say the Prince George Native Friendship Centre is one of the organizations using the holistic approach as a driving force behind any strategies or interventions we develop on behalf of our constituents. This one-stop shopping approach ensures we can provide services to the entire family in all areas of their lives.

Representation on this committee is from the Carrier-Sekani Tribal Council, the friendship centre, United Native Nations, and the Métis community. Although this committee is still in its infancy...we have been successful just because we have started to communicate.

Dan George
Prince George Native Friendship Centre
Prince George, British Columbia, 31 May 1993

Our community-centred approach reflects the following four philosophies: holistic learning, empowerment, relevance and healing.

Mary Clifford
Director, Health Services,
Prince George Native Friendship Centre
Prince George, British Columbia, 31 May 1993

Some services could be delivered from a number of different sites. Each community will require its own tailor-made solution. However, we wish to underscore the importance of integrating the delivery of services, whatever the physical arrangements for housing them might be.

Healing lodges

To complement the work of community-based healing centres we propose that a network of healing lodges be developed for residential treatment oriented to family and community healing. We are acutely aware of the need for facilities that can provide both treatment and lodging for the many people who become overwhelmed by social, emotional and spiritual problems. There has been a significant development of Aboriginal treatment facilities under the NNADAP program, with approximately 50 treatment facilities currently planned or in operation, and there are some outstanding examples of Aboriginal residential treatment facilities. The Nechi Institute and Poundmaker's Lodge in Alberta, for example, both have an excellent reputation for training counsellors and treating addictions. Yet most First Nations people and Inuit suffering from addictions and substance abuse continue to receive treatment in urban medical facilities, isolated from their communities and cultures. Existing healing lodges are also constrained by narrow funding policies that focus on individual therapy for substance abuse and exclude broader social, emotional and spiritual approaches to healing.

Although we regard the community healing centre as the foundation for transforming the health and social services system, we heard from many presenters that residential healing lodges are also required as 'safe havens' for individuals and families who require some respite from community pressures when they commence their healing journey. Some of our presenters articulated the need for lodges situated in the community:

> We need to do after-care and build after-care resources on the bands to deal with First Nations people coming now, but at the same time we still need a family-oriented treatment centre, so that I don't think it's an either/or situation. I think there is a very great need for both of them.
>
> Sara Williams
> Native Outpatient Centre
> Meysncut Counselling Centre
> Merritt, British Columbia, 5 November 1992

Commissioners also heard that there are a variety of needs for residential treatment and that they cannot always be accommodated in one facility. In some regions, shelters for women who are survivors of domestic violence are urgently needed so that they are not forced to leave children behind and relocate in distant urban centres. It would be inappropriate to expect women in abusive relationships to receive treatment in the same facility as their husbands. Young people might also require a specialized facility where peer counselling could be provided. Young people who are detached from stable families or who have become enmeshed in street life need safe places where they can learn to build connections with caring people. Our proposal respects these diverse and specialized needs, and we urge federal and provincial governments and Aboriginal organizations to ensure that adequate facilities are available.

We also heard that healing approaches that focus on the individual might not meet the needs of Aboriginal families, who require an approach that helps them with the difficult task of rebuilding a healthy family unit. Indeed, we heard that individual approaches to treatment are sometimes as destructive as the historical forces that have created many of the problems, because they continue to isolate the individual from the family. A major concern is the situation where an individual receives treatment and then is forced to return to a dysfunctional family where problems are perpetuated.

As described in Chapter 2, the family is the core institution of Aboriginal society. It is central to all social needs, including governance, economy, education and healing. The Aboriginal view of the significance and centrality of the family is different from non-Aboriginal views, which recognize the importance of the family but often give precedence to individual rights and autonomy over family ties and obligations.

For this reason we propose that Aboriginal communities be given the necessary resources to expand the availability of family-oriented healing lodges. This proposal should not inhibit the continued development of more specialized healing facilities or the continued modification of non-Aboriginal services to meet Aboriginal needs. However, since few family-oriented healing lodges currently exist in the country, emphasis should be placed on developing these important facilities to complement the work of community healing centres.

One example of a family-oriented healing lodge was described in a presentation from the Rama First Nation, where the idea of locating these lodges away from communities was promoted:

> During the past couple of days you have heard some of our speakers talk about and support the healing lodge. Our dream of a Native way of healing. For the past few years the Rama and Area Native Women's Association have had a vision – our own healing lodge located on the Chippewas of Rama First Nation.
>
> At present, there are no Native treatment centres in any of the United Indian Council or tribal council areas. Non-Native treatment centres have little or no knowledge of Native traditional healing methods. As a result, very few Native people, if any, will attend non-Native treatment centres; therefore there is no progress in the healing process and the cycle continues, be it physical, sexual or emotional abuse – not to mention alcohol or substance abuse.
>
> We must have our own healing lodge [which would ideally take] a holistic approach to healing for all family members including extended families. The tragic cycle that many Native families find themselves in will not be broken until we can implement our own healing methods with a facility Native people will have a trust in and feel comfortable in...with our healers, our own elders, our own language, our own treatment centre where we will not be judged because we are different but will be accepted and respected for who we are. This will surely promote the trust needed to enhance our motivation to wellness as well as instill pride in our people and our traditional way of life.

The Chippewas of Rama First Nation has agreed to allocate the land for a healing lodge – a...quiet, peaceful location near the woods and the lake, and at the same time not far from our population. We must have this facility funded. As it has already been said, we have the resources; we just want to use them. We no longer want to feel like we are getting something for nothing. A dollar value is placed on everything Aboriginal people propose to do. We no longer want to feel that we are accepting charity. We must be able to feel that we are accepting our own fair share for all that we have lost. Also, we no longer want to feel that we are a burden to the taxpayers as wards of the Crown.

I don't want to dwell on things past because the past is gone, but my own son committed suicide at the age of 20 years. Last summer my sister died of alcoholism. There are many such stories as these. With our own treatment centre, perhaps some of these tragedies can be avoided. My parents were both alcoholics. We had nowhere they could accept treatment, so the cycle continued.

Until we can achieve our own on-reserve holistic healing lodge, our people will continue on the destructive path of family violence, of substance abuse, of suicides, of identity lost as well as the loss of our language and traditional values.

Joan Simcoe
President, Rama and Area Native Women's Association
Orillia, Ontario, 14 May 1993

The Gwich'in Tribal Council is using $1 million of its land claim settlement to develop the Tl'oondih Healing Camp on the Peel River, 28 miles from Fort McPherson. The camp will provide a residential 42-day substance abuse program for entire families. The healing program will rely on a mixture of traditional and modern treatment methods and involve a two-year program of follow-up counselling once families return to their communities.

Another model that could be adapted to place more emphasis on family-oriented healing is the Strong Earth Woman Lodge in Manitoba:

There is one thing that stays with us as Native people, one strength, and that is the power that comes from the Creator, the power and the strength of the traditional teachings. What we have done at Traverse Bay, together with people from this Sagkeeng First Nation, we have together built the Strong Earth Woman Lodge....

The Strong Earth Woman Lodge is a holistic healing centre based on Native spirituality and traditional teachings. Holistic healing is the healing of the mind, body, emotions and spirit. Traditionally, this is done through sweat lodges, fasting, vision quests, herbal medicines, ceremonial healing with the eagle fan and rattles, in which sacred songs and the drum are key components; traditional teachings at the sacred fire; sharing circles; individualized counselling; and guidance and direction through traditional teachings.

The Strong Earth Woman Lodge incorporates any or all of these into an individualized program based on the needs of each client. All clients are instructed in the seven sacred teachings and are encouraged to seek understanding of the four elements – fire, earth, water and air – and the four directions. The seven sacred teachings are respect, love, courage, humility, honesty, wisdom and truth. These teachings are carried by the spirits of the Buffalo, Eagle, Bear, Wolf, Sabe, which is the Giant, Beaver and Turtle respectively.

The Strong Earth Woman Lodge offers 24-hour care service towards holistic healing for grieving, loss of identity and suicide crisis intervention. Native spirituality fills the spiritual vacuum in the lives of people traumatized by residential schools and allows clients to find healing for sexual, emotional, mental and physical abuses. Strong Earth Woman Lodge is also a place for Native people just wanting to learn their culture. Although the lodge is based on Native spirituality, we welcome people from all faiths and from all nations. The recommended lengths of stay are four-, eight-, or twelve-day periods or as required.

The lodge is located on traditionally sacred grounds 70 miles northeast of Winnipeg and is run by Native women and men under the direction of the Creator.

Connie Eyolfson
Strong Earth Woman Lodge
Fort Alexander, Manitoba, 30 October 1992

The development of healing centres and healing lodges can begin now, with a commitment from federal, provincial and territorial governments to collaborate with Aboriginal community governments and organizations to make room for systematic change.

RECOMMENDATION

The Commission recommends that

Healing Centres **3.3.6**
and Lodges Federal, provincial and territorial governments collaborate with Aboriginal nations, organizations or communities, as appropriate, to

(a) develop a system of healing centres to provide direct services, referral and access to specialist services;

(b) develop a network of healing lodges to provide residential services oriented to family and community healing;

(c) develop and operate healing centres and lodges under Aboriginal control;

(d) mandate healing centres and lodges to provide integrated health and social services in culturally appropriate forms; and

(e) make the service network available to First Nations, Inuit and Métis communities, in rural and urban settings, on an equitable basis.

Transforming the service system

The current array of services

As we begin to imagine the contours of a system of healing centres and lodges, it is important to remember that we are not starting with a blank slate. There is a large and complex array of services supported by federal and provincial governments that Aboriginal communities and service personnel have modified to some extent to fit their needs. However, control of these services continues to be vested in external agencies and bureaucracies; narrow programmatic interests frustrate attempts to organize holistic responses to need; and variations in available services reflect systematic inequities rather than adaptations to community diversity.

Reserves and Inuit communities benefit from federal support of targeted health and social services. In 1994, Health Canada spent nearly one billion dollars on health care for people living on-reserve and in Inuit communities. In addition to providing non-insured health benefits, these funds supported various facilities described as health stations, nursing stations and health centres in more than 500 reserves and Inuit communities. Virtually all reserves and Inuit communities have similar facilities. Only communities with very small populations (under 100) do not have a health facility with permanent staff. These facilities are usually staffed by nurses and community health representatives (CHRs) and supported by family physicians and other specialists who visit the community periodically. Almost all CHRs and an increasing number of nurses are Aboriginal. In principle, at least, they provide a combination of primary care, public health and health promotion services to all community residents.

The federal government also supports some 50 residential treatment centres and seven hospitals scattered across the provinces, providing services almost exclusively to First Nations and Inuit patients. Many of the treatment centres are located within First Nations' territories. They are staffed largely by Aboriginal people and incorporate many of the principles of holistic, culturally based healing that we have described.

Many of the community health facilities were constructed in the 1970s or earlier. They range from old and decrepit clinics with limited capacity to provide a healing program, to modern, fully equipped health centres with an excellent capacity for primary medical care and general public health programs. In addition to requiring general renovation to meet contemporary standards, older facilities are crowded and unable to provide an expanded range of healing programs. For example, a representative of the Skidegate Caregivers' Society, speaking in Prince Rupert, British Columbia, described her community's problem with inadequate facilities:

> Skidegate has been successful in obtaining funds to address some of our health and social needs but is facing the problem of finding space. Our health centre and band office are inadequate to serve a safe, therapeutic, culturally sensitive program. There are no other rental spaces available in Skidegate and, as a result, we have had to rent facilities off-reserve....
>
> The health centre was built close to 20 years now and there is room for two CHRs, a nurse and maybe a doctor's clinic. It's in a trailer and the walls are not even – it's not a good place for counselling.
>
> When we hold workshops, we rent whatever space is available – the church, the community hall, wherever we can find space....We've had to rent office space for the counsellor out of the reserve because...the health centre's walls are so thin you can hear through the walls....There is no money for capital and there's no money for a building....
>
> Mary Anne Wilson
> Skidegate Caregivers
> Prince Rupert, British Columbia, 26 May 1993

In the majority of Aboriginal communities, there is a foundation of basic services on which to build, although adequacy varies from one community to another. However, efforts to achieve a holistic approach to healing are frustrated by fragmented delivery structures and inappropriately trained personnel who are often ill-equipped to mobilize the strengths of the community in support of whole health. The challenge in this context is to transform the current system, building on the experience and investments already in place. This will require that

- resources be provided to Aboriginal governments to identify the changes necessary to transform existing programs and facilities;
- Health Canada's transfer policy be revised to reflect this new policy focus on community healing centres;

- federal, provincial, territorial and Aboriginal governments revise current health and social services policy to facilitate integrated service delivery; and
- federal, provincial, territorial and Aboriginal governments make additional resources available to facilitate the transformation of existing health and social service facilities into community healing centres and lodges.

Métis and other Aboriginal people residing off-reserve in cities or rural communities have not benefited from federally supported service delivery, although the non-insured health benefits program has been available to some status Indians living off-reserve and Inuit outside their northern communities. For Aboriginal people living in rural areas, services are often inaccessible because of distance and inappropriate because they ignore social and cultural aspects of health and disease. A Métis presenter at Paddle Prairie, Alberta, described the situation in his district:

> The Paddle Prairie Settlement stretches almost 30 miles along the Mackenzie Highway and is the same across. With the populations of Key River and Carcajou, there are almost 1,000 people living here, all of whom have been promised by the provincial government that they can have equal access to health services as any other Albertan.
>
> But people have to travel to see a physician, dentist...[and for] all of our other needs. The health unit supplies home care visits and a nurse for two days a week to the hamlet of Paddle Prairie....
>
> All of this leaves us with some confusion and a very fragmented health delivery system. Needless to say, this means extra cost for our people in travel...accommodation and meals, and often loss of pay. That is while they have to leave their jobs to travel to Grande Prairie or Edmonton. We think this is discrimination.
>
> John Crisp
Paddle Prairie Metis Settlement
High Level, Alberta, 29 October 1992

For Aboriginal people in urban areas, the problems are more often failure to make contact with needed services, the lack of culturally appropriate services, and the absence of Aboriginal personnel who can overcome barriers to effective service.

Thus, Aboriginal people who do not live in communities that receive federally funded services tend to be served inadequately, sometimes to a severe extent. The evidence presented in our hearings and in the research studies and intervener participation reports prepared for us indicates that they suffer social and economic disadvantages that undermine health and well-being, experience social exclusion and barriers to effective service, and have the same concerns about the need for holistic, community-based services.

As noted earlier, most statistics refer only to Indian people on-reserve and those served by federal programs. Consequently, little information is available on the priority health needs of Métis and other Aboriginal people in cities, towns and rural areas. Transformation of the service system for these populations must start with needs identification and planning. Aboriginal healing centres should be designed to provide holistic, culture-based services in the context of primary health care and health promotion and co-ordinate access to other non-Aboriginal health and social services. Métis and other Aboriginal communities in urban and rural areas should have the opportunity to develop healing centres and healing lodges as part of a national effort to restore and maintain Aboriginal health. However, in view of the general lack of service infrastructure off-reserve, the first requirement is resources for needs assessment and planning.

In Volume 4, Chapter 2 we described the many initiatives undertaken by women in the area of health and healing. They struggle to survive with uncertain funding, draining the energies of volunteers and underpaid staff. Demonstration projects and short-lived programs often have a great deal to teach, through both their successes and their difficulties. New initiatives should make maximum use of them and the dedication and expertise of the women who organized them, as well as the networks that continue to channel information and support new endeavours.

The beginnings of change

In many communities, a shift in the orientation of health and social services is already under way. Earlier we documented examples of Aboriginal communities where innovations in local service delivery are beginning to reflect holistic characteristics, Aboriginal control and local diversity and extending the range of services to provide more equitable access. The push for change and the exploration of more holistic strategies have been carried forward by federal and provincial governments as well as by Aboriginal people. Here we have in mind Health Canada's transfer initiative, selected provincial initiatives, the devolution of responsibility to community governments, and a new federal program for building healthy communities, all of which have points of congruence with the systematic change we propose.

In 1986, the federal government introduced the health transfer initiative, designed to transfer administrative authority for community health services over time to reserves in the provinces. Aboriginal people in the territories became involved in a similar transfer process through the devolution of responsibility for health services to the territorial governments. Inuit and some First Nations people in Quebec achieved a considerable level of community control over health and social services through the James Bay and Northern Quebec Agreement and the Northeastern Quebec Agreement. These initiatives promise to provide opportunities for Aboriginal communities to assume greater responsibility for developing health services and programs at the community and regional levels. Views on the health transfer program were presented earlier in the chapter.

The research we commissioned and the briefs and submissions we received leave us singularly impressed with the extent to which health programs in communities that have participated in transfer initiatives increasingly reflect Aboriginal priorities. First Nations and Inuit authorities at the community and regional levels have responded creatively to a limited opportunity and have begun to transform health facilities and programs along the lines we envision. Indeed, the innovations introduced in some communities point the way to approaches we endorse in this chapter. Creativity in Aboriginal services is dampened, nevertheless, by policy and funding constraints imposed from outside Aboriginal communities.

Provincial governments have also recognized the value of decentralization, community involvement and integrated service delivery. As early as 1971, following the recommendations of the Castonguay-Nepveu commission, Quebec established a network of local community service centres for the integrated delivery of health and social services. They are intended to encourage teams of physicians, social workers, nurses, dentists, technicians and others to provide co-ordinated front-line services through facilities that ideally should have high levels of community involvement. The goal of an integrated service delivery system has never been achieved, however. Community health clinics continue to operate in most provinces, but they are at the margins rather than the centre of the health care system, which continues to revolve around the authority and professional norms of physicians.

In the past several years, provincial governments have begun to re-examine this approach to health care in an attempt to gain some measure of control over escalating expenditures. Central to these initiatives is the development of regional health authorities, with responsibility for rationalizing and administering health and social services, and the promotion of community health clinics with non-medical personnel (such as nurse practitioners, midwives and mental health counsellors) providing a full range of integrated health and social services.

Although most provincial reforms are directed to the general population, several provincial governments have recently launched similar initiatives for Aboriginal communities. Ontario announced its Aboriginal Healing and Wellness Policy in June 1994. It adopts a status-blind approach to developing health and healing centres for Aboriginal communities. Five new healing lodges and 10 new Aboriginal health access centres will be funded around the province. While this initiative will have particular benefits for Aboriginal people in urban areas, it will also provide resources to First Nations communities to enhance community healing centres. The program has brought together resources from the provincial ministries of health and community and social services, the women's directorate and the Native affairs secretariat. It fosters partnerships between Aboriginal people of various status categories on- and off-reserve and the creative use of band program funds, federal capital allocations and provincial operating grants.

In some parts of the country, Aboriginal organizations have initiated negotiations with the federal government to create new regional health systems under the jurisdiction and control of Aboriginal communities. For example, the Health Framework Agreement for First Nations People in Manitoba, negotiated in 1994 by the Assembly of Manitoba Chiefs and the federal health minister, was intended to provide a framework through which new structures and systems could be developed to implement the goal of a First Nations health system in Manitoba. It was not signed, however, because of federal reluctance to include in the agreement reference to health as a treaty right. For many First Nations, who look to treaties as the legal foundation of their relationship with Canada, the continuing refusal of the federal government to recognize health care as a treaty right will constrain further development of health and social systems. (For a full discussion of treaties as the principal instrument structuring the relationship of treaty nations with the Canadian state, see Volume 2, Chapter 2.)

At the district level, the Meadow Lake Tribal Council provides an example of how self-government and community healing are inextricably linked. In its submission to the Commission describing their plan for a First Nation-controlled health care system, the council states: "The intention is to ground the health system in a model of health that focuses on healing, personal and community development, and prevention". Programs serving nine communities will be managed by the tribal council through self-government agreements with the federal government, and community healing services will be administered through formal agreements between the tribal council and each member community.[251]

In some instances, the development of a system of healing centres and lodges could be undertaken by existing regional health organizations that have adapted already to the geographic and cultural conditions of the region and the jurisdiction and regulatory authority of the province or territory. The Nunavik regional government of northern Quebec is one example. The Labrador Inuit Health Commission is another. As of March 1996, a total of 195 tribal councils or multi-community agencies were involved in the transfer of health services. Of these, 66 projects representing 141 First Nations communities were the subject of signed transfer agreements with Health Canada, and 129 agencies or councils representing 237 communities were engaged in pre-transfer projects. In addition, Health Canada is funding special initiatives by the Labrador Inuit Health Commission, the Union of New Brunswick Indians and the Grand Council of Treaty 8 First Nations.[252]

The federal initiative announced in September 1994, Building Healthy Communities, promises to provide $243 million over five years to assist First Nations and Inuit communities in developing community health facilities and services. It also intends to provide for a more integrated approach to funding where program-specific funding can be rolled into integrated community-based health services agreements. These would enable First Nations and Inuit communities to target resources to priority needs. Health Canada has also announced that non-insured health benefits will be transferred to some First Nations and Inuit communities on a pilot-project basis, which should also provide greater flexibility in developing community-based services.

It is evident, then, that there are numerous instruments and relationships now in existence or in negotiation through which our proposals could be implemented.

However, the fragmentation of programs supported by each level of government and the lack of co-ordination between federal and provincial governments create serious impediments to the effectiveness and cost-efficiency of programs. Recognition of Aboriginal jurisdiction in health and social services will provide a basis for holistic approaches to healing services. Within current jurisdictions, barriers to integrated services and intergovernmental collaboration should be removed.

RECOMMENDATIONS

The Commission recommends that

Laws, Regulations and Funding to Support Integrated Services

3.3.7

Federal, provincial and territorial governments collaborate with Aboriginal nations, regional Aboriginal service agencies, community governments and Aboriginal organizations, as appropriate, to adapt legislation, regulations and funding to promote

(a) integrated service delivery that transcends restricted service mandates of separate ministries and departments;

(b) collaboration and shared effort between federal, provincial/territorial and local governments; and

(c) the pooling of resources flowing from federal, provincial, territorial, municipal or Aboriginal sources.

Transform Current Services

3.3.8

Aboriginal organizations, regional planning and administrative bodies and community governments currently administering health and social services transform current programs and services into more holistic delivery systems that integrate or co-ordinate separate services.

Implementing a new system

Developing healing centres to serve Métis and other Aboriginal people in rural and urban areas will involve creating new organizational structures and redistributing resources from existing provincial and municipal institutions. As well, new resources will be required to deliver services where now they are unavailable.

The development of regional healing lodges, ideally serving all Aboriginal people who share history, culture or current affiliation in a regional community, might involve a significant planning period. Current residential services could expand their duties to address a broader range of needs and partially fill the gap we have identified in family and community healing.

Table 3.14
Communities With 1,000 or More Persons Who Reported Single Aboriginal Origins, 1991

Newfoundland	Quebec	Yukon
Urban	**Urban**	**Urban**
Happy Valley-Goose Bay	Chicoutimi-Jonquière	Whitehorse*
	Gatineau	
	Hull	
	Laval	
	Montreal*	

Manitoba	Saskatchewan	Alberta
Urban	**Urban**	**Urban**
Brandon	North Battleford	Calgary*
Thompson	Prince Albert*	Edmonton*
Winnipeg*	Regina*	Fort McMurray
	Saskatoon*	Grande Prairie
		Lethbridge
Non-Urban	**Non-Urban**	**Non-Urban**
Division 19	Ile-a-la-Crosse	Improvement District 17*
Division 22	La Loche	Improvement District 18*

British Columbia	Ontario	Northwest Territories
Urban	**Urban**	**Urban**
Kamloops	Brantford	Inuvik
Port Alberni	Hamilton	Iqaluit
Prince George	London	Yellowknife
Prince Rupert	Ottawa	**Non-Urban**
Surrey	St. Catharines-Niagara	Arviat
Vancouver*	Sault Ste. Marie	Baker Lake
Victoria	Sudbury	Fort Smith
	Thunder Bay	Pangnirtung
	Toronto*	Rae-Edzo
		Rankin Inlet

Notes:
* Areas with 3,000 persons or more who reported a single Aboriginal origin.

Statistics Canada defines urban as an area with a population of at least 1,000 and a population density of at least 400 per square kilometre at the previous census. Rural is defined as small towns, villages and other populated places with populations under 1,000 according to the previous census; rural fringe areas or census metropolitan areas and census agglomerations that may contain estate lots and other non-farm land uses, as well as intensive agricultural land uses; agricultural areas; and remote and wilderness areas. Both urban and rural areas listed in this table exclude reserves and settlements.

Source: Statistics Canada, 1991 Census, Aboriginal population by census subdivisions and census metropolitan areas, 1994.

The location and catchment area for particular healing centres should be determined through a planning process involving local residents. We suggest that rural communities with an Aboriginal population of 250 should be eligible to participate in the planning process and that a more dispersed rural Aboriginal population of 1,000 should be eligible as well. In cities and towns, a base Aboriginal population of 1,000 should establish eligibility for planning purposes. A list of 44 urban communities and four non-urban districts with a minimum of 1,000 Aboriginal people who reported only Aboriginal ancestry is shown in Table 3.14.[253]

Whether urban or rural, healing centres will vary in size, level of staffing and type of services, depending on the size of the population served. For example, in Prince Edward Island and New Brunswick, provinces with small Aboriginal populations, urban centres might function more as referral and co-ordinating units with some capacity to provide culture-based services. In cities such as Montreal, Toronto, Winnipeg and Regina, centres should provide a full range of health and healing services on a more autonomous basis. In locations where on-reserve and off-reserve populations live in close proximity, services could be shared.

In our recommendations on urban service delivery (see Volume 4, Chapter 7), we propose that urban services be provided as a rule on a status-blind basis. We acknowledge, however, that the Métis Nation and treaty nations in the prairie provinces have a history of distinct development and that it might not be feasible yet to establish healing centres that serve Métis and First Nations people together. However, for reasons of efficiency and economy, as well as shared interests, we urge all Aboriginal communities to collaborate in the development of urban healing centres and regional lodges.

RECOMMENDATION

The Commission recommends that

Planning and
Needs Assessment

3.3.9

Federal, provincial and territorial governments, in consultation with Aboriginal nations and urban communities of interest, co-operate to establish procedures and funding to support needs assessment and planning initiatives by Métis and other Aboriginal collectivities, in rural and urban settings, to

(a) form interim planning groups for rural settlements with a minimum of 250 Aboriginal residents, or catchment areas, whether urban or rural, with a minimum of 1,000 residents;

(b) compile an inventory of existing services, organizations and networks directed to meet Aboriginal needs, from which to build on existing strengths and ensure continuity of effort; and

(c) prepare plans to develop, operate and house healing centres, considering the goal of equitable access by Aboriginal people wherever they reside, the historical pattern of distinct Métis and treaty nation development in the prairie provinces, the availability and adaptability of municipal and provincial services, and the cost and efficiency of services.

In developing healing lodges, it should be possible to adapt or modify existing residential programs and facilities, but clearly there will be a need for new capital development as well as incremental service delivery costs to fill the gap in services oriented to family and community healing. Early identification of pressing needs will be required, along with formation of regional planning bodies to co-ordinate effort. Long-term budget forecasting will be necessary to ensure that facilities are strategically located and, in the operational phase, adequately equipped and funded.

The number and location of healing lodges across Canada would emerge as a result of regional planning. Since we anticipate that both federal and provincial governments will contribute to establishing and operating healing lodges, it might be most feasible to carry out planning on a provincial basis or, in the case of the Atlantic provinces, on a multi-provincial basis.

Recommendations

The Commission recommends that

Regional Healing Lodges

3.3.10

Aboriginal, federal, provincial and territorial governments, as appropriate, collaborate on regional initiatives to develop healing lodges providing residential services oriented to family and community healing, with priority being given to

(a) needs assessment and planning that reflect regional Aboriginal initiative and responsiveness to the diversity of cultures and communities;

(b) services broadly inclusive of all Aboriginal people resident in a region or associated with the nations of the region;

(c) institutions that collaborate with and complement other Aboriginal institutions and services, particularly healing centres delivering integrated health and social services; and

(d) governance structures consistent with emerging forms of Aboriginal self-government in the region.

Capital and
Operating Budgets

3.3.11

Aboriginal, federal, provincial and territorial governments incorporate in funding agreements plans for capital development and operating costs of a network of healing lodges.

Governance of health and healing institutions

Health and healing institutions deliver services under the authority of provincial legislation. Implementing the healing centres strategy might require arrangements to do things differently or exemption from certain regulations. One example is legislative recognition of Aboriginal custom adoption in the Northwest Territories.[254] Another is partial exemption from confidentiality rules that have prevented adoptees of status Indian origin from learning their identity and exercising their Aboriginal rights. In some provinces, Indian adoptees are entitled to be informed of their status on reaching the age of majority, while adoptees of other origins do not have access to information that identifies their origins.

With the concurrence of the provinces and the support of the federal government in respect of Inuit and Indian people on-reserve receiving federal services, it is possible to begin to implement the healing centres strategy now. For Métis communities and Aboriginal people off-reserve in rural and urban settings, change is impeded by the policy vacuum. Provincial governments continue to resist developing or financing Aboriginal-specific programs, and the federal government declines to exercise its authority concerning off-reserve services.

In Volume 4, Chapter 7, we propose federal and provincial sharing of responsibility to break through the barriers to restructuring services for Métis and other Aboriginal people. We propose that provincial and territorial governments be responsible for financing services for Aboriginal people off-reserve that are ordinarily available to other residents. Provinces should also undertake the cost of making these programs appropriate for Aboriginal residents. The federal government would be responsible for the costs of self-government on Aboriginal territory, including health and social services delivered by Aboriginal governments. It would also be responsible for Aboriginal government services and treaty entitlements outside Aboriginal territory where these exceed benefits generally available. Given the picture of disadvantage detailed in this chapter, we propose further that the costs of affirmative action to compensate for historical disadvantage be shared by federal, provincial and territorial governments on a formula basis reflecting fiscal capacity. (For details, see Volume 4, Chapter 7.)

The urgent work of restoring the health of Aboriginal people should be undertaken without delay. The readiness of federal and provincial governments to support a new health strategy, which Aboriginal people have advocated and which we endorse, will be among the first tests of commitment to restructuring the relationship between Aboriginal people and the rest of Canada. The House of Commons Standing Committee on Health has also urged the federal government to "take the lead in co-ordinating and implementing [a comprehensive] plan of action for Aboriginal wellness" in collaboration with provincial and territorial governments and national Aboriginal organizations.[255]

Healing centres and lodges will operate under the authority of federal, provincial or territorial governments in the immediate future and will derive their authority from Aboriginal nation governments when self-government is established in relevant territories. Under any of these jurisdictions, the healing centre or lodge would be guided in the fulfilment of its responsibilities by a board of directors drawn from the community or communities served. The board should represent the diversity of community members, paying particular attention to include in decision making the voices of women, youth, elders and people with disabilities. It should ensure that ethical practices appropriate to the culture are followed by staff, administration and political bodies and that appeal mechanisms are in place so that persons who believe they have been ill-served or injured have recourse.

One of the strengths of the proposed system will be its capacity to obtain specialist services and residential care on behalf of collectivities larger than single communities, sharing expertise within the Aboriginal planning community and achieving economies of scale. Co-ordination of regional services will require the establishment of planning bodies, which should include representation from relevant governments, mainstream and other service institutions affected by regional planning, and community members, in particular women, youth, elders and people with disabilities. The components of a regional service system that should be represented in regional planning bodies are shown in Figure 3.10.

The Commission assumes that health and social services will be designated as a core area for the exercise of self-government and that they will be among the first areas of jurisdiction to be occupied by Aboriginal governments. The major difference between service delivery under provincial jurisdiction and under self-government will be that Aboriginal nations will enact the laws and draft the regulations establishing conditions and standards. Intergovernmental transfers will supplement revenues from within the Aboriginal nation to support services. With implementation of the human resources development strategy set out in the next section, we anticipate visible and progressive movement toward staffing service, administration and planning positions with Aboriginal personnel.

We urge federal, provincial and territorial governments and Aboriginal governments and organizations to support regional planning bodies, to bring together the interests and needs of communities that have the prospect of coalescing into self-governing nations or confederacies of nations. With co-opera-

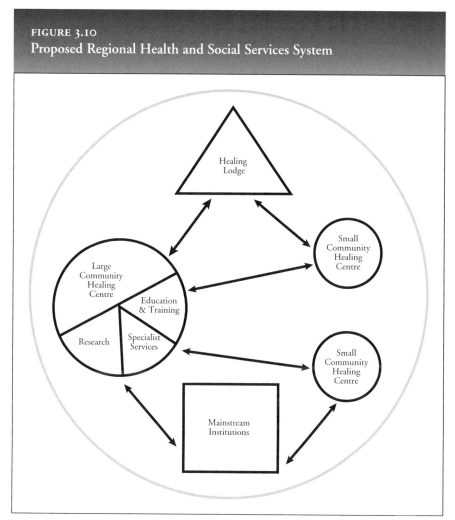

FIGURE 3.10
Proposed Regional Health and Social Services System

tion between Aboriginal and non-Aboriginal authorities and among Aboriginal constituencies, healing centres and lodges can begin to advance the long-term goal of achieving whole health for all Aboriginal people.

RECOMMENDATION

The Commission recommends that

Regional Planning **3.3.12**
Bodies Federal, provincial and territorial governments, and Aboriginal governments and organizations, support the assumption of responsibility for planning health and social services by regional

Aboriginal agencies and councils where these now operate, and the formation of regional Aboriginal planning bodies in new areas, to promote

(a) equitable access to appropriate services by all Aboriginal people;

(b) strategic deployment of regional resources; and

(c) co-operative effort between Aboriginal communities and communities of interest, consistent with the emergence of nation governments and confederacies.

3.3 Human Resources Strategy

Developing Aboriginal human resources is essential to ensure the success of the new approaches to health and healing we recommend. Without the necessary Aboriginal administrators and service providers, it will not be possible to improve Aboriginal health and social conditions. There must be a substantial and continuing commitment to develop the capacity of Aboriginal people to provide health and social services. This capacity building should be an important part of the relationship between Canadian governments, mainstream service agencies and Aboriginal governments and organizations.

As discussed more fully in the education chapter in this volume and in the governance and economic development chapters in Volume 2, several broad strategies are required to foster the development of Aboriginal human resources:

- increasing the capacity and number of education and training programs that are provided by Aboriginal institutions;
- improving the contribution of mainstream education and training programs to the development of Aboriginal human resources;
- improving Aboriginal students' ability to pursue education and training through the provision of financial and other supports; and
- improving the cultural appropriateness and effectiveness of education and training programs to meet the needs of Aboriginal students and communities.

Our purpose here is to outline some of the ways these broad strategies can be implemented to increase the number of Aboriginal people involved in the health and social service professions.[256] Progress in this sphere is vital to the well-being of Aboriginal people, and current efforts to address the problem are inadequate. Although many reports and task forces have called for improvement, progress has been very slow.[257]

While the provision of health and healing services should not be seen as the exclusive domain of health and social service professionals, many aspects of the planning, delivery and evaluation of health and healing services do require the expertise of individuals with formal training. Therefore, part of the plan for Aboriginal health and healing must consider how these needs can be met.

The current status of Aboriginal human resources in health and healing

There was unanimity among Aboriginal representatives and representatives of professional associations and service organizations appearing before the Commission that improvements are needed in the recruitment, training and retention of Aboriginal people in the health and social services professions to meet current and future needs:

> Both the federal and provincial governments need to recognize that we do need resources in order to better ourselves. We need to have the human resources – First Nations human resources.
>
> Phil Hall
> Alderman, District of Chilliwack
> Victoria, British Columbia, 22 May 1992

> We find that the key to better integration of health and social services in Aboriginal communities is an increase in the number of health professionals originating from these communities....The Royal Commission should recommend that priority be given to training programs that are accessible to and realistic for Aboriginal peoples. [translation]
>
> Huguette Blouin
> L'Association des hôpitaux du Québec
> Montreal, Quebec, 16 November 1993

> Services [are] obstructed by the shortage of necessary public health workers. The preferred avenue for the improvement of health status is an increase in the number of qualified and skilled Aboriginal public health workers in Canada providing public health services to Aboriginal communities.
>
> Janet Maclachlan
> Canadian Public Health Association
> Ottawa, Ontario, 17 November 1993

> We must seek control of our medical services and social welfare/child welfare programs. By doing so, we must also begin training of Aboriginals in all professional capacities involved with these programs. A mandate for the beginning of the next millennium must be a national educational program designed to capture the hearts, minds, and spirits of Aboriginal youth and provide them with the

way to become obstetricians, pediatricians, psychologists, nurses, social workers, [addictions] counsellors, [and] therapists of the future.

April Prince
All Nations Youth Council
Prince George, British Columbia, 1 June 1993

The Canadian Medical Association recommends that the Canadian government...increase access and support programs to encourage Aboriginal students to enter health careers.

Dr. Richard J. Kennedy
Canadian Medical Association
Ottawa, Ontario, 17 November 1993

I would like to see more emphasis on training of Aboriginal people for the health field. There have been a number of Aboriginal people who have gone into nursing. There have been some who have gone into social work, and very few who have gone into medicine.

Dr. Fred W. Baker
Canadian Paediatric Society
Ottawa, Ontario, 18 November 1993

The impact of Aboriginal hospital workers has been tested at Ville-Marie and other hospitals. The results clearly demonstrate improved accessibility of services...we support the training of Aboriginal community workers and social workers to provide community and social consultations and intervention services within the communities. [translation]

Ghislain Beaulé
Research Officer
Regional health and social services board
of Abitibi-Témiscamingue
Val d'Or, Quebec, 30 November 1992

We need to involve our own people in our own way with our own human resources.

Gerri ManyFingers
Calgary, Alberta
26 May 1993

Regrettably, very little information has been collected systematically about the number of Aboriginal professionals involved in health and healing services. The Canadian Public Health Association, for example, in a recently published study on the recruitment and training of public health workers, described the current state of information in the following terms:

"We're Not Sure." This was the common response when key informants were asked if they knew the current numbers of Aboriginal
public health workers and/or Aboriginal students studying health care
in Canada.[258]

Nonetheless, the Commission has been able to collect some information, and
it confirms that there is significant and widespread under-representation. Several
examples illustrate the point.

In 1990, it was estimated that fewer than 20 Aboriginal physicians practised in Canada.[259] In 1993, there were about 40 Aboriginal physicians,[260] and
22 Aboriginal students were enrolled in medical schools.[261] The Native Physicians
Association reports 51 self-identified Aboriginal physicians.[262]

We estimate that the ratio of Aboriginal physicians to Aboriginal population is approximately 1:33,000. The corresponding ratio in the general population is about 1:515.[263] We estimate that only about 0.1 per cent of physicians
in Canada are Aboriginal. These figures show that Aboriginal people are seriously
under-represented in the medical profession.

Figures on medical school enrolment indicate that there will be about 35
Aboriginal physicians graduating over the next five years. While many will
practise medicine, others will serve as consultants and administrators. While these
new graduates will almost double the number of Aboriginal physicians in
Canada, it could take five decades at the present rate of change to achieve equitable representation of Aboriginal people in the medical profession. This disparity
must be addressed.

Similar under-representation is evident in other health and social services
professions. In nursing, for example, a recent survey conducted by the Aboriginal
Nurses Association of Canada revealed only about 300 Aboriginal registered
nurses in Canada, although other estimates have been higher.[264] The number does
not appear to have changed much over the past few years. According to recent
statistics provided by the Canadian Nurses Association, there are 264,339 registered nurses in Canada, of whom 235,630 are employed in nursing.[265]
Therefore, only about 0.1 per cent of registered nurses in Canada are Aboriginal.
Moreover, there are only three Aboriginal dieticians in Canada,[266] and only
about 70 Aboriginal dental therapists.[267] Similar information is unavailable for
many other professional groups, because most do not keep records of the
number of Aboriginal practitioners.

The medical services branch of Health Canada, which supports the
employment of substantial numbers of Aboriginal people in health services, combines the staffing numbers of Aboriginal and non-Aboriginal personnel, with the
result that Aboriginal participation cannot be stated definitively. However, we
know that most community health representatives and most counsellors
employed in the National Native Alcohol and Drug Abuse Program are

Aboriginal. Field staff in these two programs in 1993-94 numbered 616 and 465 respectively.[268] During the same period, 521 nurses were also in the field, the majority employed directly by the medical services branch and 118 employed by Indian bands. An additional 381 field staff were employed as clerk/interpreters, caretakers and housekeepers.

The concentration of Aboriginal personnel in paraprofessional positions is indicated in data collected by Statistics Canada in the 1991 Aboriginal peoples survey (see Table 3.15). Of 6,645 Aboriginal persons reporting that they were employed in medicine and health, 5,535 cited nursing/therapy related assistants as their occupation. If the figure from the Aboriginal Nurses Association survey is taken as definitive (about 300 Aboriginal nurses), then we can infer that the vast majority of Aboriginal people in this category are related assistants.

Just over 3 per cent of the Aboriginal labour force reported occupations in medicine and health, compared to 5.2 per cent of the Canadian population. An additional 3.3 per cent – 6,980 persons – reported social work occupations. These include welfare administrators, child welfare, day care and home care workers, and the staff of women's shelters and family violence projects. When we examine the proportion of the Aboriginal labour force involved in the combined categories of health and social services by industry, including all occupations associated with medical and social services, we see 8.8 per cent of the Aboriginal labour force, compared to 9 per cent of the Canadian labour force as a whole.

Another analysis treats education and health services as a single category. When persons employed in these sectors are considered as a proportion of the employed labour force, we see that 15.8 per cent of the Aboriginal labour force and 15.4 per cent of the non-Aboriginal labour force is employed in health and education services.[269] When we consider that professional employment in these sectors requires higher education, that most services staffed by Aboriginal people are on-reserve or in Inuit communities, that only 0.9 per cent of Indian people on-reserve hold degrees, and that the number of Inuit holding degrees is too small to register statistically,[270] it is clear that a major effort is needed in education and training.

The practical experience and cultural awareness of Aboriginal CHRs and NNADAP counsellors are highly valued by Aboriginal people. They realize, however, that if they want to assume control of health and social services at all levels, they will need greater access to higher education and professional training. If half the Aboriginal people in health and social service occupations were to advance their qualifications to assume professional and supervisory roles now filled by non-Aboriginal personnel, training would be needed for some 6,700 persons.[271]

Since most Aboriginal services are currently located on-reserve and in Inuit communities, staffing new Aboriginal services in urban and rural off-reserve settings will require more trained personnel. To be more responsive to

TABLE 3.15
Participation in Health and Social Services, Aboriginal and Non-Aboriginal Populations Age 15+, 1991

	Aboriginal Identity		Non-Aboriginal	
	#	%	#	%
By major field of study				
Health professions/science/technology	8,825	10.4[1]	884,490	11.8
Social sciences[2]	9,745	11.5[1]	659,950	8.6
By occupation				
Medicine and health	6,445	3.3[3]		5.2
Nursing/therapy-related assistants	5,535			
Health diagnosing and treating	115			
Other occupations in medicine and health				
Social services	6,980	3.3[3]		—
By industry				
Health and social services		8.8[4]		9.0

Notes:

— = not available.

1. Population base is Aboriginal people age 15 or older who have completed a post-secondary program of any type.

2. Including anthropology, archeology, area studies, economics, geography, law, environmental studies, political science, psychology, sociology, social work.

3. Population base is Aboriginal people age 15 or older in the labour force.

4. Includes clerks, drivers, support staff.

Source: Statistics Canada, Major Fields of Study of Postsecondary Graduates, catalogue no. 93-329, p. 8; Statistics Canada, 1991 Census and Aboriginal Peoples Survey, custom tabulations; and Kerr et al., "Canada's Aboriginal Population, 1981-1991", research study prepared for RCAP (1995), Tables 4.1 and 4.2.

Aboriginal clientele, mainstream institutions will also require an increase of Aboriginal personnel. Raising the number of Aboriginal people employed in mainstream institutions depends on raising the number of appropriately trained candidates. An additional 6,500 trainees to staff urban and off-reserve services and to fill positions in mainstream institutions is a reasonable projection. We therefore propose that governments and educational institutions undertake to train 10,000 Aboriginal people in health and social services, including professional and managerial roles, over the next decade.

Health and social sciences are already prominent among the courses of study chosen by Aboriginal people pursuing post-secondary education. Our analysis indicates that of Aboriginal people who have completed a post-secondary program, 8,825 (10 per cent) have studied in the field of health sciences, and

9,745 (11.5 per cent) have studied social sciences (see Table 3.15). The challenge is to shift the level and length of study from short-term certificate training to long-term professional degree training.

Over time, Aboriginal institutions will become more involved in developing training programs or modules of study to complement technical training. Non-Aboriginal institutions and governments that fund them will continue to play a major role in meeting the goals of Aboriginal human resources development.

Difficulties created by the low number of Aboriginal professionals are compounded by the manner in which these scarce resources are distributed. Two problems are of particular concern to us. First, for a variety of personal and professional reasons, many Aboriginal professionals do not practise in Aboriginal communities.[272] The Native Physicians Association estimates that only 20 to 25 per cent of their members has a practice involving 50 per cent Aboriginal clients or more.[273] Of the estimated 60 Aboriginal nurses in Quebec, only one-third work with Aboriginal people.[274] We believe that similar patterns of distribution exist throughout Canada. They affect Inuit particularly. For example, we were told that there were no Inuit registered nurses serving on Baffin Island.[275] In addition:

Among the Inuit [in Northern Quebec], we still have no Aboriginal social workers. [translation]

Francine Tremblay
Montreal, Quebec
16 November 1993

In the eastern Arctic, there are no professional social workers that are university trained who are Inuit. Nor are there any Inuit doctors, nurses, architects, dentists, [or] lawyers.

Bill Riddell
Iqaluit, Northwest Territories
25 May 1992

Every year we have different nurses, we have different doctors coming in. This is really hard on the people, having to see different nurses and having to see different doctors, and telling your story all over again has been really hard on a lot of people here in the community.

Mary Teya
Community Health Representative
Fort McPherson, Northwest Territories, 7 May 1992

It is apparent that efforts to increase the number of Aboriginal health and social services professionals must be combined with efforts to encourage them to provide services to their communities.

Second, Aboriginal professionals are often concentrated in the lower ranks of organizations rather than in supervisory, management or policy positions.[276] To the extent that this situation prevails, Aboriginal people do not have the opportunity to influence program design, program delivery or resource allocation.

Governments, professional associations and service delivery organizations rarely collect information about the participation of Aboriginal people in the health and healing professions. We believe this reflects the low priority accorded to developing Aboriginal human resources.[277] The absence of this vital information is an obstacle to planning. The need for better information about Aboriginal human resources was highlighted in a presentation by the Canadian Public Health Association:

> To undertake appropriate health human resources planning for Aboriginal communities, complete and comprehensive data sets are needed regarding the current number of and projected need for trained Aboriginal public health workers working in the field....A complete inventory of all professional and para-professional health-related training programs for Aboriginal students is needed to assess the availability, accessibility and relevancy of these programs.
>
> Elaine Johnson
> Canadian Public Health Association
> Ottawa, Ontario, 17 November 1993

A comprehensive human resources plan for Aboriginal health and healing is needed. Developing it will not be easy, because the range of direct service work related to health and healing is broad. Within the field of public health alone, for example, some 50 different specialities have been identified in home care, inspection, medical care, dental health, pharmacy, nursing, nutrition, occupational health and safety, primary care, therapy, environmental health, ophthalmology, rehabilitation, medical research, and other areas.[278] Because of the holistic concept of health that Aboriginal people hold, we also want to emphasize the important contributions to be made by other practitioners: community animators and planners, traditional healers, midwives,[279] family and child support workers, mental health workers, specialists in environmental health and community infrastructure, substance abuse specialists, interpreters, translators, and many others.[280]

When systems are being redesigned and reshaped in the way we have recommended, where there is a need for the effective management of scarce resources, and where creative solutions based on new approaches must be found, the work of many others will be needed to complement that of direct service personnel: community leaders, administrators, planners, evaluators, researchers, public education specialists, community development practitioners, and others. A comprehensive human resources development plan should consider these needs as well.

Support for Aboriginal training in health and social services has been targeted generally to entry-level positions in direct service delivery and local administration.[281] Although these programs are important, the emphasis needs to be shifted to educational opportunities in the areas of program design, evaluation and senior management skills. While this type of training has sometimes been made available to those employed by governments, few Aboriginal staff reach the levels where senior management skills are learned and practised.

RECOMMENDATIONS

The Commission recommends that

Canada-Wide Human Resources Strategy

3.3.13

The government of Canada provide funds to the national Aboriginal organizations, including national Aboriginal women's organizations, to permit them to prepare a comprehensive human resources development strategy in health and social services that

(a) facilitates and draws upon regional initiatives, integrates information from diverse sources, and is structured to incorporate regular updating;

(b) builds an inventory of Aboriginal human resources currently available in health and social services, identifying where, in what field and at what level Aboriginal personnel are currently practising;

(c) assesses current and future Aboriginal human resources needs and identifies the actions needed on the part of governments, educational institutions and others to address these needs;

(d) assesses requirements for direct service personnel as well as for planners, researchers and administrators;

(e) collates an inventory and available evaluative data on training and education options;

(f) explores recruitment, training and retention issues;

(g) examines the personal and professional supports required to encourage Aboriginal professionals to practise in Aboriginal communities;

(h) develops proposals for a system to monitor the status of Aboriginal human resources; and

(i) develops an analysis of how, to the maximum extent possible, Aboriginal human resources development can be brought under Aboriginal control.

Commitment to
Train 10,000
Professionals

3.3.14

Federal, provincial and territorial governments commit themselves to providing the necessary funding, consistent with their
jurisdictional responsibilities,

(a) to implement a co-ordinated and comprehensive human
resources development strategy;

(b) to train 10,000 Aboriginal professionals over a 10-year
period in health and social services, including medicine,
nursing, mental health, psychology, social work, dentistry,
nutrition, addictions, gerontology, public health, community development, planning, health administration,
and other priority areas identified by Aboriginal people;

(c) to support program development in educational institutions providing professional training, with preference given
to Aboriginal institutions; and

(d) to ensure that student support through post-secondary
educational assistance, scholarships, paid leave and other
means is adequate to achieve the target.

We recognize that national Aboriginal organizations will not always be in the
best position to implement the recommendations that emerge from the development strategy. Communities, nations and other Aboriginal organizations and
institutions will also make an important contribution. However, it is our view that
national Aboriginal organizations are in the best position to conduct a country-
wide assessment of current resources and future requirements, beginning immediately and during the transition to self-government. Given the multifaceted
needs and the extensive resources required to address them, we have concluded that
a high level of co-ordination on a Canada-wide basis is warranted. Once needs and
development strategies have been assessed, Aboriginal nation governments, regional
planning bodies, federal, provincial and territorial governments, educational institutions and professional associations will be in a much better position to see how
they can contribute to achieving the goals of the comprehensive strategy.

While a strategy will provide the detailed framework needed to advance
Aboriginal human resources development, efforts must also begin immediately
to address critical shortages of resources. Planning and research cannot be used
as an excuse to delay action. Expanded training and professional development
opportunities are urgently needed for personnel now in the field and for new
roles already being defined. They must be provided as soon as possible.

As discussed in Chapter 5 of this volume, an important means of promoting Aboriginal human resources development is to increase the support available

for education and training institutions under Aboriginal control. Here, however, we discuss some of the important contributions that can be made by mainstream education and service delivery institutions. We focus on programs that are already having a positive impact and that can provide a foundation for new initiatives.

Building on success

The Community Health Representative Program

One of the most successful programs involving Aboriginal people in promoting the health of Aboriginal people is the community health representative program. We believe CHRs can play an important role in developing healing centres and providing other health and healing services. In particular, they can help Aboriginal individuals and communities learn to exercise personal and collective responsibility with regard to health matters.

The duties of CHRs include health promotion and education and participation in assessing health needs. CHRs have been successful in extending health and healing services to many Aboriginal communities and have helped improve the quality of services available from mainstream service providers. Through liaison between medical staff and community members, they have been particularly important in promoting sensitive treatment of community members and preventing unnecessary institutionalization.[282]

Despite the significant accomplishments of the CHR program, it has faced a number of challenges. An evaluation of the program, conducted by the medical services branch of Health Canada and the National Indian and Inuit CHR Organization, summarized a number of these problems.[283] Although CHRs are often called upon to provide assessment, treatment and emergency services, particularly in smaller communities where there are no resident medical staff, their training focuses on health promotion and education. Therefore, they might be ill-equipped to provide medical services if requested by the community. When they do provide these services, issues of competence and liability arise. Although a number of educational institutions are involved in providing CHR training, there are no Canada-wide standards. Furthermore, training has suffered from a lack of financial support from governments and educational institutions. Also, because of the involvement of communities and Aboriginal and non-Aboriginal governments and organizations, CHRs often have no clear lines of accountability. There is a need, therefore, to increase the number of CHR co-ordinators and supervisors. Finally, there are simply not enough CHRs to meet the demand for their services.

It has also proved difficult to retain CHRs. In part, this is because of the high job demands and isolation that CHRs often experience. They do not have access to the support systems available to urban practitioners. We were told:

> The CHR program has not reached its full potential. While we are fortunate that our CHRs have received basic training...we have been unable

to get ongoing refresher training programs for them. This is very important for a group of health workers who are operating alone in isolated communities....Our CHRs have not been recognized as full, participating members of the health care team by health professionals. This situation is improving, but we have to continue to promote our CHRs as key community health workers who have local knowledge that many of the health professionals lack. An introduction to the CHR program could also be geared into the training of health care professionals before [they] work in northern communities.

Iris Allen
Labrador Inuit Health Commission
Nain, Newfoundland and Labrador, 30 November 1992

In the absence of respite, professional support, and opportunities for professional enrichment, CHRs often find themselves unable or unwilling to carry on. Related to these concerns, upgrading can be difficult, because their education and experience often are not recognized by mainstream educational programs or professions.

CHRs and other professionals can face additional frustrations when they relocate from northern and other remote regions. There they had a broader scope of practice and fewer restrictions than in the south, where common practices can come under careful scrutiny from professional bodies, employers and other practitioners. This can and does lead to situations where practitioners from the north are made to feel they are unqualified to fulfil responsibilities in areas where, in fact, they have developed a good deal of expertise.

One of the most serious limitations of the current CHR program is that CHR services are available only to First Nations people and Inuit living on their traditional lands. While the health and social status of urban Aboriginal people indicate that they also need access to health education and promotion services of the type provided by CHRs, the program is not available to them.[284]

We do not see the CHR program as a substitute for increasing the number of Aboriginal people in nursing, medicine, health administration, social work or other professions. However, this type of program is an important component of effective and accessible Aboriginal health and social services systems. Moreover, CHRs have extensive experience and a strong commitment to improving the health of Aboriginal people. Therefore, we would like to see much more attention paid to developing programs and policies that would enable CHRs to gain more experience and advance their professional training.

While we have called for a reorientation of the health and social programs available to Aboriginal people, and while we believe there is a need to train many more Aboriginal health and social service professionals, we do not foresee the need to displace existing staff. We believe Aboriginal people currently involved in providing a range of health and social services, even though they might not have formal professional training, are the building blocks of future initiatives.

Some should have the opportunity to pursue professional training, while others should have the opportunity for advancement to positions involving planning, training and administration. Many, however, should continue to provide primary care and education and promotion to Aboriginal communities.

The National Native Alcohol and Drug Abuse Program

Another program that has successfully involved Aboriginal people in health and social services delivery is the National Native Alcohol and Drug Abuse Program (NNADAP, now often referred to as addictions and community-funded programs). This program, which employed some 465 people in 1993-94, has made an enormous contribution to the development of Aboriginal human resources in the addictions and mental health fields. O'Neil and Postl have observed:

> [NNADAP] has been responsible for the creation of hundreds of community-based alcohol prevention and treatment projects across the country. Since the early eighties, this program has contributed to the emergence of some of the most significant Aboriginal health initiatives in the country, including the Four Worlds Development Project, the Nechi Institute, the Alkali Lake prohibition strategy, and the more recent Healing the Spirit Worldwide conference in Edmonton.[285]

NNADAP was established some 20 years ago by the department of Indian affairs.[286] Its purpose remains

> To support Indian and Inuit People and their communities in establishing and operating programs aimed at arresting and offsetting high levels of alcohol, drug, and solvent abuse among their populations on-reserve.[287]

It seeks to achieve this through three interrelated strategies: reducing the incidence of substance abuse; reducing the prevalence of substance abuse; and training prevention and treatment workers. The range of initiatives funded under NNADAP is very broad. It includes employing staff who provide prevention and treatment services, providing funding for treatment programs, including residential treatment programs, and providing resources to those involved in educating and training addictions workers. To date, the program has funded some 400 community-based alcohol and drug abuse treatment projects and 51 First Nations treatment centres across Canada. The annual budget of the program exceeds $50 million.[288]

Staff involved in services delivery at the community level are generally employed directly by local Aboriginal governments. As with other programs that have been the subject of health transfer or alternative funding agreements, however, only program delivery, not program design or management, has been transferred to Aboriginal control.

NNADAP has been controversial; there is not universal agreement about the extent to which the program has achieved its objectives. In the latest evaluation of the program, conducted by the Addiction Research Foundation in 1989, concerns were expressed about the effectiveness of many of the prevention and treatment programs funded by NNADAP. However, even this critical evaluation concluded that the training component of the program was successful in preparing Aboriginal people to provide treatment services in the addictions field.[289]

Some stakeholders have been concerned that the program has not been as responsive to community needs as it should be because of the highly centralized approach to funding and contract administration. As a result of this centralization, limits are placed on the number of different services and on the way they are provided. This approach discourages innovation and sometimes has made it difficult to adapt programs to meet local priorities.[290] For example, echoing the concerns of other individuals and organizations,[291] one Aboriginal leader told us:

> NNADAP...submitted a new submission to the Treasury Board...that was to address the alcohol and drug abuse needs of Aboriginal people in Canada. That process was to establish where grassroots people got involved in advising government on what the issues were. What happened with that process is that First Nations people got involved. We got involved and advised the government that these are our needs. Then our needs weren't recognized. The process was taken over by the bureaucrats. The NNADAP program now is run under Health and Welfare Canada and is run by bureaucrats without Native consultation. There has to be a change where consultation is continuing and...Native people have an opportunity to voice themselves.
>
> Phil Hall
> Alderman, District of Chilliwack
> Victoria, British Columbia, 22 May 1992

NNADAP workers encounter many of the challenges associated with working in rural and northern areas that CHRs face. Many of the issues concerning CHR training, retention, career advancement, and recognition also affect NNADAP workers.[292] These must be addressed if the effectiveness of the program is to be improved.

Two additional concerns about NNADAP were raised in presentations to the Commission: the program does not extend beyond reserves to provide services to Aboriginal people living in urban centres; and it provides services to First Nations people and Inuit but not to Métis people. As we point out in Volume 4, Chapter 7, the quality of services for Aboriginal people in urban areas is a particular concern to the Commission.

> [A]nother issue is off-reserve Native people, youth. NNADAP is an effective program, but it is only geared to on-reserve people. There is really nothing for off-reserve people...people in the urban centres....I have had

a lot of confrontations with off-reserve youth organizations within the city saying, "It is for Native people, isn't it? Why can't we go?" And we say: "Well, it is not your money"....[F]unding must become available through the government; I am not sure, Health and Welfare Canada or the other governments. I am not sure where it would come from.

Cheryl Starr
Saskatchewan Indian Youth Advisory Committee
Saskatoon, Saskatchewan, 27 October 1992

Since a substantial percentage of Aboriginal people live in urban centres and it is not currently possible for them to have access to the same resources as those available in Aboriginal communities, this situation must be rectified. The problems of drug abuse are just as prevalent in the cities as they are on the reserves. Why not have a NNADAP officer in the cities? [translation]

Louis Bordeleau
Native Aid and Friend Centre of Senneterre
Val d'Or, Quebec, 1 December 1992

There should also be an alcohol abuse program (like NNADAP) for Métis people.

Sydney McKay
Manitoba Metis Federation
Thompson, Manitoba, 31 May 1993[293]

Provincial and territorial governments should co-operate with the federal government to provide services for treating and preventing substance abuse to Aboriginal people who do not reside on their traditional lands and to Métis people. Urban youth, particularly the increasing number who are coming into conflict with the law, and those living on the streets, detached from any stable community, are frequently involved in substance abuse. Services should be adapted to fit their needs and be under Aboriginal control.[294]

RECOMMENDATION

The Commission recommends that

Adaptation of
Current Programs

3.3.15

Federal, provincial and territorial governments and national Aboriginal organizations, including Aboriginal women's organizations, explore how training approaches and personnel complements of current health and social services, including the

> community health representative and drug and alcohol abuse programs, can contribute to a more comprehensive, holistic and integrated system of services, while helping to maintain continuity and adequacy of Aboriginal community services.

Earlier in this chapter, we outlined our proposals for developing Aboriginal healing centres and lodges. We believe some residential treatment centres currently funded through NNADAP will want to continue focusing on the treatment of addictions. We concluded that there is a need for many more such programs across Canada. At the same time, other residential treatment centres want to expand the scope of their services, but they have been constrained by the terms of reference for NNADAP funding. We believe these centres should be given the opportunity to become part of the network of holistic healing lodges we propose.

Health Canada is considering a review of NNADAP to clarify how it works best and what directions it should pursue in the future. Such a review is warranted, because many concerns have been expressed about the program, and an evaluation has not been conducted for seven years. The issues raised here should form the basis of the evaluation and any future program planning.

Training in other areas

The CHR program focuses on health education and promotion services, while NNADAP focuses on services in the addictions field. While we have suggested a number of improvements to both, we believe the programs have had a significant effect on the health and social conditions of Aboriginal people already. Their success in promoting Aboriginal human resources development is particularly welcome. However, there are many other areas where improved services are still needed, where success will depend on the availability of qualified Aboriginal health and social service professionals, but where there is no program like NNADAP or the CHR program.

We are concerned about the current status of Aboriginal human resources in such important fields as social services, child welfare, mental health and social assistance administration.[295] There are no systematic, organized programs of support for training and professional development in these areas among federal and provincial government departments, post-secondary educational institutions, or Aboriginal and non-Aboriginal service agencies. Individual Aboriginal communities have had to find the funding for these activities from within their already limited program administration budgets.

Formal training programs at Aboriginal and non-Aboriginal post-secondary educational institutions will play a very important role in increasing the number of Aboriginal professionals. However, there is a need to co-ordinate training and education with opportunities for employment and advancement that serve the particular needs of Aboriginal communities, both urban and rural. (For a full discussion of job-related training strategies, see Volume 2, Chapter 5.)

An example of the limitations of current approaches to training and retraining is found in a study of a Manitoba Aboriginal child welfare agency and its workers conducted for the Commission (see box).

While planning for integrated and holistic approaches to service development and delivery, governments and the national Aboriginal organizations should also consider Aboriginal human resources development programs – like NNADAP and the CHR program – in other areas that are critical to the health and well-being of Aboriginal people.

University-based initiatives

Program-specific training, such as that developed in the NNADAP and CHR programs, is important, but attention also needs to be focused on attracting Aboriginal students to post-secondary institutions and keeping them there for the duration of a degree program. As discussed more fully in Chapter 5 of this volume, Aboriginal education and training institutions are ready to take on more responsibility in this area, and they should receive the increased support needed to expand the range, quality and capacity of their programs. As well, some non-Aboriginal post-secondary educational institutions have made great strides in attracting and keeping Aboriginal students. Unfortunately, many others have made no measurable headway. Successful programs deserve recognition and support, and other institutions should be encouraged to implement them.

The progress made by several medical schools is noteworthy. Graduates of the University of Alberta, for example, will contribute a 35 per cent increase in the total number of Aboriginal physicians in Canada over the next five years. In addition, the university attracts Aboriginal students to programs in health administration, pharmacy, physiotherapy, occupational therapy and nursing. A significant proportion of practising Aboriginal physicians is made up of graduates of the University of Manitoba, which has had a pre-medical studies program for Aboriginal students since 1979. As well, the University of Toronto has a support program for Aboriginal medical students.

The Canadian Association of University Schools of Nursing presented a brief to the Commission about many innovative programs in nursing schools across Canada that are intended to attract and graduate Aboriginal nurses.[296] For example, Yellowknife has developed a registered nurses program; Dalhousie University in Halifax offers an outpost nursing program and a northern clinical program; the University of Saskatchewan has offered the National Native Access Program to Nursing since 1985; and Lakehead University in Thunder Bay, Ontario, has a Native Nurses Entry Program. Similar programs for other health and social service professions are also beginning to emerge. For example, the

Saskatchewan Indian Federated College offers a Bachelor of Indian Social Work program, and McGill University offers a certificate program in northern social work practice. St. Thomas University, in Fredericton, and Dalhousie University have offered bachelor of social work programs with modified content and schedules to accommodate Aboriginal people already employed. These are welcome developments.

Successful participation in professional programs often depends on students receiving financial and academic support as well as personal and family support. This requires a commitment from the educational institutions involved and from government. The University of Alberta, for example, has established an Office of Native Health Care Careers, and similar support programs exist at a number of other Canadian universities.

In the past, the adaptation of professional programs has usually depended on limited-term grant funding. We believe that it is the obligation of mainstream institutions to provide culturally appropriate services, including the education of personnel to staff such services.

Because of funding limitations and other restrictions, some training programs have had to place limits on the number of new admissions. In other instances, however, the existing infrastructure of faculty and other resources could support a larger number of students. We urge post-secondary institutions and funding bodies to explore creative ways to realize this potential. While there may be enough non-Aboriginal professionals in some fields and too many in others, for Aboriginal people there are serious shortages in every health and social service profession.

Although some mainstream institutions and government programs have shown leadership in improving educational opportunities for Aboriginal students pursuing professional training, others have shown little interest. It is difficult to see how a continuation of current practices alone will result in the significant increases in Aboriginal human resources that are required. While current supporters must increase their commitment, new ones should also be enlisted.

Educational institutions, governments, and provincial and national professional organizations, acting together with Aboriginal organizations, can do much more than they do now to address the shortage of Aboriginal professionals. Moreover, if the will is there, much can be accomplished within existing mandates and budgets. In this regard, it would be useful to examine the following questions:

- What barriers exist that prevent Aboriginal students from participating in professional training programs, and how can these barriers be removed?
- How can Aboriginal people become more fully involved in the development and delivery of professional education programs?
- How can Aboriginal organizations and governments, mainstream educational institutions, professional organizations, and Canadian governments work together more effectively to increase the number of Aboriginal people in the health and social service professions?

Planning for Success – Overcoming Barriers

Human services agencies, as well as other employers, customarily obtain their staff 'ready-made' as graduates of post-secondary education programs offered outside the workplace and paid for mostly from general revenues. Such is not the case with First Nations and other Aboriginal employers. This is true, first, because they rightly want to employ First Nations people as far as possible. Second, in the local communities, even without any positively discriminating hiring policy, the only staff available are First Nations people....First Nations graduates of the same programs from which non-Aboriginal employers draw their staff are in seriously short supply.

A full range of responses, sustained over a considerable number of years, is required to attend to this shortcoming. These should include everything from in-service training to community college certificates; from degree programs to specially designed training programs. Some may require periods of study away from the community; others may be designed in a more decentralized fashion, enabling community-based part time study. Content and duration will vary depending upon the needs of the individual and the agency....

It is observed that quite unrealistic expectations are placed upon post-secondary institutions and training programs in terms of what they can deliver in what time frame. For example, a typical middle class non-Aboriginal student, entering a bachelor of social work program with all the academic pre-requisites, takes four years of full-time study to complete. This assumes no major financial or other interruptions to the student's program. The First Nations agencies on the other hand depend, at least for most of their local staff, on programs (degree or otherwise) in which existing staff can enrol. In other words, assuming half-time work and half-time study, it would take each worker/student eight years to complete. Granted, a degree program is at the high end of the continuum, and some short-cuts and accommodations can be made even in a degree program (practicums in the workplace, for example), but the time frames and sustained commitment from the agency, employee and funders outlined here far exceed any discussions on the subject of training this author has seen or heard.

Furthermore, the typical student referred to here hardly exists in First Nations communities....[V]ery few local staff have the usual prerequisites. Completing the necessary remedial work may add yet more time to the study period....[M]any Aboriginal students enroled in programs offered by mainstream institutions speak of the difficulties they experience with cultural dissonance. This is experienced in both the content and process of instruction. It leads often to withdrawal, and at best, frequent time-outs to deal with their doubts....[I]n the foreseeable future, heavy reliance on the mainstream institutions for trained staff will continue. Planning for the necessary time frames, staffing patterns...and funding will need to be predicated on this fact.

Even if a period of apprenticeship with elders, and/or a more culturally relevant program at an Aboriginal-controlled post-secondary institution (of which there are few at present) were seen as appropriate, other sorts of crises conspire to disrupt the continuity of the period of study....

[T]he content of the journey of inquiry in human services training is more likely than for other students to trigger in the Aboriginal student memories of past abuse or other damaging experiences....When the individuals themselves feel whole and free of the crisis in their own identity, they are rarely free of the crises experienced by family members and others close to them. Deaths, births, family violence, suicide, ill-health, job loss, economic hardships of other kinds, are life events, most of a stressful kind, that are experienced by Aboriginal people more than the typical middle class student....Add to the elements listed above, the usual staff profile of a mature person (usually female), with extensive family responsibilities now combined with those of worker and student, and one begins to more fully appreciate the challenge to the individual, the employer, and the training institution....

This section of the report concludes with two thoughts. The first is that...none of the three parties [to the Manitoba Aboriginal tri-partite agreements, that is, Canada, Manitoba, and the Aboriginal organizations involved] have developed a serious long-term training plan that would be commensurate with the degree of importance attached· to the issue....Second, none of the training programs provided to date, have planned for very many of the barriers to success which have been listed here. Time frames need to be planned in a more realistic fashion, staffing patterns need to be changed to allow for educational leave at the same time as the agency is obliged to deliver services, and a high level of supports of varied kinds need to be provided to the students. Where even some of these elements have been present, completion rates have markedly improved.

Source: Pete Hudson "Politics and Program: A Case Study of a First Nations Child and Family Service Agency", research study prepared for RCAP (1994).

Some institutions may conclude that they have little to offer, but others will discover that they can make a significant contribution.

We believe it is important to review the curricula of professional education programs to improve their cultural appropriateness and effectiveness for Aboriginal and non-Aboriginal students alike. We are persuaded also that the success of Aboriginal students in mainstream education programs is improved when there is a core group of Aboriginal students who can provide personal and professional support to one another. Where this is occurring, benefits for non-Aboriginal students are also being reported. Opportunities for the cross-fertilization of Aboriginal and non-Aboriginal knowledge, experience, and practice enrich the educational experience for all. (These ideas are discussed more fully in Chapter 5 of this volume.)

Circumstances across the country vary to such a degree that a single prescription cannot apply. However, when some answers to these questions have been pursued in the past, they have led to a remarkable number of creative approaches that have improved educational opportunities for Aboriginal people. Some of them have included

- establishing specific admission and retention targets for Aboriginal students;
- re-examining entry requirements;
- establishing pre-professional and pre-admission preparation programs;
- developing an organized system of financial, academic, personal and family supports for Aboriginal students;
- initiating innovative strategies to provide continuing support for Aboriginal practitioners in the field;
- creatively using mentors, secondments, and exchanges;
- supporting program innovation in colleges and universities;
- adopting alternative modes of delivering professional education programs that increase access and effectiveness; and
- involving Aboriginal people in program planning.

Many successful programs are already in place. (For more details, see Chapter 5 of this volume.)

If the participation of Aboriginal people in mainstream professional training programs is to increase, post-secondary institutions should also examine the nature of current professional training, who provides it and how. Many programs are not well suited to Aboriginal students or to the challenges that Aboriginal professionals will face in providing services to their communities.

Aboriginal participation in professional training is not simply a matter of fitting Aboriginal students into mainstream programs. These programs should be changed to attract Aboriginal students, to value Aboriginal knowledge and experience, and to provide culturally relevant information and skills that will prepare Aboriginal students to work in their communities. We believe that mainstream educational institutions can accomplish this transformation by forging new relationships with Aboriginal organizations, governments and communities, as well as with Aboriginal students and professionals. We return to these issues in Chapter 5 of this volume.

Many presentations during our public hearings focused on the need to make professional training more relevant and effective for Aboriginal and non-Aboriginal students who will be providing services to Aboriginal people.[297] We were told:

> Our education system is a model that appears quite incompatible with the reality, culture and traditions of Aboriginal people....[T]he Commission should make representations to the various educational groups to include in their educational programs for health profession- als concepts related to the various... cultural approaches. [translation]
>
> Dr. Paul Landry
> Association des hôpitaux du Québec
> Montreal, Quebec, 16 November 1993

> Training of social work staff should become inclusive of cultural issues as they apply to Aboriginal people. I feel that this is something we all need...training on subjects that we don't have as much knowledge on as we should.
>
> Rhonda Fiander
> St. John's, Newfoundland
> 22 May 1992

> Presently, many Native counsellors are trained through bachelor of social work programs, programs which fail to serve the specific needs of Aboriginal students and communities. We accept that some aspects of the BSW program are immensely helpful; however, Native coun- sellors require a broader range of training.
>
> John Sawyer
> Ontario Native Education Counselling Association
> Toronto, Ontario, 18 November 1993

> [We recommend] that cross-cultural training and preparation be mandatory for non-Aboriginal persons working amongst Aboriginal peoples. This would include those involved in policing, in correc- tional services, health and education, social services, and a variety of government agencies and departments. It is essential that such train- ing be developed and directed by Aboriginal peoples.
>
> Reverend William Veenstra
> Christian Reform Church in Canada
> Vancouver, British Columbia, 15 November 1993

I think it is essential to develop training, for example, in cross-cultural nursing or training for doctors who are going to work in the North and all personnel who are going to work in the North, to work within a cross-cultural perspective of communication with Aboriginal communities that helps view the culture not as a risk factor but as a coherent and intelligent system. For that, obviously much remains to be done....It requires more than open-mindedness and receptiveness; it also requires that the researchers innovate in providing the content of those approaches. [translation]

Rose Dufour
Department of Community Health,
Laval University Hospital Centre
Wendake, Quebec, 18 November 1992

Ultimately, there is an unavoidable need to re-examine thoroughly the professional training of non-Aboriginal socio-health staff while encouraging Aboriginal people through the use of approaches and practices that respect their culture and diversity. [translation]

Francine Tremblay
Montreal, Quebec
16 November 1993

There is abduction of our children because non-Aboriginal social workers have no understanding of the values and traditions of our people.

Doris Young
Founding President, Indigenous Women's Collective
Winnipeg, Manitoba, 22 April 1992

Cross-cultural training for health/hospital personnel and professionals [is required] – for example, physicians, optometrists, dentists, assistants, receptionists, ambulance drivers....All levels of government should enhance the knowledge and sensitivity of health care providers with respect to Native customs and traditions.

Gloria Manitopyes
Calgary Aboriginal Urban Affairs Committee
Calgary, Alberta, 26 May 1993

We received many briefs and presentations from those involved in post-secondary education telling us of steps being taken to develop more culturally sensitive approaches to professional training for Aboriginal students. A professor at McGill University summed up her view of the changes needed in universities in this way:

Universities must open their gates to Aboriginal communities, to their students, seek their counsel, instantiate their ideas, build programs and practices that will empower rather than marginalize, that will underline the strength and dignity of Aboriginal students' identities, their cultural holdings, their remaining languages, as well as recognize their struggles and serve to enrich the wider community and the populations of Aboriginal communities.

Martha Crago
McGill University
Montreal, Quebec, 2 December 1993

RECOMMENDATIONS

The Commission recommends that

Increase Number of Graduates

3.3.16

Post-secondary educational institutions providing programs of study leading to professional certification in health or social services collaborate with Aboriginal organizations to examine how they can

(a) increase the number of Aboriginal students participating in and graduating from their programs;

(b) provide support for students to promote completion of programs;

(c) develop or expand specialized programs; and

(d) modify the curriculum of programs leading to certification so as to increase the cultural appropriateness and effectiveness of training provided to Aboriginal and non-Aboriginal students who will be providing services to Aboriginal people.

Continuing Professional Education

3.3.17

Post-secondary educational institutions and professional associations collaborate with Aboriginal organizations to ensure that professionals already in the field have access to programs of continuing professional education that emphasize cultural issues associated with the provision of health and social services.

A related issue (already discussed in relation to the CHR program and NNADAP) is the failure of mainstream educational institutions and professional organizations to recognize and affirm Aboriginal knowledge, skills and experience. This is a barrier to entry into professional training and into employment where professional skills can be developed further. It is also a barrier to advancement. Formal credentials and work experience with non-Aboriginal organizations – even if they are not directly applicable to the needs of Aboriginal people – are often valued more than Aboriginal knowledge and experience working in Aboriginal communities.[298] In Chapter 5 we discuss a number of strategies to overcome these barriers.

As Aboriginal educational and professional institutions continue to develop, and as self-government proceeds, Aboriginal people will take a much more active role in recognizing and certifying Aboriginal professionals, based on Aboriginal standards and accreditation processes. However, mainstream educational institutions and professional organizations should examine how they can recognize the legitimacy and value of what Aboriginal people have learned through their education and life experience. There is an opportunity and a challenge for the organizations representing post-secondary educational institutions and university and college teachers to encourage their members to embrace the spirit and intent of our recommendations and to help bring about needed changes.

RECOMMENDATIONS

The Commission recommends that

Recognize Aboriginal Knowledge

3.3.18

Post-secondary educational institutions involved in the training of health and social services professionals, and professional associations involved in regulating and licensing these professions, collaborate with Aboriginal organizations and governments to develop a more effective approach to training and licensing that recognizes the importance and legitimacy of Aboriginal knowledge and experience.

AUCC and CAUT Provide Leadership

3.3.19

The Association of Universities and Colleges of Canada and the Canadian Association of University Teachers encourage their members to implement the Commission's recommendations with respect to professional training of Aboriginal people for health and social services, and that these organizations provide leadership to help ensure that the recommendations are implemented.

The need for government support

Post-secondary educational institutions will be unable to move forward in the directions we have recommended without the support of the governments on which they rely for much of their funding. We believe that governments have an obligation to participate in these efforts. Existing programs have proven effective, but their scope needs to be expanded significantly if the problems we have outlined are to be overcome.

The Indian and Inuit Health Careers Program is one example of how governments, Aboriginal communities and post-secondary educational institutions can work together to promote Aboriginal professional development.[299] Established in 1984 by the medical services branch of Health Canada, the program is intended to encourage and support Aboriginal participation in educational opportunities leading to professional careers in the health field. The program also seeks to overcome the social and cultural barriers that inhibit the educational achievement of Aboriginal students. Originally funded as a three-year pilot project, the program was approved for continuing funding in 1986.

The program provides support at the student, institutional and community levels. Some 80 per cent of its budget supports post-secondary education institutions in developing student support and counselling services, curriculum enhancements, and access programs for Aboriginal students entering health studies. Programs that receive support include the Native Nurses Entry Program at Lakehead University, the National Native Access Program to Nursing at the University of Saskatchewan, and the Native Health Care Careers Program at the University of Alberta.

At the local level, the program supports Aboriginal communities, efforts to encourage students to choose health careers through activities such as career fairs, workshops, role models and field trips to health facilities. It also provides orientation and on-the-job training for students pursuing health studies.

A small but important part of the program involves providing direct financial assistance to Aboriginal students. Since 1984, the program has awarded 200 bursaries and 70 scholarships to First Nations, Inuit and Métis students.

The Indian and Inuit Health Careers Program is an example of what government agencies can do to help Aboriginal people pursue professional training. We believe other government agencies – federal, provincial and territorial – should consider how they can encourage increased Aboriginal participation in a variety of health and social services professional training and develop other such programs.

It is regrettable that the Indian and Inuit Health Careers Program has not been expanded over the years. The program's original annual budget was $3.1 million in 1984; however, the annual budget stood at $2.6 million in 1994-95. As a result, funding for some program components has been reduced, while for others it has been eliminated altogether. A further limitation of the program is that institutional support is committed for only three years at a time. This has been a serious obstacle to long-term planning.

Given the critical shortage of Aboriginal professionals and the importance of increasing their numbers, we consider the reductions in the scope of the Indian and Inuit Health Careers Program ill-advised. We believe that such initiatives should be expanded and transferred to Aboriginal control.

The Indian and Inuit Health Careers Program is one type of initiative that warrants support. The approaches validated by experience in the program should be expanded: support to educational institutions, direct assistance to Aboriginal students, and promotion of health careers through building community awareness.

Governments have also been involved in providing work-related training opportunities for Aboriginal people through the programs of the federal department of human resources development and other agencies. These programs have prepared some Aboriginal people for involvement in health and social services programs, but training is provided in many other areas as well. Some steps have been taken to involve Aboriginal people more directly in needs assessment and in the design and delivery of programs. However, as discussed more fully in Volume 2, responsibility for these programs must be in the hands of Aboriginal people if the needs of Aboriginal communities and nations are to be met.[300]

Community-based training and education

A comprehensive approach to the development of Aboriginal human resources must look beyond programs of study offered at post-secondary educational institutions, which by themselves will not be enough to meet the need we have identified.

In developing our ideas about community-based training, we considered a number of needs. A realistic and effective plan for developing Aboriginal human resources must provide for community participation and for recognition of traditional practices. Many of the most effective health and healing initiatives that have come to our attention have been instituted by Aboriginal community leaders who do not have the type of education or experience that would be recognized by mainstream educational and professional bodies. Therefore, any plan for developing Aboriginal human resources must consider how to support the efforts of community leaders to improve health and social conditions in their own communities.

Aboriginal communities and nations also need opportunities to share their ideas, to learn from one another, and to develop collaborative approaches to assessing and addressing education and training needs. They must also be able to voice their needs directly and seek their own solutions.

As discussed earlier in this section and in Chapter 5, structured programs requiring full-time study over a number of years at institutions far from Aboriginal communities are not accessible to many potential Aboriginal students. While innovations such as distance education are helping, it will be some time before a full range of professional training programs is available to most Aboriginal communities in Canada. Even in urban areas, where an increasing number of Aboriginal people reside, social, cultural and economic barriers inhibit access to mainstream post-secondary programs.[301] While these barriers are being removed, community-based training initiatives can be adapted to address community priorities and help to create a climate that prepares and supports Aboriginal people planning to pursue professional training.

Aboriginal professionals, particularly those practising in rural and remote areas, have a variety of needs with regard to continuing education and professional development once they have completed their initial training. With support, they can often make a significant contribution to the development of human resources in their communities. Support to those already in the field, so that they can promote awareness and training in their own communities, is another important reason to provide for local training in a human resources development plan.

Aboriginal people are in the process of redefining professional training to make it more holistic, more grounded in Aboriginal experience, and more relevant to Aboriginal circumstances. Much of what constitutes the Aboriginal knowledge and experience base is not recognized in formal programs of instruction or training, although, as noted earlier, some institutions are making progress in this area. To provide for the preservation and enhancement of Aboriginal knowledge and practices, Aboriginal people must have the opportunity to engage in knowledge development and transmission.

No top-down or centralized approach to education or training will be able to respect the diversity of needs and opportunities at the local community level. In fact, the quality of Aboriginal education and training will depend to a large degree on how knowledge and expertise currently available at the community level are used. Enhancing the ability of communities to participate in the design of education and training programs can only contribute to the quality of the programs that are developed.

Aboriginal education and training institutions, controlled by Aboriginal people, can make a very important contribution to addressing these needs over the coming years, as they evolve in tandem with other structures under self-government. However, we believe that additional measures are required now.

In 1994, the government of Ontario introduced an Aboriginal health policy and subsequently initiated an Aboriginal Healing and Wellness Strategy.[302] This strategy was developed jointly with the Aboriginal people of Ontario. Under the policy, the health ministry undertakes to provide funding for training Aboriginal personnel and volunteers engaged in programs related to Aboriginal family healing and health. Funding is available to Aboriginal communities or organizations, and collaborative projects involving several communities or organizations are particularly encouraged. The cost to organizations of analyzing policy and participating in the planning and management of initiatives is explicitly recognized. Eligible projects are those that will build Aboriginal knowledge and skills, such as projects to develop curriculum, training resources and materials, training programs or strategies, and specific training events. Funding is limited, but enhanced funding is available for collaborative projects and for projects in remote locations. Project results are to be shared with other communities through an Aboriginal health clearinghouse.

We believe that the approach adopted by the Ontario government will encourage the creative energies of Aboriginal organizations and communities. Funding to communities will give them an opportunity to proceed with training and education activities that they consider priorities. We are also confident that the Ontario approach will result in new partnerships between Aboriginal organizations and communities and with mainstream educational institutions.

Other governments are also recognizing the importance of community-based education and training. For example, the community wellness program adopted by the government of the Northwest Territories contains a significant community education and training component. The directions document points out:

> When education and training programs are developed and delivered by outside experts, and held outside the community, not as many people are able to take advantage of the training opportunities. Some simply do not complete their training. Education and training programs must be culturally appropriate, delivered by Aboriginal people, and offered as close to home as possible. It is crucial they be relevant to community members for them to assume responsibility for their own care.[303]

Education and training also figure prominently in the Alberta government's 1995 strategy to improve Aboriginal health.[304]

While our earlier recommendations were aimed primarily at providing support for Aboriginal participation in formal courses of study at educational institutions, we believe that widespread adoption of the Ontario approach would result in the development of many worthwhile community training and education initiatives, such as

- education and training activities to support traditional healing and the knowledge on which it is based;
- special training measures in northern and isolated communities for social workers, nurses, police officers, CHRs, and community organizations to assist them in dealing with substance abuse, suicide, violence in families and other problems;
- in some regions, specially trained crisis response teams of health professionals who can react to emergencies;
- distance education and support programs to advance the training of students and practitioners in remote areas;

- well-qualified translators, interpreters and escorts trained to accompany people to medical appointments, because the services provided by these individuals can have a profound effect on the accuracy of diagnosis and the effectiveness of treatment;[305]
- specialized training to help Aboriginal and non-Aboriginal professionals deal with the challenges facing Aboriginal people in urban areas;
- assistance in transferring ownership and responsibility for health and social services systems because of the long history of government control with limited community input;
- training and professional development opportunities for board members and staff in areas such as needs assessments, program planning, program evaluation, administration, community organization, and organizational development as new Aboriginal-controlled programs (such as healing centres and healing lodges) are developed;
- the opportunity for Aboriginal communities, organizations and governments involved in health and social services development to come together, to share ideas, and to profit from one another's experience and expertise; and
- assistance and support to reorient segmented service systems so that they are more holistic and more responsive to community needs.

The needs are diverse, and the priorities are best determined by the communities themselves.

As in the Ontario plan, any new approach should be flexible enough to respond to the full range of training needs identified by Aboriginal communities. It should also reward co-operation and collaboration – if Aboriginal communities or governments within a region see that there are benefits to collaborating with one another to address common needs, the program should be flexible enough to respond to these opportunities.

RECOMMENDATION

The Commission recommends that

Support for Community Participation

3.3.20

Federal, provincial and territorial governments, in collaboration with Aboriginal organizations and governments, allocate funds to support Aboriginal community participation in planning, program development, training, and promoting community awareness in relation to human resources development in health and social services.

Traditional healing and traditional healers

Our analysis of Aboriginal health and social conditions, and the strategy for Aboriginal health and healing based on this analysis, focused attention on the importance of promoting traditional Aboriginal healing practices as one of the essential components of effective Aboriginal health and healing systems. Many issues have to be addressed if traditional healing is to make a greater contribution to the well-being of Aboriginal people, including access to existing services, protection and promotion of existing skills and knowledge, regulation of traditional healing practices by traditional healers themselves, and co-operation between traditional Aboriginal and western practitioners. Our recommendations will encourage and support traditional practices, but here we want to provide some further thoughts about this important subject.

Traditional practices have survived years of ridicule, denunciation and prohibition, though a great deal of traditional knowledge was no doubt lost in the years of suppression. It would be easy to downplay the importance of traditional practices, because Aboriginal communities have often hidden them from non-Aboriginal eyes in order to protect them. In fact, some Aboriginal people might not be aware of the opportunities offered by traditional healing, and they might not even know about healing practices available in their own communities. It is important, therefore, that surviving practices be protected from further loss and misrepresentation, and that they be strengthened and adapted to contemporary conditions. Interested readers will find a more detailed discussion of traditional knowledge in Volume 4, Chapter 3.

To preserve existing traditional knowledge and explore its application to the health and social problems facing Aboriginal people today, a number of issues will have to be discussed and resolved by governments, health authorities and healers. (See Appendix 3A for elaboration of issues related to traditional healing practices.) The number of active healers, midwives and elder-advisers is unknown, but it is not likely to rise as fast as the demand for their services. This suggests the need for training and/or apprenticeship programs.

Along with a shortage of healers, intolerance of alternatives to bio-medicine in the United Sates and Canada over the last hundred years has led to a decline in traditional practices. They are little known and only superficially understood, except among a small number of traditionalists – some of them elders, but many of them younger. Resistance to an increased role for traditional health and healing comes from those who believe Christian values conflict with traditional values, from the non-Aboriginal population, and from the bio-medical community. It will take consistent effort in public and professional education to change these views.

Traditional healing has endured major and deliberate assaults on its validity. To protect and preserve existing skills and knowledge, and at the same time develop and extend their application, active support – not just increased tolerance – is required. In non-Aboriginal society, this falls under the heading of 'research and development', an accepted and well-funded requirement of bio-medicine. An equivalent support structure, fully controlled by Aboriginal people, is needed to preserve and advance the potential of traditional healing.

These matters are primarily the business and responsibility of Aboriginal healers, communities and nations. As responsibility for the planning and delivery of health and social services is taken on by Aboriginal nations, it will fall to them to decide the place of traditional healing. Nevertheless, there is a role for governments – they can and should provide funds to help Aboriginal people now, and in the long-term they must establish financing frameworks to enable Aboriginal health and social services to develop traditional healing practices in the way and to the extent they see fit.

RECOMMENDATION

The Commission recommends that

Protect and Extend Traditional Healing

3.3.21

Governments, health authorities and traditional practitioners co-operate to protect and extend the practices of traditional healing and explore their application to contemporary Aboriginal health and healing problems.

Implementing this recommendation will require immediate steps, such as conservation of the oral tradition by compiling written or video records, encouraging apprenticeships, and other means; patent protection for traditional pharmacological knowledge and substances; and controlled access to traditional knowledge that is considered sacred.

In addition, government and non-government funding bodies, such as the Social Sciences and Humanities Research Council, the Medical Research Council, equivalent funding agencies of provincial and territorial governments, and private foundations concerned with health and social well-being, should designate funds for the study, preservation and extension of traditional health and healing practices. These funds should be administered by a committee consisting of a majority of Aboriginal people and chaired by a qualified Aboriginal person.

Aboriginal governments, health authorities and traditional healers should also co-operate in exploring the history, current role, and future contribution of traditional health and healing practices.

Finally, mainstream institutions should consider and implement strategies to extend understanding of and respect for traditional health and healing practices. These might include roles for

- schools, especially where there is a significant Aboriginal population, to explore the values and practices of traditional medicine as part of inculcating in students an overall sensitivity to Aboriginal cultures;
- Aboriginal health and social service professionals and their associations to explore the applicability of traditional values and healing practices to their area of endeavour and to work with non-Aboriginal professional associations to create a supportive environment for their use;
- social service agencies, especially those serving an Aboriginal population with persistent social problems, to explore the possibility of incorporating the values and practices of traditional healing in current programs.

A policy of enhancing the role of traditional healing in Aboriginal and mainstream health and social services will require co-operation between conventionally trained personnel and traditional practitioners. This has important implications for the training of non-Aboriginal health and social services professionals.

Institutions involved in training health and social services professionals, as well as professional associations, should develop ways to sensitize practitioners to the existence of traditional medicine and to the possibilities for co-operation and collaboration across boundaries. In addition, Aboriginal and non-Aboriginal health care organizations and associations should continue to discuss the benefits of and barriers to collaboration and co-operation through periodic meetings or conferences, by the initiation of one or more demonstration projects to explore models of partnership, and through other means.

RECOMMENDATIONS

The Commission recommends that

Dialogue Between Aboriginal and Bio-Medical Practitioners

3.3.22

Aboriginal traditional healers and bio-medical practitioners strive actively to enhance mutual respect through dialogue and that they explore areas of possible sharing and collaboration.

Educational Institutions Respect Traditional Practices

3.3.23

Non-Aboriginal educational institutions and professional associations involved in the health and social services fields sensitize practitioners to the existence of traditional medicine and healing practices, the possibilities for co-operation and collaboration, and the importance of recognizing, affirming and respecting traditional practices and practitioners.

There have been some important developments in these areas, particularly in recent years. But a more dedicated effort is required on the part of all concerned to increase the level of understanding and respect and to safeguard the traditional knowledge and practices that are so vital to the well-being of many Aboriginal people.

Conclusion

Human resources development is one of the most important aspects of building the capacity of Aboriginal peoples and nations to address pressing health and social needs. It is clear to us that more services, if imposed by outside agencies, will not lead to the desired outcomes.

There is very little current information about the status of Aboriginal human resources in health and social services in Canada, but what is available indicates shortages in critical areas. While information should be collected on a more systematic basis, and while a comprehensive plan for Aboriginal human resources should be developed, these activities should not be allowed to delay the immediate action needed to increase the number of Aboriginal people who can design and deliver health and social services.

We have proposed a multi-faceted approach to the development of Aboriginal human resources in the health and social services fields. Educational institutions must increase their capacity to train Aboriginal students and make the training they provide more relevant to Aboriginal needs, but Aboriginal students must also be assisted to take advantage of the opportunities that become available. Mainstream institutions must lend their support, but there is also an increasingly important role for Aboriginal institutions. Formal courses of study are needed, but more flexible, community-based options for increasing competence and capacity are also required. Existing programs that have proved their value must be expanded, but other institutions must also become involved in expanding opportunities for Aboriginal students. Aboriginal people must have the opportunity to pursue professional studies, but it is also important that traditional knowledge and practices be preserved and enhanced.

By working together, Aboriginal and mainstream educational institutions, professional associations and service delivery organizations can make a difference. Many models of effective co-operation exist, but the scope of current initiatives must be broadened significantly to address present and future needs.

The health and social conditions facing Aboriginal people in Canada today constitute a crisis and a tragedy. No amount of external intervention, however well intentioned, will return Aboriginal people to the state of well-being they once enjoyed. What external forces cannot bring about, however, Aboriginal people can achieve for themselves. We firmly believe that a commitment to developing Aboriginal human resources will help to bring about the significant improvements in the health of Aboriginal people that are so desperately needed.

3.4 Enlisting the Support of the Mainstream Service System

It has become clear to us that more effective responses to the health and social needs of Aboriginal people will have to be achieved through two complementary strategies: the continuing development of health and healing systems under the control of Aboriginal people; and the transformation of the mainstream service system so that it can make a more positive contribution to the well-being of Aboriginal people. Having discussed our ideas about Aboriginal institutional development, we turn now to the steps that should be taken concerning the mainstream health and social service system, including government programs, hospitals, health centres, drug and alcohol programs, family violence programs, child welfare programs, programs for persons with disabilities, public health programs, mental health programs and residential treatment programs.

Some might suggest that mainstream services have little to contribute to the improvement of Aboriginal health and social conditions. They have often failed Aboriginal people in the past, and if Aboriginal institutions and governments continue to develop as we recommend, there is no doubt that many Aboriginal people will look to institutions of their own design to provide services. Nonetheless, we believe mainstream health and social programs will continue to have a significant effect on the lives of Aboriginal people and that it is important to enlist the positive support of these programs.

These programs will continue to influence the well-being of Aboriginal people for several reasons. There will always be Aboriginal people who choose mainstream services, even if programs under Aboriginal control are readily available. This should not be surprising, because the element of choice is no less important to Aboriginal people than it is to other Canadians. No matter how good a particular service is, or how competent the service provider, it will not be the most effective or desirable option for every individual in all circumstances. In Canada, we value being involved in decisions that affect our well-being, and this involvement can have a significant bearing on the effectiveness of the services we receive.

Having choices among services and service providers, however, is likely to remain a distant dream for many Aboriginal communities. Owing to the small population and remoteness of many Aboriginal communities, some health and social services, particularly specialized services, may be available only from mainstream providers. In these instances, the well-being of the Aboriginal people who must use these services will depend on what the mainstream system has to offer. Especially in the period when Aboriginal health and social programs are being developed more fully across the country, reliance on mainstream services will continue.

The prospects for Aboriginal people who live in urban centres are similar. At our public hearings, many organizations pointed out that an increasing number and proportion of Aboriginal people reside in urban areas, that they require health and social services, that the Aboriginal service infrastructure is not adequate to meet their needs, and that the services available from mainstream agencies are often not appropriate or effective. As discussed more fully in Volume 4, Chapter 7, the health and social needs of Aboriginal people in urban centres are multifaceted, and they arise for a variety of different reasons. In part, they result from the poverty that Aboriginal people often experience in urban centres. While many Aboriginal people come to cities in search of jobs, housing, educational opportunities, and a better life, the reality can be very different. Poverty brings with it an increased risk of a broad range of health and social problems. In addition, the culture shock of adjusting to life in a new, and culturally alien, environment can lead to social or health problems requiring attention from service providers.

Many Aboriginal people come to urban centres with needs that arose from health and social problems experienced in their own communities. For example, we learned that some Aboriginal women move to the cities to escape violence. In other instances, Aboriginal people move to urban areas to obtain health or social services not available in their own communities. We were told that elderly people often have to relocate to urban centres to obtain needed services.[306]

To address these concerns, we set out a plan for the development of urban-based Aboriginal services in Volume 4, Chapter 7. However, even with the development of these services, reliance on mainstream services is likely to continue for the foreseeable future.

The resources allocated to the mainstream health and social services systems are vast, particularly when compared with the resources under Aboriginal control. In considering options for the future, therefore, it is only reasonable to consider how the mainstream system can help. This is all the more important since incremental resources will be very scarce in the current climate of fiscal restraint.

Aboriginal and mainstream healing systems have much to offer one another. It would be detrimental to the development of both systems, and to those they served, if ways to co-operate and collaborate were not fully explored and encouraged.

For these reasons, we conclude that the potential of mainstream health and social service programs to contribute positively to the well-being of Aboriginal people is great, even though it has not always been developed effectively in the past.

Reforming mainstream systems: the limitations of past approaches

In recognition of the fact that non-Aboriginal health and social programs have not served Aboriginal people very effectively, and in response to pressure from Aboriginal organizations, the courts, and human rights authorities, policy makers have instituted a number of strategies over several decades in an attempt to sensitize mainstream health and social services providers to the needs and aspirations of Aboriginal peoples. It is instructive to examine some of these approaches, to analyze why they have generally produced such limited results, and to explore what can be done differently in the future.

Initiatives to improve the effectiveness of mainstream health and social service programs have taken many forms, including

- affirmative action and employment equity hiring policies;
- specialized Aboriginal units staffed by Aboriginal employees within larger mainstream programs;
- cross-cultural education programs for non-Aboriginal staff;
- Aboriginal input into mainstream programs and decisions; and
- Aboriginal customary practices included in the services offered by mainstream agencies.

Affirmative action

One strategy to make non-Aboriginal health and social programs more responsive to the needs of Aboriginal people has been affirmative action. A general discussion of affirmative action appears in Volume 2, Chapter 5; here we review some of the implications for health and social services.

Most agencies serving Aboriginal people report that they make a special effort to recruit Aboriginal staff. Some agencies have gone to considerable lengths and, in a number of instances, formal programs have been approved by human rights authorities. Even for agencies not involved in providing services directly to Aboriginal communities, federal, provincial and municipal laws and policies often call for equitable employment practices.

Most affirmative action programs involve the design and implementation of specialized recruitment strategies. These might consist of recruiting at educational institutions with high Aboriginal enrolment, advertising in Aboriginal publications, asking Aboriginal leaders to identify suitable applicants, and using specialized recruitment firms. These and other methods have been used to recruit Aboriginal social assistance workers, family services staff, corrections staff, police officers, health workers, and many others.

Many presentations to the Commission discussed affirmative action. A full array of perspectives on this controversial subject was evident. Some felt that affirmative action had been beneficial, and they called on employers to make a stronger commitment to such initiatives:

> Affirmative action hiring policies for staff and professors and administrators would be one area [where] non-Aboriginal peoples can start to share the power and the resources that they hold.

> James Murray
> Brandon University Student Union
> The Pas, Manitoba, 20 May 1992

Industry and public service require quotas, employment equity and affirmative action programs. Some people are against them, but I believe...[they] will make an impact.

Raymond Laliberté
Métis Addictions Council
La Ronge, Saskatchewan, 28 May 1992

How do we eliminate systemic racism? The answer is that we begin with systemic change. In our opinion, three ways to start that process are cross-cultural training, affirmative action, and strong and effective anti-racism policies with teeth to them....[T]he [Saskatchewan Human Rights] Commission recommends mandatory implementation of affirmative action.

Theresa Holizki
Chief Commissioner
Saskatchewan Human Rights Commission
Saskatoon, Saskatchewan, 28 October 1992

We may have to start with affirmative action programs to get more [Aboriginal] women represented in the justice system within the government, but I think that eventually women would naturally be there. Women just need a chance to get their foot in the door.

Reana Erasmus
Yellowknife, Northwest Territories
7 December 1992

If you are going to make any headway, there has to be a strong, mandatory affirmative-action type of program to bring Aboriginal people into the workforce and promote them.

Dick Martin
Canadian Labour Congress
Ottawa, Ontario, 15 November 1993

Many other presenters provided a more critical assessment of what affirmative action has achieved to date. Some also raised questions about the underlying purpose of affirmative action and suggested that such programs may have a limited role in correcting existing inequities:

It has been abundantly clear and plainly evident...that the federal government has [attempted] to assimilate and otherwise integrate Indian people into the mainstream of Canada. This included an attempt to destroy our nations, lands, cultures and values, and to make us municipal governments made up of ethnic minorities whose proper place is within the multi-cultural minorities framework assisted and recognized by policies of affirmative action.

Chief Carl Quinn
Saddle Lake Band
Hobbema, Alberta, 10 June 1992

Basically, my position is that affirmative action has failed Native people in Canada. It was designed to facilitate their entry...in the workforce, and this has not been achieved anywhere in Canada....There is a danger in affirmative action....[T]he very fact we have affirmative action programs, the larger society seems to believe that they are doing something....[I]t makes them feel good.... These affirmative action programs can go on for years and make the larger society feel good and no Natives are being hired.

John Hart
Saskatoon, Saskatchewan
28 October 1992

Affirmative action initiatives have not gone far enough. Many more of our women and people are graduating from high school and university, yet they are unable to find meaningful employment. Most affirmative action programs establish ridiculously low target levels and after hiring one or two Aboriginal people, no further efforts are made to increase the Aboriginal representation among their staff. Nor do they expend much effort to retain the staff they did hire. Many Aboriginal staff leave in frustration, tired of often single-handedly fighting ethnocentric attitudes on the part of their employers and co-workers.

Kula Ellison
Aboriginal Women's Council
Saskatoon, Saskatchewan, 28 October 1992

According to the Aboriginal employees, the affirmative action program and efforts are not working. Aboriginal employees perceive that progress is painfully slow....[W]e are low in numbers and we are compressed and concentrated at the bottom level of the civil service.

Louise Chippeway
Chairperson, Aboriginal Advisory Council
Roseau River, Manitoba, 8 December 1992

What about affirmative action? I don't know what it has done for Native people.

Bobby Bulmer
Yellowknife, Northwest Territories
9 December 1992

Most of us object to affirmative action programs on principle and because we believe that such programs fail to achieve their intended goals. Although affirmative action programs may succeed in allocating people of a given description into the workplace, by and large it is felt that legislative requirements to hire what may be unqualified or minimally qualified people achieves nothing positive in the long run for either the employer or the employee.

Bill Gagnon
Hay River Chamber of Commerce
Hay River, Northwest Territories, 17 June 1993

You know, they talk about employment equity all the time. Let's practise it.

Chief Walter Barry
Benoit's Cove Band
Gander, Newfoundland, 5 November 1992

Employers claim that they are committed to increasing the number of Aboriginal people they employ and, generally, we believe they are. With a few exceptions, however, their efforts have been largely ineffectual. Even after these programs have been in place for some time, very few Aboriginal people are employed. As a result, employers have little evidence that affirmative action works. After more than two decades of affirmative action, the vast majority of Aboriginal health and social services in Canada continue to be provided by non-Aboriginal people working in non-Aboriginal agencies.

Although most affirmative action programs have met with limited success in recruiting, retaining and promoting Aboriginal employees, a few have made noteworthy progress. Moreover, the success of some employment equity programs for other under-represented groups (for example, programs to increase the number of women on university faculties) leads us to conclude that affirmative action programs can achieve much more for Aboriginal people than their record to date would indicate.

Many reasons for the failure of affirmative action programs have been identified.[307] During economic downturns, employers have few vacancies and, consequently, few opportunities to recruit Aboriginal staff.[308] Employers also say that Aboriginal applicants often fail to meet the requirements for positions that do become available. This is a valid concern, and it is why we believe it is necessary not only to provide employment opportunities for Aboriginal people but also to train more Aboriginal people in the health and social services professions. However, we also believe there are other reasons for the low number of Aboriginal employees in health and social services agencies.

Position requirements may be difficult for some Aboriginal applicants to meet, even if they are not strictly relevant to the duties of the position. Other requirements may be unreasonable or inappropriate to apply to Aboriginal applicants, for cultural or other reasons. Insistence that applicants meet such requirements may amount to a form of systemic discrimination. We were given many examples during the course of our public hearings. We were told how high school completion, aptitude test scores, and other measures that are subject to cultural bias are used to screen out potential Aboriginal employees, even before an interview.[309]

As we have discussed, there are no generally accepted methods or systems in place to recognize and accredit Aboriginal knowledge and experience. Rather, the focus in hiring is usually on formal credentials and experience that can be obtained only from mainstream educational institutions and employers. This may serve to discriminate unfairly against Aboriginal applicants.

Another reason for limited employment numbers could lie in Aboriginal people's experiences with health and social services agencies. Aboriginal people might question the programs and policies of the agencies trying to recruit them, for example, particularly if the agency has shown a reluctance to examine the effects of its programs and policies on Aboriginal people. They may have had unhappy personal experiences themselves, or they may have seen the consequences of inappropriate or inadequate services in their communities. This happens particularly when the potential employer exercises a social control function, as in the case of child welfare agencies. Given the historical impact of non-Aboriginal child welfare policies and services, it is understandable that Aboriginal people have shown considerable reluctance to work for non-Aboriginal child welfare agencies. They might also feel that their families or communities would criticize them for becoming part of a system that has been unresponsive to Aboriginal needs or rights in the past. They might not want to put themselves in the position of having to continue agency practices that are ineffective or culturally inappropriate.

Aboriginal candidates for positions with mainstream agencies might feel uncomfortable accepting and keeping employment in an environment where they are in the minority, or where no support system is apparent to help them deal with the stresses of the workplace. It is sometimes difficult even to apply to a non-Aboriginal agency for employment when, as is usually the case, the recruitment process is presided over by non-Aboriginal people. When agencies have no record of employing, retaining, promoting and valuing Aboriginal staff, potential candidates may not see a job with a mainstream agency as a viable career option.

When Aboriginal people do join non-Aboriginal organizations, they often feel an absence of support for the personal and professional challenges they face in professional practice. There is evidence that some Aboriginal employees in non-Aboriginal agencies do not derive the sense of fulfilment from their work that they are seeking. Instead, they seek other employment, often with Aboriginal agencies, thus leading to high turnover rates and a perception of Aboriginal employees as unreliable or lacking the requisite loyalty to the employer.

There is nothing wrong with Aboriginal staff gaining experience in mainstream agencies and then moving on to play leadership roles in Aboriginal organizations and governments. Indeed, many Aboriginal leaders have had this type of experience. It is a positive result of the initiatives of some mainstream agencies to hire, train and promote Aboriginal staff. Our concern, however, is that the experience of Aboriginal employees in mainstream agencies is often far less rewarding than it should be. We do not believe Aboriginal staff should feel compelled to leave mainstream agencies because the working environment is not supportive.

Perceptions of Aboriginal employees as unreliable may influence future hiring practices. Likewise, when reports of bad experiences circulate within Aboriginal communities, other potential applicants are discouraged from coming forward.

In addition to these concerns, there are problems with employment equity related to the depth of commitment by employers, the adequacy of existing legislation, and the lack of effective monitoring. These issues are discussed more fully in Volume 2, Chapter 5.

A number of these concerns were summarized in a presentation to the Commission from the Canadian Auto Workers:

> There is a lengthy list of problems and obstacles to be addressed before Aboriginal people in Canada gain equitable access to secure, well-paying jobs. Identifiable issues are lack of commitment of employers, beginning with top management; weak administration and enforcement of employment equity programs; bias and racism directed at Aboriginal workers; hiring procedures that discriminate; unreasonable demands for qualifications; and work arrangements that affect the ability of Aboriginal workers to settle into a job and retain it.
>
> Debbie Luce
> Canadian Auto Workers
> Toronto, Ontario, 19 November 1993

Aboriginal units within mainstream institutions

Recognizing some of the problems with affirmative action, some service providers have established specialized Aboriginal units, staffed by Aboriginal employees, within larger non-Aboriginal programs and agencies. Perhaps the best known example of this approach was the RCMP's Indian Special Constable Program (now reorganized). Similar programs have been established for employment counsellors, social assistance workers, substance abuse counsellors, health care providers, and many others. This approach has also been used with success outside the health and social services field. The National Film Board, for example, established an Aboriginal studio based in Edmonton. Its purpose is to involve Aboriginal people more fully in the Canadian film industry and to ensure better representation of Aboriginal perspectives in Canadian films.

Some of these initiatives have been quite successful in attracting and retaining Aboriginal staff and in delivering quality services to Aboriginal people. However, they have encountered many of the same problems as affirmative action, although not always to the same degree. Often they are not accorded the same status as equivalent mainstream programs, resource levels may be inferior, and staff do not always have the same latitude as mainstream staff to carry out the responsibilities of their positions. As a result, they are often seen as 'second class' programs by administrators and the public.

This was certainly the case, for example, with the Indian Special Constable Program. 'Special' meant that Indian constables were not full-fledged RCMP constables – they did not receive the same level of training or remuneration as regular constables, and they were not permitted to wear the red serge, the ceremonial uniform of the RCMP. The drawing of these sorts of distinctions is not at all uncommon in the types of programs discussed here.

Cross-cultural awareness

Another approach to improving the effectiveness of mainstream health and social service programs has focused on promoting greater awareness among non-Aboriginal staff of the needs and circumstances of their Aboriginal clients. These initiatives have usually involved ad hoc programs of cross-cultural awareness, as well as related training and education programs. Such programs have been adopted widely in non-Aboriginal agencies with a large Aboriginal caseload.

The available evidence indicates that the effectiveness of these initiatives depends heavily on the program design and the knowledge and skills of the resource persons that deliver them. Results are not always positive; in fact, some programs have had the opposite effect. As the Assembly of First Nations pointed out in their brief to us:

> Optional, ad hoc approaches to training, such as voluntary, one-day workshops – once a year seminars in response to misunderstandings – accomplish very little.[310]

The AFN has expressed concern that these types of programs could solidify stereotypes and cause friction in the workplace, leaving the impression that people of other cultures are 'difficult'.

Cross-cultural input

Other initiatives have taken the form of inviting Aboriginal input in decision making in non-Aboriginal programs. Elders are consulted about treatment options; the band council is asked about the apprehension of a child; committees are established to provide community input in the work of hospitals and other non-Aboriginal agencies.

These measures to secure Aboriginal input often result in improved relations between Aboriginal communities and those responsible for service delivery. In addition, there is some evidence that the effectiveness of some programs has improved because Aboriginal input has led to better decisions and greater community acceptance of decisions. Yet, the improvements in program effectiveness are often far from dramatic. Moreover, opportunities for Aboriginal input often rely on informal arrangements that depend on the interest and goodwill of individual officials in mainstream agencies. Because they seldom become institutionalized, these arrangements often remain in effect for only a limited time.

Introducing traditional Aboriginal practices into non-Aboriginal programs has also become fairly commonplace. Child welfare and young offender institutions, for example, sometimes permit sweat lodges, sweet grass ceremonies, and the attendance of elders and spiritual leaders; hospitals sometimes make provision for the services of traditional healers. At least in some instances, however, officials may not be fully committed to these efforts. Moreover, programs may not be accorded the same importance or respect as corresponding programs for non-Aboriginal clients. They may even be cancelled or modified to comply with the requirements of mainstream policies or programs.

During the Aboriginal Justice Inquiry of Manitoba, for example, Commissioners Hamilton and Sinclair found that elders and traditional healers were discouraged from visiting Aboriginal inmates in correctional facilities because they and their sacred articles were not accorded proper respect by the correctional staff.[311] Meanwhile, non-Aboriginal clergy and health professionals were not required to undergo the same security procedures.

We heard about one program that introduced Aboriginal practices into non-Aboriginal programs:

> Native social workers do indeed show up to help Native offenders cope with white man's justice. Similarly, all correctional facilities have social groups for members of the First Nations. We view these and most current programs, however, as only a token and reluctant recognition of our [Aboriginal] origins. All such programs fail to provide any significant recognition of the deeper cultural, spiritual and communal traditions at the First Nations level.
>
> Brian Espansel
> Vice-Chair, Native Sons
> Toronto, Ontario, 25 June 1992

Imbalance in relationships

Although the kinds of initiatives described often involve considerable effort and expense, they have not always achieved the desired results. While some improvements in the effectiveness of health and social services have been brought about, the gains have usually been modest. Even with these types of reforms, non-Aboriginal programs do not usually achieve the level of effectiveness or acceptance in Aboriginal communities that these same programs enjoy in non-Aboriginal communities.

We believe these strategies have not had a greater effect primarily because they do not address the underlying imbalance in relations between Aboriginal people and the broader society. In fact, these approaches have sometimes been used to justify the continuation of this imbalance and to avoid more fundamental reforms. We have concluded that programs based on values and beliefs that may not be shared by Aboriginal people cannot be transformed into programs that are effective and culturally appropriate through the adoption of these types of approaches alone.

Remarkably little attention has been directed to promoting real Aboriginal involvement in and control of health and social services in Canada, or to creating true partnerships involving Aboriginal and non-Aboriginal organizations and governments, although this has certainly begun to change in recent years. Rather, the programs and policies developed by mainstream agencies have too often been assumed to constitute the best possible approach to delivering services to all, including Aboriginal people. Various initiatives, such as those we have described, have then been implemented to help Aboriginal people fit in, accept, or adjust to non-Aboriginal programs and to the values and beliefs on which they are based.

This history constitutes the backdrop against which future plans must be laid. We believe the lesson of this history is clear: the types of initiatives we have described cannot succeed unless they are accompanied by more fundamental reforms that recognize and support Aboriginal self-determination. As one presenter told us,

> This new relationship [between Aboriginal people and Canada] cannot be a mere tinkering with the status quo by way of affirmative action or employment equity.
>
> Clem Chartier
> Saskatoon, Saskatchewan
> 12 May 1993

The types of initiatives we have described can make an important contribution to improving the effectiveness of mainstream services, provided that they are accompanied by more fundamental reforms. The imbalance in relations must be addressed, the inherent right of Aboriginal people to govern their own affairs must be recognized, and Aboriginal institutions must be allowed to flourish. If these changes do not proceed, attempts to improve the effectiveness of mainstream health and social programs for Aboriginal people through these approaches will continue to lead to frustration and disappointment.

New approaches based on a renewed relationship

Mainstream programs and service providers can contribute to improving Aboriginal health and social conditions in two important ways: by encouraging and supporting the development of health and social service systems under Aboriginal control; and by improving the appropriateness and effectiveness of mainstream services provided to Aboriginal people.

Support for the development of health and social programs under Aboriginal control can be provided in many ways. Mainstream organizations can examine how to transfer programs to Aboriginal control; they can encourage collaboration involving Aboriginal and western healing systems; and they can support Aboriginal organizations' efforts to develop plans, standards, and processes for accrediting their programs and staff. Other steps could include supporting the development of Aboriginal networks, creating resource centres with Aboriginal materials, and negotiating partnership agreements that strengthen Aboriginal organizations involved in service delivery.

During our hearings we learned about many examples of this type of collaboration. In Inukjuak, northern Quebec, we were told that an explicit part of the mandate of non-Aboriginal health and social workers is to pass their knowledge along to Inuit fellow workers, thereby promoting the development of Aboriginal human resources in Aboriginal communities. In Winnipeg, we heard of co-operative efforts on the part of government, non-government and Aboriginal organizations to establish an urban health and social services centre for Aboriginal people, staffed entirely by Aboriginal people. In Val d'Or, we learned about steps taken by a health and social services board to assist Aboriginal people in developing a community health promotion strategy. A number of professional associations told us about their involvement in cross-cultural exchanges and collaboration among Aboriginal and non-Aboriginal health and healing experts.[312]

In Montreal, we learned about a unique research and education initiative involving the Centre for Indigenous Nutrition and Environment at McGill University. The centre is a university program whose activities are overseen by a governing board made up of six Aboriginal organizations representing Inuit, First Nations and Métis people. The participatory research model used by the centre directly involves Aboriginal communities in defining research needs and carrying out research. The centre's program specifically recognizes the importance of cultural issues and indigenous knowledge and seeks to improve the capacity of Aboriginal communities to deal with issues affecting their nutrition and environment. In northern Quebec, the mainstream public health authorities have entered into an agreement with the Cree and Kativik boards of health to provide backup tertiary care and referral services and to support these boards in the areas of health programming and evaluation. These agencies and organizations are showing leadership, and we encourage others to learn from these positive examples of what can be accomplished.[313]

There can be no doubt about the importance of good will. However, relations must be developed in a true spirit of partnership, with the levels and types of support provided by mainstream organizations determined by Aboriginal peoples themselves. Anything less will not succeed. One non-Aboriginal educator expressed the spirit of partnership this way:

> As non-Aboriginal people, we must be tolerant and accepting of political and social agendas which are not of our own making. Aboriginal peoples must govern themselves in their own ways. We must also, however, recognize that we need 'bridging institutions' to cross cultural divides. These institutions must be built jointly and from both directions toward the middle, instead of from one side to the other.
>
> Douglas A. West
> Thunder Bay, Ontario
> 27 October 1992

The second way that mainstream health and social service agencies can contribute to improving the health and well-being of Aboriginal people is by taking steps to improve the quality of their services. Some examples of the steps that can be taken include

- increasing Aboriginal staffing and other forms of Aboriginal involvement in the day-to-day operations of mainstream programs;
- developing and implementing plans to provide for the structured, organized and systematic involvement of Aboriginal people in the design of programs and in the governance of mainstream agencies;
- examining the barriers that prevent the provision of traditional health and healing services, and implementing measures to overcome these barriers;
- developing and implementing a plan to combat racist behaviours;
- providing the services of interpreters and making literature available in Aboriginal languages;
- carrying out assessments of Aboriginal health and social needs and redesigning services to meet these needs;
- bringing needed promotion and prevention services to Aboriginal communities on a proactive basis, rather than waiting until there is a crisis;
- establishing a clear point of contact for Aboriginal people so that they can easily obtain any information or assistance they require about access to mainstream services;
- developing a protocol to ensure that any concerns or suggestions about services provided are acted on promptly; and

- developing a monitoring system to ensure that the quality and effectiveness of services provided to Aboriginal people are assessed regularly.

In every instance, Aboriginal communities and organizations should be engaged in designing and guiding initiatives.

We are particularly concerned about levels of Aboriginal staffing in non-Aboriginal health and social service agencies. We have already discussed measures to increase the number of trained Aboriginal professionals, but recruitment practices and workplace policies will also have to change if trained Aboriginal professionals are to be attracted to work for mainstream agencies.

Aboriginal staffing levels in mainstream organizations should be at least proportional to the percentage of Aboriginal people served by the organization. Moreover, proportional Aboriginal representation should be achieved throughout the agency hierarchy, from entry levels to the most senior positions. Where the number of applicants or the qualifications of applicants are not sufficient to achieve these objectives, there is a positive onus on mainstream organizations to institute measures to overcome barriers to Aboriginal employment. For example, organizations can develop pre-training and apprenticeship programs, provide bursaries and other forms of support, and institute educational leave and professional development policies to address inequities in opportunities.

A renewed commitment to employment equity is required on the part of mainstream health and social service agencies. This must entail the widespread adoption of practices that have proved effective.[314] These include developing a long-term plan; shifting the approach from individual applicants and positions to one that focuses on strategic partnerships and alliances with Aboriginal communities and institutions; adopting a more proactive approach to forecasting human resources requirements and how they will be met in the future; and strengthening auditing, monitoring and enforcement mechanisms to ensure that the goals of employment equity are achieved.

At least in the short term, and likely for some time, there will be a critical shortage of Aboriginal human resources. These resources are desperately needed in Aboriginal organizations and in the mainstream system. Therefore, one of the most important steps to improve Aboriginal health and social conditions is to accelerate training and professional development opportunities for Aboriginal people.

Earlier we referred to the limited results of many cross-cultural awareness programs, yet there is no denying the importance of cross-cultural sensitivity for personnel providing services to Aboriginal people. Therefore, we believe that mainstream agencies must renew their commitment to fostering cultural sensitivity. The risks and consequences of failure are such that cross-cultural training must be planned and implemented to provide reasonable assurance of achieving the desired outcomes. Initial cross-cultural training in the curricula of professional education programs, as well as continued training through staff orientation and professional development, will help to ensure success. It is also important to involve Aboriginal people in designing and implementing these programs. In addition, success will be influenced by the climate of support provided by the organization and by the commitment of the organization's senior administrators to provide culturally appropriate services.

Cross-cultural training should not be seen as a panacea. In the absence of the many other improvements required in mainstream agencies, cross-cultural training cannot be expected to achieve miracles. Rather, a comprehensive approach to transforming the policies and programs of mainstream agencies is required; cross-cultural training is only one component, albeit an important one.

During our hearings we heard several examples of the types of initiatives discussed here. Some of these initiatives are fully operational, while others are in various stages of planning. In St. John's, we heard about an innovative partnership between the friendship centre and a psychiatric hospital to provide interpretation services to improve the quality of mental health care for Aboriginal people.[315] In Nain, we heard about the efforts of the Melville Hospital in Happy Valley-Goose Bay to ensure that Labrador Inuit referred to other hospitals had access to an interpreter who could help them get the services they needed.[316] In the Yukon, we were informed about one hospital's efforts to hire an Aboriginal social worker and the tremendous improvements in the quality of care for Aboriginal patients that had been achieved as a result.[317]

In Montreal, the Association des hôpitaux du Québec, which represents hospitals in the province, told us about encouraging its members to allow Aboriginal people to practise their cultural traditions in the hospital setting.[318] Also in Montreal, we heard of proposals to have health and social services personnel complete apprenticeships in Aboriginal languages, to improve communication with Aboriginal clients, and we learned of special admissions criteria at one educational institution linked to the applicant's commitment to practise in a region with a significant Aboriginal population following graduation.

In several presentations in northern and southern Canada, we heard about the importance of midwifery services for Aboriginal people and learned about apprenticeship programs to train Aboriginal midwives.[319] A number of municipalities told us about steps they had taken to improve the range and appropriateness of health, social, recreational, and other services for Aboriginal people. We were also told about partnerships that municipal governments had developed with Aboriginal organizations.[320]

In Alberta, we heard about plans for mentorship programs for non-Aboriginal mental health workers, where mainstream personnel would have the opportunity to become cognizant of Aboriginal cultures, languages and traditional practices.[321] In New Brunswick, we heard about proposals to bring non-Aboriginal service providers in health and social services together with urban Aboriginal organizations to improve services for Aboriginal people residing in the city. In Saskatoon, we heard about the efforts of one human rights authority to improve the cultural appropriateness of services and Aboriginal staffing levels in mainstream agencies. In Prince George, we heard about the development of plans for the involvement of Aboriginal and non-Aboriginal agencies in a co-operative effort to meet the multiple needs of victims of fetal alcohol syndrome and fetal alcohol effect.

Finally, in Sault Ste. Marie, we heard how Aboriginal agencies are providing cross-cultural training for non-Aboriginal agencies, organizations and service providers involved in support services for Aboriginal women.[322]

We wish to recognize those involved in bringing about these creative improvements in service delivery, and we call on others to follow in their footsteps.

Plans developed by mainstream service institutions should contain a number of common elements. They should set out the organization's goals with reference to

- attracting, retaining, and promoting Aboriginal people;
- overcoming barriers to Aboriginal involvement at all levels in the organization (for example, service delivery, program management and design, and agency governance) and how these obstacles will be overcome;
- ensuring that non-Aboriginal staff are equipped to provide culturally sensitive and effective services to the Aboriginal people;
- improving the availability of effective services to Aboriginal clients;
- monitoring Aboriginal health and healing issues; and
- supporting Aboriginal institutional development.

The specific components of each action plan will vary with the responsibilities of the organization concerned and the service environment in which it operates.

Other groups

In addition to educational institutions and mainstream health and social services agencies, the support and leadership of many others will be needed to implement the directions we have outlined. While space does not permit a detailed examination, we would like to discuss professional associations, the voluntary sector, and the labour movement.

During our hearings, we received presentations and briefs from a number of professional associations in the health and social services field – organizations such as the Canadian Medical Association, L'Association des hôpitaux du Québec, the Canadian Paediatric Society, the Ontario Psychological Association, the Canadian Public Health Association, the Ordre des infirmières et infirmiers du Québec, the Corporation Professionelle des Médecins du Québec, and others.

These organizations are involved in the design of initial and continuing professional education, and in some instances they license and set standards for their members. They advise governments and service providers on professional practice issues, they conduct research on the efficacy of services and on other issues, and they take an interest in issues that affect the development and effectiveness of their members. These organizations told us they are deeply concerned about the health and social status of Aboriginal people. They advised us on the critical issues to be addressed, they outlined the steps they had taken already in their own professions, and they told us about their genuine desire for partnership with Aboriginal people.

Professional organizations can make a significant contribution to improving the health and social conditions of Aboriginal people. In addition to the extensive resources and experience at their disposal, they are strategically placed to help overcome barriers to improved services. In a number of areas, including professional training, licensing, standard setting, accreditation, and the recognition of Aboriginal knowledge and experience, professional organizations have the opportunity to play an important leadership role.

The contributions of non-profit, voluntary agencies to the health and well-being of Canadians is immeasurable. These organizations provide direct services, raise public awareness, promote research, advocate for the needs of their members, and participate in the design of health and social programs. During our public hearings, we received presentations and briefs from many such organizations, including the Canadian Diabetes Association, the Canadian Association for Community Living, the National Anti-Poverty Organization, the Canadian Mental Health Association, St. John's Ambulance, the Canada Safety Council, and many others. As discussed earlier in this chapter, several of these organizations have taken significant steps to become more informed and involved in the issues of Aboriginal health and social conditions. These organizations want to participate in finding and implementing more effective strategies to address Aboriginal health and social issues, and we believe they have an important role to play.

Some of Canada's leading labour organizations, including the Canadian Labour Congress, the Canadian Auto Workers, and the United Steelworkers, also made presentations during our public hearings. As with the organizations already mentioned, the unions are genuinely concerned about the health and social conditions of Aboriginal people. They rightly believe they have an important role in promoting social justice for Aboriginal people. For example, labour leaders told us:

We come here to express our solidarity and our support and our concerns about government inaction to resolve Aboriginal issues that have been plaguing our country for such a long time.

Hassan Yussuff
Canadian Auto Workers
Toronto, Ontario, 19 November 1993

We went and got Aboriginal members and Aboriginal leaders from our union and formed a small working group. With them, we studied two areas that we thought were important, where we would be able to get a first-hand view of the shortcomings of the union in dealing with our Aboriginal members and to get input from our Aboriginal members about things that we could do to start down the path....We are doing a lot of work to change what has been primarily a white, male-dominated union, to create opportunities for all of the people in our society....[O]ur goal is eventually to have our organization and its staff and employees and leadership reflect the make-up of our society....I think one of the important roles that this Commission could play is to recognize the important role of the trade unions....The experience of the last several years in our union is a real desire to be allies with the Aboriginal community, in particular with Aboriginal workers.

Leo Gerard
National Director, United Steelworkers of America
Toronto, Ontario, 19 November 1993

We wish to begin by reiterating the labour movement's support for the inherent right of Canada's Aboriginal peoples to self-determination, including the right of self-government and jurisdiction over lands and resources. We outlined this position in a major policy statement at our last 1992 Vancouver convention which is included with our brief....Aboriginal people are starting to move into staff and executive positions within labour. Unions have begun organizing in Aboriginal communities....The improvement of Aboriginal employment opportunities is a primary area for coalition building between labour and Aboriginal people and organizations.

Dick Martin
Canadian Labour Congress
Ottawa, Ontario, 15 November 1993

Many health and social agencies, whether they are government agencies or agencies operated by quasi-governmental or non-governmental authorities, are governed by collective bargaining agreements. As a result, the way they hire, retain and promote staff is often influenced in important ways by the provisions of these agreements. Given the low representation of Aboriginal professionals in the labour market, a number of presentations to the Commission expressed concern that these agreements, and particularly the provisions related to seniority, could have the effect of denying Aboriginal people employment and promotion opportunities.[323] However, in several presentations to the Commission, we learned that labour representatives are actively seeking ways to overcome these barriers, and they are committed to improving employment prospects for Aboriginal people.

Other mainstream organizations could be added to the list of stakeholders discussed here – municipal governments, churches, private sector organizations, and many others. Although we do not discuss these sectors separately, all have an important contribution to make.

RECOMMENDATION

The Commission recommends that

Action Plans of
Mainstream
Institutions and
Voluntary
Organizations

3.3.24

Non-Aboriginal service agencies and institutions involved in the delivery of health or social services to Aboriginal people, and professional associations, unions, and other organizations in a position to influence the delivery of health or social services to Aboriginal people

(a) undertake a systematic examination to determine how they can encourage and support the development of Aboriginal health and social service systems, and improve the appropriateness and effectiveness of mainstream services to Aboriginal people;

(b) engage representatives of Aboriginal communities and organizations in conducting such an examination;

(c) make public an action plan appropriate to the institution or organization involved, outlining measurable objectives and a timetable for achieving them; and

(d) establish means to monitor and evaluate implementation of the plan by the institution or organization itself and by Aboriginal representatives.

In addition, in Volume 5, Chapter 4, we discuss the need for a public education strategy to promote awareness of and respect for the history and cultures of Aboriginal nations and peoples and their role in the life of Canada. The initiative outlined there will help to heighten awareness about current health and social conditions and about the challenges that lie ahead for mainstream institutions in developing a renewed relationship with Aboriginal peoples.

Implementation strategies

We urge every mainstream agency, educational program and professional body involved in health and social services for Aboriginal people to take up the challenges outlined in this chapter. Some have already done so, but the present level of commitment is not sufficient to bring about all the changes that are needed.

Federal, provincial and territorial governments provide significant funding for health and social services through mainstream agencies, and there are many professional bodies with the authority to accredit professional education programs. The time has come for these influential funding and professional bodies to provide leadership. Incentives can be provided by allocating financial and other resources to organizations willing to implement reforms. But this alone will not overcome intransigence and resistance in some quarters. Therefore, we believe granting and funding bodies as well as professional associations should actively encourage the development and implementation of action plans of the type just discussed. Where the agency serves a significant number of Aboriginal clients, the existence of an action plan, and regular evidence that the plan is being implemented, should be required.

RECOMMENDATION

The Commission recommends that

Enforcement of
Service Standards

3.3.25
Governments responsible for funding and professional bodies responsible for accrediting non-Aboriginal institutions and agencies engaged in the delivery of Aboriginal health and social services

(a) establish as a criterion for continuing funding and accreditation the preparation and implementation of goals and standards for services to Aboriginal people; and

(b) require that Aboriginal people, communities and nations affected by such services be fully involved in the development, implementation and evaluation of such goals and standards of practice.

Mainstream health and social programs continue to fail Aboriginal people on a massive scale. If the crisis in Aboriginal health and social conditions is to be addressed, mainstream programs must be reformed in a meaningful way to ensure that they make a much more positive contribution to finding and implementing the solutions that are needed so urgently.

Given the magnitude of the problems to be overcome, and the high human and economic cost of failure, we believe our recommendations are entirely appropriate to the circumstances. (An analysis of the costs of maintaining the status quo is presented in Volume 5, Chapter 2.) Agencies involved in service delivery, as well as bodies responsible for funding and licensing or accrediting these agencies, must come together to demonstrate the commitment that is required. Anything less will prove a recipe for insupportable human and financial costs.

3.5 Housing and Community Infrastructure

The fourth component of our strategy to transform the health status of Aboriginal people is the resolution of the long-standing, debilitating and worsening crisis in Aboriginal housing and the eradication of threats to public health posed by unsafe water supplies and inadequate waste management in rural and remote Aboriginal communities.

In Chapter 4 of this volume, we set out our analysis of the magnitude of the problems, the obligations of federal, provincial and territorial governments to take action on the problems, the barriers to resolution, and a strategy to achieve adequate community infrastructure within five years and an adequate housing supply within 10 years. While a substantial investment is required to achieve these ends, the payback in terms of improved health and well-being and stimulation of Aboriginal economic activity will quickly generate offsetting gains.

Implementing the four components of our strategy will do much to foster whole health in Aboriginal populations, but maintaining health improvements over the long term will depend on a much broader transformation of the conditions of Aboriginal life. We urge action now on health concerns, because a healthy citizenry is essential to building vital nations. At the same time, effective government and productive economies are equally essential to sustaining the health of the people.

4. THE JOURNEY TO
WHOLE HEALTH

To identify a sound basis for the re-establishment of health and well-being among Aboriginal people, we have tried to come to a new and deeper understanding of what makes people well. We had the benefit of carefully considered proposals from frontline caregivers and health administrators (both Aboriginal and non-Aboriginal) and of new insights from health researchers who are reconceptualizing the determinants of health. From their collective wisdom, we have concluded that good health is not simply the outcome of illness care and social welfare services. It is the outcome of living actively, productively and safely, with reasonable control over the forces affecting everyday life, with the means to nourish body and soul, in harmony with one's neighbours and oneself, and with hope for the future of one's children and one's land. In short, good health is the outcome of living well.

Whole health, in the full sense of the term, does not depend primarily on the mode of operation of health and healing services – as important as they are. Whole health depends as much or more on the design of the political and economic systems that organize relations of power and productivity in Canadian society. For Aboriginal people, those systems have been working badly; before whole health can be achieved, they must begin to work well.

Some Aboriginal leaders despair of the continuing tunnel vision of non-Aboriginal authorities who insist on the capacity of bio-medical and social welfare regimes to bring health to Aboriginal people. At a circumpolar health conference in 1984, Peter Penashue, an Innu leader from Labrador, spoke about freedom from domination as the route to improved health for his people:

> The Innu are sick and dying because of a well-documented syndrome of ill health brought on by the enforced dependency and attempted acculturation of an entire people. This ill health will improve or worsen not according to the...level of health care funding, but only as a result of a political choice by those now engaged in the extension of control over Innu land and Innu lives....
>
> The fact is, that for the Innu, health and ill health are profoundly political issues, inseparable from social and economic considerations. The arrival of an elaborate health care system among the Innu has coincided with a rapid worsening of Innu health. This is not to imply that one has led to the other but rather to emphasize that the health or ill health of the Innu has been [determined] by factors that have very little to do with the health care system. We feel that those who are sincere in wanting to promote Innu health rather than merely developing a larger, self-serving medical system must be prepared to address problems to which traditional medical disciplines do not have the answers.
>
> The World Health Organization has recognized that individual good health can best be assured through maintenance of healthy socioeconomic and cultural systems, and that, conversely, the exploitation and humiliation of societies will inevitably lead to both collective and individual ill health.
>
> For the Innu, the real health system will be one which will allow Innu society to function properly again, one which will remove foreign domination, and one which will offer the Innu respect as a distinct people.[324]

Thus, the sum of Aboriginal experience, population health research and World Health Organization analysis adds up to the same conclusion: health, like every facet of human experience, is the handmaiden of power. What happens to the ill health conditions described in this chapter depends as much on the allocation of power in Canada as on the reorganization of health and healing systems.

The reorganization of health and healing systems can do much to improve the well-being of Aboriginal people. And good health, in turn, can contribute to the political and economic renewal of Aboriginal people to a degree that has long been underestimated by Aboriginal and non-Aboriginal people alike. Whole health may depend on politics and economics, but the dependence is mutual. The new political and economic systems that Aboriginal people are now struggling to build will not achieve the peaks of creativity, efficiency and integrity of which they are capable unless and until the health of all the people becomes a contributing force:

> Self-reliance, self-determination, self-government and economic development will not be achieved unless the people enjoy health and wellness, be this on an individual, family or community basis....[The Meadow Lake Tribal Council's vision of health] calls for achieving balance and harmony in the physical, mental, emotional and spiritual aspects of life....The vision...is to build services for Indian people by Indian people, giving them the power to make positive change in their communities. This power will only come from well adjusted individuals, who have pride in themselves and their communities.[325]

In a sense our entire report is about restoring and maintaining whole health among Aboriginal people. In Volume 1 we considered the evidence of efficacy and equilibrium in Aboriginal cultural systems when Europeans first encountered them, along with the tragic errors that undermined relations of mutual respect and benefit between Aboriginal and non-Aboriginal peoples and compromised the political, economic, social and spiritual well-being of Aboriginal nations. In Volume 2 we proposed structural changes that can set the relationship on a different course, freeing Aboriginal people to pursue well-being in ways they determine freely and restoring the lands and resources to make that possible. The subject of the present volume is the range of practical steps that can be undertaken to start the journey to whole health. Volume 4 articulates the particular visions of well-being held by different Aboriginal constituencies. Volume 5 makes the argument that restoring the political, economic and social health of Aboriginal people will enhance the well-being and vitality of the whole of Canadian society.

In this chapter we have proposed an Aboriginal health strategy with four essential components to promote health and healing in Aboriginal nations, communities, families and individuals. The strategy is relevant and urgently required no matter which government is in charge. It can be implemented immediately by federal, provincial and territorial governments in consultation with Aboriginal people. This chapter also sets out challenges that Aboriginal nation governments will have to take up when they assume jurisdiction.

The costs of inaction are too great to be borne any longer. The potential rewards of resolute action are limitless. The time to begin is now.

NOTES

1. United Nations Development Programme, *Human Development Report 1994* (Toronto: Oxford University Press, 1994), p. 93. In the three UNDP reports published from 1991 to 1993, Canada was ranked either first or second.

2. Health and Welfare, *Health Indicators Derived from Vital Statistics for Status Indian and Canadian Populations, 1978-86* (Ottawa: Supply and Services, 1988). Most statistics collected by the federal government refer only to registered Indians (as defined by the *Indian Act*) and sometimes to Inuit living in the Northwest Territories. These are the categories of Aboriginal people most likely to be served by the programs of the department of Indian affairs and the medical services branch of the federal health department. Statistics may differ significantly between regions. For example, Simard and Proulx specify that for Northern Quebec, the variation from national standards of life expectancy is three years for Crees and 10 years for Inuit (Jean-Jacques Simard and Solange Proulx, "L'état de santé des Cris et des Inuit du Québec nordique: quelques indicateurs statistiques de l'évolution récente", *Recherches amérindiennes au Québec* XXV/1 (1995), pp. 5-6).

3. Calculating the infant mortality rate (IMR) for any population is a complex procedure. This generalization summarizes a picture in which the IMR is from one-and-a-half to three times greater for Aboriginal than non-Aboriginal people, depending on whether we are referring to infant, neonatal or post-neonatal deaths; and whether we are referring to registered Indian people or Inuit. The rate is greater in all categories among Inuit.

4. Royal Commission on Aboriginal Peoples [RCAP], *Discussion Paper 2: Focusing the Dialogue* (Ottawa: Supply and Services, 1993).

5. 'Whole health' is the term we have adopted to signify the concept of health used most often by Aboriginal people, encompassing the physical, emotional, intellectual and spiritual dimensions of the person and harmonious relations with social and environmental systems that are themselves functioning in a balanced way.

6. Nicholas Denys (1672), quoted in Cornelius J. Jaenen, *Friend and Foe: Aspects of French-Amerindian Cultural Contact in the Sixteenth and Seventeenth Centuries* (Toronto: McClelland and Stewart, 1976).

7. Historian George Wharton James (1908), quoted in R. Obomsawin, "Traditional Indian Health and Nutrition: Forgotten Keys to Survival into the 21st Century", in Thomas Berger (Commissioner), *Selected Readings in Support of Indian and Inuit Health Consultation*, Volume II (Ottawa: Health and Welfare, 1980), p. 44.

8. Virgil J. Vogel, *American Indian Medicine* (Norman, Okla.: University of Oklahoma Press, 1970), p. 159.

9. Olive Patricia Dickason, *Canada's First Nations: A History of Founding Peoples from Earliest Times* (Toronto: McClelland and Stewart, 1992), pp. 43-44. The quotation is from Chrestien Le Clercq, *New Relation of Gaspesia: With the Customs and Religion of the Gaspesian Indians*, William F. Ganong, ed. (Toronto: Champlain Society, 1910), p. 296.

10. See P.M. Ashburn, *The Ranks of Death: A Medical History of the Conquest of America*, ed. Frank D. Ashburn (New York: Coward-McCann, 1947); Henry F. Dobyns, *Their Numbers Became Thinned: Native American Population Dynamics in Eastern North America* (Knoxville, Tenn.: University of Tennessee Press, 1983).

11. See Robert Larocque, "L'introduction de maladies européennes chez les autochtones des XVIIᵉ et XVIIIᵉ siècles", *Recherches amérindiennes au Québec* XII/1 (1982), pp. 13-24.

12. Vogel, *American Indian Medicine* (cited in note 8), p. 154.

13. See also Denys Delâge, "Epidemics, Colonization, Alliances: Aboriginal Peoples and Europeans in the Seventeenth and Eighteenth Centuries" (translation, unpublished, 1993).

14. Denys Delâge, *Le pays renversé: Amérindiens et Européens en Amérique du nord-est, 1600-1604* (Montreal: Boréal Express, 1985), p. 101.

15. Roger Gibbins and J. Rick Ponting, "Historical Overview and Background", in J. Rick Ponting, ed., *Arduous Journey: Canadian Indians and Decolonization* (Toronto: McClelland and Stewart, 1986), pp. 18-57.

16. George F.G. Stanley, "As Long as the Sun Shines and Water Flows: An Historical Comment", in A.L. Getty and Antoine S. Lussier, eds., *As Long as the Sun Shines and Water Flows: A Reader in Canadian Native Studies* (Vancouver: University of British Columbia Press, 1983).

17. E. Brian Titley, *A Narrow Vision: Duncan Campbell Scott and the Administration of Indian Affairs in Canada* (Vancouver: University of British Columbia Press, 1989). The legacy of these assimilationist policies is still evident today among some older people in First Nations communities who fear that if they participate in traditional ceremonies they will be arrested.

18. James B. Waldram, D. Ann Herring, and T. Kue Young, *Aboriginal Health in Canada: Historical, Cultural and Epidemiological Perspectives* (Toronto: University of Toronto Press, 1995), pp. 156-158; Health and Welfare, *Aboriginal Health in Canada* (Ottawa: Supply and Services, 1992), pp. 12-13.

19. Waldram et al., *Aboriginal Health in Canada*, p. 164.

20. Corinne Hodgson, "The Social and Political Implications of Tuberculosis Among Native Canadians", *Canadian Review of Sociology and Anthropology* 19/4 (1982), pp. 502-512; John D. O'Neil, "The Politics of Health in the Fourth World: A Northern Canadian Example", *Human Organization* 45/2 (1986), pp. 119-127;

W. Vanast, "The Death of Jennie Kanajuq: Tuberculosis, Religious Competition and Cultural Conflict in Coppermine, 1929-31", *Études/Inuit/Studies* 15/1 (1991), pp. 75-104.

21. John D. O'Neil and Patricia Leyland Kaufert, "*Irniktakpunga!*: Sex Determination and the Inuit Struggle for Birthing Rights in Northern Canada", in Faye D. Ginsberg and Rayna Rapp, eds., *Conceiving the New World Order: The Global Politics of Reproduction* (Los Angeles: University of California Press, 1995), pp. 59-73.

22. See John D. O'Neil, "The Cultural and Political Context of Patient Dissatisfaction in Cross-Cultural Clinical Encounters: A Canadian Inuit Study", *Medical Anthropology Quarterly* 3/4 (1989), pp. 325-344; Dara Culhane Speck, *An Error in Judgement: The Politics of Medical Care in an Indian/White Community* (Vancouver: Talonbooks, 1987); Joseph M. Kaufert and John D. O'Neil, "Biomedical Rituals and Informed Consent: Native Canadians and the Negotiation of Clinical Trust", in George Weisz, ed., *Social Science Perspectives on Medical Ethics* (Dordrecht, The Netherlands: Kluwer Academic Publishers, 1990).

23. Health and Welfare, Communiqué 1979-88, "Statement on Indian Health Policy" (19 September 1979).

24. *Report of the Advisory Commission on Indian and Inuit Health Consultation*, Thomas R. Berger, Commissioner (Ottawa: 1980).

25. Health and Welfare Canada, *Discussion Paper: Transfer of Health Services to Indian Communities* (Ottawa: Health and Welfare, 1981).

26. Interested readers may wish to consult a comprehensive bibliography on this subject compiled by David E. Young and Leonard L. Smith, *The Involvement of Canadian Native Communities in their Health Care Programs: A Review of the Literature Since the 1970's* (Edmonton: Circumpolar Institute and Centre for the Cross-Cultural Study of Health and Healing, 1992).

27. The agreement was later formalized by a special act of the Quebec National Assembly passed in 1984 (*An Act to ratify the Agreement concerning the building and operating of a hospital centre in the Kahnawake Territory*, R.S.Q. c.13). For more details on its history and current operations, see Ann C. Macaulay, "The History of Successful Community-Operated Health Services in Kahnawake, Quebec", *Canadian Family Physician* 34 (October 1988), pp. 2167-2169; and Louis T. Montour and Ann C. Macaulay, "Editorial: Diabetes Mellitus and Atherosclerosis: Returning Research Results to the Mohawk Community", *Canadian Medical Association Journal* 139 (1988), pp. 201-202.

28. For contrasting perspectives on this debate, see Richard F. Salisbury, *A Homeland for the Cree: Regional Development in James Bay 1971-1981* (Montreal: McGill-Queen's University Press, 1986); Sally M. Weaver, "Self-Government Policy for Indians 1980-1990: Political Transformation or Symbolic Gestures", revised version of a paper presented at the 1989 UNESCO Conference on Migration and the Transformation of Cultures in Canada (Calgary, April 1991); and Daniel Beauvais,

"Autochtonisation des services de santé: réalité ou utopie?", in *James Bay and Northern Québec: Ten Years After*, ed. Sylvie Vincent and Garry Bowers (Montreal: Recherches amérindiennes au Québec, 1988), pp. 98-101.

29. When Newfoundland joined Confederation in 1949, the government of Canada did not apply the terms of the *Indian Act* and the services of the department of Indian affairs to the Aboriginal people of Labrador. Instead, an agreement was signed whereby the provincial government would be responsible for Aboriginal people and the federal government would provide most of the program funding. No Aboriginal people or nations were signatories to the agreement. In recent years, the federal government has entered into direct funding arrangements with Aboriginal people in Labrador, but on an inconsistent basis that the people view as arbitrary and capricious. (For more discussion of the circumstances of Labrador Aboriginal peoples, see Volume 4, Chapters 5 and 6.) For further information on LIHC, see I. Allen "Community Health Representatives Working in Labrador Inuit Communities", in *Circumpolar Health 90: Proceedings of the 8th International Congress on Circumpolar Health, Whitehorse, Yukon*, May 20-25, 1990, ed. Brian Postl et al. (Winnipeg: University of Manitoba Press, 1990), pp. 151-152.

30. For a description of history and activities see the AIHCC reports (1983-1992) and Richard N. Nuttall, "The Development of Indian Boards of Health in Alberta", *Canadian Journal of Public Health* 73/5 (September/October 1982), pp. 300-303.

31. See Anishnawbe Health Toronto, *A Proposal to Establish a Community Health Centre* (Toronto: Anishnawbe Health, 1988); V. Johnston, "Health: Yesteryear and Today", in *Multiculturalism and Health Care: Realities and Needs*, ed. Ralph Masi (Toronto: Canadian Council on Multicultural Health, 1990); and C.P. Shah, "A National Overview of the Health of Native People Living in Canadian Cities", in *Inner City Health – The Needs of Urban Natives: Proceeding of the Ninth Symposium on the Prevention of Handicapping Conditions*, ed. W. Yacoub (Edmonton: University of Alberta, 1988).

32. Young and Smith, *Involvement of Canadian Native Communities* (cited in note 26), p. 19; Linda C. Garro, Joanne Roulette and Robert G. Whitmore, "Community Control of Health Care Delivery: The Sandy Bay Experience", *Canadian Journal of Public Health* 77 (July/August 1986), p. 281; Waldram et al., *Aboriginal Health in Canada* (cited in note 18), p. 236.

33. The non-insured health benefits program provides funds to registered Indian people and Inuit for a variety of health-related goods and services that are not covered under medicare. The main items covered are dental care, vision care, transportation out of community for necessary medical procedures, payment of provincial medical insurance premiums and the cost of prescription drugs. The program is administered by the medical services branch of the federal health department, but its administration is currently under review, with the apparent goal of shifting responsibility to Aboriginal hands.

34. Dara Culhane Speck, "The Indian Health Transfer Policy: A Step in the Right Direction, or Revenge of the Hidden Agenda?" *Native Studies Review* 5/1 (1989), pp. 187-213.

35. Waldram et al., *Aboriginal Health in Canada* (cited in note 18), p. 238.

36. G. Connell, R. Flett and P. Stewart, "Implementing Primary Health Care Through Community Control: The Experience of the Swampy Cree Tribal Council", in Postl et al., eds., *Circumpolar Health 90* (cited in note 29), pp. 44-46. In our public hearings, spokespersons from the Mohawk First Nation at Kahnawake explained why they made the decision *not* to enter the transfer process. See, for example, Rheena Diabo, Kahnawake Shakotii'takehnhas Community Services, transcripts of the hearings of the Royal Commission on Aboriginal Peoples [hereafter RCAP transcripts], Kahnawake, Quebec, 5 May 1993.

37. Information supplied by Health Canada, Medical Services Branch, Program Transfer, Policy and Planning, March 1996.

38. Meredith A. Moore, Heather Forbes and Lorraine Henderson, "The Provision of Primary Health Care Services Under Band Control: The Montreal Lake Case", *Native Studies Review* 6/1 (1990), pp. 153-164; Waldram et al., *Aboriginal Health in Canada* (cited in note 18), p. 237; and Benita Cohen, "Health Services Development in an Aboriginal Community: The Case of Peguis First Nation", research study prepared for RCAP (1994). For information about research studies prepared for RCAP, see *A Note About Sources* at the beginning of this volume.

39. For a critical evaluation of the situation in Quebec, see André Tremblay, "L'organisation de la santé dans une réserve montagnaise" and Francine Tremblay, "Complexité des discours et des pratiques de développement et de gestion dans le réseau Kativik de la santé et des services sociaux", both in *Recherches amérindiennes au Québec* XXV/1 (1995), pp. 21-40 and pp. 85-94 respectively.

40. As well, the Commission notes growing evidence that infectious diseases are not in fact well controlled in the world generally. (See, for example, Laurie Garrett, *The Coming Plague: Newly Emerging Diseases in a World Out of Balance* (New York: Farrar, Straus and Giroux, 1994.) Most but not all of the newly emerging diseases originated outside North America. However, since poverty, poor housing and social dysfunction are considered to contribute to their emergence, the Commission is concerned about the vulnerability of some Aboriginal communities.

41. In fiscal year 1992-93, federal, provincial and territorial governments together spent approximately $2 billion on health care and $2.2 billion on social development programs for Aboriginal people.

42. T. Kue Young, *The Health of Native Americans: Towards a Biocultural Epidemiology* (Toronto: Oxford University Press, 1994), pp. 37-38.

43. Health and Welfare, *Aboriginal Health in Canada* (cited in note 18), p. 33.

44. Young, *The Health of Native Americans* (cited in note 42), p. 37. According to Young, this was a "most remarkable achievement" because it has taken other populations much longer to make equivalent gains.

45. Health and Welfare, *Aboriginal Health in Canada* (cited in note 18), p. 33. See also note 2.

46. Because of small numbers of Aboriginal people in some measured categories, as well as the peaks and troughs in particular disease conditions over time, the statistical picture for any one year may differ from the picture resulting from statistics averaged over several years, as was done to create Table 3.1 (and others). Furthermore, data collection in relation to Aboriginal people is uneven. Most often, it encompasses only registered (status) Indian people and Inuit living in the Northwest Territories. In most reporting regions, only registered Indian people living on-reserve are included, while in others, data pertaining to those living off-reserve are collected as well. No data on the health of Aboriginal people in British Columbia or the Northwest Territories have been collected since 1985.

    See Volume 1, Chapter 2 (particularly the endnotes) for a general discussion of the sources of data used by the Commission in this report.

47. For data specific to Inuit in Quebec, see Tremblay, "Complexité des discours" (cited in note 39).

48. We discussed comparative rates of suicide in RCAP, *Choosing Life: Special Report on Suicide Among Aboriginal People* (Ottawa: Supply and Services, 1995. We discussed violence in families in Chapter 2 of this volume.

49. Canadian Medical Association, "Canada's Doctors Call on Government to Improve Health of Aboriginal Peoples", news release, Ottawa, 17 November 1993.

50. Abdel R. Omran, "The Epidemiological Transition: A Theory of the Epidemiology of Population Change", *Milbank Memorial Fund Quarterly* 49/4 (October 1971, Part 1), pp. 509-538.

51. The transition from the second to the third stage began in the 1940s. At that time, about 70 per cent of (U.S.) health care dollars were spent controlling infectious diseases. Now more than 80 per cent of the available dollars are spent on managing chronic diseases and their complications. See D. Etzweiler (President, International Diabetes Center), "International Concerns about Diabetes and Indigenous Peoples", in A. Kewayosh, ed., *Sociocultural Approaches in Diabetes Care for Native Peoples: Proceedings of the Second International Conference on Diabetes and Native Peoples* (Ottawa: First Nations Health Commission, Assembly of First Nations, 1993), p. 14.

52. These data are an average calculated over the 1986-1990 period. See T. Kue Young, "Measuring the Health Status of Canada's Aboriginal Population: A Statistical Review and Methodological Commentary", research study prepared for RCAP (1994). In the 1950s, when the network of federal health facilities first began to reach the Northwest Territories, the infant mortality rate (IMR) for Inuit was 240 deaths per 1,000 live births. Despite rapid and remarkable improvement,

the IMR for Inuit living in the Northwest Territories today is still the highest of all Aboriginal peoples.

53. Canadian Institute of Child Health (CICH), *The Health of Canada's Children: A CICH Profile*, 2nd Edition (Ottawa: CICH, 1994), p. 143.

54. J. Fraser Mustard and John Frank, *The Determinants of Health*, CIAR Publication No. 5 (Toronto: Canadian Institute for Advanced Research, 1991), pp. 18-19.

55. David J.D. Barker, "Rise and Fall of Western Diseases", *Nature* 338 (30 March 1989), pp. 371-372.

56. CICH, *Health of Canada's Children* (cited in note 53), p. 37.

57. See, for example, the testimony of Anne Rochon Ford and Vicki Van Wagner of the Interim Regulatory Council of Midwifery describing community consultations with Aboriginal women in Ontario, RCAP transcripts, Toronto, Ontario, 2 November 1992. See also John D. O'Neil and Penny Gilbert, eds., *Childbirth in the Canadian North: Epidemiological, Clinical and Cultural Perspectives* (Winnipeg: Northern Health Research Unit, University of Manitoba, 1990).

58. Health and Welfare, *Strengthening Prenatal Health Promotion for Disadvantaged Families* (Ottawa: Supply and Services, 1994), p. 1.

59. Nancy Waters and Denise Avard, *Prevention of Low Birth Weight in Canada: Literature Review and Strategies* (Ottawa: Canadian Institute of Child Health, 1992).

60. For more ideas about action in this field, see the testimony of Marlene Thio-Watts, RCAP transcripts, Prince George, British Columbia, 1 June 1993, as well as Waters and Avard, *Prevention of Low Birth Weight in Canada* (cited in note 59); and Health and Welfare, *Strengthening Prenatal Health Promotion* (cited in note 58).

61. Marilyn Van Bibber, "FAS Among Aboriginal Communities in Canada: A Review of Existing Epidemiological Research and Current Preventive and Intervention Approaches", research study prepared for RCAP (1993).

62. There has been some dispute about the validity of the research demonstrating a causal link between alcohol consumption and the constellation of defects labelled 'fetal alcohol syndrome'. A minority of researchers have suggested that other factors, including maternal malnutrition, may be the cause. However, the most recent research demonstrates clearly that alcohol has independent effects on the fetus, and prenatal alcohol exposure is now thought to be the leading cause of birth defects and intellectual disability in North America. See "Fetal Alcohol Syndrome", *Alcohol Alert* 13/PH297 (July 1991) (Washington: National Institute on Alcohol Abuse and Alcoholism, U.S. Department of Health and Human Services); and Kenneth Lyons Jones, *Smith's Recognizable Patterns of Human Malformation*, 4th edition (Toronto: W.B. Saunders Co., 1988).

63. Van Bibber, "FAS Among Aboriginal Communities in Canada" (cited in note 61). See also Mary Jane Ashley, "Alcohol-Related Birth Defects", in *Aboriginal Substance Use: Research Issues*, ed. Diane McKenzie (Ottawa: Canadian Centre on Substance

Abuse, 1992), pp. 69-73. We note that small sample sizes in the studies of FAS and FAE in Aboriginal communities make generalizations tentative at best.

64. House of Commons, Report of the Standing Committee on Health and Welfare, Social Affairs, Seniors and the Status of Women, *Foetal Alcohol Syndrome: A Preventable Tragedy* (Ottawa: June 1992).

65. Van Bibber, "FAS Among Aboriginal Communities in Canada" (cited in note 61).

66. For further discussion of the particular needs of women in combatting addiction, see testimony before the Commission by Jackie Adams of Urban Native Women of the First Nations, RCAP transcripts, Port Alberni, British Columbia, 20 May 1992; Charlotte Ross of La Ronge Native Women's Council, RCAP transcripts, La Ronge, Saskatchewan, 28 May 1992; Catherine Brooks, Executive Director of Anduhyaun, RCAP transcripts, Toronto, Ontario, 26 June 1992; Della Maguire of the Micmac Native Friendship Centre, RCAP transcripts, Halifax, Nova Scotia, 4 November 1992; and Nancy van Heest of Urban Images for First Nations, RCAP transcripts, Vancouver, British Columbia, 2 June 1993.

67. Standing Committee on Health and Welfare, *Foetal Alcohol Syndrome* (cited in note 64), pp. 27-28.

68. Van Bibber, "FAS Among Aboriginal Communities in Canada" (cited in note 61).

69. See public testimony given by Betsy Jackson and Lorraine Stick of the Alcohol Related Birth Defects Committee, RCAP transcripts, Whitehorse, Yukon, 18 November 1992; Della Maguire of the Micmac Native Friendship Centre, RCAP transcripts, Halifax, Nova Scotia, 4 November 1992; Joyce Goodstriker of the Blood Tribe Education Board, RCAP transcripts, Calgary, Alberta, 26 May 1993; Marlene Thio-Watts of the Northern Family Health Society, RCAP transcripts, Prince George, British Columbia, 1 June 1993; Marie Baker, Aboriginal Women's Council, RCAP transcripts, Vancouver, British Columbia, 2 June 1993; and Ian Hinksman, President, B.C. Aboriginal Network on Disability Society, RCAP transcripts, Vancouver, British Columbia, 4 June 1993. See also Van Bibber, "FAS Among Aboriginal Communities in Canada" (cited in note 61).

70. In some places, the policy came some time later. In northern Quebec, it was not until the 1970s that evacuation of pregnant women to hospitals in Moose Factory or Montreal became routine. In the Northwest Territories, the policy did not come into effect until the late 1970s. Christopher Fletcher, "The Innuulisivik Maternity Centre: Issues Around the Return of Midwifery and Birth to Povungnituk, Quebec", research study prepared for RCAP (1994).

71. For details of traditional birthing practices and their role in family and community solidarity, see Lesley Paulette, "Midwifery in the North", research study prepared for RCAP (1995); Laura Calm Wind and Carol Terry on behalf of Equay Wuk (Women's Group), *Nishnawbe-Aski Nation Traditional Midwifery Practices* paper presented to the Ministry of Health of Ontario concerning the exemption of Aboriginal traditional midwives from the *Regulated Health Professions Act, 1991* (Sioux Lookout, Ontario: August 1993); Rose Dufour, *Femmes et enfantement –*

sagesse dans la culture Inuit (Quebec City: Éditions Papyrus, 1988); and the testimony of Dr. Bernard Saladin D'Anglure of the department of anthropology, Laval University, RCAP transcripts, Wendake, Quebec, 17 November 1992.

72. Fletcher, "The Innuulisivik Maternity Centre" (cited in note 70). Lesley Paulette, in her research study "Midwifery in the North" (cited in note 71), told us, "Elders have suggested that in the days when families gave birth together in the traditional way, the bonds between family members were stronger than they are today. In particular, men seem to have had a different kind of appreciation for their wives and a closer relationship with their children".

73. Vicki Van Wagner, Ontario Interim Regulatory Council on Midwifery, RCAP transcripts, Toronto, 2 November 1992. See also Paulette, "Midwifery in the North"; and Sarah Robinson, "The Role of the Midwife: Opportunities and Constraints", in Iain Chalmers, Murray Enkin and Marc J.N.C. Keirse, eds., *Effective Care in Pregnancy and Childbirth* (Toronto: Oxford University Press, 1989).

74. See Ginette Carignan, *Pregnancies and Births Among the Inuit Population of Hudson Bay, 1989-91* (Quebec City: Community Health Department, Laval University Hospital Centre, 1993); and François Meyer and Diane Bélanger, *Évaluation des soins et services en périnatalité, Hudson et Ungava : Volet épidémiologie – Grossesses et naissances dans deux populations inuit du Nouveau-Québec* (Quebec City: Community Health Department, Laval University, 1991).

75. Nunavik comprises 14 communities in all. Eight are served by the primary care hospital in Povungnituk and six are served by a similar facility in Kuujjuaq. There is no similar maternity care program in Kuujjuaq.

76. Fletcher, "The Innuulisivik Maternity Centre" (cited in note 70). See also the testimony of Ineaq Korgak of the Baffin Regional Health Board, (RCAP transcripts, Iqaluit, Northwest Territories, 26 May 1992; Ipeelee Kilabuk of the Health Committee, RCAP transcripts, Pangnirtung, Northwest Territories, 28 May 1992; Martha Greig, Vice-President of Pauktuutit, RCAP transcripts, Ottawa, Ontario, 2 November 1993; and Rose Dufour, Laval University Hospital Centre, Wendake, Quebec, 18 November 1992.

77. This analysis is most closely associated with Thomas McKeown, *The Origins of Human Disease* (Oxford: Basil Blackwell, 1988); *The Modern Rise of Population* (London: Edward Arnold, 1976); and *The Role of Medicine: Dream, Mirage or Nemesis?* (Princeton: Princeton University Press, 1979).

78. John F. Marchand, "Tribal Epidemics in the Yukon", *Journal of the American Medical Association* 123/16 (1943), pp. 1019-1020.

79. A.F.W. Peart and F.P. Nagler, "Measles in the Canadian Arctic, 1952", *Canadian Journal of Public Health* 45 (1952), p. 146.

80. Ales Hrdlicka, *Physiological and Medical Observations Among the Indians of Southwestern United States and Mexico*, Bulletin 34 (Washington, D.C.: Smithsonian Institution, Bureau of American Ethnology, 1908); and David A. Stewart, "The

Red Man and the White Plague", *Canadian Medical Association Journal* 35 (1936), pp. 674-676.

81. G.C. Brink, *Across the Years: Tuberculosis in Ontario* (Willowdale, Ontario: Ontario Tuberculosis Association, 1965).

82. Tuberculosis killed 24 per cent of the children who attended residential schools in western Canada during the 15-year period investigated by the government's own medical superintendent (western region), Dr. Peter Bryce. See P.H. Bryce, *The Story of a National Crime: An Appeal for Justice to the Indians of Canada* (Ottawa: James Hope & Sons, 1922). For more discussion of the history and impact of residential schooling on Aboriginal people, see Volume 1, Chapter 10, and John S. Milloy, "Suffer the Little Children: The Aboriginal Residential School System, 1830-1992", research study prepared for RCAP (1996).

83. Kathryn Wilkins, "Tuberculosis Incidence in Canada in 1992", *Health Reports* 6/2 (1994), Statistics Canada Catalogue No. 82-003, pp. 301-309.

84. Young, *The Health of Native Americans* (cited in note 42), p. 63.

85. Young, *The Health of Native Americans,* pp. 56-57.

86. The work of Imrie and Newhouse suggests that the incidence of sexually transmitted diseases among Aboriginal people is relatively high. Robert Imrie and David Newhouse, "Aboriginal People and HIV/AIDS in Canada", research study prepared for RCAP (1994). See also the testimony of Glen Ross of the Cree Nation Tribal Health Centre RCAP transcripts, The Pas, Manitoba, 20 May 1992; and Maggie Saunders, RCAP transcripts, Yellowknife, Northwest Territories, 10 December 1992.

87. Health Canada, "Information: HIV/AIDS and Aboriginal People in Canada" (Ottawa: 1994), p. 2. More recent figures indicate that as of January 1996 Health Canada was aware of 176 cases of AIDS among Aboriginal people. See Warren Goulding, "Behind the Statistics", *Maclean's,* 15 July 1996.

88. Risk factors for HIV/AIDS among Aboriginal people were discussed in our public hearings by Glen Ross, Cree National Tribal Health Centre, RCAP transcripts, The Pas, Manitoba, 20 May 1992; Linda Day and Frederick Haineault, B.C. First Nations AIDS Society, RCAP transcripts, Vancouver, British Columbia, 2 June 1993; and Maggie Saunders, RCAP transcripts, Yellowknife, Northwest Territories, 10 December 1992.

89. Alan Kennard, vice-president of the Vancouver Native Health Society, warned us that "TB and AIDS [together] could be the deadliest combination to Aboriginal people since smallpox" (RCAP transcripts, Vancouver, British Columbia, 4 June 1993).

90. Imrie and Newhouse, "Aboriginal People and HIV/AIDS in Canada" (cited in note 86). See also the testimony of Joylenne Shade, RCAP transcripts, Lethbridge, Alberta, 25 May 1993; and Cheryl Starr of the Saskatchewan Indian Youth Advisory Committee, Saskatoon, Saskatchewan, 27 October 1992.

91. See the testimony of Linda Day and Frederick Haineault of B.C. First Nations AIDS Society, RCAP transcripts, Vancouver, British Columbia, 2 June 1993; Susan Beaver, RCAP transcripts, Toronto, Ontario, 25 June 1992; and T'mas Young, Micmac AIDS Task Force, RCAP transcripts, Halifax, Nova Scotia, 4 November 1992.

92. Susan M. Beaver, RCAP transcripts, Toronto, 25 June 1992.

93. Imrie and Newhouse, "Aboriginal People and HIV/AIDS in Canada" (cited in note 86).

94. See, for example, Farkas et al., "Impact of HIV Infection/AIDS on Social Service Agencies Serving Children and Youth in Toronto", *Canadian Journal of Public Health* 81 (July/August 1990), p. 297.

95. Imrie and Newhouse, "Aboriginal People and HIV/AIDS in Canada" (cited in note 86). See also Alan Kennard, RCAP transcripts, Vancouver, British Columbia, 4 June 1993; and T'mas Young, RCAP transcripts, Halifax, Nova Scotia, 4 November 1992.

96. For discussion of recommended public health responses to HIV/AIDS, see the research study prepared for RCAP by Imrie and Newhouse, "Aboriginal People and HIV/AIDS in Canada" (cited in note 86), and RCAP transcripts of the testimony given by Glen Ross, The Pas, Manitoba, 20 May 1992; Linda Day, Vancouver, British Columbia, 2 June 1993; Maggie Saunders, Yellowknife, Northwest Territories, 10 December 1992; Tom Iron, Wahpeton, Saskatchewan, 26 May 1992; and T'mas Young, Halifax, Nova Scotia, 4 November 1992.

97. Report of the Second International Conference on Diabetes and Native Peoples (Honolulu, Hawaii, 19-21 May 1993). See Alethea Kewayosh, ed., *Sociocultural Approaches in Diabetes Care for Native Peoples* (Ottawa: Assembly of First Nations, 1993).

98. Staff communication, Sue Boyd, manager, Community Access Network, Canadian Diabetes Association, 6 July 1995.

99. See also Paul Brassard, Elizabeth Robinson and Claudette Lavallée, "Prevalence of Diabetes Mellitus Among the James Bay Cree of Northern Quebec", *Canadian Medical Association Journal* 149/3 (1993), pp. 303-307.

100. Expert Committee of the Canadian Diabetes Advisory Board, "Clinical Practice Guidelines for Treatment of Diabetes Mellitus", *Canadian Medical Association Journal* 147/5 (1992), p. 707.

101. *Sociocultural Approaches in Diabetes Care* (cited in note 97).

102. For a detailed discussion see T. Kue Young et al., "Prevalence of Diagnosed Diabetes in Circumpolar Indigenous Populations", *International Journal of Epidemiology* 21/4 (1992), pp. 730-736; and T. Kue Young, Emoke J.E. Szathmary, Susan Evers and Brian Wheatley, "Geographical Distribution of Diabetes Among the Native Population of Canada: A National Survey", *Social Science & Medicine* 31/2 (1990), pp. 129-139.

103. Maureen I. Harris, Wilbur C. Hadden, William C. Knowler and Peter H. Bennett, "Prevalence of Diabetes and Impaired Glucose Tolerance and Plasma Glucose Levels in U.S. Population Aged 24-74 Years", *Diabetes* 36 (April 1987), pp. 523-34.

104. See Donnell Etzweiler "International Concerns about Diabetes and Indigenous Peoples", pp. 13-19, in *Sociocultural Approaches in Diabetes Care* (cited in note 97); and Young, *The Health of Native Americans* (cited in note 42), p. 146.

105. Young, *The Health of Native Americans*, p. 139.

106. Quoted in *Sociocultural Approaches in Diabetes Care* (cited in note 97), pp. 55-56.

107. *Sociocultural Approaches in Diabetes Care* , pp. 5-8, 32-35, 76-79.

108. *Sociocultural Approaches in Diabetes Care*, p. 6, based on research by M. Yvonne Jackson and Brenda A. Broussard, "Cultural Challenges in Nutrition Education Among American Indians", *The Diabetes Educator* 13/1 (1987), pp. 47-50; and L. Tom-Orme, "Diabetes in a Navajo Community: A Qualitative Study of Health/Illness Beliefs and Practices", PH.D. dissertation, University of Utah College of Nursing, 1988.

109. *Sociocultural Approaches in Diabetes Care*, pp. 76-79.

110. Both diabetes prevention programs are described in *Sociocultural Approaches in Diabetes Care*.

111. For further information, see the testimony of Dr. Louis T. Montour of the Kateri Memorial Hospital Centre, RCAP transcripts, Kahnawake, 5 May 1993; Ann C. Macaulay, Nancy Hanusaik and Deborah D. Delisle, "Diabetic Education Program in the Mohawk Community of Kahnawake, Quebec", *Canadian Family Physician* 34 (July 1988), pp. 1591-1593; Ann C. Macaulay, Louis T. Montour, and Naomi Adelson, "Prevalence of Diabetic and Atherosclerotic Complications Among Mohawk Indians of Kahnawake, PQ", *Canadian Medical Association Journal* 139 (1988), pp. 221-223.

112. See, for example, RCAP transcripts of the testimony of Isabelle Smith, Saskatoon, Saskatchewan, 27 October 1992; Judi Johnny, Whitehorse, Yukon, 18 November 1992; Gary Tinker, Ile-a-la-Crosse, Saskatchewan, 8 December 1992; Valerie Monague and Leonore Monague, Orillia, Ontario, 12 May 1993; Connie Laurin-Bowie and Bob Walker, Toronto, Ontario, 2 June 1993; James Sanders and Wanda Hamilton of the Canadian National Institute for the Blind, Ottawa, Ontario, 15 November 1993; Doreen Demas, Winnipeg, Manitoba, 17 November 1993; and James "Smokey" Tomkins, Ottawa, Ontario, 17 November 1993.

113. Statistics Canada, *The Daily*, News Release, "Disability and Housing, 1991 Aboriginal Peoples Survey" (25 March 1994). The APS depended on self-reports, which are subjective. However, the APS asked a number of questions designed to confirm or contradict the subject's perception by revealing behavioural consequences. Questions reflected the World Health Organization's definition of disability as "any restriction or lack (resulting from an impairment) of ability to perform an activity in the manner or within the range considered normal for a human being."

114. House of Commons, Special Committee on the Disabled and the Handicapped, *Obstacles: The Third Report* (Ottawa: Supply and Services, 1981).

115. National Aboriginal Network on Disability, "Aboriginal Disability", brief submitted to RCAP (1993), p. 5. For information about briefs submitted to RCAP, see *A Note About Sources* at the beginning of this volume. See also Volume 4, Chapter 7 for further discussion of urban Aboriginal people with disabilities.

116. David A. Randall, John A. Fornadly and Kevin S. Kennedy, "Management of Recurrent Otitis Media", *American Family Physician* 45/5 (May 1992), pp. 2117-2123; Rose Dufour, "Prêtez-nous l'oreille! Anthropologie de l'otite moyenne chez les Inuit", PH.D. dissertation, Quebec City, Laval University (1989).

117. J.D. Baxter, "What Have We Learned About Otitis Media and Hearing Loss by Studying the Native Peoples of Canada?", *Journal of Otolaryngology* 19/6 (1990), pp. 386-388; and Peter D. Eimas and James F. Kavanagh, "Otitis Media, Hearing Loss, and Child Development: A NICHD Conference Summary", *Public Health Reports* 101/3 (May-June 1986), pp. 289-293.

118. Jan Allison Moore, "Delivery of Audiologic Service and Prevalence of Hearing Loss in the Western Canadian Arctic", in *Circumpolar Health 90* (cited in note 29), pp. 630-633.

119. See "Tips from Other Journals", *American Family Physician* 49/7 (1994), p. 1654.

120. Healthy Inuit Babies Working Group, *Community Programs for Healthy Inuit Babies: Guidelines* (Ottawa: Pauktuutit, 1994); and Bernice L. Muir, *Health Status of Canadian Indians and Inuit: 1990* (Ottawa: Health and Welfare, 1991).

121. Healthy Inuit Babies Working Group, *Community Programs.*

122. David W. McCullough, "Chronic Otitis Media in the Keewatin Area of the Northwest Territories", *Journal of Otolaryngology* 19/6 (1990), pp. 389-390.

123. James Baxter, "An Overview of Twenty Years of Observations Concerning Etiology, Prevalence, and Evolution of Otitis Media and Hearing Loss Among the Inuit in the Eastern Canadian Arctic", in *Circumpolar Health 90* (cited in note 29), pp. 616-619; Baxter, "What have we learned?" (cited in note 117), pp. 386-388.

124. Baxter "An Overview" (cited in note 123); Baxter, "What have we learned?" (cited in note 117).

125. In relation to audiology and otolaryngology, the special services normally involved in identifying and treating otitis media, Salloum and Crysdale have documented the problems of securing reliable services in Sioux Lookout. Sharon Salloum and William S. Crysdale, "Ear Care for a Canadian Native Population", *Journal of Otolaryngology* 19/6 (1990), pp. 379-382.

126. House of Commons, Special Committee on the Disabled, *Obstacles* (cited in note 114); House of Commons, Special Committee on the Disabled and the Handicapped, *Follow-up Report, Native Population:* Fourth Report (Ottawa: Supply and Services, 1981).

127. House of Commons, Standing Committee on Human Rights and the Status of Disabled Persons, *Completing the Circle: A Report on Aboriginal People with Disabilities,* Fourth Report (Ottawa: 1993).

128. See, for example, the testimony of Mary Lou Fox, RCAP transcripts, Sudbury, Ontario, 31 May 1992; Louise Chippeway, RCAP transcripts, Roseau River, Manitoba, 8 December 1992; and Darlene Kelly, RCAP transcripts, Vancouver, British Columbia, 2 June 1993. See also Fernande Lacasse, "La conception de la santé chez les Indiens montagnais", *Recherches amérindiennes au Québec*, XII/1 (1982), pp. 25-28.

129. See, for example, RCAP, *Choosing Life* (cited in note 48); *Bridging the Cultural Divide: A Report on Aboriginal People and Criminal Justice in Canada* (Ottawa: Supply and Services, 1996); and Chapter 2 in this volume.

130. These are not aberrant figures. In the 1986-1988 period, injury also appeared as a leading cause of death in statistics gathered by the federal government. Health and Welfare Canada, *Aboriginal Health in Canada* (Ottawa: Supply and Services, 1992), p. 30.

131. According to the Canada Safety Council, the significant decrease in motor vehicle fatalities achieved during the last 20 years in Canada as a whole has not been equalled in the Aboriginal population. Canada Safety Council, "Submission to the Royal Commission on Aboriginal Peoples" (1993), p. 3. See also the testimony of the Canada Safety Council, given by Émile-J. Thérien, president, and Ethel Archard, manager of marketing and production, RCAP transcripts, November 1993.

132. See, for example, the 10-step model described by William Haddon, Jr., in "Advances in the Epidemiology of Injuries as a Basis for Public Policy", *Public Health Reports* 95/5 (1980), pp. 411-421. One of its applications to Aboriginal risk was explored by B. Friesen. See "Haddon's Strategy for Prevention: Application to Native House Fires", in *Circumpolar Health 84: Proceedings of the Sixth International Symposium on Circumpolar Health*, ed. Robert Fortuine (Seattle: University of Washington Press, 1985), pp. 105-110.

133. Telephone communication, Dr. Gordon Trueblood, Epidemiology and Community Health Specialties, Medical Services Branch, Health Canada, Ottawa, 20 July 1995.

134. The project is in its pilot phase. Written communication, Dr. Gordon Trueblood, Epidemiology and Community Health Specialties, Medical Services Branch, Health Canada, Ottawa, June 1995.

135. Fermented beverages were used, mostly for spiritual and ceremonial purposes, by some southern Aboriginal peoples but apparently by none who lived north of the 49th parallel. Lurid stories of Aboriginal drunkenness abound in the historical literature on the fur trade, but it is important to acknowledge that many Aboriginal people abstained from drinking; many opposed the consumption of alcohol by others, and many welcomed the arrival of the Northwest Mounted Police as a defence against the whisky traders from the United States. Furthermore, little alcohol was consumed except on visits to trading posts, where European traders

encouraged its use and joined in its consumption. Waldram et al., *Aboriginal Health in Canada* (cited in note 18), pp. 137-140.

136. Alcohol is the addictive substance presenting the greatest number of problems to Aboriginal people and communities in Canada. However, solvent and inhalant use is inflicting grave damage to young people in some places, particularly in northern and isolated communities, where it is has been observed in children as young as six years old (Laurence Kirmayer et al., "Emerging Trends in Research on Mental Health Among Canadian Aboriginal Peoples", research study prepared for RCAP, 1994). The extreme toxicity of solvents and inhalants means that permanent injury to the brain and other organs may occur, even during a short period of use. The federal health minister has announced funding for six solvent abuse treatment centres for First Nations and Inuit (Donald Macdonald, "Aboriginals gain six treatment centres", *The [Ottawa] Citizen*, 12 May 1995, p. A10).

Less visible action has been taken in relation to the very high rates of tobacco use among Aboriginal people. According to Thomas Stephens, well over half (57 per cent) of Canada's Aboriginal adults are smokers (Thomas Stephens, *Smoking Among Aboriginal People in Canada 1991* [Ottawa: Supply and Services, 1994]). Most (62 per cent of smokers) consume 11 to 25 cigarettes per day. More Inuit than First Nations or Métis people smoke, in a ratio of about three to two. Tobacco is generally understood by non-Aboriginal Canadians to be a highly addictive substance with a wide range of ill health implications. This public health message should be communicated more effectively to Aboriginal people. Santé Québec, *A Health Profile of the Inuit*, Report of the Santé Québec Health Survey Among the Inuit of Nunavik, 1992, Volume 1: Health Determining Factors, ed. Mireille Jetté (Montreal: Santé Québec, 1994).

137. Testimony of Jacques LeCavalier, Chief Executive Officer, Canadian Centre on Substance Abuse, RCAP transcripts, Ottawa, Ontario, 2 November 1993.

138. Most data describing substance abuse in Canada (and elsewhere) is self-report data. Telephone communication, Dr. R. Smart, Head of Social Epidemiology, Addiction Research Foundation of Ontario, Ottawa, 14 July 1995.

139. Yukon Government, *Yukon Alcohol and Drug Survey*, Volume 1: Technical Report (Whitehorse: Yukon Government Executive Council Office, Bureau of Statistics, 1991).

140. Santé Québec, *A Health Profile of the Cree*, Report of the Santé Québec Health Survey of the James Bay Cree, ed. Carole Daveluy et al. (Montreal: Santé Québec, 1994). See also Johanne Laverdure and Claudette Lavallée, *User Profile and Description of Mental Health Services Provided to the James Bay Cree* (Montreal: Montreal General Hospital, Department of Community Health, 1989).

141. See J. David Kinzie et al., "Psychiatric Epidemiology of an Indian Village: A 19-Year Replication Study", *Journal of Nervous and Mental Disease* 180/1 (1992), pp. 33-39.

142. The prevalence of medically defined psychiatric disorders among Aboriginal people is impossible to establish with confidence because of the reluctance of many Aboriginal people to seek help from mainstream services for such conditions, the varied professional definitions of what 'counts' as a mental illness when people do seek help, and the rarity of aggregated records analysis. When records have been examined, they have shown two common conditions in the distress patterns of Aboriginal people: depression or suicidal thoughts and behaviour, and alcohol and drug abuse. In most studies, the co-incidence of more than one condition and of related social problems is high. For further discussion, see Laurence J. Kirmayer et al., "Emerging Trends in Research" (cited in note 136); and Steering Committee on Native Mental Health, *Agenda for First Nations and Inuit Mental Health* (Ottawa: Health and Welfare Canada, 1991).

143. Until 1982, the program was called the National Native Alcohol Abuse Program (NNAAP).

144. Young and Smith, *Involvement of Canadian Native Communities* (cited in note 26), p. 15.

145. In our public hearings, the Commission was addressed by scores of people concerned about addictions. Those who spoke from direct program experience included Maggie Hodgson of the Nechi Institute on Alcohol and Drug Education; Patrick Shirt, Deanna J. Greyeyes and Wilson Okeymaw, all of the National Native Association of Treatment Directors; Henoch Obed and Robin Dupuis of the Labrador Rehabilitation Centre's Alcohol and Drug Abuse Program; Apenam Pone, Innu Alcohol Program; Andrea Currie, Stepping Stone Street Outreach Program; Gordon King and Marie Francis, MicMac Native Friendship Centre; Donald Horne, Kahnawake Shakotii'takehnhas Community Services; Tommy Keesick and Roy Assen, Grassy Narrows First Nation Solvent Abuse Program; Winston McKay, Metis Addictions Corporation of Saskatchewan; Joyce Racette, Metis Addictions Council of Saskatchewan; Donald Favel, Northwest Drug and Alcohol Abuse Centre; John Loftus, Action North Recovery Centre; Matthew McGinnis, Calgary Alpha House; and Tom George, Drug and Alcohol Counsellor, Stoney Creek Band.

146. Recently, some analysts have considered the possibility that Aboriginal people may suffer from 'post-traumatic stress disorder' as a result of long-term exposure to violence and the risk of sudden death, as well as multiple loss of family members, ways of life, lands and cultures. Kirmayer and his colleagues have pointed out that this possibility is appealing scientifically because it yields a single explanation for a diverse set of phenomena; clinically, because it leads to a strategy of disclosing, reliving and transforming traumatic memories; and morally, because it shifts the blame from self to others. Kirmayer et al., "Emerging Trends in Research" (cited in note 136). It is not clear how effective the technique of psychological 'purging' by means of personal and collective narrative is in resolving the social and emotional ill health experienced by Aboriginal people today, but we were informed by leading Aboriginal caregivers that they have found the approach useful.

147. Kirmayer et al., "Emerging Trends in Research" (cited in note 136).

148. Steering Committee on Native Mental Health, *Agenda for First Nations and Inuit Mental Health* (cited in note 142).

149. Steering Committee on Native Mental Health, *Agenda For First Nations and Inuit Mental Health*, p. 6.

150. See Michèle Therrien, "Corps sain, corps malade chez les Inuit, une tension entre l'intérieur et l'extérieur – Entretiens avec Taamusi Qumaq", *Recherches amérindiennes au Québec* XXV/1 (1995), pp. 71-84.

151. Kirmayer et al., "Emerging Trends in Research" (cited in note 136); and staff communication, Dr. Stephen Hodgins, head of the department of public health, Nunavik regional board of health and social services, 25 July 1995.

152. See, for example, Douglas Black et al., *Inequalities in Health: The Black Report* (New York: Penguin Books, 1982); George Davey-Smith, Mel Bartley and David Blane, "The Black Report on Socioeconomic Inequalities in Health 10 Years On", *British Medical Journal* 301 (1990), pp. 373-377; and Clyde Hertzman, "Where are the Differences Which Make a Difference?", Canadian Institute for Advanced Research, Population Health Working Paper No. 8 (Toronto: CIAR, 1990).

153. Hertzman, "Where are the Differences?", p. 5.

154. Russell Wilkins and Owen B. Adams, *Healthfulness of Life: A Unified View of Mortality, Institutionalization, and Non-Institutionalized Disability in Canada* (Montreal: Institute for Research on Public Policy, 1985).

155. British Columbia, *A Report on the Health of British Columbians: Provincial Health Officer's Annual Report, 1992* (Victoria: Ministry of Health and Ministry Responsible for Seniors, 1993), p. 25.

156. Federal, Provincial and Territorial Advisory Committee on Population Health, "Strategies for Population Health: Investing in the Health of Canadians", paper prepared for the meeting of Ministers of Health, Halifax, 14-15 September 1994, p. 14.

157. Human Resource Development, *Improving Social Security in Canada: Income Security for Children, A Supplementary Paper* (Ottawa: Supply and Services, 1994); and CICH, *The Health of Canada's Children* (cited in note 53); Gail Aitken and Andy Mitchell, "The Relationship between Poverty and Child Health: Long-Range Implications", *Canadian Review of Social Policy* 35 (Spring 1995), pp. 19-36.

158. R. Shillington, "Estimates of the Extent of Child Poverty: Census 1986" (cited in Aitken and Mitchell, "The Relationship between Poverty and Child Health").

159. Sharon Kirsh, *Unemployment: Its Impact on Body and Soul* (Ottawa: Canadian Mental Health Association, 1992).

160. The Honda Foundation, *Prosperity, Health and Well-being*, Proceedings of the 11th Honda Foundation Discoveries Symposium, 16-18 October 1993 (Toronto: The Canadian Institute for Advanced Research).

161. At least as recipients of social assistance experience it, there is no single system of social assistance in Canada. Provinces and territories have their own policies and guidelines, which are in turn open to regional and local interpretation. In some provinces, municipal governments are responsible for establishing and administering programs. The result is that there are, in effect, hundreds of welfare systems in Canada. National Council of Welfare, *Welfare Incomes 1993* (Ottawa: Supply and Services, 1994).

Social assistance to Aboriginal people is administered by different levels of governments depending on the 'status' of the recipients, that is, whether they are registered or non-registered Indian people living on- or off-reserve, Inuit living in or outside the Northwest Territories, or Métis people. For more details on the administration of social welfare programs, see Volume 2, Chapter 5, and Volume 4, Chapter 6. See also Allan Moscovitch and Andrew Webster, "Social Assistance and Aboriginal People: A Discussion Paper Prepared for the Royal Commission on Aboriginal Peoples" (1995).

162. Moscovitch and Webster, "Social Assistance and Aboriginal People".

163. National Council of Welfare, *Welfare Incomes 1993* (cited in note 161).

164. National Council of Welfare, *Welfare Incomes 1993*.

165. CICH, *The Health of Canada's Children* (cited in note 53).

166. National Council of Welfare, *Welfare Incomes 1993* (cited in note 161), p. ii.

167. CICH, *The Health of Canada's Children* (cited in note 53), p. 113.

168. Representatives of the National Anti-Poverty Organization described the need for a productive place in society as a general human drive and pointed out that the western nations and their restructuring economies are, at present, unable to provide that opportunity to growing numbers of their citizens. See RCAP transcripts, testimony of Lynne Toupin, Executive Director, National Anti-Poverty Organization, Ottawa, Ontario, 16 November 1993.

169. World Bank, *World Development Report 1992: Development and the Environment* (New York: Oxford University Press, 1992).

170. Canadian International Development Agency, *Water, Sanitation and Development: Water and Sanitation Sector*, Development Issues Paper (Ottawa: Supply and Services, 1988).

171. On a world scale, diarrheal diseases that result from contaminated water kill about two million children and cause about 900 million episodes of illness each year. See *World Development Report 1992* (cited in note 169). More recent figures suggest that one billion people lack access to an adequate supply of water and 1.7 billion do not have adequate sanitation facilities. (See Ismail Serageldin, *Water Supply, Sanitation, and Environmental Sustainability: The Financing Challenge* (Washington, D.C.: World Bank, 1994), p. 1.

172. Mani Shan Andrew brief submitted to RCAP (1992). Ms. Andrew described herself as a 26-year-old Naskapi Mushuau woman living in Davis Inlet, Labrador, a

mother of five, and a member of the Innu Nation and the Innu Skueuts Committee.

173. DIAND Technical Services, *Community Water and Sewage System Profiles 1994 (Preliminary Report)* (Ottawa: DIAND, February 1995). The figures in the report refer to 'community systems' only. Individual household systems (wells, pails, septic fields, privies) are known to have problems too.

174. DIAND Technical Services, *Community Water and Sewage System Profiles*, p. 4.

175. DIAND Technical Services, *Community Water and Sewage System Profiles*, p. 7.

176. CIDA, *Water, Sanitation and Development* (cited in note 170).

177. World Health Organization, *Improving Environmental Health Conditions in Low-Income Settlements: A Community-Based Approach to Identifying Needs and Priorities* (Geneva: UNEP & WHO, 1987).

178. The number of fires on reserves poses a serious health and safety problem. The average number increased from 174 in the period from 1970 to 1979 to 295 in the period from 1980 to 1989. Property damage was estimated at about $12 million during the 1980-89 period (measured in 1989 dollars). Young and his colleagues have estimated that the mortality rate from house fires among Aboriginal people is six to 10 times higher than for other Canadians. T. Kue Young et al., *The Health Effects of Housing and Community Infrastructure on Canadian Indian Reserves* (Ottawa: Supply and Services, 1991), p. 60.

179. Young et al., *Health Effects of Housing*.

180. Young et al., *Health Effects of Housing*.

181. Ted Rosenberg et al., "The Relationship of the Incidence of Shigellosis to Crowded Housing, Lack of Running Water and Inadequate Sewage Disposal", report prepared for the Department of Health and Welfare, Medical Services Branch, Manitoba Region, completed in 1995 [unpublished]. The same study notes that, in the period for which records were studied, 81 per cent of the cases of hepatitis A were First Nations people.

182. Trevor Hancock, "The Future of Public Health in Canada: Developing Healthy Communities", *Canadian Journal of Public Health*, 79/6 (November/December 1988), p. 416.

183. This voluminous literature stretches back to the classic study by Rachel Carson, *Silent Spring* (Cambridge, Mass.: Riverside Press, 1962). More recently it has included World Commission on Environment and Development, *Our Common Future* (Oxford: Oxford University Press, 1987); World Health Organization, *Potential Health Effects of Climatic Change: Report of a WHO Task Group* (Geneva: World Health Organization, 1990); John M. Last, "Global Environment, Health and Health Services", in Maxcy, Rosenau and Last, eds., *Public Health and Preventive Medicine* (Norwalk, Conn.: Appleton and Lange, 1992), p. 677; Daniel Stokols, "Establishing and Maintaining Healthy Environments: Towards a Social Ecology of Health Promotion", *American Psychologist* 47/1 (January 1992), p. 6;

and Price Waterhouse, *Canada Health Monitor: Highlights Report, Survey 6* (Toronto: Price Waterhouse, 1992).

184. Ontario, Premier's Council on Health, Well-Being and Social Justice, *Our Environment, Our Health: Healthy Ecosystems, Healthy Communities, Healthy Workplaces* (Toronto: Queen's Printer for Ontario, 1993).

185. Given the high degree of urbanization of Aboriginal people in recent years, such a land-based lifestyle is no longer the norm, though it might be the choice of more Aboriginal people if fish and game were still plentiful and uncontaminated.

186. Charles Dumont and Tom Kosatsky, "Évolution de l'exposition au mercure chez les trappeurs cris de la Baie James", in *Les enseignements de la phase 1 du Complexe La Grande*, ed. Nicole Chartrand and Normand Thérien (Montreal: Hydro-Québec, 1992), pp. 79-90.

187. Unwarranted fears about contaminated fish and game in some Aboriginal communities may be steering people away from traditional foods that are safe and nourishing toward fatty foods, junk foods and other products of little nutritional value.

188. For one example, see Ellen Bielawski, "The Desecration of Nánúlá Kúé: Impact of the Taltson Hydroelectric Development on Dene Sonline", research study prepared for RCAP (1993).

189. This point of view is increasingly acknowledged by researchers. See in particular Georges E. Sioui, *For an Amérindian Autohistory: An Essay on the Foundations of a Social Ethic*, trans. Sheila Fischman (Montreal: McGill-Queen's Press, 1992). For a discussion of this and related issues, see Kirmayer et al., "Emerging Trends in Research" (cited in note 136), pp. 59-62, as well as Volume 4, Chapter 6 of this report.

190. See, for example, Pierre Trudel, "La Compagnie de construction crie prise à partie par un Cri", *Recherches amérindiennes au Québec* XXV/1 (1995), pp. 95-96.

191. Canadian Wildlife Federation, "Submission to the Royal Commission on Aboriginal Peoples" (1993), p. 2.

192. Ingestion of methylmercury to a blood concentration of more than 100 parts per billion is considered unsafe for human health. At higher concentrations, mercury poisoning can lead to Minamata disease, named after the community in Japan where 1,800 people suffered brain and nerve damage, and some ultimately died, from the effects of methylmercury. See Leonard T. Kurland, Stanley N. Faro, and Howard Siedler, "Minamata Disease: The Outbreak of a Neurological Disorder in Minamata, Japan, and its Relationship to the Ingestion of Seafood Contaminated by Mercuric Compounds", *World Neurology* 1/5 (1960), pp. 370-395. The ill health effects of mercury have been recognized at least since the time of the historian Pliny, who lived in the first century A.D. The phrase 'mad as a hatter' refers to the disastrous ill health effects on hat-makers from using mercury to improve the felting quality of wool and fur, up to and during the nineteenth century. See Warner Troyer, *No Safe Place* (Toronto: Clarke, Irwin & Co., 1977).

193. Dr. Stephen Levin of the Occupational Medical Clinic at Mount Sinai Hospital in Toronto has explained some of the difficulties faced by epidemiologists trying to establish the links between exposure to environmental contamination and later human health effects. Stephen Levin, "Akwesasne Environment: The Limits of Science", *Northeast Indian Quarterly* (Fall 1988), pp. 30-34.

194. Harriet Kuhnlein, "Global Nutrition and the Holistic Environment of Indigenous Peoples", in RCAP, *Path to Healing: Report of the National Round Table on Aboriginal Health and Social Issues* (Ottawa: Supply and Services, 1993), pp. 251-263.

195. James B. Waldram, "Hydroelectric Development and Dietary Delocalization in Northern Manitoba, Canada", *Human Organization* 44/1 (1985), pp. 41-49.

196. Shkilnyk, *A Poison Stronger Than Love* (cited in note 192); Sean McCutcheon, *Electric Rivers: The Story of the James Bay Project* (Montreal: Black Rose Books, 1991); Waldram, "Hydroelectric Development"; and Larry Krotz, "Dammed and Diverted", *Canadian Geographic* III/1 (February/March 1991), pp. 36-44. A few studies report little change in diet as a result of industrial projects. See, for example, Robert M. Bone, "Country Food Consumption During the Norman Wells Project, 1982-1985", *Polar Record* 25/154 (1989), pp. 235-238; and Charles W. Hobart, "Impacts of Industrial Employment on Hunting and Trapping among Canadian Inuit", in Milton M.R. Freeman, ed., *Proceedings: First International Symposium on Renewable Resources and the Economy of the North* (Ottawa: Association of Canadian Universities for Northern Studies, 1981).

197. Waldram, "Hydroelectric Development".

198. Dave Stieb and Katherine Davies, *Health Effects of Development in the Hudson Bay/James Bay Region* (Ottawa: Canadian Arctic Resources Committee, 1993); David DesBrisay, "The Impact of Major Resource Development Projects on Aboriginal Communities: A Review of the Literature", research study prepared for RCAP (1994); and Thomas R. Berger, *Northern Frontier, Northern Homeland: The Report of the Mackenzie Valley Pipeline Inquiry,* Volumes I and II (Ottawa: Supply and Services, 1977), p. 204.

199. Kuhnlein, "Global Nutrition" (cited in note 194), p. 259.

200. Stephanie Pfirman, Kathleen Crane and Peter deFur, "Arctic Contaminant Distribution", *Northern Perspectives* 21/4 (Winter 1993-94), pp. 8-15.

201. Matthew Coon-Come, Grand Chief of the Cree Nation of Quebec, "Speech to the New York State Legislative Hearings", New York City, 30 September 1991.

202. Peter Usher, "Socio-Economic Effects of Elevated Mercury Levels in Fish in Sub-Arctic Native Communities", paper presented to the conference on Contaminants in the Marine Environment of Nunavik, Montreal, 12-14 September 1990.

203. B. Wheatley, "A New Approach to Assessing the Effects of Environmental Contaminants on Aboriginal Peoples", paper presented to the 9th International Congress on Circumpolar Health, Reykjavik, Iceland, 1993.

204. Berger, *Northern Frontier, Northern Homeland* (cited in note 198), p. 155-157.

205. Usher, *Socio-Economic Effects of Elevated Mercury Levels* (cited in note 202); Shkilnyk, *A Poison Stronger than Love* (cited in note 192).

206. Geoffrey York, *The Dispossessed: Life and Death in Native Canada* (Toronto: Lester & Orpen Dennys, 1989).

207. DesBrisay, *The Impact of Major Development Projects on Aboriginal Communities* (cited in note 198); Sylvie Vincent, "Consulting the Population: Definition and Methodological Questions", trans. Harriet Wichin (Montreal: Great Whale Review Support Office, 1994).

208. The five-year allocation of funding for water quality enhancement on reserves under the Green Plan (1989) was the first foray into formal programming.

209. Some ideas were conveyed to us in testimony. See RCAP transcripts for the following testimony: Joan Scottie, Rankin Inlet, Northwest Territories, 19 November 1992; Reg Whiten, Fort St. John, British Columbia, 19 November 1992; Jane Tennyson, Timmins, Ontario, 5 November 1992; Henry Lickers, Akwesasne, Ontario, 4 May 1993; Bob Moore, Brantford, Ontario, 13 May 1993; and Chief Clarence T. Jules, Ottawa, Ontario, 5 November 1993.

210. Robert Moore, Program Manager, Six Nations of the Grand River Forestry Program Project, RCAP transcripts, Brantford, Ontario, 13 May 1993.

211. Henry Lickers, Director, Department of the Environment, Mohawk Council of Akwesasne, RCAP transcripts, Akwesasne, Ontario, 4 May 1993.

212. Albert Saddleman, Canadian Indian Water Rights Commission of B.C., RCAP transcripts, Kelowna, British Columbia, 16 June 1993.

213. Peter Stevens, Eskasoni First Nation Community, RCAP transcripts, Eskasoni, Nova Scotia, 7 May 1992.

214. Joan Feather, *Social Health in Northern Saskatchewan: Discussion Papers for Working Group on Social Health* (Saskatoon: University of Saskatchewan Northern Medical Services, 1991), pp. 1-2.

215. Barbara Barnes, director of the National Association of Cultural Education Centres, told us that although there is no 'pan-Indian' culture, there is a commonality of values and philosophical outlook shared by First Nations people from across the country (RCAP transcripts, Orillia, Ontario, 4 May 1993). Lesley Malloch drew a similar conclusion from her research (Lesley Malloch, "Indian Medicine, Indian Health: Study Between Red and White Medicine", *Canadian Woman Studies* 10/2 & 3 (1989), p. 10). Neither of them assumed the inclusion of Métis people or Inuit. In Volume 1, Chapter 15, we suggest that life on the land and understandings of spiritual and natural law generate a commonality of world view that is, nevertheless, given diverse expression in different nations and cultures.

216. Criticism of the 'lifestyle choice' analysis has been persistent. The themes of the criticism are that much of what is termed individual choice is in fact a result of social and economic factors and not easily changed as a matter of individual will, and that this analysis shifts responsibility from the public health system to the individual,

which may result in the withdrawal of state services where they are in fact still necessary.

217. Robert G. Evans and Gregory L. Stoddart, "Producing Health, Consuming Health Care", *Social Science and Medicine* 31/12 (1990), p. 1347.

218. OECD Secretariat, *Health Care Financing Review: Annual Supplement* (Paris: Organization for Economic Cooperation and Development, 1991).

219. Quoted in Lorenz K.Y. Ng, Devra Lee Davis, Ronald W. Manderscheid and Joel Elkes, "Toward a Conceptual Formulation of Health and Well-Being", in Lorenz K.Y. Ng and Devra Lee Davis, eds., *Strategies for Public Health: Promoting Health and Preventing Disease* (New York: Van Nostrand Reinhold, 1981), p. 46. The Commission is persuaded by the general conclusion, without necessarily endorsing the 90:10 ratio.

220. According to Toshiyuki Furukawa, soap helped bring disease-causing microbes under control, and glass permitted sunshine to enter interior spaces, which also decreased harmful micro-organisms (Toshiyuki Furukawa, "A Transactional Comparison of Life Expectancy", a paper given at the Honda Foundation Conference on Prosperity, Health and Wellbeing, Toronto, October 1993). For a lengthy discussion, see McKeown, *The Modern Rise of Population* (cited in note 77).

221. Michael C. Wolfson, Geoff Rowe, Jane Gentleman and Monica Tomiak, "Career Earnings and Death: A Longitudinal Analysis of Older Canadian Men", Analytical Studies Branch, Statistics Canada, 1992; and R. Wilkins, O. Adams and A.M. Brancker, "Changes in Mortality by Income in Urban Canada from 1971 to 1986: Diminishing Absolute Differences, Persistence of Relative Inequality" (Ottawa: Health and Welfare Canada and Statistics Canada, 1991).

222. Furukawa, "A Transactional Comparison" (cited in note 220).

223. M.G. Marmot and George Davey Smith, "Why Are the Japanese Living Longer?", *British Medical Journal* 299/23-30 (July to December 1989), p. 1547.

224. Kirsh, *Unemployment: Its Impact on Body and Soul* (cited in note 159); G. Westcott et al., eds., *Health Policy Implications of Unemployment* (Copenhagen: World Health Organization, 1985); and Lars Iverson et al., "Unemployment and Mortality in Denmark, 1970-80", *British Medical Journal* 295 (10 October 1987), p. 879.

225. Carl D'Arcy, "Unemployment and Health: Data and Implications", *Canadian Journal of Public Health* 77/Supplement 1 (May/June 1986), p. 124.

226. Hans Selye, ed., *Selye's Guide to Stress Research*, Volume 1 (New York: Van Nostrand Reinhold, 1980); and Robert Dantzer and Keith W. Kelley, "Stress and Immunity: An Integrated View of Relationships Between the Brain and the Immune System", *Life Sciences* 44/26 (1989).

227. Other social factors are discussed in the following sources: Michael H. Robinson and Lionel Tiger, eds., *Man and Beast Revisited* (Washington, D.C.: Smithsonian Institution, 1991); Lisa F. Berkman and S. Leonard Syme, "Social Networks, Host Resistance and Mortality: A Nine-Year Follow-up Study of Alameda County

Residents", *American Journal of Epidemiology* 109/2 (1979); and James S. House, Karl R. Landis and Debra Umberson, "Social Relationships and Health", *Science* 241/4865 (29 July 1988), p. 540.

228. M.G. Marmot, Geoffrey Rose, M. Shipley and P.J.S. Hamilton, "Employment Grade and Coronary Heart Disease in British Civil Servants", *Journal of Epidemiology and Community Health* 32 (1978), p. 244.

229. Leonard Syme, "The Social Environment and Health", paper presented at the Honda Foundation Conference on Prosperity, Health and Wellbeing (cited in note 160).

230. Gus Thompson, *Mental Health, The Essential Thread* (Edmonton: Alberta Department of Health, Division of Mental Health, 1993), p. 5.

231. Kirmayer and his colleagues discuss a selection of research literature that draws similar conclusions. See Kirmayer et al., "Emerging Trends in Research" (cited in note 136), pp. 66-72.

232. Clyde Hertzman, "The Lifelong Impact of Childhood Experiences: A Population Health Perspective", a paper presented at the Honda Foundation Conference on Prosperity, Health and Wellbeing (cited in note 160).

233. Daniel P. Keating and J. Fraser Mustard, "Social Economic Factors and Human Development", in *Family Security in Insecure Times* (Ottawa: National Forum on Family Security, Canadian Council on Social Development, 1993).

234. Task Force on Human Development, *The Learning Society*, CIAR Publication No. 6 (Toronto: Canadian Institute for Advanced Research, 1992).

235. Max Cynader, "Biological Pathways that Contribute to Variations in Health Status: The Role of Early Experience", a paper presented at the Honda Conference on Prosperity, Health and Wellbeing, Toronto, October 1993.

236. CICH, *The Health of Canada's Children* (cited in note 53).

237. Thompson, *Mental Health, The Essential Thread* (cited in note 230).

238. W. Dewi Rees and Sylvia G. Lutkins, "Mortality of Bereavement", *British Medical Journal* 4 (October to December 1967), p. 13.

239. Marcia Barinage, "Can Psychotherapy Delay Cancer Deaths?", *Science* 246/4929 (27 October 1989), p. 448; and David Spiegel, "Therapeutic Support Groups", in Bill Moyers, ed., *Healing and the Mind* (Toronto: Doubleday, 1993), pp. 157-176.

240. Thompson, *Mental Health, The Essential Thread* (cited in note 230).

241. Thompson, *Mental Health, The Essential Thread*. For a more detailed discussion of the effects of stress on human health, see John Zawacki, "Stress Reduction", in Moyers, *Healing and the Mind* (cited in note 239), pp. 145-156.

242. See, for example, Moyers, *Healing and the Mind*, especially section III, "The Mind/Body Connection".

243. Dantzer and Kelley, "Stress and Immunity" (cited in note 226); Cynader, "Biological Pathways" (cited in note 235).

244. This aspect of convergence was foreseen in the definition of health put forward by the World Health Organization: "a state of complete physical, mental and social well being, not merely the absence of disease or injury".

245. For a discussion of the paradigm shift that has begun in relation to human health, see Rosemary Proctor, "Challenging the Way We Think about Health", in *The Path to Healing* (cited in note 194), pp. 49-55.

246. The jurisdictional terrain is complex, and terms of access vary from program to program. Generally speaking, the federal government's 'Indian' and Inuit health and social development programs are not open to Métis people or non-status Indians, and only sometimes open to registered Indians living off-reserve or to Inuit living outside their northern communities.

247. The Commission notes the similar finding of the House of Commons Standing Committee on Health in its report, *Towards Holistic Wellness: The Aboriginal Peoples* (Ottawa: July 1995).

248. One notable Canadian example was the forward-thinking analysis of health and social services done by M. Claude Castonguay and his colleagues in Quebec some 25 years ago. The Castonguay-Nepveu Commission (the commission of inquiry on health and welfare, 1970) called for a holistic, community-based approach to health care, based on an inclusive concept of 'social health'. Local community health and social service centres were proposed as the principal means of delivering integrated services. Many of the recommendations of the Castonguay-Nepveu Commission report were implemented in Quebec, but the report had little impact on governments outside Quebec.

249. Marcia Nozick, *No Place Like Home: Building Sustainable Communities* (Ottawa: Canadian Council on Social Development, 1992).

250. L. Bird and M. Moore, "The William Charles Health Centre of Montreal Lake Band: A Case Study of Transfer", in Postl et al., *Circumpolar Health 90* (cited in note 29), pp. 47-53. The authors report that fewer people have required hospitalization in a nearby town since the community health centre was established.

251. Meadow Lake Tribal Council, "Vision of Health and Wellness of the Nine Meadow Lake First Nations People", brief submitted to RCAP (1993).

252. Information provided by Health Canada, Medical Services Branch, Program Transfer, Policy and Planning, March 1996.

253. The Commission normally uses figures from the Aboriginal Peoples Survey [APS]. However, because the coverage of APS does not allow us to identify Aboriginal population numbers in every community, we took 1991 census figures showing Aboriginal ancestry and screened out those who reported more than one ancestry. The single-ancestry respondents should approximate the number of persons who would identify themselves as Aboriginal for purposes of service planning.

254. *Aboriginal Custom Adoption Recognition Act*, S.N.W.T. 1994, c. 26.

255. House of Commons, Standing Committee on Health, *Towards Holistic Wellness* (cited in note 247), p. 59.

256. See also Dianne Longboat, "Pathways to a Dream: Professional Education in the Health Sciences", in *The Path to Healing* (cited in note 194), p. 171; and Rick Krehbiel, RCAP transcripts, Fort St. John, British Columbia, 19 November 1992.

257. See, for example, Federal/Provincial/Territorial/National Aboriginal Organizations Working Group on Aboriginal Health, *Report to the Ministers of Health and National Aboriginal Organizations* (Ottawa: Health Canada, 1993).

258. Canadian Public Health Association [CPHA], "The Training and Recruitment of Aboriginal Public Health Workers", Issues Identification Paper (draft for discussion), Ottawa, 27 August 1993, p. 56.

259. Anne Gilmore, "Canada's Native MDs: Small in Number, Big on Helping their Communities", *Canadian Medical Association Journal* 142/1 (1990), p. 52.

260. Anne-Marie Hodes, Native Health Care Careers Program, Faculty of Medicine, University of Alberta, RCAP transcripts, Edmonton, Alberta, 15 June 1993.

261. Margo Rowan, physician, Canadian Medical Association, RCAP transcripts, Ottawa, Ontario, 17 November 1993.

262. CPHA, "Training and Recruitment" (cited in note 258).

263. Hodes, RCAP transcripts (cited in note 260).

264. The Canadian Public Health Association, for example, recently estimated that there may be 3,000 Aboriginal graduate RNs. See CPHA, "Training and Recruitment" (cited in note 258), p. 33. This wide discrepancy between estimated and identifiable personnel is indicative of the inadequacy of data on Aboriginal human resources.

265. Information provided by the Canadian Nurses Association, 6 January 1995.

266. Louis T. Montour, Kateri Memorial Hospital Centre, RCAP transcripts, Kahnawake, Quebec, 5 May 1993.

267. CPHA, "Training and Recruitment" (cited in note 258).

268. Health Canada, Medical Services Branch, Workload Increase System, May 1993. By January 1996 CHR numbers had risen to 671 and NNADAP workers to 700 (staff communication with MSB, January 1996).

269. See Stewart Clatworthy, Jeremy Hull and Neil Loughran, "Patterns of Employment, Unemployment and Poverty, Part One", research study prepared for RCAP (1995).

270. Statistics Canada, 1991 Aboriginal Peoples Survey, and 1991 Census, custom tabulations prepared for RCAP.

271. 6,445 persons in health occupations, plus 6,980 in social service occupations, equals 13,425 x 0.5 = 6,712.5.

272. Important among these reasons is the isolation often experienced by Aboriginal and non-Aboriginal health and social service professionals who practise in rural and remote communities. These conditions were described in a brief to RCAP by the Ordre des infirmières et infirmiers du Québec, RCAP transcripts, Montreal, Quebec, 16 November 1993.

273. Quoted in CPHA, "Training and Recruitment" (cited in note 258).

274. Ordre des infirmières et infirmiers du Québec, RCAP transcripts (cited in note 272).

275. See Ipeelee Kilabuk, RCAP transcripts, Pangnirtung, Northwest Territories, 28 May 1992. According to the census, the population of the Baffin Region was 11,385 in 1991. Of this number, approximately 9,100, or 80 per cent, were Inuit.

276. See, for example, RCAP transcripts of testimony from George Gillies, Inuvik Regional Hospital, Inuvik, Northwest Territories, 5 May 1992; Isabelle Impey, Saskatoon, Saskatchewan, 12 May 1993; and Lisa Allgaier, University College of the Caribou, Kamloops, British Columbia, 15 June 1993.

277. Employers may have legitimate concerns that collecting some types of information about their employees could constitute an invasion of privacy or a violation of human rights. At the same time, employers have appropriate means available to measure progress toward employment equity.

278. CPHA, "Training and Recruitment" (cited in note 258).

279. For a detailed discussion of training issues for Aboriginal midwives, see Fletcher, "Innuulisivik Maternity Centre" (cited in note 70).

280. The case for a human resources development plan was also made forcefully in a presentation by the Native Council of Canada (now the Congress of Aboriginal Peoples). See RCAP transcripts, Ottawa, Ontario, 8 June 1993.

281. One small but helpful step in systematically collecting and disseminating information about training opportunities has been taken by the department of Indian affairs, which has prepared an inventory of training opportunities. See Department of Indian and Northern Development [DIAND], "Indian/Inuit Training Opportunities, 1993-1994" (Ottawa: Supply and Services, 1993).

282. Chris Durocher, Canadian Medical Association, RCAP transcripts, Ottawa, Ontario, 17 November 1993.

283. National Working Group on Community Health Representatives Scope of Duties, *Final Report* (Ottawa: Health and Welfare, 1993).

284. There have been many proposals to extend the CHR program to urban centres. We were informed about one such proposal in a presentation by the Calgary Aboriginal Urban Affairs Committee. See Gloria Manitopyes, Native Committee Assistant, Calgary Aboriginal Affairs Committee, RCAP transcripts, Calgary, Alberta, 26 May 1993.

285. John D. O'Neil, and Brian D. Postl, "Community Healing and Aboriginal Self-Government: Is the Circle Closing?", in John H. Hylton, ed., *Aboriginal Self-Government in Canada: Current Trends and Issues* (Saskatoon: Purich, 1994), p. 75.

286. See DIAND, Indian and Eskimo Affairs Program, "National Native Alcohol Abuse Program: Information Manual and Project Guidelines" (Ottawa: 1975).

287. Addiction Research Foundation, *Final Report of the Evaluation of Selected NNADAP Projects* (Ottawa: Health and Welfare, 1989).

288. See Health and Welfare, *Aboriginal Health in Canada* (cited in note 18).

289. Addiction Research Foundation, *Final Report* (cited in note 287).

290. Presenters at the public hearings told us that the current structure of NNADAP has led to a good deal of inflexibility, including a per-bed funding formula for residential treatment that does not recognize the importance of prevention or aftercare. See, for example, National Native Association of Treatment Directors, RCAP transcripts, Calgary, Alberta, 27 May 1993. See also Addiction Research Foundation, *Final Report* (cited in note 287).

291. See Four Worlds Development Project, "Survival Secrets of NNADAP Workers", *Four Worlds Exchange* 2/1, pp. 24-39.

292. See Four Worlds Development Project, "Survival Secrets".

293. See also the presentation by Winston McKay, Metis Addictions Corporation of Saskatchewan, RCAP transcripts, La Ronge, Saskatchewan, 28 May 1992.

294. For further detail, see RCAP, *Bridging the Cultural Divide* (cited in note 129); and Chapter 2 of this volume.

295. The need for Aboriginal mental health workers was highlighted in many presentations made to the Commission. See, for example, Ghislain Beaulé, Quebec Regional Health and Social Services Board, Abitibi-Témiscamingue, RCAP transcripts, Val d'Or, Quebec, 30 November 1992. A comprehensive study of the mental health needs of the Aboriginal people of Quebec has also been completed. See Bella H. Petawabano et al., *Mental Health and Aboriginal People of Quebec* (Boucherville, Quebec: Gaëtan Morin Éditeur, 1994).

296. Penny Ericson, Canadian Association of University Schools of Nursing, RCAP transcripts, Moncton, New Brunswick, 14 June 1993.

297. There are encouraging signs that non-Aboriginal health and social service professionals are developing a greater interest in Aboriginal knowledge and practices. For example, we were told about two cross-cultural training workshop organized by the Manitoba Division of the Canadian Medical Association that attracted almost 250 people, including physicians and other health care workers. Chris Durocher, Canadian Medical Association, RCAP transcripts, Ottawa, Ontario, 17 November 1993. See also Schuyler Webster, RCAP transcripts, Sudbury, Ontario, 31 May 1993.

298. This concern was addressed in a number of presentations made to the Commission. See, for example, John Sawyer, Ontario Native Education Counselling Association, RCAP transcripts, Toronto, Ontario, 18 November 1993.

299. This description of the Indian and Inuit Health Careers Program is based on information provided to the Commission by Health Canada on 16 March 1995.

300. Progress is being made in some areas. Pathways to Success, for example, is a federal program to promote training for Aboriginal people. Initially it provided very little opportunity for Aboriginal people to influence the structure and design of the programs being provided, their involvement being restricted largely to administering existing programs. A recent review of the program, however, has recommended a consolidation of several training support programs and a new structure that would recognize the primacy of Aboriginal authority and decision making. See Human Resources Development Canada, "Pathways to Success Strategy" (Ottawa: 1995).

301. A number of presentations to the Commission addressed these issues. See RCAP transcripts for the following: Anne-Marie Hodes, Native Health Care Careers Program, University of Alberta, Edmonton, Alberta, 15 June 1993; Dr. David Skinner and Dr. Chris Durocher, Yukon Medical Association, Teslin, Yukon, 27 May 1992; and Ineaq Korgak, Iqaluit, Northwest Territories, 26 May 1992.

302. Ontario Ministry of Health, *New Directions: Aboriginal Health Policy for Ontario* (Toronto: 1994).

303. Northwest Territories, *Working Together for Community Wellness: A Directions Document* (Yellowknife: Government of the Northwest Territories, 1995).

304. See Alberta, "Strengthening the Circle: What Aboriginal Albertans Say About Their Health" (Edmonton: 1995).

305. The case for more and better qualified interpreters and translators, and the importance of the services they provide, was outlined in a brief presented by the Association des hôpitaux du Québec, RCAP transcripts, Montreal, Quebec, 16 November 1993. Similarly, we received several briefs on the importance of having escorts available to help Aboriginal people obtain needed medical services. We were told that escorts are needed especially for seniors, persons who are not fluent in the language of service providers, and for people from rural and remote areas who must travel to urban centres for treatment. See RCAP transcripts for the following: Tonena McKay, Big Trout Lake First Nation, Big Trout Lake, Ontario, 3 December 1992; Senator Edward Head, Metis Senate of Manitoba, Winnipeg, Manitoba, 21 April 1992; Samaria Reynolds, Winnipeg, Manitoba, 21 April 1992; and Herb Manak, Makkovik, Newfoundland and Labrador, 15 June 1992.

306. See RCAP transcripts for the following presenters: Tom Iron, Vice-Chief, Federation of Saskatchewan Indian Nations, Wahpeton, Saskatchewan, 26 May 1992; Eric Robinson, President, Aboriginal Council of Winnipeg, Winnipeg, Manitoba, 22 April 1992; Debra Alvisatos, Fredericton Native Friendship Centre, Kingsclear, New Brunswick, 19 May 1992; and Douglas Crosby, Secretariat of the Oblate Conference of Canada, Montreal, Quebec, 25 May 1993.

307. For a detailed discussion of these reasons, see *Report of the Aboriginal Justice Inquiry of Manitoba* (Winnipeg: 1991). See also Corinne Jetté, "The Dynamics of Exclusion: Discrimination and Other Barriers Facing Aboriginal People in the Labour Market", research study prepared for RCAP; and Ontario Native

Employment Equity Circle, "Honouring the Difference: A Challenge Paper" (Toronto: ONEEC).

308. Interestingly, however, the Canadian Labour Congress, in its presentation to the Commission, identified several large corporations that had hired significant numbers of additional staff. Very few of them were Aboriginal people. See Dick Martin, Canadian Labour Congress, RCAP transcripts, Ottawa, Ontario, 15 November 1993.

309. See Debbie Luce, Canadian Auto Workers, RCAP transcripts, Toronto, Ontario, 19 November 1993.

310. See Assembly of First Nations, "Reclaiming our Nationhood, Strengthening our Heritage", brief submitted to RCAP (1993), p. 62.

311. *Aboriginal Justice Inquiry of Manitoba* (cited in note 307).

312. See RCAP transcripts for the following presenters: Johnny Naktialuk, Inukjuak, Quebec, 8 June 1992; Wayne Helgason, Director, Ma Mawi Wi Chi Itata Centre Inc., Winnipeg, Manitoba, 23 April 1992; and Ghislain Beaulé, Quebec Regional Health and Social Services Board of Abitibi-Témiscamingue, Val d'Or, Quebec, 30 November 1992. We were also told about similar efforts, although less developed, where Aboriginal participation in the development of a regional health plan was described. See Peter Squires, Chairman, Nisga'a Valley Health Board, RCAP transcripts, Terrace, British Columbia, 25 May 1993. See also Dr. Richard Kennedy, Canadian Medical Association, Ottawa, Ontario, 17 November 1993.

313. See Timothy Johns, Centre for Indigenous Nutrition and Environment, McGill University; and Joyce Pickering, Northern Quebec Module, McGill University, Montreal, Quebec, RCAP transcripts, 2 December 1993.

314. See Aboriginal Employment Equity Consultation Group, *Completing the Circle: First Report to the Secretary of the Treasury Board* (Ottawa: Treasury Board, 1992).

315. Rhonda Fiander, Waterford Hospital, St. John's, Newfoundland; and Danny Pottle, St. John's Native Friendship Centre, St. John's, Newfoundland, RCAP transcripts, 22 May 1992.

316. See Iris Allen, Labrador Inuit Health Commission, RCAP transcripts, Nain, Newfoundland and Labrador, 30 November 1992.

317. See Dr. Chris Durocher, Yukon Medical Association, RCAP transcripts, Teslin, Yukon, 26 May 1992.

318. See RCAP transcripts for the following presenters: Huguette Blouin, Association des hôpitaux du Québec, Montreal, Quebec, 16 November 1993; Emmanuel Stip, Montreal, Quebec, 3 December 1993; and Louis Cossette, Corporation professionelle des médecins du Québec, Montreal, Quebec, 19 November 1993.

319. Earlier in the chapter, we discussed the maternity centre in Povungnituk, a leading example of how Aboriginal and non-Aboriginal providers can work together to extend culturally appropriate health services to Aboriginal people. See also

Anne Rochon Ford, Interim Regulatory Council on Midwifery, RCAP transcripts, Toronto, Ontario, 2 November 1992; and Martha Greig, Vice-President, Pauktuutit, RCAP transcripts, Ottawa, Ontario, 2 November 1993.

320. See Cheryl Ogram, City of Saskatoon Race Relations Committee, RCAP transcripts, Saskatoon, Saskatchewan, 27 October 1992; and Al Adams, Deputy Mayor, City of Thompson, RCAP transcripts, Thompson, Manitoba, 1 June 1993.

321. See RCAP transcripts for the following presenters: Tom Erasmus, Alberta Mental Health Association, Lac La Biche, Alberta, 9 June 1992; Debra Alvisatos, Fredericton Native Friendship Centre, Kingsclear, New Brunswick, 19 May 1992; Theresa Holizki, Chief Commissioner, Saskatchewan Human Rights Commission, Saskatoon, Saskatchewan, 28 October 1992; and Marlene Thio-Watts, Prince George, British Columbia, 1 June 1993.

322. Lorrie Boissoneau-Armstrong, Phoenix Rising Women's Centre, RCAP transcripts, Sault Ste. Marie, Ontario, 11 June 1992. Many Aboriginal organizations told us about partnerships with mainstream service agencies to provide cross-cultural training to their non-Aboriginal staff. See, for example, Doug Maracle, RCAP transcripts, Brantford, Ontario, 13 May 1993.

323. See, for example, RCAP transcripts for Dan Highway, Aboriginal Advisory Council, Roseau River, Manitoba, 8 December 1992; Celeste McKay, Aboriginal Women in the Canadian Labour Force, Winnipeg, Manitoba, 17 November 1993; and Denney Grisdale, District No. 70 School Board, Port Alberni, British Columbia, 20 May 1992.

324. The speech delivered by Peter Penashue was published with the following citation: Ben Andrew and Peter Sarsfield, "Innu Health: The Role of Self-Determination", in Fortuine, ed., *Circumpolar Health 84* (cited in note 132).

325. Meadow Lake Tribal Council and St. John Ambulance, brief submitted to RCAP, (1993), p. 14, Appendix A, p. I.

APPENDIX 3A

TRADITIONAL HEALTH AND HEALING

Traditional healing has been defined as "practices designed to promote mental, physical and spiritual well-being that are based on beliefs which go back to the time before the spread of western, 'scientific' bio-medicine".[1] When Aboriginal people in Canada talk about traditional healing, they include a wide range of activities, from physical cures using herbal medicines and other remedies, to the promotion of psychological and spiritual well-being using ceremony, counselling and the accumulated wisdom of the elders.[2]

Even those who are sympathetic to Aboriginal perspectives often see traditional Aboriginal healing methods as unsophisticated or 'primitive' versions of bio-medical principles. Apart from being paternalistic, this view ignores fundamental philosophical differences between the two systems, including the essential dimension of spirituality in Aboriginal healing and its much more comprehensive goal of restoring balance to individuals and communities.

Many of those who testified before the Commission called for protection and extension of the role of traditional healing, traditional values and traditional practices in contemporary health and social services. These calls were particularly strong in relation to psycho-social and 'mental health' problems (such as substance abuse and other forms of self-destructive and violent behaviour), and in relation to childbirth. Proponents called for a more tolerant regulatory environment to protect and encourage use of the 'old ways'. Indeed, many said that the integration of traditional healing practices and spirituality into medical and social services is the missing ingredient needed to make those services work for Aboriginal people.

Support for traditional Aboriginal healing and medicine was expressed to the Commission from many sources:

- In our public hearings, the majority of presentations on health and social issues by First Nations presenters mentioned the potential contribution of traditional healing values and methods to improving health outcomes.[3]
- Inuit presenters were less likely to refer to traditional practices, but many talked about the importance of past lifestyle practices – such as the traditional diet and the physically active hunting way of life, as well as other beliefs about life and living that were embedded in their cultures – to help meet current health needs.[4]
- Métis presenters said little about traditional health and healing practices in open testimony; however, a background paper prepared for the Commission

argued that Métis interest in traditional knowledge and practices inherited from their First Nations ancestors is experiencing a rebirth.[5] This paper called for Commission recommendations to support and enhance the role of traditional approaches to wellness promotion in future health and social services provided to Métis as well as other Aboriginal peoples, and the development of culturally based health services.

• The Aboriginal peoples survey found that 10.1 per cent of respondents living on-reserve, 4.6 per cent of the urban sample and three per cent of the Métis sample had consulted a traditional healer in the previous year.[6]

Reasons given for this widespread support included both direct effectiveness and the more subtly empowering effect of promoting health in culturally familiar ways:

> I remember once sitting down with [a clan leader], and he was telling me that all the people were going down to the nursing station...because they were sick with either chest pains or colds. But while they were walking down there, they were stepping over all the medicine from the land. They were walking over the medicine that they needed!...When we go to the doctor and the nurse, we give them our power to heal us when we should have the power within ourselves to heal us.
>
> Eric Morris
> Teslin Tlingit Council
> Teslin, Yukon, 27 May 1992

> [A]s European society became more and more imposing on our society...the traditional type of healing that existed was [practically] wiped out. Today, in 1992, we are looking again at the possibility of going back to some of the traditional healing techniques that were used in the past....[If we had the funds], we would like to bring in a lot more people who would assist us in traditional healing.
>
> Lionel Whiteduck
> Director, Health and Social Services
> Kitigan Zibi Anishinabeg Council
> Maniwaki, Quebec, 2 December 1992

Support came from non-Aboriginal sources as well:

> It is our belief that because our white man's medicine is very technical-oriented, very symptom-oriented, very drugs- and surgery-oriented, that it lacks something that Native medicine has, which we desperately need but don't practise: spirituality....In many of these things we are talking about – family violence, alcohol abuse, trauma,

suicide – I believe that the Native public health nurses, Native nurses, Native doctors would have that in their approach as well – a spiritual component. Then we get on into that area of the question of traditional Native medicine and things that [only] Native people will do; it is not the white man who will ever do them, it is the Native traditional medicine [man/woman].

Dr. David Skinner
Yukon Medical Association
Teslin, Yukon, 27 May 1992

With regard to traditional medicine...we wish to state that we fully respect the desire of Aboriginal peoples to use traditional medicine because we understand that this is truly an integral part of their culture and traditions. We therefore believe Aboriginal people are rightly entitled to access to holistic medicine which considers the physical, mental and spiritual aspects of a person....We find great worth in Aboriginal peoples' current reaffirmation of their attachment to and trust in their traditional medicine. [translation]

Huguette Blouin
Director, Groupe des centres hospitaliers
et des centres de réadaptation
L'Association des hôpitaux du Québec
Montreal, Quebec, 16 November 1993

Culturally responsive and holistic health care delivery and health promotion are prerequisites to improved health for Aboriginal peoples. This requires...an openness and respect for traditional medicine and traditional practices such as sweat lodges and healing circles....

Dr. Richard J. Kennedy
Canadian Medical Association
Ottawa, Ontario, 17 November 1993

The Power of Traditional Healing

Values and practices adopted or adapted from Aboriginal healing traditions offer immediate and long-term positive benefits to health status. These benefits are accessible through direct collective participation in ceremonies, one-to-one client consultation with elders and other healers, and the participation of traditional elders and healers in new program design. Areas of health care in which their contribution might be of greatest value are as follows:

Non-Physical Determinants of Health

Traditional healing and healers can provide insight into the mental, emotional and spiritual aspects of Aboriginal health and well-being, especially with regard to social problems that involve the mental, emotional and spiritual aspects of living, such as violent and abusive behaviour and self-destructive behaviour, including substance abuse; the management of chronic illness and pain; preparation for death; and the experience of grief.

Health Promotion

The values and teachings of traditional medicine can contribute to health promotion and disease prevention, directly by encouraging healthy lifestyles and indirectly by suggesting culturally appropriate approaches to health education. Hagey, for example, documented the success of a diabetes education program using the Ojibwa story of Nanabush and the Pale Stranger as a metaphor to explain the effects and management of diabetes.[7]

Support for Increased Personal Responsibility

The values of traditional medicine encourage self-care and personal responsibility for health and well-being. This contribution is particularly important at a time when Aboriginal people are emphasizing the need to find their own solutions for persistent personal and social problems.

Treatment

Numerous traditional medicines have been adopted as pharmaceuticals or have pointed the way to synthesizing drugs for treatment. Investigation of other such herbal remedies continues. Many Aboriginal people attest as well to the efficacy of non-pharmaceutical treatments and prescriptions.

Care System Reorientation

Traditional practices and healing philosophies, such as those relating to holism and balance in personal and social life, can help create health and social services that Aboriginal people feel more comfortable consulting.

Bridging the Cultures

Traditional healers may be able to serve as a bridge between Aboriginal clients and mainstream health and social service facilities, and thus assist in cross-cultural communication.

Cost Savings

A more active role for traditional healing could lower the cost of bio-medical care, thus freeing resources to improve other determinants of health such as economic status, environmental conditions, child and maternal health, and so on.

Traditional Healing and Commission Recommendations on Health Care

An extended role for traditional medicine and healing practices (where this is wanted by Aboriginal nations and their communities) can contribute to the four cornerstones of Aboriginal health and social service reform advocated by the Commission:

- The practices of traditional medicine and healing are rooted in holism as a fundamental value.
- The appropriate use of traditional medicine and healing techniques will assist in improving outcomes in a variety of ill health and social conditions, ranging from the physical to the spiritual. It will thus contribute to equity in health status for and between Aboriginal peoples.
- The recognition of traditional healing and healers by Canadian authorities will respect the diversity of approaches to health and social services taken by Aboriginal people.
- The application of traditional practices to contemporary health and social problems is a manifestation of Aboriginal control and self-determination and will lead to a care system shaped more fully by Aboriginal cultures, beliefs and values.

The call to re-establish traditional healing is part of the drive to recover indigenous ways of solving problems that have been suppressed and devalued by the dominant culture. Re-traditionalization, in all its forms, is part of a general ferment of ideas now contributing to the renewal of Aboriginal cultures.[8] As such, it is valid and valuable in its own right. It will help Aboriginal cultures retain their integrity in the face of severe pressures to yield to Euro-Canadian culture and will help individuals develop strong, proud identities as Aboriginal people.

The possibility of an enhanced role for traditional medicine and healing has special significance in relation to Aboriginal self-determination. The Aboriginal right of self-determination implies the right of First Peoples to manage their own needs and affairs, including those now met by mainstream health and social service systems. Commitment to full self-determination and self-government requires the federal and provincial governments to allow for – indeed to encourage – institutional development in Aboriginal nations and communities that differs from mainstream practice. Thus, Aboriginal governments and health agencies must have the authority to decide what place traditional health and healing will have in their care services.

Arguments based on Aboriginal rights and preferences are a powerful basis for recommending an enhanced role for traditional medicine and healing practices. An equally powerful basis is found in scientific research on the determinants of health, which shows that western bio-medicine is not the only valid or effective system of preventing and treating disease. Indeed, the greatest strengths of bio-medicine appear to lie in its treatment of acute illness and injury. Other approaches offer complementary strengths in health promotion, disease prevention and the management of chronic illness – not to mention social, mental and spiritual 'dis-ease'. Western practitioners' suspicion of and hostility to traditional approaches might be waning. Recent ground-breaking discoveries, particularly in the field of psycho-neuroimmunology, lend credence to the insights of eastern and traditional medicine. Complex bio-chemical links among body, mind, emotions and spirit, for example, can now be demonstrated.

After more than a century of well-funded dominance by bio-medicine of the institutions of health and healing in our societies, the western world is now beginning to evaluate the potential contributions of other approaches. The World Health Organization's goal of health for all is still far out of reach. Traditional medicine and healing practices are a source of ideas that may ultimately benefit not just Aboriginal peoples, but all peoples.

Commissioners understand that not all Aboriginal people share this view of the potential of traditional values and practices. Some are simply not interested. Others, who see a conflict with either Christianity or modernity, are actively opposed. Proponents of traditional healing are not advocating the imposition of traditional healers or practices where they are not wanted. Nor are they proposing to reduce Aboriginal people's access to nurses, doctors, hospitals and necessary medical services. Proponents advocate choice in medical and social services and the adaptation of health and healing systems to reflect Aboriginal preferences. This is not a simple matter of recognizing a fully developed alternative to existing services. Traditions must be thoroughly assessed and adapted to modern conditions. No one who spoke to the Commission proposed a nostalgic or uncritical approach to traditional healing. Rather, they sought an open exploration of its rich possibilities.

Policy Issues

If traditional healing and medicine are to make a larger contribution to the well-being of Aboriginal people, the following policy issues will have to be addressed:

- access to existing services;
- protection and promotion of existing skills and knowledge;

- regulation of traditional healing practices and services; and
- co-operation between traditional Aboriginal and mainstream western practitioners.

Access to Services

Current federal health policy does not reliably cover the costs incurred by those who wish to consult or work with a traditional healer.[9] First, as the Peguis case study indicates,[10] the medical services branch of Health Canada does provide some support, but that support is problematic.[11] At present, it is arbitrary, unsystematic and controlled (through the referral process) by doctors who may be unsympathetic or ignorant. The possibility of support may at any time be restricted or eliminated. Second, costs recognized by medical services branch are reimbursed under the Non-Insured Health Benefits (NIHB) program, which is fundamentally inequitable, open only to registered Indians and Inuit. Third, given the small number of traditional healers now practising, and their degree of specialization, NIHB is underfunded to pay the full cost of consultation with traditional healers. Federal support must be clarified and systematized until traditional healers become self-regulating and access to their services is controlled by Aboriginal health authorities.

There are no guidelines or systematic measures in place to support the costs incurred by traditional healers themselves, including the cost of living while practising the healing arts. Indeed, the norms of Aboriginal cultures generally forbid the payment of healers. In general, it is an obligation on the Aboriginal healer to exercise his or her gifts freely for the benefit of the community. The healer's good practice creates a reciprocal obligation on the part of the healed (and his or her family) to protect and support the healer. This obligation cannot be discharged through payment, but only through continuing respect and spontaneous material aid (such as gifts of food). Thus, healers are discouraged from acting out of narrow self-interest, and at the same time, provided with sustenance by the community so they can do their work.

Travel expenses in relation to services provided outside the home community (for example in an urban setting, or a community without its own traditional healer) may be covered by medical services branch. If so, they fall under the same inadequate NIHB program. Even when travel costs are covered, the larger problem of fees (or the equivalent) remains. Since traditional healers have not lobbied to make their income a matter of public policy, it might seem as if the Commission should be silent on the subject. However, if traditional healers are to offer their services more widely, participate in the redesign of Aboriginal health and social services, and attract apprentices, the matter of ensuring adequate income becomes a public policy concern.[12] Similarly, if traditional services are to be developed and extended, the means of traditional practice, such as the ceremonial uses of tobacco, other plants and animal parts, must be protected.

Protection and Promotion of Existing Skills and Knowledge

It is neither possible nor appropriate for non-Aboriginal people or governments to speculate on the amount of effective knowledge that has survived the years of denunciation and criminalization of traditional practices. Aboriginal communities have hidden their practices and practitioners from non-Aboriginal eyes in order to protect them. Indeed, some Aboriginal people may themselves be untutored in the possibilities offered by traditional healing skills and unaware of continuing practice in their own communities. Still, the knowledge and skills base was undeniably undermined in the course of Canada's colonial and post-colonial history. It is thus important that surviving practices be protected from further loss and misrepresentation and that they be strengthened and adapted to contemporary conditions.

As discussed in this chapter, these matters are primarily the business and responsibility of Aboriginal healers, communities and nations. As authority for the planning and delivery of health and social services is taken on by Aboriginal nations, it will fall to them to decide the place of traditional healing. The role for governments in the short term will be to provide funds to help Aboriginal people begin to take the steps described. In the long term, governments must establish financing frameworks for Aboriginal health and social services that include an allowance for the development of traditional healing.

Regulation of Traditional Healing Practices and Services

Many traditional healers are strongly opposed to formal regulation. Yet there are good arguments in favour of it. In times past, customary practice and informal norms were enough to safeguard Aboriginal people against fraudulent practitioners and to provide acknowledged healers with a livelihood through gifts and community support. But times have changed. Forms of self-regulation and community control that once operated through religious, spiritual or medicine societies or simply through local reputation are, in some places, weakened or non-existent. Clients are more vulnerable to fraudulent claims and practices – and perhaps to abuse (including sexual abuse) by people who claim healing abilities. Traditional controls that operated in the context of stable kin-based communities are unsuitable in the context of the increasing urbanization of Aboriginal people.

Issues of client protection, healer protection, healer payment and/or support and the protection of traditional medicines and ceremonial substances must be addressed in a more formal way if traditional healers, midwives and elder-counsellors are to play a significant role in Aboriginal health and social services. For traditional healing to come out of the shadows, issues of professional accountability and public trust must be addressed.

In the wider society, regulation of health professionals is achieved through a combination of provincial and federal law and self-regulation by the professions. It is, in fact, the mark of an established profession to be self-regulating. Traditional healers who accept the need for some means of control and account-ability would consider only a self-managed form.[13]

Provincial and federal laws designed to regulate bio-medical practitioners and protect their clients do not serve the interests of traditional midwives and healers. Indeed, quite the reverse is true: these laws render traditional practitioners vulnerable to a number of civil and criminal charges. The *Food and Drugs Act* makes it an offence to advertise any substance as a treatment for a disease or ill-ness unless it has been approved by Health Canada. In all provinces, the statutes governing the medical professions make it an offence to practise medicine, broadly and inclusively defined, except under licence from the self-governing body of physicians and surgeons. Provincial and municipal laws and regulations prohibit the use of tobacco in public places, generally with no exemptions for ceremonial use. Under the *Indian Act*, First Nations on-reserve might pass their own by-laws permitting and regulating traditional practice, but they would run the risk of challenge.[14] We prefer a more systematic approach.

The approach taken by other alternative health practitioners (such as mid-wives and chiropractors) has been, first, to develop their own codes of conduct and self-management, then to negotiate with provincial and territorial govern-ments for recognition and a defined scope of practice. The first of these steps is a requirement that must apply to all health practitioners, including traditional healers, in order to reassure and protect the public. As to the second, it is desir-able that provincial authorities immediately exempt traditional midwives, heal-ers and healing practices from legal restriction, as Ontario has recently done. Further regulation is a matter for negotiation by regional and provincial associ-ations of healers or their appointed spokespeople in provincial-territorial Aboriginal organizations.

The new policy in Ontario is to make clear exemptions in law for the prac-tice of traditional Aboriginal medicine. The *Regulated Health Professions Act, 1991* contains a section excepting "aboriginal healers providing traditional heal-ing services to aboriginal persons" and "aboriginal midwives providing traditional midwifery services to aboriginal persons" from prosecution under the act.[15] The *Midwifery Act, 1991* declines to regulate Aboriginal midwives, in effect giving them leave to practise without interference or legal sanction.[16] The *Tobacco Control Act, 1994* acknowledges the use of tobacco as part of Aboriginal culture and spirituality, permits Aboriginal youth under 19 to use tobacco for ceremonial purposes, allows the ceremonial use of tobacco in otherwise smoke-free areas, and requires health facilities to provide space where traditional uses of tobacco are possible.[17]

It is usual (though not guaranteed) for bio-medical practices to be subject to peer review and other forms of evaluation. It is also normal for governments to require the evaluation of health and social service programs to which they contribute funds. Traditional medicine and healing practices are therefore likely to come under pressure to accept external review. This will be problematic, because traditional healers generally object to the application of external controls.

Kaufert reports that, at a recent conference, the question of how to document and evaluate traditional practices, when raised by bio-medically trained people, provoked a furious reaction among traditionalists. These speakers argued that it would be utterly inappropriate to measure traditional, holistic healing and its results using reductionist bio-medical methods. They proposed standards of evaluation that would be generated, monitored and controlled within Aboriginal communities.[18]

Co-operation Between Traditional and Mainstream Practitioners

A policy of enhancing the role of traditional healing practices in Aboriginally controlled and mainstream health and social service facilities will require increased co-operation between conventionally trained personnel and traditional practitioners. Some people who testified at Commission hearings, and some international health policy experts, have gone so far as to advocate integration of the two healing systems.

Support for traditional medicine as an integrated part of the health care system has been a feature of international health policy for more than two decades. The World Health Organization (WHO) has recognized that traditional medicine and healing resources are the main means of providing care to the majority (80 to 90 per cent) of the world's population.[19] However, WHO and Pan American Health Organization policy documents tend to treat such services as a stop-gap or transitional measure for developing countries and disadvantaged sub-populations until such time as adequate bio-medical services can be provided.[20] This approach assumes the superiority of western bio-medicine and the gradual eclipse of traditional health and healing.

This approach is rejected by proponents of traditional health and healing in Canada, who regard it as an expression of colonial assumptions.[21] Further, this view is not supported by the Commission's analysis of the literature on the new determinants of health, which suggests that bio-medicine and illness care are over-valued and that a more inclusive approach to health and wellness is preferable. It supports many of the practices and approaches of traditional medicine, including the holistic inclusion of mental, emotional and spiritual aspects in the overall design of health and healing services.

In fact, there are a number of possible relationships between traditional and mainstream practitioners. They vary by type and degree of co-operation. We present four approaches that have been suggested.

Hub-spoke integration

In hub-spoke integration, traditional healers (the spokes) are trained to deliver primary health care under the supervision of a medically trained doctor or nurse (the hub). Traditional practitioners are viewed as auxiliaries in an under-funded health system. Their expertise is minimized, and their scope for independent practice is quite limited. In this model, the long-term goal of the care system is to increase the availability of bio-medical and tertiary health and illness care services.

Support service provision

Traditional healers work with bio-medical personnel and social workers, providing specific support services. Their services might be limited to interpretive assistance,[22] or widened to include psycho-therapeutic and/or ceremonial functions. Within a narrow range of secondary functions, this model gives traditional healers an independent role in the care system. It posits that this role will be lasting (except in so far as traditional practices lose value for Aboriginal people), but it does not protect or promote traditional practices for their own sake.

Respectful independence

In a respectful independence model, traditional and bio-medical health and healing services are developed and offered separately, in parallel systems whose practitioners have respect for one another, make referrals to one another, and may occasionally co-operate in treating clients or responding to community problems (for example, a cluster of suicides).[23] Each system is considered to have value, and traditional healing is thought of as one specialty field among many others in health care. In this model, the choice to consult one or the other of the two systems – or both simultaneously – rests with the client.[24]

New paradigm collaboration

In the new paradigm collaboration model, traditional and bio-medical practitioners would work together to develop techniques and practices to promote and restore health, using the best elements from both systems or recombining those elements into wholly new ways of approaching health and healing. This model does not advocate melding or synthesizing the two traditions into a single, integrated alternative. Rather, it imagines that both systems would be changed irrevocably by co-operation with the other, while continuing to maintain spheres of independent practice. It also imagines the possibility that new methods of healing, new treatments and new therapies could emerge from cross-fertilization.

The last model is attractive to many analysts, Aboriginal and non-Aboriginal alike. Indeed, some traditional healers support new paradigm collaboration as an immediate strategy to achieve human health and well-being, on the grounds that Aboriginal philosophies of health and healing have so much to offer a sick and de-spiritualized world.[25]

> There [should be] no doubt by any individual in the world that a drastic transformation must be developed if humanity is to reverse the course of its own destruction. Recent authorities predict that if the present course of consumption and destruction is not reversed widespread human and environmental collapse will occur....Those interested in the environment seek Native philosophy and wisdom about how to live in relation to the natural world. Indigenous people are increasingly being called upon to assist others in understanding spirituality. There is a huge emptiness within most individuals within Western civilization.
>
> Dave Courchene, Jr.
> Mother Earth Spiritual Camp
> Fort Alexander, Manitoba, 30 October 1992

Not all practitioners agree. The Aboriginal Nurses Association of Canada was given funds through the Commission's Intervener Participation Program to formulate a "strategic plan for the integration of traditional medicine within a primary health care framework".[26] Group participants were unable to reach consensus on controversial aspects of the assignment. There was a polarization of views, not only between traditional and bio-medical practitioners, but also among traditionalists. Of the latter, some were positively disposed to explore and expand areas of commonality and potential collaboration, while others were sceptical, opposed to regulation and preferring to remain independent of mainstream medicine.

Thus, the potential for co-operation between health and healing systems can be exaggerated. Traditional medicine and orthodox bio-medicine differ in profound ways. The idea of increased co-operation has strong opponents among current practitioners of traditional medicine. Concern about the possibly negative results of integrating traditional and conventional health care systems too quickly or too rigidly was expressed at Commission hearings at Orillia, Ontario, by Yvon Lamarche, whom we quoted earlier in the chapter.

Historically, practitioners of bio-medicine have argued the general superiority of their methods, showing little regard for alternatives or complementary practice. It is not surprising, then, that many traditional healers see co-operation as code for co-optation and domination.[27] As bio-medicine changes in response to pressure for reform, the grounds for two-way, respectful co-operation may widen. The Canadian Medical Association (CMA), for example, has called on members to show "openness and respect for traditional medicine and traditional healing practices such as sweat lodges and healing circles".[28] It will take an active program of professional education by organizations such as CMA to achieve this goal.

Based on these considerations, the appropriate goal for public policy in the short and medium term appears to be the third approach: respectful independence. To achieve this goal, traditional healing will require a period of internal development and self-regulation by its practitioners. Bio-medicine will require strong professional leadership to encourage respect for and develop codes of co-operation with Aboriginal healers, midwives and elder-advisers. In the long term, it will be up to future governments, to practitioners in both healing systems, and to the clients who have the greatest stake in an effective wellness system, to negotiate the terms of co-operation between traditional and bio-medical practitioners.

Conclusion

If traditional healing and healers are to assume a respected place in health-promoting systems of the future, a period of internal development and planning is needed. During this time, the four critical issues we have identified should be addressed by the parties concerned: access to the services of traditional healers, protection and extension of the existing skills and knowledge base, self-regulation by existing practitioners, and the need for dialogue between traditional healers and bio-medical (and related) personnel.

Access to the services of traditional healers, midwives and other practitioners should be assured for Aboriginal people who choose to consult them. This will require, in the short term, clarification of the provisions of the Non-Insured Health Benefits program, including guidelines for Aboriginally controlled referral. In the longer term, it will require consideration in the self-government agreements that will ultimately cover all Aboriginal nations and their communities. Both now and in the future, it will require action by mainstream health and social service providers to ensure that Aboriginal clients have the opportunity to consult a traditional practitioner, if they so desire.

Health authorities, traditional practitioners and other concerned parties should co-operate to protect and extend the practices of traditional health and healing and explore their application to contemporary health and healing problems. This will require that governments, health and education authorities, and traditional healers co-operate in taking steps to safeguard existing traditional health and healing knowledge, skills and practices. Such steps will probably centre on protecting the oral tradition by compiling written records, through apprenticeships and other means. The extension of traditional healing practices will require that governments, health and education authorities, and traditional healers co-operate in exploring the history, current role and future contribution of traditional health and healing practices in their care services and systems. In the future, they may wish to study and assess traditional cures and publicize the results of their investigations.

Traditional healers and related practitioners need to develop their existing means of self-regulation and discuss the need to develop and publish codes of conduct to govern their relations with Aboriginal clients, health authorities and governments, and with mainstream health practitioners and institutions. This will require financial assistance from Aboriginal, federal, provincial and territorial governments so that traditional healers can form national (or several regional) associations to encourage the exchange of information and build toward more formalized self-regulation. In the long term, these organizations should become self-financed and operate under the authority of Aboriginal governments.

Finally, traditional and bio-medical practitioners should continue to engage in dialogue with two objectives in mind: to enhance mutual respect and to discuss areas of possible collaboration. This will require active outreach by mainstream health professionals and their associations to initiate contact, demonstrate their respect for traditional practitioners, and show their willingness to take steps to sensitize their members and prospective members (students in professional training programs) to the value of traditional healing practices.

NOTES

1. Velimirovic quotes a more formal definition, which is often cited in World Health Organization and related literature: "[Traditional medicine is] the sum of all the knowledge and practices, whether explicable or not, used in diagnosis, prevention and elimination of physical, mental or social imbalance, and relying on practical experience and observation handed down from generation to generation, whether verbally or in writing". AFRO Technical Report Series 1976, 3-4, cited in B. Velimirovic, "Is Integration of Traditional and Western Medicine Really Possible?", in J. Coreil and J.D. Mull, eds., *Anthropology and Primary Health Care*, (Boulder, Colorado: Westview Press, 1990). RCAP uses the term 'healer' to include a wide range of people whose skills, wisdom and understanding can play a part in restoring personal well-being and social balance, from specialists in the use of healing herbs, to traditional midwives, to elders whose life experience makes them effective as counsellors, to ceremonialists who treat physical, social, emotional and mental disorders by spiritual means.

2. Traditional approaches to health and well-being are many and various, albeit containing some consistent principles and values. Historically, there were many differences between the medicine societies of the Kwakwạ kạ'wạkw of coastal British Columbia and the Anishnabe (Ojibwa) of woodland Ontario. The family-based Inuit *angatquq* (shamans) were different again. Although specific ceremonies and practices have survived, at least in some places, the general principles and values of traditional healing are more important in today's movement toward 're-tradi-

tionalization'. Cohen's research on the role of traditional healing in the Peguis First Nations community includes a brief discussion of its contemporary meanings. Benita Cohen, "Health Services Development in an Aboriginal Community: The Case of Peguis First Nation," research study prepared for RCAP (1994).

3. It is not surprising that extended presentations were rare; traditional healers have had good reason to be secretive about their practices. Many have gone underground in order to keep working. Sometimes their presence is unknown even in their own communities. See Jesse Leahy, "Kenora's Native Healer Program: By Anishnaabee, for Anishnaabee", term paper, University of Manitoba, Department of Community Medicine, Winnipeg, 1993.

4. The Inuit of Povungnituk have demonstrated the contemporary value of integrating traditional and 'western' approaches to midwifery. See Christopher Fletcher, "The Innuulisivik Maternity Centre: Issues Around the Return of Inuit Midwifery and Birth to Povungnituk, Quebec", research study prepared for RCAP (1994).

5. Diane Kinnon, "Health is the Whole Person: A background paper on health and the Métis People", research study prepared for RCAP (1994).

6. Joseph M. Kaufert, "Health Status, Service Use and Program Models Among the Aboriginal Population of Canadian Cities", research study prepared for RCAP (1994).

7. Kaufert, "Health Status, Program Use and Service Models".

8. See the discussion of re-traditionalization offered by David Newhouse, RCAP transcripts, Toronto, 3 November 1992.

9. Kaufert, "Health Status, Service Use and Program Models" (cited in note 6).

10. Cohen, "Health Services Development in an Aboriginal Community" (cited in note 2).

11. As of the mid-1980s, referral to a traditional healer became a service available 'on request' at Peguis. Costs are met under the non-insured health benefits program. There has been a growing number of referrals and requests for service since that time, especially in relation to the management of emotional problems. Requests for information about traditional healing, especially from young people, have also increased. The situation came about as a result of pressure from local health administrators, who feel vulnerable to the possibility that the interpretation of MSB policy that has permitted it may change. See Cohen, "Health Services Development in an Aboriginal Community".

12. Shestowsky indicates that the historical practice of unpaid service may be changing. Some informants in her study indicated willingness to accept remuneration, and some practitioners are already charging for services rendered. Aboriginal Nurses Association of Canada, "Traditional Aboriginal Medicine and Primary Health Care", brief submitted to RCAP (1993).

13. McCormick, a health care consultant in Calgary, notes that self-regulation is the goal of all alternative practitioners, not only to protect the public, but also to protect themselves against attempts to discredit them by the bio-medical professions. When traditional healing becomes more visible and/or more self-promoting, it seems likely that its practitioners will want protection as well. See James S. McCormick, "To Wear the White Coat: Options for Traditional Healers in a Canadian Medical Future", in D.E. Young, ed., *Health Care Issues in the Canadian North* (Edmonton: University of Alberta, Boreal Institute for Northern Studies, 1988), p. 8.

14. James C. Robb, "Legal Impediments to Traditional Indian Medicine", in Young, *Health Care Issues*, p. 134.

15. *Regulated Health Professions Act, 1991*, S.O. 1991, c. 18, s. 35.

16. *Midwifery Act, 1991*, S.O. 1991, c. 31, s. 8(3).

17. *Tobacco Control Act, 1994*, S.O. 1994, c. 10, s. 13.

18. Kaufert, "Health Status, Service Use and Program Models" (cited in note 6).

19. Kaufert, "Health Status, Service Use and Program Models".

20. M. Dion Stout and C. Coloma, "Indigenous Peoples and Health", background document for the Winnipeg workshop on indigenous peoples and health (Winnipeg: Canadian Society for International Health, 1993).

21. IDRC (1994) as discussed in Kaufert, "Health Status, Service Use and Program Models" (cited in note 6).

22. Interpretive services are a more inclusive concept than translation services. See John D. O'Neil, "Referrals to Traditional Healers: The Role of Medical Interpreters", in Young, ed., *Health Care Issues* (cited in note 13), p. 29; and Joseph M. Kaufert, John D. O'Neil and William W. Koolage, "Culture Brokerage and Advocacy in Urban Hospitals: The Impact of Native Language Interpreters", *Santé Culture Health* 3/2 (1985), p. 3.

23. This is the model practised in Nepal, where the national government has formally recognized both western medicine and traditional healing. Both are funded by the state and offer parallel services through parallel institutions. See Chief Ron Wakegijig, Alan W. Roy and Carrie Hayward, "Traditional Medicine: An Anishinabek Nation Perspective", *Environments* 19/3 (1988), p. 122.

24. There is evidence that a considerable number of Aboriginal people in Canada do consult practitioners in both systems concurrently even now. See O'Neil, "Referrals to Traditional Healers" (cited in note 22); James B. Waldram, "Access to Traditional Medicine in a Western Canadian City", *Medical Anthropology* 12/1 (1990), pp. 325-348; James B. Waldram, "The Persistence of Traditional Medicine in Urban Areas: The Case of Canada's Indians", *American Indian and Alaska Native Health Research* 4/1 (Fall 1990), pp. 9-29; and David Gregory and Pat Stewart, "Nurses and

Traditional Healers: Now is the Time to Speak", *The Canadian Nurse* 83/8 (September 1987), p. 25.

25. Young, *Health Care Issues in the Canadian North* (cited in note 13). See also the complete testimony of Dave Courchene, Jr., RCAP transcripts, Fort Alexander, Manitoba, 30 October 1992.

26. Aboriginal Nurses Association of Canada, "Traditional Medicine and Primary Health Care" (cited in note 12).

27. See Aboriginal Nurses Association of Canada, "Traditional Medicine and Primary Health Care"; and Kaufert, "Health Status, Service Use and Program Models" (cited in note 6).

28. Dr. Richard Kennedy, Canadian Medical Association, RCAP transcripts, Ottawa, Ontario, 17 November 1993.

4

HOUSING

ABORIGINAL HOUSING AND COMMUNITY SERVICES are in a bad state, by all measures falling below the standards that prevail elsewhere in Canada and threatening the health and well-being of Aboriginal people. The inadequacy of these services is visible evidence of the poverty and marginalization experienced disproportionately by Aboriginal people. Our terms of reference call for us to consider these problems, particularly the issue of "sub-standard housing".

Housing policy is a tough challenge, so daunting that it has been under review by the federal government since 1988 with no sign of resolution. But the situation has not been static over the past eight years: needs have been increasing, and governments have been withdrawing progressively from the field. The impasse must be broken; otherwise, the demoralizing and debilitating effects of the housing crisis could undermine efforts to improve relations between Aboriginal people and the rest of Canadian society and impede the move to greater self-reliance in other areas.

The problem is threefold: lack of adequate incomes to support the private acquisition of housing, absence of a functioning housing market in many localities where Aboriginal people live, and lack of clarity and agreement on the nature and extent of government responsibility to respond to the problem. On reserves, the application of the *Indian Act* and collective systems of land tenure complicate the situation. For Aboriginal people not living on reserves, the inconsistent and declining support from federal and provincial governments is threatening to undermine gains made over the past 20 years.

In this chapter we propose a 10-year strategy. We argue that removal of barriers and steady, strategic investments can bring community services and the housing stock to a level of adequacy over five years and 10 years respectively. We also project that the economic status of communities will improve through the structural changes recommended elsewhere in our report, and this will reduce public costs for housing in the longer term. Most important, the injection of capital and the integration of housing objectives with other social and economic activities in Aboriginal communities will create a synergistic effect, making housing a source of community healing and economic renewal.

This chapter begins with a description of housing conditions, followed by a discussion of principles that provide a firm foundation for policies ensuring Aboriginal people have adequate and safe shelter. The urgency of upgrading community services in locations where water supply and waste management present serious health hazards is considered next. Housing programs and policies on- and off-reserve are treated separately, and an overview of government expenditures required for the proposed strategy is presented. Finally, we explore how housing and community services can contribute to community renewal and economic growth.

1. The Intolerable Housing and Living Conditions of Many Aboriginal People

1.1 Aboriginal and Canadian Housing Conditions

Well over $2 billion of public funds have been spent and many new dwellings built in Aboriginal communities over the past decade.[1] However, standards of housing available to many Aboriginal households remain measurably below what is required for basic comfort, health and safety. This situation is documented in detail by the Aboriginal peoples survey (APS), the first comprehensive study of Aboriginal housing and living conditions, undertaken in 1991 by Statistics Canada.[2] It is confirmed for registered Indians living on reserves by 1994 data from the Department of Indian Affairs and Northern Development (DIAND). Combining these data sources provides a reasonably complete picture of the current situation among all Aboriginal groups.

Data from the APS omit a substantial number of registered Indian households on reserves, resulting in a count of 39,870 occupied private dwellings on reserves, compared with 73,659 housing units according to DIAND figures. Although it is possible to adjust the APS data to account for refusals and under-reporting on reserves, a substantial difference remains even in the adjusted figures. In this chapter, we use APS data for Indian people living off-reserve, Métis people and Inuit. The source for housing conditions on reserves is DIAND documents, except where extensive comparisons are drawn, as in Tables 4.1 and 4.2.

In Table 4.1, APS data are compared with indicators of the housing situation for the Canadian population as a whole.[3] We can see that

- houses occupied by Aboriginal people are twice as likely to need major repairs as those of all Canadians. Almost 20 per cent of dwellings – 47,000 homes – are in poor condition according to assessments by occupants. These conditions are present despite the fact that Aboriginal-occupied housing is generally newer than that occupied by other Canadians.

TABLE 4.1
Comparison of Canadian and Aboriginal Housing Indicators, 1991

	Canada	Aboriginal[1]	Aboriginal Position
Occupied dwellings	10,018,265	239,240	2.4% of Canadian households[2]
In need of major repairs	9.8%	19.6%	2 times as many in need of major repairs
Built before 1946	17.7%	13.6%	25% less than the Canada-wide proportion
No piped water supply	0.1%	9.4%	More than 90 times as many with no piped water
No bathroom facilities	0.6%	3.2%	More than 5 times as many
No flush toilet	0.5%	5.3%	More than 10 times as many
Average number of persons per dwelling	2.7	3.5	About 30% higher than the Canadian average
Average number of rooms per dwelling	6.1	5.8	Slightly smaller
Tenant-occupied dwellings	37.1%	48.7%	Almost 1/3 more tenants, not counting band-owned housing
Average gross rent per month	$546.00	$495.00	$51 per month lower on average
Owner-occupied dwellings	62.6%	41.2%	About 34% fewer owners
Owner's major payment per month	$682	$603	$79 per month lower on average

Notes:

1. According to the 1991 Aboriginal Peoples Survey (APS).

2. The actual figure is closer to 2.7 per cent of Canadian households, owing to under counting in the APS. Canada data include only non-farm, non-reserve dwellings. The Aboriginal data include all non-farm dwellings, including those on reserves, where at least one of the occupants self-identifies as an Aboriginal person. Note that tenant-occupied dwellings do not include band-owned housing, which is treated as a separate category (see Table 4.2). Owner's major payment per month refers to the average monthly payments made by the owner to secure shelter.

Source: See notes 3 and 5 at the end of the chapter.

TABLE 4.2

Housing Conditions of Aboriginal People, 1991

	North American Indians		Métis	Inuit
	On-reserve[*]	Non-reserve		
Occupied dwellings	39,870	137,580	65,005	9,655
Average number of persons per dwelling	4.3	3.3	3.3	4.3
Average number of rooms per dwelling	5.5	5.9	5.9	5.4
Tenant-occupied dwellings	5,435 (13.6)	77,445 (56.3)	33,535 (51.6)	7,125 (73.8)
Average gross rent per month ($)	362	517	505	318
Owner-occupied dwellings	10,755 (27.0)	60,025 (43.6)	30,893 (47.5)	2,510 (26.0)
Average owner's major payment per month	207	670	607	538
Band-owned dwellings	23,675 (59.4)	—	570	—
Available water not suitable for drinking	9,575 (24.0)	27,620 (20.1)	10,855 (16.7)	2,430 (25.2)
No electricity	2,585 (6.5)	9,645 (7.0)	3,682 (5.7)	445 (4.6)
No bathroom facilities	4,595 (11.5)	10,530 (7.7)	1,425 (2.2)	85 (0.9)
No flush toilet	7,715 (19.4)	2,880 (2.1)	2,230 (3.4)	496 (5.1)
In need of major repairs	15,445 (38.7)	21,420 (15.6)	10,965 (16.9)	1,770 (18.3)
Needs of residents not adequately met	15,610 (39.2)	22,905 (16.6)	12,090 (18.6)	3,175 (32.9)
Residents on waiting list for housing	5,545 (13.9)	10,065 (7.3)	4,070 (6.5)	1,255 (13.0)
Dwellings not covered by insurance	19,180 (48.1)	30,710 (22.3)	15,200 (23.4)	2,760 (28.6)

Notes:

Data pertain to dwellings where at least one of the occupants identifies as a member of an Aboriginal group.

Numbers in parentheses indicate percentage of total number of dwellings for that group.

[*] Data from the APS are deficient because of under-reporting but are the only data suitable for comparisons between Aboriginal groups. See note 5 at the end of the chapter.

— = not applicable.

Source: Statistics Canada, 1991 Aboriginal Peoples Survey, catalogue no. 89-535. See also note 3 at the end of the chapter.

- On reserves alone, DIAND estimates that some 13,400 homes need major repairs and close to 6,000 require replacement, amounting to 26 per cent of the total, or two and a half times the proportion of Canadian dwellings in need of major repairs.
- Some of the most dramatic disparities between the Aboriginal and non-Aboriginal populations occur in the community services associated with dwellings. For example, Aboriginal households are more than 90 times as likely as other Canadian households to be living without a piped water supply. Indeed, most Canadian households without a piped water supply are probably Aboriginal households. On reserves, DIAND data show more than 10,500 dwellings still without indoor plumbing, or 14 per cent of the total.
- Turning to how many people live in each dwelling, the APS finds houses occupied by Aboriginal households are smaller on average than those of Canadians as a whole, yet they tend to have more occupants. Also, 25,890 dwellings (almost 11 per cent) occupied by Aboriginal households require additional bedrooms to accommodate the number of occupants. (There are no comparable figures for Canadian households as a whole. However, other housing indicators suggest that the proportion would be substantially lower.) On reserves, 4.9 per cent of band-owned housing units contain multiple-family households, compared to 1.2 per cent of all occupied dwellings, or more than four times the country-wide proportion.
- Aboriginal people are substantially more likely to be tenants than Canadians as a whole, and this understates the situation on reserves, where 59 per cent of households live in band-owned housing and tenure is uncertain. Whereas home ownership is the largest single form of wealth enjoyed by the majority of Canadians, it is much less common among Aboriginal people. This reality affects everything from their incentives to upgrade and their ability to modify their dwellings to their future legacy to their children.

The primary source of the gap between Aboriginal and non-Aboriginal housing is affordability, or the difference between household incomes and the costs of adequate, suitable housing. In 1992, between 11 and 12 per cent of Canadian households – owners and renters – could not afford their dwellings or could not afford to upgrade their living conditions to a reasonable standard of adequacy. These households are said to be 'in core housing need', that is, their housing does not meet today's standards for adequacy, suitability and affordability. These households do not have sufficient income to afford rental accommodation that meets minimum standards, and they spend or would have to spend more than 30 per cent of their income to obtain adequate and suitable accommodation. By contrast, DIAND estimates that, based on household income, only about 16 per cent of the 74,000 on-reserve households can afford the full cost of adequate accommodation. This amounts to about 12,000 households. Of the other 62,000 households on reserves, 15,000 are in houses subsidized by the Canada Mortgage and Housing

Corporation (CMHC) that meet their needs. Thus, about 47,000 households on reserves probably cannot afford the full cost of adequate accommodation.

Using data from the 1991 Aboriginal peoples survey, CMHC estimates the total number of Métis, Inuit and off-reserve Indian households that are in core need at 63,000.[4] Combining this estimate with the estimate of on-reserve households that cannot afford the full cost of adequate accommodation suggests that Aboriginal people account for about nine per cent of all Canadian households in housing need, that is, 110,000 out of 1.16 million.[5] However, Aboriginal households comprise only about 2.7 per cent of all Canadian households. In other words, even though Aboriginal people tend to be living in housing that is cheaper and of poorer quality, they are more than three times as likely as other Canadian households to be unable to afford it.

The statistics on housing and living conditions are confirmed by the daily experience of Aboriginal people as presented in testimony to the Commission. Again and again, they told of the problems of overcrowded and substandard dwellings in their communities. For example, Valerie Monague, a social service administrator from Christian Island, Ontario, told Commissioners, "We have families that are doubled and tripled up. We have up to 18 and 20 people sometimes living in a single unit built for one family".[6] Martin Heavy Head, chairman of the Treaty 7 Urban Indian Housing Authority, noted that "low-income Native families...have no other place to go. The slum landlords in town are doing a great business".[7] Matthew Stewart, speaking in Vancouver on behalf of the National Aboriginal Housing Committee, said that for people living off-reserve "the biggest single problem...is affordable housing".[8]

Aboriginal housing conditions have been improving gradually, and the conditions described by the statistics are better than they were a decade ago. But the differences between these conditions and those of the general Canadian population remain great.

1.2 Contrasts Among Aboriginal Groups and Within Communities

Not all Aboriginal people face the same living conditions. A visit to a First Nations reserve near Montreal or in southern Ontario, a Métis community in Saskatchewan, a Denendeh community in the western Arctic, an Inuit community in Labrador, and an Aboriginal neighbourhood of a prairie city would yield an immediate impression of contrasts within the Aboriginal population itself.

In First Nations communities, 60 per cent of dwellings meet the needs of their occupants, in the opinion of the occupant (see Table 4.2). Among the occupants of these dwellings are those who have adequate incomes and finance their homes themselves or who, at their own expense, have made improvements to homes supplied by the band. Also in this group are households that have gained access to the full range of subsidies available. But the other 40 per cent are not so well provided for. In many First Nations communities, a small number of reserve residents are fortunate enough to secure a house each year, but it may be poorly built and they must struggle to maintain it amidst depressed economic circumstances and insecure tenure. There are also a substantial number of people on waiting lists for band-supplied housing.

Among those with at least one household member self-identifying as a North American Indian and not living on-reserve, just under 17 per cent are living in dwellings that do not meet their needs adequately. For Métis people, the number of households in dwellings that do not meet their needs is just under 19 per cent of the total (Table 4.2).

Among Inuit in the North, 33 per cent of households are in dwellings that do not meet their needs, which is close to the rate for Indian people on-reserve, who experience the worst conditions. In the context of a severe winter climate, the several hundred Inuit dwellings without adequate heating or fire protection systems are especially dangerous to the health and safety of their occupants (Table 4.2).

The disparities between and within Aboriginal groups and communities are primarily a result of poverty. Government assistance has provided considerable relief, but in an incomplete manner.

CMHC social housing programs – whether in Métis settlements, First Nations communities, remote communities, the North or cities – offer substantial subsidies to construct dwelling units newly built to National Building Code standards of size and construction quality. These are better built than most others in Aboriginal communities. They are then usually better maintained because mechanisms and funds for maintenance are provided as part of the package. However, they are a minority of the dwellings made available in any given locality.[9] Moreover, about half of all First Nations communities have completely rejected CMHC involvement as a route to housing adequacy.

The government recently terminated new CMHC funding for Aboriginal housing programs off-reserve and reduced the number of new, fully financed homes on-reserve from 1,800 in 1991 to 1,350 in 1994 and to 700 in 1995. (See note 61 regarding new on-reserve housing proposals released by the federal government on 25 July 1996.) Unless economic conditions improve rapidly or program funding is reinstated and increased, fewer Aboriginal people will see their housing needs fully met, and disparities in living conditions between Aboriginal people and non-Aboriginal Canadians will increase.

2. POLICY FOUNDATIONS

2.1 Housing and Community Services as Basic Human Needs

The homes where people are trying to raise families, the water they drink daily, a quiet place for study – these things are vital to health and happiness. Judging by their statements and resolutions at regional and national meetings, Aboriginal leaders recognize that adequate housing and living conditions are vital to solving many other social, economic and political problems. They know that in many rural, remote and northern Aboriginal communities, substandard housing and community services are among the chief contributors to difficulties with health, morale, safety and the environment. These problems in turn create division and sap the capacity to act collectively and decisively. Aboriginal people see housing improvements as means of simultaneously increasing control over their own lives, developing increased capacity to manage complex programs and businesses, providing meaningful jobs, sustaining Aboriginal lifestyles, cultures, and generally better health, and strengthening Aboriginal communities.

The current state of Aboriginal housing and community services poses acute threats to health. Diseases spread by inadequacies of water, sanitation and housing (tuberculosis and infections, for example) are more common among Aboriginal people than among non-Aboriginal people.[10] Dwellings are unsafe, and there is a lack of fire protection services. On reserves, DIAND figures show that 200 dwellings are lost because of fire each year.[11] In the North, solid waste dump sites and lack of sewage treatment create environmental hazards that contaminate country food consumed by Aboriginal people. Such direct threats to health would not be tolerated in other Canadian communities. They must not be allowed to persist among Aboriginal people either.

Since housing and related facilities are so closely intertwined with the rest of life, their quality and appearance are important indicators of a culture as a whole. Many cultures around the world are distinctive because of their immediately recognizable housing forms and styles and for the integration of their housing and community services with other patterns of daily living, economic and social activity. In Canada, unfortunately, the vibrant past of Aboriginal cultures, as embodied in housing, has been largely lost as a result of considerations of cost and administrative convenience. For example, housing designs have often been more typical of suburbia than the rain forests of the British Columbia coast, the tundra of the high Arctic, or the woodlands of rural Quebec. Only in the past decade have designers and builders paid specific attention to the lifestyles and traditional patterns of use for Aboriginal households. (CMHC recently held the first-ever national design competition for housing uniquely suited to the needs of Aboriginal peoples.)

As part of its research program, the Commission undertook case studies in four urban communities where urban Aboriginal housing corporations operate.[12] Tenants in these four communities indicated in interviews that their accommodation had the greatest impact on the following areas of their lives:

• Family stability – access to affordable accommodation and basic amenities and a sense of permanence, providing roots in the city while maintaining ties with reserve or rural communities.

- Access to education – the opportunity for children to get a good education in a stable environment, that is, not having to change schools frequently.

Tenants also saw the preservation and reinforcement of cultural identity as a very important need being met within these communities. While meeting basic housing needs, these corporations have allowed other needs such as employment, education and cultural retention to be addressed. In effect, the communities became more identifiable and could be contacted more readily to participate in various social, cultural and recreational activities. In addition, these housing corporations have had, for the most part, a positive impact on relations between Aboriginal and non-Aboriginal people.

An underlying Aboriginal expectation is that better housing and community services, as well as the processes and activities leading to them, will improve community morale and increase every individual's sense of self-worth and identity, and that these services will be a central part of the healing process as people rebuild their lives and their cultures simultaneously, in both social and physical forms.

That adequate housing is a basic human need has also been recognized by the federal government. The 1990 discussion paper, *Laying the Foundations of a New On-Reserve Housing Policy*, states that "the Government *does* firmly believe that all Indian people should have access to adequate, suitable and affordable housing".[13] More recently, the Liberal Party of Canada proposed that "Adequate shelter is a fundamental need of any society and a basic prerequisite for community prosperity....A Liberal government will work with Aboriginal peoples to develop an approach to housing that emphasizes community control, local resources, and flexibility in design and labour requirements".[14]

Housing policy must begin with the determination to meet the need for a healthy and suitable environment for all families and households. The removal of acute threats to health and safety is the most urgent requirement.

2.2 A Right to Housing

The combination of a sense of crisis and the inadequacy or failure of past policies has contributed to demands to transfer both authority and resources for housing and community services to Aboriginal governments. For some years, organizations representing First Nations have contended that housing is part of compensation owed to them in return for giving up effective use of the bulk of the Canadian land mass, either through formal treaties or by other less formal means.

For instance, in a submission to the Standing Committee on Aboriginal Affairs in 1992, the Assembly of First Nations (AFN) asserted that "housing is a federal responsibility which flows from the special relationship with the federal Crown created by section 91(24) of the British North America Act of 1867 and treaty agreements themselves".[15] In its brief to this Commission, the AFN called for a process to address housing rights: "The federal government must work jointly with First Nations to establish a forum for bilateral discussion to resolve issues relating to Aboriginal and treaty rights to housing".[16]

The Federation of Saskatchewan Indian Nations stated that

> [S]helter in the form of housing, renovations, and related infrastructure is a treaty right, and forms part of the federal trust and fiduciary responsibility. [This position derives] from the special Indian-Crown relationship dating back to the *Royal Proclamation of 1763*, enhanced by section 91(24) of the *Constitution Act, 1867* and sections 25 and 35 of the *Constitution Act, 1982*.[17]

These organizations argue that, if the resources associated with the lands now occupied by non-Aboriginal Canadians were still in the hands of its original possessors, there would be few serious housing problems among Aboriginal people today. They would have the resources to solve the problems themselves.

To date, the federal government has not recognized a universal entitlement to government-financed housing as either a treaty right or an Aboriginal right. It has taken the position that assistance for housing is provided as a matter of social policy, and its Aboriginal housing policy has been based on this premise. Thus, assistance has been based on 'need'. Federal, provincial, territorial and local governments have made a major commitment to assistance for housing for all Canadians, and as recently as 1993-94 they spent $3.9 billion on housing policy, most of it on assistance to Canadians in need.[18]

That the government has not recognized a general Aboriginal right to housing is an important issue in the minds of many Aboriginal people that has important practical consequences today. Many First Nations communities do not participate in the CMHC social housing program because it requires financial contributions by occupants and the assumption of long-term financial obligations for repayment of loans by the band. Some First Nations individuals living in CMHC-subsidized social housing also refuse to pay rent, because they believe they have an entitlement to housing provided by the government. The result of this outlook is that less money is available for housing on-reserve than is possible or desirable, and fewer homes are built. The lack of progress in developing a new housing policy for residents of reserves can be traced in part to these different perspectives on the part of First Nations leadership and the federal government regarding what constitutes treaty and Aboriginal rights.[19]

Therefore, we believe it is essential to start our discussion of solutions to Aboriginal housing problems by sorting through the factors and consequences associated with a right to housing or a right to shelter. We share the view that Aboriginal people have a right to housing, based on two complementary arguments.

First, adequate shelter has been recognized as a fundamental social right. In its brief to the Commission, the National Aboriginal Housing Committee stated that "the federal government has a moral, ethical and legal responsibility to continue funding Native housing both on- and off-reserve, until at least such time as parity in living conditions between Natives and non-Natives is achieved".[20] The committee pointed out that Canada is a signatory of the International Covenant on Economic, Social and Cultural Rights, adopted by the General Assembly of the United Nations on 16 December 1966. Article 11 of the covenant recognizes "the right to an adequate standard of living...including adequate food, clothing and housing; and the right to the continuous improvement of living conditions".[21] In fact, the covenant is one of several international instruments such as the Universal Declaration of Human Rights (United Nations, 1948) and the conventions of the International Labour Organization that express social and economic rights, including a right to housing. The covenant is a treaty and as such is part of international law. Implementation of the covenant is based on the principles of 'progressive realization'. States undertake to take steps, within available resources, progressively to achieve full realization of the rights.[22]

The provisions of these international agreements are not necessarily enforceable in a court of law, but they have moral force. They serve as an expression of shared values and aspirations. Social and economic rights are also found in the constitutions of a number of countries, and some go so far as to impose specific legislative measures and social programs. Section 36(1) of the *Constitution Act, 1982* provides that "Parliament and the legislatures, together with the government of Canada and the provincial governments, are committed to (a) promoting equal opportunities for the well-being of Canadians; (b) furthering economic development to reduce disparity in opportunities; and (c) providing essential public services of reasonable quality to all Canadians". Since housing is an important aspect of well-being and an instrument for improving opportunity for the disadvantaged, it is reasonable to read section 36(1) as affirming a right of Canadians to decent and adequate housing.

Second, in this report we have emphasized that governments have a duty to work toward the economic self-reliance of Aboriginal people. At the root of the housing problem is the poverty that has resulted from the dispossession of Aboriginal people from their ancestral lands and their exclusion from mainstream economic activity, with the added complications on reserves of a lack of clarity about ownership rights and ineffective government programs. In Volume 2, Chapter 4, we argued that because of the Crown's historical obligation to protect Aboriginal lands and resources, governments have an obligation to restore a land and economic base for Aboriginal people. In Volume 2, Chapter 2 we concluded that a fiduciary obligation exists on the part of all Crown institutions to reverse the condition of dependency and foster self-reliance and self-sufficiency among Aboriginal nations.[23] The evident failure of governments to make such an economic base available to Aboriginal people, in accordance with their obligations, adds force to the argument that governments should bear the main burden of financing adequate shelter for these communities until such time as this economic base is restored.[24]

In addition to this general obligation on the part of the governments to ensure that Aboriginal people have the means to afford adequate housing, there may be obligations with respect to housing based on specific treaties. At this time, apart from provisions reached in recent land claims agreements, no such obligations are being recognized by governments. The treaties process proposed by the Commission provides an avenue for treaty nations to pursue entitlement to housing related to treaties (see Volume 2, Chapter 2).

In our view, the particular duties of governments to Aboriginal people and the notion of housing as a fundamental social right impose an obligation on governments to ensure that Aboriginal people have adequate shelter. This obligation remains unfulfilled. Not only have governments failed to create the circumstances for Aboriginal people to become economically self-reliant and meet their own housing needs, but the federal government has not provided assistance to the same degree as to other Canadians. First, specific needs of Aboriginal people, whether on- or off-reserve, were recognized only in 1974, more than two decades after social housing programs began in Canada in 1949. Second, First Nations people on-reserve have not enjoyed the same degree of support in relation to need as other Canadians. Specifically,

- capital subsidy support to low-income Aboriginal people living on reserves has not been sufficient to provide adequate housing, whereas the needs of other Canadians for adequate housing have generally been met;
- the shelter component of social assistance has been withheld from the poorest reserve residents except those occupying social housing; and
- financial support for social housing to meet the needs of low-income reserve residents has not been as generous as that offered elsewhere in Canada since 1986.

One result is that the actual housing conditions of Aboriginal people, in particular on reserves, remain well below Canadian standards. To remedy these conditions we propose that governments adopt new policies and carry out their responsibility to provide housing to Aboriginal people within the following framework.

- Governments have an obligation to ensure that Aboriginal people have adequate shelter.
- Governments should ensure that Aboriginal people have the means to provide for their own housing needs by restoring a land and economic base that will enable Aboriginal people to become economically self-reliant.

- In the meantime, and to complement economic development measures, governments should provide financial assistance to all Aboriginal people and communities according to need so that all will have their housing needs met.
- At the same time, Aboriginal people have a responsibility to contribute to the cost of building and maintaining their own dwellings, whether as individuals or collectively, according to their ability to do so.
- The federal government has a responsibility to clarify with treaty nations a modern understanding of existing treaty terms as they apply to housing.

At a practical level this framework implies that governments should finance a catch-up program based on need to make adequate housing available to all Aboriginal people within a given period of time. We believe it is possible and desirable to achieve adequate housing for Aboriginal people in 10 years. In the remainder of this chapter, we examine what needs to be done to accomplish this. We have concluded that, with the right level of financial assistance from governments, Aboriginal people will be able to expand, repair and maintain their housing stock and to develop the necessary strategies and institutions. We believe that governments can provide the financing needed. We consider Aboriginal housing a priority for governments for several reasons: governments have important obligations to Aboriginal people and people in need; and improvement and expansion of the housing stock will contribute to better health and greater opportunities, as well as to healing and revitalizing Aboriginal households and communities. Moreover, as they assume jurisdiction, Aboriginal governments should not have to take over a stock of physical assets that is too small and in poor repair. They deserve a better start.

2.3 Aboriginal Self-Government

The advent of Aboriginal self-government provides a unique opportunity to recast Aboriginal housing policies. Housing is among the core areas of self-government jurisdiction for Aboriginal governments on their own territories because it is a matter of vital concern to the life and welfare of Aboriginal peoples and has no major impact on adjacent jurisdictions; nor is it otherwise the object of compelling federal or provincial concern. Future policies should be based on this principle.

As in other areas of policy, Aboriginal people feel constrained by the administrative criteria and processes of DIAND and CMHC, and many briefs from organizations expressed the view that Aboriginal institutions could do a better job of designing and delivering programs. We see potential for improvement and consider the advantages of Aboriginal control of housing in the following sections. Particularly significant is the opportunity afforded by self-government to clarify arrangements relating to home ownership and land tenure on First Nations territories.

In practice, individual communities will probably deal with day-to-day housing and community services matters. However, many Aboriginal communities are too small to maintain the full range of technical capabilities for effective housing program design, delivery and management. The development of expertise at the level of the Aboriginal nation or region will make for greater effectiveness and provide an important building block in the development of governments of Aboriginal nations. In other situations, particularly in urban centres, existing Aboriginal housing institutions can be the vehicle for greater Aboriginal control.

RECOMMENDATIONS

The Commission recommends that

Commitment to
Adequate Housing

3.4.1

Federal and provincial governments address Aboriginal housing and community services on the basis of the following policy principles:

(a) Governments have an obligation to ensure that Aboriginal people have adequate shelter, water and sanitation services.

(b) Governments have a responsibility to restore an economic base to Aboriginal people that enables them to meet their needs.

(c) Aboriginal people, individually and collectively, are responsible for meeting their housing needs according to their ability to pay or contribute in kind.

(d) Governments must supplement the resources available to Aboriginal people so that their housing needs are fully met.

(e) Aboriginal nations should assume authority over all housing matters as a core area of self-government jurisdiction.

(f) Acute risks to health and safety should be treated as an emergency and targeted for immediate action.

3.4.2

The government of Canada clarify with treaty nations a modern understanding of existing treaty terms regarding housing.

3.4.3

The government of Canada make resources available over the next 10 years to ensure that housing for Aboriginal people on-reserve is fully adequate in quantity and quality and engage the governments of the provinces and territories to reach the same goal in rural and northern communities and in urban areas.

3. COMMUNITY SERVICES: A HEALTH HAZARD

There is authoritative evidence that community services in First Nations communities are a direct threat to health. In July 1995, Health Canada and DIAND issued a special survey assessing the adequacy of water and sewage systems in First Nations communities.[25] Of the 863 community water systems examined, 211 were defective:

- 20 per cent (171) have the potential to affect the health and safety of the community if problems are not addressed; and
- another 5 per cent (40) are in need of repair or improved maintenance because they could pose a health risk should they malfunction before the problem is addressed.

Of the 425 community sewage systems examined, 64 were deficient:

- 9 per cent (39) were defective and had the potential to affect the health and safety of the community; and
- another 6 per cent (25) were in need of equipment repairs or improved maintenance practices and could pose a health risk if a malfunction were to occur.

The source of the problems ranges from inadequate or overloaded facilities to poor operations and maintenance.

In the vast majority of Canadian communities, specialized municipal departments or agencies are charged with installing and maintaining adequate water and sewage services, funded by the property-tax base. This is not the case in most First Nations communities. Physical infrastructure is built at considerable expense to the federal government[26] – more than $90,000 per dwelling unit in some cases – but subsequently systems may not perform adequately because of insufficient attention to effective operating systems and procedures. Devolution of service delivery to communities appears to have left a vacuum: the government withdrew without ensuring that communities had the awareness, resources and skills to take over.

Missing or inadequate services of one type often affect the performance of another. For example, a community water source may be affected by the lack of solid waste disposal or by improperly operated sewage treatment facilities. Fire services may be hampered by the lack of piped water at sufficient levels of pressure.

In Chapter 3 we examined the health problems associated with poor water quality and supply and inadequate sewage treatment. While there have been few studies of the relationship between substandard water supplies and sanitation facilities for Aboriginal people in Canada, it is well-established that people living in Aboriginal communities experience more illness and death from infectious diseases than do Canadians generally. A recent study of a shigellosis epidemic in Manitoba, which affected First Nations people disproportionately (69 per cent of the cases, even though only 8 per cent of the provincial population are registered Indians), concluded that 90 per cent of infections would have been preventable if water, sanitation and housing facilities had been adequate.

In addition to concerns about human health, environmental effects are also a problem. In the North, for example, some communities discharge raw or primary-treated sewage into the aquatic environment. Others have sewage lagoons or holding ponds, but these frequently overflow, or sewage leaches into surface drainage systems. These wastes take years to degrade because of the extremely slow rate of decomposition in the Arctic environment. In addition, virtually all Arctic communities are coastal, resulting in the potential for leaching of contaminants into the marine environment and affecting the quality of country foods consumed by Aboriginal people.[27] Apart from sewage lagoons, there are 1,246 solid waste dump sites in Canada's North, 200 of which are suspected of containing hazardous waste.[28] Again, these tend to persist and to pose continuing hazards to people and wildlife.

During fiscal years 1991-92 to 1994-95, some progress was made in improving community facilities under the Green Plan initiative, which provided $275 million above and beyond previous levels of funding for water and sewage services on reserves.[29] The government spent $487.6 million in total during these years to install systems as well as to expand existing facilities, and the number of homes with adequate water and sewage facilities increased by more than 15,000.[30] In 1990-91, 86.4 per cent of houses on-reserve had water services, rising to 92.1 per cent in 1993-94. The population of households with sewage services rose from 80 per cent to 85.6 per cent.[31]

The 1995 Health Canada-DIAND study *Community Drinking Water and Sewage Treatment in First Nations Communities* suggests the need for continuing funding to correct inadequacies. With respect to the 211 communities where water systems were found to be deficient, the study estimates that, to complete remedial work to correct drinking water quality will require $214 million for 99 communities where work is either now under way or the required engineering studies have been completed. Work has been completed or operating and maintenance problems are being addressed in 36 communities. The remaining 76 water systems require engineering studies before estimates can be prepared.

With regard to the 64 sewerage systems found to be deficient, remedial measures for 36 systems where projects are under way or engineering studies have been completed are estimated to cost $57 million. Work has been completed or operations and maintenance problems are being addressed in 12 communities, and engineering studies for the remaining 16 sewage systems are required to determine the cost of remedial work.

These estimates suggest a cost in the order of $460 million or more for remedial measures for all systems, including installation of adequate systems where they do not exist.[32] The government intends to spend more than $500 million over the next three years for remedial action and to meet growth requirements. With approximately one-third of expenditures going to inadequately performing systems, it will take up to nine years to complete remedial measures at this rate of spending.[33] We regard this delay as too long, given the threats to health, and urge that remedial work be completed in five years at an estimated extra cost of $50 to $60 million per year.

Sanitation facilities that remain to be installed will probably be more expensive to construct than the ones already in place.[34] Therefore, it is important that all opportunities to make community services more cost-effective be pursued. Community services technologies – for water, sewers, electricity and garbage collection – have not always been appropriate to the practical needs and environmental circumstances of Aboriginal communities. For example, in several regions, full suburban-style services have been constructed in dispersed settlements at great cost per dwelling serviced.

There is scope for innovation in the construction and management of community services to reduce costs without compromising quality and to free funds for remedial work or extension of services to more dwellings. In the United States, for example, a wide range of new and less costly technologies are being developed for purifying water, treating sewage, and managing solid waste in smaller centres. Aboriginal people will need to acquire this kind of expertise and apply it to their own needs if they are to avoid continuing problems of health, safety and costs. Strategic alliances could be formed with the U.S. organizations engaged in work on 'small community flows',[35] building on the one that already exists between Environment Canada and the Water Environment Federation of the United States.

The lack of sewage treatment facilities is not the only challenge. There are serious operating and maintenance problems. What is needed is regular, competent operation and maintenance coupled with periodic testing. Health Canada currently tests water every three months, and sewage systems are monitored by DIAND on request from First Nations communities. The results from the Health Canada-DIAND survey suggest a need for improvement. The survey report observes:

> While the most common problem is the absence of adequate systems, a significant problem in small communities is a lack of adequate training for the systems operators of water treatment and sewage treatment facilities. Many of the operators are people with some technical background but not necessarily with a strong background in the requirements for water treatment or sewage plant operations.[36]

Community services technologies have become more complex and difficult to maintain without investments in organization and staff training to manage and operate them. In addition to funding operations, DIAND funds tribal councils to provide advice and expertise to communities on planning, construction and maintenance of water and sewage systems.[37] Under Health Canada's drinking water safety program, a Green Plan initiative with $25 million in funding over six years, sampling and testing of water has been increased, health awareness is being promoted, and advice is being given to First Nations communities and DIAND. A number of initiatives have been launched in collaboration with First Nations, including

- a pilot project to train water treatment plant operators in 14 First Nations communities in northern Ontario;
- the creation of the Ontario First Nations water treatment plant operators association by the chiefs of Ontario;
- the establishment of a training centre by the Split Lake Cree community in Manitoba for water-quality technicians; and
- a computerized system to track drinking water quality, and numerous pilot projects to enable tribal councils to use the system.[38]

This is a good start. The government should move quickly from pilot projects to comprehensive action and continue to apply resources after the drinking water safety program expires. The Commission agrees with the recommendations of the Health Canada-DIAND survey to give high priority to training First Nations personnel and strengthening co-operation among First Nations, DIAND and Health Canada. We would, however, go further than what is recommended in that report. We see a significant need to build the capacity of First Nations to operate and maintain water and sewage systems. This could be done through the creation of a First Nations community services corporation to fulfil much the same functions in First Nations communities that the Ontario Clean Water Corporation does in smaller municipalities in that province. OCWC helps small communities with technical expertise and financing for the planning, development and implementation of water systems and encourages joint projects between communities. It operates on a cost-recovery basis. Another option would be for Aboriginal communities to link up with provincial and territorial agencies like OCWC, which may be a cost-effective option for these technical services.

Adequate housing, sewer, water and waste management services at the community level do not happen by accident or as a result of on-again-off-again arrangements. Most Aboriginal people now live in communities of at least a few hundred people. Such communities do not require large-scale complicated housing and community services technologies or organizations, but they do require attentive and knowledgeable people and dedicated expert organizations to operate safe and reliable systems.

RECOMMENDATIONS

The Commission recommends that

Water and Sewage Systems **3.4.4**

The government of Canada provide additional resources for construction, upgrading and operation of water and sewage systems to ensure that adequate facilities and operating systems are in place in all First Nations communities within five years.

3.4.5

The government of Canada provide funding and technical support to First Nations governments to operate and maintain community water and sewer systems and to establish technical support institutions as required.

4. HOUSING ON RESERVES

Obstacles to ensuring an adequate housing stock on reserves are embedded in the structures of governance, land tenure and subsidy programs. Unless there are fundamental changes in all of these, progress will be difficult, and every initiative will start out with three strikes against it. What is required is clarification of authority and responsibility, establishment of effective ownership or lease arrangements, and renewed efforts to marshall sufficient resources to address the housing problem. This means reform of government policy as well as new approaches and greater responsibility for Aboriginal people.

To recap, there are about 74,000 dwellings on reserves. Of these, 6,000 are unsalvageable and need replacement; 13,000 need major repair (that is, an investment of up to $30,000 for a new roof or exterior shell, insulation, electrical or plumbing systems); and 21,000 need minor renovations. In addition, 11,000 more dwellings are needed to meet pent-up demand.[39] That these conditions have been allowed to persist is evidence of serious inequities in programs and policies.

Although DIAND provided subsidies to build and repair over 45,000 dwellings between 1988-89 and 1993-94, by the end of that period, fewer than 9,000 additional units were assessed as adequate by DIAND staff. The proportion of dwellings in this category rose from 42 per cent to just 46 per cent of the total stock, instead of 95 per cent as might have been expected given the number of units financed. It appears that 36,000 homes either did not achieve adequacy or fell below it during the five-year period. This points to serious deficiencies in the quality and maintenance of dwellings.

4.1 Federal Housing Programs on Reserves

The government provides assistance through two agencies, DIAND and CMHC:

- DIAND provides funding for housing on reserves in the form of subsidies for capital costs (construction of dwellings and renovations), certain operating costs for persons on welfare, and program administration costs borne by First Nations communities. It does not make loans for housing, but it guarantees loans by private lenders insured by CMHC and also loans made directly by CMHC.

- CMHC's on-reserve rental housing program provides First Nations with a subsidy up to an amount that would bring the interest rate on housing loans down to two per cent. First Nations borrow from private lending institutions for the cost of construction minus DIAND capital subsidies, at prevailing interest rates and with a typical repayment period of 25 years. The loans are insured under the *National Housing Act* and are guaranteed by the minister of Indian affairs. First Nations enter into agreements with CMHC that stipulate the levels of rents to be charged and the maintenance regime to be followed. Also available from CMHC is the homeowner residential rehabilitation assistance program (homeowner RRAP), which provides loans of up to $25,000, of which a maximum of $5,000 to $8,250 can be forgiven, depending on income and geographic zone.[40]

The base budget for DIAND's capital subsidy housing program was set at $93 million in 1983 and has not changed since. This amount is supplemented by funding related to Bill C-31 ($43 million in 1994). These amounts are intended to support construction of 3,600 homes and 3,900 renovations.

CMHC assistance declined from 1,800 new units in 1991 to 1,350 units in 1994 and an expected 700 units in 1995. In addition, 1,200 units were repaired each year with CMHC subsidies; in 1995, the number was 600. As a rule, assistance from CMHC is added to the capital subsidy from DIAND to increase the amount available per dwelling rather than to finance more dwellings. In combination with a limited number of homes that are financed without government subsidies, this means that each year up to 4,000 new homes are constructed and a similar number are repaired or renovated. The programs are discussed more fully below.

Table 4.3 provides a picture of DIAND and CMHC funding as of 1994-95 and cumulatively over the past 12 years.

Capital subsidies

DIAND offers different amounts of per unit capital subsidies toward the cost of building homes for registered Indians. The amounts range from $19,000 to

TABLE 4.3
Federal Government Expenditures on Housing in First Nations Communities

	1994-95
	$ millions
DIAND	
Housing construction and renovation (base budget of $93 million, $43 million related to Bill C-31)	136
Heating and utilities cost for social assistance recipients	66
Shelter component of social assistance for rents paid by those in loan-financed (CMHC-insured and other) housing	38
Support for administration of program and training costs of First Nations	5
Total[1]	245
CMHC	
On-Reserve Rental Housing Program	94
Residential Rehabilitation Assistance Program on reserves	9
Total	103
Cumulative program activity by the federal government, 1982-1993	
DIAND housing construction subsidies	$935 million, 33,000 units
DIAND housing rehabilitation subsidies	$200 million, 38,000 units
CMHC social housing subsidies on-reserve	$543 million, 16,000 units built and 22,000 renovated
Total[2]	$1,678 million

Notes:
1. The amounts paid through the social assistance program are estimated. DIAND also incurs expenditures for site preparation and servicing relating to construction of dwellings and installation of new water and sewer systems. These are included in its capital budget for infrastructure.
2. The total number of units is smaller than the sum of the units under each program, since DIAND and CMHC subsidies are often combined for the same units, and some units have been built and repaired.

Source: Data obtained from various DIAND documents.

$46,000, with an average of $30,000. They are set according to the different regions of the country established by DIAND, with more for northern and remote locations to reflect higher transportation and other costs. These amounts have not changed since 1983 and today can buy just over half what they could then. Today, the price of a standard newly constructed home is $90,000 or more. A basic kit of materials alone would cost about $35,000, without shipping, interior finishing materials or basic household equipment. (This amount is based on commercial quotations for housing kits shipped to locations in central Canada.) The DIAND capital subsidy, therefore, pays for only part of the cost of a home.

Another DIAND program offers subsidies of $6,000 per unit for rehabilitation, an amount that was also set in 1983. As most Canadian homeowners are aware, substantial renovation jobs today would cost about $20,000 or more.

The result is that there is often not enough money to build a solid, durable dwelling unit. Unless additional funding is available through CMHC-backed loans or from revolving loan funds, the community has to draw on other resources such as job creation programs and training funds to cover labour costs. Access to commercial financing has been restricted because of the inalienability of Indian property on-reserve. (Barriers to access to capital are discussed more fully in Volume 2, Chapter 5.)

Since 1983, all DIAND-subsidized units are supposed to have been constructed according to National Building Code standards. However, neither adequate financing nor enforcement and inspection systems were in place, other than for CMHC social housing projects. Therefore, it is unlikely that dwellings with only DIAND subsidies were up to standard in all or even a majority of cases. Moreover, the code is intended to provide a minimum that is insufficient for durable homes in all parts of the country and does not anticipate the intensity of use resulting from larger households in Aboriginal communities. Most reputable Canadian builders claim to build well in excess of code requirements.

If the cap of $46,000 on the DIAND subsidy were removed, it might be possible to build fully adequate homes. Although fewer houses would be built, this might be better in the long run than building a larger number of dwellings that do not last.

A handful of communities in Ontario and Quebec have set up revolving loan funds to finance construction. DIAND subsidies and loan payments from owner-occupants are deposited in these funds. The legal status of such mechanisms is unclear, but they have been successful in creating community-based capital pools for housing loans.

Social assistance and inadequate maintenance

DIAND pays $66 million annually to social assistance recipients for the cost of utilities. It also provides $38 million in subsidies for debt servicing ('shelter allowances') to households dependent on social assistance who live in dwelling units financed by loans. Almost all of these units are CMHC units.[41]

In presentations to the Commission it was suggested that a federal social policy commitment to equality of benefits for those whose degree of need is similar has not been honoured. People receiving welfare off-reserve are given a shelter component to cover the cost of rent, including maintenance and insurance. People receiving social assistance who live in dwellings financed only with DIAND construction subsidies (about 30 per cent of on-reserve households)[42] are effectively not eligible for contributions to the maintenance and insurance costs of their homes.

The main argument for this policy, which dates from 1983, is that bands do not charge rent for band-owned housing and thus cannot be paid rent on behalf of social assistance recipients by DIAND.[43] DIAND has indicated that it will consider paying the shelter component of social assistance if a band charges rent for all its units. However, this policy has not been designed in detail or promoted with First Nations communities, partly because on-reserve housing policies have been under review since 1988 and no major changes have been made since that time. The feasibility of introducing rents has not been tested through pilot projects. Clearly, simply withholding maintenance and insurance funds from so many social assistance recipients on reserves will not push bands into community-wide rental charges. Meanwhile, the housing stock is deteriorating because no resources are being mustered for maintenance and repair. Even simple repairs, such as replacing roof tiles to prevent leaks, are not being done.

Overall, this policy has had the perverse effect of providing the least amount of financial support to those with lowest incomes living in the worst housing. Within the last decade alone, several hundred million dollars that would otherwise have been provided to social assistance recipients for their housing costs were withheld, causing people to suffer and resulting in a rapid deterioration of capital assets because of lack of maintenance.[44] Governments that have generally looked after the housing requirements of Canadians in need, in particular in urban centres, have failed to provide for this basic human need on reserves.

It is little wonder that houses on reserves have been estimated to last, on average, half as long as houses built elsewhere in Canada.[45] If this is to change, certain conditions are essential: dwellings must meet standards of completion and durability appropriate for their location and use technologies that are related to local skills and resources; residents need sufficient income from earnings or social assistance to finance maintenance; and questions of ownership and responsibility must be resolved.

Financial difficulties for bands using CMHC'S Rental Housing Assistance Program

Figures published by DIAND show that dwellings financed by CMHC and receiving continuing subsidies of operating and maintenance costs have likely represented the bulk of real improvements in recent years. However, many bands that used the CMHC program have become mired in financial problems.

In part, this is a result of the way the CMHC subsidy is determined and because of a decline in interest rates. Funding arrangements for CMHC social housing units on reserves are not as favourable as those for identical dwellings elsewhere in the country. Since 1986, CMHC has subsidized social housing, including non-profit housing and co-operative housing, in such a way as to cover the gap between actual operating costs and revenues received from tenants or co-operative members. Under the old program that remained in place on reserves, CMHC subsidies, both for debt servicing and for operating costs and maintenance, were tied to interest rates. As the inflation rate dropped in the latter part of the 1980s, so did interest rates. Average subsidies from CMHC dropped substantially as a result. Many social housing projects on reserves – perhaps half – were pushed into financial difficulty because of these reduced subsidies.[46]

There were other problems as well. Some of the projects were barely viable financially to begin with, with little or no margin for error. Bands also experienced difficulties in collecting rents. Arrears have now mounted into the hundreds of thousands of dollars in several cases and have stymied any further activity by these bands, as well as threatening other band programming.[47]

Thus, the chief mechanism for fully financing housing on reserves fell into disrepute in a number of First Nations communities, some of which had entered into loan-financing arrangements only reluctantly in the first place. About half of all bands have been placed in debt management arrangements by DIAND at one time or another, and excessive housing debts were a key factor in a majority of cases. As noted already, about half of all bands, including some of the poorest with the greatest housing need, have simply refused debt financing and thus failed to gather sufficient finances to meet their requirements.

Conclusion

We have shown that the full cost of building and maintaining adequate housing was not addressed by DIAND. The department limited itself to setting a formal requirement that housing built with its subsidies must meet the National Building Code, without determining how this could be accomplished in practice and without effective enforcement. The program was such that moneys for construction of dwellings and major repairs were spread thinly over many units, which generally were poorly built and deteriorated quickly. Nor, as we have seen, did DIAND settle as a matter of policy exactly how people receiving a fraction of the full cost of maintaining, repairing and insuring their homes would cope. Given the structure of the program on reserves and the late arrival of full financing through CMHC, many reserve residents came to expect that cheaply built housing was simply a stop-gap measure for which no significant maintenance support was available. The results are evident: on-reserve housing conditions are worse than those of any other Aboriginal group, despite the construction of many housing units.

We have pointed to two specific instances of inequitable treatment of households on-reserve: the lack of shelter allowances for social assistance recipients and the manner in which the CMHC subsidy is calculated. The former alone implies a shortfall of financial support of hundreds of millions of dollars during the past decade. What is disturbing about these two aspects of government programs is that they have been so counter-productive by limiting resources for maintenance and discouraging loan financing. More effective programs would have gone a long way to addressing the housing challenge on reserves with the amount of funding made available.

The ineffectiveness of programs and the attitudes they have fostered have combined with another problem – the lack of a clear legal regime to define rights and obligations relating to dwellings on reserves – to worsen the housing problem.

4.2 The Legal Regime and Tenure

Formal authority for virtually everything associated with housing and residential development on reserves remains in the hands of either the governor in council or the minister of Indian affairs. The minister's responsibilities under the *Indian Act* include ownership of land and real property and control over their use, regulations concerning housing conditions, and financing and programming relating to housing and community services. First Nations lack the legal capacity to regulate land use, dwelling possession and use, landlord-tenant relations, buying and selling, site servicing and a host of other matters taken for granted by provinces and municipalities.

The department of Indian affairs is not fully exercising its current wide authority under the law. The department is reducing staff with expertise in housing. But a process to give First Nations greater authority and responsibility in housing and community services is lacking. The result is an absence of effective governance, a policy vacuum that has led in turn to a lack of clarity about ownership and the respective responsibilities of occupants, bands and the government. DIAND's discussion paper, published in 1990, put the issues this way:

> The lack of clarity of housing occupancy and ownership rights of individuals and First Nations prevents some communities and individuals from investing in new and better housing. People are reluctant to invest in housing if they cannot be sure that they can live in the housing for as long as they want, or sell or transfer it to someone else when they wish. Bands themselves are uncertain about their authority to regulate the development, construction, allocation, occupancy, use and maintenance of housing on their reserves. Many bands do not have clear review or appeal mechanisms by which individuals can appeal band decisions affecting their security of tenure. These problems are standing in the way of Indian people

taking control of housing assets, and making investments that will improve housing conditions and increase the durability of the stock.[48]

At present, band members can gain possession of a house and use a defined portion of reserve land according to the custom of the band or by being allotted a portion of land by the band council and given a certificate of possession or occupation by the minister. Many reserves in British Columbia and central and eastern Canada have opted to use these certificates, which amount to deeds. Among First Nations like the Dene, the Crees of Quebec, the Algonquin and the Six Nations, individual ownership is common, with positive results. Even so, certificates are generally used for only a fraction of the houses in the community. Other residents live in band-owned dwellings, without defined rights and responsibilities. Certificates of possession are not widely used in northern Ontario and the prairie provinces, where occupants' rights are defined by custom. Customary rights have not been legally tested and remain uncertain. For the majority of houses on reserves, the rights of the occupant and the band are only vaguely defined.

Individual home ownership does not guarantee care and maintenance of a dwelling. But where there is no clear responsibility and accountability, either individual or collective, it is not surprising if little care is taken. At a time of serious resource constraints, it is essential to create certainty to ensure that needed investments will occur, whether by individuals, bands, Aboriginal housing authorities or other sources in addition to the federal government's contribution.

Because of the desire to preserve and indeed expand the Aboriginal land base, First Nations may need to explore home ownership regimes that do not threaten to alienate the land. Over the past two decades, various instruments of ownership that are detached from clear title to the land underneath a building have been developed in non-Aboriginal communities. The range of possibilities includes condominiums, equity co-operatives and leasehold arrangements. Provinces have passed legislation to separate title to land from title to structures on it to permit condominium ownership arrangements. Similar legislation could be developed for reserves. Within the framework of such instruments, it would be possible to encourage home ownership on reserves through innovative approaches like the development of an equity stake through rental payments over time and buy-back guarantees by the band where the re-sale market is limited. For those who cannot afford to own homes or where there is a preference for communal property, rental regimes will be needed to clarify tenants' rights (security of occupancy, regular upkeep) and responsibilities (for example, provisions for sanctions when obligations such as rent and care of the rental unit are not met).

The key aspects of security of tenure have to do with the dwelling unit itself rather than the land on which it rests. Owners cannot be evicted as long as they meet their financial obligations. Owners can typically make major changes to the unit they occupy entirely at their own initiative. They can determine who will occupy their home in the future. They can benefit from a difference between purchase or construction price and sale price. They can capture the financial benefits of renovations and improvements if the buyer is willing. All these benefits of home ownership could be conferred on reserve residents, even though they cannot hold title to a specific piece of land.

Under landlord and tenant legislation and common or civil law, tenants also have certain rights, such as the right not to be evicted without notice and due process. They can decorate their dwellings and generally use them as they see fit, as long as others are not bothered. All of these positive features of security of tenure can be provided by Aboriginal governments on reserves using a variety of tenure options such as those mentioned above.

Greenland may provide some examples of the kinds of arrangements that may be possible. There we see collective ownership of land, but because improvements to the land can be bought and sold, there is an active market in housing and commercial properties.

The Commission believes that Aboriginal self-government offers an unprecedented opportunity for First Nations to assume full authority with respect to housing and land use. Under self-government, Aboriginal nations should have clear legal powers to regulate tenure and home ownership, and they can then create an environment favourable to investment in housing and maintenance by establishing effective ground rules. First Nations should prepare for the future by examining alternative tenure regimes and making choices among them, and by building capacity at the level of the nation to exercise their powers over housing and implement effective regimes. The federal government should actively support such measures.

As explained in Volume 2, Chapter 3, Aboriginal nations can exercise law-making capacity in core areas. We would expect housing and tenure to be among the first areas to be taken up as nations begin to govern themselves. To prepare themselves and to clarify tenure as much as possible in the interim, we suggest that First Nations communities move forward in ways they judge appropriate. Greater certainty about tenure can be created by extending the use of certificates of possession. First Nations can introduce maintenance charges or rental fees on the basis of their current powers under the *Indian Act*.[49] It may be possible to clarify the rights and responsibilities of tenants and First Nations communities by introducing a system for the registration of leases, as suggested in the 1990 DIAND discussion paper.[50] Such approaches will work best where there is broad support in the communities and where there is a strong sense that the new approaches are a step toward self-government. The federal government can offer encouragement by providing financial incentives for communities that institute rental and maintenance regimes, for example, by contributing on behalf of social assistance recipients. More generally, the government could express support for communities that introduce more explicit tenure systems and indicate that it will not interfere with such systems.

4.3 Rallying Resources to Meet the Need for Adequate Shelter

Debt financing

Mortgages are used so universally to finance construction of dwellings that their advantages seem too obvious to mention. What people need from a house, first and foremost, are shelter and comfort. They receive these over time, so it makes sense to pay for them as they are being enjoyed by the occupant, whether through rents or monthly instalments on a loan. Few households anywhere have enough capital to pay cash for a home before they move in.

Debt financing also has considerable appeal as a way to address shortages of adequate housing on-reserve. It would make it easier to launch a campaign to make on-reserve housing stocks fully adequate to the needs of Aboriginal people. Construction can be accelerated if it is financed by loans and if program funds are then applied as needed to repay loans and interest over time. In fact, if construction were financed entirely by loans, the amounts DIAND now provides in the form of capital subsidies would be sufficient to launch a catch-up program. Only several years from now would the budget need to be increased to meet rising debt payments. A loan financing approach enables the government to do more in the short run while it faces fiscal constraints.

Both the federal government and First Nations are reluctant to adopt a debt financing strategy. To make the long-term commitments required in the face of uncertainty about future economic growth and pressing fiscal problems is difficult for the government. For their part, First Nations communities have analogous concerns about their economic base. As well, they have experienced financial difficulties with the CMHC program or are aware of other communities having such problems, and the view that housing is a treaty right also holds them back.

In our view, this reluctance to use debt financing should be overcome. As we have argued, housing is so important to individual and community well-being that effective approaches must be found. If tenure arrangements are clarified and all parties assume their responsibilities, a catch-up strategy in which debt financing plays an important role will be quite feasible.

But debt financing alone is not the answer. The amount of debt relating to housing would keep on increasing over the years, and so would debt servicing payments. Faced with limited resources and many competing demands, the government would at some point be forced to refrain from adding to the budget for housing. Construction would then be sharply reduced, and improvements in housing conditions might be eroded over time. Only economic development will generate the Aboriginal incomes and savings required to keep on constructing dwellings and to reduce the burden on governments in the longer run. We believe that progress can and should be made to strengthen First Nations' economic base and that economic development will follow. We have concluded that a catch-up program for housing on reserves, financed in part through loans, is feasible and attractive on that basis. Properly managed to secure maximum local involvement, housing construction and repair can be a leading economic activity that helps to galvanize the energies of communities and the move toward greater self-reliance.[51]

Rallying local resources

First Nations can generate more resources for the housing sector in three main ways: reducing capital costs through contributions of labour and materials; increasing the financial contributions made by individuals through rental charges; and giving people the option of carrying a mortgage as an alternative to paying rent.

In Aboriginal communities, it is often possible to substitute local materials for standard construction supplies, log homes being the most obvious example. If communities work together to create larger markets, take advantage of new technologies and produce their own designs, they may be able not only to meet their own housing needs more efficiently but also to gain access to larger markets.

A greatly underused resource is the ample pool of unemployed labour in many communities. Although not everyone has the skills required in the construction trades, many can contribute in some fashion. Self-building and self-maintenance will reduce borrowing requirements and increase Aboriginal equity in projects.

First Nations communities frequently combine the inadequate DIAND housing subsidy with other program funds, such as training allowances, to cobble together the resources to build houses. In some cases, members of the community contribute their time without compensation. But this practice is not as common as it could be. A generation or two ago, communities often worked together to build homes for those who needed them. For instance, in 1963, 20 log houses were built by welfare recipients in a single construction season in La Loche, Saskatchewan, with the use of a sawmill supplied by the local church.[52] The homes are not luxurious, but they are adequate and durable and a source of considerable community pride. We heard similar stories elsewhere, stories of resourceful people putting together the building materials and trades like electrical wiring and plumbing by bartering their own skills. Today, such practices are less common. Prospective occupants may contribute their own labour and family members may help out. But others often expect to be paid, as they were paid when housing subsidies were more adequate in the early 1980s, and through a succession of make-work and training programs available on reserves, such as the Work Opportunities Program and the New Employment Expansion Development Program. Thus, Habitat for Humanity, a charitable organization that provides low-cost housing to those in need by relying on volunteer labour and donated materials, has had a mixed reception in some communities. The homes constructed were adequate, but the process was not seen to generate sufficient economic benefit. In urban areas, the experience of Habitat for Humanity with Aboriginal people has been different, with notable successes. This initial experience does not mean that Aboriginal communities have given up on the Habitat for Humanity approach.[53]

There may be some scope for securing greater contributions from prospective occupants. 'Sweat equity' contributions could be encouraged by giving priority to those who undertake to make large contributions, something that is already being done. And financial charges to the occupants can be adjusted to reflect the effort they have put in. If tenure is clarified, occupants may be more willing to contribute to the construction and upkeep of their dwellings, since they would have a clear claim on the benefits.

But to elicit greater contributions from community members generally, First Nations communities will need to have the freedom to adjust social assistance to their own particular circumstances. Until now they have not been allowed to do so. Social assistance in First Nations communities has to conform to the rules and criteria of the province in which the community is located. Thus, communities have not been able to use income support transfers to mobilize labour for activities such as housing construction and maintenance. In First Nations communities, there have been various training and employment programs over the years, funded in part by transfers of funds from the social assistance budget. However, the communities have not had the authority to reallocate funds or change the rules for social assistance.

We believe that the proposals for social assistance reform presented in Volume 2, Chapter 5 will enable First Nations to make much greater use of local labour in a catch-up effort over 10 years to construct houses in Aboriginal communities. There we examined two approaches to reforming social assistance, both of which could be used to provide income support while generating economic and/or social development. The first approach retains the existing basis of individual entitlement with modifications to permit individuals to participate in economic or social development and personal development activities. The second approach is based on community entitlement, which would enable Aboriginal governments to use social assistance dollars to generate employment through economic and social development projects.[54] With either approach, the key would be to combine housing and social assistance funds to stimulate productive contributions to housing from members of the community.

Such approaches would build equity with money that is already coming into communities in the form of welfare payments. They would build the skills base needed for continuing maintenance and for spin-off businesses. And they would create a sense of greater control over the well-being of the community and of ownership of the housing stock as a valuable asset and source of pride.

The second way Aboriginal communities can generate more resources is to increase the financial contributions made by the community and individual households. At present, apart from CMHC units, two extremes coexist: homes that are entirely or largely financed by the occupants, either independently or with a guarantee from the band, and the majority of houses for which the band charges no rent. (Charges covering part of the cost of community services and utilities are common.) Rental charges of 25 per cent of income – a standard approach used in social housing in non-reserve communities[55] – with a maximum reflecting rents in the regional market should be used to build up capital for major renovations and new homes. An exemption could be provided for a substantial base amount of earnings in a manner analogous to a personal income tax exemption to ensure that people are not discouraged from becoming self-reliant.

Introducing rental charges where none apply today will not be easy for First Nations communities. Charges could be introduced gradually, with an initial emphasis on maintenance and repair, so that occupants enjoy some immediate benefits as a result of their contributions.

Maintenance fees and rents would become a far more attractive proposition if the federal government paid shelter allowances for social assistance recipients living in band houses. In fact, this would amount to a continuation of a policy that is now in abeyance because of budgetary pressures. We believe the government should be offering to supplement community resources with shelter allowances for social assistance recipients. The government could encourage the staged approach that many communities may want to take by offering to pay shelter allowances up to a level required to create a financial reserve for maintenance of existing homes. Timely maintenance will slow the deterioration of the housing stock and is a most effective way of improving living conditions. Shelter allowances for maintenance and insurance would cost approximately $40 million a year (see Table 4.4, later in the chapter).

A third way to rally resources would be to give people who can and wish to exercise it the option of carrying a loan and acquiring an ownership interest in the home they occupy. Many households may be willing to invest more in their home if they can be sure of enjoying the benefits of doing so or realize a gain upon transfer of ownership. At the same time, many households will need financial assistance, and this could be provided in the form of incentives for ownership. Many approaches are possible in this regard, such as interest subsidies, partly forgivable loans and up-front equity subsidies.[56] We recommend that such approaches be actively pursued by First Nations and governments.

Success stories

To meet their housing needs, First Nations communities have to put together funding, labour and supplies from a variety of sources. They can learn from each other how to make the most of their situation. Some communities have been quite creative.

In Quebec, the Gesgapegiag community has developed an active housing program using DIAND housing subsidies and CMHC funds, as well as credit from the local Caisse populaire Desjardins.[57] The band government secures loans for candidates who demonstrate an ability to repay long-term mortgages. It also provides local labour through unemployment insurance funds for on-the-job training. The community has developed a training program in building trades such as plumbing, carpentry, and electrical work.

The First Nations community of Westbank in British Columbia finances its housing through DIAND, the CMHC rental housing program and owner equity. An Aboriginal-owned company in Alberta provides pre-fabricated homes for the community. Community services funds and contributions from the homeowner cover the expense of building the foundation, and local labour is hired to assemble the houses delivered from Alberta. While this interdependent arrangement has been successful thus far, it is not without risk, as each stage requires the co-operation and delivery of every partner.

The housing program of the Oujé-Bougoumou Cree Nation in Quebec was established as part of the agreement that created the Oujé-Bougoumou village. The DIAND housing subsidy and CMHC social housing funds were used to establish a capital fund that represented the equivalent of 117 houses. This pool of funds enabled the community to develop realistic housing construction plans that included bulk-purchasing and a cost-effective construction schedule. The savings from these measures were used as the basis for a revolving loan fund. The housing program at Oujé-Bougoumou consists of two parts: the home ownership program, which builds affordable, energy-efficient homes for families with an annual income of $21,000 or more, and the rental program, available to individuals on fixed incomes, welfare recipients and those with low incomes.

Looking at another approach, the Old Masset Development Corporation (OMDC) in British Columbia has a plan to build 200 houses in the next seven years. The plan is based on the provincial government confirming the Old Masset community's access to 1,000 hectares in Haida Gwaii that it has used traditionally for harvesting timber. OMDC would be entitled to harvest logs for export as well as for milling purposes. This would enable them to establish a housing capital fund and provide them with cheaper timber, reducing the cost of housing construction in their community. Spin-off economic activity is also expected to flourish under such an arrangement.

A few First Nations communities in Ontario, Quebec and Alberta have devised programs using government funds as a starting point, chiefly geared to fostering individual home ownership. Several communities, such as the Six Nations, Gesgapegiag and the Oujé-Bougoumou Cree, have been successful in financing housing through revolving funds, capitalized initially with DIAND housing subsidies and replenished continuously through housing loan repayments from members of the community.

These and other examples involve the exercise of effective community leadership, the creative use of existing programs, and the co-ordination of many different actors and resources to achieve results. These success stories, and others from Métis, Inuit and urban Aboriginal housing organizations, suggest what can be achieved by increasing Aboriginal control and by using housing as a means of wider community development and renewal.

In July 1995, the minister of Indian affairs announced a welcome demonstration program, to take place on five reserves across Canada, to investigate alternative approaches to house construction. The purpose of the program is to enhance the use of local resources to build lower-cost quality housing, allowing the community to be less dependent on outside contractors, suppliers and trades people. DIAND will support the construction of a maximum of five houses in five communities with a contribution of $50,000 per unit. Projects must make use of local resources, including materials produced in the community such as logs, timber, sand and gravel, and hire unemployed workers from the community who are receiving social assistance benefits. These are the kinds of directions that should be explored more widely.

An estimate of government expenditures required

A 10-year program, starting in 1997, to bring the housing stock on reserves up to standard, accommodate those now waiting for a home, and provide for future population growth will require an investment of $5.1 billion. The bulk of this spending would go toward building new dwelling units. Present needs include replacing 6,500 houses and meeting a backlog of 11,000 houses; future needs consist of 30,100 units for new households and 4,000 units that will need to be replaced before better maintenance puts an end to the rapid deterioration of the existing stock.[58] Should implementation of this catch-up effort be delayed, its cost will increase, as the stock would deteriorate further.

Major repair and renovation is a further requirement. An estimated 14,000 units need major work at an average cost of $30,000. This proposed activity would in part replace the current minor repairs of some 4,000 units per year, and it would ensure that units are brought up to standard. The cost of minor repairs would be met out of funds for regular maintenance of existing stock as well as contributions by households.

There is also a cost associated with operating newly constructed homes. At a cost of $2,100 per dwelling for heating and utilities, 5,160 new units per year will result in $11 million in additional expenses for heating, electricity and utilities. There is also a need for more funding for program delivery.

How can these resources be generated? It is estimated that First Nations communities generate about $140 million per year for housing costs at the present time. This includes charges for heat and utilities as well as rental and mortgage charges. Included in this amount is the contribution of about 6,000 households who assume full responsibility for housing and services costs. In addition, First Nations contribute to the cost of construction through training funds and sweat equity.

According to calculations by DIAND based on the 1991 census, only 16 per cent of households on reserves are able to pay the full cost of housing services. Of the other 84 per cent, half can contribute something toward the cost of housing, whereas the other half cannot. Clearly, First Nations communities are extremely dependent on government assistance for housing. For our projections we assume that First Nations people will be able to contribute one-third of the cost of construction and repair for a catch-up program and one-third of the cost of operating and maintaining the newly built dwellings. This estimate assumes that First Nations people will creatively use all resources at their disposal, as we have discussed. (The estimate is also global and approximate. The contribution will vary greatly from community to community, depending on the level of employment and income and the availability of materials, skills and other factors.)

For the purpose of estimating government expenditures, we further assume that the government will pay half its contribution to the capital costs of construction and repair in the form of capital subsidies and commit to making instalment payments on debt for the other half.[59] We are making this assumption since we do not want to propose that the government share of the catch-up program be financed entirely by loans. This would defer too large a share of the cost and result in First Nations incurring a very large debt.

On the basis of these data and assumptions, and if construction of new homes and repair take place steadily over the next 10 years, the government expenditures required are as set out in Table 4.4. The amount of capital subsidies required for new construction and major repair, $169 million per year, is constant over time and a moderate increase from the $136 million DIAND spends at present. However, additional funding is needed to service debts and to operate and maintain newly built stock, and the amounts needed escalate over time as the newly built stock grows. Finally, a constant annual amount of funding is required to maintain and insure existing stock. These estimates underscore the point that the housing challenge in First Nations communities lies not so much in the volume of new construction as in the quality of new dwellings and the maintenance of existing stock. New construction also requires site prepara-

TABLE 4.4
Additional Annual Federal Expenditures Required to Achieve Adequate Housing On-Reserve over 10 Years with Partial Debt Financing

	1997	2006	2007
	$ millions		
Construction of new dwellings and major repairs			
1. Capital subsidies	169	169	90
2. Debt servicing (including maintenance)	23	230	242
3. Heating, electricity and utilities ($1400 per unit)	7	72	75
4. Program delivery	15	15	15
5. Government expenditures on new and repaired dwellings (1+2+3+4)	214	486	422
6. Maintenance and insurance on existing stock	40	40	40
Total federal expenditures (5+6)	254	526	464
Less existing expenditures	(141)	(141)	(141)
Increase in federal expenditures	113	385	323

Notes: The cost of constructing a new dwelling is assumed to be $90,000; major repair or renovation, $30,000; and heating, electricity and utilities, $2,000. These assumed costs of construction, repair and operations of dwellings are similar to those presented by DIAND in *Laying the Foundations of a New On-Reserve Housing Program*, discussion paper (Ottawa: Supply and Services, 1990). The amounts in the table reflect only the federal share, which is two-thirds of total costs. Maintenance and insurance costs are assumed to be $1,800 per year per new unit. Debt servicing combined with maintenance and insurance is calculated at one per cent of the amount of the loan per month. Subtracted from total federal expenditures are amounts the federal government spends on new housing on-reserve: capital subsidies by DIAND ($136 million) plus an estimated $5 million in loan subsidies by CMHC during 1995-96. Note that DIAND and CMHC will also incur costs related to debt servicing, maintenance and operation of the existing stock of dwellings on-reserve during the next 10 years, in the amounts indicated in Table 4.3.

tion and servicing. As the number of new units under the catch-up program is somewhat higher than at present (approximately 4,000 homes are built annually), an increase in the budget for construction of municipal service infrastructure is required.

After the 10-year period, when the backlog has been eliminated and the housing stock is of good quality and well-maintained, construction is required only to provide dwellings for new households. The volume of construction thus falls to somewhat less than half the annual level during the catch-up period. Capital subsidies drop sharply, and so does the amount of new commitments for housing loans and utilities.

4.4 Institutional Development

Delivery of housing programs has been devolved to First Nations communities, but limited resources have been made available by DIAND to create and maintain managerial and administrative structures to operate programs. Based on an overhead cost ratio of 10 per cent of capital for administration, the amount provided by DIAND should be in the order of $14 million annually. In reality, only $5 million is allocated for this purpose. CMHC has devoted considerably more attention and resources to program delivery and housing stock management and maintenance. Subsidies for this purpose are built into the monthly transfers from CMHC to the bands as non-profit housing corporations. However, only about half of First Nations communities have taken up the CMHC program, and the stock covered by it amounts to only 20 per cent of the total located on-reserve.[60]

The most active tribal council and band organizations appear to be at work in southern Ontario, Saskatchewan, British Columbia and Quebec, with more isolated pockets in Alberta, Manitoba and Atlantic Canada. Elsewhere, housing is an adjunct of band council operations. In our view, the focus for developing new institutions or strengthening established ones should be at the nation level or above. Many First Nations communities are too small to maintain the full range of technical capabilities for housing program design, delivery and maintenance. There has been some movement among First Nations communities to develop broader regional or province-wide organizations, for example, in British Columbia (the First Nations Housing Society of B.C.) and Saskatchewan (the Saskatchewan Indian Housing Corporation under the Federation of Saskatchewan Indian Nations).

In British Columbia, the Commission received a presentation from the Secwepemc Nation, which recommended that housing programs be transferred to levels of government such as their own organization, which represents 17 communities.

> It is a large enough organization that there is some flexibility there to be able to handle long-term programs or major projects. It is large enough to be administratively effective, but at the same time it is small enough to be accountable. It can meet on a regular basis. The communities can feel involved.
>
> Bruce Mack
> Secwepemc Nation
> Kamloops, British Columbia, 14 June 1993*

The Commission is of the view that there is a need for regional institutions to work with managers at the community level to design programs and develop the capacity for housing construction, maintenance and community services.

---

* Transcripts of the Commission's hearings are cited with the speaker's name and affiliation, if any, and the location and date of the hearing. See *A Note About Sources* at the beginning of this volume for information about transcripts and other Commission publications.

Under self-government, the natural locus for such organizations is at the nation level, but nations may want to join forces and develop capacity at a higher level of aggregation. Governments have a vital role to play in working with Aboriginal organizations to build up existing centres of strengths and, where they are absent, to assist their formation.

Such institutions may be able to develop particular expertise in arranging financing and brokering building materials supply as well as in providing technical support for housing and community services. Through the secondment of staff from CMHC and other housing resource groups, effective organizations could be put into operation very quickly. (Opportunities to develop financial institutions and building supply stores and production are examined later in the chapter when we discuss economic development.)

4.5 Conclusions and Recommendations

On-reserve housing policy and programs have been under review since 1988. In 1990, DIAND issued a discussion paper, *Laying the Foundations*, and in 1992, the Standing Committee on Aboriginal Affairs published its report, *A Time For Action: Aboriginal and Northern Housing*. Policy proposals have apparently been brought to cabinet a number of times, but little changed until the proposals announced on 25 July 1996.[61] In the communities, while houses are being built and renovated, sound regimes to ensure maintenance of existing homes and build up resources for new construction are still lacking.

There is a way out of this deadlock. The parties have to make housing a priority and assume their responsibilities. Our main purpose in this chapter has been to exhort governments and First Nations households and governments to do so, to clarify their roles and to show how they can be fulfilled in an effective way.

Progress will be made only step by step. The need for adequate shelter is too pressing to wait for full self-government and economic self-reliance, although these are the basis for policy in the longer term. Much can be accomplished if the government removes program constraints and establishes conditions to enable better maintenance and repair of existing stock and the accumulation of capital for replacement. Communities that want to tackle their housing problem must be supported.

RECOMMENDATIONS

The Commission recommends that

Housing in First
Nations
Communities

3.4.6

The government of Canada and First Nations governments and people undertake to meet the need of First Nations people for adequate housing within 10 years.

3.4.7

The government of Canada complement the resources supplied by First Nations people in a two-to-one ratio or as necessary to achieve adequate housing in 10 years by
- providing capital subsidies and committing to loan subsidies for construction of new homes and renovations;
- providing funds for property insurance and regular maintenance for home occupants receiving social assistance or with low earned incomes;
- paying rental subsidies for those receiving social assistance or with low earned incomes in amounts that are equitable compared to off-reserve programs; and
- offering financial incentives for private home ownership.

3.4.8

First Nations governments and people make every effort to marshall more resources for housing and community services, through financial contributions from residents in the form of maintenance fees, rents or mortgage payments, and contributions in kind, such as sweat equity and local materials.

3.4.9

First Nations governments assume jurisdiction over housing at the earliest opportunity, enact clear laws regarding housing tenure, and pursue authority to adjust other programs such as social assistance with a view to marshalling more resources for housing.

3.4.10

First Nations governments develop institutions at the nation level or through inter-nation agreements to administer housing and tenure regimes and deliver housing programs with financial and technical support from the government of Canada.

3.4.11

The government of Canada support the efforts of First Nations communities to develop and implement their own tenure systems and housing programs, innovative uses of social assistance to stimulate contributions to housing, and institutions above the community level.

5. Housing in Non-Reserve Communities

The main impediments to creating adequate and affordable housing for Aboriginal people living in non-reserve communities are poverty and discrimination.

5.1 Policies and Programs

CMHC's Rural Housing Program for Aboriginal People was introduced in 1974 to address the needs of rural low-income non-Aboriginal people and Aboriginal people living in non-reserve communities of less than 2,500. The main program provided for home ownership (suspended in 1991) and for rental and lease-to-purchase options in which the client made a payment based on household income and the government covered the difference between that payment and the full cost of shelter. One-time grants for emergency repairs were also available. From 1992 to 1995, CMHC provided a self-help program that enabled clients to build their own homes in return for reduced monthly payments. The Residential Rehabilitation Assistance Program, also available on reserves, was still available in 1995 to Aboriginal people living in non-reserve communities.[62]

The corporation's urban housing program for Aboriginal people supported the acquisition of housing units by non-profit housing organizations for rental on a rent-to-income basis (25 per cent of gross income). CMHC subsidizes the difference between the housing organization's revenues from rents and its operating costs.

CMHC has also long acted as a lender of last resort in rural and remote areas. However, this function has declined somewhat as private lenders have shown greater willingness to lend. Still, their loans are provided at market rates, and relatively few Aboriginal people have the incomes to qualify.

CMHC stopped making commitments for new units under these programs as of 1 January 1994. Delivery of renovation units continued in 1994 and 1995. Thus, expenditures in 1994-95, shown in Table 4.5, are related almost entirely to social housing projects built in previous years. The lion's share of the monthly subsidy bill goes to repay loans insured or provided directly by CMHC; the remainder goes to maintenance of the stock and operations of the housing institutions.

At 31 December 1994, 9,088 of the 24,815 units under adminstration under the rural housing program were estimated to be occupied by Aboriginal people, most of them home-ownership units, and there were 10,301 units under the urban Aboriginal program. Table 4.6 provides a picture of spending under the various programs between 1986 and the termination of new commitments for construction of units in 1994.

TABLE 4.5 CMHC Expenditures on Housing for Aboriginal People Not Living on Reserves, 1994-95	
	$ millions
Rural and Native Housing Program	75.5
Urban Native Housing Program	94.8
Remote Housing Program	2.1
Emergency Repair Program	1.1
Total	172.5

In addition to the program support listed earlier, CMHC provides assistance in program delivery, including training. CMHC does not support community infrastructure to provide water and sewerage services as such, but it finances site services to individual units, such as wells, septic tanks and hook-ups to subdivision services.

Most provinces and territories have participated in funding social housing. Since 1985, the urban Aboriginal program has been cost-shared by Newfoundland, Quebec, Manitoba and Saskatchewan. Also since 1985, Newfoundland, New Brunswick, Quebec, Ontario, Manitoba, Saskatchewan (partly), Alberta and the Northwest Territories have cost-shared the Rural and Native Housing Program. The province of Alberta had two housing programs serving predominantly Aboriginal households, but new delivery has been terminated.

Aboriginal people are eligible for general housing programs. However, almost all provincial housing programs have been substantially reduced or eliminated in the past few years, and competition for new and existing housing units is intense. The government of the Northwest Territories delivers housing assistance through an access to home ownership program. Aboriginal people con-

TABLE 4.6 CMHC Expenditures on Housing for Aboriginal People Not Living on Reserves, 1986-87 to 1994-95	
	$ millions
Rural and Native Housing Program	446
Urban Native Housing Program	538
Renovation	42
Total	1,026

stitute such a large proportion of the population that they are the key clientele of this program.

Of the 645,000 non-reserve social housing units under CMHC administration as of 31 December 1994, 19,389 were identified by the corporation as being exclusively for Aboriginal people. Thus, about three per cent of all social housing has been assured to non-reserve Aboriginal households in need, who make up five to six per cent of the Canadian population in core need. Aboriginal people can gain access to the general social housing stock by meeting the relevant criteria in different localities. Aboriginal people are known to do so, but the extent to which they do is not known.

No official data on use of general social housing by Aboriginal people are available, but some indications can be found. In Saskatchewan, according to an unpublished survey by the provincial government, Aboriginal people live in public housing at a rate in excess of their share of the population but not in proportion to their share of households in need. As well, in 1994 CMHC paid more than $32 million in housing subsidies to Inuit in northern Quebec under general non-profit and housing programs.

Hence, it is not possible to say how well Aboriginal people's needs are met relative to those of other Canadians. What is clear, however, is that programs targeted to Aboriginal people have made a major contribution to meeting the need for adequate housing, without meeting it fully.

5.2 The Institutional Base for Self-Reliance

Rural, remote and northern housing

In an urban setting, most economic activity occurs through the market system. People build houses as investments as well as to provide shelter. The whole process is shaped by potential resale when a household decides to move.

But in rural, remote and northern locations, few of the rules governing housing in a market-driven context apply. There is not enough cash income, and the communities are too small to have a market for housing. Homeowners have little or no hope of a good return on their investment through rental or resale. At the same time, rural and remote communities face substantially higher unit costs for construction and operation. Costs of sewer and water servicing in particular can be dramatically higher than in heavily settled southern areas because there are no economies of scale for central plants and trunk lines.

Cash incomes in remote areas are often very low, especially where people engage in traditional activities, and the cost of goods is higher than in urban and most southern areas. For these reasons, many groups representing Aboriginal people in rural and remote areas were critical of CMHC's requirement that rent and loan repayments under its lease-to-purchase option be paid at the rate of 25 per cent of gross income. By the same token, Inuit Tapirisat of Canada has indicated that the Northwest Territories Housing Corporation's home ownership assistance program (HAP) is of interest to Inuit but that they are often too poor to afford their own share of costs.[63] In his presentation to the Commission, Don Morin, minister of housing for the Northwest Territories, indicated that only one applicant out of 100 was qualified for a unit under HAP.[64]

Various ways of meeting housing needs have been tested. Between 1985 and 1990, CMHC offered a self-build alternative to the lease-to-purchase option under a rural and Aboriginal housing demonstration program. This enabled people to build their own homes as partial payment for ownership in lieu of paying 25 per cent of income over 25 years. This option proved quite successful in northern areas of the country.[65]

In our hearings, we were told of some frustration people felt with the lack of flexibility in housing programs that were ill-suited to the circumstances of rural and remote communities. For instance, Jacqueline Ellsworth, the manager of the housing program for off-reserve Aboriginal people in Prince Edward Island, asked why CMHC requires that their organization participate in a national competitive process when the first five-year term of a mortgage is up for renewal. They have found that services cannot be provided as effectively from a distance and that designated contact persons are sometimes practically impossible to reach. CMHC's rigid rules for distinguishing between market and non-market areas were also criticized as inappropriate to Prince Edward Island. CMHC reacted unfavourably to a proposal to use the home ownership component of the rural housing program for Aboriginal people to help build a small village, stating that it would not qualify because the site was in an area designated as a market area. Ellsworth took issue with CMHC's position: "The fact is that the national market versus non-market policy...leaves virtually no area in Prince Edward Island that is not designated as a market area".[66]

Tony Andersen, chairman of the board of directors of the Torngat Regional Housing Association in Labrador, told us that houses built in the 1960s and '70s based on southern designs without regard for the northern environment immediately showed structural deficiencies and had at best a life expectancy of 20 years without expensive structural upgrading. He went on to say:

> The design is still very much dictated to us, especially when it comes to delivering dollars from *National Housing Act* programs...by engineers from other parts of the world or other parts of Canada at least. The association maintains that the units designed from the foundation to the finish must have our input to gain the respect of the people who live in them.
>
> Tony Anderson
> Torngat Regional Housing Association
> Nain, Newfoundland and Labrador, 30 November 1992

Aboriginal control and the institutional base to exercise that control are seen as essential to the improvement of programs so that they meet the needs of local communities. Substantial progress has been made in the development of an institutional base over the past decade, but this achievement is now seriously threatened. In rural and remote areas, institutions delivering programs on a fee-for-service basis predominate. With the end of off-reserve housing programs, their existence is threatened as revenues dry up.

The oldest of these housing organizations belongs to the Manitoba Metis Federation. In its brief to the Commission, the federation indicated that it has been active in housing since it was formed in 1967 and it helped to create the rural and Aboriginal housing program.[67] It established a housing branch in 1979 and, since then, has delivered the rural and Aboriginal housing program. For seven years, it has delivered housing programs under tripartite arrangements with CMHC and the Manitoba Housing and Renewal Corporation. In 1992, income from fee-for-service arrangements was $1,731,245, and the federation had one or more housing development officers and housing counsellors in each of its six regional offices. In 1995, however, virtually no income was earned.

In his presentation to the Commission, the minister of housing for the Northwest Territories documented the series of cutbacks in the N.W.T. since 1991 and the government's difficulties in meeting housing needs. He pointed out that their housing backlog in 1993 was 3,500 units, and there is a need to build at least 400 to 500 units a year just to keep up with the growth.

> We have a plan on how to end the dependency on the federal government as well as the territorial government, to create more home ownership for our people and so our people can take care of their own problems. The problem is with any plan you need some capital funding and that's what we don't have.
>
> Don Morin
> Minister of Housing,
> Government of the Northwest Territories
> Hay River, Northwest Territories, 17 June 1993

Over the past two decades, the federal government has provided significant leadership in social and Aboriginal housing and has engaged provincial governments in this effort through cost-sharing agreements. The federal government's withdrawal from this area, at the same time as many provinces are also reducing support for social housing, threatens to halt progress and undermine gains already made in meeting the basic shelter needs of Aboriginal people not living on reserves.

There is a clear need for joint strategies and concerted support from all governments and Aboriginal housing organizations to marshall the resources needed for the major catch-up effort we propose in this chapter. We call upon all parties to commit resources, including those that could be available through self-build initiatives, to this effort.

Urban markets

Adequate and affordable housing has long been, and continues to be, a priority concern and need for Aboriginal people living in urban environments. As many presentations to the Commission stressed, the core problem in urban centres is clearly the lack of supply of inexpensive, adequate housing from the private sector, coupled with discrimination by private landlords.[68]

The past three decades have seen a large increase in Aboriginal migration to cities. In 1991, 25.6 per cent of all Aboriginal people lived in the census metropolitan areas of Halifax, Montreal, Ottawa-Hull, Toronto, Winnipeg, Regina, Saskatoon, Calgary, Edmonton, Vancouver and Victoria.[69] Rural-urban migration of Aboriginal people will continue, creating mounting pressures for affordable accommodation. Aboriginal people often move to specific areas of cities where landlords are willing to rent to them. Some of these areas have the characteristics of urban ghettos. with aggressive policing, barred windows, and routine drug- and alcohol-related violence. They are not good neighbourhoods in which to raise a family.

Efforts to address Aboriginal concerns about adequate and affordable housing in urban areas began in the late 1960s and early '70s. In 1970, Kinew Housing was formed as a non-profit corporation to begin meeting the housing needs of Aboriginal people in Winnipeg, and this was followed by other programs in Toronto, Fredericton, Edmonton and Saskatoon. CMHC's urban housing program for Aboriginal people was established in 1978 to provide assistance to non-profit housing corporations or co-operatives to acquire, build, renovate and operate subsidized rental housing. There are now 92 Aboriginal urban housing corporations in Canada, with assets estimated at more than $500 million.[70] At 31 December 1994, these corporations administered 10,301 units, according to CMHC data.

The accommodation provided through these housing corporations, as revealed in tenant interviews, has had considerable benefits, including family stability, access to education opportunities, the preservation and reinforcement of cultural identity and, for the most part, a positive impact on relations between Aboriginal and non-Aboriginal people. In addition, the stable environment provided by these corporations has enabled tenants to take advantage of employment opportunities, to further their education and, in some instances, to buy their own homes. Through counselling services, the corporations have also helped tenants gain access to government and other resources to increase their chances for self-reliance.

Housing corporations face several challenges, as the government has ceased making new commitments under the urban Aboriginal housing program. The immediate consequence is that the corporations cannot meet the continuing need for social housing. Representatives of urban Aboriginal groups appearing before the Commission told us they have long waiting lists and expressed concern that these lists will grow.

A lack of new funding is not an immediate threat to the survival of the corporations, as they have assets and income from rents and government subsidies on existing units. They do not have much equity, however. For instance, the Gabriel Housing Corporation in Regina, the subject of one of four case studies carried out for the Commission, has assets of $13 million and mortgage debt amounting to 96 per cent of the value of assets, with replacement reserves making up the remaining four per cent.[71]

The age of the housing stock is a problem. About 23 per cent of the 11,000 units managed by these corporations were purchased between 1971 and 1983, when few subsidies were available. The corporations often purchased older homes that were more affordable and fell within the maximum unit prices defined by CMHC, resulting in more maintenance and repair costs.

Current CMHC regulations prevent housing corporations from selling a house that is not cost-effective, since the mortgage on the house cannot be transferred to a different unit. If corporations were also allowed to move earnings around within a portfolio of units and to apply surpluses to buying new units, they could expand their housing stock at a modest rate without additional subsidies. (Over time, the loans for these projects are paid off, and non-profit corporations find themselves in the same fortunate position as any other debt-free owner.) We believe that the government should relax current restrictions to give social housing corporations greater freedom to manage their assets and thus maximize the services they provide.

Urban Aboriginal housing corporations should be encouraged to expand their mandate in a way that increases individual self-reliance through home ownership. Additional activities to serve the needs of the growing Aboriginal population in urban areas could include self-build initiatives for low-income people who wish to become homeowners, lease-to-purchase options for tenants, and the direct sale of properties to tenants. With a broader mandate, the corporations would continue to meet social needs through the provision of subsidized, affordable rental accommodation. But they would also open doors to the future self-reliance of urban Aboriginal people.

Self-reliance and home ownership can also be promoted through approaches like that of Habitat for Humanity. We believe that this approach holds promise in urban areas as well as in Aboriginal communities and urge Aboriginal people, particularly youth, to work with this organization in meeting their housing needs (see also Volume 4, Chapter 4).

Aboriginal housing corporations face other challenges.[72] Few resources have been allocated for staff and board training and development. A report prepared for CMHC in 1988 stated:

> There was no start-up management training provided to the Native institutions – some staff were encouraged by CMHC to attend local Real Estate Board courses, but generally speaking, the Native groups had to make it on their own within the tight financial and time constraints of the program.[73]

The portfolios of many urban Aboriginal housing corporations may not be large enough to achieve efficient management systems. (A critical mass, in the view of professional property management firms, ranges from 250 to 400 units.) In addition, these corporations have tended to purchase widely dispersed single units, increasing their administrative load.

While social housing provided through Aboriginal non-profit corporations is a viable and productive approach to meeting Aboriginal needs in urban areas, it is unlikely that it could meet all the need in a reasonable period of time. A rapid solution to urban Aboriginal housing problems must make use of private rental stock. In many regions with substantial Aboriginal populations, there is a large supply of reasonably priced rental accommodation. For example, in October 1994, the following vacancy rates existed in major urban centres in western Canada: Calgary – 5.1 per cent; Edmonton – 8.7 per cent; Regina – 3.1 per cent; Winnipeg – 5.6 per cent. A three per cent rate is considered sufficient to provide for healthy competition in the rental market. Rent subsidies are a cost-effective way to make adequate accommodation available to low-income households in urban areas. Households whose main source of income is social assistance receive shelter allowances as a supplement. However, households with low earned incomes may not be able to afford adequate housing, and these households need assistance.

Rent subsidies can be attached to particular dwelling units, or they can be made available to households in the form of shelter allowances that bridge the gap between the market rent of adequate accommodation and what the household can afford. The latter type of assistance leaves maximum choice to the household. This approach has been tested in several provinces, with generally favourable results.

Shelter allowances are at least a partial response to the problem of discrimination in rental housing markets in that they give landlords greater assurance that rents will be paid. It is generally acknowledged that discrimination exists and that Aboriginal people as a group rarely find what they need in the private housing market.[74] However, as protection against discrimination is ineffective, there will remain a need for social housing corporations.[75]

5.3 An Estimate of Government Expenditures Required

According to a preliminary estimate by CMHC, based on data from the 1991 Aboriginal peoples survey (APS), approximately one-third of Aboriginal households off-reserve are in core need: adequate housing does or would take up more than 30 per cent of these households' income, and assistance from government is generally required for them to have their needs met. The amount of assistance required varies and is generally higher in the North.

According to the APS and population projections prepared for the Commission, an estimated 17,000 new units are required to meet the needs of those who do not live in their own dwelling, and 37,000 dwellings need major repair. In addition, population growth over the next 10 years will add 21,600 households in need of assistance.[76]

As discussed in the previous section, the form of assistance will vary by location. In urban centres where there is a rental market, needs can be met by rent subsidies, obviating the need for new construction. This could meet the needs of about one-third of those in need. For the other two-thirds, housing assistance will take the form of mortgage subsidies. If it is assumed that households in need can afford to pay one-third of the cost, government funding for a ten-year catch-up program will amount to $37 million in the first year, rising to $366 million by the tenth year.[77] After the 10-year period, new construction is required only to keep up with new household formation, that is, 2,160 instead of 3,860 units per year. New loan commitments will also drop sharply, and rental and mortgage subsidies will rise by $10 million per year from then on, instead of by $31 million as during the catch-up period.

5.4 Conclusions and Recommendations

There is clearly a need for subsidized housing for Aboriginal people living in non-reserve communities. Whatever differences may exist about details, the Commission found broad agreement among leaders, experts, and community representatives that CMHC programs directed to Aboriginal people who do not live on-reserve need to be restored, with appropriate modifications for greater effectiveness and to stimulate individual self-reliance.

Over the past decade, Aboriginal people have made significant progress in developing the institutional capacity to address housing problems in non-reserve communities. The Commission is concerned that the federal government, having helped to create the institutional base for housing programs, is now undermining that base with the elimination of key CMHC programs. We understand that the federal government's 1994-95 program review was based on the principle of reducing program activities that are not core functions of the federal government. Many programs, in addition to CMHC's social housing programs, have been affected.

However, the Commission believes that the federal government's withdrawal from this area is unrealistic and at odds with one of its responsibilities to Aboriginal people. Governments have a duty to ensure that Aboriginal people have the means to afford their own housing and, failing that, to supplement the resources Aboriginal people can supply. A major catch-up effort requires collaboration by all parties. In this constrained fiscal environment, the federal government cannot assume that its withdrawal from CMHC programming in non-reserve communities will mean that provinces will take over. If anything, the federal withdrawal creates a vacuum and loss of the critical mass of resources needed to leverage other resources, private sector and Aboriginal, necessary for a catch-up effort.

RECOMMENDATIONS

The Commission recommends that

Housing in Non-Reserve Communities

3.4.12
The government of Canada and the governments of the provinces and territories undertake to meet fully, in co-operation with Aboriginal people and within 10 years, the need for adequate housing of Aboriginal people not living on reserves.

3.4.13
Aboriginal people not living on reserves make every effort to marshall more resources for housing in a variety of ways, through contributions in kind, use of local materials, and effective housing organizations.

3.4.14
The government of Canada engage the provincial and territorial governments in a strategy to meet the housing needs of Aboriginal people living in non-reserve communities by
- reinstating and increasing funding for new social housing and mortgage subsidies under the Aboriginal off-reserve programs of CMHC;
- providing greater autonomy and flexibility to Aboriginal organizations delivering the program in rural areas and to urban social housing corporations; and
- providing rental subsidies as a cost-effective option where rental markets exist.

6. GOVERNMENT EXPENDITURES TO ACHIEVE ADEQUATE HOUSING FOR ABORIGINAL PEOPLE IN 10 YEARS

To summarize the financial implications of our approach to the Aboriginal housing challenge, we propose that governments and Aboriginal people undertake to meet fully the needs of the Aboriginal people for adequate and suitable shelter by the year 2007. This means that sufficient new dwelling units are provided to accommodate new household formation, to supply homes to those on waiting lists, and to replace unsalvageable units on-reserve. In addition, all major repairs and renovations currently needed should be completed within 10 years. In First Nations communities, the federal government would complement the resources brought to bear by people in the communities by supplying funds covering two-thirds of the cost of new construction and major repair – half of it through capital subsidies, the other half to be financed by loans. The federal government would also pay for regular maintenance and insurance of newly built stock and the cost of heating and utilities. In addition, the federal government would immediately supply funds for regular maintenance and insurance of existing dwellings whose residents are dependent on social assistance. Elsewhere, federal, provincial and territorial governments would provide two-thirds of the cost of upgrading and expanding the housing stock or, where rental markets exist, of rental subsidies for households in core need. Clearly, the federal government would have to take the lead and supply all the necessary finances on reserves and a major share of the off-reserve requirements.

As shown in Table 4.7, implementation of this 10-year catch-up program will require additional government spending of $228 million in the first year, rising to $774 million by the tenth year. If the federal government maintains the capital subsidy on reserves at about its present level, new funds are needed for payment of mortgage or rental subsidies for newly built and renovated dwellings (in the first year, $23 million on-reserve and $37 million off-reserve). These payments double in the second year and increase by the same amount every year over the 10-year period. New funds are also needed for acceleration of installation and repair of water and sewage systems in communities that have unsafe and inadequate systems. These extra expenditures, however, come to an end after five years.

By the end of the 10-year period, the backlog will have been eliminated and major repairs will no longer be needed. Accordingly, the level of construction and repair activity on-reserve will have dropped by about one-half, and capital subsidies will have been reduced by the same proportion, as will expenditures for expanding infrastructure. The expenditures for infrastructure investment in Table 4.7 are estimated on an assumed cost of $20,000 per unit. After the year 2006, the number of new homes constructed annually on-reserve is projected

TABLE 4.7

Additional Government Expenditures Required to Achieve Adequate Housing for Aboriginal People over 10 Years

	1997	2006	2007
	$ millions		
On-Reserve			
Construction of new dwellings and major repair (5,160 units per year, dropping to 3,000 units after 2006)			
Capital subsidies	169	169	90
Debt servicing (including maintenance)	23	230	242
Heating, electricity and utilities	7	72	76
Program delivery	15	15	15
Government expenditures related to new and repaired dwellings	214	486	423
Maintenance and insurance on existing stock	40	40	40
Total federal housing expenditures on-reserve	254	526	463
Less existing expenditures	(141)	(141)	(141)
Net new federal housing expenditures on-reserve	113	385	322
Net new federal expenditures on water and sanitation systems on-reserve	78	23	(20)
Off-Reserve			
Mortgage and rental subsidies (federal, provincial and territorial governments; 3,860 units per year, dropping to 2,160 units after 2006)	37	366	382
Total incremental government expenditures for housing, water and sanitation	228	774	684

Note: The estimate for water and sewer systems includes $55 million to make existing systems adequate and safe and $23 million to accommodate the increase in the annual volume of new construction.

to decline by 2,150 units, from 5,160 to 3,010 units. Expenditures for debt servicing and heating, electricity and utilities on-reserve and for mortgage and rental subsidies off-reserve are related to the size of the stock of subsidized dwellings and will continue to be required after the catch-up period. Amounts required will increase over the years as more dwellings are added but at a lower rate than during the catch-up period.

On the basis of these projections, additional government expenditures related to housing for Aboriginal people would resume an upward trend after a one-time reduction at the end of the catch-up period. Two other factors need to be considered, however. First, loans for dwellings built before 1996 will be paid off at some point, and subsidies for payments on this debt will no longer be required. Further into the future, loans for construction during catch-up will be repaid. Hence, total government expenditures for Aboriginal housing will not keep rising inexorably in the future.

Second, and more important, if the economic circumstances of Aboriginal people improve, they will assume a larger share of housing costs, and the government share will be reduced accordingly. As noted elsewhere in this report, little progress is evident in this regard, but much greater economic self-reliance certainly is possible if policies are changed. We are convinced that on the basis of policies recommended in this report, significant economic gains are possible for Aboriginal people within 10 to 20 years. This is a key objective of our proposals. If poverty among Aboriginal people were eradicated, not only would expenditures on housing programs be sharply reduced, Aboriginal people would also contribute more revenues to governments. The implications of increasing economic self-reliance for government finances are examined in Volume 5, Chapter 3.

7. Revitalizing Aboriginal Communities Through Housing

7.1 Economic Development

Housing construction and maintenance provide excellent opportunities for Aboriginal employment and business creation because of their high local labour content. It is assumed that construction of a new unit requires 1.5 person-years, and major renovations 0.5 person-years. Needs are as estimated in this chapter, including all 42,700 new dwellings needed off-reserve to accommodate population growth off-reserve. A 10-year effort to meet housing needs will generate approximately 178,000 person-years of employment in the construction sector alone – not counting employment from maintenance and minor renovations and repair – or 17,800 full-time, full-year jobs. This would be close to twice the present level of Aboriginal employment in the sector.[78] To maximize benefits to Aboriginal communities, a focused effort to exploit new economic opportunities must accompany the building program. There will be opportunities to establish new businesses and acquire skills not just in construction, building supplies and financing but also in many other lines of business as more income earned in construction activity is spent in communities.

Considerable Aboriginal capacity already exists. In 1991, 6.1 per cent of Aboriginal adults reported an occupation in the construction sector, compared to 4.0 per cent of Canadians.[79] The proportion of construction businesses in Canada owned by Aboriginal people exceeds the Aboriginal share of the adult population. These businesses provide a wide range of services, from excavation to drywalling, road grading and paving to landscaping.[80] But they tend to be small, counting about three employees per firm, compared to five for other construction firms, and have low revenues per employee. In relation to the distribution of the Aboriginal population, private construction businesses are rather numerous in British Columbia and off-reserve and less common elsewhere.[81] On-reserve one finds more community-owned businesses and independent trades persons.

In isolated Aboriginal communities the construction sector tends to be locally oriented. On remote reserves, a small number of homes are built year after year, and because of the lack of alternative employment opportunities, band governments try to maximize the amount of paid work and on-the-job training. Often, geographic isolation means that there are few opportunities for businesses to expand and for tradespeople to earn income outside the community.

In more densely populated areas, Aboriginal businesses are participating increasingly in the larger markets. At the same time, Aboriginal governments are aiming to get the best value for their housing budgets and will give preference to local contractors only if they are competitive.

A boom in housing construction and repair would do more than create jobs and higher profits. It would enable contractors to take on larger projects and gain experience before venturing into the wider regional market. The Aboriginal construction industry would be able to acquire the more advanced technical and large-project management skills in which it still lags. (See Volume 2, Chapter 5 for a discussion of specialized knowledge and skills needed for economic development.)

Greater gains are possible if communities work together, pooling their resources. For instance, through pooling, construction activity may reach the threshold at which acquisition of specialized equipment becomes profitable. Communities could own and operate businesses jointly or agree to rely on each other's specialized tradespeople, in particular if there is no regional market that offers opportunities for growth and specialization of Aboriginal businesses. An example of the potential for joint action, and one cited in Volume 2, Chapter 5, is the Cree Construction Company (Quebec), established in 1976 with a mandate to construct houses in Cree communities. It later expanded into road construction and maintenance, infrastructure and renovation works, and environmental projects. The company reached just under $66 million in business volume in 1993-94, with a profit of $4,253,000 before taxes and a net profit of $2,678,082. During the peak season that year, 250 Cree were employed throughout the territory.[82]

A similar approach could be taken with building supplies. As almost all Aboriginal communities are too small to have a building supply store and sawmill, pooling of local demand that is boosted by catch-up construction activity will create new opportunities to establish businesses and factories or to make them more competitive. For instance, in Wikwemikong on Manitoulin Island, a building supply store is jointly owned by the First Nations communities in the region. Some communities have not been satisfied with the service and cost-competitiveness of the store, but these problems are now being addressed. There are plans to open a store in Sioux Lookout to supply communities in the region, but it is feared that this might trigger a price war with current suppliers. An increase in demand for materials flowing from greater housing activity will make this store and others like it more viable. There is also potential for spin-off businesses, as illustrated by the community-owned construction company in Fort Chipewyan, which has developed an equipment rental operation.

There is growing interest in using locally produced materials in home construction, and some communities are looking into design and pre-fabrication as a way to provide year-round employment. With building materials, building kits, log homes and prefabricated dwelling components, possibly with Aboriginal designs, it may be feasible to break into national or international markets. In the past decade, the technology of pre-engineered dwellings in Canada has advanced tremendously, to the point where companies are exporting the majority of their products, especially log houses, to the most demanding markets in the world. A Canada-wide Aboriginal building materials corporation could be created to assemble and ship housing kits at lowest cost and with maximum Aboriginal content.

The indirect effects of a housing construction boom on the economic development of Aboriginal communities could far outweigh the opportunities in sectors directly related to housing. A housing boom would bring much more income into communities, which, together with income now spent outside communities, could provide a sufficient market for new local services such as general stores, repair of automobiles and equipment and other services. In Volume 2, Chapter 5 we cited a study conducted for the Shuswap Nation Tribal Council in British Columbia, which found that 81 per cent of all consumer expenditures in the six communities studied were made off-reserve. At an average of $16,700 per household, the 457 households in these communities inject $7.3 million annually into the non-Aboriginal economy.[83] This indicates the potential for developing services in the communities, a potential that would be larger still with the incomes generated by an intensive housing program. Communities would also be able to accumulate savings and build capital for further investment.

To maximize business development, capital needs to be available. As construction activity accelerates, the government should stand ready to supply equity capital to new and expanding businesses. It is unfortunate that business development programs have taken the brunt of federal expenditure restraint; this should be reversed. In Volume 2, Chapter 5 we recommended that the federal government restore funding for programs that provide equity contributions to businesses to the highest level experienced in the last decade.

Small Aboriginal construction firms as a rule are unable to obtain performance bonds, making it difficult for them to break into the wider market and undertake larger projects. Governments sometimes waive the bonding requirement, and some Aboriginal capital corporations have provided a line of credit on occasion, but no general remedy is available. It appears that specific support of Aboriginal firms at strategic moments is necessary. These firms can boost their own preparedness through joint ventures or subcontracting on larger projects.

Throughout our hearings, organizations involved in housing argued that an Aboriginal financing institution should be created to capitalize on opportunities related to housing and ensure that the substantial profits from interest on loans remain within the Aboriginal community. At present, there is only a minimal Aboriginal presence in the financial sector. A few communities have caisses populaires and credit unions involved in local lending activities. The largest independent Aboriginal financial institution is Peace Hills Trust, a full-service trust company.

In Volume 2, Chapter 5 we argued that banking services should be made available in or be accessible within a reasonable distance of all Aboriginal communities, through the establishment of credit unions and bank branches. The demand for mortgage loans, especially during a catch-up housing construction program, will make establishment of credit unions or bank branches more feasible. In a number of First Nations communities, private mortgages without ministerial and band guarantees are a realistic possibility, as methods now exist to use real property on-reserve effectively as security for loans without violating the *Indian Act* or risking alienation of reserve land.[84] Such opportunities may multiply in the future as economic development proceeds and arrangements for housing tenure are clarified.

For many First Nations communities, band governments will continue to deliver housing, and the financing of CMHC-subsidized units will remain the model for some time. This involves loans centrally financed by CMHC or by private institutions or capital market funds. (An example of a private fund is the proposal to create a First Peoples trust, as described in Volume 2, Chapter 5.) Here too opportunities for Aboriginal involvement exist. Two Aboriginal capital corporations (ACCs) have recently begun to act as agents for CMHC. One of these, All Nations Trust of Kamloops, B.C., is incorporated as a trust company and could evolve to become a full-service deposit-taking financial institution. Other ACCs are not so well-positioned, and their small capital base and high-risk lending for small business development do not constitute a good starting point for becoming banking or trust companies. However, involving ACCs and similar Aboriginal institutions in the delivery of mortgage loans makes good business sense, and we believe governments should expand participation of Aboriginal institutions in financing residential mortgages and other loans as opportunities to do so increase and Aboriginal financial and institutional capacity grows.

For maintenance and repair of housing, small-scale solutions that reflect the smaller amount of capital involved may be appropriate. A community savings institution could be involved in lending for renovation projects or new pieces of household equipment, with repayment over a shorter period and with community 'loan circle' repayment schemes. (For more information on community loan circles, see Volume 2, Chapter 5.)

RECOMMENDATION

The Commission recommends that

Economic
Development

3.4.15

The government of Canada help Aboriginal people exploit the economic development opportunities arising from an increase in construction, repair and maintenance of dwellings for Aboriginal people

- by providing funding and support through training and business development programs; and
- by actively expanding the involvement of Aboriginal financial institutions in mortgage financing as agents of CMHC and as mortgage lenders.

7.2 Political, Social and Cultural Benefits

To conclude this chapter, we return to one of its leading themes: the significance of housing for community activity, self-expression and healing. To illustrate this theme, we look at the story of a community that was relocated and obtained funding to rebuild. While most communities will not be able to focus on their housing needs in the same intensive way, the example is nonetheless instructive.

The Cree community of Oujé-Bougoumou, Quebec, chosen by the United Nations as one of 50 exemplary communities around the world, provides a vivid example of how traditional values and culture can be combined with modern design and technology, providing the basis for cultural renewal.[85] Forced out of their homes seven times over five decades to make way for mining developments, deprived of their independent status as a band in 1936, and finally dispersed in 1974 to other communities or relegated to living in shacks beside logging roads, the living conditions of the Oujé-Bougoumou Cree had degenerated by 1986 to a state described in a report prepared for the Grand Council of the Crees of Quebec as the worst in the developed world.

In 1982, they began a long and difficult campaign to regain their rights to their land. An agreement with Quebec was concluded in 1989, though only after a high profile blockade of the main logging road to Nemaska. The agreement provided surface rights to 167 square kilometres of land, together with $25 million toward the construction of a village for their 525 community members and the development of socio-economic programs. In 1992, the federal government contributed an additional $50 million.

The design of the village takes into account more than physical accommodation and encompasses concerns about cultural renewal, economic development, environmental sustainability and social healing. The depth of the feeling about this new village is captured in the words of three of its residents, as recorded by John Goddard:

> I still shiver when I say the word 'home'.
>
> I can't find the words to describe the joy, the happiness, the love I feel in this community.
>
> The hurt and pain is in the past now. I am happy that my two children will not grow up with a lonely feeling in their hearts like I did.[86]

Goddard reports that when Chief Abel Bosum opened the medical clinic, he said that he thinks of the entire village as a healing centre, a place of learning, physical sustenance and spiritual renewal, an environment that produces healthy, secure, confident and optimistic people.

The village, designed by Aboriginal architect Douglas Cardinal, with extensive involvement of community members, has a number of features to foster renewal:

- central buildings that combine teepee shapes with modern forms, houses designed to echo the style of the central buildings and a layout reflecting traditional Cree settlement patterns;
- an open pavilion or *saptuan*, a longhouse-style meeting place that doubles as a skating rink in the winter;
- an innovative district heating system that uses waste sawdust from nearby mills;
- a home ownership program with payments geared to income;
- a school that functions as a place for both learning and recreation and that has become a centre of village life;
- regular workshops to discuss the roles and responsibilities of community living to make the transition from 23 years of dispersion to a significantly altered way of life; and
- a summer work program for youth to help foster a new attitude toward personal effort and wealth creation.

Deciding to develop their village with a district heating system was one of the major decisions the community had to make, because it required a substantial capital investment and the building of energy-efficient homes, while the revenues expected from those houses would be so low that the viability of the district system was not assured. The Oujé-Bougoumou community report, *On the Road to Self-Reliance*, documents their reason for proceeding with the system:

> The key to understanding the community's decision is that they viewed the district heating system as an integral part of the future socio-economic development of the community, and thereby, having an impact on local employment, on future community projects and on their innovative housing program. They were not looking strictly at short-term economic return. They had instead adopted a pro-foundly comprehensive view of community economics and were convinced that the community as a whole would reap substantial benefits from the installation of a district heating system.

Over the long term, the Commission sees an increasing capacity to make housing and community services a centrepiece of cultural and community renewal because they are so tangible and visible. Indeed, we believe housing can and should be a key part of community healing and of cultural revival and self-definition among Aboriginal peoples. Aboriginal design and environmental technologies could reflect the rich history and the deep environmental sensitivity of communities and regions.

The opportunities range from actual use of heritage designs to new versions of housing that capture the spirit of historical dwelling designs and carry it forward in a contemporary way. Distinctive Aboriginal housing could make a significant contribution to a more vibrant and liveable Canada.

Because poor quality housing and community services are reflections of poverty and a deeper malaise as well as contributors to them, appropriate actions to improve living conditions are a vital part of community building. However, when provided without participation or close attention to individual and community needs, housing and community services become yet another message of dependency and subordinate status. The lessons of Oujé-Bougoumou underscore this point. In the words of Chief Abel Bosum:

> Now we are no longer the 'forgotten Crees'. We are no longer the passive victims of industrial forces, no longer the pathetic, oppressed people seeking the sympathy of others. Instead, we have become daring innovators and self-confident planners.
>
> Instead of winning people's sympathy, we are now gaining their respect.[87]

NOTES

1. To place these expenditures in context, in 1993-1994, all governments combined spent $3.9 billion on housing for Canadians in need. (Statistics Canada, "Public Sector Finance, 1994-1995: Financial Management System", catalogue no. 68-212, Table 1.33.) Expenditures on social housing (assistance to households in need that cannot obtain affordable, suitable and adequate shelter in the private market) by the Canada Mortgage and Housing Corporation (CMHC) were in excess of $2 billion in the same year. In addition, governments provide shelter allowances to households dependent on social assistance.

2. Statistics Canada, Aboriginal Peoples Survey (APS), "1-Disability, 2-Housing", catalogue no. 89-535.

3. The source of the figures for Canada as a whole is Statistics Canada, "Household Facilities and Equipment, 1995", Catalogue No. 64-202. Caution must be used in comparing data from this catalogue with APS figures since categories and samples used are somewhat different. (For a general discussion of the sources of data used by the Commission in this report, see Volume 1, Chapter 2, particularly the endnotes.) However, overall patterns seem clear enough. Since the Canadian data include Aboriginal households (except those living on reserves), disparities may appear somewhat smaller than if Aboriginal households were excluded. In Table 4.1 and Table 4.2, the general Canadian data include only non-farm, non-reserve dwellings. The Aboriginal data include all non-farm dwellings, including those on reserves, where at least one of the occupants self-identifies as an Aboriginal person. Note that tenant-occupied dwellings do not include band-owned housing, which is treated as a separate category (see Table 4.2). 'Owner's major payments per month' refers to the average monthly payments made by the owner to secure shelter.

4. DIAND and CMHC made their estimates of housing need available to the Royal Commission on Aboriginal Peoples.

5. The estimate of Canadian households in core need was published by CMHC in *Research and Development Highlights*, Socio-Economic Series "Canadian Housing Need, 1991", Issue 11 (Ottawa: CMHC, 1993). This estimate is based on the household income, facilities and equipment data base at Statistics Canada (which contains data from several sources, including the household facilities and equipment survey, on which the Canadian data in Table 4.1 are based), whereas the estimate for Aboriginal people off-reserve is based on the Aboriginal peoples survey. The two sources are not consistent, and the number given for the Aboriginal share of households in core need must therefore be treated with caution.

6. Transcripts of the Royal Commission on Aboriginal Peoples [hereafter RCAP transcripts], Orillia, Ontario, 12 May 1993.

7. RCAP transcripts, Lethbridge, Alberta, 25 May 1993.

8. RCAP transcripts, Vancouver, British Columbia, 3 June 1993.

9. According to 1993-94 data from *Canadian Housing Statistics, 1994*, CMHC social housing made up about 20 per cent of housing on reserves, 13 per cent of urban Aboriginal housing, and less than 9 per cent of Aboriginal housing in rural areas and smaller communities. DIAND also provides assistance for housing in First Nations communities, but its program has tended to deliver poorly built, rapidly deteriorating dwellings.

10. Chapter 3 of this volume documents the higher rates among Aboriginal people of illness and death due to infectious diseases. Press reports continue to add to the body of evidence. For example, the Mathias Colomb Cree Nation in northern Manitoba recently reported 300 cases of hepatitis and 12 cases of TB among the 1,960 residents of the reserve, and several other health problems. Among the probable causes are overcrowding (few homes have been built in the past few years because of large debts), a water supply contaminated by seepage from a sewage lagoon, toxic gases from an old industrial site over which a school gymnasium was built, and methane gas build-up from a deteriorated sewer line under one of the homes. "Home, horrible home", *Winnipeg Free Press*, Sunday, 5 November 1995, p. A5; and "Indians blame polluted land for epidemic of hepatitis, TB", *Globe and Mail*, 23 November 1995, p. A3.

11. The Aboriginal rate of deaths from fire is 3.5 times the non-Aboriginal rate, as reported in House of Commons, Fourth Report of the Standing Committee on Aboriginal Affairs, *A Time for Action: Aboriginal and Northern Housing* (Ottawa: December 1992).

12. Obonsawin-Irwin Consulting, "Aboriginal Self-Determination: The Role of Aboriginal Urban Housing Initiatives", research study prepared for the Royal Commission on Aboriginal Peoples [RCAP] (1994). For information about research studies prepared for RCAP, see *A Note About Sources* at the beginning of this volume. The four case studies (research studies prepared for RCAP) are MEWS Corporation (Stan Willox), "Urban Aboriginal Housing Project, Case Study: Gabriel Housing Corporation" (1993); H.P. Consultants, "Skigin-Elnoog Housing Corporation" (1993); George W. Miller, "Inuit Non-Profit Housing Corporation of Ottawa: A Case Study"; and Obonsawin-Irwin Consulting, "A Case Study of Urban Native Homes Inc. of Hamilton" (1993).

13. Department of Indian Affairs and Northern Development [DIAND], *Laying the Foundations of a New On-Reserve Housing Program, Discussion Paper* (Ottawa: Supply and Services, 1990), pp. 1-2.

14. Liberal Party of Canada, *Creating Opportunity: The Liberal Plan for Canada* (Ottawa: Liberal Party of Canada, 1993), p. 100.

15. Assembly of First Nations, Presentation to the Standing Committee on Aboriginal Affairs on First Nations' Housing, 18 February 1992, as quoted in *A Time for Action*, Standing Committee on Aboriginal Affairs (cited in note 11), p. 23.

16. Assembly of First Nations, "Reclaiming Our Nationhood, Strengthening Our Heritage: Report to the Royal Commission on Aboriginal Peoples (1993), rec-

ommendation 92. For information about briefs submitted to RCAP, see *A Note About Sources* at the beginning of this volume."

17. Tony Coté, director, Saskatchewan Indian Housing Corporation, in House of Commons, *Minutes of Proceedings and Evidence of the Standing Committee on Aboriginal Affairs*, Issue No. 23 (Ottawa: Queen's Printer, 1992), p. 9.

18. Statistics Canada, "Public Sector Finance" (cited in note 1).

19. The first steps toward a review of the on-reserve housing policy were taken in 1988. The discussion paper *Laying the Foundations* (cited in note 13) was issued in 1990. To date, no new policies have been announced.

20. National Aboriginal Housing Committee, "First Our Lands, Now Our Homes...A Response to the Urban and Rural Native Housing Crisis Created by Canada's Federal Budget Cutbacks", brief submitted to RCAP (1993), p. 5.

21. National Aboriginal Housing Committee, "First Our Lands, Now Our Homes", p. 8.

22. See also Attorney General of Ontario, "The Protection of Social and Economic Rights: A Comparative Study", Staff Paper, Constitutional Law and Policy Division, Ministry of the Attorney General of Ontario, 19 September 1991.

23. The right of Aboriginal people to a land and economic base is also beginning to be asserted in international law. A Draft Declaration on the Rights of Indigenous Peoples is being developed by the United Nations Working Group on Indigenous Populations and recognizes Indigenous peoples' rights to territory and to "freely pursue their economic, social and cultural development".

24. This obligation of governments is also being asserted in international forums. Article 22 of the UN Draft Declaration on the Rights of Indigenous Peoples states: "Indigenous peoples have the right to special measures for the immediate, effective and continuing improvement of their economic and social conditions, including in the areas of employment, vocational training and retraining, housing, sanitation, health and social security."

25. Health Canada and DIAND, *Community Drinking Water and Sewage Treatment in First Nations Communities* (Ottawa: Public Works and Government Services, 1995).

26. The federal government pays about 80 per cent of the cost of installing and operating sewage systems; service charges cover the remaining 20 per cent.

27. Government of Canada, *The State of Canada's Environment* (Ottawa: Supply and Services, 1991).

28. DIAND, *Arctic Environmental Strategy Progress Report* (Ottawa: 1995).

29. The Green Plan funds have been integrated into the annual budgets for DIAND and are not identified separately in the estimates or the public accounts. See DIAND and Canadian Polar Commission, *1995-96 Estimates*, Part III: *Expenditure Plan* (Ottawa: Supply and Services, 1995).

30. Health Canada and DIAND, *Community Drinking Water and Sewage Treatment* (cited in note 25), pp. 10 and 13. Probably close to two-thirds of the amount spent was for site preparation and servicing of new dwellings. At an average investment of $20,000 per dwelling (an average reflecting recent experience) and approximately 4,000 dwellings per year, $320 million would have been needed over four years for new dwellings. Thus, $167.6 million or just over one-third of the total of $487.6 million would have been available for improvement of inadequate systems. This is confirmed by data from the *Housing and Infrastructure Report, 1994*, and the main estimates of 1991-92 to 1995-96, showing that $98 million out of $270 million for water and sewer projects was spent in communities lacking adequate systems or having only partial systems, while the other two-thirds was used to hook up newly built homes. (Only projects with a total value of more than $1 million are listed in the estimates.)

31. DIAND and Canadian Polar Commission, *1995-96 Estimates* (cited in note 29). No comparable data are available for Canadian homes.

32. This estimate is based on the assumption that the systems for which no engineering studies have been completed will cost as much, on average, as those costed. As costs of construction and repair vary widely among systems, this figure is only an approximation. On 10 July 1996 the government announced that it would reallocate $98.5 million within the existing DIAND budget to accelerate work on First Nations community water and sewage systems.

33. Approximately one-third of capital spending on sewer and water systems over the past four years was on sites with inadequate facilities.

34. See Figure 40, Details of Major Capital Projects, in *1995-96 Estimates* (cited in note 29).

35. 'Small community flows' refers to miniaturized water and sewage systems. Facilities in dwellings are designed to minimize use of water and accumulation of wastewater. Water is supplied and wastewater collected by small haul tanks pulled by tractors, snowmobiles or all-terrain vehicles.

36. Health Canada and DIAND, *Community Drinking Water and Sewage Treatment* (cited in note 25), p. 14.

37. In 1994-95, DIAND allocated $27.5 million to operating water systems and $12.6 million for wastewater. Almost half the funds relates to water delivery and wastewater removal by truck plus payments to municipalities for services. In addition, DIAND allocated $1.2 million to management and training related to community service systems. Information provided by Finance Branch, DIAND.

38. Health Canada and DIAND, *Community Drinking Water and Sewage Treatment* (cited in note 25), p. 19.

39. These numbers are based on data provided by DIAND and differ from Tables 4.1 and 4.2, which are based on the Aboriginal peoples survey (APS).

40. As of 1995, the maximum loan size was $27,000, and the forgivable portion ranged from $12,000 to $18,000. A supplement of 25 per cent for both the loan and forgivable portion is provided in areas defined as remote. Between 1988 and 1995, CMHC also delivered an initiative to counter violence within families, in which forgivable loans were provided for emergency and interim accommodation for victims of family violence, with expenditures of $7.2 million in Aboriginal communities.

41. The cost of maintenance and loan repayment for CMHC units is covered by three sources: rents paid by occupants based on their income; shelter allowances from DIAND for social assistance recipients; and the CMHC rental subsidy. A large majority of households in CMHC units on-reserve are dependent on social assistance. DIAND had also made commitments to pay shelter allowances for social assistance recipients living in housing projects that are privately financed without CMHC subsidies, but only when most of the cost of the project was met by charges to the occupants. However, DIAND is now making virtually no new commitments to pay shelter allowances as there is no guarantee it can meet these obligations under its present budget.

42. Approximately 32,000 households on-reserve receive social assistance (43 per cent of 74,000). Of these, about 10,000 are in CMHC-subsidized social housing (two-thirds of 15,000) and receive shelter allowances. The residual, 22,000 households, accounts for 29.7 per cent of the 74,000 households on-reserve.

43. Among other arguments made to defend this policy is the government's opposition to 'double dipping' into two types of DIAND subsidies, that is, for both construction and maintenance costs. However, the construction subsidies offered by DIAND do not cover the cost even of building an adequate dwelling for a low-income household, much less provide for maintenance and insurance costs. The full construction cost of an adequate dwelling on a typical reserve is between $80,000 and $90,000, with annual maintenance and insurance costs of around $1,200 to $1,500. Against this total, DIAND contributes from $19,000 to $46,000 (with an average of $30,000) on a one-time basis. Moreover, there is no provision against such double-dipping for social housing elsewhere or for dwellings on reserves built with CMHC assistance, where many people on social assistance live.

    It is also argued that people should be accountable for the funds they are given for rent. It may be that these funds are not being used for housing at all but for other purposes according to decisions made by the chief and council. This of course can be addressed by developing maintenance systems and keeping separate accounts.

44. This statement concerns only the cost of maintenance and insurance of dwellings. The average cost of maintaining a dwelling is $1,000 per year, according to Statistics Canada figures, and a modest insurance package may cost $300 per year. To pay the 22,000 households dependent on social assistance and not living in CMHC-subsidized homes a shelter allowance of $1,000 would cost approximately $40 million annually, or $400 million over 1983 to 1992.

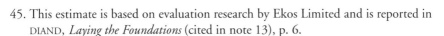

45. This estimate is based on evaluation research by Ekos Limited and is reported in DIAND, *Laying the Foundations* (cited in note 13), p. 6.

46. Housing corporations on reserves either did not actively seek or failed to obtain the benefits of greater social housing subsidies made available in 1986, when the overall design of CMHC's programs was modified. From 1979 to 1986, the aim of Canada's social housing policy was to foster an income mix in housing developments, and CMHC provided a subsidy related to the interest cost of financing projects. This policy continued to apply on reserves after 1986. The subsidy reduced the cost of financing eligible capital cost from market rates of interest to interest at two per cent. As the DIAND capital subsidy and a nominal value for land could be included in eligible capital, the actual loan amount taken out by bands was often much lower than the amount on which the subsidy was based. When interest rates declined, the CMHC subsidy dropped more sharply than the cost of loan servicing and operations related to social housing on reserves.

47. Bands take out loans in connection with CMHC projects and are responsible for meeting monthly debt payments. CMHC pays its subsidy to the band. If a band fails to meet its loan payments, the lender has the right to demand payment under the ministerial guarantee. DIAND will then pay the lender and recover funds from the band. CMHC may withhold its subsidy if the band fails to meet terms of its agreements with CMHC and may also cease to undertake new housing projects with that band.

48. DIAND, *Laying the Foundations* (cited in note 13), p. 19.

49. Section 83(1)(a) of the *Indian Act* provides that the council of a band may, subject to the approval of the minister, make by-laws for "taxation of interests in land in the reserve of persons lawfully in possession thereof...".

50. DIAND, *Laying the Foundation* (cited in note 13), p. 19.

51. Greater economic self-reliance will also generate extra government revenues that can help cover the cost of housing assistance programs. See Volume 5, Chapter 3 for further comments on the fiscal effects of greater economic self-reliance of Aboriginal people.

52. "Historic housing program a lesson for La Loche", letter from Dennis Strom, *The Northerner*, La Ronge, Saskatchewan, 12 September 1995.

53. Habitat for Humanity is a non-profit, charitable organization that over the past 20 years has built and renovated homes for low-income families in need in more than 40 countries. The organization has been active in Canada for more than 10 years and has 46 affiliates. From its Canadian headquarters in Waterloo, Ontario, the organization assembles volunteers, uses many donated materials, and offers preferential loans to homeowners and prospective homeowners, who must contribute a substantial amount of time (500 hours) to building their own and other homes. In Volume 4, Chapter 4 we advocate the Habitat for Humanity approach as a way of bridging the wage and non-wage economies and empowering youth, who by vol-

unteering labour can learn marketable skills and acquire credits that can be put toward home ownership.

54. Under the Australian community development program introduced in 1977, remote Aboriginal communities can initiate economic and social development projects that are funded in part by social assistance payments to members of the community. Social assistance recipients become employees of the community in these projects, which have to be approved by the Aboriginal and Torres Strait Islanders Commission.

55. It should be noted that this standard approach was criticized throughout the Commission's hearings as being too inflexible in remote areas, where cash incomes are low and many people are engaged in traditional activities.

56. For instance, in *Laying the Foundations* (cited in note 13), DIAND raised the possibility that the government would make payments to match the equity contributions of home buyers.

57. Gesgapegiag (population, 400) is a Mi'kmaq community located in the Gaspé on the Baie des Chaleurs, 60 kilometres east of Restigouche.

58. Of the approximately 74,000 dwelling units counted in 1993-94, 6,000 needed to be replaced and 13,000 needed major repair, according to DIAND data. There was also a backlog of 11,000 people wanting their own homes.

It is expected that 7,800 more units will have been built by the end of 1995-96, of which 1,800 will be financed with CMHC assistance. Over the same period, 1,500 units will be lost (one per cent of the stock per year). The net result is that the housing stock will have increased to just over 80,000 by the spring of 1997. Assuming that the need for replacement and major repair is proportional to the size of the stock and that the backlog will remain the same, by 1997 17,500 new units and major repairs to 14,000 units will be needed. These are current needs.

To assist in assessing future needs, the demographic projections prepared for RCAP foresee the on-reserve population aged 15 to 64 increasing from 184,100 to 245,900 by the year 2006. With 91,000 households in 1996 (80,000 dwelling units plus a backlog of 11,000 homes), 30,100 more units will have to be built over the 10 years from 1997 to 2006 if household formation keeps pace with the increase in the population aged 15 to 64. It is further assumed that one per cent of the stock will be lost or fall into disrepair every year for five years, after which regular maintenance programs, and in particular funding by DIAND of regular maintenance for social assistance recipients, will prevent homes being lost. We also assume that no further major renovations are necessary as a result of improved maintenance. Hence, future needs consist of 30,100 units to accommodate the growth in the number of households on reserves and 4,000 replacement units, for a total of 25,000.

Thus, over the period 1997-2006, the value of construction is 51,600 new units at $90,000 each, for a total of $4,644 million, plus major repairs at $30,000 each to 14,000 units for $420 million. Spread out over the ten years, the value of construction would be $506 million per year.

It is worth noting that these estimates reflect a very high standard: a fully adequate housing stock in excellent condition. For instance, we assume that all major repairs and renovations required will be made by the year 2006. Compare this with the fact that in 1991 eight per cent of the Canadian housing stock was in need of major repair or renovation.

59. The government could make this contribution by maintaining the DIAND capital subsidy and adding CMHC-subsidized loan financing for the large majority of new homes built on-reserve. Alternatively, it could rely on loans to a greater extent and reduce the amortization period below the usual 25 years so that loans are repaid faster.

60. CMHC has supported First Nations communities and tribal councils in establishing a capacity to conduct Native Housing Inspection Services inspections on a fee-for-service basis.

61. This chapter is based on housing conditions and government policy as of mid-1995. On 25 July 1996, just before this report was printed, the government announced a new approach for on-reserve housing that includes some of the directions we propose in this chapter and an increase in the budget for on-reserve housing of $140 million over the next five years. The amount will be found through reallocations within existing DIAND and CMHC budgets.

62. On the whole, CMHC programs cannot be restricted according to the ethnic or racial origin of recipients. Accordingly, only the Urban Native Housing Program provides assistance exclusively to Aboriginal people. It is estimated that, between 1986 and 1993, 44 per cent of the funding in the Rural and Native Housing Program was directed to Aboriginal people, and for the Emergency Repair Program Aboriginal people received 51 per cent. Aboriginal people accounted for about seven per cent of the Residential Rehabilitation Assistance Program in rural areas.

63. Inuit Tapirisat of Canada, *Towards an Inuit Housing Policy*, paper prepared for CMHC (1994).

64. RCAP transcripts, Hay River, N.W.T., 17 June 1993.

65. See Tony Andersen, Chairman, Board of Directors, Torngat Regional Housing Association, RCAP transcripts, Nain, Newfoundland and Labrador, 30 November 1992.

66. RCAP transcripts, Charlottetown, Prince Edward Island, 5 May 1992.

67. Manitoba Metis Federation, "Submission to the Royal Commission on Aboriginal Peoples", Intervenor Participation Program report to RCAP (1992).

68. See presentation by the National Aboriginal Housing Committee, RCAP transcripts, Vancouver, British Columbia, 3 June 1993.

69. Statistics Canada, 1991 Aboriginal Peoples Survey, custom tabulations, 1994.

70. Obonsawin-Irwin Consulting, "Aboriginal Self-Determination" (cited in note 12).

71. MEWS Corporation (Stan Willox), "Case Study: Gabriel Housing Corporation" (cited in note 12).

72. The discussion on Aboriginal housing corporations draws from the research study prepared by Obonsawin-Irwin Consulting, "Aboriginal Self-Determination" (cited in note 12).

73. Peter Holland, DEL Support Centre, "Management Training Needs of Urban Native Housing Projects", research project prepared for CMHC (1988).

74. See for instance CMHC, *Strategic Plan, 1992-1996* (Ottawa: Canada Mortgage and Housing Corporation, 1991), p. 26.

75. There has never been a successful case under provincial human rights legislation of proven discrimination by a private landlord on the grounds of the applicant's poverty. Few cases have been brought to human rights tribunals on the basis of racial discrimination. The reality has been that, by the time lengthy inquiry and hearing processes are completed, the dwelling in question has long since been rented to another household. Evicting the new occupants would lead to further legal challenges if they are reliable tenants. Moreover, in the case of other forms of discrimination in housing – such as not providing adequate services or living conditions – recourse has rarely been sought by Aboriginal people, who have been too concerned about keeping the dwelling they have, regardless of its condition, or unaware of their rights as tenants.

76. According to the APS, of householders with at least one member identifying as an Aboriginal person, there were 199,400 households not living on reserves. Of the dwellings they occupied, 31,600 were in need of major repair, and 14,400 respondents indicated that there were people living in the dwellings who were on a waiting list for housing. As of 1996, these numbers are assumed to be 17.5 per cent larger, reflecting population growth and adjustment for the APS population for underreporting. This Aboriginal population is expected to grow by 26 per cent over the 10 years from 1996 to 2006, from a base of 251,300 units (234,300 units plus a backlog of 17,000). Thus, to accommodate household formation resulting from population growth, 64,800 units will be required. One-third of the new households are assumed to be in core need.

77. At a cost of $90,000 per new dwelling and $30,000 for a major repair, the total capital cost of 38,600 new units and 37,000 major repairs is $4,584 million. It is assumed that rent or mortgage payments plus the cost of maintenance and insurance are one per cent of these capital values per month, and that construction takes place evenly over the 10 years. Note that the estimate of construction and repair needs includes only dwellings with major deficiencies and households that are in core need or do not have a home of their own. This narrow definition of needs warrants a high government share of cost. It is assumed that households will meet the cost of heating, electricity and utilities of new dwellings.

As mentioned earlier in the chapter, in the case of housing on reserves, these estimates reflect a high standard, one that exceeds the present quality of the Canadian housing stock as a whole. To realize the proposed program, governments will probably also have to provide more assistance to non-Aboriginal people in housing need. By contrast, part of the backlog in housing can possibly be met by renovating existing homes, at considerable savings.

78. See Informetrica, "Aboriginal Construction Sector Capability Study", final report prepared for DIAND (1995), note 3.

79. 1991 Aboriginal Peoples Survey, custom tabulations; and Statistics Canada, "Occupation – The Nation", catalogue no. 93-327.

80. Examples provided by the federal department of industry, drawn from a list of more than 300 projects funded by Aboriginal Business Canada since 1989.

81. See Informetrica, "Aboriginal Construction Sector Capability Study" (cited in note 78).

82. Cree Regional Economic Enterprises Company (CREECO), *Annual Report*, 1993-94.

83. André LeDressay, "A Brief Tax(on a me) of First Nations Taxation and Economic Development", in *Sharing the Harvest: The Road to Self-Reliance*, Report of the National Round Table on Aboriginal Economic Development and Resources (Ottawa: RCAP, 1993), p. 215.

84. The caisse populaire at Kahnawake has involved members of the community as trustees who take over assets from the borrower in case of default. This model is now being applied at Akwesasne by the Bank of Montreal.

85. The story of the Oujé-Bougoumou is recounted in Volume 1, Chapter 11. This section is based on John Goddard, "In from the Cold", *Canadian Geographic* 114/4 (July/August 1994), p. 39; and *On the Road to Self-Reliance: The Impact of Alternative Energy Technology on Community Development,* An Oujé-Bougoumou Community Report (1993).

86. Goddard, "In from the Cold", p. 39.

87. Goddard, "In from the Cold", p. 47.

5

EDUCATION

Among the Dene, it is said the child is born with a drum in its hand...

The child is born with integrity.

The child has worth.

It is the birthright of the Dene child to be acknowledged and respected for this.

The child who is not respected cannot become what it is meant to be.[1]

IN ABORIGINAL SOCIETIES, as in many societies, children are regarded as a precious gift. Control over the education of their children has been a pressing priority of Aboriginal peoples for decades. This is not surprising. The destiny of a people is intricately bound to the way its children are educated. Education is the transmission of cultural DNA from one generation to the next. It shapes the language and pathways of thinking, the contours of character and values, the social skills and creative potential of the individual. It determines the productive skills of a people.

Aboriginal peoples are diverse in their histories, environments and cultures, but their deep commitment to education cuts across all boundaries. In our public hearings, Aboriginal parents, elders, youth and leaders came forward to tell us of the vital importance of education in achieving their vision of a prosperous future. Education is seen as the vehicle for both enhancing the life of the individual and reaching collective goals.

For more than 25 years, Aboriginal people have been articulating their goals for Aboriginal education. They want education to prepare them to participate fully in the economic life of their communities and in Canadian society. But this is only part of their vision. Presenters told us that education must develop children and youth as Aboriginal citizens, linguistically and culturally competent to assume the responsibilities of their nations. Youth that emerge from school must be grounded in a strong, positive Aboriginal identity. Consistent with Aboriginal traditions, education must develop the whole child, intellectually, spiritually, emotionally and physically.

Current education policies fail to realize these goals. The majority of Aboriginal youth do not complete high school. They leave the school system without the requisite skills for employment, and without the language and cultural knowledge of their people. Rather than nurturing the individual, the schooling experience typically erodes identity and self-worth. Those who continue in Canada's formal education systems told us of regular encounters with racism, racism expressed not only in interpersonal exchanges but also through the denial of Aboriginal values, perspectives and cultures in the curriculum and the life of the institution.

The human costs of this failure are immense. It saps the creative potential of individuals, communities and nations. Yet, despite the painful experiences Aboriginal people carry with them from formal education systems, they still see education as the hope for the future, and they are determined to see education fulfil its promise.

Aboriginal people rightly expect education to serve as a vehicle for cultural and economic renewal. But this will not happen without critical changes in education processes and systems. To grasp the directions education should take in the future, we must first understand how the present situation came to be. This chapter provides the historical context of Aboriginal education and presents some of the important initiatives introduced in Aboriginal education in recent years as a foundation for goals and strategies for the future.

1. BACKGROUND

The introduction of European-style education to Aboriginal people varied by geographical location, by the timing of contact, and by the specific history of relations between various peoples and Europeans. In some regions, schools operated by religious missions were introduced in the mid-1600s. In other locations, formal education came much later. But if there were many variations in the weave of history, a single pattern dominated the education of Aboriginal people, whatever their territorial and cultural origins. Formal education was, without apology, assimilationist. The primary purpose of formal education was to indoctrinate Aboriginal people into a Christian, European world view, thereby 'civilizing' them. Missionaries of various denominations played a role in this process, often supported by the state.

Under its constitutional responsibility for "Indians, and Lands reserved for the Indians", the federal government enacted provisions in the *Indian Act* applying to the education of status Indians. In the late 1800s and early 1900s, the numbered treaties were signed, and tribal leaders negotiated education provisions as part of the treaties. In the provinces, the federal government gradually withdrew from funding the education of Aboriginal people not residing on reserves, but not without protests from some of the provinces, which were reluctant to assume these costs.

In carrying out its responsibilities for Indian education, the federal government turned to the churches, which shared the government's goal of imparting Christian, European values. In Volume 1, Chapter 10, we recounted how residential schools were used deliberately to break down the transmission of culture and language from one generation to the next. For nearly a century, parents and grandparents in reserve communities were legally compelled to turn their children over to the custody of residential school authorities. Children were beaten for speaking their own language, and Aboriginal beliefs were labelled 'pagan'. In many schools, sisters and brothers were forbidden social contact, and the warmth of the intergenerational Aboriginal family was replaced with sterile institutional child rearing. Many residents endured sexual and physical abuse. Hard labour and hunger were part of the experience of many children. Those who tried to run away were returned to be punished and rehabilitated. The effects of these coercive efforts at social engineering continue to be felt generations later. (See Chapter 2 in this volume, particularly our discussion of the inter-generational effects of state interventions in Aboriginal family life.)

From early contact, education for Métis people emphasized religious studies, with some basic arithmetic and writing. Métis people in some areas attended residential schools, and in the northwest, the sons of affluent Métis received the formal education of the privileged, often being sent to eastern Canada or England for higher education. Missionaries provided limited instruction to the children of Métis people who followed the migration of the buffalo. However, most Métis in rural and northern areas had little access to more than primary school until the 1950s. According to the report of Alberta's Ewing Commission in 1936, 80 per cent of Métis children in the province had no schooling at all.[2]

Among Inuit, formal education in the north arrived at various times. In Labrador, the first school was begun by the Moravians in 1791. From the age of five years, children were taught to read and write in their own language. By the early 1800s, the New Testament and hymn books had been translated into Inuktitut and were used to teach children and adults alike. Christian Inuit were required to send their children to school, and by 1840 most Christian Inuit could read and write in Inuktitut.[3] When Newfoundland joined Confederation in 1949, the language of instruction became English, eroding Inuktitut language use.

In other parts of northern Canada, formal schooling of Inuit began much later. Contrary to the experience of Inuit in Labrador, teaching in the local language was not commonplace elsewhere in the north. Inuit attended residential schools in some areas and missionary-run schools in others. In the 1950s, Inuit were encouraged to move into permanent settlements by making school attendance by children compulsory.[4]

With few exceptions, assimilationist education predominated in schools established under government or church authority. Although elementary day schools supported by the federal government continue to be a characteristic of schooling on-reserve, in the 1960s the federal government pursued a policy of integrating children from reserves into nearby provincial schools or boarding children with families in urban centres to attend high school. Also in the 1960s, provincial governments in the west formed large school districts in northern areas of their provinces with some Aboriginal representation. At the same time, a growing number of Aboriginal people moved from employment-starved rural areas into urban centres, expanding the number of Aboriginal students in city schools. Residential schools continued to operate into the 1970s.

In 1972 the National Indian Brotherhood (the forerunner of the Assembly of First Nations) produced a policy statement, "Indian Control of Indian Education", which marked a watershed in Aboriginal education. This statement sent a clear, unequivocal call for local control of education by First Nations communities and parents. It recognized the failure of federal, provincial and territorial governments to implement appropriate policies to address First Nations goals for education. From 1972 on, discussion between First Nations and the state shifted to restoring control of education in all its dimensions to First Nations parents and communities. Inuit and Métis people voiced similar concerns.

In the next section we review briefly what has happened since 1972 and consider current arrangements for the education of Aboriginal children on reserves, in the Northwest Territories and the Yukon, in contexts where modern treaties have already been concluded, and in provincial schools.

1.1 First Nations Reserves

The federal government's response to "Indian Control of Indian Education" was to adopt a 'devolution' approach, transferring the administration of education to Aboriginal education authorities in reserve communities. This has been a slow process, still under way more than twenty years later. Since 1972 residential schools have been phased out, federal day schools have dropped in number, and the number of schools under Aboriginal administration has grown proportionately. Aboriginally controlled schools have hired more Aboriginal teachers, enhanced curriculum to include cultural elements and introduced language classes. Yet Aboriginal education bodies report that their authority over education is limited. The federal government has generally insisted that schools conform to provincial regulations with respect to curriculum, school year and so on, thereby restricting schools' ability to include innovative, culture-based curriculum. Funding is very basic, with little money for Aboriginal curriculum development and few resources to address special needs. While the number of band-operated schools has grown steadily (51 per cent of federally funded schools in 1993-94[5]), almost half of First Nations children whose parents live on reserves attend provincial schools off the reserve. The federal government transfers funding to provincial schools to provide these services. Until recently, First Nations have had no control over these transfers and no opportunity to influence how education services are delivered. More recently, they have gained some involvement in negotiating agreements for education service delivery by outside authorities. There was a significant shift toward more Aboriginal control of education in 1994 when the Mi'kmaq Education Authority concluded an agreement with federal authorities for more autonomy.[6]

1.2 The Northwest Territories and the Yukon

An effort is being made to revise the education acts of the Northwest Territories and the Yukon through consultation with Aboriginal people. Aboriginal languages have recognition in the Northwest Territories generally. In the school system, two culturally based curriculum projects have been undertaken with extensive community involvement: Dene Kede and Inuuqatigiit. Among youth proceeding to higher levels of education, Aboriginal students continue to be under-represented. Although Métis people speak the Dene languages, their own language, Michif, has not been incorporated into the school system, nor has a culturally based Métis curriculum been developed.

In the Yukon, local autonomy has been very limited. However, under the provisions of the Umbrella Final Agreement negotiated with the Council of Yukon Indians, education now falls within the legislative powers that can be exercised by First Nations.[7]

1.3 Modern Claims Settlement Areas

Education has been a priority in the settlement of some modern land claims. The James Bay and Northern Quebec Agreement (1975) provided for the creation of the Kativik and Cree school boards, each considered a special school board in the legislation adopted subsequently by the province of Quebec. The Kativik school board is controlled and operated by Inuit of Nunavik (14 communities) and has jurisdiction and responsibility for elementary, secondary and adult education for all people, including non-Inuit, living in the territory. While it exercises a high degree of control over education, it is still obliged to follow the Quebec provincial curriculum. The Cree school board performs a similar function for the Crees of northern Quebec and operates with parallel constraints.

Other claims settlements, such as the Yukon agreement, have also addressed education concerns. For communities under the Inuvialuit agreement, education is administered by the government of the Northwest Territories. In 1999, Nunavut is expected to assume jurisdiction for education from the government of the Northwest Territories.

1.4 The Provinces

The majority of Aboriginal children outside of the territories – First Nations, Métis and some Inuit – attend provincial schools. Métis children attend provincial and territorial schools almost exclusively. As shown in Table 5.1, about 42 per cent of First Nations people lived off-reserve in 1991, and in almost all instances, their children attended provincial schools.[8] In the same year, 46 per cent of students residing on reserves attended provincial schools.[9] Thus, 68.7 per cent of First Nations students were in provincial school systems.

Provincial schools have varied in their receptivity to Aboriginal children. In some locations where there are many Aboriginal children, schools have opened their doors to Aboriginal parents and developed vibrant community/school programs. In Toronto, Saskatoon and Winnipeg, school boards have negotiated to establish Aboriginal schools. These are the exception. Most Aboriginal students attend schools where there is no special effort to make them or their families feel part of the life of the school. Aboriginal parents say they are excluded from their children's education. There is a gap between the culture of the home and that of the school. In very few instances are Aboriginal people among the representatives on school boards.

Except in a few northern areas where they constitute a majority of residents, Métis people have had minimal influence on the schooling of their children. Their history and languages have received only limited attention in school curricula. Where there have been special initiatives, First Nations culture, languages and issues are often given more prominence than those of Métis. In the prairie provinces, there has been more government recognition and respect for Métis concerns in education.

There have been many important initiatives by provincial governments and school boards to create a more positive learning environment for Aboriginal children. Aboriginal support staff have often been hired, curriculum has been reviewed to eliminate obvious racism, alternative programs have been established to assist students at risk, and Aboriginal teachers are being hired, particularly at the elementary school level. Aboriginal youth are staying in school longer. There have been gains, but these have been too modest. As shown in Figure 5.1, in 1981, 63 per cent of Aboriginal people 15 years or older no longer attending school had completed primary school, and 29 per cent had completed high school. A decade later, 76 per cent of Aboriginal people over 15 had completed primary school, and 43 per cent had completed high school.[10] In 1991, even though Aboriginal youth were staying in school longer, the majority were still leaving before completing high school (see Volume 2, Chapter 5). The gap

TABLE 5.1
Adjusted Aboriginal Identity Population, 1991

Location of Residence	Total Aboriginal		Registered North American Indian		Non-Registered North American Indian		Métis		Inuit[3]	
	#	%	#	%	#	%	#	%	#	%
Total[1]	720,600	100	438,000	100	112,600	100	139,400	100	37,800	100
Reserves	254,600	35	254,600	58	–[2]		–[2]		–[2]	
Non-Reserve	466,100	65	183,500	42	112,600	100	139,400	100	35,600	100
Urban	320,000	44	148,500	34	77,800	69	90,100	65	7,900	22
Rural	146,100	20	35,000	8	34,900	31	49,300	35	27,700	78

Notes:

1. Approximately 95,000 was added to the APS count to compensate for the population on unenumerated reserves and undercoverage in participating reserve and non-reserve areas.

2. Actual APS counts for non-status Indians, Métis people and Inuit living on reserves were 3,600 (3.5%), 4,535 (3.4%) and 620 (1.7%) respectively. Because of the small numbers, these were added to non-reserve counts.

3. Non-reserve, urban and rural, adjusted counts for Inuit were derived by applying the percentage of urban and rural Inuit from the APS actual counts to the total adjusted Inuit count.

4. As a result of multiple Aboriginal group identity responses, the sum of individual group populations may be greater than the number in the total column.

5. Urban is defined as a population concentration of at least 1,000 with a density of at least 400 persons per square kilometre.

6. The urban and rural counts do not include reserves.

7. Figures may not add to totals because of rounding.

Source: M.J. Norris et al., "Projections of Canada's Aboriginal Identity Population, 1991-2016", research study prepared for RCAP (1995).

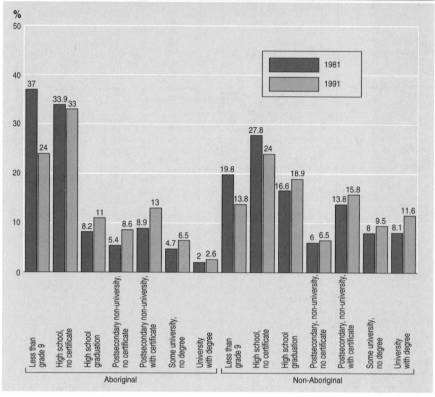

FIGURE 5.1
Highest Level of Education, Aboriginal and Non-Aboriginal Populations Age 15+, 1981-1991

Note: Includes persons still attending school.

Source: Statistics Canada, 1981 Census, 1991 Census, and 1991 Aboriginal Peoples Survey, custom tabulations.

between Aboriginal and non-Aboriginal people in terms of high school completion had narrowed only slightly. We must ask why schooling has continued to be such an alienating experience for Aboriginal children and youth.

For nearly 30 years, Aboriginal leaders have made policy recommendations to governments, and governments have conducted internal studies. The Commission examined 22 reports on Aboriginal education written between 1966 and 1992.[11] The recommendations of these reports, many of them excellent, show remarkable consistency (see box).

What we find most disturbing is that the issues raised at our hearings and in interveners' briefs are the same concerns that Aboriginal people have been bringing forward since the first studies were done. As we examine each one, we

Recommendations in Past Reports and Studies

- Aboriginal control of education.
- School courses in Aboriginal studies, including history, language and culture.
- Training and hiring of more Aboriginal teachers.
- Inclusion of Aboriginal parents, elders and educators in the education of Aboriginal children.
- Special support programs for Aboriginal students, for example, counselling, substance abuse education, remedial education and retention programs.
- Funding of support services for students in post-secondary studies.
- Aboriginal language instruction from pre-school to post-secondary education.
- The resolution of federal, provincial and territorial jurisdictional conflicts over responsibilities, or recognition by the federal government of its funding responsibility for education.
- Training Aboriginal adults for teaching, para-professional and administrative positions in education.
- More emphasis on pre-school and kindergarten education.

see that there has been progress, but it has unfolded at a snail's pace and falls far short of the goal. We have to question why, with so many sincere efforts to change the quality of Aboriginal education, the overall results have been so disappointing. From our analysis, we offer the following observations.

- Federal policy has been moving in the right direction since 1972, but federal authorities have failed to take the decisive steps necessary to restore full control of education to Aboriginal people.
- Nearly 70 per cent of Aboriginal education has been in the hands of provincial or territorial authorities, with few mechanisms for effective accountability to Aboriginal people and involvement of parents.
- Aboriginal people have been restricted in their efforts to implement curricula that would transmit their linguistic and cultural heritage to the next generation.
- Financial resources to reverse the impact of past policies have been inadequate.

It is readily apparent that Canadian society has not yet accomplished the necessary power sharing to enable Aboriginal people to be authors of their own education. This suggests that there are persistent barriers to be addressed if education for Aboriginal people is to change significantly.

1.5 The Need for Fundamental Change

We believe that Aboriginal parents and Aboriginal communities must have the opportunity to implement their vision of education. Aboriginal children are entitled to learn and achieve in an environment that supports their development as whole individuals. They need to value their heritage and identity in planning for the future. Education programs, carefully designed and implemented with parental involvement, can prepare Aboriginal children to participate in two worlds with a choice of futures. Aboriginal people should expect equity of results from education in Canada.

This will not happen if the education system continues unchanged. For significant change to occur, Aboriginal people must have the authority to organize their own education and to influence how their children are educated. We see this happening through a number of avenues.

Education is a core element of jurisdiction in Aboriginal self-government. Aboriginal people must have the opportunity to exercise self-governance in education. In so doing, they would resume control of their education in its entirety, passing their own legislation and regulating all aspects of education. Aboriginal nations, public governments and community of interest governments could all establish their own educational institutions under their own jurisdiction.

Although there were positive moves toward Aboriginal control under the James Bay and Northern Quebec Agreement, the Kativik and Cree school boards are still governed by the rules of the provincial department of education. With the recognition of self-government, Aboriginally controlled school authorities would operate under an Aboriginal nation's law-making authority. We see Aboriginal self-governance in education applying to Aboriginal education institutions at all stages of life from early childhood on. Elementary and high schools, Aboriginal colleges and universities would all function as part of an integrated system of lifelong education.

In urban areas where there are Aboriginal people from various nations, they may choose to combine their efforts and exercise governance through collective structures such as Aboriginal school authorities, deriving their mandate from Aboriginal community of interest governments or provincial or territorial governments. Participation by parents in Aboriginal education systems in urban settings would, of course, be by choice. Aboriginal people could also continue to send their children to public schools and other provincial and territorial educational institutions by preference or because they are the only available option.

Numerous studies of education have identified changes required to improve the quality of education for Aboriginal children attending public education institutions. In the discussion that follows, we repeat many of these recommendations, because they remain relevant. It is vital that Aboriginal parents and families be able to become involved, articulating and shaping the education they want for their children. Where there are larger numbers of Aboriginal children, Aboriginal people have sometimes been able to establish their own schools with the sponsorship of local school boards. Such schools create a venue for innovative programs and active community involvement. In addition, there have been specific initiatives by provincial and territorial governments and local school boards to improve the quality of Aboriginal education; it is imperative that these continue.

In some public post-secondary institutions, Aboriginal people have become more involved in governance and decision-making structures. This positive development strengthens the capacity of colleges and universities to serve Aboriginal constituents. In this chapter we outline other steps that should be taken to increase the capacity of public post-secondary institutions to respond to Aboriginal students' needs.

Changes in the public school system have been incremental and often far too slow. In schools administered by Aboriginal people, there have been serious constraints on their capacity to transform education. Aboriginal people will continue to negotiate an ever-widening space to implement their vision, pushing against the confines of such restrictions. Recognition of Aboriginal peoples' right to govern their education will be a major watershed. Aboriginal governments and education authorities will be positioned to implement the bolder vision they have developed. There will be many variations in the configuration of these changes. Some may resemble existing public school systems. Others will entail reorganization of the school year, the curriculum and school personnel. Aboriginal people remain committed to giving their children a range of options for the future and will, no doubt, negotiate avenues for children to move between Aboriginal and mainstream systems.

As discussed in Volume 2, Chapter 3, we anticipate that the assumption of jurisdiction by Aboriginal governments will proceed through three stages:

- the introduction of self-starting initiatives by Aboriginal nations for which they negotiate financial support within existing legislation;
- a transitional phase during which Aboriginal nations recognized under an Aboriginal Nations Recognition and Government Act exercise law-making powers on their existing territories in core areas, with financing, commensurate with the scope of jurisdiction, provided by the federal government; and
- the conclusion of treaties between Aboriginal nations and Canada (the federal government and the provinces) defining the scope of self-government and the role of Aboriginal governments as a third order of government in Canada.

Our recommendations are designed to open the door to fundamental changes in the practice of Aboriginal education that can be implemented within present jurisdictions, during the transition to self-government, or by self-governing Aboriginal nations.

RECOMMENDATIONS

The Commission recommends that

Education and **3.5.1**
Self-Government
Federal, provincial and territorial governments act promptly to acknowledge that education is a core area for the exercise of Aboriginal self-government.

Transitional **3.5.2**
Control of
Education
Federal, provincial and territorial governments collaborate with Aboriginal governments, organizations or education authorities, as appropriate, to support the development of Aboriginally controlled education systems by
  (a) introducing, adapting or ensuring the flexible application of legislation to facilitate self-starting initiatives by Aboriginal nations and their communities in the field of education;
  (b) mandating voluntary organizations that are endorsed by substantial numbers of Aboriginal people to act in the field of education in urban and non-reserve areas where numbers warrant until such time as Aboriginal governments are established; and
  (c) providing funding commensurate with the responsibilities assumed by Aboriginal nations and their communities, or voluntary organizations, given the requirements of institutional and program development, costs of serving small or dispersed communities, and special needs accruing from past failures of education services.

In the pages that follow, we assume a path of education with Aboriginal self-governing institutions and Aboriginal participation in public schools, colleges and universities. Many of the issues should be considered by Aboriginal education authorities as well as public institution officials. We also address establishing the institutional capacity to enable Aboriginal peoples to be self-governing in education at all stages of life.

2. THE FRAMEWORK:
LIFELONG, HOLISTIC EDUCATION

> Education is a lifelong, continuous process requiring stable and consistent support. First Nations people of every age group require appropriate formal and informal opportunities for learning and for teaching. The education provided must be holistic. Education processes and institutions must address the intellectual, spiritual, emotional and physical development of participants.[12]

Our discussion of education issues proceeds according to four stages of the life cycle: the child, the youth, the adult and the elder.[13] To organize the discussion, we use the Medicine Wheel, a teaching and communication tool borrowed from the traditions of First Nations people of the plains – Blackfoot, Cree, Dakota and others (see also Volume 1, Chapter 15). Although it is not a part of all Aboriginal traditions, it is nevertheless useful for understanding perspectives that are shared by many Aboriginal peoples. The Medicine Wheel is used to discuss relationships and values. Representing the circle of life, the wheel has no beginning and no end.

The first set of relationships of interest here is the connection between learning and the life cycle (Figure 5.2). Learning goes on throughout the life cycle, from infancy and early childhood to old age. Aboriginal people see education as a process that begins before birth and continues long after formal education is over. Learning at one stage has implications for subsequent stages. An adult who has not had the opportunity to develop fully may have to address growth needs later in life. As individuals mature and perhaps attain the status of elder, they are able to transmit to younger generations the knowledge and wisdom acquired through a lifetime of learning. As we will see, the integrity of the lifelong learning cycle in Aboriginal societies has been broken and must be restored.

The second set of relationships is the connection between dimensions of learning and development. In Aboriginal educational tradition, the individual is viewed as a whole person with intellectual, spiritual, emotional and physical dimensions. Each of these aspects must be addressed in the learning process. Holistic education is the term used to describe the kind of education traditionally used by Aboriginal peoples. Such education is organized to develop all aspects of the individual. In western countries, similar learning models have evolved, but they have been eclipsed by models of education that place primary emphasis on intellectual development, with this focus intensifying as the individual moves into higher levels of education.

Lifelong learning and learning aimed to balance all dimensions of the person are intermeshed. At each stage of life, learning should develop the whole human being. Intellectual, spiritual, emotional and physical learning depends upon the success of development at previous stages.

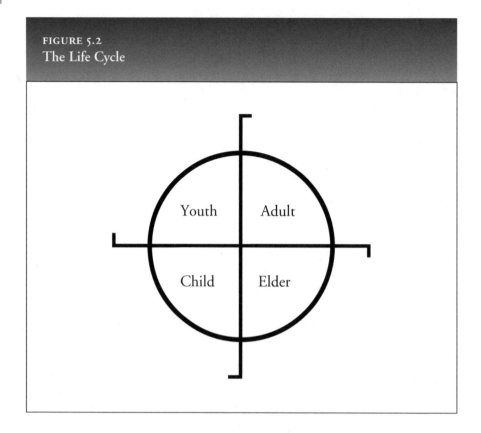

FIGURE 5.2
The Life Cycle

Youth | Adult

Child | Elder

The circularity of the medicine wheel urges us to keep the whole picture in mind, even though the individual component parts may be compelling. As we wrestle with issues in the education of the child, the youth, the adult, and the elder in turn, we will be reminded that the problems encountered by adults today are rooted in education processes in the past. We will see that educational innovation at each stage of the life cycle gives us the opportunity – and indeed the responsibility – to bring about profound and significant changes in the lives of generations to come.

3. THE CHILD

Childhood is the foundational stage of life. Within the family, the child acquires language, develops trust, becomes aware of self and others, establishes bonds with family members, develops intellectual and social skills and values. This important foundation prepares the child to enter society's formal system of education, the other distinct context in which the child must function. During this important early stage of life, the child's intellectual, spiritual, physical and emotional capacities must be developed and his or her special gifts identified and nurtured.

FIGURE 5.3
The Child's Capacities to be Developed

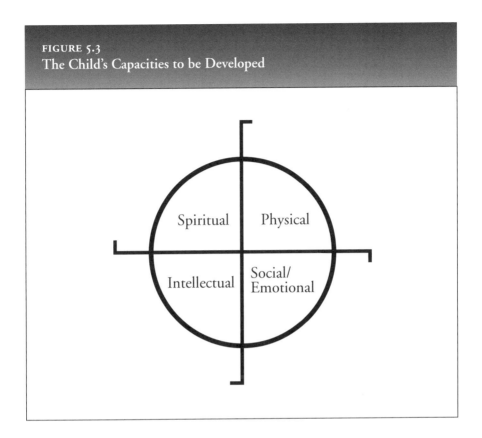

Spiritual | Physical

Intellectual | Social/ Emotional

3.1 Early Childhood Education

Young children absorb information at a rate greater than at any other stage of life. They make sense of the world around them, deciphering a whole language system in order to communicate. They learn to label objects, perceptions and emotions. They form bonds with the significant people upon whom they are dependent and develop trust. They are curious, exploring, receptive and vulnerable.

Early childhood is one of the most important points in the learning process. In recent decades, research has confirmed the critical importance of infancy and early childhood as a foundation upon which identity, self-worth and intellectual strength are built. Trauma, dislocation and inconsistency in early childhood can affect the rest of the individual's life.[14] But if the child's environment is rich in love, intellectual stimulation and security, the capacity to grow is invigorated. Because early childhood is regarded as so important to later development, educators have turned a spotlight on learning before formal education normally begins.

Traditional Aboriginal life provided the conditions for a solid childhood foundation. Babies and toddlers spent their first years within the extended family where parents, grandparents, aunts and uncles, brothers and sisters all shared responsibility for protecting and nurturing them. Traditional Aboriginal child-rearing practices permitted children to exert their will with little interference from adults.[15] In this environment, children were encouraged to develop as thinking, autonomous beings. At the same time, they acquired language and were integrated into the rhythms of daily life in the family and community.

In this early stage of development, children learned how to interpret and respond to the world. They learned how to walk on the land, taking in the multiple cues needed to survive as hunters and gatherers; they were conditioned to see the primacy of relationships over material possessions; they discovered that they had special gifts that would define their place in and contribution to the family and community. From an early age, playing at the edge of adult work and social activities, they learned that dreams, visions and legends were as important to learning as practical instruction in how to build a boat or tan a hide. (See Volume 1, Chapter 15 for more discussion of patterns of socialization that contribute to the formation of distinctive Aboriginal world views.)

Traditional child-rearing practices survive in many Aboriginal families, and they are consciously being revived in others. Some parents are fortunate to have the continuing support of an extended family, with grandparents and other family members available to share the responsibilities of parenting and to pass on knowledge and skills that support a strong sense of identity and self-esteem.

However, social change, the stresses of poverty, and disruptive interventions in Aboriginal family life over generations have taken a severe toll on the capacity of many Aboriginal families to provide this kind of positive environment for raising children. As discussed in Chapter 2 of this volume, family violence scars the lives of far too many Aboriginal children. Families who live in urban areas often find themselves far from the company of relatives who can give support on a daily basis. Access to elders is particularly difficult in cities. The lives of many young parents are economically precarious as they try to survive on the brink of crisis. Many children are being raised by a single parent, usually the mother, who receives no outside help besides social assistance.

If stresses interfere with the development of a child's capacity for health, self-esteem and intellectual growth before beginning school, the schooling experience soon accentuates the child's 'weaknesses'. Once they have entered the formal education system, children may never recover the ground lost in these early years.

The link between early childhood experience and success in the formal schooling system has been studied intensively by researchers since the 1960s. At that time, programs such as Head Start in the United States were implemented to help children develop the skills needed to tackle the demands of formal education. After three decades of examining early childhood interventions, there is strong evidence that such programs do make a difference, particularly if they are continued into the elementary school system. There is substantial research showing that children who participate in high quality early childhood development programs are more likely to finish high school and to be employed.[16] The Carnegie Institute, for example, has called for the United States Congress to expand family leave rights, improve the training of daycare workers and extend Head Start programs even further.[17]

In 1994, Ontario's Royal Commission on Learning found the arguments for early childhood intervention so compelling that they recommended giving all parents the option of sending their children to early childhood education programs from age three. They were particularly concerned about the increasing number of children growing up in poverty:

> Children who come through a carefully planned process of early education gain significantly in competence, coping skills, and (not least important) in positive attitudes towards learning....We're convinced that early childhood education significantly helps in providing a level playing field of opportunity and experience for every child, whatever her background.[18]

Testimony from Aboriginal parents, grandparents, educators and organizations indicated Aboriginal people's appreciation of the importance of the early years. Studies by the Assembly of First Nations, the Congress of Aboriginal Peoples, and the National Association of Friendship Centres have all advocated early childhood education and child care under Aboriginal control.[19]

Aboriginal people want to prepare their children for stronger academic performance, but their concerns go beyond a singular focus on cognitive development. They recognize the need of families for support and respite while they struggle with personal and economic problems. They want to see early identification of children with special needs and provision of appropriate care and parent education in the community. They see high quality child care as a necessary service for parents undertaking training or gaining a foothold in the work force. Most important, they see early childhood education as a means of reinforcing Aboriginal identity, instilling the values, attitudes and behaviours that give expression to Aboriginal cultures. (For a closer look at child care in support of training and employment, see Volume 2, Chapter 5, and our discussion of employment development.)

Formal education, as we will see later, is still predominantly the domain of non-Aboriginal professionals even though inroads into the teaching profession are being made by Aboriginal people. Initiatives by Aboriginal people to implement their priorities in early childhood education have therefore taken shape typically in daycare services on-reserve, where a substantial degree of community control can be maintained, and in grant-funded projects on- and off-reserve engaging the energies of parents and volunteers. Many Aboriginal par-

Splats'in Daycare Centre

In 1991 the Splats'in daycare centre was initiated by the Spallumcheen First Nation community in British Columbia. The program design was based partly on the Te Kohanga Reo model from Aotearoa (New Zealand) and used an extended family model, with elders and children participating in everyday activities together. Through daily exposure to the use of the Shuswap language, the children absorbed the language quickly. The elders introduced the children to traditional activities, such as caring for animals, cultivating a garden, and making traditional crafts. The whole daycare environment reflected the traditional rhythm of Shuswap life and social relationships. When funding for the two-year program ended, the community tried to continue it using volunteer resources, but momentum for the language and cultural component were lost. Program staff believe that this kind of program needs long-term program stability to be effective.

ents are resistant to the idea of sending their children to school at progressively earlier ages, particularly when schools have so often proven to be a hostile environment for the development of Aboriginal identity.

The incorporation of Aboriginal language in early childhood programs has been a focal point for the drive to ensure that learning in such settings has a distinctly Aboriginal character.[20] One of the models of great interest to Aboriginal communities in Canada has been the Maori language 'nests', or *Te Kohanga Reo* (discussed later in this chapter). This total immersion program involves trained staff, parents and elders and uses local community facilities, and aspects of it have already been adapted by Aboriginal communities in Canada, with impressive results. In British Columbia, the Splats'in daycare program in Enderby (see box), the Gitksan immersion program in Kispiox, the Kyah Wiget education society in Moricetown, and the Gitwangak education society in Kitwanga have all been influenced by Te Kohanga Reo. In our hearings, Aboriginal presenters from all over Canada expressed interest in the model. There have also been programs in tribal communities in the United States, for example, the Lummi of Washington state, where parents have created programs based on their linguistic and cultural traditions.

The development of language skills is an important dimension of early childhood education. There is an increasing body of research supporting the importance of fluency in a primary language before entering school.[21] Research with bilingual students indicates that the primary language becomes the vehicle for acquiring more complex learning, but fluency levels must be strong. Students who are switched from their primary language to another language before they have strong fluency levels have more difficulty with learning. This is particularly important for Aboriginal children living in predominantly English- or French-speaking environments who do not speak an Aboriginal language, English or French with any depth. Purposeful intervention at this early stage will provide the language base upon which future learning takes place.

The accumulation of convincing evidence that early childhood is a strategic intervention point to enhance healthy development and learning has prompted government initiatives to invest in this stage of learning. Aboriginal initiatives in early childhood education, many of them including Aboriginal language components, have received a major boost from the Child Care Initiatives Fund, introduced by the federal government in 1988 to support community-based initiatives in early childhood development. The program committed $98 million over five years and was extended for an additional two years. Almost a hundred Aboriginal child care and daycare projects received funding, demonstrating the range of approaches to pursuing community objectives: Aboriginal language immersion programs, in-home daycare, free-standing daycare facilities, Head Start programs, toy lending libraries for parents, training programs for local caregivers, and manuals to help non-Aboriginal caregivers respond sensitively to the needs of Aboriginal children.

This spectrum of programs underlines the desirability of having a variety of options available to parents, to respond to varying circumstances and preferences. Early childhood education can take many forms, some institutionally based and others focused on the family and the home. Some parents may reject institutional forms of early childhood education, preferring to work with their own children at home, with support or resources from child care workers or educators. Others, including working parents, may prefer to see a centralized facility where children come together under one roof. Since any intervention at this critical age for cultural transmission will have a profound, long-term impact on the child's life, it is imperative that early childhood strategies be fully under the control of parents, who can make strategic choices about shaping their child's future.

In 1992 the federal government introduced the Brighter Futures program with a mandate to support projects in child development and community mental health. There is a First Nations and Inuit component in Brighter Futures for on-reserve and Inuit communities. Aboriginal people off-reserve are eligible to apply for project funds available to the general public.

In 1995, Health Canada introduced an Aboriginal Head Start program that will disburse $83.7 million over four years for about 50 projects. The program is directed to Aboriginal people primarily in the western provinces and northern regions and not living on-reserve. Community programs are expected to contain Aboriginal Head Start's five components: culture and language; education; health promotion and nutrition; social support programs; and parental involvement. The program is not intended to focus on day care.

In December 1995 the minister of human resources development announced the First Nations and Inuit Child Care Initiative, to take effect in fiscal year 1995-96, funded at $72 million over three years, with $36 million in ongoing funds thereafter. Its focus is child care to support participation in employment as well as child development. Both Aboriginal Head Start and the human resources development initiative consulted Aboriginal people in their design. The programs have separate administrations and advisory structures.

Provincial governments, which have constitutional responsibility for child care as a social support measure and early childhood education as an educational service, have recognized the importance of early childhood education. In British Columbia, the Royal Commission on Education (1988) recommended that bands and councils, school authorities and government agencies take steps to improve the language capabilities of Aboriginal children in pre-school and in the early years of elementary schooling.[22] The prominence given to early childhood education in the report of the Ontario Royal Commission on Learning (1994) is another indication that this period of development has emerged as an important field of intervention for policy makers.

We acknowledge the importance of programs that commit substantial resources to support early childhood development. Community experience with these programs has already established a strong base from which future programming can evolve. However, problems remain to be addressed.

First, early childhood programs are variously defined as child care to support parental employment; as mental health or prevention initiatives to enhance the life chances of children at risk; and as cultural programs to reinforce cultural identity and educational programs to foster intellectual achievement. We consider these distinctions irrational. Aboriginal parents and educators consistently press for holistic programs that address the physical, intellectual, social, emotional and spiritual development of children. This priority should guide the design and operation of all early childhood programs.

Second, programs with differently defined objectives and eligibility criteria, directed to various target groups, are initiated by different departments and different levels of government. The lack of co-ordination between programs and the maze of regulations governing them constitute an impediment to rational planning and equitable access to services at the community level.

Third, early childhood programs for Aboriginal children are funded predominantly as special projects of limited duration. The newly announced Indian and Inuit Child Care Initiative (enhancing daycare services already in place under Indian affairs sponsorship on-reserve and in Inuit communities) addresses the need for continuity. On the other hand, the highly regarded Child Care Initiatives Fund has been terminated and with it many of the creative projects for which it provided seed funding. Stop-and-start program support is wasteful of resources and community effort and demoralizing to Aboriginal people. It is also difficult to acquire or construct appropriate facilities without secure funding.

In our recommendations for health and healing centres in Chapter 3 of this volume, we urged that the full range of health and social services be brought under Aboriginal control through a reorganized service system. Early childhood program needs could be addressed within this system, or they could be dealt with as an extension of the education system. The requirements for support of holistic child development are the same in either case.

As Aboriginal nations are recognized and negotiate fiscal transfers to support community services, they will be positioned to introduce services that respond to community priorities in an integrated, equitable and consistent manner. Within current jurisdictions, a strong commitment from federal, provincial and territorial governments is needed to provide stable support to early childhood programs that serve all Aboriginal children, regardless of their status and residence.

The strategy supported must give parents and communities the opportunity to exercise choice across a spectrum of high quality, culturally appropriate early childhood education options. These include support for parents and families in the home, language immersion, co-operative arrangements, in-home daycare, daycare centres, involvement with elders, and other community activities. Aboriginal governments should place a priority on early childhood education in formats appropriate to the community and ensure that resources for early childhood education are negotiated in self-government agreements.

Many presentations before the Commission emphasized the importance of restoring the role of elders in early childhood and elementary education. The legacy of elders is precious, unique and irreplaceable. In the models of early childhood education adopted by some communities, elders have been able to resume their role in intergenerational teaching. Again, it takes parent- and community-controlled initiatives to implement such an approach.

RECOMMENDATION

The Commission recommends that

Early Childhood Education Support

3.5.3

Federal, provincial, and territorial governments co-operate to support an integrated early childhood education funding strategy that

(a) extends early childhood education services to *all* Aboriginal children regardless of residence;

> (b) encourages programs that foster the physical, social, intellectual and spiritual development of children, reducing distinctions between child care, prevention and education;
> (c) maximizes Aboriginal control over service design and administration;
> (d) offers one-stop accessible funding; and
> (e) promotes parental involvement and choice in early childhood education options.

3.2 The Child in the Formal Education System

At the age of six, children are required to enter the formal education system.[23] From that point on, children spend most of their daytime hours in classrooms. What happens there will have a profound impact upon their whole lives. While the family and other forces in society also shape the child, the education system is a compelling and compulsory presence in the child's life. In the classroom, children must absorb what is being taught, and their performance is evaluated continuously through a system of rewards and penalties.

The success of transition to the more regimented school system depends, in part, on the continuity between the child's home environment and the classroom. The elements of this continuity include language, the presence of familiar respected persons, and the consistent application of values that govern daily life.

Values and traditions of Aboriginal peoples and nations are diverse, but there are common elements that often conflict with those dominant in the conventional classroom. For example, Aboriginal children may be raised in a home environment where co-operation and non-competitiveness are emphasized. They may be taught that intellectual and other gifts are meant to be shared for the benefit of others rather than for personal gain. In some Aboriginal cultures, the principle of non-interference predominates; the child's will is respected, and adults do not interfere in the choices made by the child. The imposition of the adult's will on the child is considered inappropriate except, of course, in instances where the child may encounter harm.[24] By contrast, the regimentation of the classroom experience, the emphasis on individual achievement, and the exertion of the teacher's authority constitute a rupture with the child's home environment. This process of cultural conflict is described by Elsie Wuttunee:

> A common concern of parents is when schooling becomes a threat to their developing child's identity, primarily when the values and world view that prevail at school contradict or ignore the existence of a different perspective the child lives with at home. In the case of students of Aboriginal ancestry, this situation is all too common. The

result can be that the child experiences serious conflict and doubt about the validity of his or her own identity. When an Aboriginal child's identity has been threatened, they will withdraw into themselves; become silent and refuse to participate as a means of protecting themselves from criticism and rejection; attempt to abandon their previous identity and mould themselves to the culture which they perceive as more valid or acceptable; they may take on non-productive and rejecting attitudes which generally culminate in failure or dropping out.

Elsie Wuttunee
Calgary Catholic Separate School District No. 1
Calgary, Alberta, 27 May 1993*

Today, the efforts of Aboriginal educators and communities are directed to restoring continuity between the Aboriginal home environment and the school. The teaching of Aboriginal languages, the staffing of schools with Aboriginal teachers, the inclusion of elders as teachers, and the development of curriculum rooted in the values, history and traditions of Aboriginal peoples are all attempts to fit formal education into a broader learning process that begins in the family.

Educational change is now under way, but within strict limits. Where modern treaties have been concluded, as under the James Bay and Northern Quebec Agreement, there has been some latitude to reshape the education process and experiment with alternatives. In the Northwest Territories, public education is being adapted to reflect the language base and values of Aboriginal residents. Gains have been made in southern Canada as well, where some First Nations administer education under an arrangement with the department of Indian affairs. Staff are hired by local school authorities, language classes can be introduced, and Aboriginal materials can be incorporated into the curriculum. Provinces, territorial governments and local school boards have also directed financial resources to assessing curriculum, employing Aboriginal support workers, making language classes available, and increasing the opportunities for students to learn about Aboriginal history and values.

These efforts represent important changes in the environment for Aboriginal children. But data as recent as the Aboriginal peoples survey (1991) showed that a large percentage of Aboriginal youth was not completing high school. As discussed later in this chapter, of Aboriginal youth aged 15 to 24 years who left school, 68.5 per cent did not have a diploma.[25] There are local variations and success stories of keeping students in school until graduation. Researchers who

---

* Transcripts of the Commission's hearings are cited with the speaker's name and affiliation, if any, and the location and date of the hearing. See *A Note About Sources* at the beginning of this volume for information about transcripts and other Commission publications.

study retention issues maintain that leaving school is not a sudden event. Rather, it is a process that begins much earlier. In the education of Aboriginal children, the seeds of the future are being planted in early school experience.

Many complex, interrelated factors contribute to creating the conditions for successful education for children. We cannot hope to deal with all of them here. We know, too, that parents hold differing hopes and dreams for their children, depending on a host of cultural, family and personal expectations. In this section, we consider three concerns that Aboriginal people raised repeatedly as fundamental issues in education of children and youth: a curriculum that instils a proud Aboriginal identity and competence as an Aboriginal person; language education; and Aboriginal control and parental involvement.

Innovations in curriculum

Modest improvements have been made to school curricula over the last 15 years. There is more Aboriginal content, particularly in schools where the majority of the students are Aboriginal. Careful scrutiny of textbooks has meant that fewer texts portray Aboriginal people in negative terms. In some linguistic communities, Aboriginal language curriculum materials are being used in the school system. These are important accomplishments to which many elders, educators and parents have contributed.

However, improvements have been far too slow and inconsistent. Revisions often gloss over or avoid tackling the fundamental changes that are necessary to create curriculum that is rooted in an Aboriginal understanding of the world, in subjects such as history, art, health, mathematics and sciences. To substantiate this assessment in the face of efforts to improve the education of Aboriginal children, it is necessary to focus on some of the obstacles that continue to block the attainment of Aboriginal goals. To do so, we present an example of a successful education program that is community- and culturally based. We examine what makes it appealing and ask why similar education initiatives are not more widespread.

Akwesasne is a Mohawk community at the intersection of the Ontario, Quebec and New York state borders. The Akwesasne Science and Mathematics Pilot Project was begun in 1988 to reverse the pattern of student alienation from science and mathematics as it is taught in most curricula (see box). The Mohawk people started with the assumption that all jobs of the twenty-first century would require a solid science and mathematics base and that everyone serving the community would require such training. In addition, the community requires the skills of health and science professionals in its self-governing structures. It was also considered critical that the curriculum should not supplant Aboriginal values and knowledge.

The Aboriginal health professions program of the University of Toronto, the board of education of the Mohawk Council of Akwesasne, and General Vanier Secondary School of the Stormont, Dundas and Glengarry Public School

Board (Ontario) joined together to carry out the project, which they call the "Mohawk Way to Go to School". A curriculum for grades seven to nine has been developed, with extensive involvement of Mohawk health and science professionals, elders, spiritual leaders, parents and community members. Other advisers, Aboriginal and non-Aboriginal, are consulted from time to time. Throughout this process, Mohawk contributions to science and mathematics, historically and in the present, have been elaborated. Working with these contributors, staff have been able to develop science themes integrating earth, trees, animals, birds, agriculture, food, water, cosmology and Mohawk ways of knowing. Similarly, they have developed mathematics themes incorporating Mohawk number systems, cultural values, sacred circles and references to ceremonies. Mohawk concepts of space, time, measurement and distance, puzzles and games are used. Applications of mathematics to agriculture, forestry, geography and conservation are studied.

The science and math *content* is not the only focus of the pilot project. Teaching and learning methods are also being analyzed to determine what works best for the children. The approach of successful traditional Mohawk teachers is observed carefully because it is so effective. Career promotion is a component of the project. Students are given opportunities to meet Aboriginal science and math professionals in Canada and the United States to learn about various careers.

Much can be learned by examining the characteristics of the Akwesasne science and maths curriculum and the process followed to develop and implement it:

- The curriculum makes Mohawk knowledge, values and beliefs its central focus, not a supplement to a western science and mathematics curriculum.
- The curriculum does not reject western science and mathematics concepts, but it does not attempt to assimilate students into the logic of western beliefs. It makes visible the underlying values and assumptions of Mohawk and western concepts. These are different ways of looking at the world, with complementary strengths.
- The curriculum is holistic. Rather than separating the earth and water into component parts from a single disciplinary perspective, it looks at the interconnections from a multitude of perspectives. This construction of the curriculum reflects a whole way of thinking about the world.
- The curriculum includes experiential components that link the theory learned in the classroom to the life of the community. The involvement of students in monitoring serious environmental problems in the community is immediate and engaging. Students do not have to ponder the possible connection between what they are learning and its value to the well-being of their community.
- The curriculum development process used community involvement in an optimal way. The resources of the whole community, including those not cur-

Akwesasne Science and Mathematics Pilot Project
"Mohawk Way to Go to School"

At Akwesasne, we are using the Mohawk Thanksgiving Address, which has been recited for centuries. It acknowledges and expresses appreciation for the natural world and the duties that are fulfilled in order to maintain existence. This forms the basis of the science curriculum design and embraces the Mohawk concept of the relatedness of all creation while exploring the internal and external environments of all living things. The Aboriginal concept of 'ecology' is examined and compared to the dominant culture theories.

Our Mother Earth is studied through the discovery of what constitutes earth, or soils, and Aboriginal uses of soils are explored from an agricultural perspective as well as from an Aboriginal potter's perspective. Plant life is surveyed from a holistic Aboriginal perspective – their assistance to Mother Earth, people and animals (ecology); medicinal characteristics; uses as natural dyes; the Haudenosaunee [Iroquois] connection of the Three Sisters – corn, bean and squash – and the cultural significance they play. The characteristics of western classifications are incorporated into the units.

Water is looked at from an Aboriginal ecological perspective, while also incorporating the study of the chemical composition and properties...An activity being incorporated into the grade 8 curriculum is a water quality project that monitors the water life and the water conditions along the heavily polluted St. Lawrence River. Local universities and governmental agencies participate in assisting the students to conduct the various testing and analysis required. This activity is incorporated into the draft

rently resident at Akwesasne, were tapped to bring this curriculum to fruition. Elders, spiritual leaders, historians, science and math professionals, and others with specialized knowledge contributed to the project. Parents and community leaders invested in the project. In short, this is a unique Mohawk design, built from the bottom up and owned by the community.

- The essential role of elders and spiritual leaders in teaching the young is clearly evident. The knowledge of elders and spiritual leaders is integral to the curriculum and its teaching process.
- Children shaped by this curriculum will have a better chance of operating comfortably in two worlds.
- Non-Aboriginal educators and school authorities collaborated to provide support to strengthen the resources of the project, but control of the project is firmly under Mohawk leadership.

mathematics and science curriculum for grade 8. Haudenosaunee and First Nations beliefs permeate the exercise to ensure that the values of Aboriginal people are reinforced. Another project being designed for grade 8 curriculum is a joint effort with the Akwesasne Environmental Division that will design and implement an indoor aquaculture project, including historical Mohawk fishing practices.

Animals form the basis of the Haudenosaunee 'clan system' or family organization. This significant practice is incorporated into the curriculum while also studying classification, characteristics, cell and cell functions. The study of 'Energy' includes units on the Haudenosaunee teachings of the four winds, Thunder, Lightning, Sun and overall conservation, while also examining the 'western' science. The cosmos is incorporated by providing experiential teaching in the Aboriginal and Haudenosaunee concept of oneness with the universe. The moon, stars and other galaxies are intertwined with Aboriginal cosmos mythology to demonstrate the intricate thought of our ancestors relative to cosmology.

Field trips and experiential programming are integrated into the science curriculum to demonstrate incorporation of Aboriginal and 'western' concepts.

Source: Excerpted from Brenda Tsioniaon LaFrance, "Culturally Negotiated Education in First Nation Communities, Empowering Ourselves for Future Generations," paper presented at the National Round Table on Education, Royal Commission on Aboriginal Peoples, Ottawa, July 1993.

- Careful attention is paid to what works and why. The evaluation of each component of the project, as a way to improve it and to understand its dynamics, will make an important contribution to this and other Aboriginal curriculum and teaching projects.

The Akwesasne science and maths project is not the only model of innovation in Aboriginal education in Canada (see box). But these are the exception rather than the rule. Most Aboriginal children in Canada do not have the opportunity to experience the excitement of science, maths and other subjects grounded in the concepts of their respective nations. Although the National Indian Brotherhood articulated the principle of "Indian control of Indian education" in 1972, more than two decades later, Aboriginal children are still consuming the standard curricula of mainstream educational institutions. Adding Aboriginal content to curriculum usually consists of adding units designed to

Examples of Culture-Based Curriculum

- The Dene Kede Curriculum in the Northwest Territories is the culmination of a major community-based effort to produce a cultural curriculum for children in kindergarten through to grade six. It is a holistic curriculum built around the four key relationships that are central to a full life: the land, the spiritual world, other people and the self. The teaching approach is based on experiential learning using key cultural experiences. Analysis, practice, review, reflection and basic academic skills are offshoots. This innovative curriculum makes extensive use of community participation, the children's personal experience and the resources of elders. The curriculum, with its 50 thematic units, can be adapted by each community to establish its own unique community curriculum. To assess student progress, the curriculum emphasizes individual development and student self-evaluation rather than comparative measures.

- The Inuuqatigiit curriculum, also in the Northwest Territories, is intended for Inuit children from kindergarten to grade 12. In its draft stage in 1994-95, the curriculum adopted three dimensions of Inuit life as its foundation: the circle of belonging (to the family, to the community and to the world); the cycle of life; and the cycle of the seasons. All of these are infused with Inuit values and beliefs. Thematic units have been prepared to elaborate these concepts in relation to other people and the environment.

- SIMA7, Come Join Me, is an intercultural curriculum produced in British Columbia for pre-adolescent Aboriginal and non-Aboriginal youth. It begins with a series of lessons for understanding stereotyping and then introduces students to a summer camp attended by First Nations youth from across Canada and Central America. During the four-day camp, the young people share important dimensions of their cultural traditions. The student reader, teacher's guide and video are published by Pacific Educational Press. *SIMA7* (pronounced 'shee-ma' with a glottal stop at the end) is a word in the Lil'wat language. SIMA7 is adapted from DIMA7WI, meaning 'Come join us, you all'.

'enrich' existing curriculum content rather than changing the core assumptions, values and logic of the curriculum itself. Language and culture classes may be added to a school's program without altering the basic English or French curriculum, the science curriculum, the maths curriculum and the social studies curriculum.

Why has there not been more curriculum innovation when Aboriginal educators and communities and their allies have worked so hard for more than two decades to improve Aboriginal education? The experiences presented to the Commission suggest why progress has been stalled.

One of the main reasons is that First Nations schools (reserve schools) have been required to sign funding agreements specifying that programs must conform to provincial standards.[26] While many Aboriginal parents and educators would willingly follow parts of a provincial curriculum, there must also be room for creative curriculum design, as at Akwesasne.

The concern of parents is that the child's education will not be recognized by provincial school systems if the child must transfer from one school to another. To the credit of the Ontario government, the Akwesasne science and maths project is provincially accredited. In many communities, however, efforts at curriculum innovation have met negative responses. Curriculum innovation is risky: it is much safer to make modifications that are unlikely to attract attention from outside authorities.

The experience of Kitigan Zibi Education Council, which has insisted on curriculum control in local education, illustrates the tensions of trying to make curriculum innovation work with the current systems:

> We would decide what would be best. Now, we are not fools. We knew that our kids would be going to college and university so we would prepare our curriculum in [light of] that....If our students decide to transfer from our system...into the Quebec [CEGEP] system, the Ministry of Education doesn't recognize [our program]. The higher institution [university] does [recognize it]; the lower level doesn't. No logic.
>
> Gilbert Whiteduck
> Maniwaki, Quebec
> 2 December 1992

Innovative Aboriginal programming is not a question of watering down standards. The fundamental question is whether Aboriginal people can represent their values in the design of education programs. Aboriginal people have operated from a position of weakness with respect to provincial governments and their educational institutions. Even in Nunavik, where the James Bay and Northern Quebec Agreement has assigned the Kativik school board considerable authority and flexibility, the imposition of standards from external educational authorities has interfered with the attainment of local goals. Sheila Watt Cloutier of Makivik Corporation and the Nunavik educational task force writes:

> We accepted the southern institutional programs as the standard, because that is what schooling meant to us – it was what southern society did in their schools. In addition our School Board was

accountable to the Quebec Government through its Ministry of Education, and not to our own emerging regional government. As a result, what our school system provided was a watered down, superficially adapted version of the official Quebec Curriculum. This has little to do with the real challenges our people are facing. The result is a system that does not adequately prepare our youth for life in either the North or the South.[27]

The right of Aboriginal people to articulate and apply their own standards of excellence in education is at stake in this debate. Tension is likely to intensify as provinces and territories move to implement Canada-wide testing of students. The goals of education embodied in such testing are defined by non-Aboriginal authorities. Some Aboriginal parents and communities may share these goals, but it should not be assumed that they will place them above their own goals for the education of their children. Self-determination in education should give Aboriginal people clear authority to create curriculum and set the standards to accomplish their education goals. Aboriginal and non-Aboriginal authorities must negotiate agreements that show mutual recognition of each other's curriculum decisions and standards. As self-governance in education is implemented, agreements should demonstrate respect and recognition of Aboriginal competence in the area.

Lack of funding resources has been another significant deterrent to developing systematic, integrated Aboriginal curricula. The Akwesasne science and mathematics pilot project is exactly that – a pilot project. The organizers were able to assemble project funding from a variety of government and private sources. Securing assured funding after the pilot project phase ends is critical to sustaining the approach in the longer term.

The community-based process that produced the Mohawk Way to Go to School is costly in time and resources, but there is no other way to undertake this kind of innovation. Standard Canadian curricula are developed by teams of scholars, researchers and writers, not only in Canada but in a large, international textbook industry. Aboriginal communities and educators have performed the same important work on very low budgets and have produced some remarkable work.[28] Where cultural education centres exist, they have assisted with and sometimes spearheaded curriculum development. But often curriculum development is left to the Aboriginal teacher, who must produce it on the spot. This is an inefficient approach with no permanent public record of methods or materials when staff move on. Moreover, the process is ad hoc, lacking integration with a broader vision of what Aboriginal parents want education to accomplish.

The government of the Northwest Territories has sponsored curriculum development to support Dene and Inuit cultures. Such projects involve extensive consultation and considerable research and development costs. Resource materials are needed to support the curriculum and must be developed in their entirety. Once the core curriculum is developed, training for implementation and revision can be carried out through existing processes.

The Akwesasne science and maths curriculum helps us to glimpse what is possible. Holistic, culturally and community-based curriculum development is achievable and is an investment that must be made for present and future generations.

RECOMMENDATIONS

The Commission recommends that

Transfer Between **3.5.4**
Education Systems Aboriginal, provincial and territorial governments act promptly to reach agreements for mutual recognition of programs provided by their respective educational institutions so as to facilitate the transfer of students between educational systems while protecting the integrity of cultural dimensions of Aboriginal education

Curriculum **3.5.5**
Development Federal, provincial and territorial governments collaborate with Aboriginal governments, organizations and educators to develop or continue developing innovative curricula that reflect Aboriginal cultures and community realities, for delivery
  (a) at all grade levels of elementary and secondary schools;
  (b) in schools operating under Aboriginal control; and
  (c) in schools under provincial or territorial jurisdiction.

Language education

Aboriginal people speak about language and culture in the same breath. (For a more generic discussion of Aboriginal language conservation, see Chapter 6 of this volume.) Fluent speakers, particularly elders, are certain that without their languages, their cultures will be lost, because it is impossible to translate the deeper meanings of words and concepts into the languages of other cultures. Linguists agree that language shapes the way people perceive the world as well as how they describe it. The intimate relationships between language, culture and thought underlie the insistence of Aboriginal people that language education must be a priority. Mi'kmaq educator Marie Battiste describes this interrelationship and what it means to have another language imposed on one:

Cognitive imperialism...is [the attempt to change] a whole way in which people see things. I think it is important at this point to tell you a little bit about the Mi'kmaq language. It is a beautiful language. It has many, many ways of expressing things. There are more ways to express things in Mi'kmaq than there are in English and the language is built around relationships....

The language is the cement and the bonds. It provides the moral communion, if you will, of the community. And when we begin to take that language away from the people, when we replace it with this other language called English, we tear the people away from the very rudiments of that language in terms of the relationships of people to each other, the relationship to their universe, their relationships to the animals and the plants. We take away their interconnectedness and we leave them empty, lost and alone. This is a tremendous loss that people feel, as I have felt...

> Marie Battiste
> Cultural Curriculum Co-ordinator
> Eskasoni School Board
> Eskasoni, Nova Scotia, 7 May 1992

The eradication of Aboriginal languages was one prong of the federal government's overall attempt to erase Aboriginal cultures. In some parts of Canada, Aboriginal language use remains strong, particularly in the north and in the province of Quebec.[29] Linguists consider Inuktitut, Anishnabe (Ojibwa) and Cree to be the most robust languages today, while the everyday use of many other Aboriginal languages diminished substantially with the rise of schooling in English and French. Teaching Aboriginal languages in schools has been a priority of Aboriginal education authorities in their efforts to give schooling an Aboriginal cultural base.

How a language is taught depends on whether the Aboriginal language is the child's first or second language. Teaching language skills is complex:

In Eskasoni we do have language instruction going on in the school. We do provide cultural integration into the curriculum and we do a lot of things toward cultural enhancement, enrichment and appreciation. And those have had many kinds of positive outcomes. But one area still remains sort of vague, and that is the whole element of English as a second language. How do we begin to help students make the transition from their Native Aboriginal language into English? We haven't got the right formula yet.

> Marie Battiste
> Cultural Curriculum Co-ordinator
> Eskasoni School Board
> Eskasoni, Nova Scotia, 7 May 1992

The Kativik school board in Nunavik has developed curriculum materials to support oral and written language instruction. Inuktitut is used in early grades as the language of instruction and is taught in upper grades as a subject. There is strong family and community support for the use of the language. Inuktitut is heard up to six or seven hours a day on radio, and the Inuit Broadcasting Corporation co-operates with regional bodies to produce five and a half hours a week of television programming in Inuktitut. Regional magazines, official reports and community newsletters are printed in Inuktitut.

Language education is perhaps easier to implement in the home territory of Aboriginal people where there are large numbers of students from a single linguistic tradition. In urban centres where there are Aboriginal people of many linguistic backgrounds, it is more challenging to provide solid language support for everyone. British Columbia's education policy is that Aboriginal parents living in Vancouver who want their children to learn Aboriginal languages through the education system can approach the school board with an application and curriculum for a locally developed course. They suggest the name of a fluent member of the linguistic community who can be recognized as an Aboriginal language teacher by the British Columbia College of Teachers. The course can be given in a regular classroom or in a home-based or community setting.[30]

When should Aboriginal language instruction begin? When should a second or third language be introduced? These are questions asked by many Canadian parents who want their child to learn a heritage language. Researchers in language learning say that every child is born with the capacity to pronounce every sound of every human language. Children learn from the acoustic environment starting at birth. As a baby hears sounds in the environment, it selects these sounds from the vast possibilities of human speech. The period up to three years of age is a critical time for laying the child's template of sounds and language acquisition is easiest when the child is young.

Lynn Drapeau, who has conducted studies of Aboriginal languages in Quebec, advises that it is important for the child to start school in its mother tongue. The argument is that well-developed fluency in the child's first language is necessary to achieve facility in reading and writing. First Nations, Inuit, and Métis children who enter public school speaking an Aboriginal language are typically immersed in English or French, with no attention paid to retention of the primary language or to helping them gain fluency in the second language. This submersion strategy may result in impaired fluency in both languages. Drapeau's studies suggest that the current practice of shifting from the Aboriginal language (first language) to English or French (the second language) upon entering school prevents the establishment and transfer of strong literacy skills.[31]

Most Aboriginal children are not offered the option of schooling in an Aboriginal language. English and French are the only choices. This sends a powerful message to Aboriginal children that their languages are not important.

Maori Language Nests
Te Kohanga Reo

One of the innovative language approaches comes from the Maori of Aotearoa (New Zealand). The language nest is a total immersion program from birth. Elders, parents and children meet in a small, home-like setting and conduct their everyday activities, all in the Maori language. While the elders provide the knowledge of the language and traditional ways, the task of caring for the children is done by the parents. This strengthens the extended family unit while teaching the language and Maori values, beliefs, knowledge and ways of doing things. By the time children reach school age, they can speak the language. Children who have been involved in Te Kohanga Reo are able to continue using Maori in the elementary school system, Kura Kaupap Maori, an offshoot of the language nests. The teachers for this program are trained at the Auckland College of Education.

In the Maori culture, song is a vital form of communication. The language nest teachers place great emphasis on songs and acting out the words. As part of language development, teachers use traditional customs and ways of living with the land.

Te Kohanga Reo resulted from a meeting of Maori elders and leaders in 1982. They were concerned because their language was endangered. They trained 25 teachers the first year to return to their communities and establish language nests. Each year, 25 more teachers come to learn. The original teachers are now learning more complex and deeper expressions of the Maori language.

Volunteerism has been a keystone of Te Kohanga Reo. Elders and parents have given freely of their time because of a deep desire to retain Maori language and culture. The Te Kohanga Reo concept continues to evolve. Initially, there were few guidelines. Today language nests receive state funding and there are national guidelines that pertain to provision of resources.

Source: New Economy Development Group, "Maori Language Nests (Te Kohanga Reo)", in *First Nations Children: Success Stories in Our Communities* (Ottawa: Health and Welfare Canada, Children's Bureau, 1993).

The dominance of English or French in the school environment diminishes the vitality of the Aboriginal language in the child's communication world.

It is clear from the declining use of Aboriginal languages that informal acquisition will not result in the preservation and vitality of Aboriginal languages. Aboriginal communities and parents have several options. They may choose primary use of the Aboriginal language at all stages of schooling. They may decide to support the use of the Aboriginal language as a second language with bilingual fluency and literacy. A further choice is to provide early immersion in the Aboriginal language with transition to English or French after the child has strong fluency. Parents whose children speak an Aboriginal language when they start school may not realize how important it is to reinforce these language skills in the first years of schooling.

Much curriculum development and teacher education is needed to support effective language instruction. In some cases, language research is needed. Aboriginal languages usually require 'lexical elaboration' to add words to the language for concepts encountered later in the child's education. Some languages have dialects that must be documented. There has been very little research on Michif, the Métis language and its dialects, which have been mainly oral languages. The prospects for preserving Michif are discussed in Volume 4, Chapter 5. The language is in a fragile state, since only one per cent of Aboriginal people over the age of 15 reported speaking Michif in 1991.

One of the barriers to teaching Aboriginal languages in the public schools has been the lack of recognition by educators (at the elementary, high school and post-secondary levels) of the competence of elders and other fluent speakers as teachers in the school system. Because elders and other potential teachers do not hold formal qualifications, their unique expertise has not been acknowledged. They have been barred from teaching opportunities and compensation commensurate with their expertise. Some Aboriginal language teacher certification programs have now been established – for example, at Lakehead University in Thunder Bay, Ontario, and in the Northwest Territories – but we did not discover whether these programs have increased elders' access to the classroom. In Chapter 6 in this volume, we discuss the critical importance of restoring intergenerational language transmission using the expertise of fluent speakers, who are often older people.

The preservation and continued vitality of Aboriginal languages are unlikely to be assured by the education system alone. This requires individual, family and community commitment to use language as a source of collective wealth in all forms of communication: newsletters, radio and television broadcasting, public events, ceremonies and, most important, in everyday life. Political and community leaders should encourage the conduct of community business in their own language to the greatest extent possible. The formal education system can be an essential resource in a community-wide effort to ensure the vitality of Aboriginal languages for future generations. Te Kohanga Reo is one model that has attracted the attention of Aboriginal language educators and whole communities (see box). It offers evidence that grassroots community mobilization can be highly successful in saving a language where the will for language survival is widely shared.

RECOMMENDATION

The Commission recommends that

Priority of **3.5.6**
Aboriginal Aboriginal language education be assigned priority in
Language Aboriginal, provincial and territorial education systems to com-
Education plement and support language preservation efforts in local
communities through

   (a) first- or second-language instruction or immersion pro-
       grams where parents desire it and numbers warrant;

   (b) recognition of Aboriginal language competence for second-
       language academic credit whether competence is acquired
       through classroom or out-of-school instruction;

   (c) involving elders and fluent Aboriginal speakers in programs
       to enhance Aboriginal language acquisition and fluency;

   (d) developing instructional materials; and

   (e) encouraging and rewarding language teaching as a career
       path and language research in lexical elaboration, structural
       analysis and cultural contexts as professional and academic
       specializations.

Aboriginal control and parental involvement

Aboriginal control of education and parental involvement are two principles first
advocated in the National Indian Brotherhood's landmark paper, "Indian
Control of Indian Education". Many Aboriginal leaders speak of *resuming* control of education, since First Nations and Inuit exercised complete control of education for countless generations. Rather than being a new responsibility,
self-determination in education was practised by families and communities in
earlier times.

Certainly, Aboriginal involvement in the direct delivery of education has
increased substantially since the early 1970s. Through its devolution policy, the
federal government has delegated administrative authority to First Nations for
most of the schools that serve reserve communities. In a few instances where First
Nations and Métis people constitute a majority in a school district, they have
gained a majority on local school boards, for example, in the Northlands school
division in northern Alberta, the Frontier school division in northern Manitoba,
and the Northern Lights school division in northern Saskatchewan. Apart from
these exceptions, however, and despite traditions of local control and parental

involvement in Canadian education, representation of Aboriginal parents on boards of education and other education authorities is limited. This is true for both provincial and territorial public schools, where almost 70 per cent of all Aboriginal children attend school. In Ontario and New Brunswick, legislation provides for Aboriginal representation on school boards, but we did not find any data to indicate whether this approach has been successful in bridging the gap between Aboriginal parents and the education system.

Even where Aboriginal people are in the majority, they may be marginal-ized in school governance. We were told that in some communities in the Northwest Territories, Aboriginal parents are underrepresented or absent from local school bodies, even where the community is largely Aboriginal. Yellowknife education district #1 has had no Aboriginal members on the school board.[32]

Until recently, First Nation communities in British Columbia, Ontario and New Brunswick whose children attend provincial schools were subject to master tuition agreements. The federal government provided funds directly to provincial authorities on a per student basis: parents and communities had no power to set standards or require accountability from school boards receiving the funds. As these agreements have expired one by one, the First Nations communities have used funding negotiations to obtain appropriate education for their children. Again, the Commission did not find any information on whether this mechanism is improv-ing Aboriginal education. However, representatives of the Nuu-chah-nulth Tribal Council on Vancouver Island and Port Alberni school district no. 70 described the evolution of their positive working relationship, following the signing of a local agreement, and the benefits to Nuu-chah-nulth children.[33]

Even where education authorities are Aboriginal, there must be a contin-uing effort to involve parents in the education of their children. The Kativik school board found that parents felt removed from the decision making of local schools. The board and local school committees have begun a consultation process that will involve parents in defining the outcomes they want for their chil-dren through the education system. They will participate in decisions that will guide the design of education in the future.

In some urban centres, Aboriginal consultants and advisers act as the focal point for co-ordinating Aboriginal initiatives in the school system. Calgary and Vancouver have such positions (see box). City-wide advisory committees are sometimes established to work with the Aboriginal consultant. Where there are many Aboriginal students in a school, parent groups may also be set up. In many cases, however, Aboriginal parents are far removed from the school. Unless there is a critical mass of Aboriginal people involved, the school culture may be simply too difficult to penetrate.

Elders in particular are absent from the classrooms where Aboriginal chil-dren are being educated. In Aboriginal societies, elders are key teachers of the young. Elders must be restored to their place of influence in teaching the young.

Vancouver School District No. 39

Vancouver School District No. 39 has established First Nations education programs and infrastructure to serve an estimated 2,000 Aboriginal students from varying cultural backgrounds in 130 district schools. A First Nations education specialist provides leadership and support to the entire program. At the school level, 19 First Nations school support workers are deployed to encourage parent participation, to problem-solve with teachers, parents and students, and actively to facilitate culturally relevant learning experiences for Aboriginal students.

Involving Aboriginal parents has been an important focus of the First Nations education program. Some parents become involved in the school consultative committees established in each school for all parents. In three schools where there is high enrolment of Aboriginal students, the schools have established Aboriginal parent groups. At the district level, there is a First Nations advisory committee in which parents and urban-based Aboriginal organizations are represented. This advisory committee, which reports to the Vancouver school board, plays a critical role in advancing Aboriginal education issues and initiatives in the district. The First Nations education specialist also sits on other district-wide advisory committees, for example, race relations, employment equity and inner city. While there have been no Aboriginal trustees on the Vancouver school board,

The doors of the school need to be opened to Aboriginal people. The absence of parents and elders from educational processes is an expression of the lack of Aboriginal influence in the school.

In a study of First Nations and provincial schools to determine the status of First Nations control of their education, Kirkness and Bowman report a number of ways for parents to become involved with the school, including "being guest speakers, working as volunteers in the classroom, assisting in cultural activities, elders' visits, assisting on field trips, tutoring, noon hour supervision, project planning, participating in social events, coaching sports".[34] In addition, school personnel visit reserves to meet with parents or with local education authorities. Parents can also become involved in specific committees and programs, including in-service training for teachers.

One of the strategies employed by schools to bridge the gap between home and school has been the hiring of support workers or liaison workers. These workers can be crucial in promoting an understanding of Aboriginal values, providing support for children in the school, resolving difficulties, and serving as an advocate

Aboriginal parents and school staff are attempting to have an impact at various levels of the district school system.

The district has a number of support programs for Aboriginal students at the elementary, junior high and secondary levels. Students are assisted if they require a lower teacher-student ratio, if their learning styles differ from methods used in the conventional classroom, or if they are deemed to be at risk. There are three alternative school programs for grades six to 10, the grades at which Aboriginal students most frequently drop out. The ARIES street kids program operates out of the Vancouver Aboriginal Friendship Centre for Aboriginal students who have been on the street and want to continue their education.

The district has pioneered the use of Fuerstein's instrumental enrichment and dynamic assessment approach in its support programs, not only with Aboriginal students but with all students in the district. Over 700 district staff and teachers have been trained in implementing this approach in their classrooms. The First Nations education specialist has been acknowledged internationally for her leadership and expertise in this field.

In 1995, the Vancouver school board approved a feasibility study on the establishment of a First Nations school.

for children and parents. However, the important work of liaison workers is not a substitute for real participation by Aboriginal parents in the school's strategic decision-making processes and the day-to-day education of the children.

RECOMMENDATIONS

The Commission recommends that

Involvement in Decision Making

3.5.7

Where Aboriginal children attend provincial and territorial schools, provincial and territorial governments take immediate steps to ensure that Aboriginal people are involved fully in the decision-making processes that affect the education of their children. Aboriginal control of education and parental involvement should be implemented through a variety of actions:

(a) legislation to guarantee Aboriginal representation on school boards where population numbers warrant;

(b) recognition of Aboriginally controlled schools under the jurisdiction of Aboriginal community of interest governments;

(c) establishment of Aboriginally governed schools affiliated with school districts, if requested by Aboriginal people; and

(d) creation of Aboriginal advisory committees to school boards.

Involvement in **3.5.8**
School Activities All schools serving Aboriginal children adopt policies that welcome the involvement of Aboriginal parents, elders and families in the life of the school, for example, by establishing advisory or parents committees, introducing teaching by elders in the classroom, and involving parents in school activities.

Positive directions for the future

Aboriginal people, federal, provincial and territorial governments, school authorities and individual teachers have all taken important and positive steps to improve the education of Aboriginal children. Much more must be done if these gains are to be expanded.

We have discussed four key issues: early childhood education, culturally based curriculum, language education, and Aboriginal control and parental involvement. Many other themes appeared in the hearings: the lack of Aboriginal teachers and education leaders in public school systems; inadequate funding to deal with special needs of children with disabilities in Aboriginal schools; racism in classroom interactions and in curriculum; the use of intelligence and scholastic tests that take non-Aboriginal populations as their norm; learning styles of Aboriginal children and teaching styles to accommodate them; the streaming of Aboriginal children away from academically rigorous programs. The list could be extended.

Aboriginal education can follow two paths: Aboriginal governance and improved public education systems. Many issues could be resolved quickly if Aboriginal people had effective control of education and sufficient resources to develop and implement education systems that reflect their needs. Aboriginally controlled institutions will be best situated to create a learning environment in which Aboriginal values, beliefs and traditions are imbedded in the culture of the school. Aboriginal people will choose and design the programs that reflect their aspirations for their children. Aboriginal control and parental involvement will provide mechanisms for Aboriginal people to identify problems and become

Education Equity in Saskatchewan

The goal of education equity is to provide a supportive learning environment for Aboriginal children. There are five components to an education equity plan.

1. The first is to recruit more Aboriginal teachers in all of our schools.
2. The second is to involve Aboriginal parents in the education of their children. And that means a lot of things. That means making schools more friendly. That means teachers being available to parents on a very flexible basis. That means encouraging parents to participate in all aspects of school life, including school boards, division boards, that kind of thing. The Commission did not go so far as to order participation on school division boards, although it is our opinion that we have that authority.
3. The third component of an education equity plan is to put more Aboriginal content into the curriculum. The Department of Education has had a task force and has had some curriculum. The Commission has gone further. We have prepared and had sent out to all school divisions, all schools in the province, lesson plans that deal with Aboriginal history and deal with the problems of discrimination....
4. The fourth component of education equity is providing cross-cultural training for all school staff and for school administrators. That, to me, is a crucial part of education equity. Many school divisions have gone a long way to providing excellent cross-cultural training for their teachers. Unfortunately, all school divisions have not done that and it is something that the Commission is seriously considering mandating. It is at the point where some school divisions are going to have to be ordered to do that in the near future.
5. The final component to education equity is a review of all school policies to make sure [that even if] they appear neutral they do not [in fact] discriminate; again to remove systemic discrimination....All school policies are reviewed.

Many school divisions have taken this to heart and have gone right to Aboriginal organizations to improve their policies. Some have not. That kind of affirmative action program fights against systemic discrimination. We know that changing the system is a slow process. Our position is that the process has to start now. We have to do something.

Source: Theresa Holizki, Chief Commissioner, Saskatchewan Human Rights Commission, RCAP transcripts, Saskatoon, Saskatchewan, 28 October 1992.

involved in the solutions. At the same time, increased participation should not relieve provincial and territorial governments of the responsibility to take an aggressive and proactive stance against discrimination and barriers to the achievement of equitable outcomes in education for Aboriginal peoples.

The experience of Saskatchewan is instructive in this regard. In 1985, the provincial Human Rights Commission (HRC) issued a report, *Education Equity: A Report on Indian/Native Education in Saskatchewan*. The HRC requires every school board whose enrolment of Aboriginal students exceeds five per cent to prepare a plan of action for education equity. When she appeared at our hearings, Chief Commissioner Theresa Holizki noted that 18 school districts had action plans in place. She described the program and reported on its results, as detailed in the accompanying box. The HRC monitors the implementation of measures to improve the education of Aboriginal people in the province.

Other provinces and territories may have their own monitoring mechanisms, or they may have none. Except where Aboriginally run schools have been established, there is no real accountability of provincial and territorial school systems to Aboriginal parents and communities for the quality of education. This needs to change. Provincial and territorial schools receive funding to provide quality education to Aboriginal students. More than two decades after the demand for Aboriginal control of Aboriginal education, it is apparent that equity of outcomes will not be achieved without focused, determined efforts to make things change.

RECOMMENDATION

The Commission recommends that

Required School
Board Strategy

3.5.9

Provincial and territorial ministries require school boards serving Aboriginal students to implement a comprehensive Aboriginal education strategy, developed with Aboriginal parents, elders and educators, including

(a) goals and objectives to be accomplished during the International Decade of Indigenous Peoples;

(b) hiring of Aboriginal teachers at the elementary and secondary school level, with negotiated target levels, to teach in all areas of school programs, not just Aboriginal programs;

(c) hiring of Aboriginal people in administrative and leadership positions;

(d) hiring of Aboriginal support workers, such as counsellors, community liaison workers, psychologists and speech therapists;

(e) curriculum, in all subject areas, that includes the perspectives, traditions, beliefs and world view of Aboriginal peoples;

(f) involvement of Aboriginal elders in teaching Aboriginal and non-Aboriginal students;

(g) language classes in Aboriginal languages, as determined by the Aboriginal community;

(h) family and community involvement mechanisms;

(i) education programs that combat stereotypes, racism, prejudice and biases;

(j) accountability indicators tied to board or district funding; and

(k) public reports of results by the end of the International Decade of Indigenous Peoples in the year 2004.

4. YOUTH

Aboriginal youth today straddle two worlds. The non-Aboriginal world has become a fast-paced, competitive, changing environment in which ever higher levels of education and new skills are required to survive. These are powerful cultural forces that necessitate a secure, solid identity to balance the conflicting messages and demands created where the Aboriginal and non-Aboriginal worlds meet.

The medicine wheel (Figure 5.4) illustrates the cultural implications of this convergence of worlds. Some youth, whose aboriginality has been nurtured in the family and through childhood schooling, function comfortably as bicultural individuals. Others have been raised in environments where their Aboriginal heritage is peripheral to daily life, and they live primarily in mainstream society. Social scientists use the term 'assimilated' or 'acculturated' to describe this pattern. In some communities, young people have had exposure to Aboriginal lifeways and are grounded in traditional Aboriginal value systems and beliefs.

The vast majority of Aboriginal youth, however, are simply struggling to survive. They are caught between the expectations, values and demands of two worlds, unable to find a point of balance. Their despair is manifested in early school leaving, substance abuse, suicide attempts, defiance of the law, and teen pregnancies. As shown in Figure 5.1, 57 per cent of Aboriginal people age 15 and over had less than a grade 9 education in 1991 or did not graduate from high school.[35] The comparable figure for non-Aboriginal people was about 37 per cent.[36] Shocking as these figures may seem, dropping out may be an understandable choice if attending school feels like a jail sentence. Unfortunately, those who leave school have few employment options. The rate of unemployment among Aboriginal youth who have not completed high school is notoriously high. If they try to return to school, they face many barriers in an education system that is not geared to mature students.

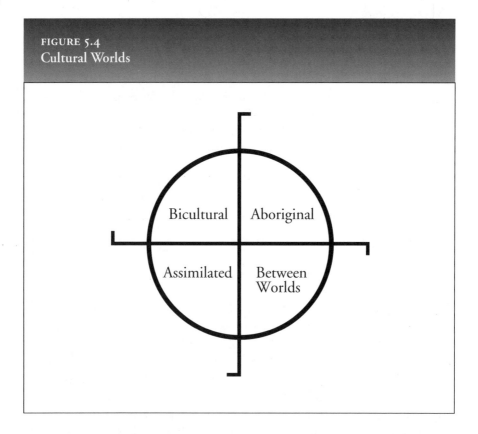

FIGURE 5.4
Cultural Worlds

The experience of Aboriginal youth today stands in sharp contrast to the heritage of Aboriginal peoples. Traditional education prepared youth to take up adult responsibilities. Through apprenticeship and teaching by parents, grandparents, aunts and uncles, skills and knowledge were shaped and honed. In the past, the respective roles of men and women in community life were valued and well established, with continuity from generation to generation, so that youth saw their future roles modelled by adults and elders who were respected and esteemed within their world.

The transition from childhood to youth was, and continues to be for some, a time marked by traditional ceremonies recognizing the emotional, spiritual, physical and intellectual upheavals young people experience as they grow into their adult bodies, emotions and roles. The importance of the individual within the community is stressed with rites of passage – fasts, vision quests and ritual dances. The unique identity of the youth in the broader community is thus established and recognized. Through participation in community life from an early age, the youth observes and absorbs the knowledge and behaviour required to function successfully in adult roles in Aboriginal society. This is part of the lifelong learning process.

By the time they enter high school, many Aboriginal youth have spent eight years or more in an education system from which they and their parents feel alienated. In public schools, the absence of support for Aboriginal identities is overwhelming: no Aboriginal high school teachers; only a limited curriculum dealing with contemporary Aboriginal languages, cultures, history and political issues; an emphasis on intellectual cognitive achievement at the expense of spiritual, social and physical development; and the marginalization of youth in decision making about their education.

At the high school level, most parents are even less involved in their children's education than at elementary school levels. Their exclusion from decision making is intensified where there are no local high schools, where teachers and administrators are non-Aboriginal, and where Aboriginal parents are in a minority. Issues of culturally appropriate curriculum, language education, parental involvement, and funding for curriculum development and culture programs are all present in the education of youth, as in the education of the child. Additional challenges are encountered in the education of youth are the need for youth empowerment; the need for local high schools; the opportunity to return to high school; and the transition from high school to economic activity and careers.

4.1 Youth Empowerment

Parents are not the only ones who feel unable to shape the education process significantly. Youth themselves are excluded. The Commission heard testimony from youth that, although their present and future are at stake, they are rarely involved in decisions about their education. The same difficulties are present in public and Aboriginally controlled schools alike. This sense of disempowerment signals that the experience of youth is out of alignment with statements by Aboriginal leaders who place hope and trust in youth as the next generation of leaders.

What processes are needed so that youth can influence their environment and change the circumstances they find distressing? Schooling, in its organization and content, can help to foster students' potential as active, engaged Aboriginal citizens and leaders.

An extensive and soul-searching evaluative study of the education system in Nunavik in northern Quebec lends support to these voices. In 1992, the final report of the Nunavik Educational Task Force pointed out that the Kativik school board had implemented many of the changes that other Aboriginal people are advocating. They had offered Inuktitut classes and opportunities for cultural programs in the school. Yet their young people were continuing to leave the education system before completion and were becoming entangled in self-destructive behaviour such as substance abuse and suicide.

The report recommended a number of changes, including the development of an integrated and systematic culturally based curriculum; adopting high academic standards; moving to a 12-month school year; adopting the community school model; implementing relevant programs for youth; offering high-impact heritage adventure programs; and providing an alternative 'culture track' school program through the Land College. To promote youth empowerment, the study recommended the following:

> Student initiated programs should be encouraged to involve students in school operations, to give them real responsibilities, and to involve older students in the creation and implementation of programs for all ages. This is to provide them with effective training, tools, and resources. Students should become a respected and responsible partner in maintaining an active community for learning. Student councils and committees, school host and monitor programs, peer and cross-age tutoring, and special projects such as travel and school exchanges and community volunteer service programs, are all examples of activities that student councils should take on to demonstrate that they have some real responsibility in the school.[37]

Presentations made to us emphasized the importance of empowering youth. (Empowerment was a recurring theme in presentations from Aboriginal youth at our hearings; see Volume 4, Chapter 4.) There have been specific efforts to do this using a variety of approaches, or several approaches in combination, including cultural approaches, skills development and support programs, sports and outdoor education programs, and transformative education. We describe several programs that are under way. While the Commission found few formal evaluations of the strengths and weaknesses of these initiatives, it is important to report the efforts of dedicated educators, elders, community members and leaders.

Cultural approaches

Cultural approaches start from the belief that if youth are solidly grounded in their Aboriginal identity and cultural knowledge, they will have strong personal resources to develop intellectually, physically, emotionally and spiritually. The ability to implement culture-based curriculum goes hand in hand with the authority to control what happens in the school system. Cultural programs can be added to the school curriculum, or the whole curriculum can be developed around a cultural core. The most established cultural programming can be found in the schools governed by Aboriginally controlled boards, for example, Kativik school board and the divisional boards of the Northwest Territories. They have been able to implement curriculum changes that communities in other parts of the country are still struggling to achieve. But there is progress in other locations, and we sample a few of them.

- Joe Duquette High School is an Aboriginally managed high school in Saskatoon, established under the jurisdiction of the separate school board. It has strong cultural programming, and there is a culture camp at the end of each year. It has been difficult to establish a strong language program because the students come from many nations with diverse languages. Joe Duquette is operating at maximum capacity.

- Children of the Earth is a high school in Winnipeg school division no. 1. In its few years of existence, it has grown rapidly. The school offers a strong cultural core as well as specific support programs that are provincially funded. Students from Children of the Earth who appeared before the Commission spoke about the school with commitment and with enthusiasm about completing their high school education.

- Ile-a-la-Crosse School in northern Saskatchewan is operated by a board composed of local people. It offers education from junior kindergarten to grade 12. Métis values, history and culture are an integral part of all subject areas, and Michif is taught as a language credit. The school building houses a daycare facility, dental clinic and public library, and the gym and classrooms are used in the evenings for public events.

- The Kahnawake Survival School (Quebec) began more than 20 years ago when Mohawk students and parents fought to establish their own school. Today, it has 170 students, from grades 7 to 11. Haudenosaunee history and culture are part of the curriculum, and the students study Mohawk language in class daily. The students' council is modelled on the traditional Mohawk government. Students sit in clans and make decisions by consensus. The council has been able to influence the school's policies.

In addition to Aboriginally run schools, provincial and territorial governments have launched important curriculum initiatives resulting in Aboriginal curriculum in the classroom. Curriculum for Dene Kede and Inuuqatigiit in the Northwest Territories are examples. In British Columbia, a First Nations studies curriculum has been developed for grade 12. Ontario has also implemented a Native As Second Language Program and produced an Aboriginal studies curriculum for grades 7 to 10.

Despite the positive contribution of culturally based programs to the lives of youth, students may have problems obtaining credit for traditionally based education. Representatives from the Nutshimiu Atusseun training centre told the Commission that the traditional wilderness skills taught by elders as part of their youth training program are not recognized by the department of education in Quebec. The department does not recognize the elders as teachers, so youth do not receive credit for the training, although they receive credit for components not taught by elders, such as first aid and job search skills. The centre has faced funding difficulties, particularly since funders of job-related skills increasingly emphasize accreditation.[38]

The use of Aboriginal role models is another approach that uses Aboriginal identity to motivate youth. Health Canada has been a major sponsor of a role model program based in part on posters featuring the accomplishments of Aboriginal people. Many of the role models travel across the country and speak to Aboriginal youth. Teachers could also serve as role models, but there are few Aboriginal high school teachers in education systems today.

Skills development and support programs

Some education programs help youth develop the skills they need to complete their academic work successfully. Through tutoring, counselling and skills development, they help to strengthen the individual's capacity for achievement. Career counselling and fairs help expose youth to career possibilities. Other programs target at-risk youth, often providing alternative programming or specific information programs that might reduce youth involvement in risky lifestyle choices such as substance abuse, unprotected sexual activity or gangs. These programs are sometimes combined with cultural approaches to tackle root issues of identity and alienation.

The Vancouver school board has introduced a program called Instrumental Enrichment, based on the work of Israeli educator Reuven Feuerstein. By working through a structured set of exercises, students develop problem-solving strategies that can be used in classroom work. They are also encouraged to apply the same principles and processes of problem solving to concerns in their daily lives. While the program serves both non-Aboriginal and Aboriginal students, the First Nations specialist employed by the Vancouver school board has played a leading role in developing and implementing this program. Many Aboriginal students have discovered for themselves that they are competent and creative learners.[39]

As well as offering a strong cultural program, Children of the Earth High School in Winnipeg offers a variety of support programs. PRIDE is an early detection and prevention program designed to prevent chemical dependency. Witchi-ak-kan-nak (partnerships) offers alternatives to students who might be attracted to gang-related violence.

Vincent Massey Collegiate in Fort Garry school division no. 5 has implemented an Empowering Aboriginal Students program. To enhance the self-concept of youth, it has introduced more Aboriginal history, language and culture in the curriculum and has increased staff awareness of the social and political concerns of students. It has also established a mentorship program between Aboriginal youth and adults.

In 1992 the First Nations House of Learning at the University of British Columbia initiated the Synala Honours Program, which offers grade 11 students a six-week on-campus experience in the summer to introduce them to university life. The students are encouraged to pursue professional careers through a program that addresses intellectual, physical, emotional and spiritual dimensions of learning. The program has a strong focus on Aboriginal identity.

Sports and outdoor education programs

Sports provide a vehicle for physical and emotional development, the nurturing of pride and Aboriginal identity, and the fostering of leadership skills. Sports can be integrated into school programs or friendship centre programs or sponsored by other community organizations. Team sports have been very popular in Aboriginal communities across the country, as have traditional sports.

The potential of traditional sport and games as a form of youth empowerment is described by Alwyn Morris, a member of the Mohawk nation and 1984 Olympic gold and bronze medallist in kayaking:

> [T]raditional sports are a recreation activity as well as a method of enhancing cultural retention. Many of the games promote values that were practised traditionally. Some games promote a spiritual value, others identify the high level of respect the people displayed for all humans, specifically women. Still others had a dispute settling purpose. Traditional training respects and fosters strength; spiritually, mentally, physically and emotionally, traits needed to be instilled in our youth today for their personal growth.[40]

Popular Canadian culture often emphasizes the elite athlete. While individual excellence is highly valued in Aboriginal cultures, there is also a strong collective tradition. The Arctic Games are a good illustration. The games include seal skinning, tea boiling, fish cutting, one- and two-foot kicks and head pulls – and competitors actually teach each other during the competition!

Sports have provided an important mechanism for youth development, as illustrated in the following examples.

The First Nations Ski Team in Calgary was established by Cort Gallup, a Cree who reached the top ranks in the Alberta skiing world. His experience taught him to believe that the physical challenge of skiing could help Aboriginal youth rediscover the superb mental and physical conditioning required of warriors and hunters in traditional societies. Twenty young people between the ages of six and 16 now train year-round for the team. Their school work has improved, their alcohol and drug consumption is non-existent, and their self-esteem has soared. The skiers have started a traditional drumming and dancing group that pulls in elders and other youth who do not wish to ski. Local merchants donate equipment, families raise money, and ski hill operators offer slope time for training. This initiative is entirely community supported.[41]

On the west coast, the annual all-Aboriginal basketball tournament attracts youth and adult teams in all age categories, male and female, from First Nations villages up and down the coast. Tribal reputations are put to the test in a week-long competition each January in Prince Rupert. Traditional entertainment is provided by students of various nations. Teams put in months of local fundraising to participate in this popular event.

Outdoor education programs have also been a vehicle for youth empowerment by combining outdoor skills, traditional land-based skills, and cultural and environmental awareness. Elders are often the primary teachers. On-the-land programs, survival camps and other culturally based outdoor programs have been initiated by some schools. The Rediscovery summer camps, for example, bring together young people between the ages of eight and 17 to spend seven days on the land learning traditional knowledge and skills. The program content differs according to the ecosystem: in Fort McMurray in northern Alberta, students canoe, hunt for small game, fish in fresh water and learn to set up camp. In coastal British Columbia, the young people develop skills related to the ocean. The Canadian Outward Bound School has also worked with Aboriginal schools in various parts of the country to run youth programs.

In Big Trout Lake, Ontario, community members have created their own land-based program. Elders take about 40 young people out on traditional land for several weeks at a time during each of the four seasons. Since 1982, the Nutshimiu-Atusseun training centre on the north shore of the St. Lawrence in Quebec has offered a 16-week youth program, of which eight weeks are spent with elders on the land. The Avataq Cultural Institute in Nunavik operates a traditional Inuit summer camp in Inukjuak each year, and a similar summer camp is operated by the community of Kuujjuaq. In New Brunswick, a summer camp provides cultural enrichment for Mi'kmaq and Wuastukwiuk (Maliseet) students.

Transformative education

Many of the youth who spoke before the Commission expressed their deep desire to be involved in their communities, to see the school joined to the real issues of their lives, to see relevance in what they are learning, to make a difference. Education as they experience it is something removed and separate from their everyday world, their hopes and dreams. This sense of distance between learning in the school and the world around them does not have to exist. It can be bridged in a number of ways.

One way is to cast aside the walls of the school and to treat the whole community as the site of education. We saw an example of this in the Akwesasne science and maths project. As part of the learning process in that curriculum, youth became involved in examining water quality. A real community issue became the focus for learning about biology, chemistry, geology and mathematics. The potential to learn citizenship skills can be woven into this learning, as well as the spiritual and ethical dimensions of the issue. For students, this is engaging learning that connects them to the whole of community life.

Another way to transcend this divide between the school experience and daily life is to take as the focus of learning the issues that are most relevant to youth. Excellent study and practice in education have emerged from other parts of the world where people have also experienced colonialism or racial oppression.[42] This form of education – called by a variety of names, including transformative education, popular education and critical pedagogy – acknowledges that the educational process is one of unequal power relationships. Students should be active creators of knowledge rather than passive recipients. The teacher is perceived as a facilitator who can guide the educational process without dominating.

By connecting their experiences to the broader picture, students are able to develop an understanding of the political, social and economic forces that shape their lives. This kind of understanding is critical for youth. The pain experienced in everyday life – racism, violence, poverty – is raw and real. Most youth do not yet have an interpretive framework that helps them understand their own experiences as part of the larger struggle of Aboriginal peoples for their rights. Many blame themselves for life conditions over which they have little control and, as a result, gravitate to risky, self-destructive lifestyles.

Transformative education uses the students' personal experiences as the springboard for deeper analysis and understanding. School courses in history, literature, Aboriginal studies, social studies, geography, art, theatre arts and other subject areas have the potential to transform experiences into an intelligible pattern with local, regional and global aspects. This educational process is participatory and may use experiential learning, research projects, oral histories, theatre, drawing techniques and other forms of creative expression to do analysis. An important dimension of the learning is the sharing of knowledge by all participants: everyone contributes and there is no competitive ranking of performance.

Youth must become active agents capable of taking action to transform the imperfect world they encounter. This is the basis of active, responsible citizenship. Youth who spoke before the Commission talked about the importance of confronting the problems they face. They came forward with examples and proposals:

> The youth in this community should organize a youth group with the express goal of combatting racism. The group could be called Kids Against Racial Discrimination and should work with a number of community organizations to develop programs to make people feel welcome, not excluded, and to educate all people in the community on the need for equality of support and of treatment. Schools must include programs against racism in curricula at all levels. Schools must provide opportunities for all students to learn about the values and beliefs of other people. The study of Native culture, for example, should be compulsory for non-Aboriginal students also.
>
> Dawn Campbell
> North Battleford Comprehensive High School
> North Battleford, Saskatchewan, 29 October 1992

As recommended in *Silatunirmut: the Pathway to Wisdom*, a study discussed earlier, youth must have opportunities to assume positions of leadership. Student councils, peer teaching, youth conferences and recreation leadership training are all options for expanding the capacities of youth for future leadership. In high

> ### "They Look A Lot Like Us"
>
> In May 1987, 12 students from Coppermine, Northwest Territories, 10 of them Inuit, travelled to China to explore a different culture and way of life. Their journey took them to Mongolia where they were to encounter a people with a culture and lifestyle that bore remarkable similarities to Inuit life. Their journey is documented in a film, "They Look A Lot Like Us – A China Odyssey" (Kudluk Productions, 1987), which has won several awards.

schools where Aboriginal students are in the minority, proactive approaches may be required to invite Aboriginal youth into leadership roles.

Also important are youth exchanges and travel. School exchanges expand learning, understanding and possibilities. Some schools already hold such trips. International exchanges should also take place. A few Aboriginal young people have travelled internationally with programs like Canada World Youth, and others have attended international gatherings of Indigenous peoples. There should be more opportunities for Aboriginal youth to make connections with Indigenous youth in other parts of the world. Transformative education, used in conjunction with travel, would help youth to analyze the links between their experience and the broader patterns of social and political life they encounter in the world.

Electronic adventures are also opening the door to exchange as students are introduced to the Internet and are able to chat with their counterparts in other parts of the world. Discussions have linked classrooms of Indigenous youth from Australia, New Zealand, the United States and other countries. Through the SchoolNet project, opportunities for electronic communication could open up significantly in the next decade.

RECOMMENDATION

The Commission recommends that

Youth
Empowerment
3.5.10

Aboriginally controlled, provincial, and territorial schools serving Aboriginal youth develop and implement comprehensive Aboriginal youth empowerment strategies with elements elaborated in collaboration with youth, including

(a) cultural education in classroom and informal settings;

(b) acknowledgement of spiritual, ethical and intuitive dimensions of learning;

(c) education to support critical analysis of Aboriginal experience;

(d) learning as a means of healing from the effects of trauma, abuse and racism;

(e) academic skills development and support;

(f) sports and outdoor education;

(g) leadership development; and

(h) youth exchanges between Aboriginal nations, across Canada and internationally.

4.2 Need for Local High Schools

The highest drop-out rate for Aboriginal students is between grades nine and 10. Where there is no local Aboriginally controlled high school, entering high school outside an Aboriginal community may be the youth's first direct experience with the attitudes of mainstream society. At this vulnerable age when there are intense social pressures, youth in public schools frequently encounter racist attitudes and behaviour that undermine their self-esteem. Presenters pointed out schooling practices that discriminate without malice on the part of teachers:

> We put Mi'kmaq [language] into kindergarten and then switch them in primary level to English with the hope that they'll start getting it....So little is understood [about the length of time] it takes to be able to think in the second language. Our students leave Eskasoni at grade 10. By that time they have been given English language instruction in school, but they are still thinking in Mi'kmaq when they leave here to go to Riverview High School. There they are subjected all day to English, at a pace that assumes they should know what is happening. Questions are given to them...and by the time the student has thought about what was asked, and what needs to be said based on what he read last night, and by the time he comes up with the right words in English to express his Mi'kmaq thinking, the teacher has long gone, moved on to someone else.
>
> Marie Battiste
> Cultural Curriculum Co-ordinator
> Eskasoni School Board
> Eskasoni, Nova Scotia, 7 May 1992

For many youth in geographically isolated communities, there are no local high schools. To continue their education, they must relocate to urban centres or spend many hours commuting. The transition to high school demands massive disruption of their family and community life, and they experience intense isolation and loneliness.

Wahsa Distance Education High School

Wahsa is a radio high school that was established in 1989 by the Northern Nishnawbe Education Council in northwestern Ontario. It serves 23 First Nations communities, most of which have only fly-in access. Radio classes are broadcast on the FM band two or three times a week, and students meet in a local community learning centre under the supervision of a local community facilitator who is responsible for creating a positive learning environment. The students hold audio-conferences with the teacher by using a telephone convener that brings students from different communities on-line at the same time for discussion with the teacher. The 'Wahsa Express' is a plane service that carries students' assignments back and forth to Sioux Lookout for marking once a week. A free tutoring hot-line and fax service gives the students additional contact with their teachers. On-site tutors help students four to eight hours a week. At least once a term, a teacher visits students in each community. Wahsa also offers Ontario correspondence courses, with the same support services as for its radio courses.

One of the important contributions of Wahsa is its creative organization of student enrolments. The school takes in students six times a year, to complete seven-week terms, each worth half a credit. Through this flexible system, students who have to leave school temporarily can resume their studies without significant loss of time or credit.

Technological difficulties have hampered Wahsa's programming. The Wahsa-serviced communities use analogue telecommunications equipment rather than the more recent digital equipment. Some communities are equipped only with radio phones. Students in some communities have had to attend a teleconference by crossing the lake in the middle of winter to use a radio phone installed outside on a screened porch. Education funding shortfalls have also limited the program's operations.

Our children, before they actually grow up...have to leave their parents to go down south, but they cannot survive in the big cities, so they just end up coming back to their own people because they get very lonely in the bigger cities, and it is a very different type of life and this is what happens. They come back to the communities and they are not hunters any more because they were not properly trained by the elders.... [translation]

Johnny Epoo
President, Avatuck
Winnipeg, Manitoba, 21 April 1992

The availability of high school education in remote or isolated communities varies from region to region. In band-controlled schools, 27 per cent go to grade 12; 59 per cent of them have grade 9, 10 or 11. The Northwest Territories has a goal of establishing high school services in every community.[43] In the Baffin Island region, early secondary education (grades 9 and 10) is available in all communities, and in Nunavik, high school can be completed in almost all of the 14 communities.

The greatest deterrent to extending high school education to all Aboriginal communities has been the high cost of offering local services where there are small numbers of students. For parents, it is also a dilemma: should they lobby for local high school services when course options will be limited, or should they send them to a regional centre where there are more choices?

Fortunately, alternatives are emerging. Some distance education projects geared to high school education have shown promising results. With a focus on youth education, the Wahsa Distance Learning High School, initiated by the Northern Nishnawbe Education Council in northwestern Ontario, has innovative ideas to encourage completion of high school programs (see box). While distance technologies in Aboriginal education still require much cultural refinement, early results suggest they are a viable option when carefully established under Aboriginal control.

There are also other options. One is to establish regional schools for Aboriginal students in Aboriginal communities. Another is to combine study in the home community with seasonal institutes that bring students from small communities together for short-term intensive instruction in some subject areas where more specialized facilities are needed. Flexibility and creativity may produce some unique combinations of educational services. The Wahsa Distance Learning High School demonstrates that flexible timetabling can expand the options available for young people.

RECOMMENDATION

The Commission recommends that

Community High
School Programs
3.5.11

High school programs be extended to communities, using cost-effective options agreed upon by parents and families, including

(a) complete school facilities for local high school delivery;

(b) regional high schools in Aboriginal communities;

(c) culturally appropriate, interactive distance education; and

(d) seasonal institutes.

4.3 High School Re-entry

If large numbers of Aboriginal youth leave the education system, what happens if they want to return? Young people leave school for a variety of reasons. When they find that a low level of formal education blocks their economic opportunities, young people sometimes decide to return to school. However, they frequently find that the road back to school is blocked. Only 22 per cent of drop-outs aged 15 to 24 return to high school; another 11 per cent take adult upgrading. About 63 per cent do not return at all.[44]

Young people who have left school may not have as strong an academic preparation as their peers, but they have acquired considerable life experience. Their particular needs may not be met by rejoining a classroom where the students are younger and less experienced. Young women returning to school may be raising children with a partner or alone. Young men may be working to support a family. To apply the principle of lifelong learning to youth, it is important to establish secondary education programs that invite youth to return to formal education and that acknowledge that their circumstances differ from those of younger students.

Unfortunately, even established programs considered successful by the Aboriginal community are not immune to education cutbacks. In Calgary, we were told about the plight of the Plains Indian Cultural Survival School (PICSS):

> In 1993 funding for the over-age students at the Plains Indian Cultural Survival School, otherwise known as PICSS, may be discontinued. This development would affect half the student population. As an alternative high school, PICSS has successfully met the challenge of enhancing the educational, cultural and personal enhancement of Aboriginal students. Students over the age of 19 need specialized programs if they are to complete grade 12.
>
> Allan Giroux
> Calgary Aboriginal Urban Affairs Committee
> Calgary, Alberta
> 26 May 1993

In consultation with youth, appropriate programs can be developed, including relevant curriculum and co-op programs. Other support may be required, such as flexible timetabling, on-site child care and outreach services such as counselling and peer support groups.[45] In some instances, income support may be required where the young person is living independently and has no other income. Youth should be involved in developing programs that address their needs.

RECOMMENDATION

The Commission recommends that

Secondary Study   3.5.12
Re-entry   Aboriginal authorities and all provincial and territorial ministries of education fund programs for Aboriginal youth who have left secondary school before graduation to enable them to resume their studies with appropriate curriculum, scheduling, academic and social support.

4.4 Economic Activity and Careers

The Canadian job market is part of a global economy. Across the country parents and business people have expressed concern about the tenuous relationship between school and the workplace. Provincial and territorial governments are considering better ways to prepare students for the work that will be available in the twenty-first century. Economic analysts predict that in the future, the available jobs will be either low-skill and low-paying, or require 16 years or more of formal education.

Aboriginal parents, elders and leaders are concerned about the job prospects of youth and the preparation of students for these jobs. Young people are worried too. In some regions there is a strong job market for trained Aboriginal graduates. To implement self-government, Aboriginal professionals will be needed. Traditional activities, the arts and trades represent important career options in some regions.

Co-operative education, which combines school studies and related work placements, has a good track record in preparing students for job opportunities. It helps them sample a variety of job options and expand their knowledge of work possibilities. Co-op education introduces students to the demands of the workplace and offers them an opportunity to establish contacts. Co-op programs have kept many high school students in school. These programs are relevant and provide training, particularly in hi-tech fields, that schools cannot match. Both male and female students are exposed to career opportunities that broaden their horizons. In some small communities, it may be more difficult to implement co-op education where there is a shortage of paid employment. Work placements might include non-wage employment, including resource-based activities and training in traditional crafts.

RECOMMENDATION

The Commission recommends that

Co-op Education   **3.5.13**
Federal, provincial and territorial governments encourage co-op initiatives by offering funding inducements to secondary schools that develop active co-op education programs for Aboriginal young people.

5. TEACHER EDUCATION PROGRAMS

Inuit teachers, Inuit culture. To help fully meet our students' educational and cultural needs, we need more Aboriginal teachers from the region within our school system. Right now, just under 20 per cent of our teachers are Inuit and an increased number of Inuit teachers is important for a variety of reasons. Not only will Aboriginal teachers serve as role models for the Inuit youth, but they will have a better understanding of the Inuit student and his or her background and thus be better able to reach our Aboriginal students.

> Larry Aknavigak
> Kitikmeot Board of Education
> Cambridge Bay, Northwest Territories, 17 November 1993

Teachers are central to the education experience. An inspiring teacher can set an individual on a path of discovery that lasts a lifetime. An insensitive teacher can scar an individual irreparably. Teachers are so pivotal to what happens in the classroom that Ontario's Royal Commission on Learning termed teachers one of the four engines that will transform the quality of schooling, learning and teaching:

> We make the point repeatedly that no positive changes to the system can happen without the enthusiastic co-operation of teachers – a central fact perversely ignored in many attempts at reform – and that teachers simply can't be expected to perform their many functions adequately unless they are properly prepared.[46]

It has been recognized for decades that having Aboriginal teachers in the classroom represents the first line of change in the education of Aboriginal children and youth. The Hawthorn report of 1966 talked about the importance of

Aboriginal teachers and non-Aboriginal teachers with cross-cultural sensitivity.[47] The training of Aboriginal teachers has been a top priority for Aboriginal people since the 1960s when they began to lobby for programs that would bring Aboriginal teachers into the classroom. Since the first programs were launched in Ontario and the Northwest Territories in the mid-1960s, there have been at least 34 Aboriginal teacher education programs across the country, many of which continue today.

Aboriginal teacher education programs have registered some important gains. In 1981, about 4,490 Aboriginal people were in teaching and related occupations. By 1991, there were 8,075.[48] While there are many more Aboriginal teachers in Aboriginal and non-Aboriginal school systems today than a decade ago, the numbers remain far too low relative to the current and projected need. At least three times as many are needed to achieve parity with the number of non-Aboriginal teachers serving non-Aboriginal children.[49] Recognizing that systematic steps must be taken if things are going to change, several jurisdictions have established targets to boost the number of Aboriginal teachers. The Northwest Territories aims to have 50 per cent Aboriginal teachers by the year 2000, up from 23 per cent in 1991. The Northern Lights school division in Saskatchewan expects to move from 24 per cent in 1992 to a target of 75 per cent Aboriginal teachers, reflecting the proportion of Aboriginal people in the region. As seen earlier, since 1985 the Saskatchewan Human Rights Commission has required school districts with an Aboriginal population of five per cent or more to establish an action plan in Aboriginal education, including the recruitment of Aboriginal teachers.

5.1 Quality of Teacher Education Programs

Unfortunately, there has not been much systematic evaluation of teacher education programs for Aboriginal people. As a result, it is difficult to comment on the comparative quality of programs or on the degree to which specific teacher education programs have developed specialized curricula to train Aboriginal teachers. What we learn from communities is that not all teacher education programs prepare teachers for the cultural dimensions of teaching in Aboriginal classrooms.

Teaching is a complex transmission of values, behaviours and knowledge. If we recall the teaching traditions of Aboriginal nations, elders are respected teachers with access to knowledge that extends back through countless generations. In oral traditions, stories are a particularly important medium for transmitting knowledge. They contain layers of meaning that listeners decode according to their readiness to receive certain teachings. In the classroom and out on the land, the teacher conveys to students the acceptable rules of behaviour and the values to be honoured through subtle verbal and non-verbal communication. Education is holistic and addresses not only the intellectual but the spiritual, emotional and physical aspects of the individual. The teacher is a role model whose own behaviour and attitudes are absorbed by students. At the same time, the teachers encourage each individual to use the special gifts they have been given and to do so in a way that benefits everyone, not just themselves.

Scholars in Aboriginal education are still studying the subtleties of the knowledge-transmission process. What is certain is that teacher education programs vary in their attention to the dynamics of teaching in Aboriginal cultural contexts. Many Aboriginal community members and education leaders have expressed frustration that Aboriginal teachers are not fully grounded in the teaching traditions of their nations. They argue that there should be stronger components in teacher education programs to address the language, history, pedagogy and traditions of Aboriginal peoples. It is important to ground teacher education programs in the cultural traditions of the communities in which teachers will eventually be working.

5.2 The Need for More Elementary School Teachers

While the number of Aboriginal elementary school teachers has been growing steadily, the majority of Aboriginal children are still not schooled in classrooms with Aboriginal teachers. This under-representation is acutely apparent in provincial and territorial school systems that serve Aboriginal children. Even where the majority of students are Aboriginal, the number of Aboriginal teachers is far too low. We have recommended that school districts increase their hiring of Aboriginal teachers. The hiring target levels set by the government of the Northwest Territories, the Northern Lights school division, and the Saskatchewan Human Rights Commission are all indicators of the need to focus attention on training more elementary school teachers and getting them into the classroom.

The immediate concern of this section is increasing the number of Aboriginal teachers being trained. The numbers can be boosted through a strategy that combines an increase in institutional capacity with enough financial and counselling support for students. Many existing Aboriginal teacher education programs have survived through short-term funding that leaves their future uncertain. The federal government, as well as provincial and territorial governments, should intervene to increase funding for teacher education programs that have good track records in the Aboriginal community and that are prepared to train more Aboriginal teachers.

Aboriginal people and post-secondary institutions have entered into partnerships to train Aboriginal teachers, with some remarkable successes. However, Aboriginal teacher education programs are not the same throughout the country. Some have been designed with or by Aboriginal people, with considerable attention paid to Aboriginal styles of pedagogy, Aboriginal history, traditions and values, and Aboriginal language instruction. Others offer teacher practicums to help Aboriginal people already working in education acquire teaching credentials. Some programs are delivered in Aboriginal communities or in regional centres. Still other programs are campus-based and offer the regular teacher education programs with some enrichment units. It is important to build on the models that represent successful collaboration between Aboriginal people and educational institutions. These programs can be assisted to increase their capacity to train and graduate more Aboriginal teachers.

RECOMMENDATION

The Commission recommends that

Expanded Teacher
Education
Programs

3.5.14

Federal, provincial and territorial governments expand financial support to post-secondary institutions for existing and new Aboriginal teacher education programs, contingent on

(a) evidence of Aboriginal support for the program;

(b) Aboriginal participation in the governance of the program;

(c) the incorporation of Aboriginal content and pedagogy into the program; and

(d) periodic evaluations that indicate that the quality of teacher education conforms to standards of excellence expected by Aboriginal people.

5.3 The Need for More Secondary School Teachers

Most of the Aboriginal teachers trained to date have been trained for elementary education. Many more are needed. At the same time, the number of Aboriginal teachers certified to teach at the secondary school level is abysmally low. This is a serious problem. In the grades where Aboriginal youth are most at risk of dropping out, Aboriginal teachers are unlikely to be among the school staff. Even in band-operated schools committed to hiring Aboriginal staff, non-Aboriginal staff are often hired because there are so few Aboriginal candidates. Attracting more Aboriginal people to secondary teaching careers is crucial in improving high school retention rates, which in turn is necessary to develop community skills for self-government. (See Volume 2, Chapter 3 for more discussion of strategies to enhance capacity to implement self-government.)

Secondary school teaching programs require that students have a university undergraduate degree in a subject provincial or territorial authorities designate as 'teachable', that is, in an area of concentration that is taught in secondary school.

This subject requirement has shut out many potential Aboriginal candidates, either because they have not completed a degree or because their degree is not in a teachable subject. Aboriginal studies is now available as a degree program in at least 10 universities, but Aboriginal studies and Aboriginal languages generally have not gained recognition as teachable subjects in faculties of education.

The lack of Aboriginal teachers at the secondary level inhibits the development of appropriate curricula and pedagogy and deprives students of role models. Youth alienation from the high school experience leads to early school-leaving and a lack of candidates for university education who could in turn become high school teachers. It is a repeating cycle.

Interrupting this cycle requires commitment and urgent co-ordinated action on several fronts simultaneously. We can suggest several ways to produce more teachers in secondary education:

- Special efforts must be made to attract Aboriginal people to secondary school teaching as a career. As early as grades seven and eight, young people must be made aware of secondary school teaching as a career option and the academic requirements necessary to reach that destination.
- Aboriginal educators already in the teaching system who wish to pursue secondary school teaching must be given the opportunity to complete the teachable subject requirements they need for certification at senior grade levels. Community-based delivery of arts and sciences courses coupled with job leaves would improve access of Aboriginal educators to subject concentrations required for teaching at the secondary level. The Northern Professional Access Program (NORPAC) program in northern Saskatchewan offers the first two years of arts and science in La Ronge, which allows adults with family responsibilities to study closer to home. Community-based delivery allows candidates to complete their teachable subject requirements at the beginning or end of their education training.
- Financial incentives can be used to encourage both young people and Aboriginal educators to pursue secondary school teaching careers. Aboriginal education authorities could offer scholarships and forgivable loans to those committed to completing programs in secondary school education. In the section on education for self-government in this chapter, we recommended that Aboriginal education authorities establish incentive and bonus programs. Aboriginal educators already in the school system would benefit from job leaves with financial incentives. Such support would make it possible to increase the number of teachers at the secondary school level.
- Teacher education programs could encourage education students to acquire the subjects needed to teach at the secondary level. A flexible option could be developed for students who decide after they enter education that secondary school teaching would be of interest to them. For example, programs

might allow students to complete subject requirements concurrently with their education studies or after completing education courses.

For further elaboration of training strategies, see Volume 2, Chapters 3 and 5.

RECOMMENDATION

The Commission recommends that

Aboriginal Secondary School Teachers

3.5.15

Canadian governments, Aboriginal education authorities, post-secondary institutions and teacher education programs adopt multiple strategies to increase substantially the number of Aboriginal secondary school teachers, including

 (a) promoting secondary school teaching careers for Aboriginal people;

 (b) increasing access to professional training in secondary education, for example, community-based delivery of courses and concurrent programs; and

 (c) offering financial incentives to students.

5.4 Community-Based Teacher Education

Faculties of education have developed some flexible partnerships with Aboriginal people. Many of these post-secondary teacher education programs have field or community components so that students can learn without leaving their communities. The programs are designed to increase the professional qualifications of those with considerable classroom experience as teaching assistants, language teachers, special needs assistants and so on. Following are some examples of post-secondary education programs that go directly to the people.

The Native Indian Teacher Education Program at the University of British Columbia (UBC) started in 1974. Today it delivers its bachelor of education programs on the UBC campus and at four field centres where students can complete the first two years of their degree. Its newest program is the Vancouver field centre, which trains teachers to work in multicultural cosmopolitan communities such as Vancouver. The students take courses in Aboriginal education and urban studies.

Since 1975 the Kativik school board has worked with McGill University to train elementary school teachers, Inuktitut language specialists, and elementary school teachers working in a second language. Students train in their home communities, and after two years they graduate with a provincial teaching diploma and a certificate in Native and northern education. They can complete a bachelor of education degree by taking additional courses on the McGill campus. McGill has used this model to deliver similar programs to train Algonquin, Cree, Mi'kmaq, and Mohawk teachers.

The Northern Teacher Education Program (NORTEP) in northern Saskatchewan has been a key element in transforming education in a region where 85 per cent of the student body is Aboriginal. It was started in 1977 with the aim of having northern teachers in northern schools. NORTEP offers a community-based program where students can take their classes in La Ronge and practice teaching is done in local community schools. The program initially focused on training elementary school teachers. In 1989 it expanded to include the Northern Professional Access Program (NORPAC), a university bridging program that offers counselling, tutoring, and two years of arts and science university courses that students can take in La Ronge. NORTEP also delivers a bridging program to Dene communities in northern Saskatchewan. As part of their professional development, teachers with many years of experience may also return to classes and upgrade their skills to a B.ED. or M.ED. level. With a strong Aboriginal voice in the governance of these programs, teacher education has a solid component of course work directly related to the cultural aspirations of the region. Cree and Dene languages, northern essential learnings, Aboriginal pedagogy, and field trips such as trapping school or cultural camp are part of the curriculum.

The Gabriel Dumont Institute, in conjunction with the University of Saskatchewan and University of Regina, offers SUNTEP (Saskatchewan Urban Native Teacher Education Program). Initiated in 1980, this very successful four-year bachelor of education program is delivered in Regina, Saskatoon and Prince Albert. The students are primarily Métis and non-status First Nations people.

In 1984 the Inuit communities of Povungnituk and Ivujivik entered into a partnership with the University of Quebec at Abitibi-Témiscamingue (UQAT) to deliver community-based teacher education and to participate in a school and curriculum project. Three Inuit instructors work under the direction of six UQAT faculty to deliver the courses in Inuktitut. Each 45-hour course is usually delivered in three blocks of 15 hours, with three visits by the faculty member to the community. Inuktitut has had to be extended to include concepts for which there was no existing vocabulary. The students and the faculty members communicate in English – their common second language.

We commend these efforts to deliver teacher education in communities. They extend accessibility to Aboriginal people who cannot pursue post-secondary education by conventional means. We urge the continuation of such programs and encourage post-secondary institutions that have not already done so to consider this form of delivery. If the number of Aboriginal teachers is to increase, community-based education will be an essential facilitator.

RECOMMENDATION

The Commission recommends that

Teacher Education Accessible in Communities

3.5.16

Federal, provincial and territorial governments provide support to increase the number of Aboriginal people trained as teachers by

(a) expanding the number of teacher education programs delivered directly in communities; and

(b) ensuring that students in each province and territory have access to such programs.

5.5 The Need for Other Educational Professionals

The number of Aboriginal people with graduate degrees in education is still small. First Nations House of Learning at the University of British Columbia offers the Ts''kel Program at the master's and doctorate levels in education. Blue Quills College in Alberta offers a part-time master of education program in conjunction with San Diego State University. Blue Quills college students spend six weeks in the summer in San Diego and complete the rest of their work in Alberta. The institution established this program with San Diego because of the American university's willingness to work with them to meet their needs. There continues to be a need for more Aboriginal education administrators, counsellors, psychologists, speech pathologists and other professionals in education-related fields. The certification of language teachers has been a problem because many of the candidates who are richly qualified in their cultural and linguistic backgrounds do not have the academic qualifications required in Canadian teaching systems.

As part of their community-based teacher education initiative, the government of the Northwest Territories is tackling one of the major criticisms of past programs in the N.W.T. and elsewhere – many para-professional courses were offered that do not open career paths to undergraduate degrees or other options.[50] They have implemented a new co-ordinated system of educator training so that Aboriginal language specialists, classroom assistants and special needs assistants can earn course credits from Arctic College and McGill University during their two-year basic teacher training program. These credits can then be applied to teacher education and undergraduate programs. Educators call this 'articulation'; it means that course credits can be counted toward a number of different career programs or toward more advanced certification in the same career area. Further work is being done to articulate courses for school and community counsellors, early childhood educators and interpreter-translators.

The lack of articulation of educator programs is widespread, with many implications for the individuals involved and for the advancement of Aboriginal education as a whole. Representatives of the Ontario Native Education Counselling Association (ONECA) told us about their concerns.[51] Since 1977 ONECA has offered the Native Counsellor Training Program, in collaboration with the Ontario ministry of education and the department of Indian affairs. In 1985 ONECA took over the administration of the program. Despite its success in training counsellors for Aboriginal education programs, it lacks the academic and provincial recognition given other guidance and social counsellor training programs.

The experience of ONECA, which is not uncommon, points to the need for co-ordinated planning in the training of educators. Aboriginal authorities will have to co-operate with deliverers of teacher education programs to overcome obstacles in education career paths and to map out better articulated educator programs.

RECOMMENDATION

The Commission recommends that

Career Paths   **3.5.17**

Teacher education programs, in collaboration with Aboriginal organizations and government agencies that sponsor professional and para-professional training, adopt a comprehensive approach to educator training, developing career paths from para-professional training to professional certification in education careers that

(a) prepare Aboriginal students for the variety of roles required to operate Aboriginal education systems; and

(b) open opportunities for careers in provincial education systems.

5.6 The Education of Non-Aboriginal Teachers

Teacher education programs also have a role in preparing non-Aboriginal teachers and school professionals to provide education services. Many Aboriginal children and youth in provincial and territorial schools will spend most of their time in classrooms with non-Aboriginal teachers. The values reinforced by the teacher, the inclusion or exclusion of Aboriginal materials and perspectives in the course, the type of interaction in the classroom, and the relationship between teachers and parents will all affect the comfort of the Aboriginal student. Other education staff – principals, counsellors and psychologists – make professional decisions every day that affect the lives of children. All these educators must be able to fulfil their professional responsibilities with sensitivity and energy to help their students blossom.

The quality of education Aboriginal students receive in provincial and territorial schools depends on the willingness of school personnel to create a supportive learning environment for them. This will not happen in a vacuum. School staff in various education roles must have the opportunity to develop this commitment to high-quality education, based on understanding of Aboriginal culture and values and on issues in Aboriginal-Canadian relations. We emphasize the need to correct erroneous assumptions and to dispel stereotypes that still abound in the minds of many Canadians, distorting their relationships with Aboriginal people. Accurate information about the history and cultures of Aboriginal peoples and nations, the role of treaties in the formation of Canada, and the distinctive contributions of Aboriginal people to contemporary Canada should form part of every Canadian student's education.[52] A presenter at Cranbrook, British Columbia, articulated the goal of Aboriginal educators and many other Aboriginal people:

> When we speak of education it is not only meant that the Aboriginal person must become better educated in the non-Aboriginal school of thought. The non-Aboriginal person must be made aware of our history, our traditional lifestyle and the downfall and resurgence of our peoples as history has evolved today. This information must become a compulsory component in the teaching of all Canadians.
>
> Gwen Phillips Clement
> Ktunaxa Independent School System
> Cranbrook, British Columbia, 3 November 1992

Teachers cannot convey accurate information about Aboriginal people and instil respectful attitudes unless they have been prepared to do so. In training future educators, a compulsory component focused on Aboriginal people will allow students to develop a deeper understanding of what is at stake in their relationships with Aboriginal students and will prepare them to teach Aboriginal subject matter. Educators already in the school systems must have an opportunity to learn about Aboriginal people through professional development programs that foster cultural sensitivity.

RECOMMENDATION

The Commission recommends that

Aboriginal Component in All Teacher Education Programs

3.5.18

Provinces and territories require that teacher education programs
(a) in pre-service training leading to certification include at least one component on teaching Aboriginal subject matter to all students, both Aboriginal and non-Aboriginal;

(b) develop options for pre-service training and professional development of teachers, focused on teaching Aboriginal students and addressing Aboriginal education issues; and

(c) collaborate with Aboriginal organizations or community representatives in developing Aboriginal-specific components of their programs.

6. THE ADULT

By adulthood an individual attains status as a responsible member of the family and community, contributing to economic, social, political and spiritual life. Many adults, however, reach this stage ill-prepared to be active participants in the economy. Some still lack the education and skills needed to take available employment or, as we suggest in Volume 2, Chapter 5, to create their own employment through business development.

Assuming there are jobs, one solution to under-employment is for people to return to school for more education and training. Those who have completed high school and technical, college or university programs stand a much better chance in the job market. But it is not only the individual who reaps the rewards of higher education. Communities are attempting to build the local skills pool they require for Aboriginal self-government. Education, then, is an investment with long-term benefits for the individual, for Aboriginal communities, and for Canadian society.

Over the past 10 years, the number of Aboriginal people attending and completing post-secondary education programs has increased. Most of the increase is in the non-university post-secondary category, as shown in Figure 5.1. Unfortunately, current statistical information does not distinguish between someone who has completed a six-week certificate in a preparatory course and someone who has received a two-year diploma in a technical subject. The figure also demonstrates that, although more Aboriginal students are attending university, the proportion completing university programs has risen by only one per cent over the last decade. The figure is around three per cent – one-quarter of the proportion of non-Aboriginal persons who receive a university degree.

Obstacles continue to block Aboriginal people from achieving higher levels of education. Adults who left high school without graduating may be admitted to post-secondary studies as mature students, but they usually have to complete qualifying or bridging programs. Many students live in remote or isolated areas that require them to relocate for education programs; this may not be feasible if a person has family responsibilities and financial obligations. Any individual or family living at the edge of survival requires solid financial assistance to make a significant life change, and few people who live in poverty will risk taking out loans for post-secondary education.

In addition to these barriers, there is the question of the training and education programs themselves. Many ignore Aboriginal perspectives, values and issues and give scant attention to the work environment in which students will use their professional knowledge and skills. In the informal culture of the institution, there may be little or no affirmation of Aboriginal identity, and the environment may replicate the negative features that led students to drop out of school in the first place. Aboriginal support systems – peer networks, family activities, financial, personal and academic counselling, or daycare services – may not be in place. The lack of institutional readiness to develop these supports is a significant deterrent to the completion of programs for students who do enrol. Lack of Aboriginal control, strongly evidenced in the education of children and youth, is also encountered in the education of adults.

We envisage a world where the representation of Aboriginal people among doctors, engineers, carpenters, entrepreneurs, biotechnologists, scientists, computer specialists, artists, professors, archaeologists and individuals in other careers is comparable to that of any other segment of the population. Aboriginal leaders who signed treaties earlier in our history sought education that would give their children the knowledge and skills to participate as equals in the Canadian economy that was emerging. We are still far from realizing that goal. We have not achieved equal opportunity or equal results in the post-secondary education now available to Aboriginal people.

Removing barriers is urgently needed. Over the past two decades, Aboriginal populations have been rebounding, following a growth pattern similar to the non-Aboriginal population but about 10 years behind. Between 1991 and 2016, the population aged 15 to 24 is expected to grow from 142,400 to 175,500 as the children of today's young adults become youths and young adults. Within the next decade, they will reach an age when post-secondary education and job opportunities must be accessible. The demand is expected to expand even further until the year 2011, when the 20-to-24 age group will be the largest segment of the Aboriginal population. After that, growth rates should decline and gradually converge with those of the non-Aboriginal population. (For further discussion of population projections and employment needs, see Volume 2, Chapter 5.)

In the next section we discuss difficulties in access to and completion of higher levels of education and training, the strides made in recent years, and the directions that need to be pursued to advance the education of Aboriginal adults. We also analyze how post-secondary institutions are responding to the educational needs of Aboriginal adults and how they can contribute in the future.

6.1 Getting in the Door

Academic upgrading, adult basic and literacy programs

After being out of school for some years, returning to the classroom takes courage and determination. The pursuit of further training and education represents a big step for Aboriginal adults whose own school experience was negative and degrading. Many adults go back only to provide a better life for their children.

When taking training and higher education programs, adults who left school must usually begin with academic upgrading, adult basic or literacy programs. Most of these programs, unfortunately, are not designed with the particular needs of Aboriginal people in mind. Métis people feel especially affronted:

> Métis...people are students in programs but their particular needs have not been recognized nor addressed. The input of the Metis...organizations has not been sought nor have programs designed and proposed by them been supported....It became clear in speaking with officials involved with literacy programming that the distinctions between the needs of Metis...people were often confused with needs of Status Indian peoples.[53]

Where Aboriginal-run programs do exist, they survive on unstable project funding. This discourages program and curriculum development. Student funding is frequently a problem. Because of past schooling history, the student may have considerable ground to cover for which the training period is simply too short. Training allowances that sustain the student and dependents during the program period come to an end, and the student is unable to continue.

Aboriginal programs in academic upgrading, adult basic education and literacy often include elements that strengthen Aboriginal identity and self-esteem and build support networks among the students. These elements appear to be essential components of successful programs. They begin to heal the wounds the individual has accumulated over years of failed schooling, and they establish a stronger basis for the individual to pursue further training and education. Aboriginal adult programs must have the resources to include these components. The testimony of a student in an Aboriginal literacy program explains why such programs are so significant in forming new attitudes toward education:

> This year at Nokee Kwe we have been able to have the opportunity to experience a brief look back into our past and saw what we have lost as Native people and what we have maintained to survive this far. We have upgraded our math, English, communications and work skills, and some of us have learned computer skills for the very first time. The staff and instructors of Nokee Kwe have taught us all that and more....
>
> We are not savages as some have been led to believe. Our land was taken, promises were broken, and our children were stolen from

their homes to be taken to schools far away. At these schools they were robbed of their heritage, they were beaten for speaking their own language....We were even led to believe that it was bad to be an Indian. We have had to endure so much since Columbus landed here 500 years ago; yet, we still have to endure a lot, but still we survive and we will continue to survive. Our language is still alive as well as our culture, and we are very proud to be Indian.

Roly Williams
Nokee Kwe Adult Education Centre
London, Ontario, 12 May 1993

Those who work in academic upgrading, adult basic and literacy services have been consistent in criticizing

- the absence of Aboriginal control over the design of programs;
- fragmented, project-by-project funding for programs;
- fragmented funding sources for student training allowances;
- inadequate community facilities to support programs;
- the lack of financial support for Aboriginal language literacy; and
- the arbitrary separation of literacy, adult basic education, and academic upgrading from job training services.

All these difficulties can be traced to the single reality that adult education services are not under the direction of Aboriginal self-governing authorities. A variety of Aboriginal agents have emerged to deliver specific programs in either the literacy or upgrading field or job training services. Many of them survive precariously, exercising administrative responsibilities devolved from federal, provincial and territorial authorities.

In contrast, it seems that most of the problems described above have been overcome in Nunavik, where the Kativik school board has been responsible for adult education and job market training.[54] Through control of these services, school authorities have been able to blend academic and job skills creatively, responding to the needs of the adults they serve. Literacy is also offered in English, French and an Aboriginal language.

The Kativik experience suggests what changes must take place. Aboriginal people must be able to design adult education services that meet the needs of students.[55] Students must be able to obtain training moneys at one access point rather than negotiate a maze of federal and provincial programs, all with their own regulations. Program agents need a stable funding base and must have the flexibility to combine adult education and job training in locally appropriate ways. (We speak more about this in the section on job training.) Community learning centre facilities are crucial to creating an environment where adult students can reconnect with formal learning processes. And finally, Aboriginal people must be able to obtain literacy services in the language of their choice.

There are many organizations with the capacity and desire to assume responsibility for integrated adult education services, much as Kativik has done. Other communities and organizations may move more slowly toward full control. Federal, provincial and territorial governments should move quickly to negotiate the delivery of integrated adult education services through the Aboriginal organizations and governments that are ready for them. Multi-year agreements, with control over the design of programs, could be negotiated in the transition to self-government.

RECOMMENDATION

The Commission recommends that

Aboriginal Delivery of Integrated Adult Training

3.5.19

Federal, provincial and territorial governments collaborate with Aboriginal governments and organizations to facilitate integrated delivery of adult literacy, basic education, academic upgrading and job training under the control of Aboriginal people through

(a) delegating responsibility for delivery of training under current jurisdictions by concluding agreements with Aboriginal governments, their mandated education authorities, or voluntary organizations representing Aboriginal communities of interest;

(b) supporting adaptation of program design, admission criteria, language of instruction, and internal allocation of funds by Aboriginal delivery agents, to accommodate Aboriginal culture and community needs;

(c) acting promptly to conclude agreements for multi-year block funding agreements to enable Aboriginal nation governments, during the transition to self-government, to assume primary responsibility for allocating funds to meet training needs through programs of Aboriginal design.

Access and university or college preparation programs

Students who complete high school may find college and university still beyond their reach. Many students will have been streamed into non-academic programs in secondary school. Their skills, course completions or grade point standing may not satisfy entry requirements to post-secondary institutions. Courses needed may include

University of Alberta's Access Program

The University of Alberta has developed perhaps the most comprehensive access program in public post-secondary education. They have established quotas of five per cent for Aboriginal enrolments in all faculties, representing the proportion of Aboriginal people in the Alberta population. They have also established a transition year that opens access to eight programs: arts, agriculture and forestry, business, education, engineering, Native studies, nursing and science. All credits earned in the program are transferable. New students are required to have an average of at least 50 per cent in all prerequisite high school subjects and a minimum overall average of 60 per cent. Through the Office of Native Student Services, students can obtain personal, academic, financial and career or employment counselling.

communications, mathematics, science and computing skills; knowledge of Aboriginal history and issues to build a strong base for Aboriginal identity; and exploration of career possibilities to which the student has not yet been exposed.

Aboriginal and non-Aboriginal institutions are increasingly offering such programs under a variety of labels – university and college entrance programs, access programs, transition programs, bridging programs. They may be general in nature, or they may have a specific focus, for example, access to health careers, science or engineering. They may be offered in the local community through learning centres or at regional centres through a college or Aboriginal institution. Sometimes a program requires attendance at the host institution in an urban setting. The recent proliferation of such programs indicates that they are making a difference in preparing people for further studies.

The admission as mature students of Aboriginal applicants who do not necessarily have secondary school diplomas has allowed many older people to enter college and university. It is not unusual for parents and grandparents to return to school, sometimes at the same time as their children and grandchildren.

Student funding

Financial support for post-secondary education is a key issue. Concerns are likely to escalate as more Aboriginal youth and adults search for promising career and job options. The next decade and a half will be crucial, as larger numbers of young people reach the age for post-secondary education and the job market. At the same time, more Aboriginal adults over 25 can be expected to return to education and job training to improve their financial opportunities.[56] These demographic trends highlight the importance of strategic policy interventions to increase access to post-secondary education now.

The federal government has been the most important source of financial assistance for First Nations and Inuit students. The Northwest Territories has funded university education for all residents, including First Nations, Métis, Inuit and non-Aboriginal students. The Yukon also provides funding subsidies for all residents, but at a lower rate than the Northwest Territories. But for Métis people and for First Nations people without strong ties to their communities of origin, funding is extremely limited. Most must take out loans to pay for their education. In some instances, Métis organizations, provincial governments and corporate donors have established bursaries and scholarships, but these are minimal relative to tuition and living costs.

One funding issue that arouses passionate and bitter debate is treaty rights to education. The numbered treaties promised education. Treaty nations and the federal government have been locked in a battle grounded in two widely divergent views of history. For treaty nations, education is a right that was negotiated in exchange for giving up large tracts of traditional territory. In their view, this includes all levels of schooling, and that understanding is strongly embedded in the oral history that has come down from Aboriginal elders who were present at treaty negotiations and signings.

The federal government has denied that post-secondary education funding is a treaty right. It has applied the *Indian Act* provisions and its post-secondary education funding policy to treaty nations on the same basis as First Nations that did not sign the numbered treaties. Students who do not live on a reserve often do not receive post-secondary education funding. Treaty nations argue that every treaty member should be entitled to the benefits, regardless of residence – in other words, that the right to education is guaranteed and portable.

Over the past two decades, the Supreme Court of Canada has ruled in various cases that broad, just and liberal interpretation of treaties is in order, with due regard for the historical context in which they were signed. The historical context for Aboriginal peoples was one in which the buffalo and other animals that had sustained a migratory land-based economy were disappearing. Oral history tells us that Aboriginal leaders negotiating treaties were seeking education that would provide a livelihood sufficient to put them on an equal footing with the settlers in the new economy. Treaty nations argue that they were guaranteed an outcome from education that is not being honoured. Pauline Pelly, a Saskatchewan elder, voiced this view at the Federation of Saskatchewan Indian Nations treaty rights education symposium in October 1991:

> Education was given to us. They promised us that you will be very smart, like the cunning of the white man. The highest education that you can get, that is what they promised to us. That is what we wanted.

First Nations maintain that the spirit and intent of the treaties are as significant as the actual wording. The promise of a 'schoolhouse on every reserve' represented what was state-of-the-art education when the treaties were signed. And elders maintain that it was state-of-the-art education that Aboriginal peoples negotiated. Supreme Court interpretations have lent support to Aboriginal contentions that the representations of government at the time are as important as the actual words written down.

RECOMMENDATION

The Commission recommends that

Treaty Promise of **3.5.20**
Education   The government of Canada recognize and fulfil its obligation to treaty nations by supporting a full range of education services, including post-secondary education, for members of treaty nations where a promise of education appears in treaty texts, related documents or oral histories of the parties involved.

Federal government policy has been to contribute post-secondary education funding for First Nations students who have status under the *Indian Act*, whether or not they have treaty entitlements. Inuit in northern Quebec and Labrador and other Inuit living outside the Northwest Territories and the Yukon are also eligible for assistance under this policy. Nevertheless, some Inuit have not been able to obtain funds, particularly if they have no ties to the organization administering the funds or if they have lived away from their community for some time. In the late 1980s and early 1990s, federal government funding was capped for First Nations and Inuit students, and many were unable to find other sources of funding to pursue post-secondary education.

Aboriginal education authorities and post-secondary institutions told the Commission they simply could not serve the students who wanted to attend programs but could not find funding assistance. This suggests that Aboriginal enrolments in post-secondary education have been limited because there has not been enough financial support. Demand rose when First Nations students who regained status under Bill C-31 became eligible for post-secondary education benefits. The inadequacy of education funding was one of the most pressing concerns youth and many leaders brought before the Commission.

Our analysis of federal expenditures on Aboriginal people indicates that the budget for the post-secondary education assistance program in 1992-93 was

$201 million. (See Volume 5, Chapter 2 for our discussion of economic disparities, government expenditures and the cost of the status quo.) This was increased by $20 million in 1994-95 and by a further $14 million in 1995-96.

The challenge over the next 20 years will be to find adequate support for the larger numbers of youth who will require post-secondary education in order to become productive in the labour force. As career opportunities with Aboriginal self-governments open up, as Aboriginal colleges and training institutions extend services closer to home, and as the impact of Aboriginal control over education takes root, more youth will be using post-secondary education as a path to a better future. Demand for services will certainly rise.

The policy environment for funding will merit careful monitoring. The federal government has reduced support for post-secondary education in federal-provincial transfer payments, and the impact of this has yet to be assessed.[57] Should it result in higher tuition fees, as many observers anticipate, fewer Aboriginal people will be able to attend post-secondary institutions unless there is more financial assistance. Métis and other Aboriginal students who are not now eligible for federal funding will be even further removed from the possibility of a post-secondary education. The needs will be far beyond what can be supplied by the organizations that currently provide small bursaries for these students.

Students with no other recourse – particularly Métis and other Aboriginal students who cannot obtain assistance through their communities of origin – have sometimes turned to student loans. The resulting level of debt has been crushing:

> Upon graduation as a teacher, [the Métis person] will not be joining the middle class but will be in the ranks of the working poor. A single student with no dependents in the B.Ed. program in 1990 with no other source of income would accrue $13,008 of debt that was eligible for remission and $21,138 to be repaid in full. Another student in the same class, single with three children, deemed to be more in need, would incur an even greater debt load. This individual would owe $17,280 eligible for remission and $56,260 to be repaid in full.[58]

About 50 per cent of full-time Aboriginal students and 72 per cent of part-time students are over the age of 24. A majority have family responsibilities and many – mostly women – are single parents. The cost of tuition has been far outweighed by the cost of daily living, at least until now. Reliable child care and other support services are often essential to a student's academic success. The cost of attending a post-secondary institution is much higher in an urban setting where housing is more expensive. Most Aboriginal students do not come from socio-economic backgrounds where their parents can be expected to contribute financially.

Having to rely on student loans to finance their education is a serious disincentive for many potential students. Already functioning at the margins financially, and with family responsibilities, they simply cannot countenance the prospect of assuming debt in an atmosphere of such uncertainty. If a mature student is to borrow enough to sustain the family through years of study, the debt burden will be overwhelming, regardless of the student's job circumstances later on.

The numbers of Aboriginal youth and young adults will increase over the next 15 years, and they will be prime candidates for post-secondary education services. The next generation should have the chance to break the cycle of poverty that has confined Aboriginal people to the margins of Canadian society. Post-secondary education is a critical link in the chain of transformation. We must encourage the momentum that is gathering. In years to come, we expect to see Aboriginal people in every valued occupation and profession in the country.

The preparation of human resources for Aboriginal governments must accelerate. The persistent gap between Aboriginal and non-Aboriginal people in access to post-secondary education completion must be erased. Without adequate student funding, that gap could increase rather than diminish as a larger number of Aboriginal youth come of working age and proportionally fewer have access to post-secondary education.

RECOMMENDATION

The Commission recommends that

Federal Support of Post-Secondary Students

3.5.21

The federal government continue to support the costs of post-secondary education for First Nations and Inuit post-secondary students and make additional resources available

(a) to mitigate the impact of increased costs as post-secondary institutions shift to a new policy environment in post-secondary education; and

(b) to meet the anticipated higher level of demand for post-secondary education services.

We recognize that present assistance does not extend to all Aboriginal people. Métis students have great difficulty obtaining funding, as do First Nations people and Inuit who do not have sustained communication with their communities of origin. The financial assistance programs already established by Aboriginal organizations, provincial governments and corporations are desperately needed, but they are clearly not enough.

A scholarship fund could extend benefits so that Aboriginal people not covered by the current federal program would have improved access to post-secondary education. Funding for this should come from federal and provincial sources, corporate sponsors and individual contributors. It is beyond the Commission's scope to determine the best way to establish such a fund – for example, whether a trust fund or some other vehicle would better suit long-term needs. It will be important to establish an administrative structure that optimizes the use of existing programs and structures rather than overlapping or duplicating them. The planning work for the fund will best be undertaken by Métis and other Aboriginal education leaders and students for whom it is intended.

RECOMMENDATION

The Commission recommends that

Métis and Aboriginal Scholarship Fund

3.5.22

A scholarship fund be established for Métis and other Aboriginal students who do not have access to financial support for post-secondary education under present policies, with

(a) lead financial support provided by federal and provincial governments and additional contributions from corporate and individual donors;

(b) a planning committee to be established immediately,

    (i) composed of Métis and other Aboriginal representatives, students, and federal and provincial representatives in balanced numbers;

    (ii) given a maximum two-year mandate; and

    (iii) charged with determining the appropriate vehicle, level of capitalization, program criteria and administrative structure for initiation and administration of the fund; and

(c) provisions for evaluating demand on the fund, its adequacy and its impact on participation and completion rates of Métis and other Aboriginal students in post-secondary studies.

Location of program delivery

Many Aboriginal adults simply cannot relocate to the urban centres where most post-secondary education opportunities are available. Offering studies in the community or closer to home has been one way to improve access. In an increasing number of communities, there are adult or community learning centres that provide adult education at many levels. Literacy, adult basic and academic upgrading courses, job training courses, university and college entrance programs, and college or university courses may all be offered at the community learning centre or at a nearby regional centre to which the student can commute. Some of these community and regional centres have become highly organized post-secondary institutions operated by Aboriginal people with an admirable degree of success in seeing students through to completion of their programs.

Such centres have also been established in large urban areas. Some universities have begun to deliver courses and programs through their continuing education departments using local delivery centres, although these arrangements inevitably require a minimum enrolment of students.

Although still in its infancy, distance education is also proving useful for delivering post-secondary education services.[59] Not all distance education formats are effective; correspondence education, for example, does not have high completion rates. Interactive approaches have been quite successful, however, particularly those using video and television. The problem with many distance education programs is that they offer standard Canadian content with little or no adaptation to the values, perspectives or issues of Aboriginal peoples. Most courses are taught in English or French rather than in Aboriginal languages, even in regions where an Aboriginal language is widely used in the community. Nevertheless, distance education has shown promise, and it is now a matter of finding appropriate configurations of technology, instructional methods, instructors and curriculum content. We return to distance education in the section on education for self-government later in this chapter.

Credit for Aboriginal language competency

Earlier in this chapter, we discussed the marginalization of Aboriginal languages in the education systems of Canada. We recommended that Aboriginal language competency be recognized for course credits in the public school system. It is equally important that it be recognized for credits at the college and university level. High school credits in Aboriginal languages should be considered equivalent to other modern language credits for entrance into post-secondary programs. Where students are seeking higher level credits for language competence, appropriate procedures should be established to verify fluency and grant credits in a way that ensures equality with other modern languages.

Aboriginal languages are already being taught at some universities, as regular course offerings or as special courses where Aboriginal people from specific linguistic communities come together to study. Recognizing these languages by granting credits not only affirms the knowledge and self-worth of those who speak them but also accords them their rightful place as the original languages of the Americas.

RECOMMENDATION

The Commission recommends that

Aboriginal **3.5.23**
Languages Canada's post-secondary institutions recognize Aboriginal lan-
Equivalent to guages on a basis equal to other modern languages, for the pur-
Modern Languages pose of granting credits for entrance requirements, fulfilment of
second language requirements, and general course credits.

Conclusion

Over the past two decades there have been positive advances in access to education for Aboriginal students. These include the establishment of bridging
mechanisms; more programs offered closer to students' homes; more local facilities for community learning; and the introduction of interactive distance education. There are other issues still to be resolved, however, such as the need for
stable, adequate financing for adult education services; recognition of the treaty
right to post-secondary education; continuation and enhancement of funding
support for post-secondary students; the extension of funding to Métis and other
Aboriginal students now excluded from post-secondary benefits through a scholarship fund; increased support for community learning centres; and Aboriginal
control of adult services and job training so they can be blended in appropriate
ways to prepare adults to live productive economic lives.

Some Aboriginal educators have warned that increasing exclusivity of university education for the general population of Canadians may mean restricted
access for Aboriginal people. Any policy changes that have the effect of limiting Aboriginal people's access to post-secondary education must be promptly
counterbalanced by policies to secure access, if equitable participation of
Aboriginal people in Canadian society is to be achieved and maintained.

6.2 Inside the Door: Institutions
Serving Aboriginal Adults

Once Aboriginal students have begun post-secondary education, what are their
experiences? Do they complete their studies? How relevant is their education to
the job opportunities and professional demands they will face?

Figure 5.1 shows that more students completed non-university programs
in 1991 (13.3 per cent) than in 1981 (8.9 per cent), although the 1991 figure
is still below that of non-Aboriginal people (15.8 per cent). The proportion of
the Aboriginal population undertaking university programs increased to 8.6 per

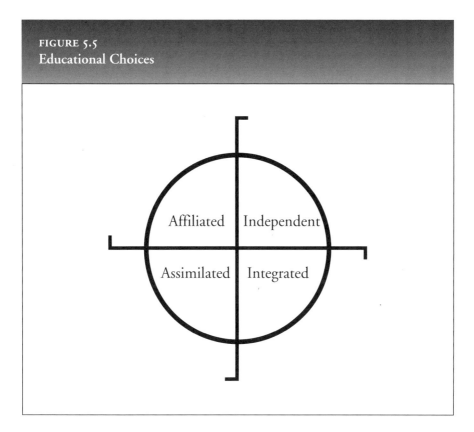

FIGURE 5.5
Educational Choices

Affiliated | Independent

Assimilated | Integrated

cent by 1991, but the record of completion was very low (three per cent) and increased by only one per cent between 1981 and 1991.

These results raise questions about how Canada's post-secondary institutions are accommodating the needs of Aboriginal students. Dr. Ray Barnhardt, a professor at the University of Alaska-Fairbanks, has classified universities according to the degree of control Aboriginal people have over the education offered. He puts post-secondary institutions into three categories – assimilative, integrative and independent.[60] We use these categories to examine the post-secondary arrangements that serve Aboriginal students in Canada, and we add a fourth category – affiliated – to describe an organizational variation that offers an enhanced degree of autonomy for Aboriginal institutions short of full independence. The four options – assimilated, integrated, affiliated and independent – are displayed in Figure 5.5.

Mainstream and public post-secondary institutions

Barnhardt's first category is assimilative – that is, the post-secondary institution offers a fixed menu of programs, courses and services. Everyone is expected to fit in. This accurately describes post-secondary education as it was constituted two decades ago, and much professional training still follows this model. But gradually the assimilative approach has been giving way to more integrative approaches. Within their education mandate, integrative institutions recognize Aboriginal peoples as a distinct group, and many have made significant shifts in their program offerings.

For example, there are now Aboriginal studies (or Native studies) departments in at least 10 universities across Canada. Faculties of law have instituted courses and programs that address the legal issues and concerns of Aboriginal peoples. Teacher training programs have been implemented in most provinces, the Northwest Territories and the Yukon. As these programs have demonstrated their value, additional ones have been developed in Aboriginal management, business and economic development, and social work. Access programs are being designed to attract Aboriginal students to health sciences, engineering and science. Distinct co-ordinating mechanisms have also been implemented; for example, the First Nations House of Learning at the University of British Columbia is the home away from home for Aboriginal students and has contact with students in all departments of the university.

Post-secondary institutions have also entered into arrangements with Aboriginal people to deliver courses in regional centres and at the community level. Several such arrangements were mentioned earlier in the chapter, and there are many other examples. For small communities, this kind of arrangement becomes difficult if the number of students falls below the institution's minimum numbers for delivery.

Aboriginal peoples are still vastly under-represented in the sciences and mathematics. Many spokespersons have signalled the need to attract more students to technical professions that are increasing in importance in the global economy.

The last two decades have taught us about the environment and support systems that can help Aboriginal students succeed. Involvement in the governance of the institution is a significant symbol of intent and a vital force shaping program development. Programs tailored to the values and needs of Aboriginal people are the starting point for inviting students to follow a successful path. The recruitment of Aboriginal faculty and instructors, the presence of elders, the sponsorship of Aboriginal cultural events, and appropriate counsellors and support staff are all ingredients for success.

The students must have opportunities to give voice to their concerns and to develop leadership skills. A growing number of institutions have an Aboriginal students' union that not only represents students within the institution but also links Aboriginal student groups regionally and nationally.

The government of Ontario's Aboriginal post-secondary policy, initiated in 1991, is a good example of strategic intervention to promote education partnerships. Its goals are to increase the participation of Aboriginal students in Ontario's public post-secondary education institutions and to optimize completion rates. Grants are available to offset the special costs of designing and delivering Aboriginal programs. Funds are also designated to increase the number of Aboriginal counsellors and special support services. Institutions that receive grants are expected to integrate funded initiatives into regular program delivery and base budgets by the end of the funding period to maintain continuity. Representation of Aboriginal organizations on governing bodies and establishment of an Aboriginal committee to guide programs and services are also required. Costs of participation by Aboriginal organizations are offset by the program (see Appendix 5A).

Post-secondary institutions in all jurisdictions are reeling from funding cutbacks imposed by governments in pursuit of deficit reduction. It might be argued that they are in no position to introduce Aboriginal-specific initiatives without special funding. We acknowledge these pressures, and later in this chapter we propose that federal, provincial and territorial governments allocate resources for new initiatives by post-secondary institutions in fields of study related to the implementation of self-government.

We maintain, however, that recognition of the distinct place of Aboriginal nations in the Canadian federation and accommodation of Aboriginal culture and identity should be regarded as a core responsibility of public institutions rather than as a special project to be undertaken after other obligations are met. Educational institutions have a pivotal role in transforming the relationship between Aboriginal peoples and Canadian society.

RECOMMENDATION

The Commission recommends that

Mainstream Post-Secondary Initiatives

3.5.24

Public post-secondary institutions in the provinces and territories undertake new initiatives or extend current ones to increase the participation, retention and graduation of Aboriginal students by introducing, encouraging or enhancing

(a) a welcoming environment for Aboriginal students;

(b) Aboriginal content and perspectives in course offerings across disciplines;

(c) Aboriginal studies and programs as part of the institution's regular program offerings and included in the institution's core budget;

(d) Aboriginal appointments to boards of governors;

(e) Aboriginal councils to advise the president of the institution;

(f) active recruitment of Aboriginal students;

(g) admission policies that encourage access by Aboriginal applicants;

(h) meeting spaces for Aboriginal students;

(i) Aboriginal student unions;

(j) recruitment of Aboriginal faculty members;

(k) support services with Aboriginal counsellors for academic and personal counselling; and

(l) cross-cultural sensitivity training for faculty and staff.

There are many accounts of students feeling isolated in a hostile environment where professors and fellow students express racist attitudes and opinions. Aboriginal students are silenced by unthinking remarks in the college or university classroom:

> My English teacher said, when one of the students put up her hand and asked "Are Indian people really vicious and barbaric like these journals say?"...she said, "Yes, most are all accurate and correct....The journals are correct. Anthropologists and sociologists knew what they were saying and recording."[61]

Daily encounters with racism are emotionally exhausting, particularly when the student is in the minority and feels too vulnerable to challenge the views expressed.

Within the integrated environment, the establishment of Aboriginal colleges may provide a way to mobilize effective supports in some locations.[62] Colleges are a time-honoured tradition in many universities. Sometimes the whole campus is organized into colleges; in other instances, just a few colleges exist, organized according to religious affiliation. The purpose of a college is to provide a community environment conducive to academic and social life. Colleges are usually residential, with their own faculty, visiting scholars, libraries and other facilities. Faculty and students are in an atmosphere that promotes personal interaction. This environment would be attractive to some Aboriginal students, providing social support and fostering academic success. It would also be a suitable base for offering cultural programs, which could be made available to students regardless of their academic specialty.

RECOMMENDATION

The Commission recommends that

Residential University Colleges

3.5.25

Where there is Aboriginal support for an Aboriginal college within a university, and where numbers warrant, universities act to establish an Aboriginal college to serve as the focal point for the academic, residential, social and cultural lives of Aboriginal students on campus, and to promote Aboriginal scholarship.

Innovative directions in Aboriginal program delivery must continue to be implemented. Funding, however, is often tenuous. Some post-secondary institutions have expressed their commitment to Aboriginal programs and support services by integrating the costs into operational budgets. Too often, however, programs or services depend on external funding that is available for a limited period, after which there is no guarantee of institutional funding. Many Aboriginal programs have foundered as a result of this instability. The Ontario Aboriginal post-secondary education funding policy has encouraged institutions to start new programs in partnership with Aboriginal peoples and gradually to absorb the costs into their budgets.

Aboriginally controlled post-secondary institutions

Canada's post-secondary institutions are important players in education for Aboriginal adults, but increasingly vital are the Aboriginally controlled colleges, institutes and community learning centres that have developed over the past two decades. In Barnhardt's categorization, these fit best into the category of independent arrangements. The fourth category, affiliated, describes the most common arrangement, however, whereby Aboriginal institutions establish links with institutions recognized by provincial and territorial ministries of higher education. Aboriginal institutions delivering post-secondary education, like American tribal colleges, have their roots in the determination of communities and nations to see relevant education services offered close to home.

Four identifiable types of institutions have evolved. The first resembles a full-fledged college. It attracts students from many nations and offers a wide range of programs, usually accredited through a partnership or affiliation with one or more post-secondary institutions. The largest and best known of these is the Saskatchewan Indian Federated College (SIFC), controlled by the Federation of Saskatchewan Indian Nations. SIFC offers its own bachelor programs that include language studies, fine arts, Aboriginal studies and business. All SIFC courses are provincially accredited through a federation agreement with the University of Regina. In 1995, SIFC, in partnership with the Business College of the University of Saskatchewan, launched the first Aboriginal M.B.A. program in Canada. With more than 1,200 students from nations across Canada, SIFC offers a unique opportunity to study in an Aboriginally defined environment. The Association of Universities and Colleges has recently accepted SIFC as a member.

Other large and well-established colleges are Blue Quills, Maskwachees Cultural College, and Old Sun at Gleichen in Alberta, Gabriel Dumont Institute in Saskatchewan, Secwepemc Cultural Education Society and Nicola Valley Institute of Technology in British Columbia, and Yellowquills in Manitoba. The Association of First Nations Post-Secondary Institutions in British Columbia has

Yellowhead Tribal Council

The Yellowhead Tribal Council in Spruce Grove, Alberta, serves the post-secondary needs of its five member tribes. At its central campus at Spruce Grove, it houses administration offices, classrooms, a computer laboratory and a student lounge. It has offered a variety of on-site programs, including a 40-week university and college entrance preparation program, a university transfer program with the University of Alberta and Athabasca University, a health development administration program delivered by Athabasca University, a bachelor of social work program from the University of Calgary, a social worker diploma program from Grant McEwen Community College, and a business administration certificate program from Athabasca University. The centre offers a full range of support services to students, including tutoring, financial and peer counselling, financial support, emergency funding, library facilities and an orientation week. In 1992-1993, it had a student body of 268.

recently been formed (with 14 full members and two upcoming members) to co-ordinate efforts to secure the resources and policy structures these institutions need to operate effectively and independently.

The second type of affiliated institution is smaller and more locally focused. It serves primarily the members of a tribal council or a regional area. One example is the Yellowhead Tribal Council in Alberta, which represents a joint effort to offer preparatory and university programs close to home in a comfortable supportive setting (see box). The key to the success of smaller Aboriginally controlled institutions is having cash in hand to shop for the best programs for their students. They can approach a variety of mainstream post-secondary institutions, outline their needs, and negotiate for the educational services they want. Colleges and universities, eager to increase their student counts, tend to respond positively when there is financial assistance to support non-conventional delivery of courses. This type of institution, for example, the Wilp Wilxo'oskwhl Nisga'a in British Columbia, often crosses the conventional boundaries of universities, colleges and technical institutes by offering a wide range of courses.

The third type of Aboriginal institution is the community learning centre. These are the hub of local adult education in the communities they serve. A variety of institutions deliver programs in the learning centre, including adult basic education, academic upgrading, distance education courses, language courses, vocational training, and community-delivered programs from larger institutions. Some programs are accredited and others are not. The local community controls the learning centre, but its operations are usually dependent on external grants in connection with program services. Sometimes the facility is owned by an outside college and sometimes by the community. Course sponsors often pay for someone from the community to act as a site co-ordinator, program facilitator or course tutor. The campuses of Alberta Vocational Centre – Lesser Slave Lake, located in Aboriginal communities in northern Alberta, started out as local adult centres offering upgrading and short courses. They have since evolved into a network of campuses offering a variety of education services, including distance education courses. In Ontario, Contact North delivers courses using a network of community learning centres. Similar centres exist in the Northwest Territories, the Yukon and elsewhere.

The fourth type of Aboriginal institution, which comes closest to Barnhardt's independent model, is the non-profit institute that offers training in communities or to a group of communities. There are many of these under Aboriginal control in all parts of Canada; they offer training relevant to Aboriginal self-government. Some operate province- or territory-wide, and some nationally. Some specialize in particular types of training. Unfortunately, the training they offer is often not accredited. They may also act as brokers for programs in partnership with public post-secondary institutions. Examples of these training institutes include the First Nations Technical Institute in Tyendinaga, Ontario, and the First Nations Justice Institute in Mission, British Columbia.

Aboriginally controlled post-secondary institutions of all four types enjoy strong grassroots support. They offer programs valued by Aboriginal communities and they provide a supportive environment that encourages students to persist with their studies. Many programs are custom-designed to address the priorities and values of Aboriginal communities. The number of colleges and institutes continues to multiply, but they share two serious problems: chronic lack of funding and the reluctance of mainstream post-secondary institutions and professional organizations to recognize their courses and the degrees or certificates they offer.

Funding Aboriginally controlled post-secondary institutions

Aboriginal post-secondary institutions live on precarious federal and provincial funding. The department of Indian affairs provides the only stable financial support received by the Saskatchewan Indian Federated College. But as the college has documented repeatedly, this funding is far less than that received by comparable public post-secondary institutions.[63] The other schools depend on small program grants, which are short-term, often project-specific and always subject to change. This instability unsettles operations and makes long-term planning difficult. Aboriginal post-secondary institutions must be recognized and given stable funding.

Accreditation and transfer of credit

The second difficulty is the struggle to get recognition from other institutions for the courses students complete. While Aboriginal colleges may accept the students' learning, conventional post-secondary institutions have been reluctant to recognize programs they have not developed and that depart from standard college or university course design. So their students can earn transfer credits, Aboriginal institutions have been compelled to enter into agreements with colleges to grant concurrent credit with the Aboriginal institutions. This arrangement is far from ideal, as one presenter explained to the Commission:

> We've utilized a variety of affiliation models with our local community college. This has required surrendering some autonomy, but it has allowed students to gain some transfer credits. This is one of our dilemmas in the area of affiliation and accreditation. Presently, in order for our courses to be accredited, we have to turn over control to one of the local colleges or universities....We are frustrated by our inability to fully accredit our programs. We have designed some excellent and innovative programs which have no precedent. Indeed, other community colleges are modelling some of their programming after our approach....
>
> Christie Clifton
> North Coast Tribal Council Education Centre
> Prince Rupert, British Columbia, 26 May 1993

The ability to design and offer relevant programs is one good reason to promote Aboriginally controlled institutions. There is another: their success rate in seeing students through to completion of their programs far surpasses that of mainstream post-secondary institutions. The Gabriel Dumont Institute reports a program completion rate of 70 per cent; the North Coast Tribal Council Education Centre stated at our hearings that 80 per cent of students complete their courses; and the Secwepemc Program at Simon Fraser University reported that 80 per cent of its students graduate.[64]

The U.S. experience is very similar to Canada's. There are 24 tribal colleges in the United States funded under the *Tribally Controlled Community Colleges Assistance Act.* They offer baccalaureates or shorter programs. Despite chronic funding shortages, tribal colleges produce graduates who go on to good jobs or further studies in non-Aboriginal institutions.[65]

Aboriginally controlled education institutions normally build student support mechanisms into their operations. Most of their staff are Aboriginal and serve as role models for students. They have strong ties with local Aboriginal communities, elders and resource people, and they collaborate with these groups in cultural programs. We heard about several proposals to start Aboriginal post-secondary institutions. For example, Inuit Tapirisat of Canada believes there should be an independent Inuit post-secondary educational institution. Métis people in Manitoba are establishing a multi-purpose institution they call the Louis Riel Institute.

Aboriginal post-secondary institutions play a unique role in the education of Aboriginal adults. For 20 years, they have shown durability and resilience. They will not supplant the services of non-Aboriginal institutions, which many Aboriginal students will continue to attend. Canadian post-secondary education institutions provide a wide range of programs that Aboriginal post-secondary institutions could not possibly replicate. Canadian colleges and universities should continue their efforts to create a more hospitable environment for Aboriginal students. At the same time, Aboriginal institutions offer a milieu that supports student success and offers programs that reflect the distinct perspectives and values of First Nations, Inuit and Métis peoples. As Aboriginal governments come forward with unique needs for service programs, Aboriginal institutions will be able to respond to these requests with innovative programs defined by Aboriginal people.

Governments and the Canadian educational community should recognize Aboriginally controlled post-secondary institutions by supporting them and giving them the opportunity to gain the same respect accorded public post-secondary institutions. This recognition should be translated into core funding for the services they provide and accredited status within provincial and territorial post-secondary systems so that students can transfer between Aboriginal and provincial or territorial institutions without penalty. Such arrangements already exist between institutions in different provinces, each of which has its own standards.

We are aware that respect has to be won, not legislated. However, policies can secure the resources and establish the conditions in which Aboriginal people can develop credible, autonomous post-secondary institutions. In our view, these institutions have the greatest potential for erasing the education gap between Aboriginal and non-Aboriginal people discussed in this chapter and in our analysis of economic issues in Volume 2, Chapter 5.

To move ahead with the development of autonomous Aboriginal institutions, co-operation between Aboriginal and mainstream educators and institutions will be essential. We urge professional organizations such as the Association of Universities and Colleges of Canada and professional associations of college and university teachers to encourage their members to enter into collaborative relationships with Aboriginal planners, educators and institutions. (See Chapter 3 in this volume for elaboration of the role we recommend for mainstream institutions and voluntary organizations in the development of Aboriginal institutions.)

RECOMMENDATIONS

The Commission recommends that

Fund Aboriginal **3.5.26**
Post-Secondary
Institutions
Federal, provincial and territorial governments collaborate with Aboriginal governments and organizations to establish and support post-secondary educational institutions controlled by Aboriginal people, with negotiated allocation of responsibility for

(a) core and program funding commensurate with the services they are expected to provide and comparable to the funding provided to provincial or territorial institutions delivering similar services;

(b) planning, capital and start-up costs of new colleges and institutes;

(c) improvement of facilities for community learning centres as required for new functions and development of new facilities where numbers warrant and the community establishes this as a priority; and

(d) fulfilment of obligations pursuant to treaties and modern agreements with respect to education.

Regional and **3.5.27**
National
Aboriginal Boards
Aboriginally controlled post-secondary educational institutions collaborate to create regional boards and/or a Canada-wide board to

(a) establish standards for accrediting programs provided by Aboriginal post-secondary institutions;

(b) negotiate mutual recognition of course credits and credentials to facilitate student transfer between Aboriginal institutions and provincial and territorial post-secondary institutions;

(c) establish co-operative working relationships with mainstream accreditation bodies such as the Association of Universities and Colleges of Canada and professional associations such as the Canadian Association of University Teachers; and

(d) pursue other objectives related to the common interests of Aboriginal institutions.

6.3 Preparing for the Job Market

We discussed job market and training issues in some detail in Volume 2, Chapter 5, where we noted that Aboriginal communities experience high levels of unemployment and that Aboriginal people, even in urban areas, endure higher rates of unemployment than other Canadians. Job training often provides what an individual needs to find and keep a job.

Non-university training has been used effectively by Aboriginal people in recent years. More than 13 per cent of Aboriginal people 15 years of age and older have a post-secondary certificate or diploma, compared with about 16 per cent of the total Canadian population. As shown in Figure 5.1, the gap between Aboriginal and non-Aboriginal completion rates narrowed between 1981 and 1991, from 4.9 per cent in 1981 to 2.5 per cent in 1991.

Presenters before the Commission spoke of continuing barriers, however, to securing training and matching skills with jobs:

- In small communities, often there are simply no jobs available and no opportunities for individuals after they complete their training.
- Individuals sometimes lack the academic pre-requisites for training and need first to complete these courses. Adults find this separation of academic and job training very frustrating. For mature students, it is often harder to get into apprenticeship and college programs than it is to gain access to university courses because of the academic pre-requisites for some training programs.
- There are gaps in the availability of training support and a confusing array of sources for training funds, differing for First Nations (status and non-status, on-reserve, off-reserve), Inuit and Métis people. Funding periods for training programs may be too short for students to complete their programs. Federal programs are seldom co-ordinated with provincial and territorial programs.[66] For an individual searching for funding support, it is hard to know where to go.
- Training programs are not flexible. Program guidelines prevent Aboriginal delivery agents from engaging in creative custom-designed programs such as combining academic and job training components or setting up work-study or co-op programs.
- Individuals who want to tackle long-term studies at colleges and universities are excluded from funding support. If they want the support, they are locked into studying in short-term programs, which may not suit their needs or lead to well-paying jobs in the long run. Deeply entrenched in current government mandates are sharp distinctions between employment-oriented training and college and university programs.

The interrelationship of job training and upgrading, as well as the complicated dynamics of funding, were described by one presenter:

We have many members wanting to go into upgrading classes in order to qualify for post-secondary schooling. This is where the biggest problem arises. The band does not receive any funding to support these students. They are told to see Canada Employment and Immigration Centre or go to Alberta Vocational Training for their support or any type of training allowance. AVT will not help students living on-reserve and going to school on-reserve. So that leaves CEIC. CEIC has limited seats available. Then, again, that is only a solution for a handful of our students.

Clarence Fournier
Beaver First Nation
High Level, Alberta, 29 October 1992

Employment training programs have been important sources of training for many Aboriginal people. In the 1990s, the federal government has attempted to fine-tune its employment programs so that Aboriginal people have more say in decisions about training in their communities. The Pathways to Success program, initiated in 1990 with a five-year mandate, is the most recent initiative in decentralized administration of federal programs. Under this program, national, regional and local decision-making boards were set up with equal numbers of Aboriginal people and federal officials. The Pathways interim evaluation indicated that although the involvement of Aboriginal people in decision making was positive, programs funded under Pathways have remained the same as previously, with little flexibility for the redesign of programs to meet community needs.[67] More recently, the federal government completed a consultation process with program users and decided to develop a subsequent program that recognizes Pathways as a transitional phase leading to more Aboriginal control of employment development services. The successor program, to take effect in fiscal year 1996-97, is the Aboriginal Labour Force Development Strategy.

The Commission was told that Kativik Regional Government in Nunavik has overcome the restrictive structures in most job training with control over adult education and training under the James Bay and Northern Quebec Agreement.[68] This has enabled Inuit to design community training programs, including those that combine academic and work skills, and literacy training in the language of the individual's choice (Inuktitut, French or English). Their experience suggests that Aboriginal people will be best served by programs that place under their control the design of adult education and job training. More flexibility is required so that communities can do what is best for their citizens.

Another concern in training for the job market has been the under-representation of Aboriginal peoples in the trades, in technology programs, and in the sciences and maths. One of the barriers has been a funding gap, as communities have been unable to direct funds where they are needed. The following quotation is representative of many presentations that addressed this problem:

People assume that we get all kinds of dollars to run our programs. The reality is that it doesn't even get close to the mark. There are many, many different gaps in the post-secondary area. The tribes don't even get funded to provide assistance to vocational and trade students, for example. Students who are in trades programs, in electrical programs at SAIT [Southern Alberta Institute of Technology], and so on, for example, quite often never know where to turn because our post-secondary departments and adult education departments do not get that kind of funding.

Vivian Ayoungman
Director of Education, Treaty 7 Tribal Council
Calgary, Alberta, 27 May 1993

Again, with an adequate pool of funding for human resources development and with the ability to use it according to local priorities, communities would be able to address training concerns. The need to establish a flexible approach to training is echoed in the following submission.

In a Pathways introduction workshop...one participant stood up and asked in regards to the limited education offered that 'You mean to say that you'll make my son a welder but you won't make him a doctor?' Pathways to Success, then, has the ability to appear racist in the eyes of many of the grassroots people.[69]

We have already made recommendations to address some of these concerns, such as our recommendation earlier in this chapter for Aboriginal control of job training services, with the flexibility to integrate delivery of literacy, adult basic education and academic upgrading. In Volume 2, Chapter 5, we recommended a 10-year special training initiative involving partnership among Aboriginal nations, governments, private sector employers, and education and training institutions, with an emphasis on closely linking training with real, sustainable jobs. The careful matching of training with jobs, the use of co-operative education with alternating study and work terms, and the emphasis on training for Aboriginal people in science-based and technological fields are all essential elements of a strategy to prepare Aboriginal people for the job market. We elaborate on these themes and others in our discussion of education for self-government later in this chapter.

7. ELDERS

As we turn our attention to the role of elders in education, we complete the life cycle displayed in the medicine wheel introduced at the beginning of our analysis. Elders have always played a central role in Aboriginal education, which is fundamentally an inter-generational process. Elders are keepers of tradition, guardians of culture, the wise people, the teachers. In Aboriginal societies, elders are known to safeguard knowledge that constitutes the unique inheritance of the nation. They are revered and respected. While most of those who are wise in traditional ways are old, not all old people are elders, and not all elders are old (see Volume 4, Chapter 3).

To interpret the perspectives of elders and other Aboriginal people who testified before the Commission, it is critical to understand the meaning and significance of traditional knowledge. Traditional knowledge is a discrete system of knowledge with its own philosophical and value base. Aboriginal peoples hold the belief that traditional knowledge derives from the Creator and is spiritual in essence. It includes ecological teachings, medical knowledge, common attitudes toward Mother Earth and the Circle of Life, and a sense of kinship with all creatures.

Each nation also has its own body of knowledge that encompasses language, belief systems, ways of thinking and behaving, ceremonies, stories, dances and history. Through thousands of years in the Americas, nations have evolved intricate relationships with their lands and resources. While western academics and intellectuals have begun to give some credence to Aboriginal understandings of the universe, including ecological knowledge in particular, the gatekeepers of western intellectual traditions have repeatedly dismissed traditional knowledge as inconsequential and unfounded. They have failed to recognize that their approach to knowledge building is also defined by culture and that Aboriginal intellectual traditions operate from a different but equally valid way of construing the world. Aboriginal people have particular difficulty with the western notion that knowledge can be secular or objective, divorced from spiritual understanding and deeply imbedded values and ethics.

Traditional knowledge also has its own forms of transmission. Rooted in an oral tradition, knowledge is frequently passed on in the form of stories, which are rendered in accurate detail to preserve their authenticity. These stories, often simple on the surface, are multi-layered and address complex moral and ethical issues. Traditional knowledge is also transmitted through one-to-one instruction and by modelling correct behaviours. Often, traditional knowledge is intended to be conveyed only at particular times or locations and in specific contexts.

Elders expressed deep concern to Commissioners about the current state of education. While they do not reject participation in Canadian education, they question the exclusion of traditional knowledge and its methods of transmission. They see that young people and adults emerge from school with a confused sense of Aboriginal identity and without the basic cultural knowledge to participate fully in the traditions of their society.

To the despair of the elders, when they try to become involved in the education process, they find many obstacles. There have been few resources in the school systems to support the involvement of elders. The fact that they are not given compensation comparable to that of other teachers and professionals sends a clear message that their knowledge and expertise are not valued. The programs where they teach are underfunded, with few resources to support their efforts in curriculum development and for supplies and teaching materials. Elder Rhoda Karetak, an Inuk, expressed her frustration:

> The Aboriginal people and the elders, we know that they are not recognized in terms of the education, in terms of their knowledge....Also as the climate here is as much as 50 or 60 below, we are not to teach our own children as to how they are to start making their own clothes that are warm because we have no papers which would recognize that we have abilities. There are still people out there today who are still alive who can teach these things. Because we don't have papers or maybe because of our lack of education, it seems that is the way it is. [translation]
>
> Rhoda Karetak
Rankin Inlet, Northwest Territories
19 November 1992

Innu Elder Simeo Rich spoke of the indignity of seeing non-Aboriginal people in the school system taking over the teaching of traditional activities:

> As a matter of fact, the Innu kids are not taught by the elders how to make a canoe, how to do traditional skills. Non-Native people are teaching our kids how to do the traditional skills, the things that the elders know. There is another rumour going around in Happy Valley that there is a program going to be run, how to make snowshoes. Non-Native people are stepping all over our lives and we're unable to do such things, to teach the younger generation these things....Half of the elders are all gone and you know it could have been the elders teaching us sufficiency skills that we could have learned from them.
>
> Simeo Rich
Sheshatshiu, Newfoundland and Labrador
17 June 1992

In other instances, teachers are not experienced in involving elders effectively in their classrooms. They are bound by their own schedules and lesson plans, and elders report that they are not able to teach what they would like to share with the children. Often, school timetables conflict with the proper time to transmit traditional knowledge and skills, for example, in ceremonies or in land-based activities.

A further insult has been difficulties in getting non-Aboriginal school boards, colleges and universities to recognize the qualifications of elders to teach in areas where they have unique cultural knowledge.[70] The insistence of education authorities on paper qualifications has prevented many elders from becoming instructors in formal education systems. The Northwest Territories has taken a lead in developing a certification program for teachers of Aboriginal languages, but the program has not been operating long enough for this Commission to determine whether it has opened the classroom door to more language teaching by elders. Education authorities mandated by self-governing Aboriginal nations will determine the qualifications required for specialists in Aboriginal languages, culture and history in their own schools and education institutions. Their expertise in establishing standards of competence and excellence in these areas undoubtedly would be of value to mainstream institutions as well.

If intergenerational education processes are to be restored, obstacles to elders' participation must be overcome. Elders must become an integral part of the learning process for Aboriginal children and youth. This will require changes in the way Aboriginal and non-Aboriginal school systems approach elders and traditional knowledge. They could reach out to elders by

- asking elders for their advice;
- establishing a place in the school that elders can call their own, where they can meet, conduct ceremonies and counsel students;
- reviewing and amending school policies to ensure that elders are valued and respected;
- consulting with elders to ensure that traditional activities and ceremonies are given appropriate recognition, time and significance in the school calendar;
- providing support and resources to record, publish and disseminate materials elders provide for the school;
- dedicating a portion of the space in school resource centres to traditional knowledge under the direction of the elders in the community;
- initiating traditional knowledge workshops for school staff;
- involving elders in planning for curriculum projects; and
- in collaboration with elders, conducting community discussion groups to reach consensus between the school and the community on the role of elders.

RECOMMENDATIONS

The Commission recommends that

Elders' Role in Education **3.5.28**
Elders be reinstated to an active role in the education of Aboriginal children and youth in educational systems under Aboriginal control and in provincial and territorial schools.

Elders' Compensation **3.5.29**
Elders be treated as professionals and compensated for their education contribution at a rate and in a manner that shows respect for their expertise, unique knowledge and skills.

Recognize Aboriginal Knowledge 3.5.30

Provincial and territorial education ministries, boards of education and educators recognize the value of elders' knowledge to all peoples' understanding of the universe by

(a) giving academic credits for traditional Aboriginal arts and knowledge whether acquired in the classroom or through non-formal means in cultural activities, camps and apprenticeships; and

(b) collaborating with elders to determine how traditional Aboriginal knowledge can be made accessible in the education of all students, whether Aboriginal or non-Aboriginal, in institutions under Aboriginal, provincial or territorial control.

Exchanges Among Elders and with Academics 3.5.31

Educational institutions facilitate opportunities for elders to exchange traditional knowledge with one another and to share traditional knowledge with students and scholars, both Aboriginal and non-Aboriginal, in university settings.

In the Aboriginal Peoples' International University, the creation of which we recommend below, elders would hold the place of honour as the keepers of knowledge of the Aboriginal world.

8. ABORIGINAL INSTITUTIONS

The Commission received submissions indicating that there are institutional gaps in education services, particularly those that support self-determination in education. While the primacy of local control in education was emphasized repeatedly in testimony to the Commission and in Aboriginal education studies for nearly three decades, certain objectives in Aboriginal education can be achieved only by co-ordinating efforts at local and regional levels. The challenge is to find the right mechanisms to support cultural, linguistic and regional diversity, to ensure accountability to Aboriginal people, and to promote exchange, communication and information-based services that require widespread co-operation among nations and organizations.

In the twenty-first century, Aboriginal peoples will live in a shrinking world of near-instantaneous exchange of information and knowledge. At the same time, the world will become more homogeneous through dissemination of a common popular culture by the mass media and transnational industries. Aboriginal communities have already joined this world culture and can be expected to continue as active participants. These trends make it even more critical to ensure that Aboriginal cultures have support to preserve and transmit the core of language, beliefs, traditions and knowledge that is uniquely Aboriginal.

Presenters before the Commission offered creative suggestions on how to do this. We address five areas: the teaching and promotion of traditional knowledge; applied research; residential schools scholarship and collective memory; information exchange; and statistical data bases.

8.1 Aboriginal Peoples' International University

The Commission must seek not only immediate solutions to current problems but also responses that will serve future generations. The Aboriginal Peoples' International University (APIU) is proposed as a twenty-first century mechanism to promote traditional knowledge and scholarship, undertake applied research related to Aboriginal self-government, and disseminate information necessary to the achievement of broad Aboriginal development goals. We see the APIU as an Aboriginal network of co-ordinated regional institutions and programs representing diverse cultural and linguistic traditions – those of First Nations, Inuit and Métis peoples.

Promotion of traditional knowledge and scholarship

Because of the geographical, cultural and linguistic diversity of Aboriginal peoples in Canada, no single institution could properly represent all traditions. Since traditional knowledge is rooted in particular parts of the biosphere, it makes sense to seek a model that draws on the strengths of regional and localized knowledge. A network of institutions and programs, affiliated as the Aboriginal Peoples' International University, would reflect local priorities, values and traditions, and at the same time, promote a broader understanding of traditional knowledge among nations. The backbone of this initiative has already solidified with the creation of Aboriginal institutions and programs and specialized fields of advanced study.

The idea of an Aboriginal Peoples' International University is not new. The Saskatchewan Indian Federated College and the Canadian Council on Aboriginal Business have proposed a national university, and elders, educators, and traditional people from Canada have been involved in meetings for a proposed International Indigenous University of the Americas. In Canada and throughout the world, there are universities dedicated to education through distance or that function with several widely dispersed campuses. An Aboriginal university is being discussed in Australia.[71] We are developing the concept here, knowing that further discussion will be needed among elders, educators and leaders in First Nations, Métis and Inuit communities to elaborate and implement it.

We have spoken about elders as the guardians and keepers of traditional knowledge, the unique philosophical and spiritual traditions of Aboriginal peoples. For thousands of years, they transmitted knowledge formulated within the ancient wisdom of indigenous values and understandings. Today, few Aboriginal people have access to this knowledge in their pursuit of learning. An APIU would create the opportunity for elders, traditional people and bicultural scholars from many Aboriginal nations to study together.

What would an APIU offer beyond courses provided in Aboriginal programs and mainstream post-secondary institutions? It would articulate a unifying vision within which diverse traditions could promote the study of traditional knowledge at its most complex levels. It would contribute to the dedicated efforts of many communities and leaders to restore elders to a place of honour as the first teachers and scholars of Aboriginal peoples. It would give Aboriginal and non-Aboriginal researchers, professionals and scholars opportunities to meet elders and study with them. It would push outward the boundaries of knowledge by developing frameworks of analysis and interpretation defined by Aboriginal values and perspectives. It would offer advanced studies, complementing Aboriginal undergraduate programs. Aboriginal graduate students, who now have few choices beyond the western intellectual tradition, would have options rooted in Aboriginal intellectual and spiritual traditions. Research undertaken in association with an APIU would address the specific concerns of implementing Aboriginal self-government.

The university would benefit not only Aboriginal people. Throughout the world, the importance of indigenous knowledge to humankind has been recognized by leading scholars in the sciences and humanities. The new university would be a place where non-Aboriginal people could study with the acknowledged experts of the Aboriginal world: the elders. Internationally, elders are already sought for their understanding of local environments and for their expertise in botany and ecological relationships. Environmental scholars and policy makers, medical researchers, healers and other scholars could meet with elders in gatherings that are respectful of their unique knowledge.

We see an APIU as a university without walls, depending largely on existing facilities in post-secondary institutions and Aboriginal communities. While a small core facility would be required, its educational activities would be undertaken in regional locations, with elders, students, scholars and others converging for agreed purposes. Through institutes, conferences and workshops, an APIU would bring together elders and Aboriginal scholars with seekers of knowledge. In addition to on-site learning, telecommunications technology would allow virtual communities to form, so that students in all parts of Canada could study with elders anywhere in Canada and the Americas.

For example, the Saskatchewan Indian Federated College and the First Nations House of Learning at the University of British Columbia might offer a summer institute with the Aboriginal Peoples' International University, linking classrooms in both locations and other parts of the world. The Mohawk Nation might offer an institute, focusing on its traditional system of governance and its international activities, with Aboriginal students across the country participating through audio- and videoconferencing. The Grand Council of the Crees might initiate a discussion group with Aboriginal law students and others across the country to share their experiences as participants in the Working Group on Indigenous Populations at the United Nations. All of these learning events could be co-sponsored by the Aboriginal Peoples' International University, which could undertake the linking work and negotiate accreditation and transfer of credits, where appropriate.

An APIU should be a co-operative venture that bolsters initiatives already under way and does not compete with them. Potential affiliates of the Aboriginal Peoples' International University might include

- Aboriginally controlled post-secondary institutions and Aboriginal units in provincial and territorial institutions, with proposed Métis and Inuit colleges as part of the network;
- the Centre for International Indigenous Studies and Development at the Saskatchewan Indian Federated College;
- the Centre for Traditional Knowledge, sponsored by the Canadian Museum of Nature, the Canadian Commission for UNESCO and the United Nations World Decade for Cultural Development;
- the Native Philosophy Project and Rockefeller Foundation visiting humanities fellowships at Lakehead University in Thunder Bay, Ontario;
- the Ts''kel program for graduate-level education at First Nations House of Learning, University of British Columbia; and
- the University of Alberta's proposed doctorate program in indigenous knowledge.

Collaborative relationships could be forged with like-spirited programs in other countries, such as the University of California at Berkeley's doctoral program in indigenous knowledge, the Centre for World Indigenous Studies in Olympia, Washington, Harvard's graduate programs in education administration, and indigenous institutions in other parts of the Americas.

Applied research

In addition to its focus on traditional knowledge, an APIU would create an important opportunity to unite its research capacity with the needs of Aboriginal governments. Joint research projects could be undertaken, both on a consultancy basis and as part of partnerships in research. For example, a community may wish to have the APIU involved in establishing a research project on economies or on education. The university would not only offer communities the very richest of Aboriginal intellectual resources; it would also enrich its own knowledge bases through learning in the community. Cadres of graduate students could work with communities on community projects while refining methods of inquiry within participatory research frameworks. In establishing an applied research capacity, the APIU should work collaboratively with Aboriginal professional organizations that share a commitment to knowledge building and community.

A planning process

The planning of the university should be mandated by national and regional Aboriginal organizations. Aboriginal education leaders from across Canada have developed considerable expertise in post-secondary institution building over the past two decades. Their assistance should be sought in developing the operating structures of the APIU and its components and preparing the plans for implementing it. The APIU will potentially have affiliates in every province and territory. With implementation of self-government, federated Aboriginal structures to charter an institution serving all regions of Canada may well emerge. In the interim, federal legislation to charter the institution and concurrent recognition of degree-granting functions by the provinces should be explored. (A precedent exists: Royal Military College in Kingston, Ontario, was established by an act of Parliament in 1874 and empowered by provincial statute in 1959 to grant degrees.)

We propose that a steering group with a three-year mandate take responsibility for consultation and design. In addition, we propose that a number of key information and knowledge functions be located in the APIU. We see the need to establish working groups to do detailed planning for these functions and to determine whether the international university would be the best location for them. The steering group would oversee the establishment of working groups and receive their reports. A two-year mandate for these working groups would allow for integrated strategic planning.

RECOMMENDATIONS

The Commission recommends that

Establish Aboriginal Peoples' International University

3.5.32

A university under Aboriginal control, which could be called the Aboriginal Peoples' International University, with the capacity to function in all provinces and territories, be established to promote traditional knowledge, to pursue applied research in support of Aboriginal self-government, and to disseminate information essential to achieving broad Aboriginal development goals.

Steering Group to **3.5.33**
Plan APIU   First Nations, Inuit and Métis leaders in collaboration with the federal government establish a steering group funded by the federal government, with a three-year mandate

> (a) to explore options, conduct consultations and prepare a plan to implement an Aboriginal Peoples' International University by the year 2000; and
>
> (b) to collaborate with other working groups in determining the appropriate location of a documentation centre and archive, an electronic information clearinghouse, and statistical data bases.

8.2 Information Exchange: An Electronic Clearinghouse

In virtually every area of the Commission's concern, there were calls for the establishment of clearinghouses and mechanisms to promote the exchange of information among agencies and communities doing similar kinds of work. Curriculum development, language projects, classroom practice, early childhood education and counselling approaches are just a few of the education-oriented fields where practitioners, academics and students are seeking to exchange information. The same thirst for information was evident in the areas of economic development, health and law, to name a few. Young people also spoke of the importance of being in touch with one another and with data bases relevant to their concerns and priorities.

Infrastructure to support these functions has begun to emerge on the Internet. The U.S.-based NativeNet is an electronic clearinghouse that illustrates some possibilities for electronic exchange. NativeNet already has lists where practitioners can exchange information about education, language, health and other topics. A list has also been established for Native American professors. In addition, there are user groups through which Aboriginal people in Canada are discussing a wide range of issues; some are seeking approaches to teaching about stereotypes; teachers want to link their classrooms with other Aboriginal classrooms around the world; Aboriginal teachers are looking for jobs; and community projects are searching for information on Aboriginal Head Start. The number of home pages of Aboriginal educational institutions, cultural education centres, businesses, museums, art galleries and resource collections is rising rapidly on the World Wide Web. In addition, the World Center for Indigenous Studies in Olympia, Washington, has established an archive that makes important documents available on-line. Political happenings, economic development, legal issues, social concerns and international indigenous events are all lively conversation topics in various user groups.

The establishment of an electronic clearinghouse would be a possibility for Canada. But would it be inclusive? There are a number of concerns. First, there is the issue of cost. At present, connecting to the Internet could be expensive for communities that are far from a service provider. Long-distance telephone charges would be prohibitive and would discourage use. This technological problem could create urban communities rich in information and rural communities shut out of the electronic information flow. Moreover, many geographically isolated communities have minimal telecommunications infrastructure that would barely support information services reliant on digital and emerging technologies. Inuit Tapirisat of Canada has presented a brief to the Canadian Radio-television and Telecommunications Commission explaining its fears that telecommunications companies will invest in research to diversify their services in large, lucrative markets rather than providing a reliable service in small, isolated communities.[72]

Second, the languages of exchange on the Internet are English and French, not Aboriginal languages. Despite the assimilative potential, a language of mutual exchange is required for dialogue across nations. This need not interfere with the goal of establishing networks in Aboriginal languages for exchange within linguistic communities.

Third, communicating through the Internet requires some computer and keyboarding skills. This may be a problem for those who have not been exposed to computer technology, but increasingly, Aboriginal children and youth are acquiring computer skills and embracing electronic technology. So have many Aboriginal professionals in all fields of work. The federal government's decision to include schools under federal jurisdiction in the SchoolNet project will accelerate access to the Internet for Aboriginal young people served by these schools. (In 1995, Industry Canada and the Assembly of First Nations launched a joint project, First Nations School Access Project, to connect First Nations schools through SchoolNet, the national network of educational contacts and resources and an entry point for the Internet.) Of course, there will continue to be other forms of exchange, including teleconferences, gatherings, conferences, workshops and seminars. For those not inclined to use the Internet, there will undoubtedly be intermediaries who extract information and feed it into community and professional circles.

An electronic clearinghouse could offer a highly decentralized network linking rural and urban communities across the country, with participation from a wide variety of leaders, grassroots workers, researchers, students, youth and citizens at large. Important resources could be available from electronic archives, and the resources of various Aboriginal centres and libraries across the country could be obtained through on-line catalogues. Users would be able to locate relevant resources and contact communities directly for material communities wish to control themselves. Within Aboriginal communities, access could be ensured by installing public computer terminals in a school, adult education building, library or other public facility.

In planning for a clearinghouse, access for geographically dispersed communities and the state of community telecommunications should be analyzed with a view to upgrading facilities where needed. The appropriateness of establishing a clearinghouse as a part of an Aboriginal Peoples' International University should also be considered.

RECOMMENDATION

The Commission recommends that

Electronic   3.5.34
Clearinghouse   An electronic clearinghouse be established to facilitate the free flow of information among Aboriginal communities, education and self-government workers and individuals, the planning and development of this clearinghouse to be carried forward by a working group
(a) established in collaboration with First Nations, Inuit and Métis leaders;
(b) funded by the federal government and given a two-year mandate; and
(c) attentive to the need for Canada-wide and international communication as well as exchange in Aboriginal languages within linguistic communities.

8.3 Statistical Data Bases

Aboriginal governments, businesses and organizations will require solid information on which to base planning, analysis and research. At present, Aboriginal data bases to support these functions are localized and fragmentary. Many existing data bases have been generated because of government reporting requirements. These requirements will change, and as self-government is implemented, it will be important to put in place a strategy to ensure that data bases provide access to information required by Aboriginal institutions.

Which institutions produce more Aboriginal graduates in given areas of study? Are Aboriginal incomes keeping pace with those in the general population? What effect are youth empowerment programs having on school completion rates? What is the state of Aboriginal language retention levels – or the housing stock, or patterns of health and disease – relative to those of other communities? If there is no co-ordinated strategy for establishing data bases, the capacity to answer these kinds of questions will shrink as non-Aboriginal governments vacate their administrative role.

The gathering of information and its subsequent use are inherently political. In the past, Aboriginal people have not been consulted about what information should be collected, who should gather that information, who should maintain it, and who should have access to it. The information gathered may or may not have been relevant to the questions, priorities and concerns of Aboriginal peoples. Because data gathering has frequently been imposed by outside authorities, it has met with resistance in many quarters. This is particularly true of the census, which is Canada's primary mechanism for gathering consistent information at regular intervals.

Aboriginal governments, businesses and organizations need reliable information, and a common strategy is needed for co-ordinating data bases. The challenge is defining what information should be collected in a consistent way across communities, who should do it, and how it can be maintained in a way that respects confidentiality. The information currently collected may not be the most relevant for community planning purposes, and it is important to plan data bases from the community level up. Timing is important, because Aboriginal governments will be putting in place management information systems, if they have not already done so.

We believe that the gathering of information should be controlled by Aboriginal people, although the co-operation of non-Aboriginal agencies and institutions such as Statistics Canada will be essential to develop a complete picture of Aboriginal life in rural and urban Canada. Access to information at a grassroots level should be maximized, and electronic and on-line data bases are the best way to achieve this. There needs to be a mechanism for gathering and maintaining this information through a small core operation. We refer to this mechanism as the statistical clearinghouse.

The statistical clearinghouse could be part of the Aboriginal Peoples' International University and could co-ordinate efforts to agree upon a standardized data base, organize periodic data collection, and develop an online electronic data base for Aboriginal communities and organizations. As proposed later in this chapter, an Aboriginal human resources inventory could be established and maintained. Communities and businesses would have access to the most up-to-date information for program and business planning, feasibility studies, operations, proposal writing and strategic decision making. Moreover, the clearinghouse could have a multiple training function: to help communities and organizations set up standardized and customized information-gathering approaches and data bases; to facilitate training of nation and community personnel in the use of statistical information in their operations; and to build a pool of Aboriginal people with skills in statistics, demography and economic analysis so that statistical data bases can be used to the fullest. Aboriginal communities could enter into agreements with the statistical clearinghouse for the mutual exchange of information. Depending on its mandate, the clearinghouse could pursue co-operative arrangements with government and with Statistics Canada in furthering shared objectives, under conditions agreed upon by Aboriginal communities. The appropriateness of establishing the clearinghouse as a function of the Aboriginal Peoples' International University should be considered.

RECOMMENDATION

The Commission recommends that

Working Group for Statistical Clearinghouse

3.5.35
First Nations, Inuit and Métis leaders establish a working group, funded by the federal government, with a two-year mandate to plan a statistical clearinghouse controlled by Aboriginal people to
  (a) work in collaboration with Aboriginal governments and organizations to establish and update statistical data bases; and
  (b) promote common strategies across nations and communities for collecting and analyzing data relevant to Aboriginal development goals.

8.4 Aboriginal Documentation Centre

The history of residential schools and of the relocation of Aboriginal people is recorded in government, church, school and corporate archives throughout the country. While their experiences are etched in the memories of thousands of Aboriginal people today, these events are only partially documented. In our discussions of residential schools and relocations in Volume 1, Chapters 10 and 11, we recommended that this unique and historically significant information should be collected, preserved and made accessible. We believe that a national Aboriginal documentation centre could provide appropriate leadership by establishing an active program of research and dissemination and by maintaining a suitable facility for such a collection.

The documentation centre would have as its focus historical information on residential schools and relocations. However, there are many important archival collections relevant to Aboriginal life in Canada that do not have an appropriate home and to which the public and scholars have limited access, if any. The documentation centre could be a repository for diverse historical collections. A plan outlining acquisition and collections priorities would need to be developed.

Today, electronic media offer the opportunity to make collections available on-line from access points around the globe. By co-ordinating its efforts with other archives that house collections important to the history of Aboriginal people and relations with Canada, the documentation centre would become a key access point for collections and electronic data bases of other institutions as well as its own holdings.

As a priority, the documentation centre should address the issue of gathering oral history on residential schools and relocations. Aboriginal people who experienced these first-hand should have the opportunity to tell their stories for the benefit of present and future generations. A video archive of testimony should be established to preserve these accounts. This will become a lasting legacy to all Canadians. In addition to initiating its own research, the documentation centre should be able to fund both community-based and scholarly projects on residential schools and relocations.

Gathering documentation will not alter Canadians' awareness of Aboriginal history; it must be complemented by public education. Many Canadians are just becoming aware of residential school and relocation policies, and even today there are few teaching materials for adults and children. The documentation centre could spearhead the production of materials, including multi-media and travelling exhibits, for public education.

The appropriateness of establishing the centre as a function of the Aboriginal Peoples' International University should be considered in the planning process.

RECOMMENDATION

The Commission recommends that

Documentation Centre on Residential Schools and Relocations

3.5.36

The federal government fund the establishment of a national documentation centre to research, collect, preserve and disseminate information related to residential schools, relocations and other aspects of Aboriginal historical experience, the planning and development of the centre to be carried forward by a working group

(a) established in collaboration with First Nations, Inuit and Métis leaders; and

(b) having a two-year mandate.

9. EDUCATION FOR
SELF-GOVERNMENT

Preparing Aboriginal people to assume the complete range of responsibilities associated with self-governance must be recognized as a top priority in post-secondary education. At this historical juncture, Aboriginal people, governments, educational institutions and professional organizations all have crucial roles in building the capacity of Aboriginal nations and their communities to exercise self-government.

Over the past two decades, as the determination to re-establish self-governing nations has gathered momentum, Aboriginal people have repeatedly stressed the importance of building their capacity to operate contemporary self-governing structures. Much of our earlier discussion of adult and post-secondary education was devoted to structural and operational barriers. We have made recommendations to increase the prospects of educational success. The recommendations focused on

- strengthening the contribution of Canada's post-secondary institutions to the education of Aboriginal people;
- increasing the number, capacity and stability of Aboriginal institutions;
- increasing access for students through financial and other supports; and
- creating culturally based, relevant learning opportunities.

These changes will not happen overnight, although many of them can advance quickly with the political determination and the resources to bring about change. On the other hand, education for self-government cannot wait. Aboriginal communities and organizations urgently require trained personnel to plan and implement self-government.

9.1 Planning for Self-Government

For more than two decades, Aboriginal administrations have been growing steadily in scale and complexity. Today, many Aboriginal communities run multi-million-dollar administrations, economic development projects and businesses. Local administrations manage social services, education, sport and recreation, health, housing, public works, public safety and security, job creation and training while at the same time planning for self-government. Aboriginal administrators contract consultants of various sorts as needed – lawyers, evaluators, specialists – much as other governments do. To the extent possible, most communities try to hire local or other Aboriginal people to fulfil these responsibilities. Where there is no land base or where communities combine their efforts, Aboriginal organizations have been established to administer a variety of services, sometimes single services like health or education and, other times, multiple services. These, too, need administrators and specialized personnel.

While the pool of trained Aboriginal people has increased in recent years, particularly with the introduction of college and university programs that better reflect the needs of Aboriginal administrations, there remains a severe shortage of skilled Aboriginal personnel for the number of jobs in Aboriginal administrations. Self-government will open up an even broader selection of jobs. Education is essential to hone the talents needed to assume the responsibilities of the present and future, as we were told in Winnipeg:

> Education – the objective of Métis self-government and economic development – cannot be achieved in the absence of educated and technically trained individuals within our Métis communities who must administer and operate the sophisticated bureaucratic systems that our political leadership will require. We will need more trained managers, engineers and technicians than we now have. We have identified the problems and the roadblocks but unless governments are prepared to work with us on this vital issue, then our deliberations will have taken us no further.
>
> Claire Riddle
> Vice-President
> Winnipeg Region of the Manitoba Metis Federation
> Winnipeg, Manitoba, 23 April 1992

The number of Aboriginal graduates in fields related to Aboriginal self-government must increase very soon. Unfortunately, as land issues are being settled – as in the Yukon and the Nunavut agreements – federal government policy has been to negotiate training dollars that are made available only after agreements have been concluded. This policy is short-sighted given the number of years of training required for many senior positions in Aboriginal governments. The experiences of Nunavut's implementation training committee and the Council for Yukon First Nations, both acting on recent self-government agreements, are instructive for understanding aspects of planning human resources for self-government.

In both the Yukon and Nunavut, self-government training funds are quite limited, so they are seen as supplementing existing human resource development programs, sponsored by the federal government, which are expected to provide the bulk of training dollars. In both instances, a systematic approach has been taken to analyzing human resource needs.

In the Yukon, provision was made for each First Nation community to examine the skills and competencies required to implement the agreement at the community level, to take stock of the trained people already available in the community, and to identify the gaps and the number of individuals required in various areas.[73] A training policy committee is responsible for helping the council and the First Nations community meet these training needs by using existing programs where appropriate or by developing new programs if necessary. The committee is charged with keeping in mind the values and cultural dimensions of First Nations communities, as well as the non-academic needs of trainees, including transportation, daycare, housing, counselling, financial and other support. In addition, the committee is to explore the feasibility of a single-window concept for training funds, that is, whether a single pot of money should be pooled from various training funding sources, much as we recommended earlier in this chapter.

In Nunavut, researchers noted that 51 different organizations and their 198 employees would be involved in implementation.[74] They examined the existing and anticipated jobs and concluded that high school and college programs were producing sufficient candidates to fill the administrative support positions in these organizations. But there was a need to train internal administrators, program administrators, scientists and other professionals, and senior executives. Training of community members to direct implementation of the agreement by serving on boards and committees is essential. While researchers recommended that on-the-job training and educational leave be used to make professional development available to current employees, they pointed out that training for youth must also be a priority, given high rates of unemployment among Inuit 15 to 24 years of age.

Taken together, the Nunavut and Yukon examples are helpful in identifying some of the dynamics involved in training for self-government that may be applicable elsewhere.

- Self-government education must be addressed in connection with two distinct groups: those now employed in community administrations and organizations, and a large population of youth who are ready to enter the labour force. These groups may have unique, if overlapping, educational needs, which may include on-the-job training, professional development, job leaves, distance education and local delivery as well as more conventional methods of education in regional and urban centres.
- Students must have adequate financial support for academic and non-academic needs if they are to be successful.
- Self-government training needs can be pinpointed through planning by local and regional organizations. This will ensure that investment in training programs and support for student choices are adapted to the particular skill requirements and contexts of Aboriginal self-government while not neglecting generic skills that can be used anywhere in the labour market.
- It cannot be assumed that Aboriginal self-government jobs will be identical to those in other government organizations. Thus, adapted training programs must be provided.
- Funding mechanisms for self-government training and education should result in easy access for workers and students and should be simple to

administer. A one-stop funding approach is preferable to the current fragmentation of program funding, involving multiple government departments, each with a narrow mandate and its own program guidelines.

9.2 Programs That Work

Aboriginal communities, tribal councils and other organizations have been inventive in providing training and education for self-government. Among the design principles that can contribute to the success of programs are these:

- Aboriginal people are central decision makers.
- The programs address the needs and priorities of Aboriginal people.
- The programs include Aboriginal perspectives and methodologies.
- They open doors for the participation of Aboriginal people.
- They emphasize partnerships and mutual understanding.
- They find creative ways to overcome obstacles.

We have discussed many of these in our examination of Aboriginal adult education, and we summarize them by offering a few examples of existing programs that are designed to foster the success of Aboriginal students in self-government education. These examples are intended to exemplify the principles and represent only a few of the programs that could be described.

Concordia University in Montreal launched an education support services project for Aboriginal students in 1992. As in other post-secondary institutions with similar services, the aim is to offer practical assistance and an environment in which students are encouraged to complete their programs in areas of study related to self-government as well as in other academic fields. Concordia's support services include an academic adviser, a study centre, tutors, computers, cultural programs, and an annual orientation program for Aboriginal students. Overseeing this project is the Concordia Council on First Nations Education, which is composed of university and Aboriginal representatives (including two elders) and Aboriginal student representatives. Concordia has a First Nations student association and a student centre that has attracted Aboriginal students not only from Concordia but from other Montreal post-secondary institutions as well. When they appeared before the Commission in November 1993, Concordia officials were considering a bridging program and more active recruitment of Aboriginal faculty. They estimated that they had 100 Aboriginal students and three Aboriginal faculty members. The previous spring, 12 students had graduated, including two masters of fine arts. For more than two decades, other public post-secondary institutions have pursued similar initiatives (as well as providing daycare) to meet the needs of Aboriginal people.

Not all Aboriginal people can leave their homes and relocate to urban centres for their education. Many are already employed in their communities. Access programs and bridging programs have reached students who need to begin their studies at home. In Saskatchewan the Northern Teacher Education Program (NORTEP) expanded its efforts through the Northern Professional Access Program (NORPAC):

> In 1989 we had to expand our program. We had been busy keeping elementary teachers trained....Our high schools were growing in the north, so now we needed to provide high school teachers. In order to provide high school teachers we needed arts and science programs. There wasn't enough high school teacher involvement or applicants, so what we did was we tied it on to a university bridging program called NORPAC. It's called professional access to college and we provide two years of arts and science in La Ronge, along with secondary teacher [education].
>
> The university bridging program provides services such as counselling, tutoring....It is also a work study program where if somebody is interested in the legal profession, we have had people at work in the prosecutor's office, we have had people work at the legal aid office. People who are interested in administration will work at village offices or band offices. If they were interested in health, they will work in medical clinics. It's a work study program that works quite sufficiently in providing University of Saskatchewan classes and also University of Regina classes.

Rick Laliberté
Chairperson, NORTEP/NORPAC Board of Directors
Ile-a-la-Crosse, Saskatchewan, 8 December 1992

NORTEP and NORPAC are examples of collaborative relationships that lead to programs attentive to Aboriginal people's varying needs. These programs open the door to a range of career options that relate to Aboriginal self-government. Other access programs were described earlier in the chapter.

Professional development programs also help those already employed in Aboriginal administrations. Six tribal councils in northwestern Ontario have joined forces with the continuing education division of the University of Manitoba to offer a certificate in the management of community, economic and organization development. The part-time program is geared to senior managers who meet 15 times for one week at a time over a two-year period.[75] The ATII pilot project experimented with the delivery of a series of management training workshops to communities across Nunavut, northern Quebec and Labrador using interactive televised instruction. Programs provided in the community, combined with distance education and periodic institutes, extend the reach of post-secondary institutions into communities.

Incentives and bonuses may be necessary to make programs viable for Aboriginal people who are the major breadwinners in their families. As part of its community-based teacher education program, the government of the Northwest Territories provides training incentives to encourage para-professional staff to earn professional credentials. Many Aboriginal people supporting families cannot afford to leave their jobs, nor can they live on the subsistence allowances paid to students. The government of the Northwest Territories has responded by offering bonuses to increase student financial assistance to 50 to 60 per cent of employees' salaries.[76]

Aboriginal people have persistently sought partnerships with Canada's public post-secondary institutions. Over the past decade, some post-secondary institutions anticipated the range of education needs associated with Aboriginal self-government. The Donner Canadian Foundation, for example, funded the start-up of Aboriginal management and economic development programs at Trent University, the University of Lethbridge and the Saskatchewan Indian Federated College. A self-government diploma program was initiated at the University of Victoria in the school of public administration. Carleton University has offered a master's degree in Aboriginal community economic development. The Saskatchewan Indian Federated College is launching an Aboriginal M.B.A. program. Since 1973, the University of Saskatchewan has operated a pre-law program that has been the first step in the academic careers of many of today's Aboriginal lawyers, and the University of Ottawa has offered a similar program for francophones in civil law since 1990. There are many examples across the country of one- and two-year certificate and diploma programs offered in a broad range of professional and technical areas relevant to self-government.

Other programs train specialized para-professional and professional staff to deliver community services such as education, health, justice and social services. In Chapter 3 of this volume, we discussed the successful community health representative model. One problem is that many more trained Aboriginal people are needed in a great variety of areas, with increasingly higher levels of formal qualifications. A second problem has been creating culturally appropriate and relevant education and training. Programs designed for mainstream settings often fail to prepare students for professional responsibilities in Aboriginal surroundings. Programs designed in close collaboration with Aboriginal people are grounded in the social, cultural, legal and political contexts that graduates will actually encounter.

Aboriginal training institutes and organizations have emerged as important providers of training in areas related to self-government. Institutes such as the First Nations Tribal Justice Institute in British Columbia, the Gabriel Dumont Institute in Saskatchewan, the First Nations Technical Institute in Ontario, and ATII Training Inc. in Nunavut are examples of Aboriginally controlled training programs in tribal policing, natural resource management, computer technology and management. These institutes and others like them have faced challenges in obtaining recognition of their programs from mainstream institutions. As a result, many have had to negotiate joint accreditation arrangements for specific programs. We have already discussed difficulties with respect to accreditation and transfer credit arrangements.[77] These institutes will continue to play an important training role, first, because of their track record in developing programs suited to the needs of Aboriginal people, and second, because they create a learning environment that nurtures Aboriginal identity. At the provincial and territorial levels, mechanisms must be found to promote more open learning systems that respect the diverse education paths chosen by Aboriginal nations.

Institutions are not the only means to prepare people for self-government. Aboriginal people and the corporate sector have developed internship and scholarship programs to increase the interchange of expertise. The internship program of the Canadian Council of Aboriginal Business has been particularly successful in allowing Aboriginal students and young people to acquire expertise and contacts highly relevant to Aboriginal self-government. Several of Canada's chartered banks have instituted training and scholarship programs that bring Aboriginal people into their organizations. Corporations in the energy sector have established scholarship and work placement programs. For example, NOVA Corporation told us:

> We participate in an educational awards program, again to assist Aboriginal students to obtain post-secondary education relevant to the oil and gas industry and to increase the number of Aboriginal professionals in the petroleum industry in general and in NOVA specifically. We provide an award each year at southern Alberta colleges. Our bursaries are $3,500 each, awarded to Aboriginal students enroled in two-year business or technical programs.
>
> Barbara Tate
Vice-President, NOVA Corporation
Calgary, Alberta, 27 May 1993

Such programs have mutual benefits: corporate sponsors can diversify their organizational culture by bringing in Aboriginal people, and Aboriginal people can gain important training and experience.

In addition, for many years Canadian Executive Service Overseas (CESO) has offered its services in Aboriginal communities. In its brief to the Royal Commission, CESO explained that the retired executives who make up the organization have often been involved in one-on-one training and have brought important skills to projects where specific expertise has been required. The transfer of skills has been an important aspect of their work in the past and will be even more so in the future as they place an added emphasis on partnerships with Aboriginal communities and organizations.[78]

Developing human resources for self-government is not simply a matter of acquiring knowledge and skills from outside the Aboriginal community.

Successful programs also help students find their own paths as Aboriginal citizens and professionals. There is Aboriginal knowledge that only elders and other people rooted in Aboriginal cultural traditions can provide. Apprenticeships, community work placements and co-operative education open avenues to integrating knowledge and skills in culturally appropriate ways.

In summary, experience over two decades has identified critical factors that contribute to the success of students and the creation of a pool of human resources suited for work in Aboriginal governments. The challenge is now to accelerate capacity building in order to produce enough graduates, particularly in fields where Aboriginal people are under-represented.

9.3 Self-Government Personnel Needs

Canada lacks a country-wide assessment of Aboriginal human resources to guide the establishment of a detailed human resources development strategy for self-government. Such data would greatly assist in planning and policy development for Aboriginal nations, regions and communities.

While national statistical requirements may be hard to specify, we know that there have been many local and regional efforts to evaluate the human resource requirements of self-government. Some of this information is available to help identify training and education priorities (see Chapter 3 of this volume and Volume 2, Chapter 5). In addition, important characteristics of Aboriginal human resources development help in setting potential requirements:

- Human resources capacity has been growing in areas where special initiatives have been launched, particularly in law, elementary education, social work, management and some areas of community health. In other fields, there have been modest gains, and in still others, Aboriginal people are virtually absent. Table 5.2, using demographic, social and economic data from the 1991 Aboriginal peoples survey, describes the post-secondary training and education received by Aboriginal and non-Aboriginal women and men. The most common training for Aboriginal women is in the commerce, management and administration field, at 30.9 per cent (29.7 per cent for non-Aboriginal women), followed by training for health services at 16.6 per cent (19.5 per cent for non-Aboriginal women), and education-related careers at 15.3 per cent (15.8 per cent for non-Aboriginal women). Aboriginal men are trained mainly in the engineering, applied science and trades fields, at 57.1 per cent (41.6 per cent for non-Aboriginal men), with the number of men trained in the social sciences at 10.4 per cent (8.3 per cent for non-Aboriginal men), and commerce, management and administration at 10 per cent (15.6 per cent for non-Aboriginal men). As we will see, the commerce, management and administration category includes clerical positions, an important point when we examine where people work after training.

- Many more Aboriginal women than men enter university programs, yet women and men graduate in approximately the same proportion. Many of the women are sole-support mothers. In the 25 to 49 age range, 9.2 per cent of Aboriginal women have some university education, and 4.2 per cent have completed a university program. Of Aboriginal men of the same age, 6.2 per cent have some university education, and 3.9 per cent have completed university programs.[79]

- Table 5.3 gives an indication of how training has translated into jobs. Aboriginal women work primarily in clerical and service positions, with only 7.6 per cent in management and administration positions in 1991. Aboriginal men are concentrated in construction (20.3 per cent), other trades and land-based activities, with others working in the service sector (11.3 per cent), and only 6.9 per cent in management and administration. These patterns reveal not only the distribution of employment but also the persistent under-representation of Aboriginal women and men in management and administrative positions, jobs Aboriginal people must hold to implement self-government. As discussed in Volume 2, Chapter 5, Aboriginal personnel are concentrated in low level clerical and administrative positions. They can, however, be trained through professional development opportunities.

- Few Aboriginal people complete university programs. We saw earlier in this chapter that the proportion of Aboriginal students graduating from university programs remained low, at around 3 per cent between 1981 and 1991, compared to nearly 12 per cent of non-Aboriginal people. However, a growing number of Aboriginal people complete post-secondary education programs at technical institutes and colleges.

- Much of the training Aboriginal people have been able to take in their communities has combined academic upgrading and short skills courses sponsored by federal and provincial human resource development programs. Many para-professional and on-the-job training programs have been closely tied to specific job requirements, such as how to administer government programs. Regardless of how useful they are in offering practical skills and knowledge, the courses are usually not recognized by educational institutions for transfer credit, nor do they advance the person along a career path or broaden opportunities for job mobility. Self-government education in the future must be forward looking, providing career possibilities for Aboriginal people and an ever widening repertoire of relevant skills.

- It is instructive to consider the kinds of skills that Aboriginal communities and organizations purchase from consultants. The fact that they contract with consultants reveals capacities that need to be developed internally, including program development specialists, program evaluators, comptrollers, auditors and economic development consultants. External staff include

TABLE 5.2
Comparison of Demographic, Social and Economic Characteristics, Total Canadian and Aboriginal Populations, 1991

Education	Total Canadian		Total Aboriginal		North American Indians				Métis		Inuit	
					Registered		Non-Registered					
	F	M	F	M	F	M	F	M	F	M	F	M
Population that quit high school (age 15–49)	–	–	92,960	83,820	57,515	50,700	11,275	10,050	18,490	17,705	6,190	5,845
Returned (%)	–	–	28.1	17.9	27.2	17.7	34.6	19.6	33.1	20.8	11.7	10.0
Took equivalency upgrading (%)	–	–	14.4	13.1	15.4	13.5	11.4	13.3	11.9	10.8	17.6	17.5
Major field of post–secondary study, population age 15+ (%)												
Education, recreation, counselling	15.8	5.4	15.3	6.4	16.5	7.4	12.2	5.3	15.2	5.3	20.4	5.2
Fine and applied arts	8.0	3.4	7.8	3.0	6.4	3.0	10.0	2.7	10.1	3.6	–	–
Humanities	7.0	5.2	3.7	2.7	3.6	2.5	4.9	4.0	2.6	2.3	–	–
Social sciences	8.8	8.3	12.5	10.4	13.5	11.2	12.3	9.5	11.4	10.2	–	5.8
Commerce/management/administration	29.7	15.6	30.9	10.0	30.1	10.8	29.6	9.8	31.6	9.5	41.9	6.9
Agricultural/biological science/technology	4.5	4.9	5.7	4.3	4.6	4.7	8.0	3.7	6.3	4.2	6.0	–
Engineering/applied sciences	0.7	6.7	–	1.3	–	1.3	–	1.8	–	1.3	–	–
Engineering/applied science technology/trades	3.5	41.6	6.2	57.1	5.9	54.2	7.8	59.6	6.3	58.0	7.6	70.5
Health science and technology	19.5	4.2	16.6	3.1	18.5	3.3	14.3	2.2	14.5	3.7	12.9	–
Math/physical sciences	2.1	4.3	0.4	1.0	–	0.8	–	1.1	0.9	0.9	–	–
Financial assistance	–	–	14,519	9,250	9,755	4,920	2,565	1,920	3,095	2,215	325	260
Applied/received (% of total)	–	–	54.7	57.2	65.2	65.8	26.3	23.3	45.5	42.4	–	–
Applied/did not receive (% of total)	–	–	7.3	10.9	5.6	9.7	13.4	14.2	9.0	8.0	–	–
Never applied (% of total)	–	–	32.6	30.4	24.3	20.7	56.3	57.0	38.0	47.1	34.0	57.9

Source: Statistics Canada, 1991 Aboriginal Peoples Survey, custom tabulations; Statistics Canada, 1991 Census, catalogue no. 93-329.

TABLE 5.3

Occupations of Aboriginal and Non-Aboriginal Populations Age 15+ in the Experienced Labour Force, 1981 and 1991

	Aboriginal				Non-Aboriginal			
	M		F		M		F	
	1981	1991	1981	1991	1981	1991	1981	1991
	%	%	%	%	%	%	%	%
Management/administration	5.8	6.9	4.1	7.6	11.3	14.0	5.5	10.3
Natural science/engineering/math	2.4	2.5	0.7	0.7	4.9	5.9	1.2	1.8
Social science	2.0	2.2	4.9	7.1	1.3	1.6	2.1	3.0
Religion	0.1	0.2	0.1	—	0.4	0.3	0.2	0.1
Teaching	1.7	1.6	5.8	6.1	2.9	2.9	6.3	6.3
Medicine and health	0.8	0.8	5.9	6.1	1.7	2.0	8.7	9.1
Arts and literature	1.8	1.8	1.4	1.5	1.5	1.7	1.4	1.7
Clerical	5.0	5.8	27.3	27.9	7.1	7.1	36.5	31.7
Sales	3.7	4.5	6.5	5.9	8.7	9.1	9.4	9.5
Service	9.9	11.3	27.4	25.6	9.6	10.1	15.6	15.8
Farming and related	4.1	3.7	1.6	1.3	5.3	4.4	2.2	2.1
Fishing/trapping	2.8	3.0	0.2	0.7	0.5	0.5	0.1	0.1
Forestry and logging	5.3	4.2	0.6	0.3	1.0	0.9	0.1	0.1
Mining and related	2.4	1.3	0.1	—	1.1	0.8	0.1	0.0
Processing	6.0	3.8	3.2	2.0	5.3	3.9	2.2	1.7
Machinery	3.8	2.6	0.5	0.3	4.1	3.2	0.5	0.3
Production/fabrication	7.5	6.3	4.5	1.8	10.2	8.8	4.9	3.2
Construction	18.1	20.3	0.9	0.7	10.8	10.3	0.3	0.4
Transportation/equipment	7.0	6.4	1.3	1.3	6.2	5.9	0.6	0.7
Material handling	4.3	3.1	1.5	0.7	2.7	2.2	1.2	0.8
Other crafts	1.1	1.1	0.8	0.8	1.7	1.5	0.7	0.6
Other	4.3	6.8	1.0	1.5	1.8	2.9	0.5	0.9

Source: Statistics Canada, 1981 Census and 1991 Aboriginal Peoples Survey, custom tabulations; Statistics Canada, 1991 Census, Major Fields of Study of Post-Secondary Graduates, catalogue no. 93-329 (1993).

teachers, education administrators, social workers, lawyers, engineers, housing consultants, nurses, doctors, dentists, optometrists and business managers. The wide range of outside expertise suggests that the building of internal capacity needs to be across many fields of expertise. (It is true that some externally hired staff are Aboriginal people from outside the community. It is unrealistic to expect small communities or organizations to supply expertise in every area.)

In summary, the human resource indicators suggest that the groundwork has been laid for Aboriginal self-government, particularly in building up administrative capacity. However, communities and organizations possess these capacities in unequal amounts. Senior and executive management skills are scarce, as are a wide range of professional skills requiring university education. At the same time, there are Aboriginal people with the relevant skills and experience to provide the backbone of Aboriginal self-government. The challenge will be to create opportunities for them to acquire a variety of skills that will support new, higher levels of responsibility.

There is an urgent need to open up opportunities for youth in Aboriginal self-government. Young people must be made aware that as Aboriginal governments resume responsibility for areas of life that have been controlled by others, new opportunities will emerge, for example, in justice administration and law enforcement, finance and investment, science and health, economic and business development, environmental and natural resources management, and technology. As noted in Chapter 3 of this volume, there are many careers in the health professions alone in which there are almost no Aboriginal people.

9.4 What Needs to Be Done

The next two decades will be critical for boosting the number of Aboriginal graduates who can work in Aboriginal governments. In this section, we outline a number of strategies for generating sufficient capacity to implement self-government.

Funding for institutional partnerships

It is important to increase the number of institutions preparing Aboriginal people for self-government. We have already recommended government funding of Aboriginally controlled post-secondary institutions as one way to do this. At the same time, we recognize the critical role of Canada's public post-secondary institutions. We believe that partnerships between Aboriginal people and public post-secondary institutions are extremely important for broadening the range of professional skills Aboriginal people will acquire.

In the immediate future, it is critical that post-secondary institutions turn out graduates in fields related to the core administrative areas of Aboriginal self-government: management (including resource management and education administration), public administration, economic development, finance and planning. Such programs should be tailored to the requirements of Aboriginal governments and designed to provide students with a number of progressively more advanced credentials at the diploma, three- and four-year bachelor's degree and master's degree levels. Executive M.B.A. and master of public administration (M.P.A.) programs geared to Aboriginal self-government should also be encouraged to produce as many graduates as possible. In some cases, multi-disciplinary programs of two, three or four years could be created with a specific focus on training for Aboriginal self-government. Wherever possible, co-operative education should be built into the program.

From experience to date, we believe that Aboriginal people must be involved as full decision makers in education processes and projects intended to address their needs. Public post-secondary institutions that enter into partnerships with Aboriginal people and demonstrate a commitment to Aboriginal self-government education deserve support.

RECOMMENDATION

The Commission recommends that

Education for Self-Government Funding

3.5.37

Federal, provincial and territorial governments establish funding programs to support education for self-government, to be available to

    (a) public post-secondary institutions that have entered into partnerships with Aboriginal people to initiate or expand training and education in areas identified as priorities by Aboriginal governments, organizations and communities for the implementation of self-government; and

    (b) Aboriginally controlled post-secondary institutions for program innovation to enhance capacity for self-government.

Incentives for students

We have identified three types of candidates for self-government education: those already employed in Aboriginal government and related services; the substantial number of young people who are in the job market but are undereducated; and those who will be joining the labour force in the next two decades.

In our discussion of capacity building for self-government (see Volume 2, Chapter 3), we noted that if 'professional' behaviours are defined to conform to the demands of non-Aboriginal bureaucracies, they may bring the Aboriginal public servant into conflict with community standards of behaviour. In our discussion of the child in the formal education system earlier in this chapter, we noted the potential for a similar conflict between the Aboriginal culture and the culture of the school. In both cases the conflicts tend to inhibit personal investment in learning, skills development and advancement to higher levels of education and responsibility. When they assume control over education and public services, Aboriginal nations have the opportunity to reinforce traditional cultural norms of achievement and excellence in roles that have been dominated for generations by non-Aboriginal people.

In traditional Aboriginal societies, each member's capabilities were considered spiritual gifts; individuals had a responsibility to discover, develop and share those gifts to sustain the life of the community. Mohawk tradition teaches that the practice of politics is the highest form of spirituality, because exercising power to affect future generations carries with it the highest spiritual responsibilities. A similar ethic can be found in the traditions of other Aboriginal nations. We believe that the most powerful incentives for adults and young people to invest in education for self-government will come from communities and kin who publicly and privately celebrate their members' diverse gifts and honour those who serve.

Young people must discover that the future holds rewarding career possibilities. Counsellors must be made aware of the career options for Aboriginal youth in self-government fields. This will require good working relationships between Aboriginal governments and career counsellors. Young people must receive early career guidance so that their school programs will contain the prerequisites they will need to realize their career goals.

Tangible rewards and incentives will also have a place in encouraging students to undertake and complete higher education and professional training in management and public administration, teacher education and education administration, recreation leadership, economics, accounting, health fields, social work, natural resource management and other programs considered important to Aboriginal self-government and self-reliance.

For Aboriginal people now employed, completion of education and training should lead to career advancement and improved compensation; program and services budgets should accommodate leave to allow people to study while they work and paid leave for more extensive training. Other strategies for capacity building and career enhancement are discussed below and in Volume 2, Chapter 5.

Although we have already addressed student funding, we believe that there should be additional incentives to reward student choice and completion of programs related to Aboriginal self-government. The funding guidelines of the

department of Indian affairs permit First Nations and Inuit education authorities to designate up to five per cent of their post-secondary funding as incentives to students enroled in studies related to self-government and for scholarships
rewarding academic excellence.[80] This is a very progressive policy in principle.
However, it assumes sufficient funds are in the authority's annual budget to meet
the basic demand for post-secondary assistance. Given the pressures on educational assistance budgets, it is unlikely that significant incentives can be provided
from existing resources.

Additional funding is required to permit First Nation and Inuit governments and education authorities to offer incentives in designated occupations
and careers. These could include scholarships to reward exceptional achievement,
top-up funds for students who must be separated from their families and therefore incur additional costs for lodging during training; and loans forgivable on
completion of a period of employment in the service of self-government. The
incentives would provide resources over and above regular student funding.
For Métis and other Aboriginal students, incentives for self-government studies could be part of the scholarship fund recommended earlier.

During the transition to self-government, Aboriginal nations with jurisdiction over education will be able to allocate funds and designate scholarships
in study areas of priority in their human resources development plans.

Recommendations

The Commission recommends that

Youth Careers **3.5.38**
Campaign Aboriginal governments and organizations collaborate to launch
a Canada-wide campaign to make youth aware of the opportunities to serve their nations that will open up with the advent
of self-government and of the tangible and intangible rewards
that accompany public service.

Student Incentives **3.5.39**
for Self- The federal government make funds available to First Nation
Government
Studies and Inuit governments and organizations to support incentives to encourage students to complete bachelor's and master's
level studies and professional training in areas of priority to self-
government, including such measures as
  (a) employee release time for concurrent work and study;
  (b) paid leave to pursue full-time study;
  (c) scholarships in studies related to self-government;

    (d) top-up of educational assistance for family needs, includ-
    ing exceptional housing costs; and

    (e) student loans that are forgivable on completion of a period
    of employment in the service of self-government.

Co-op programs, internships and executive exchanges

A 1994 study by the federal department of human resources found that students
who study in co-operative work-study programs at the college and university
levels have higher rates of employment upon graduation and earn more than
those who did not follow co-op programs.[81] These findings attest to the advantages of work placements and internships in preparing students for employment.

    Programs meant to meet self-government needs should include work
placement and internships. Efforts should be made to create opportunities for
students to work in placements related to their program of studies.

    In addition to Aboriginal governments and small businesses, Canada's
federal, provincial and municipal governments can provide important training
grounds in public administration. Corporations can also make a substantial contribution to education for self-government by offering placements and internships. We have mentioned opportunities offered by banks, resource industry
companies and other corporations. With the co-operation of the public and private sectors, Aboriginal students can sample a range of valuable work experiences.
These jobs can also be a significant source of job contacts for students, as well
as a supplement to student income.

RECOMMENDATION

The Commission recommends that

Co-op Placements
in Business and
Government

3.5.40

Canada's corporations, small businesses and governments
become active partners in Aboriginal self-government education
by identifying co-op placement and internship opportunities in
their organizations, in consultation with Aboriginal people.

    Interchanges between corporate executives and senior staff of Aboriginal
administrations can provide mutually beneficial professional development experiences. Such exchanges help to promote an understanding of the management

environments and cultural milieu in which decisions are being made, and they provide practical skills and invaluable contacts. Executive M.B.A. and M.P.A. programs should adopt such exchanges as part of their offerings.

RECOMMENDATION

The Commission recommends that

Executive 3.5.41
Interchange Canada's corporations and governments at all levels establish executive interchange opportunities in partnership with Aboriginal governments.

Leadership and professional development for Aboriginal self-government

So far, we have talked about training and educating people to work in Aboriginal governments and related services. But the Aboriginal political and public service leadership will also require professional development.

New leaders and Aboriginal leaders whose responsibilities are expanding into new areas need to develop skills in many areas, including negotiation, media relations, community development and government relations. Aboriginal leaders, like politicians everywhere, must have an opportunity to keep their skills current with their evolving responsibilities, as must members of newly established self-government institutions.

For Aboriginal people whose jobs involve the implementation of holistic, integrated service delivery, there must be a team emphasis in developing planning, management, communications and other professional skills across disciplinary boundaries. Workshops on community development, strategic planning, government relations, conflict resolution and other areas of public administration and management will increase the knowledge of staff and their ability to work toward community goals as an integrated team.

This kind of professional development can be achieved through specialized and custom-designed workshops. Participants in such training events in business and the professions are often able to accumulate credits toward professional credentials.

In Volume 2, Chapter 3, we recommended establishing an Aboriginal government transition centre to facilitate nation building and citizen participation during the transition to self-government. The centre would work in association with universities, post-secondary education facilities, and other organizations across Canada.

Professional organizations

The Commission was pleased to see the number of professional organizations that made presentations on Aboriginal issues. Many expressed their support for improving the quality of life of Aboriginal people under conditions where Aboriginal people can determine their own direction. Professional organizations in general expressed their desire to establish good working relationships with Aboriginal people. We are hopeful that doctors, nurses, teachers, professors, mental health professionals, lawyers, business people, bankers and other members of professional organizations will play an active and supportive role in seeing that our recommendations are implemented.

Some professional organizations have already established Aboriginal committees or working groups to provide direction and advice. This is an encouraging step. It shows that members of the professions recognize their role in promoting entry of Aboriginal people to their ranks. It also provides the opportunity to discuss whether professional practice in Aboriginal environments requires different kinds of training and knowledge. We encourage professional organizations that have not yet built links with Aboriginal people to do so. As noted in Chapter 3 of this volume, Aboriginal people are themselves engaged in creating definitions of professionalism, based on Aboriginal knowledge and values as well as ideas from mainstream society.

Because some professional organizations play pivotal roles in regulating and licensing practitioners, it is important that they understand Aboriginal perspectives on the bodies of knowledge they regulate. Through dialogue, professional organizations and Aboriginal people can find ways of working together to extend credentials to recognize Aboriginal knowledge. We have already recommended the organization of scholarly exchanges between elders and academics. The Aboriginal Peoples' International University could play a facilitating role in such events.

RECOMMENDATION

The Commission recommends that

Professional **3.5.42**
Associations Professional associations and self-governing bodies in the professions
Support actively support the professional training of Aboriginal people by
Aboriginal
Training (a) entering into dialogue on such issues as credentials, recruitment, mentoring, career paths linking para-professional

and professional training, education based on Aboriginal culture, systemic discrimination and racism;

(b) establishing scholarships for Aboriginal people;

(c) encouraging their members to gain an understanding of Aboriginal perspectives;

(d) spearheading initiatives to introduce Aboriginal cultural perspectives into professional training programs; and

(e) providing leadership by encouraging implementation of the recommendations in this report that are relevant to their areas of expertise.

Professional education using distance education

Options for education must expand for Aboriginal people already engaged in self-government activities in their communities who cannot leave for extended periods. It is time to push further on the promises offered by distance education technology. As discussed earlier, the ATII pilot project's cost-effective delivery of management education across four time zones provides experience upon which Aboriginal people and post-secondary institutional partners can build. We propose a more extended test of this model at a more advanced level of study, including such fields as management, health and economic development. Using curriculum developed by Aboriginal people and interactive video technologies, a program of professional studies could be delivered, perhaps in conjunction with summer institutes. The model could test various combinations of technologies and teaching methods, as well as support services intended to encourage students to complete courses. The project could create unique resources that could be shared electronically. Using videoconferencing, elders and other resource persons could participate in the program.

We see this kind of project as ideal for the applied research agenda of the Aboriginal Peoples' International University (APIU). Such a project has broad implications for Aboriginal self-government education and would establish from the outset the networking capabilities of the APIU, its multi-nation character, and its commitment to research that advances the practice of self-government. To carry out the project, it would be necessary to create a consortium of APIU members, Aboriginal governments, professional associations, media partners and Aboriginal education researchers. Members of Mokakit, an Aboriginal education research association that draws its membership from among Aboriginal educators with graduate degrees, as well as non-Aboriginal associates, could play a pivotal role in such an undertaking. A carefully documented research study would produce important data to underpin models for the future.

RECOMMENDATION

The Commission recommends that

Support of
Distance
Education Models

3.5.43

The federal government, media corporations, provincial and territorial governments and private donors provide funding and/or gifts in kind (for example, access to facilities and technology) to establish a distance education model of professional training suitable for Aboriginal people who wish to pursue post-secondary studies from their communities.

Aboriginal human resource development inventory and strategy for self-government

We emphasize again our belief that education for self-government is an urgent priority. Concerted efforts are required on many fronts to increase local capacity to implement Aboriginal self-government. The initiatives we have proposed should be launched immediately.

At the same time, it is crucial to establish a comprehensive inventory of Aboriginal people available for work across Canada that will serve as the data base for human resources planning and policy. Current labour force information does not describe Aboriginal human resources in sufficient detail, particularly because there are so few Aboriginal people in many employment categories. The data base would allow Aboriginal governments, employers, post-secondary institutions and Canadian governments to pinpoint Aboriginal human resources requirements more accurately, establish target levels in specific areas, track the number of graduates in relevant fields, and monitor progress toward human resources development goals. For example, the inventory would establish the number of Aboriginal secondary teachers, dentists, carpenters, system analysts, archaeologists, marine biologists, trappers, professional foresters, nurses, certified general accountants, and so on. Specific policy strategies can be developed to increase the number of graduates in priority areas.

The establishment of a comprehensive and accurate data base would be the first step toward that end. We believe that the national Aboriginal organizations, through their memberships, would be well-positioned to carry out this initiative. The data base could be housed at the proposed clearinghouse and could be updated regularly by the clearinghouse. For this reason, it is critical from the outset to develop a single, co-ordinated approach with mutually agreed tracking categories. The inventory should be available in formats that facilitate local, regional and Canada-wide human resource planning. (For further discussion of the human resources inventory, see Chapter 3 in this volume.)

RECOMMENDATION

The Commission recommends that

Canada-Wide Aboriginal Human Resources Inventory
3.5.44
The federal government provide funding for national Aboriginal organizations to co-ordinate establishment of a Canada-wide Aboriginal human resources inventory that is amenable to regular updating.

Education is a lengthy process. It takes time to build local capacity. Education for self-government cannot and should not wait until self-government agreements are concluded. Aboriginal communities and organizations must proceed now with preparing personnel. The pace of education and training must gather momentum so that Aboriginal nations can assume their self-governing responsibilities with a full complement of trained Aboriginal people.

10. NEW PARTNERSHIPS IN ABORIGINAL EDUCATION

10.1 A Shift in Authority

Throughout this chapter we have urged that education in all its dimensions be placed under the control of Aboriginal people. To initiate phase one of a shift in authority, we recommended that federal, provincial and territorial governments act promptly to acknowledge that education is a core area of self-government jurisdiction, that is, one in which Aboriginal nations and their communities can take initiatives. Such acknowledgement would open the door to adaptation and flexible interpretation of existing legislation and funding conditions and would allow Aboriginal nations and communities that are ready to proceed with fundamental change to get started.

In phase two, Aboriginal nations will reconstitute themselves and gain recognition under the proposed Aboriginal Nations Recognition and Government Act. They will then be able to exercise jurisdiction in core areas, preferably agreed upon with the federal and provincial governments, in the context of a Canada-wide framework agreement, or with the federal government and those provinces ready to act. We have no doubt that education will be one of the areas in which Aboriginal nations will wish to assume jurisdiction at an early date and that it will be readily recognized by federal and provincial governments as an area of vital concern to the life and welfare, the culture and identity of Aboriginal peoples.

10.2 Learning from the Past, Building for the Future

The educational reforms implemented in the past 25 years have laid a solid foundation for the shift in authority that we propose. As we have documented in this chapter, First Nations and Inuit communities have assumed administrative responsibility for local schools. They have introduced changes that have made curriculum and school culture more relevant to community experience and encouraged young people to stay in school longer. Tribal councils and regional governments have established education authorities to lead the process of change; provincial and territorial organizations have negotiated policy frameworks with provincial governments; national organizations have represented their constituents in federal forums, conducted major research projects and promulgated policy documents on education; and Aboriginal post-secondary institutions and training institutes have emerged, negotiating a variety of funding agreements with governments and affiliations with provincial institutions.

Aboriginal people have become more active in influencing provincial and territorial education, negotiating tuition agreements, forming advisory groups and seeking representation on school boards. Provincial and territorial institutions have adapted curriculum, introduced special programs and delivery methods, and in some cases have set targets for increasing student access and retention. Provincial and territorial governments have turned their attention to how policy can enhance Aboriginal participation and success in provincial institutions.

Aided by special initiatives in teacher education since the 1960s, Aboriginal people have gained a foothold in the teaching profession, and many have taken their place in schools on-reserve and in northern communities, although representation in provincial schools is still low. Education has been a prominent choice of Aboriginal people pursuing graduate studies. Educators with post-graduate credentials and those who have moved from the classroom to administrative roles now constitute a corps of mature Aboriginal professionals taking leadership in educational policy and reform.

All of these changes are welcome. But as we have shown, they are not enough to close the gap between the education obtained by Aboriginal students and that of other Canadians. As the skills requirements of a post-industrial, globalized economy rise, the marginalization, poverty and relative disadvantage of Aboriginal people are in danger of increasing unless success in education can be radically improved.

Equipping successive generations with the skills to participate in a global economy is a major goal of Aboriginal people and their educators, but it is only part of the story. Aboriginal people are determined to sustain their cultures and identities, and they see education as a major means of preparing their children to perceive the world through Aboriginal eyes and live in it as Aboriginal human beings. Aboriginal education therefore must be rooted in Aboriginal cultures and community realities. It must reinforce Aboriginal identity, instill traditional values, and affirm the validity of Aboriginal knowledge and ways of learning.

The evidence we have reviewed indicates that education under the control of Aboriginal people typically pursues the dual objectives of fostering skills relevant to participation in contemporary society and reinforcing cultural identity. It also produces better outcomes according to objective measures of academic achievement and contributions to the community and subjective assessments of personal growth and satisfaction.

10.3 New Partnerships

The implementation of Aboriginal self-government will add momentum to change already under way and will introduce a new dimension of Aboriginal control. Self-government will permit the establishment of Aboriginal education systems under the jurisdiction of Aboriginal nations and the authority of laws adopted by the nation.

Once recognized, Aboriginal nations can exercise jurisdiction in core areas of jurisdiction. They can establish education authorities to make policy on education goals and standards, the administration of community schools, tuition agreements and purchase of provincial or territorial services. Some nations will be able to develop infrastructure for autonomous policy development, access to specialist services, hiring of personnel, training and professional development of educators, curriculum development and research. Some will want to join with other nations to carry out these functions, as we describe below.

In the transition period following recognition, nations will receive federal funding according to the responsibilities they assume in core areas of self-government. When established as a third order of government, they will receive revenue from sources within the nation and intergovernmental transfers. They will allocate resources for government services, including education systems and community schools. Nations will participate in negotiating province-wide or territory-wide policy frameworks with provincial or territorial governments, normally through representation in multi-nation organizations.

Aboriginal public governments will exercise jurisdiction in education under their constitutions or the mandates negotiated to define their roles as communities or regions within provincial or territorial boundaries. Aboriginal community of interest governments, which come together in urban centres or rural districts to seek recognition and act in education, will exercise authority delegated by provincial or nation governments with which they affiliate or for which they deliver services.

Table 5.4 displays the levels of organization that might be developed in an Aboriginal education system and the way authority and responsibility might be distributed. For the sake of simplicity, the model refers primarily to nation governments.

Local Aboriginal communities would continue, as they do now, to make decisions about education: they would decide whether students would attend Aboriginal schools or provincial or territorial institutions. They would implement policy in local schools, negotiate tuition agreements for their students and participate in decision making in local school boards, post-secondary institutions and training programs under provincial or territorial jurisdiction. Under self-government, the authority to deliver education, implement policies and fund local education will derive from the Aboriginal nation. Communities will participate in policy making through representation in Aboriginal nation governing bodies and nation education authorities.

Multi-nation organizations will constitute a third level of organization in Aboriginal education systems. The rationale for a third level of organization is set out by Common and Frost in a recent publication drawing on First Nations education experience in Ontario. The authors refer to a Native Ministry of Education (NMOE) as the locus for functions we see as appropriate for multi-nation organizations.

> No single First Nation could hope to mount costly research projects, thus necessitating a regional or provincial organization to investigate such areas as: efficacious Native learning styles, language acquisition models, or intervention approaches to reduce drop-out rates. The research department should search for appropriate pupil-teacher ratios for Native schools, develop culturally appropriate intelligence tests and numerous other educational issues.
>
> The curriculum development and implementation branch would design curricula to meet locally identified needs and integrate Indian values in curricula, pedagogy and teaching materials....As well, the Ministry could also have an evaluation branch for providing audits and evaluation of First Nation-operated systems.
>
> Further, the Ministry would have an adult and continuing education branch for developing programs to meet individual First Nation's needs. The NMOE could facilitate and co-ordinate distance education approaches and use of technology to deliver secondary and post-secondary programs to remote, small, isolated Native communities (i.e., interactive television and computers).
>
> Without a third level structure, the issues of accreditation will become problematic. If a First Nation operated system declares itself independent from provincial curricula and standards, the provincial institutions and post-secondary programs may challenge or not rec-

TABLE 5.4
Model of An Aboriginal Education System

Local Community	Aboriginal Nation	Multi-Nation Organization	Canada-Wide Networks
• Participates in policy making through representation in Aboriginal nation governing bodies and nation education authority • Makes decisions on instruction of local students • Implements nation policy in local Aboriginal institutions • Negotiates tuition agreements in accord with nation policy • Participates in decision making in local institutions under provincial/ territorial jurisdiction	• Enacts or adopts laws on Aboriginal education • Establishes an education authority to make policy on education goals and means of achieving them in the nation • administration of schools and colleges within the nation • tuition agreements • purchase of provincial/ territorial services • Receives revenues and distributes funds for government services including education • Participates in establishing policy framework province-wide through representation in multi-nation organizations	• Negotiates policy framework with the province or territory • for tuition agreements • access to provincial or territorial services • transfer between Aboriginal and provincial or territorial academic programs • Develops curriculum • Monitors academic standards in Aboriginal system • May co-ordinate nation support of Aboriginal post-secondary institutions • Advises provincial ministers of education, colleges and universities and training • Provides an umbrella for representation of community of interest governments administering education	• Federated organizations reflecting nation interests • Aboriginal Peoples' International University • electronic clearinghouse • statistical clearinghouse • documentation centre • associations for standard setting and accrediting post-secondary programs and institutions

ognize the credentials of the products of First Nation-operated systems. A Native Ministry of Education could develop its own standards and inspect systems to ensure set standards are being met.[82]

Educational innovation to date has been led by community schools and nation or tribal council education authorities. These bodies may be reluctant to relinquish their autonomy to participate in larger coalitions. Common and Frost acknowledge that there could be conflicts between the interests of the local community and the priorities of a third-level organization. In our view, however, the benefits of having an agency at the provincial level that can negotiate the development of Aboriginal education systems outweighs any disadvantage to nations and their communities from sharing authority with an Aboriginal organization of broader scope.

In summary, we would see a multi-nation organization negotiating a policy framework with the province governing tuition agreements, access to provincial services and transfer between Aboriginal and provincial academic programs. It would develop curriculum, monitor academic standards in the Aboriginal education system, advise provincial ministers of education, colleges and universities, and provide training. It could also represent community of interest governments administering education in urban centres.

The fourth level of organization for which we see a need under self-government is Canada-wide networks. We anticipate that governance structures will take a federated form rather than a centralized hierarchy. At the Canada-wide level, the need for federated structures in education that reflect the interests and priorities of constituent nations and institutions is particularly important.

It is no accident that there are no examples of Canada-wide institutions of educational governance. Education in all parts of Canada is recognized as a process that must be rooted in the local community, even while global economic forces exert pressure for more uniformity. In proposing Canada-wide vehicles to support Aboriginal education in the twenty-first century, we emphasize that these institutions must sustain dialogue with and between local communities even as they test the possibilities of advanced technologies and links with other nation-states. Emerging telecommunications technologies offer an unprecedented opportunity for Aboriginal institutions to transcend distance and at the same time give primacy to grassroots priorities and participation. Local diversity and nation autonomy must be respected if Canada-wide institutions are to mobilize and sustain support and function effectively.

Our recommendations include establishing an Aboriginal Peoples' International University, an electronic information clearinghouse, a statistical clearinghouse, and a documentation centre. We also recommend the formation of a Canada-wide board or association to set standards and accredit Aboriginal post-secondary programs. In each case we see the Canada-wide institutions facilitating networking among local and regional programs and institutions and providing a broader perspective on the current status and future possibilities of Aboriginal education.

While we see Aboriginal institutions leading the way and setting the pace for innovation and increased effectiveness in Aboriginal education, we wish also to emphasize the continuing importance of provincial and territorial institutions in Aboriginal education. As Aboriginal people participate more fully in every facet of Canadian life, they will become more visible in colleges, universities and professional schools. Urban elementary schools and district high schools will continue to serve Aboriginal students in significant numbers. Employment-oriented training programs will contribute to Aboriginal people's entry or re-entry into the labour market.

Local education and training institutions under provincial or territorial jurisdiction should continue their efforts to accommodate Aboriginal students, deliver culturally sensitive services to Aboriginal communities under contract, establish Aboriginal programs, designate Aboriginal schools or delivery sites under Aboriginal management, consult with local Aboriginal communities, and engage Aboriginal representatives in governance and decision making in their institutions. In Volume 4, Chapter 7, we argued that provincial governments should ensure that their fiduciary obligations to Aboriginal people are fully honoured and respected. When the debate regarding the level of government responsible for Aboriginal services is laid to rest, we expect the provinces to support strongly the capacity of local institutions to deliver culturally appropriate Aboriginal services.

As shown in Table 5.5, provincial and territorial governments will contribute greatly to Aboriginal self-government in education. They will negotiate a policy framework with Aboriginal nations and multi-nation organizations, establish Aboriginal policy for provincial and territorial institutions, delegate authority and provide financial support for education services delivered by Aboriginal community of interest governments in urban centres and consult regularly with Aboriginal nations and multi-nation organizations.

In Volume 2, Chapter 3, we recommended the reorganization of federal government structures for the conduct of Aboriginal affairs. Even in advance of those changes, however, the federal government can act to support the implementation of self-government in Aboriginal education by accommodating initiatives by Aboriginal nations and their communities under current legislation; encouraging the development of education authorities consistent with the emergence of self-governing Aboriginal nations, confederacies and communities of interest; allocating resources to recognized Aboriginal nations during the transition to self-government for exercise of jurisdiction in education; and supporting the establishment of Canada-wide institutions serving the common goals of Aboriginal nations and communities of interest. These federal government roles, summarized in Table 5.5, will support and facilitate the work of Aboriginal governments and education authorities, extending and accelerating the move already in progress to transfer responsibility for education to Aboriginal control.

TABLE 5.5
Federal, Provincial and Territorial Roles in Aboriginal Education

Local Institutions	Provincial/Territorial Ministry	Federal Role In Aboriginal Education
• District school boards • Post-secondary institutions • Human resource training programs Roles include • accommodating students • delivering services under contract • establishing Aboriginal programs • designating Aboriginal schools, program units or delivery sites under Aboriginal management • consulting with Aboriginal community • engaging Aboriginal representatives in governance and decision making	• Negotiates policy framework with Aboriginal nations and multi-nation organizations • Establishes Aboriginal policy for implementation in provincial and territorial institutions • Delegates authority and provides financial support for service delivery by Aboriginal agencies and community of interest governments	• Accommodates self-starting initiatives of Aboriginal nations and their communities within current legislation • Encourages the development of education authorities consistent with the emergence of self-governing Aboriginal nations, confederacies and communities of interest • Allocates resources to recognized Aboriginal nations during the transition to self-government for exercise of jurisdiction in agreed-upon core areas • Supports the establishment of Canada-wide institutions serving the common goals of Aboriginal nations and communities of interest

Education is an area where considerable Aboriginal expertise, personnel and organizational infrastructure are already in place. Our recommendations build on these foundations and propose vigorous partnerships among Aboriginal, federal, provincial and territorial governments and shared effort among Aboriginal nations, governments and communities of interest to usher in a new era in Aboriginal education.

Notes

1. Northwest Territories, Department of Education, Culture and Employment, *Dene Kede – Education: A Dene Perspective* (Yellowknife: August 1993).

2. Alberta, *Report of the Royal Commission Appointed to Investigate the Conditions of the Half-Breed Population of Alberta* (Edmonton: Provincial Museum and Archives of Alberta, 1936), p. 7.

3. Tim Borlase, *Labrador Studies: The Labrador Inuit* (Happy Valley-Goose Bay, Labrador: Labrador East Integrated School Board, 1993), p. 203.

4. Bernard Gauthier, "Évaluation des interventions gouvernementales en matière d'éducation au Nouveau-Québec inuit", *Recherches amérindiennes au Québec* 19/1 (1989), p. 64.

5. Department of Indian Affairs and Northern Development [DIAND], *Basic Departmental Data – 1994* (Ottawa: Supply and Services 1995).

6. A political accord was signed by the Mi'kmaq Chiefs of Nova Scotia and the minister of Indian affairs on 4 November 1994, committing both parties to actions that will result in Mi'kmaq jurisdiction over education. A formal agreement will lead to legislation to create a Mi'kmaq education authority.

7. *Yukon First Nations Land Claims Settlement Act*, S.C. 1994, c. 34.

8. Mary Jane Norris, Don Kerr and François Nault, "Projections of the Aboriginal Identity Population in Canada, 1991-2016", research study prepared by Statistics Canada for the Royal Commission on Aboriginal Peoples [RCAP] (1995). For information about research studies prepared for RCAP, see *A Note about Sources* at the beginning of this volume. For a general discussion of the sources of data used by the Commission in this report, see Volume 1, Chapter 2, particularly the endnotes

9. DIAND, *Basic Departmental Data – 1994* (cited in note 5).

10. 23.9 per cent had less than grade 9, and 33.6 per cent had high school/no certificate, for a total of 57.5 per cent with less than high school graduation. The 43 per cent figure assumes that those undertaking post-secondary certificate programs have achieved the equivalent of high school graduation, although in fact many in the latter category participate in specialized vocational programs or studies to qualify for regular post-secondary programs.

11. The Commission consulted numerous national, provincial and community reports and studies addressing Aboriginal education concerns, contemporary as well as historical. We also commissioned a content analysis of concerns in 22 education studies contained in the Commission's review of previous commissions and task forces. (Roy Vermillion, "Chart of Previous Commissions and Task Forces Recommendations", research study prepared for RCAP (1994)). The 22 education studies can be found in the reviews undertaken by Carleton University for RCAP, *Public Policy and Aboriginal Peoples, 1965-1992*, Volume 2: *Summaries of Reports by Federal Bodies and Aboriginal Organizations*; Volume 3: *Summaries of Reports by Provincial and Territorial Bodies and Other Organizations* (Ottawa: Canada Communication Group, 1994). The studies are as follows:

Excellence in Education: Improving Aboriginal Education in New Brunswick (1992)
Closing the Gap: The Native Indian Students' Achievement Study (New Brunswick, 1991)

Literacy for Métis and Non-Status Indian Peoples: A National Strategy (1991)

You Took My Talk: Aboriginal Literacy and Empowerment. Fourth Report of the Standing Committee on Aboriginal Affairs (1990)

Report of the Provincial Advisory Committee on Post-Secondary Education for Native Learners (British Columbia, 1990)

A Review of the Post-Secondary Student Assistance Program of the Department of Indian Affairs and Northern Development (Standing Committee on Aboriginal Affairs, 1989)

Breaking Barriers: Report of the Task Force on Access for Black and Native People (Nova Scotia, 1989)

Tradition and Education: Towards a Vision of our Future (Assembly of First Nations, 1988)

Native Education in Alberta: Alberta Native Peoples' Views on Native Education) (1987)

Final Report: Working Group on Native Education, Training and Employment (Alberta, 1987)

Kwiya: Towards a New Partnership in Education (Yukon, 1987)

Speaking Out: Consultations and Survey of Yukon Native Languages: Planning, Visibility, Growth (1986)

Report of the Task Force on Aboriginal Languages (Northwest Territories, 1986)

Improved Program Delivery: Indians and Natives Study Team Report to the Task Force on Program Review (the Nielsen task force report, 1985)

Inner City Dropout Study (Saskatchewan, 1985)

Reaching Out: Report of the Indian and Métis Education Consultations (Saskatchewan, 1985)

Education Equity: A Report on Native Indian Education in Saskatchewan (1985)

Indian Education: Everyone's Concern (New Brunswick, 1984)

Learning: Tradition and Change (Northwest Territories, 1983)

Indian Control of Indian Education (1972)

Minutes of Proceedings and Evidence of the Standing Committee on the Annual Reports of the Department of Indian Affairs and Northern Development, 1967-68 and 1968-69 (1971)

Survey of the Contemporary Indians of Canada (the Hawthorn report, 1966)

12. Federation of Saskatchewan Indian Nations Education Commission, "Educational Principles", quoted by Vice Chief E. (Dutch) Lerat and Del C. Anaquod in *A Brief to the Strategic Planning Working Group of the Department of Saskatchewan Education, Training and Employment on the Future of Education, Training and Employment in Saskatchewan* (Federation of Saskatchewan Indian Nations, 1993).

13. We use the term 'elder' in two separate but inter-related senses in this chapter. First, elder refers to someone who is moving toward the end of the life cycle. In Canadian society the term 'senior' is frequently used. An elder has acquired a lifetime of experience that embodies not only the individual's own life story but also the social-political history of the nation. In general, Aboriginal societies treat the knowledge and experience of elders with great respect. We will also refer to elders in the sense of individuals trained in traditional knowledge and responsible for safeguarding and

transmitting traditional knowledge, ceremonies and beliefs from one generation to the next. In this sense, not every old person is an elder; not every elder is an old person. Elders are highly revered in Aboriginal societies. (See Volume 4, Chapter 3, for further discussion of the role of elders in various areas of community life.)

14. See Carnegie Task Force on Meeting the Needs of Young Children, *Starting Points: Meeting the Needs of Our Youngest Children* (New York: Carnegie Corporation of New York, 1994). The task force found that the influence of early environment on brain development is long-lasting and that stress during the first three years of life has a negative impact on brain function. "By ensuring a good start in life, we have more opportunity to promote learning and prevent damage than we ever imagined."

15. Clare Brant, a Mohawk psychiatrist, documented the practice of 'non-interference', a prominent characteristic of parenting and social interaction in many Aboriginal cultures. Non-interference entails not criticizing or attempting to control the behaviour of others by direct intervention. This applies not only in peer relations, but also in relations between parents and children. His work appears in Clare C. Brant, "Native Ethics and Rules of Behaviour", *Canadian Journal of Psychiatry* 35/6 (August 1990), p. 534.

16. David P. Weikart, *Quality Preschool Programs: A Long-Term Social Investment*, Occasional Paper No. 5 (New York: Ford Foundation, 1989).

17. Carnegie Task Force, *Starting Points* (cited in note 14). In 1990 the U.S. Congress passed the first legislation addressing early childhood issues in fifty years, and funding for Head Start programs had reached the highest level since their inception. See Alice S. Paul, *Early Childhood Education in American Indian and Alaska Native Communities* (Washington, D.C.: Department of Education, Indian Nations at Risk Task Force, 1991).

18. Ontario, *For the Love of Learning: Report of the Royal Commission on Learning, A Short Version* (Toronto: Queen's Printer for Ontario, 1994), p. 12.

19. Assembly of First Nations, *National Overview of First Nations Child Care* (Ottawa: Assembly of First Nations, 1989); Congress of Aboriginal Peoples (formerly Native Council of Canada), *Native Child Care: The Circle of Care* (Ottawa: Native Council of Canada, 1990); National Association of Friendship Centres, "Final Report to the Royal Commission on Aboriginal Peoples" (1993). For information about briefs submitted to RCAP, see *A Note About Sources* at the beginning of this volume.

20. For a discussion of the importance of Aboriginal language in establishing cultural patterns of perception and world view, see Volume 1, Chapter 15. See Volume 4, Chapter 3 for elders' perspectives on culture, language and values. For a discussion of the role of education programs in retaining and revitalizing Aboriginal languages, see Chapter 6 in this volume.

21. Researchers such as Ramirez, Yuen, Ramey and Pasta (1991) and Reyes (1992) emphasize the importance of fluency in a primary language, that is, a first language. See J. David Ramirez et al., "Final Report: Longitudinal Study of Immersion

Strategy, Early-Exit and Late-Exit Transitional Bilingual Educational Programs for Language-Minority Children, Volume 1", submitted to U.S. Department of Education (San Mateo, California: Aguire International, 1991); and Maria de la Luz Reyes, "Challenging Venerable Assumptions: Literacy Instruction for Linguistically Different Students", *Harvard Educational Review* 62/4 (1992), p. 427.

22. British Columbia, Royal Commission on Education, *A Legacy for Learners* (1988), is the basis for the provincial pre-school program in British Columbia. It is a child-centred, active learning approach that focuses on language development. Parents are encouraged to take an active part in their child's education.

23. There are provincial and territorial variations in this age, ranging from age five in British Columbia to age seven in Prince Edward Island, New Brunswick, Manitoba and Saskatchewan. For further information, see Austin J. Harte, *Improving School Attendance: Responsibility and Challenge* (Toronto: Canadian Education Association, 1994), pp. 17-18.

24. Brant, "Native Ethics and Rules of Behaviour" (cited in note 15).

25. Statistics Canada, custom tabulations, 1991. See Volume 2, Chapter 5, Table 5.20, which displays educational attainment of Aboriginal people no longer in school, by age group. In the 15-24 age group, 20.7 per cent of young people no longer in school had attained grade 8 or less, and 47.8 per cent had some high school education but no certificate. In the 25-49 age group the proportion with less than grade 8 remains almost constant, at 19.9 per cent, while the proportion with no certificate drops to 30.5 per cent. The proportion of the more mature group with high school certificates is comparable to the younger group (15.1 per cent of those 15-24 and 13.2 per cent of those 25-49), but fully 18.1 per cent of the 25-49 age group has a non-university certificate, indicating that re-entry to educational programs classified as post-secondary is an important avenue for raising attainment levels.

26. A standard clause in a DIAND education contribution agreement in British Columbia reads: "The Recipient shall ensure that registered Indian students ordinarily resident on reserve...have access to one or more of the following: instructional and support services in a band-operated or an independent/private school that provides provincially recognized programs of study and employs only teachers who are members in good standing with the British Columbia College of Teachers...".

27. Sheila Watt Cloutier, "Honoring Our Past, Creating Our Future: Education in Northern and Remote Communities", Discussion Paper No. 7 on Education, prepared for RCAP, National Round Table on Education (1993).

28. The Akwesasne science and maths project estimates that $200,000 a year for five years is required to undertake a similar process of curriculum development, covering three or four grade levels, with two curriculum writers. The Dene Kede project recommended a budget of approximately $130,000 a year for five years to develop the kind of framework their project created, with one curriculum writer and extensive travel and consultation. Thereafter, travel costs (50 per cent of the

budget) can be expected to decline and more costs can be assumed regionally and locally as implementation proceeds.

29. Pierre-Étienne Laporte, "Connaître la situation des langues autochtones du Québec: une préoccupation du CLF [Knowing the status of Aboriginal languages of Quebec: a concern of the CLF], *Bulletin du Conseil de la langue française* 9/3 (Fall 1992). See also Jacques Maurais, ed., *Les langues autochtones du Québec* (Quebec City: Publications du Québec, 1992).

30. RCAP staff communication with Lorna Williams, First Nations specialist, Vancouver School Board, September 1995.

31. Lynn Drapeau, "Issues in Language and Education for Native Populations in Quebec", research study prepared for RCAP (1995).

32. Information supplied by the department of education, culture and employment of the Northwest Territories, 30 March 1995.

33. Transcripts of the hearings of the Royal Commission on Aboriginal Peoples (hereafter, RCAP transcripts), Port Alberni, British Columbia, 20 May 1992.

34. Verna J. Kirkness and Sheena Selkirk Bowman, *First Nations and Schools: Triumphs and Struggles* (Toronto: Canadian Education Association, 1992), p. 47.

35. The Nunavut Implementation Training Study offers the following figures: People who do leave school do so later as demonstrated by a dramatic decline in the proportion of school leavers who leave at grade 8 level or less...For Nunavut as a whole, the decrease in the proportion of students leaving school at a grade 8 or lower level decreased from 43 per cent in 1986-87 to 2 per cent in 1990-91. In all regions and for Nunavut as a whole, there was a correspondingly large increase in the proportion for students leaving between grade 9 and grade 11...from 27 per cent to 63 per cent for Nunavut as a whole. (Nunavut Implementation Training Committee, "Nunavut Implementation Training Study: A Study on Training for Implementation of the Nunavut Land Claims Agreement", Volume 2: Main Report, prepared by Consilium (December 1994), p. 91.)

The Southwest Region of the Manitoba Metis Federation's "Report to the Royal Commission on Aboriginal Peoples" cited a 1988 study from the University of Manitoba in which 55 per cent of Métis respondents had only grade 9 or less education and a further 25 per cent had grade 10 or 11. In northern Quebec, 70 per cent of Cree and Inuit students drop out before completing high school. Bernard Lamothe and Louise Lemire, "Scolarité, développement et activité économique chez les Inuit du Québec arctique", *Recherches sociographiques* 35/3 (September-December 1994), p. 559.

DIAND's annual report, *Basic Departmental Data – 1994* (cited in note 5), "On-Reserve Students Remaining Until Grade 12 for Consecutive Years of Schooling", indicates an increase in students remaining until grade 12, from 53.6 per cent in 1991-92 to 77.7 per cent in 1993-94. We cannot confirm whether this dramatic increase in grade 12 enrolments has translated into grade 12 graduations.

Nor can we ascertain whether this sizeable change is also reflected in the schooling of other Aboriginal students, or whether perhaps there has been a change in the method of calculating statistics at DIAND.

36. Statistics Canada, "Educational Attainment and School Attendance: The Nation", 1991 Census, catalogue no. 93-328 (1993), Table 7.

37. Nunavik Educational Task Force, *Silatunirmut. The Pathway to Wisdom*, Final Report of the Nunavik Educational Task Force (Lachine, Quebec: Makivik, 1992), Recommendation 47.

38. Réginald Vollant and Bernard St-Onge, Nutshimiu-Atusseun training centre, RCAP transcripts, Sept-Isles, Quebec, 19 November 1992.

39. The significance of this approach for Aboriginal education is documented in a video entitled *The Mind of a Child: Working with children affected by poverty, racism and war*, National Film Board, 1995.

40. Alwyn Morris, untitled report (commissioned by Fitness and Amateur Sport Canada, 1992), p. 45.

41. See New Economy Development Group, *First Nations Children: Success Stories in Our Communities* (Ottawa: Children's Bureau, Health and Welfare, 1993).

42. The theoretical works of Paulo Freire in Brazil, Ira Shor and Henry Giroux in the United States, Roger I. Simon, and Rick Arnold et al. of the Toronto-based Doris Marshall Institute for Education and Action belong to the critical pedagogy and transformative education schools of thought. *Theater of the Oppressed*, founded by Brazilian Augusto Boal, is a particularly powerful tool for working with youth to explore issues that are of priority to them. Readers should consult Rick Arnold et al., *Educating for a Change* (Toronto: Between the Lines and the Doris Marshall Institute for Education and Action, 1991); Augusto Boal, *Theater of the Oppressed*, trans. Charles A. and Maria-Odilia Leah McBride (New York: Urizen Books, 1979); Paulo Freire, *Pedagogy of the Oppressed*, trans. Myra Bergman Ramos (New York: Seabury Press, 1974); Henry Giroux, *Border Crossings: Cultural Workers and the Politics of Education* (New York: Routledge, 1992); Ira Shor and Paulo Freire, *A Pedagogy for Liberation: Dialogues on Transforming Education* (Granby, Mass.: Bergin & Garvey Publishers, 1987); and Roger I. Simon, *Teaching Against the Grain: Texts for a Pedagogy of Possibility*, ed. Henry A. Giroux and Paulo Freire (Toronto: OISE Press, 1992).

43. Northwest Territories, Department of Education, Culture and Employment, "Preparing for Tomorrow: Departmental Directive on Community Senior Secondary Schooling" (Yellowknife 1994).

44. Statistics Canada, 1991 Aboriginal Peoples Survey, custom tabulations, 1994.

45. See United Nations, *Report of the Fourth World Conference on Women*, Beijing, China, 4-15 September 1995,) UN Doc. A/CONF. 177/20. The "Platform for Action" (Strategic Objective B.4) calls on governments and educational authorities to "Remove all barriers to access to formal education for pregnant adolescents

and young mothers, and support the provision of child care and other support services where necessary".

46. *For the Love of Learning* (cited in note 18), p. 1.

47. H.B. Hawthorn, ed., *A Survey of the Contemporary Indians of Canada: A Report on Economic, Political, Educational Needs and Policies*, 2 volumes (Ottawa: DIAND, 1966-1967).

48. "Population 15+ in the Experienced Labour Force Showing the Number in Teaching and Related Occupations, for the Aboriginal Identity and Non-Aboriginal Population, 1981 and 1991". These figures likely include an unknown number of individuals working with paraprofessional qualifications. See Don Kerr, Andy Siggner and Jean Pierre Bourdeau, "Canada's Aboriginal Population, 1981-1991", research study prepared for RCAP (1995).

49. In 1991 there were 612,415 non-Aboriginal people in teaching and related occupations serving 3,637,150 school children (age five to 14). At the same time, there were 8,075 Aboriginal people in teaching and related occupations and 148,135 Aboriginal school children (age five to 14). This means that there was one non-Aboriginal teacher for every six non-Aboriginal children, but only one Aboriginal teacher for every 18 Aboriginal children. To bring the ratio of Aboriginal teachers to Aboriginal children to the same level as that for non-Aboriginal people, about 24,000 more Aboriginal teachers would have to be working in the various education systems. See Kerr, Siggner and Bourdeau, "Canada's Aboriginal Identity Population, 1981-1991" (cited in note 48); and Statistics Canada, 1991 Census, "Mother Tongue: 20% Sample Data", catalogue no. 93-333.

50. Northwest Territories, *Teacher Training in the N.W.T.: Department of Education, Culture and Employment Programs* (Yellowknife: 1992).

51. Ontario Native Education Counselling Association (ONECA), "An Evaluation of the Long-Term Effectiveness of the Native Counsellor Program", brief submitted to RCAP (1993).

52. In 1994, the Royal Commission on Learning in Ontario (cited in note 18) put forward the following recommendation:
    That the province include in its requirements for pre-service and in-service teacher education a component related to teaching aboriginal students and teaching about aboriginal issues to both Native and non-Native students.

53. Gabriel Dumont Institute of Native Studies and Applied Research and Metis National Council, *Literacy for Metis and Non-Status Indian Peoples: A National Strategy* (Saskatoon: no date).

54. Staff communication with Annie Popert, former executive director, Kativik School Board, May 1994.

55. Lamothe and Lemire, "Scolarité, développement et activité économique" (cited in note 35).

56. In the year 2011, the 20 to 24 age group will represent the single largest five-year age cohort in the Aboriginal population, at a projected 98,900 persons; the 15- to 19-year-olds will be the second largest, at 90,300. In contrast, these two five-year cohorts are expected to be the seventh and eighth largest in the Canadian population as a whole.

57. *Budget Implementation Act, 1995*, S.C. 1995, c. 17.

58. This passage is quoted by Cecil King in "The State of Aboriginal Education in Southern Canada", research study prepared for RCAP (1993), quoting a paper by the Gabriel Dumont Institute, "A Post-Secondary Education for Metis People".

59. Lynne Davis, "Electronic Classrooms, Electronic Highways: A Review of Aboriginal Distance Education in Canada", research study prepared for RCAP (1994).

60. Eber Hampton and Steve Wolfson have built on Barnhardt's categories in their paper, "A Vision of First Nations Controlled University Education in Canada: The Saskatchewan Indian Federated College Model and Beyond", brief submitted to RCAP (July 1993).

61. Ethel Gardner, "First Nations House of Learning: A Continuity of Transformation", research study prepared for RCAP (1994).

62. The Saskatchewan Indian Federated College and the First Nations House of Learning, as well as academic departments of Aboriginal or Native studies, fulfil some but not all of the functions of a college.

63. Blair Stonechild, "Short Paper on Research Priorities in the Areas of Indian University and Urban Education, and Museum Training", paper prepared for RCAP (1992).

64. Giselle Marcotte, RCAP transcripts, Saskatoon, Saskatchewan, 28 October 1992; Christie Clifton, North Coast Tribal Council Education Centre, RCAP transcripts, Prince Rupert, British Columbia, 26 May 1993; and John Hart, Secwepemc Cultural Education Society, RCAP transcripts, Kamloops, British Columbia, 14 June 1993.

65. A good overview of the American tribal college system can be found in Schuyler Houser, "Underfunded Miracles: Tribal Colleges", United States Government, Indian Nations At Risk Task Force Commissioned Papers, 1991, ERIC document ED 343 772. Houser notes that while every college is locally controlled and reflects its own tribal character, the colleges have joined forces to form the American Indian Higher Education Consortium (AIHEC) to act in their common interest. By 1978, AIHEC had successfully lobbied Congress to pass the *Tribally Controlled Community Colleges Assistance Act*, which legislated funding assistance. Unfortunately, they have never been funded to the level permitted by the legislation.

66. Secretary of State for Youth and Training and Human Resources Canada, *Pathways Structural Review, Stage II: Strategic Directions, Options for Consideration* (Ottawa: 1995). This review confirms our findings that fragmentation of funding and lack

of co-ordination among training programs remain a weakness in present approaches to employment development services for Aboriginal people. The report cites the partnership between Pathways' Regional Aboriginal Management Board of Ontario and the provincial Jobs Ontario program as a promising example of trilateral approaches to human resources development.

67. Universalia, "Assessment of the Pathways to Success Strategy, Final Report to the National Aboriginal Management Board", draft #2, March 1994.

68. RCAP staff communication with Annie Popert, former executive director, Kativik School Board, May 1994.

69. South West Region of the Manitoba Metis Federation, "Report to the Royal Commission" (cited in note 35), p. 21.

70. Universities are generally reluctant to appoint elders to teaching positions because they do not have the formal qualifications normally required. Trent University in Peterborough, Ontario, has shown leadership in this area by appointing elders as regular tenured faculty members.

71. See Errol West, "Australian First Nations University: A discussion on the establishment of an Aboriginal university", *Australian Universities' Review* 2 (1994), pp. 52-54. Establishment of a national Aboriginal education institute was recommended in House of Commons, *Report of the Standing Committee on Aboriginal Affairs and Northern Development*, Sub-Committee on Aboriginal Education (Ottawa: Canada Communication Group, June 1996). The institute, as proposed, would fulfil many of the co-ordination and information functions that we envisage for the Aboriginal Peoples' International University, but it is not identified as an institution of higher learning.

72. The Canadian Radio-television and Telecommunications Commission (CRTC) has released a report, *Competition and Culture on Canada's Information Highways: Managing the Realities of Transition* (Ottawa: Public Works and Government Services, 1995), acknowledging the need for government involvement in decisions on infrastructure development in high-cost areas and the importance of the information highway in helping to deliver social and commercial services in remote areas. Further, the CRTC recognizes people's concern that there be public access to certain on-line services at minimal or no charge.

73. Council for Yukon Indians, *Umbrella Final Agreement Implementation Plan, Annex E: Arrangements for Training and the Training Policy Committee* (Ottawa: DIAND, 1993).

74. Nunavut Implementation Training Committee, *Nunavut Implementation Training Study: A Study on Training for Implementation of the Nunavut Land Claims Agreement, Final Report*, Volume 1: *Summary Report*, Volume 2: *Main Report* (September 1994). ATII Training Inc. estimates that 2,300 new jobs will be created by the establishment of Nunavut. See "Northern Education and Training Systems for Inuit: A Strategy Analysis", research study prepared for RCAP (1993).

75. DIAND, *Indian/Inuit Training Opportunities, 1993-1994* (Ottawa: Supply and Services, 1992), p. 129.

76. Northwest Territories, *Teacher Training in the N.W.T.* (cited in note 50), pp. 18-19.

77. The Institute of Indigenous Government (IIG), established by the Union of B.C. Indian Chiefs, opened its doors in Vancouver in September 1995, offering programs in political development and leadership; indigenous government administration; economic and social development; and international indigenous relations. The IIG was designated a provincial institute under the *College and Institute Act* in May 1995 and grants its own certificates and a two-year associate degree in indigenous government studies. Through a two-year arrangement with the Open Learning Agency (OLA), students can earn course credits that are recognized as open university credits and are transferrable to other post-secondary institutions with transfer credit arrangements with the OLA. Such reciprocal relationships – in which Aboriginal authority is recognized – are needed between Aboriginal and public post-secondary institutions.

78. CESO Aboriginal Services, "Lessons from the CESO Experience: Helping People to Help Themselves", brief submitted to RCAP (1993).

79. Statistics Canada, 1991 Aboriginal Peoples Survey.

80. DIAND, *Post-Secondary Student Assistance Program* (Ottawa: Supply and Services, 1989).

81. Human Resources Development Canada, Program Evaluation Branch, "Evaluation of the Co-operative Education Option: Final Report" (Ottawa: 1994).

82. See Ron Common and Lorraine Frost, *Teaching Wigwams: A Modern Vision of Native Education* (Muncey, Ontario: Anishinaabe Kendaaswin Publishing, 1994), pp. 35-36.

Appendix 5A

Native Education and Training Strategy May, 1991

Ministry of Colleges and Universities, Ontario*

I Introduction

The Ministry of Colleges and Universities (MCU) in 1988 identified the need to develop a strategy which would increase the number of Native students attending and graduating from Ontario's colleges and universities.

An MCU Native Advisory Committee was established to oversee the development of the strategy. It was comprised of staff from the Ministries of Colleges and Universities, Education, Skills Development and the Ontario Native Affairs Secretariat, one representative each from the college and university sectors and representatives from the following Native organizations:

- Chiefs of Ontario
- Association of Iroquois and Allied Indians
- Nishnawbe-Aski Nation
- Union of Ontario Indians
- Ontario Native Women's Association
- Ontario Federation of Indian Friendship Centres
- Ontario Métis and Aboriginal Association
- Grand Council Treaty #3[1]

The mandate of the committee was to make recommendations to the Minister of Colleges and Universities with respect to increasing Native participation and completion rates in Ontario's existing colleges and universities. The then Minister of Colleges and Universities agreed that the development, implementation and evaluation of the Strategy would be based on a partnership relationship between the ministry, colleges and universities and these Native organizations.

While the Native organizations acknowledged MCU's mandate to work within the existing postsecondary educational system, they stressed that the strategy process was only a short-term process that formed a small component of their efforts towards their long-term, educational agenda: Native control of Native education, including the establishment and funding of Native postsecondary institutions.

The Advisory Committee submitted its final report with recommendation to the Minister of Colleges and Universities in January, 1991. This report forms the

---

* Now called the Ontario Ministry of Education and Training.

foundation of the MCU Native Education and Training Strategy* which was approved by the Government.

II MCU Native Education and Training Strategy

Goals of Strategy

- To increase Native participation and completion rates in university and college programs;
- To increase the sensitivity and awareness of postsecondary institutions to Native culture and issues; and
- To increase the extent and participation of Native people in decisions affecting Native postsecondary education.

Key Elements of Strategy

In order to achieve the above goals, the Strategy includes the following key elements:

(a) enhancing the development and delivery of programs and services to Native students, including the following initiatives:
- increasing the level of specialized support services available to Native students;
- providing funding to Ontario colleges and universities to offset the higher costs of Native programming;
- encouraging the development of programs and curriculum that are relevant to Native people;
- facilitating flexible and innovative program delivery mechanisms to Native communities.

(b) reducing the barriers that restrict Native access to postsecondary institutions including activities with respect to admissions, access programs and Native teacher education programs;

(c) increasing Native community involvement in institutional governance, program development, and admissions criteria;

(d) establishing a Native Education Council to advise the Minister on Native postsecondary education issues;

(e) implementing and evaluating the Strategy in partnership with provincial Native organizations;

(f) providing these organizations with funding to cover costs associated with their involvement in the implementation of the Strategy.

---

* Now known as the Aboriginal Education and Training Strategy.

Specific Initiatives of the Strategy

1. Native Education Council

A Native Education Council (NEC) will be established by Order in Council to advise the Minister of Colleges and Universities on all aspects of Native post-secondary education, including those related to native programs, services and policies. The NEC would also work with MCU in the implementation and evaluation of the Strategy.

The Council will consist of one member from each of the following Native organizations, one of whom will be the Chair:

- Association of Iroquois and Allied Indians
- Nishnawbe-Aski Nation
- Union of Ontario Indians
- Ontario Native Women's Association
- Ontario Federation of Indian Friendship Centres
- Ontario Metis and Aboriginal Association
- [Grand Council Treaty #3][2]

The appointments will be made by Order in Council.

A secretariat will be established to provide the administrative support for the Council. It will have two full-time positions, a secretary and a coordinator. The coordinator of the secretariat will report to the Chair of the Native Education Council.

2. Proposal Selection Committee

A Proposal Selection Committee will be established to undertake responsibility for the review and selection of proposals to be funded under the MCU Strategy.

The composition of the committee will be as follows:

Membership:
Non-voting:

1 Ministry of Colleges and Universities
1 Council of Regents
1 Ontario Council on University Affairs

Voting:

6 Institutional representatives with Native educational expertise (3 college representatives nominated by the Council of Presidents and 3 university representatives nominated by the Council of Universities).

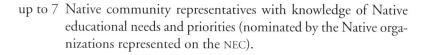

up to 7 Native community representatives with knowledge of Native educational needs and priorities (nominated by the Native organizations represented on the NEC).

3. Native Community Involvement with Postsecondary Institutions

Eligibility to receive funding under the Strategy will be dependent upon a college or university agreeing to:

(a) Ensure that a process exists which would provide local Native community[3] representatives with direct access to the governing body/senate on all aspects effecting Native postsecondary education within the institution;

(b) establish a Native committee with significant local Native community membership to oversee key Native programs and services. The committee will also assist in the determination of appropriate mature student admissions criteria for Native students and be involved in reviewing the admissions protocol affecting Native applicants;

(c) develop, in collaboration with the institutional Native committee, a comprehensive plan of action, including an evaluation process, designed to enhance the institution's sensitivity to Native issues and to increase the accessibility and retention rates of Native students within the institution. This plan should be approved by the institution's governing body/senate.

Colleges and universities which have demonstrated a previous commitment to addressing the educational and training needs of Native people through the provision of quality Native programs and services, will be given preference in terms of Strategy funding.

4. Native Program and Service Initiatives

Programs and services for Native students in colleges and universities will be improved through the provision of funding of the following initiatives:

- increasing the number of Native counsellors employed by postsecondary institutions, through a Native Support Services Core Fund;
- improving the range and quality of specialized support services provided to Native students, through a Special Projects - Native Support Services Enhancement Fund;
- supporting the development of Native curricula and encouraging innovative and flexible delivery of Native programs through a Special Projects - Program Development Fund;
- Offsetting the special costs associated with developing and delivering Native programs through a Supplementary Grant Fund.[4]

5. Access of Native Students to Post-secondary Institutions

To increase the access of Native students to postsecondary institutions:

- postsecondary institutions are encouraged to adopt guidelines for mature student admissions, which takes into consideration the prior learning experience of the candidate.
- professional schools or faculties are encouraged to implement enrolment equity policies. This should be undertaken with the advice and assistance of the institution's Native committee and/or the local Native community;
- postsecondary institutions are encouraged to establish general and/or program-specific Native access programs to improve access to postsecondary education;
- Native student recruitment for general, professional or specialized access programs should be carried out in close consultation with the institution's Native Committee;
- postsecondary institutions are encouraged to deliver culturally appropriate, distance education to Native communities through a combination of telecommunications technology and on-site academic support;
- all applications submitted to the Northern Distance Education Fund (NDEF) which concern Native-specific programs will be reviewed for recommendations on funding by the Proposal Selection Committee.

6. Native Teacher Education Programs

To improve the accessibility, appropriateness, and effectiveness of teacher education programs for Native people:

- Strategy funding will be made available under the Special Projects Fund and the Supplementary Grant Fund to Native teacher education programs which satisfy the following criteria:
  - (i) include as a central component, instruction in a Native-specific curriculum and pedagogy based upon learning modes derived from the Native cultural and linguistic heritage;
  - (ii) ensure that Native-specific curricular components and pedagogy are available as elective credit courses to all teacher education students;
  - (iii) ensure the use of indigenous resources and the recognition of regional differences;
  - (iv) ensure that all Native teacher education programs are qualitatively equal to mainstream teacher education programs;
  - (v) ensure greater curricular emphasis on NSL and NFL instruction;

- postsecondary institutions are encouraged to consider community-based education models in developing Native teacher education programs;
- postsecondary institutions are encouraged to give priority to the recruitment of Native professors to regular tenure-stream positions by recognizing Native-language ability and indigenous knowledge.

7. Education Issues - Ministry of Education

The Ministry of Education has the primary responsibility for teacher certification, teacher education programs, and policies and curricula for elementary and secondary schools. The Minister of colleges and Universities will request the Minister of Education to address teacher eduction issues which fall within MOE's responsibilities, in a manner consistent with the recommendations of the Native Advisory Committee's teacher education paper. (Refer to Appendix 1.)

8. Funding to Native Organizations

In order to achieve the objectives of the Strategy, ongoing funding will be provided to Native Organizations to ensure that they have the capacity to participate in a meaningful way in the implementation of the Strategy. Implementation costs will include such items as salaries for additional staff to be hired by the Native organizations, travel and administrative costs. The Native Education Council will be responsible for determining the distribution of these funds amongst the Native organizations.

9. Evaluation

In year four, an evaluation of the MCU Strategy will be undertaken in partnership with the Native Education Council. This will include developing the terms of reference, implementing the evaluation and preparing a report of findings and conclusions. Funding in the amount of approximately $130,000 will be allocated to cover the costs of an evaluation of the Strategy.

The Ministry will work with the NEC and the postsecondary institutions to develop a data base for self-identified Native students.

The Ministry of Colleges and Universities will report to the Cabinet Committee on Justice each year on the progress in implementing the Strategy.

10. Funding

In 1991/92, an amount of $3.1 million has been allocated to support the implementation of the strategy.

May 23, 1991

Appendix 1
Mcu Native Advisory Committee Report

Teacher Education Recommendations which Fall within MOE's Jurisdiction

1. The education and credentialling of Native People to work in all educational fields be designated a priority.
2. The curricular content of teacher education programs be reviewed to ensure that they recognize and affirm Native culture and history.
3. Priority be given to establishing Native-language immersion programs and programs to enable the achievement of bilingual fluency.
4. Alternative and flexible credentialling criteria such as utilizing prior learning assessment be established for Native people with respect to the Ontario Teacher's Certificate to recognize the expertise acquired through indigenous, non-formal education.
5. Recognition of a career path in Native education should be widely available through basic and additional qualifications.

Notes

1. As of October 1989, this organization withdrew from the Advisory Committee.

2. Grand Council Treaty #3 has a standing invitation from the MCU to be involved in this process.

3. The term local Native community, as used in this paper, refers to the local representatives of First Nation political bodies, friendship centres, Ontario Métis and Aboriginal Association, Ontario Native Women's Association and Native service organizations.

4. The Supplementary Grant Fund would provide colleges and universities with an additional .25 of a funding unit for each full-time student enroled in a designated Native program. This funding would be supplementary to the regular operating grants and it would be targeted funding which could only be used in relation to the designated program.

6

ARTS AND HERITAGE

Our focus thus far in Volume 3 has been measures to correct disparities between the quality of life of Aboriginal people and that enjoyed by other Canadians. In this chapter we discuss policy to affirm and support the cultural identity and expression of Aboriginal peoples. We begin by recalling the framework for considering cultural issues established in Volume 1 and the effects of past assimilation policies on self-expression and intercultural relations. We then present the rationale for action to support cultural expression before turning to the specific areas in which such action is required.

In Volume 1, Chapter 15, we described traditional Aboriginal culture as a way of life shaped by intimate relationships with the land, reinforced by a world view attributing life and spirit to all elements of the biosphere, and expressed in ethically ordered behaviours in social, economic and political spheres. We also described how contemporary Aboriginal people reach into their traditions for wisdom and strength to cope with the diverse responsibilities of a modern environment.

Culture, in this view, is dynamic, grounded in ethics and values that provide a practical guide and a moral compass enabling people to adapt to changing circumstances. The traditional wisdom at the core of this culture may transcend time and circumstance, but the way it is applied differs from one situation to another. It is the role of the family – that is, the extended network of kin and community – to demonstrate how traditional teachings are applied in everyday life.

In Volume 1 we discussed in some detail the interventions of the Canadian state that interrupted the transmission of culture in Aboriginal nations: the imposition of the *Indian Act*, residential school policies, and relocation of communities. The harshly assimilative policies of the past have been abandoned, but school curricula, to which virtually all Aboriginal young people are exposed, have only begun to reflect facets of Aboriginal life. Radio and television now reach into the remotest Aboriginal communities and pull Aboriginal young people toward a world view in which urban, non-Aboriginal ways are held up as models.

In our special report on suicide, we cited culture stress as a major factor in the vulnerability of Aboriginal young people to self-destructive behaviour. We linked this phenomenon to the cumulative impact of assimilative policies of the past and the failure of public institutions to reflect to Aboriginal people positive images of themselves and their cultures:

> In cultures under stress, the smooth operation of society and the sense life makes to its members can be seriously impaired. Culturally transmitted norms that once provided meaning and guided individual behaviour become ineffectual as rules for living or sustaining relationships, and the rules themselves fall into disrepute. People lose confidence in what they know and in their own value as human beings. They may feel abandoned and bewildered and unsure about whether their lives have any real meaning or purpose.[1]

As the history of Aboriginal experience over the last century demonstrates, living in a culture under stress does not lead people to abandon their identity and warmly embrace the culture of the dominant society, which is seen as the source of distress. In fact, young people in particular are likely to be caught between worlds, detached from the values of their culture of origin but not integrated into the alternative system. The confusion of these alienated young people adds to the dysfunction of their communities.

We have argued for the adoption of mutual recognition as a basic principle in a renewed relationship between Aboriginal and non-Aboriginal peoples in Canada, considering not only the negative results of culture stress but also the positive value of a firm cultural base to support participation in a liberal democratic society. The protection and enhancement of civic participation and individual freedom and responsibility have always been central concerns of liberal democracies. However, it has not always been recognized that these goals can be achieved only when people are members of viable cultures that provide a supportive context for individual participation and autonomy. People can be active and responsible members of their communities only if they have a sense of their own worth and the conviction that what they say and do in both the public and the private sphere is capable of making a significant contribution.

The legacy of our colonial history bears heavily upon Aboriginal people in the form of culture stress. It also distorts the perceptions of non-Aboriginal people, sustaining false assumptions and a readiness to relegate Aboriginal people to the margins of Canadian society. To free ourselves of this legacy we need effective means of communication within and between Aboriginal nations to allow Aboriginal people to reclaim their history and tell it in diverse forums, especially for the benefit of the youth, who are forging their adult identities. Equally important, we need channels of communication between cultures, so that Aboriginal people can communicate in authentic ways who they are and how their cultural traditions continue to be significant for themselves and for society as a whole.

Myths and misconceptions about Aboriginal identity and culture have found a home in the popular imagination. They will be dislodged only through dialogue with skilful and authentic Aboriginal communicators. The issues discussed in this chapter are therefore fundamental to achieving the mutual respect and sharing proposed as the basis for a new relationship. Knowledge of one another and shared wisdom are essential to a true partnership of peoples.

Elsewhere in this report we have recommended ways to enhance communication within Aboriginal nations and between nations and cultures. In Volume 1, Chapter 7, we recommended publication of a multi-volume history of Aboriginal peoples in Canada. In Volume 2, Chapter 3, we set out a process of communication and nation building to knit together old ties and solidify new ones, to adapt traditional practices of leadership and governance to today's requirements of self-government. In the chapters on treaties and lands and resources in Volume 2, we spoke of the need to educate Canadians about the role of treaties in the formation of Canada and the fundamental relationship that Aboriginal peoples maintain with the land. In Chapter 5 of this volume, we describe practical ways in which a cultural base can enrich and enhance education. In Volume 5, Chapter 4, we propose a detailed program of public education to add depth and commitment to a renewed relationship between Aboriginal and non-Aboriginal people.

In the present chapter, we give particular attention to the cultural institutions and programs necessary to

- identify and protect historical and sacred sites and to safeguard Aboriginal heritage from misappropriation and misrepresentation;
- conserve and revitalize Aboriginal languages;
- enhance the presence of Aboriginal people and cultures in the media; and
- support the literary and artistic expression of Aboriginal people.

1. Cultural Heritage

The cultures of Aboriginal peoples are intimately linked to the land, not just to land in a generic sense but also to the particular places given to them, according to tradition, for sustenance and safekeeping. On these lands they have made their home since time immemorial, and there the bones of their ancestors are at rest. The events of history are marked by particular features of the landscape.

Traditions of wisdom and spirituality are represented in objects dedicated to ceremonial use, which have taken on sacred significance. Territories, family lineages and entitlements are recorded in stories and songs and represented in masks and crests.

As they gradually lost control of their lands and other elements of their environment, Aboriginal people became separated from many of these symbols of history and culture. Protection of historical and sacred sites, recovery of human remains so that proper burial can be arranged, repatriation of artifacts that are the private property or sacred inheritance of particular families and communities – these are essential to the spiritual health of nations and communities. Concerns about appropriation of cultural property and uses that violate the rules of propriety in the culture in which the property originates extend beyond material objects and include intellectual property as well.

1.1 Sacred and Historical Sites

> The land was considered a mother, the giver of life. On the land were many sacred places and sites where religious ceremonies both collective and individual were visited and used. These include the mountains, rivers, hills, rocks, and lakes. The land, in addition to the plant and animal life it supported, provided sites for vision quests, burials, and places to plant special types of plants that were very important in the religious life of the Blackfoot, such as tobacco. It also provided material such as ochre used in painting and religious ceremonies, and sacred rocks used to mark sacred places such as medicine wheel and burial sites.[2]

This description of a particular people's relationship to the land applies to many Aboriginal cultures in Canada. To Aboriginal people, identity is deeply entwined with territory, the territory that has fostered their culture and ways of life.[3] A more detailed exploration of Aboriginal peoples' relationship to the land and concepts of land ownership can be found in Volume 2, Chapter 4 on lands and resources and in Volume 4, Chapter 3 on elders' perspectives. Because of this deep relationship with the land, the control of sacred sites, burial grounds and archaeological sites is important to Aboriginal people.

Territory itself is important to Aboriginal nations, but certain areas hold special significance. Ancestral burial grounds or sites for spiritual ceremonies are considered sacred land. Other areas are significant for their role in the history of peoples – for example, The Forks in Winnipeg and Batoche on the North Saskatchewan River, which are important in Métis history. Other sites are reminders of battles marking boundaries between nations and of treaties concluded to maintain peace. In the north, inuksuit, the great stone markers erected by Inuit to guide hunters across the treeless landscape, are monuments to Inuit life in their ancient homelands.

It is not uncommon for sites to hold both historical and sacred significance. This is true of the weirs at the Atherley Narrows, near Orillia, a community in central Ontario. Weirs were a network of fences that 'herded' fish to an open area where they were netted or speared. Carbon dating shows that the weirs are about 4,500 years old, which means construction began in 2500 BC. They were part of a traditional fishing camp where the Ojibwa, Mississauga and other nations would meet to socialize and conduct healing ceremonies. The area, unique in North America and possibly the world, is of considerable historical interest to the Ojibwa in the area and to archaeologists. But there are other considerations:

> More important to the site is the spirit that moved the site. The power that was in Mnjikaning [traditional name for the Ontario community of Rama] that moved the ceremonies, that made it such a clean place, such a harmonious place. It is that spirit we cannot lose....If we could ever get hold of the place, if we could ever reclaim it the power that would come from that place, the healing that would come from that place would be astounding.
>
> Rob Belfry
> Ogemawahj Tribal Council
> Orillia, Ontario, 14 May 1993[*]

Mr. Belfry's remarks convey a tone of urgency because, at the time he was speaking, the weirs were in danger of destruction. Dredging carried out years ago created currents that were causing the site to collapse. As of October 1995, negotiations to protect the site were continuing.[4]

Historical boards have limited authority to protect heritage sites from development and, in some cases, may not understand the importance of a site to an Aboriginal community. Aboriginal groups, unfortunately, often have little influence in deciding priorities. This situation exemplifies the problems Aboriginal people often experience in trying to practise their traditional spirituality today. All too often, Aboriginal people's desire or need for access to traditional sites for traditional activities has led to conflict with officials:

> All along the foothills, ceremonial leaders are spiritually guided to conduct ceremonies at specific sites, some of which are off-reserve, located on provincial or federal Crown lands. Our elders are being denied full access by the discretion of park superintendents, with the excuse that fires are not permitted. The national parks make us pay,

---

[*] Transcripts of the Commission's hearings are cited with the speaker's name and affiliation, if any, and the location and date of the hearing. See *A Note About Sources* at the beginning of this volume for information about transcripts and other Commission publications.

like common tourists, where at one time we were able to travel freely in the parks.

Alvin Manitopyes
Representative, Plains Cree people and Environmental Committee
Assembly of First Nations
Calgary, Alberta, 26 May 1993

The Commission also heard of Aboriginal people encountering problems when they tried to enter sites to pick berries or gather traditional medicines. In many cases, these people had first visited the sites with their parents, grandparents or great-grandparents.

A final threat to the integrity of sacred and historical sites comes not from development or legislation but rather from archaeological endeavours. The search for historically and culturally significant objects often leads archaeologists to burial grounds. Aboriginal people have asked that these objects be left in the ground and that graves not be disturbed out of respect for the dead and in recognition that the burial grounds remain the collective property of Aboriginal people. Concern about respect for Aboriginal interests in collective property is not limited to burial grounds. Aboriginal people have become involved only recently in the management of petroglyph (rock carving) sites and the interpretation of their significance. Aboriginal people believe it is important to document history, and in many cases they are willing to work with mainstream professionals to do so. However, control over excavation is within provincial and territorial jurisdiction. In some jurisdictions, Aboriginal groups are consulted as a matter of courtesy before excavation permits are issued, and in Nunavut any excavation permits will require Inuit approval. Generally, however, no consistent policies or laws are in place to ensure that Aboriginal people control this central element of their heritage.

In Volume 2, Chapter 4, we recommended that sites of sacred or historical significance should be considered in the reallocation of lands. For lands under the primary control of Aboriginal nations, those nations will make decisions about protection and use. For lands under the joint jurisdiction of the Crown and Aboriginal nations, protection and access can form part of co-management agreements. Where sacred or heritage sites are part of lands under primary jurisdiction of the Crown or subject to fee simple interests or ownership rights, then Aboriginal access and involvement in management will be negotiated.

There are a few concerns not addressed in these recommendations for future jurisdiction over lands. The first is a question of what can be done now. The new agreements will take time to conclude, but some initiatives can begin immediately. Indeed, given encroaching development and natural processes such as erosion that can threaten significant sites, initiatives cannot wait until agreements are concluded.

A necessary first step is for Aboriginal people and communities to identify and assess the condition of sites that are historically and culturally important to them. The legislation on historic sites must be reviewed to ensure recognition and protection of Aboriginal interests, and interim measures must be taken to protect significant sites that are endangered.

Some sacred and historical sites will be resources for all Canadians. When Aboriginal history and heritage are being represented in areas outside Aboriginal jurisdiction, Aboriginal people must be involved in designating the sites, designing interpretive materials, and managing the resource. It is also only fair that Aboriginal people share in the economic benefits deriving from historical sites.

There are examples of effective collaboration on these matters between Aboriginal people and public authorities. The Wanuskewin Heritage Park, which opened near Saskatoon, Saskatchewan, in 1992, is a good example. The project was in development for 10 years. Representatives from all five Aboriginal language groups drawn from across Saskatchewan took part in the planning. Aboriginal cultural values were respected throughout the project, and Aboriginal participants were full partners in a consensual decision-making process. The interpretive stories told at Wanuskewin are those that First Nations want told, and they are relayed by First Nations people themselves. The Commission points to this park as an example of appropriate Aboriginal involvement in a heritage project.

Finally, consideration must be given to heritage and sacred sites for Aboriginal people living in urban areas. We address this unique situation in Volume 4, Chapter 7. Land, together with the ritual, ceremony and traditions associated with it, is particularly important to the renewal and retention of Aboriginal identity. Support may therefore mean setting aside a parcel of land in urban areas as a sacred place for Aboriginal populations in cities.

1.2 Sacred and Secular Artifacts

Aboriginal people are seeking the return of artifacts held by museums and collectors as one way of reasserting control over how their cultures are depicted. These objects are the physical records of history and the physical manifestations of culture. They help define Aboriginal identity:

> Traditionally, Aboriginal cultural knowledge is transmitted and documented primarily through the oral tradition, but also through such things as dramatic productions, dance performances, and they are documented on such artifacts as wampum belts, birch bark scrolls, totem poles, petroglyphs and masks. This is the Aboriginal way of transmitting knowledge and of recording information and history.

> Greg Young-Ing
> Vancouver, British Columbia, 4 June 1993

Items taken from Aboriginal people and communities over the years may be secular or sacred. Secular objects might include tools, hunting equipment and clothing – articles of everyday use. Some objects have sacred significance, such as medicine bundles, which contain objects associated with visions and are opened only on ceremonial occasions. In the case of sacred objects, the only appropriate action is repatriation to the nation to which they belong. The same is true of human remains, which hold both secular and sacred importance. Other objects integral to the history and identity of certain nations, communities or families should also be repatriated.

In many cases, Aboriginal people consider the term 'artifact', with its connotations of dusty relics tagged and catalogued, inappropriate. Sacred objects such as medicine bundles and totems still speak to the people; they are still used in traditional ceremonies.

In 1979, two large collections of potlatch regalia were returned to the communities of Alert Bay and Cape Mudge in British Columbia. They were housed in museums built specifically to receive them and financed by the federal government. Repatriation can be a deeply spiritual and powerful experience, as indicated in the Peigan Nation response to repatriation of their cultural materials:

> When the Glenbow Museum allowed the return of these holy bundles and articles, I do not believe they realized their contribution to the total existence of Native people....We do not use the holy bundles; they use us. Our only responsibility is to show them reverence. We continually ask for their mercy and guidance. And because they are as alive as you and I...I now live with more confidence in the holistic development of my people.[5]

Some of the objects currently stored in museums were obtained through purchase; some were stolen. Legislation also played a role: laws were enacted to suppress religious practices, such as the potlatch ceremony of west coast nations, and items with spiritual import were often confiscated. Currently, in most provinces, ownership of archaeological material on both private and public land is asserted by the Crown.

The concerns of Aboriginal people centre on two issues: the illegitimate acquisition of these artifacts (even when obtained through legal means), and the inappropriate display and use of cultural items.

In 1988, the Lubicon Lake Cree organized a boycott of The Spirit Sings, the cultural showcase of the Winter Olympics in Calgary. Museums were asked not to lend objects for the display, and many people, Aboriginal and non-Aboriginal, refused to attend. The boycott did a great deal to raise awareness of the issues, and as a result of the conflict, the Assembly of First Nations (AFN) and the Canadian Museums Association (CMA) formed a task force with a mandate to "develop an ethical framework and strategies for Aboriginal Nations to represent their history and culture in concert with cultural institutions".[6] The task force report sets out guiding principles, policies and recommendations on repatriation and calls for the creation of new relationships to serve the needs of Aboriginal people and the interests of Canadian cultural and heritage institutions. (See Appendix 6A to this chapter for excerpts from the report.)

Although some change is under way, much remains to be done. Collections of Aboriginal artifacts, collection notes, and sound and photographic archives in museums are often not fully inventoried. Aboriginal people cannot easily gain access to these materials or, in some cases, even get information about them. As with sacred and historical sites, establishing inventories is an essential first step in developing repatriation policies and collaborating with Aboriginal peoples in the conservation, display and eventual return of heritage materials.

Of course, Canadian museums do not have a monopoly on Aboriginal artifacts. Some of the oldest collections are concentrated in museums and private collections elsewhere, particularly in Europe. Some Aboriginal groups have made informal inventories of European holdings or are aware of specific objects they wish to have returned. This might be one area where Aboriginal people and Canadian museums can work together to locate such items and request their return.

The *Cultural Property Export and Import Act* has been of some assistance in repatriating items.[7] Under the provisions of the act, however, an Aboriginal group seeking the return of an object or prevention of its export must first have the support of an established cultural institution. The Canadian Cultural Property Export Review Board may help qualified institutions to purchase artifacts by granting or lending up to two-thirds of the cost. A number of Aboriginal-controlled institutions, such as the Woodland Cultural Centre in Brantford, Ontario, are eligible to participate in this program. The grounds for determining whether a particular cultural item should be repatriated, however, are relatively narrow and do not always address the needs of First Peoples.

The repatriation of cultural objects has also been restrained by the limited capacity of Aboriginal cultural institutions to receive and house them. There are currently 72 cultural education centres in or close to reserves and Inuit communities across Canada. A few have museums, but most do not.

As of October 1995, there are two federal programs that support Aboriginal museums. The department of Indian affairs provides some support through the Cultural Education Centres Program. Support is also available through the Aboriginal Museums Assistance Program, part of Heritage Canada's general museum assistance program. Most applicants are band councils, although cultural education centres and friendship centres are eligible. Some provincial and territorial programs may also be a source of support for Aboriginal cultural institutions, but funding is usually quite limited and available only on a project-by-project basis.

The capacity of Aboriginal nations and communities to receive, conserve and display repatriated items and participate in the joint management of museums must be developed. This will require physical facilities, whether for displays in cultural education centres or for temporary or travelling exhibits.

For Aboriginal people living in cities, friendship centres may be the best place to locate heritage displays and activities. There are 113 Aboriginal friendship centres operating in urban centres, delivering a wide variety of services to help Aboriginal people adjust to the urban environment and to improve their quality of life in general.[8] Although the centres provide a number of cultural programs, there is limited interest in establishing museums at present. This is mainly because of a chronic lack of resources, but also because of the difficulty of doing justice to the many different Aboriginal cultures that coexist in urban settings. Our recommendation for a new urban Aboriginal cultural education program addresses this issue (see Volume 4, Chapter 7).

Even where Aboriginal museums do exist, they often operate on different assumptions from those of mainstream institutions. The difference relates to the perceived role of a museum in preserving heritage:

> We [Secwepemc Cultural Education Society] have been told that our curriculum development, language and publishing program are not museum functions and cannot be reflected in our budget for funding purposes. These discrepancies between our native concept of heritage and the established form will continue to cause concern as Indian and Inuit museums are set up.[9]

This philosophical difference extends to the use of traditional objects. Because of a different perception of why objects are important to culture, culturally significant materials stored in a museum may actually be used by community members.[10] Wampum belts held as cultural artifacts by a mainstream museum may be used in the Aboriginal community to validate claims or recall details of agreements. To Aboriginal people, labelled artifacts are often 'living' items relevant to the contemporary life of the individual, community and nation. There needs to be a reconciliation between museum policies and the traditional use of artifacts by Aboriginal communities.

Aboriginal people are not calling for museums to divest themselves of all Aboriginal artifacts. In the AFN/CMA report, *Turning the Page*, there was general recognition that collections and the museums that care for them can contribute to public education and awareness of the contributions of Aboriginal people.[11] In particular, items that have no sacred value, such as tools, can be kept and displayed with community consent. As well, objects that cannot be traced back to a specific family, community or nation of origin can remain in a museum's collection. Where repatriation is called for, however, museums must respect the wishes of the Aboriginal community.

The programs that may support repatriation are limited by a number of factors. Even where there is program funding for cultural education centres, capital funding to establish physical facilities is generally unavailable. In many communities, few cultural materials remain; the very word 'museum' is often a reminder of what has been lost to Aboriginal people, not what has been preserved for their use.[12] Above all, Aboriginal people have so many urgent day-to-day needs that establishing a community-controlled museum, although important and desirable, is often not the top priority.

This makes it all the more important that Aboriginal people have access to mainstream museums and the items they hold. Aboriginal people must be involved in cataloguing museum holdings and consulted on appropriate modes of display and interpretation. This provides an opportunity for non-Aboriginal professionals to gain more insight into Aboriginal culture. Further, these collections must be accessible to Aboriginal people. Here we do not simply mean an open-door policy on the part of museums, inviting Aboriginal people to visit the displays. Rather, any facility that benefits from the display of Aboriginal culture should put something back into the Aboriginal community. This could mean bringing all or part of the exhibit directly to Aboriginal communities. Such initiatives could be coupled with workshops and information sessions on museum skills and careers.

Ultimately, many objects will be returned to Aboriginal people and communities. Cultural institutions controlled by Aboriginal people allow communities to develop trained professionals to staff the institutions, enhance local economic development and, perhaps most important, give Aboriginal people control over their own culture and heritage.

The initial steps in this movement will involve capacity building within the Aboriginal community, including urban dwellers. This provides an opportunity for mutually beneficial co-operative arrangements between heritage institutions and Aboriginal communities. Many larger Canadian museums offer training and internship programs, and some universities and other educational institutions offer academic courses in subjects related to the management of cultural materials. These courses should be made more accessible to Aboriginal people through sponsorship programs provided by the museums.

Training programs can be developed co-operatively between museums and other cultural institutions and Aboriginal communities. Aboriginal people can assist in cataloguing, interpreting and displaying materials and participate in other museum activities. While Aboriginal trainees learn about museum technology, museum staff will be able to learn more about Aboriginal people and culture. These kinds of training ventures should be flexible; details can be worked out between the museums and communities directly. Such co-operative ventures can extend to mounting exhibits, displays and other cultural events, for example, 'living culture' such as traditional games, dances and ceremonies. Financial assistance, where needed, should be made available through federal, provincial and territorial employment and training and heritage programs.

Generally, museum training programs that reflect the needs and world views of Aboriginal peoples should be established in co-operation with museums and universities. A survey of existing programs could be undertaken by the Canadian Museums Association in consultation with Aboriginal groups, and the information could then be used to help ensure that future programs are developed and co-ordinated in a culturally appropriate manner.

In other chapters of our report, we have set out strategies for human resources development, emphasizing needs assessment, comprehensive strategy development, setting targets, and monitoring progress. In heritage conservation, as in other areas, capacity building must be part of long-range planning if Aboriginal nations wish to maintain their cultural heritage (see Volume 2, Chapters 3 and 5, and Chapters 3 and 5 in this volume).

In many Aboriginal societies there are no strict criteria for determining which objects are sacred and which are secular. An ornate carving may have been made as a gift or just to pass the time. By the same token, an ordinary stone may have been blessed in the past for use in special ceremonies. In any debate over the sacred or secular nature of a given object, Aboriginal representatives from the community of origin must be involved in making the distinction.

It is for this reason that the indiscriminate replication of Aboriginal artifacts can, in some cases, offend cultural propriety. In other cases, it violates the accuracy of reproduction or interpretation. In most cases, it ignores the legitimate interest of Aboriginal people in sharing the economic benefits from the sale of reproductions of historical items. Protective measures are needed to guard against this kind of misrepresentation. This issue borders on the subject of intellectual property rights, discussed in the next section.

1.3 Intellectual Property

Intellectual property rights should allow Aboriginal people to control representations of culture and knowledge that belong to individuals or collectives. There has been controversy recently about copyright on oral traditions, legends and songs collected for publication. The search for herbal remedies known to Aboriginal healers continues, and traditional designs are being incorporated in high fashion products. All of these activities raise questions about the appropriate means of protecting Aboriginal intellectual property.

In asserting claims to their traditional knowledge, Aboriginal people are not trying to retreat from the world or make their culture inaccessible to others. In fact, the opposite is true. Aboriginal people are willing to share the wealth of their cultures and are anxious to have their knowledge of the land and environment used for the benefit of all. At the same time, they want to ensure that their knowledge is used appropriately and their identity portrayed authentically. They also want fair remuneration when their intellectual and cultural property is turned to appropriate commercial use. In other words, Aboriginal people want to protect their intellectual property rights. In the words of D. Soyini Madison, "How we are represented by others shapes how we represent ourselves, what is real to us and the worlds we imagine; and images and representations are a formidable culture force".[13]

Profit drives commercial exploitation of intellectual property. But financial issues are only part of Aboriginal peoples' concern. Loss of control of traditional ideas and knowledge may lead not only to commercialization but also to the identification of sacred places by those who do not appreciate their significance, resulting in intrusions on customs and beliefs. Revealing spiritual knowledge to outsiders can destroy its sacredness or twist the meaning of teachings; inappropriate imitation of a community's cultural practices, such as that indulged in by some new age groups, is a blatant misrepresentation of Aboriginal culture, weakening the teachings in the eyes of both Aboriginal and non-Aboriginal people.

The cultural heritage of Aboriginal peoples should be protected, and the terms of protection must be consonant with their needs. This issue runs through discussions of Aboriginal heritage and culture:

> There ought to be developed an Aboriginal copyright law or a mechanism parallel to the Canadian copyright law, a law that would be respected and upheld by all levels of government....After all, these [are] the measures that Canada has undertaken....They were afraid of encroachment of the American culture into Canadian culture. So I think we should learn from this and take measures to protect our own Native culture.
>
> Sharon
> Stoney Creek, British Columbia
> 18 June 1992

However, existing intellectual property law is inherently unsuited to protecting the traditional knowledge and cultural heritage of Aboriginal peoples. It is premised on balancing a creator's economic interest in his or her work with the larger public interest in promoting the use of ideas to increase society's general store of knowledge. The present law seeks to achieve this by protecting rights for a defined period of time, after which the material enters the public domain. In legal terms, this means that almost all traditional Aboriginal culture and knowledge is already considered to be in the public domain and therefore beyond protection. In the few cases where the present law might apply, protection would be short-lived. This system is antithetical to the community-based cultural heritage of Aboriginal peoples in which there is often no individual economic interest.

In addition, the existing intellectual property regime recognizes rights only in individuals, not communities or entire societies. This too prevents protection of traditional knowledge and Aboriginal cultural heritage, since they have no individual owner. While artistic styles such as woodland painting or Inuit carving cannot be copyrighted, there should be protection from imitative work that trades on the reputation of Aboriginal art and artists. Finally, the existing law does not recognize Aboriginal peoples' understanding of the sacredness of knowledge. Copyright law is not broad enough to protect a song or a prayer that has a spiritual origin, the use of which should be restricted but over which individuals are reluctant to assert ownership.

Only a new approach and new legal framework can address the need to protect the collective intellectual and cultural rights of Aboriginal peoples. This need is not unique to Canada. As early as 1963, the legal vulnerability of Aboriginal arts and design was a topic at international meetings. There was an effort to fill the gap, led by the World Intellectual Property Organization (WIPO) and the United Nations Educational, Scientific, and Cultural Organization (UNESCO), which administer, respectively, the Berne Copyright Convention and the Universal Copyright Convention. Their efforts culminated in a model statute, prepared by WIPO, that in 1985 was recommended by the executive committee of the Berne Convention and the intergovernmental copyright committee of the Universal Copyright Convention as a basis for national legislation by member-states of both organizations.[14] The recommendation has not been acted upon by the Canadian government.

In its brief to the Commission, the Assembly of First Nations listed three main objectives relating to Aboriginal people and cultural heritage:

- to gain and maintain control over cultural objects, archival data and human remains held in museums;
- to participate fully in all matters pertaining to the history and culture of First Nations people; and
- to operate First Nations museums and cultural centres.[15]

These objectives capture the priorities expressed by Inuit and Métis people as well, and we have used them as guiding principles in developing our recommendations.

Although the process of repatriating cultural materials has barely begun, the path ahead is clear. The future relationship between Aboriginal peoples, their cultural institutions and Canadian museums will revolve not only around repatriation but also other collaborative efforts to preserve and protect Aboriginal heritage. Repatriating sacred objects and human remains is a priority, but inventory work is needed before this can proceed.

With regard to portable items, such as sacred and secular artifacts, museums and other cultural institutions must ensure that Aboriginal people are fully involved in all aspects of disposition, display and representation of Aboriginal heritage. Indeed, the Canadian Museums Association agreed to this in principle in *Turning the Page*, the task force report on museums and Aboriginal peoples (see Appendix 6A).

RECOMMENDATIONS

The Commission recommends that

Inventory of
Historical and
Sacred Sites

3.6.1

Federal, provincial and territorial governments collaborate with Aboriginal organizations and communities to prepare a comprehensive inventory of historical and sacred sites, involving elders as expert advisers, before negotiations on designation of lands in accordance with our recommendations in Volume 2, Chapter 4.

Urgent Protection
of Threatened
Sites

3.6.2

Federal, provincial and territorial governments review legislation affecting sacred and historical sites to ensure that Aboriginal organizations and communities have access to urgent remedies to prevent or arrest damage to significant heritage sites such as the Mnjikaning Fish Fence, whether they be threatened by human actions or natural processes.

Legislation on
Historical Sites
and Cultural
Artifacts

3.6.3

Federal, provincial and territorial governments in collaboration with Aboriginal organizations review legislation affecting historical and sacred sites and the conservation and display of cultural artifacts to ensure that

(a) Aboriginal interests are recognized in designing, protecting, developing and managing sites significant to Aboriginal culture and heritage and in conserving, repatriating and displaying Aboriginal cultural artifacts;

(b) Aboriginal people are fully involved in planning and managing heritage activities relevant to their cultures; and

(c) Aboriginal people share the economic benefits that may accrue from appropriate development of relevant heritage sites and display of cultural artifacts.

Museums and
Cultural
Institutions Adopt
Ethical Guidelines

3.6.4

Museums and cultural institutions adopt ethical guidelines governing all aspects of collection, disposition, display and interpretation of artifacts related to Aboriginal culture and heritage, including the following:

(a) involving Aboriginal people in drafting, endorsing and implementing the guidelines;

(b) creating inventories of relevant holdings and making such inventories freely accessible to Aboriginal people;

(c) cataloguing and designating appropriate use and display of relevant holdings;

(d) repatriating, on request, objects that are sacred or integral to the history and continuity of particular nations and communities;

(e) returning human remains to the family, community or nation of origin, on request, or consulting with Aboriginal advisers on appropriate disposition, where remains cannot be associated with a particular nation; and

(f) ensuring that Aboriginal people and communities have effective access to cultural education and training opportunities available through museums and cultural institutions.

Access to Cultural Education

3.6.5

Aboriginal, federal, provincial and territorial governments, in collaboration with Aboriginal elders, artists, educators and youth, develop and implement joint strategies to ensure that Aboriginal people have

(a) effective access to cultural and heritage education;

(b) resources to develop facilities for display of cultural artifacts; and

(c) means to participate in exchanges and joint undertakings with museums and cultural institutions.

Heritage Vocations Part of Capacity Building

3.6.6

Aboriginal, federal, provincial and territorial governments include heritage research, conservation and presentation in the list of skills identified as priorities in building the capacity to implement self-government.

The global economy knows few boundaries. An Inuit image can be used by a souvenir maker in Taiwan and the resulting product sold in Alaska, Moscow and Toronto. A distorted version of a Haida song can be recorded in Denver, Colorado, and broadcast to France and Senegal via German satellite. While individual countries have jurisdiction over the protection of intellectual property within their own borders, international protection requires international agreement and co-operation. This is particularly true of Aboriginal cultural rights. Canada should enact legislation affirming the obligations to Aboriginal peoples it has assumed under international human rights instruments. (See Volume 2, Chapter 3, and particularly

Recommendation 2.3.1 on the support of international initiatives and enactment of related domestic legislation.) It should also, in collaboration with Indigenous peoples, work through international bodies for the further protection of Aboriginal intellectual and cultural property rights. In particular, the goal should be the implementation of an international regime that recognizes that Indigenous cultural rights are collective, and not based primarily on economic interest.

Even within Canada's borders, much remains to be done. Governments, consumer groups, manufacturers and retailers associations, and Aboriginal groups should co-operate in educating and informing their members and the public at large about the difference between authentic and imitation Aboriginal arts and crafts. Governments should carry out a comprehensive review of labelling regulations, consumer protection legislation, controls on misleading advertising, and import-export regulations to ensure that Aboriginal peoples' heritage and culture are legally protected from misappropriation and misrepresentation.

Any new policies or legislation should be established in consultation with Aboriginal people. These new policies should recognize society- or community-based ownership of cultural property, not just individual ownership. They must encompass traditional knowledge, which under the present legal regime is generally considered in the public domain. Aboriginal people should have the authority to preserve the integrity of their cultural knowledge by determining who has access to it and how it can be used. Other countries, notably Australia and the United States, have adopted legislation that begins to address these needs.[16]

Aboriginal people should define the content of their indigenous knowledge and cultural heritage. One of the primary tasks of Aboriginal museums and cultural institutions should be documenting this knowledge and conserving it for their communities. Aboriginal people should also be supported in developing their knowledge for commercial purposes when it is appropriate and they choose to do so. When this knowledge creates benefits for others, policy and legislation should ensure that Aboriginal people share those benefits. A thorough legislative review is in order.

RECOMMENDATION

The Commission recommends that

Protect Aboriginal Intellectual Property
3.6.7
The federal government, in collaboration with Aboriginal people, review its legislation on the protection of intellectual property to ensure that Aboriginal interests and perspectives, in particular collective interests, are adequately protected.

The scientific community and the education system also have roles in ensuring that Aboriginal knowledge is recognized as legitimate and worthy of protection. Aboriginal knowledge should be incorporated in academic programs. While it is obvious to many that Aboriginal knowledge can inform such fields as ecology and the environment, it is no less true for other sciences, history and the arts. In our chapters on education (Volume 3, Chapter 5) and elders' perspectives (Volume 4, Chapter 3), we illustrate a number of ways to incorporate Aboriginal knowledge and philosophy in mainstream education.

Research systems and practices should enable Aboriginal communities to exercise control over information relating to themselves and their heritage. Research projects should be managed jointly with Aboriginal people, and communities being studied should benefit from training and employment opportunities generated by the research. Above all, it is vital that Aboriginal peoples have direct input in developing and defining research practices and projects related to them. To act otherwise is to repeat that familiar pattern of decisions being made for Aboriginal people by those who presume to know what is best for them. (This Commission, with the advice of Aboriginal and non-Aboriginal researchers, formulated Ethical Guidelines for Research to guide our research effort. The guidelines appear as an appendix to Volume 5.)

Knowledge is not static. Neither is culture. They grow and change in an ever-evolving environment. Aboriginal and non-Aboriginal cultures have changed and will continue to change as a result of contact and interaction. Aboriginal people know that growth can come from adapting other peoples' ideas and knowledge to their own needs. Growth can also result from re-exploring their own knowledge. Aboriginal people want to share what they know and create. But they want their communities and knowledge to be respected and accorded the same rights, in their own terms and cultural context, accorded other Canadians in the area of intellectual and cultural property. They want a relationship that is beneficial to all.

2. LANGUAGE

2.1 The Importance of Language

We have defined culture as the whole way of life of a people (see Volume 1, Chapter 15). Language is the principal instrument by which culture is transmitted from one generation to another, by which members of a culture communicate meaning and make sense of their shared experience. Because language defines the world and experience in cultural terms, it literally shapes our way of perceiving – our world view.

While Aboriginal peoples and nations in Canada have diverse cultures and ways of life, there are commonalities between cultures that can aptly be described as an Aboriginal world view, shaped by life close to the land and a deep appreciation of the spiritual dimension of being. For Aboriginal people, the threat that

I Lost My Talk

I lost my talk
The talk you took away.
When I was a little girl
At Shubenacadie school.

You snatched it away:
I speak like you
I think like you
I create like you
The scrambled ballad, about my world.

Two ways I talk
Both ways I say,
Your way is more powerful.
So gently I offer my hand and ask,
Let me find my talk
So I can teach you about me.

–Rita Joe[17]

their languages could disappear is more than the prospect that they will have to acquire new instruments for communicating their daily needs and building a sense of community. It is a threat that their distinctive world view, the wisdom of their ancestors and their ways of being human could be lost as well. And, as they point out, if the languages of this continent are lost, there is nowhere else they can be heard again.

Many forces are contributing to a decline in the use of minority languages around the world. With Aboriginal languages, however, an underlying reason for the decline is the rupture in language transmission from older to younger generations and the low regard many Aboriginal people have had for traditional language proficiency as a result of policies devised by government and enforced by churches and the education system. As documented in our chapter on residential schools, the use of Aboriginal languages was prohibited in those institutions expressly to dislodge from the children's minds the world view embodied in the languages. The policies were also meant to alienate the children from their families (and hence their cultures), which were regarded as impediments to civilization (see Volume 1, Chapter 10). As the Mi'kmaq poet Rita Joe described it, the communication of many Aboriginal children became a "scrambled ballad" as a result.

In this section, we examine the fragile state of most Aboriginal languages and the prospects for and means of conserving them, whether they be thriving, in decline or severely threatened. In our view, Canadian governments have an obligation to support Aboriginal initiatives to conserve and revitalize Aboriginal languages and as much as possible to undo the harm done to Aboriginal cultures by harshly assimilative policies. These measures must be undertaken, however, only after careful evaluation of what can be achieved and after developing an understanding of the roles public policy and Aboriginal communities and nations should have in pursuing language revitalization.

2.2 The State of Language

Canada's Aboriginal languages can be divided into 11 distinct language families identified with First Nations, to which must be added Inuktitut, with its several dialects, and Michif, which also has dialects drawing on several Aboriginal languages. The groupings are established by comparing languages and using a number of procedures that allow the reconstruction of a common ancestor. There are between 53 and 70 languages in these families.[18] The actual number is not clear, since the languages have not been standardized, and attempts at classification are complicated by the existence of dialects. In addition, the fact that some Aboriginal groups use distinct ethnic labels often leads to erroneous identification of their dialect as a distinct language. Table 6.1 lists Aboriginal languages by family.

Inuktitut, a group of dialects belonging to the Aleut-Eskimo family, stretches across the Canadian Arctic. Iroquoian languages are found in Quebec and Ontario. Algonquian languages extend from Alberta to the maritime provinces. The remaining eight families are found west of Lake Winnipeg only. Siouan is present in the prairies, as is Athapaskan, and the latter is also found in the Northwest Territories, the Yukon and British Columbia. Three languages, Tlingit, Haida and Kutenai, and three language families, Salishan, Wakashan and Tsimshian, are found only in British Columbia, where there is extreme linguistic complexity. None of the families is confined to Canada.

Michif, the language of the Métis Nation, cannot be tied to a specific territorial base. Métis people have settled all across Canada, with a concentration in the western provinces and the Northwest Territories. This is a hindrance to developing and promoting Michif, as there are few concentrated areas where speakers could immerse themselves in the language.

Only a small number of Aboriginal people speak Aboriginal languages. While more than a million people claimed Aboriginal ancestry in the 1991 census, only 190,165 said an Aboriginal language was their mother tongue, and 138,105 reported using their Aboriginal mother tongue in the home. Table 6.2 shows the number of people whose mother tongue is an Aboriginal language and who use that language at home. The relationship between mother tongue and

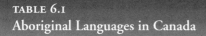

TABLE 6.1
Aboriginal Languages in Canada

Family	Language	Family	Language
Aleut-Eskimo	Inuktitut	Wakashan	Nootka
[Isolate]	Tlingit		Nitinat
[Isolate]	Haida		Kwakiutl
Athapaskan	Dogrib		Bella Bella (Heiltsuk)
	Hare (North Slavey)		Kitanat-Haisla
	Beaver	Tsimshian	Tsimshian
	Sekani		Nisga'a
	Sarcee (Sarsi)		Gitksan
	Tsilhoqot'in	Siouan	Lakota - Dakota
	Carrier (Wet'suwet'en)		Nakota (Assiniboine, Stoney)
	Chipewyan	Iroquoian	Seneca
	Slavey (South Slavey)		Cayuga
	Yellowknife		Onondaga
	Kutchin (Gwich'in or Loucheux)		Mohawk
	Kaska		Oneida
	Tahltan		Tuscarora
[Isolate]	Kutenai	Algonquian	Blackfoot
Salishan		Algonquian	
Interior	Lillooet	*Cree*	Cree
	Shuswap		Montagnais-Naskapi-Attikamek
	Thompson (Ntlakyapamuk)	Algonquian	
	Okanagan	*Ojibwa*	Ojibwa
Salishan			Odawa (Ottawa)
Coastal	Songish		Algonquin (Algonkin)
	Semiahmoo		Saulteaux
	Cowichan	Algonquian	
	Comox	*Eastern*	Delaware
	Sishiatl (Sechelt)		Abenaki
	Bella Coola		Mi'kmaq
	Squamish		Maliseet

Notes:

[Isolate] = Language not belonging to any of the recognized language families.

Italics indicate sub-groupings within a family.

Source: Adapted from Jonathan D. Kaye. "The Indian Languages of Canada", in *The Languages of Canada* ed. J. Chambers (Montreal: Didier, 1979), pp. 15-19. See also Lynn Drapeau, "Perspectives on Aboriginal Language Conservation and Revitalization in Canada", research study prepared for the Royal Commission on Aboriginal Peoples [RCAP] (1995).

TABLE 6.2

Population by Aboriginal Mother Tongue and Aboriginal Home Language

Language Family	Mother Tongue	Home Language	Ratio of Home Language to Mother Tongue (%)
Algonquian	131,330	96,230	73
Athapaskan	19,140	13,750	72
Haida	165	45	27
Inuktitut	24,995	21,905	88
Iroquoian[1]	—	—	—
Kutenai	175	40	23
Salish	2,835	835	30
Dakota (Siouan)	4,105	2,965	72
Tlingit	105	10	10
Tsimshian	395	65	17
Wakashan	3,445	1,090	32
Other Amerindian	2,925	1,065	36
Total	**190,165**	**138,105**	**73**

Notes:

1. Iroquoian language data are of little value given the refusal of Mohawk reserves to participate in the census or the Aboriginal Peoples Survey. The partial data provided by Statistics Canada for this group have therefore been omitted.

2. Mother tongue and home language numbers include single and multiple responses. The 'Other Amerindian' group reports all responses that could not (for various reasons) be included under other language families.

Source: Statistics Canada, catalogue nos. 93-317, 93-333; and Lynn Drapeau, "Perspectives on Aboriginal Language Conservation and Revitalization in Canada", research study prepared for RCAP (1995).

actual language use is an important indicator of language vitality. A discrepancy between the two indicates a language shift, since a language that is no longer spoken at home cannot be handed down to the younger generation. Table 6.2 shows that 92.5 per cent of all Aboriginal mother tongue reports originated from three linguistic groups – Algonquian, Inuktitut and Athapaskan – while the remaining 7.5 per cent stemmed from the eight other language families.

So few people speak some languages that the languages appear to be in critical condition. The linguistic isolates (languages not belonging to any of the recognized language families) – Haida (165), Kutenai (175) and Tlingit (105) – are the mother tongues of very few people. Tsimshian is the mother tongue of fewer than 400. Wakashan has five distinct languages and fewer than 3,500 people for whom it is the mother tongue. That some of these languages are also spoken in the United States does not offer much hope, as the situation there is as desperate as it is in Canada, if not worse.[19] There are at least a dozen Salishan languages, but only 2,835 people claim them as their mother tongues. The number of people whose mother tongue is in the Athapaskan family varies from 3,520 South Slavey speakers to 35 North Slavey (Hare) speakers, while the overall number of Athapaskan speakers reported in the census is 19,140.

Among the Algonquian languages, Cree is the mother tongue of the greatest number of people (82,070); Cree speakers make up 43 per cent of all those in Canada with an Aboriginal mother tongue. Cree includes several dialects, however, that not everyone who speaks Cree understands. Ojibwa is also the mother tongue of a sizeable number of people (25,255), who account for 13 per cent of all those with an Aboriginal mother tongue, but the same caveat about dialects probably applies. The Algonquian language in the most fragile state appears to be Maliseet, with 255 speakers reported.[20]

A high ratio of home language to mother tongue indicates that the language is likely to be passed to the next generation. Ratios of less than 100 per cent indicate some decline in the strength of the language, with low scores pointing to a steep decline. Table 6.2 shows that the linguistic family with the greatest vitality is Inuktitut, where the ratio is 88 per cent, followed by Algonquian, Athapaskan and Siouan, with ratios of 72 to 73 per cent. Among individual languages in the Algonquian group, Montagnais has a ratio of 97 per cent; in the Athapaskan family, Dogrib has a ratio of 87 per cent.[21]

Many language groups are experiencing a sharp decline, however. Among those whose mother tongues are Salish (30 per cent) and Wakashan (32 per cent), less than one person in three reports using the language at home. The proportion is even less for Haida (27 per cent), Kutenai (23 per cent) and Tsimshian (17 per cent), and drops to one in 10 for Tlingit. (These are global, undifferentiated statistics for language and community. A closer look needs to be taken at every community within each language group, but such a task far exceeds the limits of the present examination.)

The ratio of home language to mother tongue, combined with the number of mother tongue speakers, shows clearly that the following languages are highly endangered: Haida, Kutenai, most Salishan languages, Tlingit, Tsimshian and the Wakashan languages. In the Athapaskan family, Kutchin, North Slavey (Hare) and Tahltan are in a critical state, as are Maliseet and Abenaki in the Algonquian group.[22]

Languages spoken by only a few thousand people can also be judged endangered. Nevertheless, some such as Dogrib and other Athapaskan lan-

	Total Aboriginal	North American Indian		Métis	Inuit
		Registered	Non-registered		
	%	%	%	%	%
5-14 years	21.9	28.6	5.2	5.1	67.0
15-24	27.4	33.7	8.6	8.2	71.2
25-54	36.7	47.6	9.7	18.1	74.5
55+	63.1	74.7	24.5	43.5	90.6
% of speakers age 5+	32.7	41.8	9.0	14.4	72.5

TABLE 6.3
Speakers of an Aboriginal Language by Age Group, 1991

Source: Statistics Canada, 1991 Census and Aboriginal Peoples Survey, custom tabulations.

guages appear stable when the ratio of home use to speakers is taken into account. Attikamek, a language usually counted as a member of the Cree group, has fewer than 4,000 speakers but a very high incidence of use in the home.

Languages boasting large numbers of speakers and a high overall ratio of home use can be considered viable. Cree, Mi'kmaq, Montagnais, Ojibwa and Inuktitut seem to fall into this group, although Cree and Ojibwa may include very divergent dialects, lessening the effect of the number of speakers.

Although the 1991 census data on Iroquoian languages are unreliable because of under-reporting, other sources of information suggest that Tuscarora is on the verge of extinction in Canada. Seneca has only 25 speakers left in Canada, but a large number in the United States. From the small number of people whose mother tongue is an Iroquoian language, it appears that all such languages in Canada are in critical condition, with the possible exception of Mohawk.[23]

The analysis so far has drawn on 1991 census data and the population of just over one million reporting Aboriginal ancestry. The Aboriginal peoples survey, with adjustments for under-reporting, is based on a population of 720,000 respondents who identified themselves as Aboriginal. Data from the 1991 Aboriginal peoples survey provide information on overall Aboriginal language competence and use across Canada. Custom tabulations prepared for the Commission indicate that of respondents five years of age and over who identified themselves as Aboriginal, 50 per cent did not understand any Aboriginal language, 17.5 per cent understood one but could not speak it, and 32.7 per cent could speak an Aboriginal language. As shown in Table 6.3, the percentage who can speak an Aboriginal language is especially low among non-registered Indians

(9 per cent) and Métis people (14.4 per cent). Among Inuit, on the other hand, 72.5 per cent of a population of nearly 38,000 speak the language.

When Aboriginal language speakers are considered by age group, the decline in language transmission is starkly apparent. Even among Inuit, there is a decline of 23.6 percentage points between people 55 years old and older and those between five and 14. Among Métis people and non-registered Indians between the ages of five and 14, only one person in 20 can speak an Aboriginal language. Registered Indians, however, have suffered by far the sharpest drop in Aboriginal language transmission.

2.3 Language Maintenance and Identity

There are two essential prerequisites to devising Aboriginal language policies. First, the phenomena of language shift and language maintenance (conservation) must be thoroughly understood. Second, the relationship between language and identity must be recognized.

The extreme fragility of Aboriginal languages (and of minority languages in general) must be taken into account when considering future prospects. An understanding of language shift allows the situation to be considered in a broader context and avoids the perception that the decline in Aboriginal languages is unique in all respects. In addition, a comparative study of language maintenance efforts around the world affords valuable information about the likely success of endeavours to save Aboriginal languages.

Vulnerability

The eclipse of 'marginal' languages in favour of more dominant languages is almost as old as the world itself: politically and culturally dominant languages, spoken by greater numbers, have always overwhelmed languages that are less prestigious and spoken by fewer people. The consensus among researchers today, however, is that the phenomenon has reached acute proportions, occurring at a rate and on a scale never witnessed before.[24] Recent assessments suggest the impending extinction of as many as 90 per cent of the world's 6,000 languages.[25] Aboriginal languages in Canada are not alone; minority languages on every continent are at risk.

A better understanding of the challenges facing Canada's Aboriginal languages and the formulation of an effective response require an analysis of the causes of language disappearance in the past and the specific factors making Aboriginal languages especially vulnerable today.

Bilingualism

Is bilingualism realistically sustainable, or does it lead inevitably to assimilation by the dominant language? It is, of course, perfectly possible for an individual to master several languages. But people do not learn and use languages in a socio-cultural vacuum. The fate of a language (and the incentive to learn, use and transmit it) depends on factors that are neither linguistic nor cognitive. They are economic, socio-cultural and political. Scholars of bilingualism have come to the conclusion that bilingualism can have profoundly different consequences, depending upon whether it involves majority or minority groups, members of social elites or less advantaged groups, nation-states or stateless groups, and many other factors.

Cultural aggressiveness

Conflict with a more powerful social group is an obvious factor and the one most often encountered in language replacement situations. The resulting culture shock is characterized by demographic, socio-economic and cultural inequalities, and its effects on minority communities and their families can be devastating. The language might be replaced by that of the culturally more aggressive people or modified in pidgin form. It might be relegated to culturally inferior and unimportant roles and functions or, very occasionally, to some special uses. It might be heavily influenced, especially in its vocabulary and to some extent also in its structure, by the language of the more culturally aggressive people. Finally, the language can lose the cultural characteristics of its speakers and become an imitation of the language of the more aggressive people. It will no longer reflect the unique world view of its speakers but that of the dominant culture.[26]

The historical reasons for the decline of Aboriginal languages provide only part of the picture. Most modern western societies no longer pursue strong assimilationist policies, and some even promote multiculturalism. Yet the process of shift to the majority language and the ensuing death of minority languages continues unabated. In other words, even the best intentions of the majority group, embodied in specific efforts to promote linguistic diversity, offer no guarantee that minority languages will hold their own.

Oral tradition

Only a minority of the world's 6,000 languages have a written form and a tradition of literacy. Indigenous languages fall into the majority of so-called 'oral tradition' languages; they are essentially spoken languages. Even if most can now claim to have written forms, their use is generally infrequent. Written work is rare, and reading and writing (and transmission of these skills) are often restricted to the classroom. Research carried out for the Commission, for example, revealed that in Quebec, "despite an increase in formal schooling in the Aboriginal language and the growing number of language experts (such as Aboriginal language teachers, interpreters, techno-linguists and the like), the rate of actual spontaneous use of Aboriginal literacy skills in everyday life is quite low. Everyone somehow seems to favour reading and writing in the majority language".[27] That Aboriginal languages exist predominantly as oral tradition may have a profound impact on their survival and the nature of efforts required to strengthen them.

In concrete terms, the limited amount of writing in Aboriginal languages results in a lack of textbooks, teachers' manuals and other essential tools for language instruction. There is also a dearth of teachers trained to teach Aboriginal languages as second languages. Formal instruction to the level of full fluency is therefore difficult to find, and the only option is natural immersion in a community where the Aboriginal language is still spoken. While this may offer a culturally enriching learning experience, it is impractical for many Aboriginal people, especially for the large number living in urban areas.

Currency

Modernization is also a factor. Contact with other cultures may bring about changes that are so drastic the language is unable to adapt quickly enough to express new, everyday realities. Changing contexts have characterized indigenous life across North America. Even in the non-Aboriginal world, 50 years of socio-cultural upheaval has overwhelmed the ability of many languages to absorb and communicate new concepts and realities. Aboriginal languages have been stretched to the limit; it is therefore not surprising that Aboriginal speakers draw upon majority language resources to express these new ideas.

Linguistic enclaves

Another factor contributing to language decline is the separation of Aboriginal peoples into linguistic enclaves within an immense majority-language territory. As long as these enclaves remained isolated from the rest of the world, they stood a chance of maintaining their linguistic integrity. Geographic isolation no longer protects them, however; schools, businesses and the media have now penetrated most, if not all, communities, and the fact that speakers of Aboriginal languages are scattered rather than concentrated in geo-linguistic strongholds has become a powerful impediment to the maintenance of those languages.

Other factors

Apart from minority language fragility, several factors tend to promote a shift to the dominant language. The first is asymmetrical bilingualism, where only minority members become bilingual while members of the majority remain unilingual. The second is generalized bilingualism. As bilingual ability becomes the norm within a given group, there tends to be a shift to the dominant language simply because people will not maintain two languages indefinitely where one will suffice. Children are more likely to learn their ancestral language if a significant proportion of their community is unilingual, since inability to speak it would prevent communication, or at least make it more difficult. On the other hand, if all age groups, including elders, can understand the dominant language, any failure of younger generations to acquire the ancestral language is not socially disruptive. In the case of Aboriginal peoples, everyone is now schooled in one of the dominant languages (English or French), and it is likely that within a few generations at most, there will no longer be any unilingual speakers of Aboriginal languages. This means that there no longer will be Aboriginal language speakers whose unilingualism forces others to communicate in the Aboriginal language.

Finally, intensive use of and exposure to the dominant language in everyday life is an important element in the shift to the dominant language. Living off-reserve and in urban settings ensures constant exposure to and use of the dominant language. In Aboriginal communities, the requirements of schooling (and often the workplace), as well as the intrusion of the media, also result in intensive use of and exposure to the dominant language.

Identity and symbolism

Most people find it impossible to separate language and identity. Language is perceived as the quintessence of a culture. It expresses a unique way of apprehending reality, capturing a world view specific to the culture to which it is linked. But language is connected to identity in another important way: its presence and use in a community are symbolic of identity, emblems of group existence. Using a language is the ultimate symbol of belonging.

Language is usually seen as an essential component of ethnic identity, and it is commonly understood that the loss of a minority language automatically entails assimilation with the dominant group. But the preservation of a distinctive language may not always be essential to preservation of a distinct identity. In other words, language shift does not automatically imply ethnic assimilation. There are clear examples in Canada of Aboriginal groups who have lost their language but retain a sense of group identity and of belonging to the Aboriginal world.[28] While language is an important cultural and ethnic marker, its loss does not automatically signal a redefinition of group allegiance.

In deploring the loss of its ancestral language, an Aboriginal group may be deploring the loss of a symbol of its identity rather than an instrument of communication. Hence, the motivation to revive the ancestral language is not communication, since the dominant language fulfils that need, but stems from the desire to revive or protect a tangible emblem of group identity.

One perspective on group identification is that the group gives the individual a sense of security and continuity with the past, affirming the value of behaviours and attitudes shaped by the heritage culture and practised by the individual. The Aboriginal group or nation certainly serves the survival needs of the individual, but in many Aboriginal cultures the individual also has important obligations to contribute to the survival of the group through ethical behaviour. The nation or community, in Aboriginal thought and morality, has responsibilities of a spiritual order. Thus, maintenance of the language and group integrity has both a social-emotional and a spiritual purpose. In nations where the language has fallen into disuse, the question may have to be asked whether revival of the language in ordinary discourse is the only avenue or the most effective avenue of revitalizing the culture and fulfilling these purposes.

In our discussion of Métis perspectives (Volume 4, Chapter 5), for example, we consider the possibility that Michif as a distinct language may not be revived for daily discourse in a dispersed Métis cultural community. This prospect makes it all the more vital that the distinctive perspectives and experience embodied in the Michif language be recorded, understood and communicated in new environments so that Métis culture can continue to enrich the understanding of Métis people and all Canadians.

Throughout our report, we have emphasized the distinctive world view that characterizes diverse Aboriginal cultures. As we will see in the next section, measures can be taken to counter language shift. However, while undertaking language initiatives, Aboriginal nations will need to examine what other measures are needed to conserve Aboriginal cultures and world views, particularly for the substantial numbers of Aboriginal people whose daily activities require fluency in French or English and who are distant from the lifestyle that makes fluency in an Aboriginal language essential for survival.

2.4 Countering Language Shift

Defining objectives

Language maintenance means taking the steps necessary to ensure the survival of a language community for which the Aboriginal language is both the mother tongue and the primary vehicle of verbal exchange within the family and social networks. A language must have native speakers to survive and will remain viable only if intergenerational transmission can be maintained. It must also be used in everyday life, not just in restricted domains.

Revitalization strategies apply to linguistic groups undergoing shift to the dominant language. They usually aim to increase the number of persons with a knowledge of the Aboriginal language, but in some cases it may be possible only to slow the shift or halt further deterioration. The most common revitalization strategy is to increase the number of second-language speakers. This is at best 'palliative care' and will not by itself make the language viable. To revitalize a language, the capacity to transmit it from one generation to the next must be restored.

Stages in Reversing Language Shift

A. Ensuring Intergenerational Transmission

1. Reconstruct the language.
2. Mobilize fluent older speakers.
3. Restore intergenerational transmission through family, neighbourhood and community reinforcement.
4. Teach the language in school.

B. Extending Usage

5. Implement immersion and strong bilingual education.
6. Use the language in work environments.
7. Offer government services in the language.
8. Use the language in higher education, media and government.

Source: Joshua A. Fishman, "What is Reversing Language Shift and How Can It Succeed?", *Journal of Multilingual and Multicultural Development* 111/1&2 (1990), p. 5.

Reversal of shift involves increasing the number of first-language speakers of a language. Language revival means bringing back an extinct or near-extinct language as the medium of communication in a community.

Stages in reversing language shift

Faced with the prospect of erosion of their language, activists tend to advocate government intervention and make proposals to confer enhanced status on the receding language. The Commission has been urged to recommend that Aboriginal languages be used in educational institutions from primary school to college, that they be given official language status, and that they be used at all levels of government.

However, sociolinguists who have studied language loss and efforts to stop it generally agree that action must originate at the community level and be directed to those who can assure intergenerational transmission. Eight stages have been suggested for reversing language shift, of which the first four are the most urgent (see box).

In the first stage, the language itself must be reconstructed; this is especially critical for Aboriginal languages that are poorly researched and sparsely documented. The second stage involves the mobilization of older speakers in the community, who are often the last fluent speakers. The third stage, which lies at the heart of the process, is the promotion of family, neighbourhood and community reinforcement to restore the normal pattern of intergenerational transmission. The next stage is formal linguistic socialization, usually accomplished through literacy and schooling, but without displacing formal education in the majority language. These four stages constitute a basic, minimal program that forms the necessary foundation for the next stages.

The succeeding stages seek to extend the revived language into broader communicative and symbolic uses. The fifth stage would see the endangered language replace the dominant language in schooling through the use of immersion and other strong forms of bilingual education. The sixth would see Aboriginal languages used in the work environment. This would require considerable planning to overcome the absence of widespread literacy in Aboriginal languages.

In the second-last stage, government services offered to citizens would be provided in the Aboriginal language. Since Aboriginal communities have already begun to take responsibility for providing many services, this might be realized more easily than the preceding stage, at least within Aboriginal communities that still have a high proportion of Aboriginal language speakers and where single-language use reduces potential complexity. The final stage coincides with the recognition and implementation of cultural autonomy and contemplates use of the Aboriginal language in the upper reaches of education, media and government operations.

Formal interventions

Formal education is often viewed as the solution that will save endangered languages, but many Aboriginal language conservation and revitalization efforts remain largely symbolic in intent and achievement. Where Aboriginal languages are taught, only one or two hours of classes a week are offered.[29]

Aboriginal language immersion is popular in communities where the language is in decline. For example, to preserve Maori, the Aboriginal language of Aotearoa (New Zealand), an immersion program has been implemented at the pre-school level. In Canada, the Mohawk people are investing heavily in immersion programs. While it is clear that formal immersion can assist in the acquisition of an Aboriginal language as a second language – which is what immersion is designed to do – it is far from obvious that it will have any effect on re-establishing intergenerational transmission. It cannot be assumed that immersion students will take the language home from school; in fact, experience with French immersion programs suggests the contrary. Unless immersion is reinforced with programs to ensure that the language learned is used in family environments, the need for immersion programs will be entrenched forever, since no one will acquire the language as a first language.

There is also a danger that a heavy emphasis on immersion could encourage parents and the community to leave language transmission to teachers. Any success in formal schooling would thus be undermined, as sustained use of Aboriginal languages at home is an essential condition for their survival.

Similarly, seeking to restore a language to vitality by implementing measures at stage seven or eight of the process – that is, requiring access to a language in formal institutions – is unlikely to have broad effect if the critical stage three – reinstating or reinforcing intergenerational transmission – is neglected. Passing on the language as a first language can occur only in the family and community, in the everyday business of learning and communicating.

Experience with Canada's official languages policy is instructive regarding the impact of institutional services on language conservation. Under the *Canadian Charter of Rights and Freedoms* and the *Official Languages Act*, English and French are recognized as the official languages of Canada. Everyone has the right to use the official language of their choice in the debates and other proceedings of the Parliament of Canada and before federal courts. Section 23 of the Charter guarantees the right of minority official language citizens, where numbers warrant, to have their children receive primary and secondary school instruction in their language. Moreover, Canadians have the right to use the official language of their choice when communicating with and receiving services from federal institutions in the National Capital Region and at head offices of federal institutions located elsewhere, where there is significant demand and when the nature of the office warrants it. Canadians working in federal institutions also have the right to use the official language of their choice in designated regions. Despite all these efforts, however, the 1991 census shows that the percentage of francophones outside Quebec who speak French at home continues to decline. In fact, the data show that the percentage of francophones outside Quebec who speak English most often at home rose from 29 per cent to 35 per cent between 1981 and 1991.[30]

Declaring a language official can do little more than sanction a reality. If there is a wide discrepancy between the official status of a language and its actual use, the status will be essentially symbolic or political in intent and effect. Assigning a language official status will not guarantee intergenerational transmission.

In Aboriginal nations where the ratio of home use to mother tongue is high, making the Aboriginal language official might give impetus to its continued use in the community and to the elaboration of vocabulary to deal with contemporary inter-cultural experience. While legislation alone cannot work a reversal in language shift, its role in a multi-faceted, community-based strategy for language conservation and revitalization may be valuable.

2.5 Conclusions and Recommendations

Conservation or revitalization of a language demands maintaining or restoring intergenerational language transmission. Since intergenerational transmission depends primarily on family and community networks, the focus of language conservation and revitalization efforts must shift from formal institutions to

Aboriginal communities, families and social networks. This does not mean that other avenues should be ignored. It does mean, however, that the effect of all actions on language use and transmission in everyday communications must be taken into consideration.

It is possible to envisage a range of objectives that Aboriginal nations and their communities might adopt. The only way of ensuring survival of a language is complete cultural autonomy. In linguistic terms, this means maintaining or recreating a sizeable body of unilingual speakers of the Aboriginal language who can go about their daily lives with no more than incidental exposure to the dominant language. One step down the scale of cultural autonomy would be the maintenance of geographic areas where people, while remaining bilingual, would carry on their normal lives in the Aboriginal language, with minimum exposure to and use of the dominant language; the greater the exposure to and need to use the dominant language, the less the degree of cultural autonomy. At the other end of the scale, continual exposure to the dominant language and the necessity to use it in every facet of daily life is a powerful catalyst for the decline of the Aboriginal language.

Each nation, community and language group must decide what level of cultural autonomy it wishes and can realistically achieve. We particularly hope that communities where an Aboriginal language is still transmitted within the family will strive to maintain this situation and expand the domains in which the language is used.

Community objectives should also be established regarding the number of speakers who have achieved a satisfactory level of proficiency in the Aboriginal language and actually use it in their daily lives. Communities seeking to maintain or revitalize their language must work to increase the number of first- and second-language speakers who meet these criteria, and policies aimed at conservation or revitalization should have a demonstrable effect on attaining this goal. The ability of Aboriginal peoples to assert their inherent right to determine the status of Aboriginal languages in self-governing nations on their own territory is a first step in halting the erosion of Aboriginal languages.

RECOMMENDATIONS

The Commission recommends that

Determining
Language Status a
Core Power of
Self-Government

3.6.8

Federal, provincial and territorial governments recognize promptly that determining Aboriginal language status and use is a core power in Aboriginal self-government, and that these governments affirm and support Aboriginal nations and their communities in using and promoting their languages and declaring them official languages within their nations, territories and communities where they choose to do so.

Nations **3.6.9**
Implement a
Multi-Faceted
Language Strategy

Each Aboriginal nation in the various stages of nation building, capacity building, negotiating and implementing self-government consult with its constituent communities to establish priorities and policies with respect to Aboriginal language conservation, revitalization and documentation, including

(a) assessing the current state of Aboriginal language use and vitality;

(b) determining priorities of communities for language conservation, revitalization and documentation;

(c) consulting on the most effective means of implementing priorities;

(d) facilitating initiatives to support Aboriginal language use in families and the broader community;

(e) incorporating their Aboriginal language in education policies and programs;

(f) enhancing co-operation among nations and communities of the same language group to promote research, curriculum development and language elaboration;

(g) using their Aboriginal language in public forums and Aboriginal government business; and

(h) declaring their Aboriginal language an official language on nation territory.

In Chapter 5 of this volume, we made recommendations to enhance the recognition of Aboriginal languages in school curricula and to encourage their use as a career path for teachers and researchers. These recommendations highlight the essential role of nations, communities and families in language conservation and revitalization. We are concerned, however, about the fragile state of many Aboriginal languages and the fact that a great many of the elders who constitute the fluent speakers are also fragile with age. This is an area where restorative justice cannot wait while negotiations for a new relationship progress at a deliberate pace. Aboriginal languages have been undermined by government action. They should be conserved, restored or documented for posterity with government support. Because churches have played a critical part in the destruction of languages, we consider that practical support for the restoration of the languages would be a highly appropriate reconciliatory gesture. We are therefore proposing the establishment of an Aboriginal Languages Foundation to be endowed jointly by the federal government and private donors, both Aboriginal and non-Aboriginal.

In 1988, the Assembly of First Nations put forward a proposal for a national language foundation, legislated and endowed by the federal government and residing at Canadian Heritage. The purpose of such a foundation would be to fund local and regional language-related projects, encourage the exchange of language information, and promote Aboriginal languages. The proposal noted that a foundation would require only a small staff and that it would not be a large centralized operation. It would focus its efforts on funding community-based projects, including such initiatives as

- developing Aboriginal languages curriculum and materials;
- developing programs for training and certifying Aboriginal language teachers, linguists, interpreters, translators, curriculum developers and researchers;
- conducting research in Aboriginal languages;
- promoting traditional approaches to language learning such as language/cultural camps; and
- organizing gatherings of particular language families or groups to share ideas and experiences and make overall decisions about their languages.

The establishment of the foundation should complement, not diminish, the efforts and funding of existing cultural education centres, language institutes, language programs and curriculum projects. Support of the language foundation should be co-ordinated with provincial and territorial programs to identify gaps and ensure that all programs enhance local initiatives rather than compete with them.

As we have noted, there will be different conservation objectives for different languages depending on their state of vitality. It will not be possible to make renewal efforts on the same scale for all languages and dialects in Canada. Aboriginal nations and communities need to set priorities to determine which languages can be maintained or revitalized and which should be documented immediately because they are unlikely to be restored to regular use. As the history of western civilization has demonstrated, rich cultural knowledge need not be lost because a particular language ceases to be a vehicle for current communication.

An endowment fund – with the interest made available for annual distribution – would provide much-needed support for Aboriginal languages, and, unlike a specific program, it would be sustained over time. It will take a long-term commitment to revitalize Aboriginal languages. A fund of $100 million could provide an annual budget of four to seven million dollars for distribution and administration. In addition to federal government support and contributions from churches, an Aboriginal languages foundation could also provide a focus for corporate and other voluntary support for the revitalization of Aboriginal cultures. We propose that the Aboriginal languages foundation be capitalized at the level of $100 million, with the federal government contributing $10 million a year for five years, beginning in fiscal year 1997-98, and matching private contributions at the rate of two federal dollars for each privately donated dollar. The fund should be governed by a board of First Nations, Métis and Inuit representatives from different linguistic communities.

RECOMMENDATION

The Commission recommends that

Endowed
Aboriginal
Languages
Foundation

3.6.10

The federal government make a commitment to endow an Aboriginal Languages Foundation for the purpose of supporting Aboriginal initiatives in the conservation, revitalization and documentation of Aboriginal languages, the foundation to be

(a) capitalized by an annual federal grant of $10 million for five years, beginning in 1997;

(b) eligible to receive charitable contributions, to be matched by the federal government in a ratio of two dollars for each dollar contributed;

(c) established to support language initiatives undertaken or endorsed by Aboriginal nations and their communities;

(d) developed by a federally funded planning body, with a majority of First Nations, Inuit and Métis representatives and a two-year mandate; and

(e) directed in its operation by a board with a majority of First Nations, Inuit and Métis members.

3. COMMUNICATIONS

Portrayals of Indians as noble and savage, victim and villain are threaded throughout the narratives of Canadian culture. But the images of Aboriginal people etched in Canadian cultural narratives are largely fictional.[31] With confrontations from Oka to Ipperwash to Gustafson Lake, the events of recent history place new emphasis on improving understanding between Aboriginal and non-Aboriginal Canadians. They bring into focus the need for accurate information and realistic representations of Aboriginal peoples and create a new demand to recognize the central role of communications in building community cohesiveness within Aboriginal nations and fostering relationships between cultures.

Technology is central to Canada's social history. Like the transcontinental railroad of an earlier era, communications technologies and the cultural industries they generate shape the Canadian experience and identity. For Aboriginal people, however, the image and identity forged by the media all too often bear the traits of exclusion, stereotypical inclusion and misappropriation.

Communication is much more than a cultural glue holding a geographically vast country together. Through identifying with the images and cultural narratives that dominate our ways of seeing and representing the world, we actually construct who we are. Aboriginal perspectives in mainstream and Aboriginal media should be central factors in the formation of Aboriginal and non-Aboriginal culture, identity and community.

Particularly in the north, Canada has begun to respond to the need for Aboriginal broadcasting and newspapers. In fact, the programs and policies developed over the last two decades have served as models for indigenous communications elsewhere. Ironically, Aboriginal communications programs in Canada are now being cut back; service is far from extensive, especially in the south, and the voices of Aboriginal people are still largely absent from mainstream broadcasting and journalism. A re-examination of the role and meaning of communications media in the maintenance of Aboriginal culture, identity and community is clearly long overdue, as is a fundamental shift in the way mainstream media address and portray Aboriginal issues, culture and identity to Canadians in general.

3.1 Stereotypes and Self-Portrayal

Beverly Slapin, a non-Aboriginal person who co-wrote *Through Indian Eyes: The Native Experience in Books for Children*, has written of her childhood perception of Aboriginal people:

> Like many others outside the Native world, I grew up with the prevailing stereotypes of the people. I learned that "Indians" whoop and holler and run around in little more than war paint and feathers, brandishing tomahawks and dancing on one leg; they scalp, torture and menace innocent settlers; they beat on tom-toms and live in "teepees"; their language consists of raising one hand shoulder high and grunting "how" or "ugh!"; and they are not women, men and babies, but "squaws", "braves" and "papooses." Then, as now, Indians jumped out from comic books, greeting cards, games and toys, food packages, advertisements, movies and TV. I can still see, in my mind's eye, images of "Indians" attacking stagecoaches and covered wagons (and in my childhood nightmares, attacking *me*). The only "Indians" I remember fondly were Princess Summerfall Winterspring, whom I dearly loved, and Chief Thunderthud ("How! Kowabunga!"), both

of whom hung out with Howdy Doody and Buffalo Bob Smith....Little has changed...since my childhood. Some children who go back on their promises are called "Indian givers". "Ten Little Indians" is still a popular counting song. Non-Native children still dress as "Indians" for Halloween....And books about Native peoples are still written, published and promoted, by outsiders.[32]

Since the earliest days of contact with non-Aboriginal people, the stories of Aboriginal peoples have been constructed and disseminated by outsiders, for outsiders. The stories are told in ethnographic studies, paintings and photographs, movies, novels, in newspapers and on radio and television.[33] Aboriginal people are portrayed in a historical past reconstructed in present stereotypes: the noble Red Man roaming free in the forest; the bloodthirsty savage attacking the colony or the wagon train; the drunken Indian; the Aboriginal environmentalist; and, most recently, the warrior in para-military dress, wielding a gun.

The promulgation of negative stereotypes is offensive to Aboriginal people, and even apparently positive stereotypes can distort relationships. As with all stereotypes, there is a kernel of truth in the images, which assume a dramatic profile and become etched in the popular consciousness. But stereotypes block out complexity of context and diversity of personality and perspective. Media images that focus predominantly on conflict and confrontation make communication more difficult and reconciliation more elusive. Too often, media treatment of Aboriginal people and issues reinforces old and deeply imbedded notions of 'Indians' as alien, unknowable and ultimately a threat to civil order. Exaggerated and one-dimensional images also create problems of self-identification and cohesion within Aboriginal communities.

In the mainstream media, stories may seem to speak for Aboriginal people when the voice actually originates in the consciousness and experience of non-Aboriginal writers. The voice is 'appropriated'. Aboriginal people listen to these stories, too, and the stories confirm their dominant experience – that there is no room for authentic expression of who they are, that the choices are limited to exclusion, stereotypical inclusion or appropriation. Aboriginal media and Aboriginal participation in mainstream media offer an alternative, as one northern Aboriginal broadcaster declared:

Many of the myths and misperceptions that persist among non-Aboriginal people are perpetuated by no communication, poor communication, or one-sided communication....The depth and diversity of the Aboriginal perspectives must be communicated through both First Nations and mainstream news media, to as broad a public as possible....

Bud White Eye
Native News Network
Toronto, Ontario, 3 November 1992

Two examples of media treatment of Aboriginal experience demonstrate the effects of stereotyping and, conversely, authentic self-portrayal.

Stereotyping in the media

The common role of the media in constructing and representing Aboriginal identity, community and culture is illustrated in what some media outlets called the 'Indian summer' and others called the 'Oka crisis' or the 'Mohawk crisis' of 1990.[34]

That year, Mohawk assertions of neglected land rights led to the erection of barricades at Kanesatake and Kahnawake. Confrontations between townspeople, police, army and First Nations people focused on the immediate, local frustrations of the bridge blockade, the death of an officer of the Sûreté du Québec, and Canadian Armed Forces occupation of the area surrounding Kanesatake. The historical and national issues of Mohawk autonomy, heritage and land rights tended to be noticed only as a backdrop. When Mohawk 'warriors' barricaded themselves in the alcohol treatment centre at Kanesatake, a stand-off ensued that lasted 78 days and resulted in the deployment of 4,000 Canadian soldiers to support police at the barricades.

The events at Oka are remembered for startling media images of rock-throwing residents and scuffling Indians, staring soldiers and crying children. But in all the television, radio and newspaper coverage, one image was repeated again and again: that of the 'warriors' – bandanna-masked, khaki-clad, gun-toting Indians.[35] The image bore a remarkable resemblance to the war-bonneted warrior – the dominant film and media image of Aboriginal men in the last century.[36] As journalist Lynda Powless stated in her testimony before the Commission,

> Non-Native reporters showed us through their spotty and dismal understanding of the issues that led to and provoked Oka and subsequent coverage, that they are not as well-versed in Native issues as they pretend to be.
>
> Lynda Powless
> Native Journalists Association
> London, Ontario, 11 May 1993

When the barricades came down on 26 September 1990, 63 people left the treatment centre at Kanesatake: 27 Aboriginal men of various nations; one non-Aboriginal 16-year-old; 16 Aboriginal women; 6 children; and 10 reporters. This was the group that elicited such a powerful show of force by the Canadian state.

For many Aboriginal people, the warriors depicted by the non-Aboriginal media blurred the distinction between actively promoting Aboriginal land and treaty rights and initiating armed confrontation. For young Aboriginal men who are seeking meaning in their lives and who are impatient with the slowness of negotiated change, the role of armed defender of lands, culture and a nation's dignity has a powerful appeal.

The ideology underlying violent confrontation is not shared by all or even many in the Aboriginal community. The intensity and importance of the issues easily transforms differences into conflict, which is heightened by a lack of information addressing the complexities that Aboriginal people need to sort out:

> When you don't have an informed public, you have the kind of chaos that exists in Native communities, the kind of social rifting that is occurring and isn't being closed because people don't know what is going on. They hear the myths and the misunderstandings and misinterpretations that build, and they create problems when you don't have a free press.
>
> Lynda Powless
> Native Journalists Association
> London, Ontario, 11 May 1993

In the aftermath of Oka, books, magazine articles, and radio and television programs about Aboriginal peoples have proliferated.[37] But most of this material continues to be written and produced by non-Aboriginal people. As long as other Canadians appropriate the stories, experience, culture and spirituality of Aboriginal peoples, Aboriginal people will remain stereotyped, misunderstood and ultimately unheard. There is an urgent need therefore for Aboriginal media to assume the role that story-tellers used to fulfil, fostering the discovery and rediscovery of Aboriginal identity and community:

> There is no end to the stories that need to be told out there, and they are not being told. I think they are being told from a perspective that does not reflect Native reality. In order for Native people to achieve those goals, they have to begin to share their stories with one another and share their experiences and achievements and successes and failures, and whatever else, with one another. Along with everything else that was undermined and destroyed or wiped out were our communication methods, and our ways of speaking and telling were undermined as well. I feel that the Native media play a role in rediscovering or re-inventing those things.
>
> Miles Morrisseau
> Editor, *Native Beat*
> London, Ontario, 11 May 1993

The potential of Aboriginal media to reinforce identity and community while providing a bridge to participating in the larger society is demonstrated in the history of broadcasting in the north.

Self-portrayal in the media

> We might liken the onslaught of southern television and the absence
> of native television to the neutron bomb....Neutron bomb television
> is the kind of television that destroys the soul of a people but leaves
> the shell of a people walking around. This is television in which the
> tradition, the skills, the culture, the language count for nothing. The
> pressure, especially on our children, to join the invading culture
> and language and leave behind a language and culture that count for
> nothing is explosively powerful.[38]

The extension of television broadcasting into the Arctic in the 1960s was quickly
perceived by Inuit as a threat to their culture, vastly accelerating the process of cultural displacement that had gained momentum in the post-war period and prompt-
ing Inuit efforts to regain control of communications within their territories.

Mainstream Canadian technology and communication techniques have
played a critical role in the social history of the Indigenous peoples of the
north.[39] Technology, trade in goods, and communication techniques reinforced
non-Aboriginal authority, commercialized and restricted Aboriginal access to
information, and promoted cultural replacement. At the same time, story-
telling lost much of its function and legitimacy in Inuit society as cultural information became marginalized by the social and economic force of non-Aboriginal
society. As southern institutions moved north, they established an English or
French language 'monopoly of knowledge'.

Although radio was available in the north by the 1930s, it provided little
information for Inuit; the first Inuktitut program was not broadcast until 1960.
Television followed a similar exclusionary pattern. In 1967, television programming was introduced to a number of Western Arctic communities, but there
was no Aboriginal language programming until well into the 1970s. In 1972,
at a time when few Inuit spoke English, Canada began operating the world's first
domestic satellite communications system, established largely to bring southern
information to the north. In 1974, the Canadian Broadcasting Corporation
received funding for an accelerated coverage plan for communities of more
than 500, but no money was allocated to programming. The result was of little
relevance to northern Aboriginal people. As pointed out in a 1983 federal discussion paper on communications in the north, "Viewers in Baker Lake, N.W.T.
receive the volleyball scores from the Avalon Peninsula...and viewers in Old Crow
in the Yukon watch the crocuses blooming in Vancouver in mid-winter".[40]

But the real impact of television was far more pernicious:

> The arrival of television in the region in the 1970s presented the
> greatest danger to culture and language....[A]mong the Inuvialuit,
> everybody visited one another. Younger people like myself, years

ago, would go round and visit with the elders and sit down and listen to them talk about how they used to hunt, what sort of traps they used before the leghold traps were introduced to us here in the north. [Now,] homes in the area are bombarded with information and entertainment from the consumer-driven south, material that has little relevance to this land-based culture.

Billy Day
Inuvialuit Communications Society
Inuvik, Northwest Territories, 6 May 1992

Over the two decades following the advent of television in the north, Aboriginal people became increasingly aware of the medium's role in expanding southern cultural values and the social and economic dominance first established by earlier communications technologies.

There is evidence to indicate that oral tradition, including storytelling, has remained a basic element of Inuit culture despite its neglect in non-Aboriginal communication systems. Oral cultures tend to foster links to the past and the authority of tradition. They build consensus based on shared attitudes and values that have been affirmed by the telling and retelling of stories. Although younger Inuit who know their own language are increasingly literate in English or French, they have never completely lost the cultural features of shared information, consensus and kinship rooted in the oral tradition. It is the sharing of knowledge rooted in cultural and spiritual experience that allows Aboriginal people to adapt to a changing, often alien environment. While the pressures of cultural change may emphasize the cultural distance between younger and older Inuit and their isolation, they also increase the importance of sharing information, knowledge and values about both modern and traditional life. The oral tradition helps younger Inuit maintain a connection to the land, and it reinforces their identity and self-esteem, easily injured by the realization that they are less adept at hunting and trapping and less knowledgeable about life on the land than their elders and forebears. Television is ideally suited to either sustaining or displacing these oral traditions:

Over 90 per cent of the homes in the northern communities have a television set. As a Native journalist, I know this can definitely be one way to maintain a strong sense of Aboriginal identity in our changing environment.

Shirley Cook
Native Communications Society of the Western Arctic
Yellowknife, Northwest Territories, 8 December 1992

The establishment of an Inuit presence in northern broadcasting proceeded along both political and technological paths, as described in an essay on social change:

Throughout the 1970s ITC [Inuit Tapirisat of Canada] and other Native organizations mounted criticism of the policies and impact of public television broadcasting in the North. In 1980 the national broadcast licensing body, the Canadian Radio-television and Telecommunications Commission (CRTC) established a committee to investigate the extension of satellite television services in northern and remote regions of Canada. At the committee hearings ITC presented a proposal calling for the establishment of an Inuit broadcasting system. The CRTC supported the proposal and in 1981 the Inuit Broadcasting Corporation (IBC), serving central and eastern Arctic communities, became a reality. A federal government grant of $3.9 million provided the initial funding base for television production by several northern Native communications societies including IBC. Satellite facilities were shared with the CBC. The first IBC program was aired on January 11, 1982, reaching twenty-six northern communities.

Acquisition of the technical capability to assume responsibility for Inuit-controlled broadcasting had been proceeding in parallel with political action. Beginning in 1971 the CBC had sponsored experimental projects in community television production in northern Native communities. These typically involved training of Native personnel in the use of hand-held cameras and videotaping equipment, and providing access to community transmitters for broadcast of community events, and exchange of videotapes between communities. Another federal agency, the National Film Board, had also conducted training workshops in media techniques and equipment usage in two Inuit communities, and several other communities had been involved throughout the 1970s in projects sponsored by the federal Department of Communications, testing the use of technology to link communities interactively via satellite radio signals, rebroadcasting signals for community viewing, and producing Inuktitut language programming for broadcast by the CBC.[41]

Within a decade Inuit moved from the simplest forms of story-telling to producing television news, dramas, documentaries and children's programs. These new 'northern stories' reflect Inuit understanding of the role of contemporary media in cultural and social formation and awareness of the part played by oral tradition in constructing and confirming Inuit culture. They give Inuit the opportunity to see and hear the past they share with their elders. Although television is primarily a visual medium, it has been adapted to reflect the style and cadences of an oral tradition. The following description is typical of the network's cultural programs.

The story is told almost totally through visual elements shot in combination of subjective and objective camera perspective, predominantly through primary movement. None of the pieces has narration. Dialogue is minimal.... Synchronous natural sound predominates....The pace of the programs is slow by U.S. and southern Canadian standards.[42]

As with cultural programs, IBC's information and public service broadcasts and children's and entertainment programs reflect oral tradition through their association with Inuit history, myth and experience. Inuit television reinforces Inuit identity and cultural stability and Inuit capacity to direct social and political change in northern territories.

3.2 Aboriginal Media

Broadcasting

The modern era of Aboriginal communications began when Aboriginal peoples, uniting against the assimilative implications of the federal government's 1969 White Paper on Indian Policy, realized that they lacked channels to inform their people and to receive feedback from them. Several provincial Aboriginal organizations began communications units, which eventually formed the basis for independent Aboriginal communication societies when a core-funding program (the Native Communications Program) was established by the Secretary of State (now Canadian Heritage) in 1972. A three-year community radio pilot project, sponsored by the federal department of communications in Big Trout Lake, Ontario, and the Keewatin community of Baker Lake, was the forerunner of the Wawatay Native Communications Society. The National Film Board's Cape Dorset film workshop evolved into the Nunatsiakmiut Native Communication Society in the 1970s. By the mid-1970s, the players in the development of Aboriginal broadcasting were in place: politicized Aboriginal organizations; Aboriginal communications societies, with framework funding; government-sponsored local media projects; and initial northern broadcasting policies. The communication societies continued to increase in number and developed radio programming and newspapers in response to community and regional needs. Throughout the 1970s, they were also involved in technological innovation, particularly experimental satellite projects. At the same time, however, Aboriginal people were contending with an ever-increasing array of mainstream media bombarding their communities.

In 1980, the Canadian Radio-television and Telecommunications Commission (CRTC) issued a report on the extension of service (known as the Therrien committee report).[43] Canadian regulatory policy explicitly recognized the relationship between broadcasting and cultural and linguistic integrity, particularly with regard to Aboriginal people. The report asserted that government has a responsibility to assure the provision of broadcasting that supports Aboriginal languages and cultures and set out as principles the widespread participation of northern Aboriginal people in all aspects of media programming, in regulatory decision making, and in broadcasting distribution based on 'fair access' and 'consultation'.

Implementation of these principles led to the establishment of the Secretary of State's Northern Native Broadcast Access Program in 1983. It originally complemented the Native Communications Program, providing an additional $13.4 million per year to assist production, distribution and broadcasting by northern Aboriginal communications societies.

Another phase began in 1990. The Northern Broadcasting Policy was restructured as the Native Broadcasting Policy, with wider application of the Therrien committee principles. The federal government also approved $10 million to establish Television Northern Canada (TVNC), a satellite channel that provides television distribution for most of the northern Aboriginal communications societies. But there were two severe setbacks: the budget for the Northern Native Broadcast Access Program was drastically reduced, and the Native Communications Program was terminated. Funding for communications societies providing Aboriginal newspapers and radio in southern communities south of the 55th parallel (known as the 'Hamelin line') and for the National Aboriginal Communications Society was thus completely eliminated.[44] The impact was predictable: eight of the 21 societies were forced to close their doors. Aboriginal media, however, have established a toehold in the north:

> From early beginnings as newsletters or local radio initiatives, [Aboriginal communications] has grown to be comprised of several hundred local radio stations, 11 regional radio networks, the beginnings of a national Aboriginal radio network, six television production outlets, a pan-northern Aboriginal television network called Television Northern Canada, and numerous newspapers.
>
> Catherine MacQuarrie
> Yellowknife, Northwest Territories
> 9 December 1992

> Some of the Aboriginal communications initiatives over the years were just temporary, and others have somehow died along the way, but they all gave birth to a rather vibrant network of professionals who have become a unique element of the Canadian public communication landscape, albeit poorly paid and in some cases unemployed....I represent a dozen communications societies spanning most of the land mass of Canada and about 200 print, radio and tele-

vision professionals. I also represent Aboriginal mass media designed and developed by Aboriginal peoples, run by Aboriginal peoples and used by Aboriginal peoples. These societies are all located north of what they call the Hamelin line.

Ray Fox
National Aboriginal Communications Society
Vancouver, British Columbia, 15 November 1993

Aboriginal media today consist of a wide range of loosely knit services and resources.[45] However, they remain uneven, relatively limited, and largely restricted to regions of the north.

Biennial audience surveys indicate that Aboriginal language programming is vitally important, especially for older people who often speak neither English nor French. As a result, the percentage of respondents who watch or listen to Aboriginal programming when it is available is very high.[46] The surveys also suggest that Aboriginal audiences have acquired new knowledge and skills related to their languages, traditions and contemporary environment through Aboriginal media. There is strong interest in extending Aboriginal-language programming and in providing programs for youth, who make up the majority of the population in most communities. By increasing the presence and legitimacy of Aboriginal languages, broadcasting reinforces the interest and language competence of younger Aboriginal community members and helps slow the growing linguistic and generation gap between them and older unilingual members.

The original production guidelines for the Northern Native Broadcast Access Program set a weekly target of five hours of television and 20 hours of radio. These targets were drawn from an Irish study on the maintenance of less-used languages of the European Community. Aboriginal-language broadcasting is a clear priority for Aboriginal communications societies, and most have gone well beyond this target, especially in radio. IBC broadcasts exclusively in Inuktitut.

Language is intimately associated with culture but is not its only element. The 1990 Native Broadcasting Policy recognized this by defining an Aboriginal undertaking not only in relation to the preservation of languages and cultures but also in relation to ownership and control, target audience and programming. Shared experience is also a key element of identity, and Aboriginal media play a vital role in providing information and reflecting Aboriginal perspectives on community life and activities.

Newspapers

Five of the 13 surviving Aboriginal communications societies publish weekly, biweekly or quarterly newspapers. Others are published by Aboriginal publishers and organizations, entrepreneurs and volunteers. They range from the quarterly *Kinatuinamot Illengajuk*, an inflight magazine for Air Labrador (no longer published), to the nationally circulated *Windspeaker*. Their publication diffuses and legitimizes Aboriginal languages, provides outlets for Aboriginal voices and talents, and distributes information that facilitates Aboriginal people's participation in their own cultural, economic and political development.

Although Aboriginal newspapers and journalists play some part in providing non-Aboriginal Canadians with accurate information in its correct context, much remains unreported or grossly misrepresented:

> The depth and diversity of the Aboriginal perspective must be communicated, through both First Nations and mainstream news media, to as broad a public as possible. Current efforts to remedy inaccuracies in mainstream news coverage of Aboriginal issues are an important beginning, but they are far from enough [The] stories that are coming out that are not from a Native perspective, coming from the mainstream media, are still causing us harm.
>
> Bud White Eye
> Native News Network
> Toronto, Ontario, 3 November 1992

Aboriginal newspapers have always struggled to survive, facing problems of staffing, journalism training and funding. Before 1990, the Native Communications Program provided $3.2 million of annual funding for 11 Aboriginal newspapers; only four have survived the program's elimination.

Regional Disparities

> [W]hen the government drew that invisible line across the country and said that these communities north of this line need communication societies to preserve their languages, to preserve their songs, they gave them money for satellite networks, radio, printers for the newspapers and in the south we didn't get that. So when we started our radio station at Six Nations, we used that against the CRTC and told them that it was a form of genocide because they didn't give us the opportunity in the south to access those kinds of money so we could preserve our languages as well.
>
> Elaine Bomberry
> Association for Native Development
> in the Performing and Visual Arts
> Toronto, Ontario, 2 June 1993

However justified by the particular needs of northern Aboriginal peoples, different communications policies on either side of the Hamelin line and elimination of the Native Communications Program in 1990 have fostered inequities. Although more than half of Aboriginal people live in the south, Aboriginal communications in that part of the country received 75 per cent less funding than those in the north.[47] This has engendered understandable bitterness among southern Aboriginal media.

Aboriginal media have nevertheless developed in the south on a local level through the efforts of community volunteers and support from band councils and Aboriginal organizations. But it remains demoralizing for Aboriginal communications enterprises to operate with outdated equipment and inadequate resources alongside public broadcasters and cable operators with state-of-the-art equipment:

> For us to get access to that money and produce and distribute the programs for which the money was intended in the first place, we have to stop being broadcasters and become bureaucrats....You have to wonder how often Mansbridge and Gzowski have to go argue with Treasury Board to get a new microphone for their studio.
>
> Ray Fox
> National Aboriginal Communications Society
> Vancouver, British Columbia, 15 November 1993

The CRTC has been involved throughout the 1990s in licensing specialty broadcasting services directed to specific market segments. Seven new cable television networks began broadcasting in 1995. Still, Aboriginal programming on southern English and French networks has been sparse. On English networks, the popular CBC drama *North of 60* is one of the most visible programs featuring Aboriginal people and Aboriginal issues. A series called *The Rez* had a limited run in 1996. Current affairs programming is limited to Vision TV's *Aboriginal Voices* and rebroadcasts of *NEDAA*, the Aboriginal current affairs show produced by Northern Native Broadcasting (Yukon) on CBC Newsworld. CBC Newsworld rebroadcast *NEDAA* in marginal weekend time-slots from 1989 to 1994. *Our Native Land*, a weekly CBC radio program, was cancelled in the 1980s when the CBC reinforced regional radio programming. On the French side, with the exception of Radio-Québec's weekly television programs *Matinées autochtones* and *Nations*, most Aboriginal programming is done on an ad hoc basis.

3.3 Conclusions and Recommendations

During the past 24 years, satellites have become a driving force in Canadian communications, with fibre optics for telephone and data transmission added more recently. These will be key elements in the continuing strength of the Canadian cable industry and in trends toward competition, privatization and integration of telecommunications services. The information highway now reaches across the country, and satellites that broadcast directly to individual homes are on the horizon. Debate continues over the definition, mandate and role of public broadcasting and narrowcast, or specialty, services. And as advances in technology encourage shifts in interaction, control and culture, Aboriginal broadcasting and print media are increasingly vulnerable and increasingly important to the social and cultural well-being of Aboriginal communities.

Aboriginal broadcasting in the north has demonstrated its effectiveness as a first service for Aboriginal audiences and its ability to operate as a full partner in the Canadian broadcasting system. The communications services Aboriginal media have begun to provide are fundamental to Aboriginal access to and participation in the cultural, social, economic and political realities of both Aboriginal and non-Aboriginal life in the north and the south.

Commissioners heard many concerns from Aboriginal people regarding broadcasting and other means of communications. The most persistent and pressing related to four key issues: policy and legislative frameworks, access, training and funding.

Policy and legislation

The 1983 Northern Broadcasting Policy, rewritten as the Native Broadcasting Policy in 1990, was a vital step toward the creation of media institutions that recognize Aboriginal peoples. As a statement of principle, it established a framework to support northern Aboriginal access and representation in broadcast media. But although both policies led to legislation that recognizes Aboriginal broadcasting, current policies and legislation do not meet the requirements of Aboriginal-language broadcasting or address the needs of all Aboriginal people.

The 1986 Caplan-Sauvageau report on broadcasting policy recommended that Aboriginal-language broadcasting be entrenched in the *Broadcasting Act*: "The broadcasting act should affirm the right of native peoples to broadcasting services in aboriginal languages considered to be representative where numbers warrant and to the extent public funds permit".[48]

Aboriginal broadcasters have repeatedly requested, without success, that this recommendation be acted upon. While the new *Broadcasting Act* passed in 1991 refers to the right of Aboriginal peoples to broadcast in Aboriginal languages, the principle of fair access to Aboriginal-language programming is not included.[49] This means that the regulatory process cannot deal with access to Aboriginal-language broadcasting.

The special status of Aboriginal-language broadcasting should be recognized in legislation. Aboriginal-language broadcasting needs should be reflected in the terms of licences granted by the CRTC to public and commercial broadcasters in regions where there are significant Aboriginal populations. In addition to guaranteeing fair access, the CRTC should consider simplifying the application process for community radio, holding regular hearings in Aboriginal communities, and employing more Aboriginal people. Aboriginal broadcasters look to the CRTC to create a supportive environment for the development of Aboriginal broadcasting.

RECOMMENDATIONS

The Commission recommends that

Special Status of
Aboriginal-
Language
Broadcasting

3.6.11

The government of Canada recognize the special status of Aboriginal-language broadcasting explicitly in federal legislation.

CRTC Require
Representation of
Aboriginal
Programming

3.6.12

The Canadian Radio-Television and Telecommunications Commission include in licence conditions for public and commercial broadcasters, in regions with significant Aboriginal population concentrations, requirements for fair representation and distribution of Aboriginal programming, including Aboriginal language requirements.

Access

Aboriginal people's access to the media is closely associated with issues of policy, legislation and, ultimately, funding. The major concerns expressed to Commissioners by Aboriginal broadcast and print journalists focused on four related areas: access to mainstream media; broader access to media networks in regions of the north that do not receive TVNC; Aboriginal media for Aboriginal people living south of the Hamelin line; and assurance of access to information and media independence.

Access to mainstream media is critical to achieving wider understanding of Aboriginal identity and realities:

> The country's large newspapers, TV and radio news shows often contain misinformation, sweeping generalizations, and galling stereotypes about Natives and Native affairs. Their stories are usually presented by journalists with little background knowledge or understanding of Aboriginals and their communities. The large media outlets include shamefully few Aboriginals either on their staff or among their freelance journalists. As well, very few so-called mainstream media consider Aboriginal affairs to be a subject worthy of regular attention....The result is that most Canadians have little real knowledge of the country's Native peoples or of the issues that affect them.
>
> Charles Bury
> Canadian Association of Journalists
> Ottawa, Ontario, 15 November 1993

The Aboriginal voice will be heard only if it is included as a regular part of the Canadian media landscape. This also requires Aboriginal employees in production and management positions in southern and northern media institutions. But as the 1992 report of the House of Commons Standing Committee on Communications and Culture noted, "Employment equity is not currently afforded to Canada's aboriginal peoples...by many of our cultural industries".[50]

The past 25 years have produced many trained and experienced Aboriginal journalists and broadcasters whose talents are wasted by unemployment or under-utilized by part-time, occasional work. The media industry, including private broadcasters, must increase the number of Aboriginal people at all levels. If this is not accomplished voluntarily, the CRTC should monitor employment equity plans and, if necessary, incorporate them in licensing conditions. Moreover, those responsible for appointments should ensure Aboriginal representation on management boards and other policy agencies of Canadian public cultural industries, including the CBC and the CRTC.

Essential to countering the perpetuation of media stereotypes of Aboriginal people and neglect of Aboriginal issues and concerns is the inclusion and distribution of Aboriginal media products on a regional and national basis south of the Hamelin line. There is currently no national Aboriginal radio programming and only one television program.

The Caplan-Sauvageau report recommended creating a third national broadcasting network, an autonomous Aboriginal-language service similar to the CBC and Radio-Canada networks.[51] This would be an ideal answer to the question of southern access. But given the cost and the current economic environment, it does not seem realistic. There are, however, other options. In particular, for the relatively modest price of a satellite downlink, cable networks could carry TVNC and independent Aboriginal programming. The cost, including English or French sub-titles for Aboriginal-language productions, management, technology and distribution, could be recovered through designated fees or as part of a joint venture arrangement with public and commercial broadcasters. In addition, CBC and Radio-Canada should be mandated to purchase and broadcast Aboriginal programming, both regionally and nationally.

In many regions, Aboriginal broadcasting distribution agreements depend upon the goodwill of station or network broadcasters. CBC and commercial media that have Aboriginal broadcasting agreements almost always operate in an environment of conflicting audience and commercial interests. This has led to marginal broadcast time and limited agreements. Unless Aboriginal broadcasting and Aboriginal-language programs are given priority in regions with Aboriginal audiences, this will not change. In view of commercial pressures and perceptions of competitive disadvantage, this can probably be accomplished only by licence conditions. While the actual amount of programming time will vary from region to region, public and private broadcasters alike should be required to carry a specific quantity of Aboriginal radio and television programming that realistically reflects Aboriginal perspectives. Equally important, Aboriginal programming should receive a fair share of time slots that are attractive to Aboriginal audiences.

Finally, Aboriginal broadcasters and journalists, like their non-Aboriginal counterparts, are concerned about access to information, independence and freedom of expression. At times, they may be at odds with political leaders in communities:

> What all these stories amount to is that there is no such thing as freedom of the press in Indian country....Unfortunately, in many of our communities, our political leaders are not ready for Native journalists....Instead of seeing an article questioning a certain policy, they view that journalist's questioning as a personal attack upon themselves.

Lynda Powless
Native Journalists Association
London, Ontario, 11 May 1993

The relationship of an Aboriginal press to new institutions of self-government will require clarification to address such concerns.

RECOMMENDATIONS

The Commission recommends that

Access to Aboriginal Media Products
3.6.13
Public and private media outlets, in particular the Canadian Broadcasting Corporation, provide access to Aboriginal media products for Aboriginal and non-Aboriginal Canadians by
  (a) purchasing and broadcasting Aboriginal programming from independent Aboriginal producers; and
  (b) producing English and French versions of original Aboriginal programs for regional and national redistribution.

Employment Equity in Public and Private Media
3.6.14
Public and private media outlets address the need for training and better representation of Aboriginal people in public communications by developing and implementing employment equity plans.

Freedom of Expression for Aboriginal Media
3.6.15
Governments, including Aboriginal governments, recognize the critical role that independent Aboriginal print and broad-

cast media have in the pursuit of Aboriginal self-determination and self-government, and that they support freedom of expression through

(a) policies on open access to information; and

(b) dedicated funding at arm's length from political bodies.

Training

Journalism and broadcasting training is a long-standing concern of Aboriginal people involved in media. With the exception of a communication arts program at the University of Regina, attempts to establish Aboriginal training programs have been short-lived. The Aboriginal journalism program at the University of Western Ontario has closed, and a program planned for Arctic College has failed to materialize. A small number of Aboriginal students attend general communications, film and journalism programs at Canadian universities and colleges, but most Aboriginal journalists and broadcasters are trained on the job. Media training is an important part of the work of Aboriginal communications societies, but the Northern Native Broadcasting Access Program does not fund training. It therefore takes place on an ad hoc, in-house basis.

There is a clear need to establish stable and accessible training for Aboriginal broadcasters and journalists (see also Recommendation 3.6.14).

RECOMMENDATION

The Commission recommends that

Aboriginal Access to Media Training
3.6.16
Colleges and universities with programs in communications, journalism and film co-operate to support access for Aboriginal students by providing transition courses, scholarships and counselling services.

Funding

Commissioners heard from those involved in Aboriginal communications and media activities that the establishment of an adequate, stable financial base is critical for Aboriginal communications societies and newspapers, radio and television:

> We view ourselves as Native broadcasters in Canada. We view ourselves as part, a very critical part, of the public broadcasting system

in Canada....[W]e are part and parcel of the public broadcasting
system, and we feel that the resources are not adequate. They have
never been adequate from whatever program that's been available,
and in order for us to maintain our audience, our languages, our culture, it is critical that those resources be made available to us.

Ron Nadeau
Native Communications Incorporated
Thompson, Manitoba, 1 June 1993

Evaluations of the Northern Native Broadcasting Access Program, carried out
in 1986 and 1993, found that inadequate funding, the absence of funds for training and equipment renewal, and a greater need for independence on the part of
the broadcasters constituted basic flaws in the program structure.[52]

The extent and timing of the 1990 and 1993 cutbacks left the communications societies and Aboriginal newspapers unprepared for the necessary
financial adjustments and all but eliminated the development of new Aboriginal
initiatives, especially in the south. In 1990, $2.2 million was cut from the
Northern Native Broadcasting Access Program (NNBAP), a $3.45 million cut
eliminated the Native Communications Program, and another cut of $800,000
eliminated the Native Distribution Fund, which helped societies pay TVNC
access fees. A disproportionate share of the cuts to Secretary of State's annual
budget thus came at the expense of Aboriginal communications programs.

Although Aboriginal journalists and broadcasters recognize the economic
pressures on governments to control spending, the financial compression experienced by the journalists is particularly debilitating for a number of reasons.
First, broadcasters who are members of TVNC must balance production and distribution expenditures with those in other areas; the 1990 funding cuts require
that a greater proportion of their budgets be allocated to TVNC access, reducing
the resources available for production. Second, decreased funding has meant that
a higher proportion of funds from the NNBAP are used for administration and
less goes to the communications societies. Third, the impact of the cuts was
heightened by the societies' lack of infrastructure for revenue generation. In addition, advertising has limited revenue-raising potential in the north because of
monopolies and the small market. Fourth, aging equipment, limited and over-
extended staff, and increasing media demands were a challenge before the cuts
were announced. Finally, although northern Aboriginal broadcasters are constantly pressured to expand their services, they have never received sufficient
funding.

The elimination of funding for Aboriginal communications societies and
media south of the Hamelin line has posed even greater difficulties for many
Aboriginal communities. As noted earlier, only four of the 11 newspapers
funded by the program have survived. Funding is not available to establish or

even maintain Aboriginal radio stations, television programming or media resources in southern reserve or urban areas.

Solutions for funding Aboriginal communications must address the need for long-term, stable support of the current communications system and the development of initiatives in both southern and northern Canada. Funding strategies must reflect the central role of Aboriginal media in addressing issues of concern to all Aboriginal people and the service goals that Canada's unique system of public and private broadcasting is designed to meet. At the same time, solutions must respond to the current financial constraints on governments and Aboriginal communities and the limits of alternative sources of revenue, such as advertising.

During its deliberations, the Therrien committee discussed requiring pay-television enterprises to allocate a small percentage of the fees they collect to supporting Aboriginal broadcasting. The proposal was ultimately discarded because of the unstable nature of the pay-TV market in 1980; however, cable networks have flourished in the intervening years, and the time has come for the CRTC to re-examine supporting the broadcasting initiatives of Canada's First Peoples through the cable television fee structure. The CRTC should also examine the establishment of licensing conditions and a regulatory climate that favour production and distribution joint ventures between Aboriginal and non-Aboriginal enterprises.

RECOMMENDATIONS

The Commission recommends that

Fees and Joint Ventures to Finance Aboriginal Media Products

3.6.17

The Canadian Radio-Television and Telecommunications Commission be mandated to establish fee structures and provisions for joint ventures as part of licensing conditions to ensure a stable financial base for the production and distribution of Aboriginal broadcast media products, particularly in southern Canada.

Core Funding and Incentives for Private Support

3.6.18

Federal, provincial, territorial and Aboriginal governments provide core funding for Aboriginal media that

(a) is accessible to all Aboriginal nations and communities;

(b) builds upon existing government programs and Aboriginal media organizations;

> (c) results in long-term funding agreements that realistically reflect Aboriginal media requirements and promote self-financing; and
>
> (d) encourages private and corporate support through tax incentives.

4. PUBLISHING

Aboriginal peoples' oral traditions – transmitting cultural knowledge, history, values and world views through storytelling – can be documented in dramatic productions, dance performances, petroglyphs and artifacts such as birch bark scrolls, totem poles, wampum belts and masks. More recently, Canada has begun to see a new form of expression of the Aboriginal voice in the emergence of Aboriginal literature.

In the early years of this century, Pauline Johnson became the first Aboriginal author published in Canada. After her death in 1913, almost six decades passed before Aboriginal authors reappeared on the Canadian literary scene. In the late 1960s and early '70s, an explosion of Aboriginal literature coincided with a surge in Aboriginal political awareness and organization. Many of the books published in this period were political in content and angry in tone. Driven by social activism and written in many cases by authors who, freed from the residential school system, had successfully pursued college and university educations, these works were often marked by the presentation of distinctly Aboriginal ideas in a typically mainstream literary style.

Although the number of publications fell during the late 1970s and early '80s, an identifiably Aboriginal form of literature began to appear. While aspects of traditional story-telling had been present in earlier work, these years saw the Aboriginal voice expressed in new modes. Although this voice is certainly not monolithic, certain elements tend to recur in the new literature. It gives authority to the voices of all people in the story, rather than a principal narrator. It gives authority to the voices of animals and messages conveyed by spirits and natural phenomena. And it spans large periods of time, illustrating the Aboriginal notion that all time is closely connected and actions can transcend time.[53]

Among the literature from this period, Lee Maracle's novel *Sundogs* is written in a style that she calls "contemporary Aboriginal voice". It is not divided into chapters, and the story-line often digresses along apparent tangents whose relevance is not immediately apparent, recalling the oratorical style of elders in storytelling or ceremonial settings. Jeanette Armstrong shocked some of those preoccupied with gender politics by writing *Slash* from a first-person male perspective. She explained that this was based partly on the cultural belief that each sex is capable of assuming the characteristics of the other.[54] Tomson Highway's plays are remarkable for their ability to move from the metaphysical domain to ordinary reality, and they include characters who transcend these domains. There are many more examples.

The emergence of a distinct Aboriginal literature has not, unfortunately, been met with much openness by Canadian publishing houses and bookstores. While the major publishers have published numerous books *about* Aboriginal people, Aboriginal authors, almost without exception, have been published by small, independent presses. In major bookstores, creative works by Aboriginal authors are usually found in the Aboriginal studies section, not the literature section, leading Kim Blaeser to remark, "No, I'm not a poet, I just write Indian stuff."[55]

There are about 20 Aboriginal publishers in Canada.[56] Most are in a precarious financial situation and have had little success in obtaining funding from government programs. While almost all Canada's established non-Aboriginal publishers obtain Canada Council block grants, only two Aboriginal presses do so. In 1992, the federal department of communications established the Book Publishing Industry Development Program (BPIDP) to provide substantial annual block funding to eligible publishers, and the Publishing Distribution Assistance Program (PDAP), which provides more modest funding to help meet the costs of mailing and distribution. These are now administered by Canadian Heritage, which also offers publication project funding through its Heritage Cultures and Languages Program. According to reports from Aboriginal publishers, only one Aboriginal publisher received BPIDP and PDAP funding; in 1993-94, it lost the more substantial BPIDP grant. No funding from the Heritage Cultures and Languages Program has ever gone to an Aboriginal publisher, although an average of 12 publishers receive funding each year. Most provinces also have modest block and project funding programs, but the story is no different; only two Aboriginal presses have ever received funding.[57]

In March 1995, the Canada Council acknowledged the need to improve its support for Aboriginal arts and literature by establishing a First Peoples Secretariat and a First Peoples Committee to advise the council. It also adopted a series of objectives and initiatives intended to assist Aboriginal artists in new and traditional forms of expression. In particular, it undertook to ensure that its programs are relevant and inclusive and that Aboriginal perspectives are better reflected in the council's program guidelines and criteria and through the appointment of Aboriginal people to juries, advisory committees and staff.[58]

While the Canada Council's initiative is certainly welcome, much more needs to be done to provide an adequate and fair level of support for Aboriginal writers and publishers. Although Aboriginal languages and culture remain deeply rooted in the oral tradition, literary expression of the Aboriginal voice is vital to affirming the identities of Aboriginal peoples: first, because literature presents an authentic voice to the majority population in a medium with which it is familiar; and second, because it presents that same authentic voice and mirror for their identity to Aboriginal people themselves. To survive in the dominant culture, Aboriginal people are becoming more and more conversant with the literary tradition and the Aboriginal stereotypes with which it is replete. The dissemination of authentic Aboriginal voices is essential to educate Canadians about the rich heritage, knowledge and culture of Aboriginal peoples and to expose misrepresentation and misappropriation of Aboriginal identities.

5. VISUAL AND PERFORMING ARTS

Art is both the reflection and the extension of history, myth and spirituality. The arts are a bridge between traditional Aboriginal values and world views and contemporary Aboriginal lives. Whether they explore traditional forms, modern forms, or both, Aboriginal arts and artists are part of the evolving cultures of Aboriginal peoples. Their art not only defines distinct Aboriginal cultures but contributes greatly to the cultural definition and identity of Canada, as evidenced, for example, in the recent installation of a sculpture by Aboriginal artist Bill Reid as a focal point of the Canadian embassy in Washington, D.C.

Like Aboriginal writers, Aboriginal visual and performing artists strengthen and affirm Aboriginal identities and cultures in the eyes of Canadian society and the world at large. Their art can play an important role in destroying stereotypes. But at the same time, they must be free to explore the limits of creativity and bring its social and cultural fruits to their home communities:

> Inuit and Native settlers' arts and crafts are a functional and living expression of our cultural identity and tradition....They must be promoted and encouraged as a source of pride in our own self-reliance, skills, imagery, creativity, and as a focal point for our cultural history, our economy and our creative activities.
>
> Henoch Obed
> Labrador Inuit Alcohol and Drug Abuse Program
> Nain, Newfoundland and Labrador, 30 November 1992

The work of Aboriginal artists has not generally been represented in public galleries. Joan Vastokas observes:

> Because both traditional Native art and contemporary art by living artists of Native ancestry are stored and exhibited, not in the National Gallery as so many of us had hoped, but in the Canadian Museum of Civilization in an archaeological and ethnological context, the old debate as to where Native art more properly belongs – in the sphere of art or ethnological artifact – has been brought to a most pronounced head....By not incorporating Native art in the planning of the new National Gallery, a loud and clear statement has been made to the world that art produced by Native persons belongs not to the history of Canadian art but to ethnology.[59]

This kind of categorizing betrays an expectation that Aboriginal artists should produce traditional, or recognizably 'Aboriginal' art forms. It is yet another example of how, in most areas of their heritage and culture, Aboriginal people have often been unable to control or even influence significantly the way their artistic expressions are presented to the non-Aboriginal public. They have seldom had representatives on national or provincial arts bodies or on the boards or staff of national arts institutions.

As with most aspects of Aboriginal peoples' heritage and culture, funding is also a problem. In the performing arts, for example, grant structures and criteria have tended to favour established, mainstream companies and productions. The Department of Indian Affairs and Northern Development (DIAND) provides a reasonable level of support for the promotion of Inuit art and training in Aboriginal performing and visual arts, but little support for performing arts productions.[60] The major source of funding for the performing arts in Canada is the Canada Council. The council does not keep statistics on the ethno-cultural origins of artists it funds, but there is a widespread perception among Aboriginal artists that grant allocations to Aboriginal productions are disproportionately low. A task force on professional training for the cultural sector noted in 1991 that "Native groups often have difficulty breaking through cultural barriers to obtain grants from mainstream agencies".[61] Low Levels of grant support have a ripple effect, making private fundraising more difficult.

Historically, the Canadian arts community has had the support of individual patrons, private charitable foundations, and a variety of small, medium and large corporations. Although Canadian corporations do purchase Aboriginal visual art, their support for the performing arts is generally directed to non-Aboriginal forms of expression such as performances by symphony orchestras and ballet and opera companies. The impetus to do so is twofold. First, more and more corporations link their support to marketing of their products and services. Aboriginal people tend to be ignored as a potential market because they are a widely dispersed and economically disadvantaged minority. Second, the lack of support for Aboriginal arts from public agencies means that a corporation must make a far larger contribution to achieve the same ends. The National Ballet of Canada, for example, receives core funding from the Canada Council, the Ontario Arts Council, and local arts councils. When it produces a new ballet, it may require corporate sponsorship only for discrete items such as new sets and the choreographer's fee. It also has a substantial subscription list from which a sponsor may benefit. The ballet company and sponsor can readily agree on the value of the ballet and the level of sponsorship; in fact, market prices already exist for a variety of mainstream productions. Aboriginal companies have none of these advantages. When the Canadian Native Arts Foundation produced its major dance production, *In the Land of Spirits*, in 1988, it had to raise the entire $1 million needed to stage it.

Other barriers to recognizing and affirming the role of Aboriginal arts in defining the cultural identities of Aboriginal peoples and Canada generally are systemic. Art education, for example, should be an important part of elementary, secondary and adult education in both Aboriginal and non-Aboriginal communities. But many experienced Aboriginal artists have been excluded from teaching because they lack formal academic credentials. The artists' talents should be recognized as valuable, not wasted. One successful model to which other provincial governments might look is Alberta's Artists in Schools program.[62]

Aboriginal artists also need access to better training in an environment that nurtures and celebrates their distinct cultural endeavour. The Institute for American Indian Arts in Santa Fe, New Mexico, was often suggested to the Commission as a model by Aboriginal artists.[63]

Addressing these issues requires the support of governments, cultural agencies and institutions, and the private sector. But although the creative process needs their support, its integrity demands that patrons remain at arm's length and respect the cultural and artistic autonomy of the artists and performers. This is especially true of Aboriginal arts, which must overcome marginalization and stereotyping to become a mirror for their own peoples and an expression and affirmation of identity for Aboriginal people relative to the larger society. In other words, those who assume the role of patron also assume a responsibility to listen carefully as Aboriginal artists and performers express their experience, dreams and aspirations in their unique voices.

Because the fostering of Aboriginal artistic talent has been woefully neglected in Canadian institutions, and because the distinctive expression of Aboriginal voice, rooted in a spiritual world view and ceremonial performance, has been actively suppressed, we see the need for active support of Aboriginal arts for at least a generation while Aboriginal arts, literature and performance are being revitalized. Such support should be over and above the recognition of Aboriginal arts by mainstream cultural granting agencies.

RECOMMENDATIONS

The Commission recommends that

Aboriginal Arts Council **3.6.19**

Federal, provincial, territorial and Aboriginal governments cooperate to establish and fund an Aboriginal Arts Council, with a minimum 20-year life span and an annual budget equivalent to five per cent of the Canada Council budget, to foster the revitalization and development of Aboriginal arts and literature.

Arts Granting
Criteria Relevant
to Aboriginal Arts

3.6.20

Governments, public agencies and private organizations that provide support for the visual and performing arts, in co-operation with Aboriginal artists and performers, review all aspects of their programs to ensure that

(a) criteria for grants and awards are relevant to Aboriginal arts and artists; and

(b) Aboriginal people and perspectives are adequately represented on decision-making bodies, juries, advisory committees and staff.

Arts Training and
Facilities

3.6.21

Federal, provincial, territorial and Aboriginal governments, in co-operation with Aboriginal artists, writers and performers, support and promote the revitalization and development of Aboriginal literary, visual and performing arts through

(a) support of training programs in schools, cultural institutions and professional associations, and participation of Aboriginal students in professional studies in the arts; and

(b) accommodating requirements for appropriate display and performance of Aboriginal arts in the design of public facilities in Aboriginal communities and the community at large.

Notes

1. Royal Commission on Aboriginal Peoples (RCAP), *Choosing Life: Special Report on Suicide Among Aboriginal People* (Ottawa: Supply and Services, 1995), p. 25.

2. Leroy Little Bear, "Relationship of Aboriginal People to the Land and the Aboriginal Perspective on Aboriginal Title", research study prepared for RCAP (1993). For information about research studies prepared for RCAP, see *A Note About Sources* at the beginning of this volume.

3. This topic is also explored in some detail in RCAP, *Treaty Making in the Spirit of Co-existence: An Alternative to Extinguishment* (Ottawa: Supply and Services, 1995).

4. Staff communication with Mark Douglas concerning the Mnjikaning Fish Fence Circle, 27 October 1995.

5. A response from the Peigan Nation by Chief Leonard Bastien and Mrs. Audrey Bastien, Brocket, Alberta, to Glenbow Museum, in "Contact Continues: Museums,

First Nations and Their Changing Relationships", 25th Annual Chacmool Conference, University of Calgary, 12-15 November 1992.

6. Assembly of First Nations [AFN] and Canadian Museums Association [CMA], Task Force Report on Museums and First Peoples, *Turning the Page: Forging New Partnerships Between Museums and First Peoples* (Ottawa: 1992).

7. *Cultural Property Export and Import Act,* R.S.C. 1985, c. C-51.

8. For more information on friendship centres, see Volume 4, Chapter 7. We also set forth in that chapter recommendations to strengthen and enhance the role of friendship centres in promoting Aboriginal culture. See also National Association of Friendship Centres, brief submitted to RCAP (1993). For information about briefs submitted to RCAP, see *A Note About Sources* at the beginning of this volume.

9. Linda Jules, *Challenges and Choices: Federal Policy and Program Proposals for Canadian Museums* (Communications Canada: 1988).

10. See Deborah Doxtator, "Aboriginal People and Museum Policy in Canada", research study prepared for RCAP (1994).

11. AFN and CMA, *Turning the Page* (cited in note 6), p. 4.

12. Anne Noonan and Marc Denhez, "Native Arts, Crafts and Fakelore: Legal and Administrative Options and Recommendations", research study prepared for RCAP (1994).

13. D. Soyini Madison, "Seeing Is Believing", *New York Times Book Review* (28 February 1993), p. 23.

14. World Intellectual Property Organization, *Model Provisions for National Laws on the Protection and Expression of Folklore Against Illicit Exploitation and Other Prejudicial Actions* (WIPO and UNESCO, 1985). The provisions define four categories of folklore: verbal expression, musical expression, expressions "by action" (of the human body), and "tangible expressions" (material objects). By way of example, the last category includes "drawings, paintings, carvings, sculptures, pottery, terracotta, mosaic, woodwork, metalware, jewellery, basket weaving, needlework, textiles, carpets, costumes, musical instruments, architectural forms".

15. Assembly of First Nations, "Reclaiming Our Nationhood: Strengthening Our Heritage", brief submitted to RCAP (1993), pp. 143-144.

16. See, for example, the United States' *Native American Graves Protection and Repatriation Act,* Pub. L. 101-601, 104 Stat. 3048, 16 November 1990; and Australia's *Aboriginal and Torres Strait Islander Heritage Protection Amendment Act 1987,* No. 39 of 1987.

17. Rita Joe, "Four Poems by Rita Joe", *Canadian Woman Studies* 10/2&3 (Summer/Fall 1989), p. 28.

18. In Volume 1, Chapter 2, we identified 53 First Nation linguistic-cultural groupings. See Ruth Norton and Mark Fettes, "Taking Back the Talk: A Specialized

Review on Aboriginal Languages and Literacy", research study prepared for RCAP (1994). J.D. Kaye lists 54 'Indian' languages to which the Aleut-Eskimo languages (Inuktitut) must be added: "The Indian Languages of Canada", in *The Languages of Canada*, ed. J.K. Chambers (Montreal: Didier, 1979), pp. 15-19. Michael K. Foster identifies 53 distinct languages in "Canada's First Languages", *Language and Society* 7 (Winter/Spring 1982), p. 7; M. Dale Kinkade, "The Decline of Native Languages in Canada", also provides a list of Canadian Aboriginal languages and indicates where they are spoken, in Robert H. Robins and Eugenius M. Uhlenbeck, eds., *Endangered Languages* (Oxford: Berg Publishers, 1991), pp. 157-176. Information on linguistic affiliation can be gathered from J. Chambers, ed., *The Languages of Canada* (cited earlier in this note); Foster, "Canada's First Languages" (cited earlier in this note); and the *Handbook of North American Indians*, ed. W. Sturtevant (Washington: Smithsonian Institution), Vol. 17 (forthcoming); L. Campbell and M. Mithun, eds., *The Languages of Native America: Historical and Comparative Assessment* (Austin, Texas: University of Texas Press, 1979). See also Jacques Maurais, *Les langues autochtones du Québec* (Quebec City: Publications du Québec, 1992).

19. See Kinkade, "The Decline of Native Languages" (cited in note 18).

20. Note that the accuracy of census and Aboriginal Peoples Survey numbers is affected by under-reporting in some Aboriginal populations. See Volume 1, Chapter 2 for discussion of data sources and data used in this report.

21. Lynn Drapeau, "Perspectives on Aboriginal Language Conservation and Revitalization in Canada", research study prepared for RCAP (1995).

22. On the basis of previous census data, Kinkade had already judged the following languages near extinction: Tagish (Athapaskan), Southern Tsimshian, Abenaki (Algonquian), Han (Athapaskan), Straits Salish, Nitinaht (Wakashan), Tahltan (Athapaskan), Squamish and Sechelt (Salish), and Sarcee (Athapaskan). See Kinkade, "The Decline of Native Languages" (cited in note 18), p. 161.

23. See Kinkade, "The Decline of Native Languages"; Norton and Fettes, "Taking Back the Talk"; and Maurais, *Les langues autochtones du Québec* (all cited in note 18), which contains data indicating that Mohawk is also declining rapidly.

24. See Robins and Uhlenbeck, *Endangered Languages* (cited in note 18).

25. See Jared Diamond, "Speaking with a Single Tongue", *Discover* 14 (February 1993), p. 78.

26. Stephen A. Wurm, "Language Death and Disappearance: Causes and Circumstances", in *Endangered Languages* (cited in note 18), p. 1.

27. Lynn Drapeau, "Issues in Language and Education for Aboriginal Populations in Quebec", research study prepared for RCAP (1995). See also Peter Berliner, who noted the same attitude among Inuit in Greenland despite quite extensive development of Inuktitut literacy: "Cognitive Style and Attitudes in Bilingual Inuit",

in *Bilingualism and the Individual – Copenhagen Studies on Bilingualism*, Volume 4, ed. A. Holmen et al. (Philadelphia: Multilingual Matters, 1988), pp. 275-290.

28. Research conducted in Betsiamites, a Montagnais community in northern Quebec, has revealed that while the Aboriginal language is still flourishing there, an increasing number of people, mostly in the younger age groups, consider that speaking the Aboriginal language is not a necessary feature of their identity. In other words, it is conceivable for them to be 'Indian' without being able to speak an Aboriginal language. See Anne-Sophie Oudin and Lynn Drapeau, "Langue et identité ethnique dans une communauté montagnaise bilingue", *Revue québécoise de linguistique* 22/2 (1993), pp. 75-92.

29. S. Clarke and M. MacKenzie, "Education in the Mother Tongue: Tokenism versus Cultural Autonomy in Canadian Indian Schools", *Canadian Journal of Anthropology* 1/2 (Winter 1980), p. 205.

30. Statistics Canada, "1991 Census of Canada", *The Daily*, 12 January 1993, catalogue no. 11-001E, p. 12.

31. See Sylvie Vincent and Bernard Arcand, "L'image de l'Amérindien dans les manuels scolaires du Québec, ou Comment les Québécois ne sont pas des sauvages", in *Collection cultures amérindiennes* (Montreal: Éditions Hurtubise HMH, 1979); and Sylvie Vincent, "The Importance of Fences: Reflections on the Marginalisation of North American Indians", *Anthropologie et sociétés* 10/2 (1986), pp. 75-83. See also Donald B. Smith, "Le Sauvage: The Native People in Québec in Historical Writings on the Heroic Period (1534-1663) of New France", *National Museum of Man Mercury Series* (Ville Lasalle, Quebec: Éditions Hurtubise HMH, 1974).

32. Beverly Slapin and Doris Seale, *Through Indian Eyes: The Native Experience in Books for Children* (Gabriola Island, B.C.: New Society Publishers, 1992), p. 1.

33. For more on books for children and youth, see the following articles by Sylvie Vincent: "L'aventure et ses limites: les Amérindiens dans l'œuvre fantastique pour la jeunesse de Daniel Sernine", *Recherches amérindiennes au Québec* 17/3 (1987), p. 79; and "Les livres pour enfants, terrains de jeux idéologiques", *Recherches amérindiennes au Québec* 18/4 (1988), p. 87. Regarding films, see Martin Lefevre, "La représentation de l'Indien dans le cinéma américain", *Recherches amérindiennes au Québec* 17/3 (1987), p. 65.

34. See Volume 1, Chapter 7 for detail on the historical context of these events; and Gail Valaskakis, "Rights and Warriors: First Nations, Media and Identity", *Ariel: A Review of International English Literature* 25/1 (January 1994), p. 60. For a perspective presented by an Aboriginal film-maker, Alanis Obonsawin, see *Kanehsatake 270 Years of Resistance* (National Film Board, 1993).

35. "Rough Justice: Ottawa Buys Some of the Disputed Land, But the Mohawk Standoff at Oka Continues", *Maclean's*, 103/32 (6 August 1990), p. 18; "The Fury of Oka: The Crisis at the Barricades Lends Urgency to the Search for Solutions", *Maclean's*, 103/32 (6 August 1990), p. 16; "Mohawk Militancy", *Ottawa Citizen*, 15 September 1990, p. B1; "The Mohawk Warriors: Heroes or Thugs?", *Toronto*

Star, 24 November 1990, p. D1; "The Making of a Warrior", *Saturday Night* (April 1991), p. 30; Aislin, "Mafia Warrior" (editorial cartoon), *Montreal Gazette*, 30 April 1990, p. B2.

36. See Gail Valaskakis, "The Role, Development and Future of Aboriginal Communications", research study prepared for RCAP (1995). See also Carmen Michaud, "De l'exotisme au réel: le racisme", *Recherches amérindiennes au Québec* 21/1-2 (1991), p. 111.

37. Agnès Gruda, editorialist at *La Presse*, calculated that the number of articles written about Aboriginal issues in Quebec's French-language newspapers jumped from 200 to more than 2,000 a year for three years following the events at Kanesatake. See her editorial, "Oka, cinq ans après", *La Presse*, 7 December 1995, p. B3.

38. Rosemarie Kuptana, former president of the Inuit Broadcasting Corporation, now president of Inuit Tapirisat of Canada, cited in Debbie Brisebois, "The Inuit Broadcasting Corporation", *Anthropologica* 25/1 (1983), p. 107.

39. See Gail Valaskakis, "A Communicational Analysis of Interaction Patters: Southern Baffin, Eastern Arctic", PH.D dissertation, McGill University, 1979; and "Broadcasting and Native Northerners", in Helen Holmes and David Taras, eds., *Seeing Ourselves: Media Power and Policy in Canada* (Toronto: Harcourt Brace Jovanovich Canada Inc., 1992).

40. Communications Canada, DIAND, and Secretary of State, "Northern Broadcasting", discussion paper on northern communications, Ottawa, 18 February 1983.

41. Marlene Brant Castellano, "Aboriginal Organizations in Canada: Integrating Participatory Research", in *Voices of Change: Participatory Research in the United States and Canada,* ed. Peter Park et al. (Toronto: OISE Press, 1993), p. 148.

42. K. Madden, "The Inuit Broadcasting Corporation: Developing Video to Sustain Cultural Integrity", presented to the Annual Meeting of the International Communication Association, Dublin, Ireland, 1990.

43. Canadian Radio-Television and Telecommunications Commission, *The 1980s, A Decade of Diversity: Broadcasting, Satellites, and Pay-TV*, Report of the Committee on Extension of Service to Northern and Remote Communities (Ottawa: Supply and Services, 1980).

44. The 'Hamelin line' is drawn at the 55th parallel and defines the Canadian North for purposes of policy. See Valaskakis, "The Role, Development and Future of Aboriginal Communications" (cited in note 36), as well as Volume 4, Chapter 6.

45. For a description of the activities of the 13 Aboriginal communications societies, which are core-funded by the Northern Native Broadcast Access Program, see Valaskakis, "The Role, Development and Future of Aboriginal Communications".

46. See H. Hudson, *The Need for Native Broadcasting in Northern Canada: A Review of Research* (Ottawa: Department of Secretary of State, 1985). Native Communications Incorporated reported that 91 per cent of viewers watched its

television programs and 84 per cent listened to its radio programs. Ron Nadeau, Native Communications Inc., transcripts of hearings of the Royal Commission on Aboriginal Peoples, The Pas, Manitoba, 19 May 1992.

47. Wolfwalker Communications, "Communication Policy and Aboriginal People", research study prepared for RCAP (1994).

48. *Report of the Task Force on Broadcasting Policy* (Ottawa: Supply and Services, 1986), p. 519.

49. *Broadcasting Act*, S.C. 1991, c. 11, s. 3(1)(d)(iii).

50. House of Commons, Standing Committee on Communications and Culture, *Culture and Communications: The Ties that Bind* (April 1992), p. 46.

51. *Report of the Task Force on Broadcasting Policy* (cited in note 48).

52. Lougheed and Associates, *Report on the Native Communications Program and the Northern Native Broadcast Access Program* (Ottawa: Secretary of State, 1986); Austin Curley and Associates, *Evaluation Report: Northern Native Broadcast Access Program* (Ottawa: Secretary of State, 1993).

53. Kim Blaeser, "Papers from 'Returning the Gift': North American Native Writers' Conference", *'All of US'*/Akwe:kon 10/1 (Spring 1993), p. 35.

54. Hartmut Lutz, *Contemporary Challenges: Conversations with Canadian Native Authors* (Saskatoon: Fifth House Publishers, 1991).

55. Blaeser, "Returning the Gift" (cited in note 53).

56. Aboriginal publishers are profiled in Greg Young-Ing, "An Overview of Aboriginal Literature and Publishing in Canada", research study prepared for RCAP (1995).

57. Data collected through an Aboriginal publishing network that came together 17-20 August 1995 at Simon Fraser University for the National Aboriginal Publishers' Conference, organized by En'owkin Centre and Theytus Books Ltd.; see Young-Ing, "An Overview".

58. Canada Council, *A Design for the Future* (Ottawa: Canada Council, 1995).

59. Joan M. Vastokas, *Beyond the Artifact: Native Art as Performance*, The Fifth Robarts Lecture, 7 March 1990 (North York, Ontario: Robarts Centre for Canadian Studies, 1992), pp. 13-15.

60. The Inuit Art Section, established in 1974, provides $500,000 yearly to the Inuit Art Foundation. The Canadian Native Arts Foundation, funded partly by DIAND, disbursed over $700,000 in training grants to the Aboriginal arts community in fiscal year 1994-95. DIAND also provides minimal support for promoting First Nations visual art through the Indian Art Section, created in 1967 to establish a collection. Its initial annual acquisitions budget of $100,000 has never been increased.

61. *Art is Never A Given: Professional Training in the Arts in Canada*, Report of the Task Force on Professional Training in the Arts in Canada (Ottawa: Minister of Supply and Services Canada, 1991), p. 101.

62. Alberta Foundation for the Arts, *Artists in Schools Residency Program Guidelines*, 1994.

63. One proposal supported by a wide range of Aboriginal organizations and individuals would see a multi-purpose facility providing training and a variety of media, exhibition and performing space built on vacant land (the former Daly building site) in the heart of Ottawa, close to Parliament Hill.

Appendix 6A

Excerpts from
Turning the Page: Forging New Partnerships Between Museums and First Peoples[*]

III. Results of Consultations

The regional consultations and responses to the call for submissions have provided a national perspective on the needs and aspirations of First Peoples with regard to museums and cultural collections. The range of needs and aspirations identified reflects the cultural diversity of Aboriginal people in Canada. The level of development of thinking and action on the issues identified by the Task Force varied substantially. In some locations consideration of these issues was being undertaken, for all intents and purposes, for the first time. In other localities, cooperative relationships between museum and Aboriginal communities were well established and flourishing. Similarly, it was readily apparent that solutions, both presently operational ones and ones that were required, varied from one region to another, often substantially. However, while it was recognized that a common solution was perhaps not possible it was generally agreed that improvements, often fundamental ones, were needed in the relationship between museums and Aboriginal communities and that the Task Force was an appropriate mechanism to achieve this objective.

The consultations also demonstrated that museums and cultural institutions are well aware of the necessity and the value of working as equal partners with First Peoples. There is a strong consensus that partnerships should be guided by moral, ethical and professional principles and not limited to areas of rights and interests specified by law. The many case studies of collaborative efforts indicate that partnerships have been underway for some time in many cultural institutions across the country....

The major findings of the national consultations by the task force are outlined below.

A. The Importance of Cultural Objects in Museum Collections

The importance of cultural objects is recognized. These objects represent cultural history and values and are therefore sources of learning, pride and self-esteem. The primary concern of First Peoples is with the importance of cultural collec-

---

[*] Report of the Task Force on Museums and First Peoples (Ottawa: Assembly of First Nations and Canadian Museums Association, 1992).

tions to their own particular communities. Nonetheless, there is also a general recognition that these collections, and the institutions that care for them, serve a wider function and can contribute to greater public education and awareness of the significant cultural contributions made by First Peoples. Also, scientific investigation and reporting on museum collections are valuable means of obtaining and interpreting information on matters of culture and heritage. In the broad sense, museums are identified as having the potential to engage with living cultures, not just objects.

B. Increased Involvement of First Peoples in Interpretation

"Interpretation" as discussed in the reports and submissions includes all facets of museum administration, research, public program, and exhibition planning, and the presentations that result from such planning. There is agreement that increased involvement of First Peoples in museum work is essential in order to improve the representation and interpretation of First Peoples' histories and cultures in museums.

The major focus of discussions has been on the interpretation of First Peoples culture and history in public exhibitions. It was agreed that the role of First Peoples in Canadian history should be stressed. This approach should replace the stereotyped exhibitions that depict First Peoples as dying, primitive and inferior cultures, or as cultures isolated from Canada's history, in "pre-history" galleries. The linkage between Aboriginal heritage and the present circumstances of First Peoples should also be represented; in fact, museums should become forums for discussions of relevant contemporary issues.

C. Improved Access to Museum Collections

"Collections" include not only human remains and artifacts, but also information associated with these materials: research results, photographs, works of art, and any other information related to First Peoples culture and history held in cultural institutions.

"Access" encompasses not only physical access to collections for purposes of viewing research, making reproductions and ceremonial use, but also access to funding sources, policy development and implementation activities, as well as training and employment in museums and other cultural institutions.

There is wide agreement that enhanced access to collections related to First Peoples is appropriate and needed. Inventories of existing collections should be carried out as soon as possible and made available to the appropriate First Peoples communities. It was noted that different First Peoples have different customs and will therefore have different interests with regard to utilizing museum collections. Since narrow policies are unlikely to accommodate this diversity, cultural institutions must be flexible with regard to working out access arrangements with First Peoples. It was also recognized that some forms of access would need to be more regulated than others to take into account the selective needs of the material ranging from the religious or traditional manner of dealing with the object to its physically fragile nature.

In addition to First Peoples' access to existing ethnographic collections within museums, there was also discussion of the lack of representation of contemporary Aboriginal art in public art galleries. It was agreed that Canadian art museums should be encouraged to work with artists of First Nations ancestry to enhance their collections and exhibition programming in this area.

Access to museum jobs and training is a widely acknowledged need. Having First Peoples on staff would help to educate other museum personnel with regard to valuable Aboriginal perspectives and philosophies and would imbue a greater sensitivity to community needs and interests in non-Aboriginal museum personnel. At the same time First Peoples would gain greater access to museums and related institutions.

D. Repatriation

There was a consensus in favour of the return of human remains and illegally obtained objects along with certain non-skeletal burial materials and other sacred objects to appropriate First Peoples. In addition, there was some agreement on the return to originating communities of a selection of other objects considered to be of special significance to cultural patrimony.

It was also agreed that First Peoples communities should be able to demonstrate direct prior cultural connection and ownership with regard to collections in question. There should be Aboriginal involvement in determining who is the appropriate person or group to receive any repatriated material.

There is wide recognition that concepts of ownership vary, therefore, a case-by-case collaborative approach to resolving repatriation based on moral and ethical criteria is favoured rather than a strictly legalistic approach. The "Native American Grave Protection and Repatriation Act", recently passed in the United States, was studied by Task Force members. While not ruling out the possibility of the creation of legislation in the future, it was agreed that it was preferable to encourage museums and Aboriginal peoples to work collaboratively to resolve issues concerning the management, care and custody of cultural objects. Proposed guidelines for such a collaborative process follow in the recommendations section.

E. Training

The need for training for both First Peoples and non-Aboriginal museum personnel is critical. To work in established museums, or to develop museums in their own communities, First Peoples need training in all phases of museology.

Conversely, museum personnel need training in the cultures and values of First Peoples in order to better care for and interpret collections and to work more effectively as partners with First Peoples communities.

An inventory of active training programs in museological practice was compiled as part of the Eastern Committee report to the Task Force. Copies will be made available by late January, 1992, through the Canadian Museums Association.

F. Support for Cultural Institutions

The importance of supporting the efforts of First Peoples to manage and conserve their own cultural facilities in their own communities cannot be stressed enough. Community-based cultural centres and programs can reinforce a positive identity, help to heal cultural dislocation and improve educational opportunities for children. These improvements in turn support the realization of socio-economic goals of First Peoples communities.

G. Funding

The Task Force consultations revealed an urgent need for additional funding for projects involving First Peoples in existing Aboriginal or non-Aboriginal museums. Funding is also required to assist First Peoples in establishing their own museums.

H. International Collections

It was agreed that First Peoples need governmental assistance in gaining access to and/or repatriating cultural objects held in collections outside of Canada.

IV. Creating Partnerships: Principles and Recommendations

If museums are to achieve their goal of "interpreting the past, explaining the present and thereby illuminating choices for the future",[1] they must express accurately and in context the cultural heritage and spirit of the civilizations that they portray. In this regard, "The Spirit Sings" exhibition was a watershed in Canadian museology. It has served as a forum for identifying historical problems in the representation of Aboriginal peoples in museums and it has led to the present efforts toward establishing open and lasting partnerships between museums and Aboriginal communities.

Over the years museum exhibitions have usually been based on the assumption that Aboriginal peoples were extinct or on the verge of vanishing. A great portion of existing collections were gathered at the turn of the century when museums and private collectors rushed to collect cultural materials from

Aboriginal communities which, according to the social, scientific and political philosophy of the time, were believed to be well on the way to extinction. Some museum exhibitions reinforced a public perception that Aboriginal cultures existed only in the past and that they were incapable of change. Such perceptions continue to support the mistaken notion that Aboriginal cultures are inferior.

Museums have recognized the failings in such presentations and changes are being made. As well, a number of community-based Aboriginal cultural centres have been established instigating changes of far-reaching impact. Along with some museums the latter have begun to develop new initiatives in cultural representation. However, a great deal remains to be done to set the record straight for a museum-going public accustomed to the old-style presentations.

In order to accurately reflect within museums the fundamental and unique contribution of First Peoples to Canada, as well as the spiritual and social values of their diverse contemporary cultures, it is necessary to develop new relationships with museums based on progressive principles and policy. To quote former AFN National Chief Georges Erasmus again, "We (the Aboriginal peoples) are well aware that many people have dedicated their time, careers and their lives showing what they believe is the accurate picture of indigenous peoples. We thank you for that, but we want to turn the page...".[2]

In order to turn that page, and in the spirit of forging new partnerships, we offer the following principles and recommendations based on regional consultations, the many submissions received from organizations and concerned individuals combined with extensive and productive discussions at three national task force meetings.

A. Principles to Establish Partnerships between First Peoples and Canadian Museums

1. Museums and First Peoples will work together to correct inequities that have characterized their relationships in the past. In particular the desire and authority of First Peoples to speak for themselves should be recognized and affirmed by museums.
2. An equal partnership involves mutual appreciation of the conceptual knowledge and approaches characteristic of First Peoples, and empirical knowledge and approaches of academically-trained workers.
3. First Peoples and museums recognize mutual interests in the cultural materials and knowledge of the past, along with the contemporary existence of First Peoples.
4. First Peoples and museums must accept the philosophy of co-management and co-responsibility as the ethical basis for principles and procedures pertaining to collections related to Aboriginal cultures contained in museums.

5. Appropriate representatives of First Peoples will be involved as equal partners in any museum exhibition, program or project dealing with Aboriginal heritage, history or culture.

6. First Peoples and museums must recognize a commonality of interest in the research, documentation, presentation, promotion and education of various publics, including museum professionals and academics, in the richness, variety and validity of Aboriginal heritage, history and culture.

7. First Peoples must be fully involved in the development of policies and funding programs related to Aboriginal heritage, history and culture.

B. Specific Recommendations to Establish Partnerships between First Peoples and Canadian Museums

The range of needs and aspirations that have been identified reflect the cultural diversity of the First Peoples of Canada. Clearly, no single set of recommendations and policies will adequately address this diversity; rather, a premium has been placed on flexible approaches in the development of partnerships between First Peoples and museums.

It is also recognized that significant funding, human resources and time will be required to make the changes and implement the recommendations outlined here. Accordingly, we offer specific recommendations relating to the issues of funding and human resources in the implementation section [section 5.].

1. Interpretation

a. Museums should ensure that First Peoples are involved in the processes of planning, research implementation, presentation and maintenance of all exhibitions, programs and/or projects that include Aboriginal cultures.

b. Interpretation or representation of information related to First Peoples should conform to an ethic of responsibility to the community represented, as well as to the scholarly or professional ethics of the academic and museum communities.

c. In partnership with First Peoples, museums should refine the nature of information relating to their collections, activities and practices. Identification of items in their collections and in exhibitions using Aboriginal languages is recommended.

2. Access

a. To ensure the proper interpretation and representation of Aboriginal heritage, histories and cultures, museums should provide for the participation of Aboriginal people as members of governing structures and on boards of directors.

b. All museums and art galleries with ethnographic or Aboriginal art collections should develop programs which encompass legitimate opportunities and [encourage] the employment of Aboriginal peoples at all levels of their operations.

c. Museums should recognize the legitimate right of access by Aboriginal peoples to sacred materials, cultural objects and relevant documentation. Aboriginal peoples must also recognize the legitimate concerns of museums with respect to the care, maintenance and preservation of their holdings.

d. In concert with First Peoples museums should develop a workable process to provide full disclosure of existing information relating to Aboriginal collections. Such information will include the scope of the collection, the kinds of objects included, and the geographical location, cultural affiliation, means and period of acquisition.

e. Canadian art museums should work with artists of First Nations ancestry to enhance their collections of contemporary art.

3. Repatriation

This report considers the disposition of Aboriginal cultural patrimony, including human remains, burial objects, sacred and ceremonial objects and other cultural objects that have ongoing historical, traditional or cultural import to an Aboriginal community or culture. The Canadian Museums Association and the Assembly of First Nations should endorse and encourage the adoption of the following guidelines relating to the repatriation of Aboriginal cultural patrimony:

a. Human Remains

(i) Remains of individuals whom evidence indicates are remembered by name must be offered for disposition at the request of the families, their descendants or clan, upon notification of the appropriate First Nations, community, tribes, clan or family members.

(ii) Human remains which evidence indicates may be affiliated with a named First People must be reported to that Nation, community, clan, tribe or family.

(iii) Upon agreement and in cooperation with the museum the appropriate First Nations group may work with scientific interests for a mutually agreed upon period, and may have the remains re-interred according to the appropriate traditional or other religious practices of the First Nation or Aboriginal community.

(iv) The treatment and disposition of remains and associated burial objects that are ancient or that cannot be affiliated with a named First People shall be decided through discussion and negotiation with an advisory committee of First Peoples. The First People may work with scientific interests for a mutually agreed upon time period and may have the remains re-interred in manner consistent with local traditional practices.

(v) Museums that acquire human remains through any means must involve the appropriate First Nation in the treatment and disposition of the remains.

(vi) The retention of Aboriginal human remains for prolonged periods against the expressed wishes of First Peoples is not acceptable.

b. Objects of Cultural Patrimony

The treatment, use, presentation and disposition of sacred and ceremonial objects and any other objects of cultural patrimony should be decided on moral and ethical grounds with the full involvement of the appropriate First Nations as equal partners. In the event of disputes between individuals, between an individual and the community or between communities, the onus should be on the First Peoples to resolve the dispute according to customary practice.

Recommended options for this process include the following:

(i) Restitution or Reversion. This includes the return to an originating culture or individuals of any objects that are judged by current legal standards to have been acquired illegally. This process involves the transfer or return of legal title to an originating culture or individual from the museum, based upon existing legal mechanisms for de-accessioning.

(ii) Transfer of Title. Even in cases where materials have been obtained legally, museums should consider supporting the requests by Aboriginal communities and community-based Aboriginal museums for the transfer of title of sacred and ceremonial objects and of other objects that have ongoing historical, traditional or cultural importance to an Aboriginal community or culture. This involves a case-by-case negotiation with the appropriate communities based on moral and ethical factors above and beyond legal considerations.

(iii) Loan of Materials. Museums should loan sacred and ceremonial objects for use by Aboriginal communities in traditional ceremonies and community festivities, based on mutual agreement on the use and time period in question as well as the risk to the physical object. Again, these decisions should be based on moral and ethical considerations both from the perspective of First Peoples and from that of museum conservation ethics (i.e., respect for the physical and historical integrity of the object).

(iv) Replication of Materials. Museums and First Peoples communities should consider the replication of materials slated either for repatriation or retention by the museum for the use of the other party. Negotiations should be guided by moral and ethical considerations and the traditional knowledge and authority of the First Peoples involved, as well as the scientific knowledge of academically-trained museum personnel.

(v) Shared Authority to Manage Cultural Property. In all cases museums are urged to share management of their collections by involving the appropriate First Peoples in assisting to define access to collections, to determine storage conditions and use of collections, and to recognize traditional authority or individual ownership systems of the originating culture.

c. Repatriation of Foreign Holdings

The CMA and the AFN are urged to promote repatriation of human remains and objects of cultural patrimony held outside the country, subject to the same criteria outlined above under 1 & 2, through lobbying efforts in association with national governments, UNESCO, the International Council of Museums and other professional organizations.

4. Training

a. The CMA and the AFN, with funding provided by the Federal government, should promote the development of professional and technical training initiatives for First Peoples according to community needs and in a culturally appropriate manner.

b. Priority should be given to funding for training programs run by educational institutions and cultural centres controlled by First Peoples.

c. Non-Aboriginal museum professionals should be trained in the Aboriginal cultural knowledge and approaches relevant to museum research, conservation and interpretation.

d. Museums and other cultural institutions should recognize the legitimate credentials of certain individuals and groups within Aboriginal communities who possess knowledge of the particular culture.

5. Implementation

a. The Task Force urges the appropriate federal departments and funding programs, in consultation with the AFN and the CMA, to immediately allocate special funding over a 5 year period beginning in 1992. This funding will assist museums and Aboriginal communities to implement the principles and recommendations advocated by the Task Force. In addition to the items listed below, the initial funding will be used to study ongoing financial needs beyond the five year period. Provincial and territorial governments should also allocate increased funding for training, the development of Aboriginal run museums and cultural centres, as well as collaborative research, training, exhibitions and other special projects between existing museums and First Peoples communities.

The special funding should be allocated to a number of areas including, but not limited to the following:

- to support the proposed 1992 National Conference to discuss the findings, recommendations and implementation of this report;
- to assist in the establishment of Aboriginal-run cultural centres and museums from facility development to training of personnel;
- to assist existing museums to properly inventory their collections of ethnographic materials and to publicize same to the appropriate First Peoples;
- to assist in repatriation negotiations;
- to assist in the establishment of internship and affirmative action programs at existing museums with cultural patrimony or art collections;
- to support collaborative research, training, exhibitions and other projects between museums and First Peoples communities;
- to assist the CMA and the AFN in developing a set of national guidelines based on the principles and recommendations contained in this report;
- to assist the CMA in establishing a documentation centre, with a full-time staff position to assist museums and Aboriginal communities in implementing the recommendations of the Task Force; and
- to fund a joint committee to monitor and report developments over a five year period.

b. The CMA and the AFN are urged to lobby the appropriate federal departments to ensure that the above-mentioned funding initiative is implemented.

c. All federal and provincial funding programs for museums and related cultural institutions should establish criteria to ensure that the institutions receiving financial support adhere to the principles and recommendations contained in this report.

d. The CMA should develop a set of national guidelines with respect to interpretation, access, repatriation, training, and implementation based upon the principles and recommendations contained in this report.

e. The CMA and the AFN should recommend that principles and recommendations similar to those outlined in this report be adopted by cultural institutions other than museums, such as universities and other professional associations.

f. Museums with ethnographic or art collections should identify and publicize to the appropriate Aboriginal communities the specific personnel responsible for facilitating implementation of the principles and recommendations contained in this report.

g. The CMA and the AFN should report annually on the implementation of these principles and recommendations. In particular, the CMA is urged to ensure that a session devoted to the long-term partnerships of First Peoples and museums be an integral part of its annual conferences. These sessions will enable people to report on progress and to devise innovative and creative approaches to collaborations.

h. The CMA should establish a resource-documentation centre, with a full-
time staff position to assist museums and Aboriginal communities in implementing the recommendations of the Task Force.

i. A joint committee made up of members of the Aboriginal and museum communities should be established to monitor developments over the next
decade. The committee should be directly linked to the council of the CMA
and to the executive of the AFN or its designate organization.

j. A public review of progress made over the ten year period should be conducted in the final year to make recommendations on future needs.

NOTES

1. Communications Canada, 1988. Challenges and Choices: Federal Policy and
Program Proposals for Canadian Museums, p. 25.

2. Georges Erasmus, past National Chief, Assembly of First Nations, Opening
Address to "Preserving Our Heritage: A Working Conference for Museums and
First Peoples", Ottawa, November, 1988.

7

CONCLUSION

A GREAT MANY ABORIGINAL PEOPLE in Canada, including First Nations, Inuit and Métis people, male and female, old and young, in isolated northern communities and in urban areas, confront common problems. To an external observer, these problems consist mainly of social and economic disadvantage, and the solutions seem self-evident. Individuals are expected to seize opportunities to improve their situation by advancing their education, competing in the job market, moving from regions of slow economic activity to more promising locations, and adopting healthy lifestyles.

Many have pursued these options, as shown by statistics on education levels, labour market participation, urban migration and health. But on the whole gross disparities persist between the quality of life of Aboriginal people and that of most Canadians. The pain of deprivation and disorder in Aboriginal people's lives is intimately bound up with their identity and experience as peoples. They believe that solutions can be found by drawing together as nations and defining their collective place in Canadian life, rather than in further dispersing their communities and diluting their cultures.

1. COMMON PROBLEMS: COLLECTIVE SOLUTIONS

We are in favour of collective solutions that are complementary to individual efforts, not a rejection of them. The rationale for structural change in the relationship between Aboriginal nations and Canadian society is set out in Volume 2 of this report in terms of Aboriginal peoples' right of self-determination, in terms of justice defined by Canadian law and international norms, and in terms of sound, practical steps and policies to set the relationship between Aboriginal and non-Aboriginal people on a more harmonious and productive course.

In dealing with the social and cultural concerns of Aboriginal people, we emphasize the need to place social issues in the context of political and economic relations with the rest of Canadian society. When adults have meaningful work and a respected role in society, families will be restored to their role of nurturing and protecting their members. When Aboriginal people have a more equitable share in the wealth of the land, and regain the authority to govern themselves, they will shake off the poverty and powerlessness that sap their emotional, intellectual and spiritual vitality. Living conditions that undermine morale and physical well-being must be raised to Canadian standards through the collaborative efforts of individuals, communities, Aboriginal nations and the Canadian state. Education must affirm Aboriginal people as members of historical nations with distinctive cultures, while equipping them to reach out and participate in a global society. The authentic self-expression of Aboriginal people, as individuals and collectivities, must be heard in councils and public media and seen in history books, art galleries and on ceremonial occasions, signalling that the phase of displacement and denial of their presence in Canada has been put behind us forever.

Ideals of equality and respect have appeared consistently in public discourse on Aboriginal policy for the past 25 years.[1] A review of various policy sectors shows, however, that changes in the situation of Aboriginal people relative to the rest of Canadian society have been minimal, halting and, in some areas, retrogressive. Fundamental change will require decisive action, which we believe can be achieved best through recognition of Aboriginal jurisdiction to enact laws and implement policy, with appropriate agreements to harmonize the actions of Aboriginal, federal, provincial and territorial governments.

The social policy sectors discussed in this volume are of vital concern to the life, welfare, identity and culture of Aboriginal nations. We anticipate that these will be among the first areas where Aboriginal governments will exercise authority. It will take time to put self-government agreements in place, however, and the pace of change will vary in different nations, depending on their degree of political development. We therefore see change proceeding on three fronts:

1. negotiations to establish the scope of self-government and the institutional structures through which it will operate within the Canadian federation;
2. transitional measures mandated under the proposed recognition and government act; and
3. policy reform within existing federal, provincial and territorial jurisdictions.

The recommendations in this volume apply in any of these situations. They are based on the premise that Aboriginal people must have the authority to define their problems, establish goals, and mobilize and direct resources, whether these resources are found within their nations and communities or in federal, provincial and territorial government programs.

2. Traditional Culture and Institutions of Self-Government

Aboriginal self-government will have as its core purpose the affirmation and conservation of Aboriginal cultures and identities as fundamental characteristics of Canadian society. It will allow Aboriginal nations and communities of interest to develop institutions that reflect a distinctive world view and diverse forms of social organization. (For more detail, see Volume 2, Chapter 3, where we identify three principal models of self-government – public governments, Aboriginal nation governments, and communities of interest.) Self-government will also be the vehicle for negotiating adaptations in mainstream institutions that serve Aboriginal citizens. It therefore represents a reversal of the intent to 'civilize' and assimilate that drove public policy on Aboriginal affairs for over a century.

It should be understood that self-government does not mean bringing Aboriginal nations into line with predetermined Canadian norms of how peoples should govern themselves. It is the reinstatement of a nation-to-nation relationship. It is the entrenchment of the Aboriginal right of doing things differently, within the boundaries of a flexible *Canadian Charter of Rights and Freedoms* and international human rights standards.

The prospect of Aboriginal peoples pursuing their economic, social and cultural development in ways they freely determine[2] will raise the spectre in some minds of Aboriginal communities as backwaters of under-development, indifferent to the benefits of modernization and forever subsidized by government. This image fits better with the present reality – after more than a century of enforced assimilation – than with the perceptions Aboriginal people have of their cultures and the role their traditions will have in charting a future course.

Aboriginal peoples have survived for millennia because their cultures are dynamic and able to adapt to changing circumstances. This openness to change does not negate their traditional view of reality – that life manifests itself in repeating patterns, in the cycle of days and seasons, and in the universal experience of birth, maturation, decline, death and new birth. Life is not a linear journey in which humanity progresses to ever higher levels of enlightenment. It is a circle, with natural and spiritual laws established from the foundation of the world, and with lessons human beings have been learning throughout thousands of years of history. A good life, a fulfilling life, is gained through knowledge and ethical choice; it is not dictated by technology. A hunter in the bush can learn and abide by natural law – or violate it recklessly. An engineer can build electricity-generating devices in a way that respects the right of all creatures to share the environment – or disregard those rights. So an Aboriginal person who is instructed in and lives by traditional wisdom can live a traditional life in the bush or in the city. People who adhere to traditional ways are not hostile to change and growth; they resist systems and relationships that negate their understanding of natural and spiritual law. (For more discussion of Aboriginal cultures and their relevance to contemporary issues, see Volume 1, Chapter 15.)

Aboriginal people criticize services delivered by agencies external to their nations and communities as culturally inappropriate. Recognition of their nations' jurisdiction over social policy will pave the way for them to devise and legislate their own institutions. This will make room for creativity that does not flourish easily in the context of minority initiatives in mainstream institutions. Some nations have mature institutional arrangements in place already and require only recognition of their role in relation to other laws and authorities in Canada. Other nations will take a cautious approach, testing their capacities in specific initiatives before attempting comprehensive institutional development; still others will continue to look to mainstream institutions to meet their needs.

Distinct institutions will respond to social needs in family support, health and healing, housing, and education and will encourage cultural expression. They will honour traditional knowledge, work out new applications of old wisdom, and synthesize these with insights from mainstream science and institutional practice. The methods of problem solving developed in Aboriginal institutions will provide reference points for what is possible and desirable in mainstream services. Aboriginal institutions will not only deliver services but sustain cultures and identities in the twenty-first century.

While recognition of Aboriginal jurisdiction and development of Aboriginal institutions are central to social change, the needs are so urgent that reforming social policy within existing jurisdictions, and laying the groundwork for transition to self-government, must proceed without delay.

3. POLICY REFORM
AND TRANSITION

Aboriginal nations will be able to exercise authority in core areas of jurisdiction while new or renewed treaties are being negotiated. During the transition, community services will be delivered variously by new institutions mandated under Aboriginal authority; by agencies mandated by federal, provincial and territorial governments but directed by Aboriginal people; and by mainstream institutions that have modified their approaches to provide culturally appropriate services. While structural change is being negotiated, there is an urgent need to implement new approaches that will

1. assign a priority to social policy development;
2. adopt an integrated approach across policy areas and between different governments and government departments; and
3. create space for Aboriginal initiative.

3.1 Social Policy as a Priority

Political and legal reforms will be successful only if they make life better for the ordinary Aboriginal person. This was made very clear in our hearings, where Aboriginal people told us repeatedly that the healing of individuals, families, communities and nations must accompany self-government. Women, in particular, said that social concerns often seemed to be overshadowed by political priorities. At the Special Consultation on Suicide Prevention (convened by the Commission in Ottawa on 7 June 1993), Joey Hamelin of the Métis National Council declared, "Suicide is as important as the constitution."

Political change is essential to progress toward resolving social problems. However, progress should also be seen as an immediate priority and a powerful means of mobilizing the commitment of Aboriginal and non-Aboriginal people to support fundamental structural change. We have set out proposals for movement on social concerns in order to break down the paralyzing sense that problems are so entrenched and pervasive that nothing can be done. We amplify the voice of Aboriginal people, particularly women, who urge their leaders and Canadian governments to recognize that social concerns deserve priority and to pursue action on social policy in concert with political change.

3.2 Integrated Approaches

The way social and community services are organized now contributes to fragmentation of effort, gaps in program coverage and conflict between governments on the extent of their responsibility.

Aboriginal people say it is not helpful to categorize them as patients, parents, offenders, welfare recipients or drug abusers. They are whole human beings with strengths and weaknesses and, above all, the capacity to learn from experience how to use the resources in their environment to solve their problems. In conceptualizing the form of new Aboriginal service organizations, it will be important to avoid replicating a problem-specific group of services. Even under present regimes, however, the constraints on holistic program development can be eased. Healing centres under Aboriginal control and single-window access to adult education and training are examples of holistic services described in earlier chapters of this volume.

When services are being provided, different categories of Aboriginal status are the basis for different treatment. We maintain that, regardless of current distinctions, Aboriginal people share a common entitlement to have their presence as collectivities recognized and affirmed within Canada. They share certain experiences and needs, stemming from culture and history. Where access to appropriate services is restricted or denied because of legal status or place of residence, these inequities should be rectified. Where people experience disadvantaged living conditions because of historical policies that deprived them of resources or services, these disparities should be addressed. Where well-being is threatened by abusive or oppressive treatment implemented or permitted by misguided government policy, enriched services to counter the corrosive effects should be made available.

In Volume 4, Chapter 7, we examine the policy vacuum resulting from conflicts between federal and provincial governments over jurisdiction and responsibility for Aboriginal people living in urban areas. Social housing for off-reserve First Nations and Métis people is just one area where the various orders of government must collaborate to achieve improved levels of well-being.

Where Aboriginal governments with clear authority are established and recognized by federal and provincial governments, there is some prospect of escape from fragmentation, undercoverage and jurisdictional conflict. Even before self-government is implemented, authority and responsibility can be transferred to Aboriginal nations and to agencies mandated by Aboriginal governments and organizations. Conflicts between federal and provincial governments about the locus of responsibility for service delivery and funding support should be resolved promptly. In Volume 4, Chapter 7, we propose an approach for distributing responsibility between federal and provincial governments; even with this approach, however, resolution of conflicts will require a firm commitment to co-operative effort.

3.3 Creating Space for Aboriginal Initiative

There is currently a wealth of Aboriginal initiative and innovation in the field of community services. For example,

- language immersion and daycare involving parents, volunteers and elders in culture-based programming;
- healing circles promoting recovery from the lingering effects of violence;
- Aboriginal child and family services extending conventional limits of child welfare services;
- Métis housing corporations building a sense of community in urban centres;
- Aboriginal colleges and training institutes filling the gap between post-secondary education institutions and self-defined community needs; and
- a whole community engaged in planning a collective future after repeated displacement and years without a land base.

Many such innovations were reported in the foregoing chapters; many more are recorded in our hearings transcripts, briefs and research studies.

There is a widespread sense of anticipation among Aboriginal people that they are about to enter a new era, when their identities as peoples will be recognized, when they will regain control of their lives, and when their knowledge will count in decision-making councils. But their initiatives in social and cultural affairs are struggling for survival on the margins of institutional services that command stable support and professional recognition. Chief Gordon Peters expressed the sense of anticipation and the readiness to assume responsibility in the following words:

> Across the board, a lot is going on right now. It is given different names and takes shape in different circumstances. Some call it healing; some call it regeneration. No matter what it is called, it is the same process – people taking control of their individual lives.
>
> The route that we are going to follow is that we first need to take control of our individual lives, to be able to accept those things that are given to us by the Creator. Then we can talk to our families and then we can talk to our communities. It spreads out and continues until there is an understanding....
>
> That is when you start to have unity of people, as in the expression people coming to one mind. You won't find that in a legislative process, and you won't find it in the constitutional process.
>
> Chief Gordon Peters
Chiefs of Ontario
Toronto, Ontario, 18 November 1993*

Leslie Knight spoke in Yellowknife of the process of rebuilding capacity that must occur, and the necessity of having the resource base to achieve the transformation:

> Over the last few decades individuals and communities have almost been trained to seek solutions outside of themselves, to think that the best solutions will come from professionals, experts and agencies. I think there needs to be some retraining and some careful support of individuals and communities and groups to show them that they have the inherent skills to cope with many of the problems themselves, as long as there are appropriate resources and support given to them.
>
> Leslie Knight
Yellowknife, Northwest Territories
8 December 1992

The challenge for policy makers in the next decade will be to make room for Aboriginal initiative in the institutional life of Canada. Institutions mandated by Aboriginal governments will play a major role in extending the boundaries of what is possible. Mainstream institutions will have an equally important

---

* Transcripts of the Commission's hearings are cited with the speaker's name and affiliation, if any, and the location and date of the hearing. See *A Note About Sources* at the beginning of this volume for information about transcripts and other Commission publications.

contribution in clearing the field for Aboriginal initiative and assuming a collegial rather than a supervisory role. Aboriginal-specific adaptations in mainstream institutions may serve as transitional forms on the way to self-directing Aboriginal institutions, or adapted services may become continuing features of Canadian life.

In some cases legislative changes by federal, provincial or territorial governments will be required to redistribute effort and resources and to provide stable support for Aboriginal initiatives. In other cases, existing programs and regulations can be adjusted to achieve the same ends.

4. ACHIEVING A BALANCE

The prospect that Aboriginal and non-Aboriginal people will operate separate institutions in some cases, share services in others, and help each other to devise the most effective means of meeting social needs harks back to the nation-to-nation relationship envisaged in treaties of peace and friendship. Non-Aboriginal people might describe the change as progress toward greater justice. Aboriginal people are more likely to describe it as a second chance to establish the balanced relationship never realized fully in historical encounters. The practical steps and the financial investment required to implement the new relationship are the subjects of Volume 5.

NOTES

1. See RCAP, *Soliloquy and Dialogue: Overview of Major Trends in Public Policy Relating to Aboriginal Peoples*, volume 1 of *Public Policy and Aboriginal Peoples 1965-1992* (Ottawa: Supply and Services, 1996 (forthcoming)).

2. This is the language used in the Draft United Nations Declaration on the Rights of Indigenous Peoples, as quoted in [1994] 1 Canadian Native Law Reporter 40-47.

Appendix A

Summary of Recommendations in Volume 3

Chapter 2 The Family

The Commission recommends that

Authority for
Child Welfare

3.2.1
The government of Canada acknowledge a fiduciary responsibility to support Aboriginal nations and their communities in restoring Aboriginal families to a state of health and wholeness.

3.2.2
Aboriginal, provincial, territorial and federal governments promptly acknowledge that child welfare is a core area of self-government in which Aboriginal nations can undertake self-starting initiatives.

3.2.3
Aboriginal, provincial, territorial and federal governments promptly reach agreements on the authority of Aboriginal nations and their communities for child welfare, and its relation to provincial, territorial and federal laws respecting child welfare.

Funding Child
Welfare Agencies

3.2.4
Block funding be provided to child welfare agencies mandated by Aboriginal governments or communities to facilitate a shift in focus from alternative child care to family support.

Voluntary Agencies

3.2.5
Until community of interest governments are established in urban and non-reserve areas, voluntary agencies endorsed by substantial numbers of Aboriginal people resident in the areas be authorized under provincial or territorial law to act in the field of child welfare
(a) where numbers warrant; and
(b) with levels of funding comparable to those of agencies providing comparable services to the general population and sufficient to meet the service needs of Aboriginal people.

Leadership Stance **3.2.6**
Aboriginal leaders take a firm, public stance in support of the right to freedom from violence of all members in the community, but particularly of women, children, elders, persons with disabilities and others who may be vulnerable, as well as in support of a policy of zero tolerance of actions that violate the physical or emotional safety of Aboriginal persons.

Breadth of **3.2.7**
Representation
Aboriginal governments adopt the principle of including women, youth, elders and persons with disabilities in governing councils and decision-making bodies, the modes of representation and participation of these persons being whatever they find most agreeable.

Participation of **3.2.8**
Women
The full and equal participation of women be ensured in decision-making bodies responsible for ensuring people's physical and emotional security, including justice committees and boards of directors of healing centres and lodges.

Community Codes **3.2.9**
of Behaviour
Aboriginal leaders and agencies serving vulnerable people encourage communities, with the full participation of women, to formulate, promote and enforce community codes of behaviour that reflect ethical standards endorsed by the community and that state and reinforce the responsibility of all citizens to create and maintain safe communities and neighbourhoods.

Core Area of Self- **3.2.10**
Government
Federal, provincial and territorial governments promptly acknowledge that the field of family law is generally a core area of Aboriginal self-governing jurisdiction, in which Aboriginal nations can undertake self-starting initiatives without prior federal, provincial or territorial agreements.

Validity of **3.2.11**
Customary Law
Federal, provincial and territorial governments acknowledge the validity of Aboriginal customary law in areas of family law, such as marriage, divorce, child custody and adoption, and amend their legislation accordingly.

Consultation on **3.2.12**
Family Law
Aboriginal nations or organizations consult with federal, provincial and territorial governments on areas of family law with a view to

(a) making possible legislative amendments to resolve anomalies in the application of family law to Aboriginal people and to fill current gaps;

(b) working out appropriate mechanisms of transition to Aboriginal control under self-government; and

(c) settling issues of mutual interest on the recognition and enforcement of the decisions of their respective adjudicative bodies.

Family Law **3.2.13**
Committees
With a view to self-starting initiatives in the family law area or to self-government, Aboriginal nations or communities establish committees, with women as full participants, to study issues such as

(a) the interests of family members in family assets;

(b) the division of family assets on marriage breakdown;

(c) factors to be considered in relation to the best interests of the child, as the principle is applicable to Aboriginal custody and adoption;

(d) rights of inheritance pertaining to wills, estates or intestacy; and

(e) obligations of spousal and child support.

Chapter 3 Health and Healing

The Commission recommends that

Fundamental **3.3.1**
Principles
Aboriginal, federal, provincial and territorial governments, in developing policy to support health, acknowledge the common understanding of the determinants of health found in Aboriginal traditions and health sciences and endorse the fundamental importance of

- holism, that is, attention to whole persons in their total environment;

- equity, that is, equitable access to the means of achieving health and rough equality of outcomes in health status;

- control by Aboriginal people of the lifestyle choices, institutional services and environmental conditions that support health; and
- diversity, that is, accommodation of the cultures and histories of First Nations, Inuit and Métis people that make them distinctive within Canadian society and that distinguish them from one another.

Health: A Core Area of Self-Government **3.3.2**
Governments recognize that the health of a people is a matter of vital concern to its life, welfare, identity and culture and is therefore a core area for the exercise of self-government by Aboriginal nations.

Action to Agree on Jurisdiction and Service Delivery **3.3.3**
Governments act promptly to
(a) conclude agreements recognizing their respective jurisdictions in areas touching directly on Aboriginal health;
(b) agree on appropriate arrangements for funding health services under Aboriginal jurisdiction; and
(c) establish a framework, until institutions of Aboriginal self-government exist, whereby agencies mandated by Aboriginal governments or identified by Aboriginal organizations or communities can deliver health and social services operating under provincial or territorial jurisdiction.

Health Effects of Policy **3.3.4**
Governments, in formulating policy in social, economic or political spheres, give foremost consideration to the impact of such policies on the physical, social, emotional and spiritual health of Aboriginal citizens, and on their capacity to participate in the life of their communities and Canadian society as a whole.

Four-Part Strategy **3.3.5**
Governments and organizations collaborate in carrying out a comprehensive action plan on Aboriginal health and social conditions, consisting of the following components:
(a) development of a system of Aboriginal healing centres and healing lodges under Aboriginal control as the prime units of holistic and culture-based health and wellness services;
(b) development of Aboriginal human resources compatible with the new system, its values and assumptions;

(c) full and active support of mainstream health and social service authorities and providers in meeting the health and healing goals of Aboriginal people; and

(d) implementation of an Aboriginal community infrastructure development program to address the most immediate health threats in Aboriginal communities, including the provision of clean water, basic sanitation facilities, and safe housing.

Healing Centres and Lodges

3.3.6

Federal, provincial and territorial governments collaborate with Aboriginal nations, organizations or communities, as appropriate, to

(a) develop a system of healing centres to provide direct services, referral and access to specialist services;

(b) develop a network of healing lodges to provide residential services oriented to family and community healing;

(c) develop and operate healing centres and lodges under Aboriginal control;

(d) mandate healing centres and lodges to provide integrated health and social services in culturally appropriate forms; and

(e) make the service network available to First Nations, Inuit and Métis communities, in rural and urban settings, on an equitable basis.

Laws, Regulations and Funding to Support Integrated Services

3.3.7

Federal, provincial and territorial governments collaborate with Aboriginal nations, regional Aboriginal service agencies, community governments and Aboriginal organizations, as appropriate, to adapt legislation, regulations and funding to promote

(a) integrated service delivery that transcends restricted service mandates of separate ministries and departments;

(b) collaboration and shared effort between federal, provincial/territorial and local governments; and

(c) the pooling of resources flowing from federal, provincial, territorial, municipal or Aboriginal sources.

Transform Current Services

3.3.8

Aboriginal organizations, regional planning and administrative bodies and community governments currently administering health and social services transform current programs and services into more holistic delivery systems that integrate or co-ordinate separate services.

Planning and **3.3.9**
Needs Assessment
Federal, provincial and territorial governments, in consultation with Aboriginal nations and urban communities of interest, co-operate to establish procedures and funding to support
needs assessment and planning initiatives by Métis and other
Aboriginal collectivities, in rural and urban settings, to

    (a) form interim planning groups for rural settlements with a
minimum of 250 Aboriginal residents, or catchment areas,
whether urban or rural, with a minimum of 1,000 residents;

    (b) compile an inventory of existing services, organizations
and networks directed to meet Aboriginal needs, from
which to build on existing strengths and ensure continuity of effort; and

    (c) prepare plans to develop, operate and house healing cen-
tres, considering the goal of equitable access by Aboriginal
people wherever they reside, the historical pattern of distinct Métis and treaty nation development in the prairie
provinces, the availability and adaptability of municipal
and provincial services, and the cost and efficiency of services.

Regional Healing **3.3.10**
Lodges
Aboriginal, federal, provincial and territorial governments, as
appropriate, collaborate on regional initiatives to develop healing lodges providing residential services oriented to family and
community healing, with priority being given to

    (a) needs assessment and planning that reflect regional
Aboriginal initiative and responsiveness to the diversity of
cultures and communities;

    (b) services broadly inclusive of all Aboriginal people resident
in a region or associated with the nations of the region;

    (c) institutions that collaborate with and complement other
Aboriginal institutions and services, particularly healing
centres delivering integrated health and social services; and

    (d) governance structures consistent with emerging forms of
Aboriginal self-government in the region.

Capital and **3.3.11**
Operating Budgets
Aboriginal, federal, provincial and territorial governments incorporate in funding agreements plans for capital development and
operating costs of a network of healing lodges.

Regional Planning Bodies

3.3.12

Federal, provincial and territorial governments, and Aboriginal governments and organizations, support the assumption of responsibility for planning health and social services by regional Aboriginal agencies and councils where these now operate, and the formation of regional Aboriginal planning bodies in new areas, to promote

(a) equitable access to appropriate services by all Aboriginal people;

(b) strategic deployment of regional resources; and

(c) co-operative effort between Aboriginal communities and communities of interest, consistent with the emergence of nation governments and confederacies.

Canada-Wide Human Resources Strategy

3.3.13

The government of Canada provide funds to the national Aboriginal organizations, including national Aboriginal women's organizations, to permit them to prepare a comprehensive human resources development strategy in health and social services that

(a) facilitates and draws upon regional initiatives, integrates information from diverse sources, and is structured to incorporate regular updating;

(b) builds an inventory of Aboriginal human resources currently available in health and social services, identifying where, in what field and at what level Aboriginal personnel are currently practising;

(c) assesses current and future Aboriginal human resources needs and identifies the actions needed on the part of governments, educational institutions and others to address these needs;

(d) assesses requirements for direct service personnel as well as for planners, researchers and administrators;

(e) collates an inventory and available evaluative data on training and education options;

(f) explores recruitment, training and retention issues;

(g) examines the personal and professional supports required to encourage Aboriginal professionals to practise in Aboriginal communities;

(h) develops proposals for a system to monitor the status of Aboriginal human resources; and

(i) develops an analysis of how, to the maximum extent possible, Aboriginal human resources development can be brought under Aboriginal control.

Commitment to Train 10,000 Professionals

3.3.14

Federal, provincial and territorial governments commit themselves to providing the necessary funding, consistent with their jurisdictional responsibilities,

(a) to implement a co-ordinated and comprehensive human resources development strategy;

(b) to train 10,000 Aboriginal professionals over a 10-year period in health and social services, including medicine, nursing, mental health, psychology, social work, dentistry, nutrition, addictions, gerontology, public health, community development, planning, health administration, and other priority areas identified by Aboriginal people;

(c) to support program development in educational institutions providing professional training, with preference given to Aboriginal institutions; and

(d) to ensure that student support through post-secondary educational assistance, scholarships, paid leave and other means is adequate to achieve the target.

Adaptation of Current Programs

3.3.15

Federal, provincial and territorial governments and national Aboriginal organizations, including Aboriginal women's organizations, explore how training approaches and personnel complements of current health and social services, including the community health representative and drug and alcohol abuse programs, can contribute to a more comprehensive, holistic and integrated system of services, while helping to maintain continuity and adequacy of Aboriginal community services.

Increase Number of Graduates

3.3.16

Post-secondary educational institutions providing programs of study leading to professional certification in health or social services collaborate with Aboriginal organizations to examine how they can

(a) increase the number of Aboriginal students participating in and graduating from their programs;

(b) provide support for students to promote completion of programs;

(c) develop or expand specialized programs; and

(d) modify the curriculum of programs leading to certification so as to increase the cultural appropriateness and effectiveness of training provided to Aboriginal and non-Aboriginal students who will be providing services to Aboriginal people.

Continuing
Professional
Education

3.3.17

Post-secondary educational institutions and professional associations collaborate with Aboriginal organizations to ensure that professionals already in the field have access to programs of continuing professional education that emphasize cultural issues associated with the provision of health and social services.

Recognize
Aboriginal
Knowledge

3.3.18

Post-secondary educational institutions involved in the training of health and social services professionals, and professional associations involved in regulating and licensing these professions, collaborate with Aboriginal organizations and governments to develop a more effective approach to training and licensing that recognizes the importance and legitimacy of Aboriginal knowledge and experience.

AUCC and CAUT
Provide Leadership

3.3.19

The Association of Universities and Colleges of Canada and the Canadian Association of University Teachers encourage their members to implement the Commission's recommendations with respect to professional training of Aboriginal people for health and social services, and that these organizations provide leadership to help ensure that the recommendations are implemented.

Support for
Community
Participation

3.3.20

Federal, provincial and territorial governments, in collaboration with Aboriginal organizations and governments, allocate funds to support Aboriginal community participation in planning, program development, training, and promoting community awareness in relation to human resources development in health and social services.

Protect and Extend
Traditional
Healing

3.3.21

Governments, health authorities and traditional practitioners co-operate to protect and extend the practices of traditional healing and explore their application to contemporary Aboriginal health and healing problems.

Dialogue Between Aboriginal and Bio-Medical Practitioners 3.3.22

Aboriginal traditional healers and bio-medical practitioners strive actively to enhance mutual respect through dialogue and that they explore areas of possible sharing and collaboration.

Educational Institutions Respect Traditional Practices 3.3.23

Non-Aboriginal educational institutions and professional associations involved in the health and social services fields sensitize practitioners to the existence of traditional medicine and healing practices, the possibilities for co-operation and collaboration, and the importance of recognizing, affirming and respecting traditional practices and practitioners.

Action Plans of Mainstream Institutions and Voluntary Organizations 3.3.24

Non-Aboriginal service agencies and institutions involved in the delivery of health or social services to Aboriginal people, and professional associations, unions, and other organizations in a position to influence the delivery of health or social services to Aboriginal people

(a) undertake a systematic examination to determine how they can encourage and support the development of Aboriginal health and social service systems, and improve the appropriateness and effectiveness of mainstream services to Aboriginal people;

(b) engage representatives of Aboriginal communities and organizations in conducting such an examination;

(c) make public an action plan appropriate to the institution or organization involved, outlining measurable objectives and a timetable for achieving them; and

(d) establish means to monitor and evaluate implementation of the plan by the institution or organization itself and by Aboriginal representatives.

Enforcement of Service Standards 3.3.25

Governments responsible for funding and professional bodies responsible for accrediting non-Aboriginal institutions and agencies engaged in the delivery of Aboriginal health and social services

(a) establish as a criterion for continuing funding and accreditation the preparation and implementation of goals and standards for services to Aboriginal people; and

(b) require that Aboriginal people, communities and nations affected by such services be fully involved in the development, implementation and evaluation of such goals and standards of practice.

Chapter 4 Housing

The Commission recommends that

Commitment to Adequate Housing

3.4.1

Federal and provincial governments address Aboriginal housing and community services on the basis of the following policy principles:

(a) Governments have an obligation to ensure that Aboriginal people have adequate shelter, water and sanitation services.

(b) Governments have a responsibility to restore an economic base to Aboriginal people that enables them to meet their needs.

(c) Aboriginal people, individually and collectively, are responsible for meeting their housing needs according to their ability to pay or contribute in kind.

(d) Governments must supplement the resources available to Aboriginal people so that their housing needs are fully met.

(e) Aboriginal nations should assume authority over all housing matters as a core area of self-government jurisdiction.

(f) Acute risks to health and safety should be treated as an emergency and targeted for immediate action.

3.4.2

The government of Canada clarify with treaty nations a modern understanding of existing treaty terms regarding housing.

3.4.3

The government of Canada make resources available over the next 10 years to ensure that housing for Aboriginal people on-reserve is fully adequate in quantity and quality and engage the governments of the provinces and territories to reach the same goal in rural and northern communities and in urban areas.

Water and Sewage Systems

3.4.4

The government of Canada provide additional resources for construction, upgrading and operation of water and sewage systems to ensure that adequate facilities and operating systems are in place in all First Nations communities within five years.

3.4.5

The government of Canada provide funding and technical support to First Nations governments to operate and maintain community water and sewer systems and to establish technical support institutions as required.

3.4.6

The government of Canada and First Nations governments and people undertake to meet the need of First Nations people for adequate housing within 10 years.

3.4.7

The government of Canada complement the resources supplied by First Nations people in a two-to-one ratio or as necessary to achieve adequate housing in 10 years by

- providing capital subsidies and committing to loan subsidies for construction of new homes and renovations;
- providing funds for property insurance and regular maintenance for home occupants receiving social assistance or with low earned incomes;
- paying rental subsidies for those receiving social assistance or with low earned incomes in amounts that are equitable compared to off-reserve programs; and
- offering financial incentives for private home ownership.

3.4.8

First Nations governments and people make every effort to marshall more resources for housing and community services, through financial contributions from residents in the form of maintenance fees, rents or mortgage payments, and contributions in kind, such as sweat equity and local materials.

3.4.9

First Nations governments assume jurisdiction over housing at the earliest opportunity, enact clear laws regarding housing tenure, and pursue authority to adjust other programs such as social assistance with a view to marshalling more resources for housing.

3.4.10

First Nations governments develop institutions at the nation level or through inter-nation agreements to administer housing and tenure regimes and deliver housing programs with financial and technical support from the government of Canada.

3.4.11

The government of Canada support the efforts of First Nations communities to develop and implement their own tenure systems and housing programs, innovative uses of social assistance to stimulate contributions to housing, and institutions above the community level.

Housing in Non-Reserve Communities

3.4.12

The government of Canada and the governments of the provinces and territories undertake to meet fully, in co-operation with Aboriginal people and within 10 years, the need for adequate housing of Aboriginal people not living on reserves.

3.4.13

Aboriginal people not living on reserves make every effort to marshall more resources for housing in a variety of ways, through contributions in kind, use of local materials, and effective housing organizations.

3.4.14

The government of Canada engage the provincial and territorial governments in a strategy to meet the housing needs of Aboriginal people living in non-reserve communities by

- reinstating and increasing funding for new social housing and mortgage subsidies under the Aboriginal off-reserve programs of the Canada Mortgage and Housing Corporation (CMHC);
- providing greater autonomy and flexibility to Aboriginal organizations delivering the program in rural areas and to urban social housing corporations; and
- providing rental subsidies as a cost-effective option where rental markets exist.

Economic Development

3.4.15

The government of Canada help Aboriginal people exploit the economic development opportunities arising from an increase in construction, repair and maintenance of dwellings for Aboriginal people

- by providing funding and support through training and business development programs; and
- by actively expanding the involvement of Aboriginal financial institutions in mortgage financing as agents of CMHC and as mortgage lenders.

Chapter 5 Education

The Commission recommends that

Education and
Self-Government

3.5.1

Federal, provincial and territorial governments act promptly to acknowledge that education is a core area for the exercise of Aboriginal self-government.

Transitional
Control of
Education

3.5.2

Federal, provincial and territorial governments collaborate with Aboriginal governments, organizations or education authorities, as appropriate, to support the development of Aboriginally controlled education systems by

(a) introducing, adapting or ensuring the flexible application of legislation to facilitate self-starting initiatives by Aboriginal nations and their communities in the field of education;

(b) mandating voluntary organizations that are endorsed by substantial numbers of Aboriginal people to act in the field of education in urban and non-reserve areas where numbers warrant until such time as Aboriginal governments are established; and

(c) providing funding commensurate with the responsibilities assumed by Aboriginal nations and their communities, or voluntary organizations, given the requirements of institutional and program development, costs of serving small or dispersed communities, and special needs accruing from past failures of education services.

Early Childhood
Education Support

3.5.3

Federal, provincial, and territorial governments co-operate to support an integrated early childhood education funding strategy that

(a) extends early childhood education services to *all* Aboriginal children regardless of residence;

(b) encourages programs that foster the physical, social, intellectual and spiritual development of children, reducing distinctions between child care, prevention and education;

(c) maximizes Aboriginal control over service design and administration;

(d) offers one-stop accessible funding; and

(e) promotes parental involvement and choice in early childhood education options.

Transfer Between Education Systems 3.5.4

Aboriginal, provincial and territorial governments act promptly to reach agreements for mutual recognition of programs provided by their respective educational institutions so as to facilitate the transfer of students between educational systems while protecting the integrity of cultural dimensions of Aboriginal education

Curriculum Development 3.5.5

Federal, provincial and territorial governments collaborate with Aboriginal governments, organizations and educators to develop or continue developing innovative curricula that reflect Aboriginal cultures and community realities, for delivery

(a) at all grade levels of elementary and secondary schools;

(b) in schools operating under Aboriginal control; and

(c) in schools under provincial or territorial jurisdiction.

Priority of Aboriginal Language Education 3.5.6

Aboriginal language education be assigned priority in Aboriginal, provincial and territorial education systems to complement and support language preservation efforts in local communities through

(a) first- or second-language instruction or immersion programs where parents desire it and numbers warrant;

(b) recognition of Aboriginal language competence for second-language academic credit whether competence is acquired through classroom or out-of-school instruction;

(c) involving elders and fluent Aboriginal speakers in programs to enhance Aboriginal language acquisition and fluency;

(d) developing instructional materials; and

(e) encouraging and rewarding language teaching as a career path and language research in lexical elaboration, structural analysis and cultural contexts as professional and academic specializations.

Involvement in Decision Making 3.5.7

Where Aboriginal children attend provincial and territorial schools, provincial and territorial governments take immediate steps to ensure that Aboriginal people are involved fully in the decision-making processes that affect the education of their children. Aboriginal control of education and parental involvement should be implemented through a variety of actions:

(a) legislation to guarantee Aboriginal representation on school boards where population numbers warrant;

(b) recognition of Aboriginally controlled schools under the jurisdiction of Aboriginal community of interest governments;

(c) establishment of Aboriginally governed schools affiliated with school districts, if requested by Aboriginal people; and

(d) creation of Aboriginal advisory committees to school boards.

Involvement in School Activities

3.5.8

All schools serving Aboriginal children adopt policies that welcome the involvement of Aboriginal parents, elders and families in the life of the school, for example, by establishing advisory or parents committees, introducing teaching by elders in the classroom, and involving parents in school activities

Required School Board Strategy

3.5.9

Provincial and territorial ministries require school boards serving Aboriginal students to implement a comprehensive Aboriginal education strategy, developed with Aboriginal parents, elders and educators, including

(a) goals and objectives to be accomplished during the International Decade of Indigenous Peoples;

(b) hiring of Aboriginal teachers at the elementary and secondary school level, with negotiated target levels, to teach in all areas of school programs, not just Aboriginal programs;

(c) hiring of Aboriginal people in administrative and leadership positions;

(d) hiring of Aboriginal support workers, such as counsellors, community liaison workers, psychologists and speech therapists;

(e) curriculum, in all subject areas, that includes the perspectives, traditions, beliefs and world view of Aboriginal peoples;

(f) involvement of Aboriginal elders in teaching Aboriginal and non-Aboriginal students;

(g) language classes in Aboriginal languages, as determined by the Aboriginal community;

(h) family and community involvement mechanisms;

(i) education programs that combat stereotypes, racism, prejudice and biases;

(j) accountability indicators tied to board or district funding; and

(k) public reports of results by the end of the International Decade of Indigenous Peoples in the year 2004.

Youth Empowerment **3.5.10**

Aboriginally controlled, provincial, and territorial schools serving Aboriginal youth develop and implement comprehensive Aboriginal youth empowerment strategies with elements elaborated in collaboration with youth, including

(a) cultural education in classroom and informal settings;

(b) acknowledgement of spiritual, ethical and intuitive dimensions of learning;

(c) education to support critical analysis of Aboriginal experience;

(d) learning as a means of healing from the effects of trauma, abuse and racism;

(e) academic skills development and support;

(f) sports and outdoor education;

(g) leadership development; and

(h) youth exchanges between Aboriginal nations, across Canada and internationally.

Community High School Programs **3.5.11**

High school programs be extended to communities, using cost-effective options agreed upon by parents and families, including

(a) complete school facilities for local high school delivery;

(b) regional high schools in Aboriginal communities;

(c) culturally appropriate, interactive distance education; and

(d) seasonal institutes.

Secondary Study Re-entry **3.5.12**

Aboriginal authorities and all provincial and territorial ministries of education fund programs for Aboriginal youth who have left secondary school before graduation to enable them to resume their studies with appropriate curriculum, scheduling, academic and social support.

Co-op Education **3.5.13**

Federal, provincial and territorial governments encourage co-op initiatives by offering funding inducements to secondary schools that develop active co-op education programs for Aboriginal young people.

Expanded Teacher Education Programs

3.5.14

Federal, provincial and territorial governments expand financial support to post-secondary institutions for existing and new Aboriginal teacher education programs, contingent on

(a) evidence of Aboriginal support for the program;

(b) Aboriginal participation in the governance of the program;

(c) the incorporation of Aboriginal content and pedagogy into the program; and

(d) periodic evaluations that indicate that the quality of teacher education conforms to standards of excellence expected by Aboriginal people.

Aboriginal Secondary School Teachers

3.5.15

Canadian governments, Aboriginal education authorities, post-secondary institutions and teacher education programs adopt multiple strategies to increase substantially the number of Aboriginal secondary school teachers, including

(a) promoting secondary school teaching careers for Aboriginal people;

(b) increasing access to professional training in secondary education, for example, community-based delivery of courses and concurrent programs; and

(c) offering financial incentives to students.

Teacher Education Accessible in Communities

3.5.16

Federal, provincial and territorial governments provide support to increase the number of Aboriginal people trained as teachers by

(a) expanding the number of teacher education programs delivered directly in communities; and

(b) ensuring that students in each province and territory have access to such programs.

Career Paths

3.5.17

Teacher education programs, in collaboration with Aboriginal organizations and government agencies that sponsor professional and para-professional training, adopt a comprehensive approach to educator training, developing career paths from para-professional training to professional certification in education careers that

(a) prepare Aboriginal students for the variety of roles required to operate Aboriginal education systems; and

(b) open opportunities for careers in provincial education systems.

Aboriginal Component in All Teacher Education Programs

3.5.18

Provinces and territories require that teacher education programs

(a) in pre-service training leading to certification include at least one component on teaching Aboriginal subject matter to all students, both Aboriginal and non-Aboriginal;

(b) develop options for pre-service training and professional development of teachers, focused on teaching Aboriginal students and addressing Aboriginal education issues; and

(c) collaborate with Aboriginal organizations or community representatives in developing Aboriginal-specific components of their programs.

Aboriginal Delivery of Integrated Adult Training

3.5.19

Federal, provincial and territorial governments collaborate with Aboriginal governments and organizations to facilitate integrated delivery of adult literacy, basic education, academic upgrading and job training under the control of Aboriginal people through

(a) delegating responsibility for delivery of training under current jurisdictions by concluding agreements with Aboriginal governments, their mandated education authorities, or voluntary organizations representing Aboriginal communities of interest;

(b) supporting adaptation of program design, admission criteria, language of instruction, and internal allocation of funds by Aboriginal delivery agents, to accommodate Aboriginal culture and community needs;

(c) acting promptly to conclude agreements for multi-year block funding agreements to enable Aboriginal nation governments, during the transition to self-government, to assume primary responsibility for allocating funds to meet training needs through programs of Aboriginal design.

Treaty Promise of Education

3.5.20

The government of Canada recognize and fulfil its obligation to treaty nations by supporting a full range of education services, including post-secondary education, for members of treaty nations where a promise of education appears in treaty texts, related documents or oral histories of the parties involved.

Federal Support of Post-Secondary Students

3.5.21

The federal government continue to support the costs of post-secondary education for First Nations and Inuit post-secondary students and make additional resources available

(a) to mitigate the impact of increased costs as post-secondary institutions shift to a new policy environment in post-secondary education; and

(b) to meet the anticipated higher level of demand for post-secondary education services.

Métis and Aboriginal Scholarship Fund

3.5.22

A scholarship fund be established for Métis and other Aboriginal students who do not have access to financial support for post-secondary education under present policies, with

(a) lead financial support provided by federal and provincial governments and additional contributions from corporate and individual donors;

(b) a planning committee to be established immediately,

(i) composed of Métis and other Aboriginal representatives, students, and federal and provincial representatives in balanced numbers;

(ii) given a maximum two-year mandate; and

(iii) charged with determining the appropriate vehicle, level of capitalization, program criteria and administrative structure for initiation and administration of the fund; and

(c) provisions for evaluating demand on the fund, its adequacy and its impact on participation and completion rates of Métis and other Aboriginal students in post-secondary studies.

Aboriginal Languages Equivalent to Modern Languages

3.5.23

Canada's post-secondary institutions recognize Aboriginal languages on a basis equal to other modern languages, for the purpose of granting credits for entrance requirements, fulfilment of second language requirements, and general course credits.

Mainstream Post-Secondary Initiatives

3.5.24

Public post-secondary institutions in the provinces and territories undertake new initiatives or extend current ones to increase the participation, retention and graduation of Aboriginal students by introducing, encouraging or enhancing

(a) a welcoming environment for Aboriginal students;

(b) Aboriginal content and perspectives in course offerings across disciplines;

(c) Aboriginal studies and programs as part of the institution's regular program offerings and included in the institution's core budget;

(d) Aboriginal appointments to boards of governors;

(e) Aboriginal councils to advise the president of the institution;

(f) active recruitment of Aboriginal students;

(g) admission policies that encourage access by Aboriginal applicants;

(h) meeting spaces for Aboriginal students;

(i) Aboriginal student unions;

(j) recruitment of Aboriginal faculty members;

(k) support services with Aboriginal counsellors for academic and personal counselling; and

(l) cross-cultural sensitivity training for faculty and staff.

Residential University Colleges

3.5.25

Where there is Aboriginal support for an Aboriginal college within a university, and where numbers warrant, universities act to establish an Aboriginal college to serve as the focal point for the academic, residential, social and cultural lives of Aboriginal students on campus, and to promote Aboriginal scholarship.

Fund Aboriginal Post-Secondary Institutions

3.5.26

Federal, provincial and territorial governments collaborate with Aboriginal governments and organizations to establish and support post-secondary educational institutions controlled by Aboriginal people, with negotiated allocation of responsibility for

(a) core and program funding commensurate with the services they are expected to provide and comparable to the funding provided to provincial or territorial institutions delivering similar services;

(b) planning, capital and start-up costs of new colleges and institutes;

(c) improvement of facilities for community learning centres as required for new functions and development of new facilities where numbers warrant and the community establishes this as a priority; and

(d) fulfilment of obligations pursuant to treaties and modern agreements with respect to education.

Regional and National Aboriginal Boards

3.5.27

Aboriginally controlled post-secondary educational institutions collaborate to create regional boards and/or a Canada-wide board to

(a) establish standards for accrediting programs provided by Aboriginal post-secondary institutions;

(b) negotiate mutual recognition of course credits and credentials to facilitate student transfer between Aboriginal institutions and provincial and territorial post-secondary institutions;

(c) establish co-operative working relationships with mainstream accreditation bodies such as the Association of Universities and Colleges of Canada and professional associations such as the Canadian Association of University Teachers; and

(d) pursue other objectives related to the common interests of Aboriginal institutions.

Elders' Role in Education

3.5.28

Elders be reinstated to an active role in the education of Aboriginal children and youth in educational systems under Aboriginal control and in provincial and territorial schools.

Elders' Compensation

3.5.29

Elders be treated as professionals and compensated for their education contribution at a rate and in a manner that shows respect for their expertise, unique knowledge and skills.

Recognize Aboriginal Knowledge

3.5.30

Provincial and territorial education ministries, boards of education and educators recognize the value of elders' knowledge to all peoples' understanding of the universe by

(a) giving academic credits for traditional Aboriginal arts and knowledge whether acquired in the classroom or through non-formal means in cultural activities, camps and apprenticeships; and

(b) collaborating with elders to determine how traditional Aboriginal knowledge can be made accessible in the education of all students, whether Aboriginal or non-Aboriginal, in institutions under Aboriginal, provincial or territorial control.

Exchanges Among **3.5.31**
Elders and with Educational institutions facilitate opportunities for elders to
Academics exchange traditional knowledge with one another and to share
traditional knowledge with students and scholars, both
Aboriginal and non-Aboriginal, in university settings.

Establish **3.5.32**
Aboriginal Peoples' A university under Aboriginal control, which could be called the
International Aboriginal Peoples' International University, with the capacity
University to function in all provinces and territories, be established to promote traditional knowledge, to pursue applied research in support of Aboriginal self-government, and to disseminate
information essential to achieving broad Aboriginal development goals.

Steering Group to **3.5.33**
Plan APIU First Nations, Inuit and Métis leaders in collaboration with the
federal government establish a steering group funded by the federal government, with a three-year mandate
(a) to explore options, conduct consultations and prepare a
plan to implement an Aboriginal Peoples' International
University by the year 2000; and
(b) to collaborate with other working groups in determining
the appropriate location of a documentation centre and
archive, an electronic information clearinghouse, and statistical data bases.

Electronic **3.5.34**
Clearinghouse An electronic clearinghouse be established to facilitate the free
flow of information among Aboriginal communities, education
and self-government workers and individuals, the planning
and development of this clearinghouse to be carried forward by
a working group
(a) established in collaboration with First Nations, Inuit and
Métis leaders;
(b) funded by the federal government and given a two-year
mandate; and
(c) attentive to the need for Canada-wide and international
communication as well as exchange in Aboriginal languages within linguistic communities.

Working Group
for Statistical
Clearinghouse

3.5.35

First Nations, Inuit and Métis leaders establish a working group, funded by the federal government, with a two-year mandate to plan a statistical clearinghouse controlled by Aboriginal people to

(a) work in collaboration with Aboriginal governments and organizations to establish and update statistical data bases; and

(b) promote common strategies across nations and communities for collecting and analyzing data relevant to Aboriginal development goals.

Documentation
Centre on
Residential
Schools and
Relocations

3.5.36

The federal government fund the establishment of a national documentation centre to research, collect, preserve and disseminate information related to residential schools, relocations and other aspects of Aboriginal historical experience, the planning and development of the centre to be carried forward by a working group

(a) established in collaboration with First Nations, Inuit and Métis leaders; and

(b) having a two-year mandate.

Education for Self-
Government
Funding

3.5.37

Federal, provincial and territorial governments establish funding programs to support education for self-government, to be available to

(a) public post-secondary institutions that have entered into partnerships with Aboriginal people to initiate or expand training and education in areas identified as priorities by Aboriginal governments, organizations and communities for the implementation of self-government; and

(b) Aboriginally controlled post-secondary institutions for program innovation to enhance capacity for self-government.

Youth Careers
Campaign

3.5.38

Aboriginal governments and organizations collaborate to launch a Canada-wide campaign to make youth aware of the opportunities to serve their nations that will open up with the advent of self-government and of the tangible and intangible rewards that accompany public service.

Student Incentives for Self-Government Studies

3.5.39

The federal government make funds available to First Nation and Inuit governments and organizations to support incentives to encourage students to complete bachelor's and master's level studies and professional training in areas of priority to self-government, including such measures as

(a) employee release time for concurrent work and study;

(b) paid leave to pursue full-time study;

(c) scholarships in studies related to self-government;

(d) top-up of educational assistance for family needs, including exceptional housing costs; and

(e) student loans that are forgivable on completion of a period of employment in the service of self-government.

Co-op Placements in Business and Government

3.5.40

Canada's corporations, small businesses and governments become active partners in Aboriginal self-government education by identifying co-op placement and internship opportunities in their organizations, in consultation with Aboriginal people.

Executive Interchange

3.5.41

Canada's corporations and governments at all levels establish executive interchange opportunities in partnership with Aboriginal governments.

Professional Associations Support Aboriginal Training

3.5.42

Professional associations and self-governing bodies in the professions actively support the professional training of Aboriginal people by

(a) entering into dialogue on such issues as credentials, recruitment, mentoring, career paths linking para-professional and professional training, education based on Aboriginal culture, systemic discrimination and racism;

(b) establishing scholarships for Aboriginal people;

(c) encouraging their members to gain an understanding of Aboriginal perspectives;

(d) spearheading initiatives to introduce Aboriginal cultural perspectives into professional training programs; and

(e) providing leadership by encouraging implementation of the recommendations in this report that are relevant to their areas of expertise.

Support of
Distance
Education Models

3.5.43

The federal government, media corporations, provincial and territorial governments and private donors provide funding and/or gifts in kind (for example, access to facilities and technology) to establish a distance education model of professional training suitable for Aboriginal people who wish to pursue post-secondary studies from their communities.

Canada-Wide
Aboriginal Human
Resources
Inventory

3.5.44

The federal government provide funding for national Aboriginal organizations to co-ordinate establishment of a Canada-wide Aboriginal human resources inventory that is amenable to regular updating.

Chapter 6 Arts and Heritage

The Commission recommends that

Inventory of
Historical and
Sacred Sites

3.6.1

Federal, provincial and territorial governments collaborate with Aboriginal organizations and communities to prepare a comprehensive inventory of historical and sacred sites, involving elders as expert advisers, before negotiations on designation of lands in accordance with our recommendations in Volume 2, Chapter 4.

Urgent Protection
of Threatened
Sites

3.6.2

Federal, provincial and territorial governments review legislation affecting sacred and historical sites to ensure that Aboriginal organizations and communities have access to urgent remedies to prevent or arrest damage to significant heritage sites such as the Mnjikaning Fish Fence, whether they be threatened by human actions or natural processes.

Legislation on
Historical Sites
and Cultural
Artifacts

3.6.3

Federal, provincial and territorial governments in collaboration with Aboriginal organizations review legislation affecting historical and sacred sites and the conservation and display of cultural artifacts to ensure that

(a) Aboriginal interests are recognized in designing, protecting, developing and managing sites significant to Aboriginal culture and heritage and in conserving, repatriating and displaying Aboriginal cultural artifacts;

(b) Aboriginal people are fully involved in planning and managing heritage activities relevant to their cultures; and

(c) Aboriginal people share the economic benefits that may accrue from appropriate development of relevant heritage sites and display of cultural artifacts.

Museums and Cultural Institutions Adopt Ethical Guidelines

3.6.4

Museums and cultural institutions adopt ethical guidelines governing all aspects of collection, disposition, display and interpretation of artifacts related to Aboriginal culture and heritage, including the following:

(a) involving Aboriginal people in drafting, endorsing and implementing the guidelines;

(b) creating inventories of relevant holdings and making such inventories freely accessible to Aboriginal people;

(c) cataloguing and designating appropriate use and display of relevant holdings;

(d) repatriating, on request, objects that are sacred or integral to the history and continuity of particular nations and communities;

(e) returning human remains to the family, community or nation of origin, on request, or consulting with Aboriginal advisers on appropriate disposition, where remains cannot be associated with a particular nation; and

(f) ensuring that Aboriginal people and communities have effective access to cultural education and training opportunities available through museums and cultural institutions.

Access to Cultural Education

3.6.5

Aboriginal, federal, provincial and territorial governments, in collaboration with Aboriginal elders, artists, educators and youth, develop and implement joint strategies to ensure that Aboriginal people have

(a) effective access to cultural and heritage education;

(b) resources to develop facilities for display of cultural artifacts; and

(c) means to participate in exchanges and joint undertakings with museums and cultural institutions.

Heritage Vocations Part of Capacity Building

3.6.6

Aboriginal, federal, provincial and territorial governments include heritage research, conservation and presentation in the list of skills identified as priorities in building the capacity to implement self-government.

Protect Aboriginal Intellectual Property

3.6.7

The federal government, in collaboration with Aboriginal people, review its legislation on the protection of intellectual property to ensure that Aboriginal interests and perspectives, in particular collective interests, are adequately protected.

Determining Language Status a Core Power of Self-Government

3.6.8

Federal, provincial and territorial governments recognize promptly that determining Aboriginal language status and use is a core power in Aboriginal self-government, and that these governments affirm and support Aboriginal nations and their communities in using and promoting their languages and declaring them official languages within their nations, territories and communities where they choose to do so.

Nations Implement a Multi-Faceted Language Strategy

3.6.9

Each Aboriginal nation in the various stages of nation building, capacity building, negotiating and implementing self-government consult with its constituent communities to establish priorities and policies with respect to Aboriginal language conservation, revitalization and documentation, including

(a) assessing the current state of Aboriginal language use and vitality;

(b) determining priorities of communities for language conservation, revitalization and documentation;

(c) consulting on the most effective means of implementing priorities;

(d) facilitating initiatives to support Aboriginal language use in families and the broader community;

(e) incorporating their Aboriginal language in education policies and programs;

(f) enhancing co-operation among nations and communities of the same language group to promote research, curriculum development and language elaboration;

(g) using their Aboriginal language in public forums and Aboriginal government business; and

(h) declaring their Aboriginal language an official language on nation territory.

Endowed
Aboriginal
Languages
Foundation

3.6.10

The federal government make a commitment to endow an Aboriginal Languages Foundation for the purpose of supporting Aboriginal initiatives in the conservation, revitalization and documentation of Aboriginal languages, the foundation to be

(a) capitalized by an annual federal grant of $10 million for five years, beginning in 1997;

(b) eligible to receive charitable contributions, to be matched by the federal government in a ratio of two dollars for each dollar contributed;

(c) established to support language initiatives undertaken or endorsed by Aboriginal nations and their communities;

(d) developed by a federally funded planning body, with a majority of First Nations, Inuit and Métis representatives and a two-year mandate; and

(e) directed in its operation by a board with a majority of First Nations, Inuit and Métis members.

Special Status of
Aboriginal-
Language
Broadcasting

3.6.11

The government of Canada recognize the special status of Aboriginal-language broadcasting explicitly in federal legislation.

CRTC Require
Representation of
Aboriginal
Programming

3.6.12

The Canadian Radio-Television and Telecommunications Commission include in licence conditions for public and commercial broadcasters, in regions with significant Aboriginal population concentrations, requirements for fair representation and distribution of Aboriginal programming, including Aboriginal language requirements.

Access to
Aboriginal Media
Products

3.6.13

Public and private media outlets, in particular the Canadian Broadcasting Corporation, provide access to Aboriginal media products for Aboriginal and non-Aboriginal Canadians by

(a) purchasing and broadcasting Aboriginal programming from independent Aboriginal producers; and

(b) producing English and French versions of original Aboriginal programs for regional and national redistribution.

Employment Equity in Public and Private Media

3.6.14

Public and private media outlets address the need for training and better representation of Aboriginal people in public communications by developing and implementing employment equity plans.

Freedom of Expression for Aboriginal Media

3.6.15

Governments, including Aboriginal governments, recognize the critical role that independent Aboriginal print and broadcast media have in the pursuit of Aboriginal self-determination and self-government, and that they support freedom of expression through

(a) policies on open access to information; and

(b) dedicated funding at arm's length from political bodies.

Aboriginal Access to Media Training

3.6.16

Colleges and universities with programs in communications, journalism and film co-operate to support access for Aboriginal students by providing transition courses, scholarships and counselling services.

Fees and Joint Ventures to Finance Aboriginal Media Products

3.6.17

The Canadian Radio-Television and Telecommunications Commission be mandated to establish fee structures and provisions for joint ventures as part of licensing conditions to ensure a stable financial base for the production and distribution of Aboriginal broadcast media products, particularly in southern Canada.

Core Funding and Incentives for Private Support

3.6.18

Federal, provincial, territorial and Aboriginal governments provide core funding for Aboriginal media that

(a) is accessible to all Aboriginal nations and communities;

(b) builds upon existing government programs and Aboriginal media organizations;

(c) results in long-term funding agreements that realistically reflect Aboriginal media requirements and promote self-financing; and

(d) encourages private and corporate support through tax incentives.

Aboriginal Arts Council

3.6.19

Federal, provincial, territorial and Aboriginal governments co-operate to establish and fund an Aboriginal Arts Council, with a minimum 20-year life span and an annual budget equivalent to five per cent of the Canada Council budget, to foster the revitalization and development of Aboriginal arts and literature.

Arts Granting Criteria Relevant to Aboriginal Arts

3.6.20

Governments, public agencies and private organizations that provide support for the visual and performing arts, in co-operation with Aboriginal artists and performers, review all aspects of their programs to ensure that

(a) criteria for grants and awards are relevant to Aboriginal arts and artists; and

(b) Aboriginal people and perspectives are adequately represented on decision-making bodies, juries, advisory committees and staff.

Arts Training and Facilities

3.6.21

Federal, provincial, territorial and Aboriginal governments, in co-operation with Aboriginal artists, writers and performers, support and promote the revitalization and development of Aboriginal literary, visual and performing arts through

(a) support of training programs in schools, cultural institutions and professional associations, and participation of Aboriginal students in professional studies in the arts; and

(b) accommodating requirements for appropriate display and performance of Aboriginal arts in the design of public facilities in Aboriginal communities and the community at large.

Appendix B

Abridged Tables of Contents
Volumes 1, 2, 4 and 5[*]

Volume I
Looking Forward, Looking Back

---

[*] Tables of contents in the volumes themselves may be slightly different, as a result of final editing.

VOLUME 2
Restructuring the Relationship

3. Governance

PART TWO

4. Lands and Resources

VOLUME 4
PERSPECTIVES AND REALITIES

1. Introduction

2. Women's Perspectives

5. Métis Perspectives

6. The North

7. Urban Perspectives

VOLUME 5

RENEWAL:
A TWENTY-YEAR COMMITMENT

1. Laying the Foundations of a Renewed Relationship